Avenues of Faith

Religion and American Culture

Series Editors
David Edwin Harrell Jr.
Wayne Flynt
Edith L. Blumhofer

Avenues of Faith

Shaping the Urban Religious Culture of Richmond, Virginia, 1900–1929

Samuel C. Shepherd Jr.

The University of Alabama Press
Tuscaloosa

The University of Alabama Press
Tuscaloosa, Alabama 35487-0380
uapress.ua.edu

Hardcover edition published 2001.
Paperback edition published 2015.
eBook edition published 2009.

Typeface: Adobe Caslon

Manufactured in the United States of America
Cover photograph: St. James Church and Parish House, Richmond, 1926; courtesy of the Valentine Museum, Richmond, Virginia
Cover design: Robin McDonald

∞
The paper on which this book is printed meets the minimum requirements of American National Standard for Information Science–Permanence of Paper for Printed Library Materials, ANSI Z39.48-1984.

Paperback ISBN: 978-0-8173-5847-1
eBook ISBN: 978-0-8173-1358-6

A previous edition of this book has been catalogued by the Library of Congress as follows:

Library of Congress Cataloging-in-Publication Data

Shepherd, Samuel Claude, 1948–
Avenues of faith : shaping the urban religious culture of Richmond, Virginia, 1900–1929 / Samuel C. Shepherd Jr.
p. cm. — (Religion and American culture)
Includes bibliographical references (p.) and index.
ISBN 0-8173-1076-2 (alk. paper)
1. Richmond (Va.)—Church history—20th century. 2. Protestant churches—Virginia—Richmond—History—20th century. I. Title. II. Religion and American culture (Tuscaloosa, Ala.)
BR560.R5 S54 2001
277.55'4510821—dc21
00-011710

British Library Cataloguing-in-Publication Data available

For my parents

Dawn Hampton Shepherd
and
Samuel Claude Shepherd

Contents

Preface

My initial visits to Richmond occurred during boyhood trips to my aunt's house on the city's Southside and during family treks through town en route to my grandparents' farm in North Carolina. A native of Northern Virginia, I was fascinated by Richmond. As our car traversed the narrow "nickel bridge," I gazed downward, impressed by the surging currents of the James River cascading over the rocks below. During hot summer months, large trees shaded the handsome brick buildings that lined Richmond streets and created a quaint, enchanting atmosphere heightened by the presence of vendors selling flowers from stands at corners. The imposing Civil War monuments whetted my interest in history but implied that little of significance had occurred in the area since that ferocious conflict. Convening in the capital city, a lethargic Virginia legislature aggravated citizens of my own Fairfax County by resisting almost any measure hinting at progress and thereby reinforced the notion that Richmond was little more than the citadel of the Old Dominion. Discovering that my historical interests lay in the twentieth century, I perceived little reason to approach Richmond, a community with few discernible contributions to that period.

Yet Richmond continued to beckon. My enthusiasm for approaching twentieth-century Richmond has been kindled and fueled from afar. After a surprising sequence of events at the University of Wisconsin-Madison, I arrived in Richmond for two years of dissertation research. Upon joining the faculty of Centenary College in Shreveport, Louisiana, I shifted my attention to the closer terrain of urban Louisiana. But Richmond tugged at me again. At a National Endowment for the Humanities Summer Seminar about "Southern Religion and Southern Culture," I renewed my exploration of twentieth-century Richmond. During that summer at the University of Mississippi, the seminar director, Charles Reagan Wilson, and other participants provided fresh perspectives from which to view my previous investigation of Richmond's white Protestants. I emerged with an agenda for additional research and analysis, and I finally acknowledged the reason for Richmond's grip on me. In the twentieth century, the city had housed some remarkable citizens whose experiences reveal much about the urban South and southern religion.

Thus, in this book, I approach anew a subject I addressed in my dissertation many years ago. This work, however, is informed by an array of primary documents unavailable earlier. This account also benefits from the substantial scholarship of other historians who have expanded our understanding of a range of topics including urban reforms, the civic activism of women, race relations, Fundamentalism, and, most of all, southern religion. My dissertation adviser, John M. Cooper Jr., indulgently supported my initial Richmond expedition. Samuel S. Hill Jr. has fostered my study of southern religious history with encouragement, guidance, and incisive commentary. Wayne Flynt has stimulated my Richmond quest by exchanging ideas and information about southern leaders committed to social Christianity. At a Mellon Seminar at Rice University, John Boles prompted me to delve further into the experiences of urban southerners.

Approaching Richmond from afar has been possible only with the aid of many librarians and archivists. I wish to thank the entire staff of Centenary College's Magale Library, particularly interlibrary loan officer Sharon Chevalier for her heroic efforts on my behalf. Carolyn Tate and others at Boatwright Library, University of Richmond, provided important assistance, as did Darlene Slater of the Virginia Baptist Historical Society. At the Virginia Historical Society, Nelson Lankford and Frances Pollard made especially useful suggestions. Years ago Martha Sugg directed my initial encounter with the holdings of the Spence Library of Union Theological Seminary. At the new William Smith Morton Library, Robert Benedetto and Bill Smith have provided comparable aid. During visits to the McGraw-Page Library at Randolph-Macon College, I received assistance in my research about Richmond Methodists. At the Library of Virginia, Brent Tarter and Gregg Kimball identified valuable sources, and Ted Polk facilitated interlibrary loan access to countless crucial reels of microfilm. At the James Branch Cabell Library of Virginia Commonwealth University, Ray Bonis helped me locate important documents. The staffs of the Tompkins-McCaw Library of the Medical College of Virginia, the Richmond Public Library, and the office of the Christian Church in Virginia (the Disciples of Christ) aided my research. I wish to thank the Valentine Museum, the Library of Virginia, and the Virginia Historical Society for granting permission to publish photographs from their collections.

Some approaches to Richmond have led through other communities. In Alexandria, Virginia, archivist Julia Randle and the staff of the Bishop Payne Library, Virginia Theological Seminary, guided me in examining sources about Episcopalians. In Nashville, Tennessee, I received a cordial reception at the

Disciples of Christ Historical Society and at the Dargan-Carver Library of the Southern Baptist Convention. At Montreat, North Carolina, archivists of the Presbyterian Historical Society aided me in using essential manuscripts. I appreciate the assistance I received while using the collections of the Library of Congress, the Wisconsin State Historical Society, the Southern Historical Collection at the University of North Carolina, the Alderman Library at the University of Virginia, the William R. Perkins Library at Duke University, Prescott Memorial Library at Louisiana Tech University, and the Mamye Jarrett Library at East Texas Baptist University. The Archives of the Episcopal Church, U.S.A., in Austin, Texas, kindly responded to a long-distance request for information.

I have debts to several people for helping me in special ways. Mary Grace Taylor shared material about her father, John J. Scherer Jr. Jean B. Evans, daughter of Walter Russell Bowie, permitted me to use her father's manuscripts. Harriet Wellford, daughter of R. Cary Montague, spoke with me about her father. Ernest Trice Thompson recounted his experiences as a seminarian and as a professor at Union Theological Seminary. Winston Wright Jr. of Seventh Street Christian Church located important material about H. D. C. Maclachlan. Richard Olson of First English Evangelical Lutheran Church supplied access to documents at his church, and Benjamin Sparks of Second Presbyterian furnished me with information about his congregation. Richmonders George Glenn, Donald Traser, Patti Russell, Marion Tredway, and Kenneth Crumpton Jr. pointed the way to key sources. Several of my journeys to Richmond and to other research locations have been funded in part by summer travel grants from Centenary College, including one from the Centenary Alumni Association. For that aid I am grateful, as I am for a 1997 Summer Andrew W. Mellon Fellowship from the Virginia Historical Society. The hospitality of Barry and Eddie Westin, Rick and Alyce West, and Bertie and Bill Selvey ensured that visits to Richmond were pleasant and productive.

This work has benefited from the advice and critiques of a number of scholars. Earlier commentaries supplied by Edward M. Coffman of the University of Wisconsin and by Sam Hill have served as markers for the direction of this book. NEH seminar members Will Glass and Dan Woods offered important recommendations about expanding my earlier work. My Centenary College colleagues Alton Hancock, Ronald Dean, Rodney Grunes, Jodi Campbell, and John Peek scrutinized chapters and enhanced the manuscript with their suggestions. James T. Moore, Will Glass, Barry Hankins, James Shapleigh, Ernie Bolt, Harrison Daniel, and Robert Hohner also made discerning and helpful observations about draft chapters. Sam Hill and Sandra Treadway graciously and carefully read the entire manuscript. In preparing drafts and locating information, students Katherine Slaikeu, Dionne Procell, Tonya Jordan, Mindy Manning, Trisha Whiting, Scott Butcher, Melissa Manuel, K. C. Weeks, and Nathaniel Means rendered valuable services. Centenary faculty secretaries Bettye Leslie and Kelly Schellinger contributed their substantial typing and editing skills. Nicole Mitchell, Mindy Wilson, Kathy Swain, and Jennifer Horne of the University of Alabama Press afforded steady, genial, and appreciated guidance to ensure the production of this volume. I am also grateful for the expertise of copy editor Monica Phillips.

My scholarship has been made possible by my parents, Sam and Dawn Shepherd, and by my sister, Cora Lee Hevenor, who has kept me connected to sources about Virginia Baptist history. My most profound debt is to Julienne L. Wood, who, as a spouse and as a fellow historian, has nurtured me and my project with timely suggestions, penetrating critiques, encouragement, and loving patience.

Today, approaching Richmond generally means a speedy trip over I-95 from the north or I-64 from the west or east, and a driver is likely to be preoccupied with traffic, interchanges, and distant destinations. Arriving from the south, a visitor may glance at the striking skyline of tall, new business buildings. Even tourists coming to see historic sites will find it easy to overlook many remaining signs of Richmond's past, aside from the ones carefully identified by the visitors bureau. Yet recessed close to many of the new construction sites are imprints of Richmond's heritage, including its less-acclaimed twentieth-century history. An examination of that period reveals a dynamic community whose white Protestant leaders made their city a religious center and created a distinctively urban religious culture.

Avenues of Faith

I

The Urban Challenge

Dotting the landscape of modern Richmond, Virginia, venerable churches stand as monuments to the city's past. Less conspicuous than the numerous Civil War statues, these gentle edifices make an equally emphatic claim on the city's heritage and reflect a significant, continuing stream of community and regional culture. Yet only two Richmond churches have consistently gained historical attention. On Church Hill, in the heart of old Richmond, St. John's Episcopal Church is famous for its Revolutionary War era meetings. Near the grounds of Virginia's Capitol, St. Paul's Episcopal Church is renowned as the religious home to Confederate leaders, including Robert E. Lee and Jefferson Davis. St. John's and St. Paul's have sustained an important presence in the community in the twentieth century. Elsewhere downtown on a Sunday morning, a person may still worship in the historic buildings of Leigh Street Baptist, Second Presbyterian, and Centenary Methodist. Atop Oregon Hill farther west, Pine Street Baptist and stunningly beautiful St. Andrew's Episcopal Church stand as testimonies to vibrant working-class congregations. From Monroe Park west through the popular early-twentieth-century residential neighborhood now known as "the Fan," the contemporary faithful continue to worship in sanctuaries built in an earlier era. At such churches as First English Evangelical Lutheran, St. James's Episcopal, Hanover Avenue Christian Church, and First Baptist, Sunday services occur with a backdrop of history. To the north, along spacious streets, once-suburban Ginter Park houses Baptist, Methodist, Presbyterian, and Disciples of Christ congregations, which emerged in the century's first decades, as well as Union Theological Seminary/ Presbyterian School of Christian Education. On Richmond's northern periphery stands Emmanuel Episcopal, once a secluded rural church tied to the city as the final stop on the streetcar line and connected by its influential parishioners, the Bryan family. Across the James River in Southside Richmond, music still ascends from the area's oldest Methodist congregation, Central Methodist. In the same vicinity, once primarily an industrial community called

Manchester, Bainbridge Street Baptist remains as a link to the early twentieth century.

These active congregations provide the most direct ties to the city's religious heritage, but a circuit of Richmond offers many more opportunities to touch the town's past by visiting its churches. The former structures of Monumental Episcopal, Third Presbyterian Church, and Trinity Methodist whisper reminders of an earlier downtown prominence. And such churches as Trinity, Seventh Street Christian, All Saints Episcopal, First Presbyterian, Grove Avenue Baptist, and Second Baptist have transported their past identities to new sites. Even churches which have merged or have changed their names remember their antecedents. For example, Reveille Methodist traces its roots to an earlier downtown Union Station Methodist Church, and River Road Methodist recalls its origins in Broad Street Methodist Church of a bygone era. The buildings of the University of Richmond carry the names of its Baptist founders.

At first glance the old names and the old structures might serve as mere reminders of a seemingly simpler, distant time with its own set of delights and defects. Richmond religious leaders of the early twentieth century would have shuddered at such a verdict. They strove to adapt religious ideas and institutions to the changing environment of their urban South as well as to make their religion accessible and relevant to the inhabitants of a growing city. It is the central argument of this book that they were impressively successful in their efforts.

Today a sprawling East Coast automotive corridor threatens to submerge Richmond into a cultural landscape increasingly indistinguishable from Boston to Miami. Modern travelers arrive in Richmond after swift journeys over intricate networks of interstate highways or after rapid jet airline flights. Before penetrating to the heart of Richmond, drivers wind their way through thickets of burgeoning suburbs, with their familiar appearance and their even more familiar fast-food chains, convenience stores, and shopping malls.

By contrast, early-twentieth-century Richmond existed as an urban enclave in a rural state. After a lengthy railroad ride, some travelers entered the city at the new downtown Main Street Station. That location placed them near factories sprinkled along the nearby James River and between Church Hill to the east and Capitol Hill to the west, two residential centers steadily surrendering space to office buildings and retail stores. Country kinfolk drove their horses and wagons to the city. Local residents could reach most destinations on foot. Streetcars provided transportation to working-class suburbs like Fulton to the east, to middle-class residential areas on the West End along Franklin Street or Monument Avenue, and to some factories and amusement parks to the north and west along the city's incorporated boundaries. Wealthier citizens relied on horse-drawn carriages to carry them to evening parties. But by the 1920s, many Richmonders purchased automobiles as an expanding city dispersed more of its population and as people traveled greater distances for working, shopping, and entertainment. By then cars and buses provided an increasingly popular means of access to the state capital, and boosters proudly reported that the duration of an automobile trip from Washington, D.C., to Richmond had been reduced to little more than six hours. Recalling his youth in Charleston, South Carolina, in the late 1920s and early 1930s, literary scholar Louis Rubin declared that "a trip to Richmond" "was an event to be anticipated long in advance of departure." For him, like rural lads, Richmond was a place of "enormous sophistication" and "metropolitan splendors."[1]

The city did feature a culture decidedly different from that of the nearby countryside. Most visitors from elsewhere in Virginia would have noted a collection of characteristics setting Richmond's urban environment apart from their home places. The foremost difference was the most obvious one: masses of people resided in Richmond. Unlike rural counties with their small and scattered populations, Richmond contained almost 183,000 citizens within its approximately twenty-four square miles in 1930. Richmond was the most populated jurisdiction in the Commonwealth of Virginia, and it ranked as one of the most congested cities in the United States in the early twentieth century. Richmonders, therefore, often participated in collective experiences. Individual factories and stores employed hundreds or even thousands of workers. With many apartment leases terminating on 31 August, an estimated 15,000 Richmonders changed locations simultaneously on "moving day," 1 September. To honor Confederate veterans, dough boys, or members of labor unions, parades summoned thousands of marchers and even more spectators. Local amusement parks, sports events, and the capacious movie palaces of the 1920s drew huge crowds. Groups of male mashers periodically annoyed women at streetcar stops, boy gangs engaged in rock battles, and policemen corralled clusters of suspicious characters in dragnets. Pious people also assembled in groups. With more than fourteen hundred members, Pine Street Baptist Church formed one of the largest congregations in the South in the first decade of the twentieth century. And a person did not always gain a respite from the city at worship services. During a 1911 heat wave, Fritz Sitterdig was summoned from his church to open his ice plant because a crowd of five hundred stood "clamoring for ice." Times of suffering were also times of mass experiences. Vast throngs gazed at downtown fires, and hundreds perished in the

Spanish flu epidemic of 1918. Whether in work, play, joy, or sorrow, Richmonders had many human companions as they dwelled in a crowded urban environment.[2]

Richmond further differed from the countryside by harboring a variety of people, pleasures, institutions, and ideas. If Richmond's ethnic population was small compared to other major American cities, it was large compared to Virginia's rural counties. With a lengthy local heritage, members of the city's German-American community maintained a German-American Club, rose to prominence as business and political leaders, contributed to the city's musical life with the singing group Gesang-Verein Virginia, and worshiped—at times in German—in Lutheran, Catholic, and Jewish congregations. The city's Irish contingent remained large enough to guarantee festive St. Patrick's Days, and wealthy businessman Maj. James Dooley furnished a striking symbol of success with his extravagant Victorian mansion, "Maymont." When Richmond's Italian population climbed to almost three thousand, the Italian government assigned a consul to the city. Active in local politics, the Italian-Americans ensured the erection of a monument to Christopher Columbus, unveiled in 1927. Holding a near monopoly on shoeshine stands, Greeks disconcerted patrons when they closed their businesses to observe Easter according to the Orthodox Church calendar. A stroll on a Richmond street could lead past a Chinese laundry or to Paul Yurachek's shop on East Main Street, where this naturalized Slovakian sold his wire goods and lamp shades. Yurachek was not lonely. According to one estimate, more than 750 Czechoslovakians lived in the Richmond area, and Venable Street Baptist Church hosted a "Czecho-Slovak National Convention" in 1921. In soliciting financial support, a prominent private children's nursery proclaimed itself to be a "thoroughly cosmopolitan" institution where "Poles, Germans, Italians, French, English, Russian, and American babies can be seen every day lying side by side."[3]

The city's heterogeneity extended to its religious institutions. To be sure, evangelical Protestant churches so dominated the community that they collectively created an overarching religious culture. Southern Baptists, Methodists, Episcopalians, Presbyterians, Disciples of Christ, and Lutherans shared many religious ideas and often collaborated in religious activities. Still, the 1926 U.S. *Census of Religious Bodies* reported more than ten thousand Roman Catholics and approximately eight thousand Jews in Richmond. A single, large Greek Orthodox Church and a single, small Unitarian church occupied important places in Richmond. Quakers, Seventh Day Adventists, Christian Scientists, Mormons, Christadelphians, the Church of the Brethren, and several holiness churches provided religious options. The religious diversity touched individual lives. Young Louise Price regularly attended Episcopal services throughout the city but accompanied friends to churches of other denominations. Recording her observations in a diary, she marveled about attending a double wedding conducted in German at a "very pretty" Lutheran church. On the other hand, she seemed disconcerted by a High Mass at the new Roman Catholic cathedral and labeled the service "funny doings."[4]

The city fostered a variety of worldviews, including ideas that challenged religious beliefs. As a lecturer at the Medical College of Virginia, city coroner William Taylor repeatedly offered his personal counterpoint to religious ideas. Annually discounting the existence of the soul, he denounced the Bible as the "enigmatical statements of a book written in a semi-civilized age, at uncertain periods, by unascertainable authors in tongues unintelligible to the vast majority of living men." He added that its "interpretation by the few who can claim to understand it . . . is often in the most vital parts, irrevocably discordant and contradictory." Anyone searching for unconventional ideas or scientific knowledge could count on the faculty of the city's colleges and medical schools and could turn to the city's daily press for up-to-date information. Seeking variety in pleasures, a visitor had choices of entertainment ranging from polite restaurants to rowdy saloons, from billiard parlors to baseball games, from vaudeville or movies to operas or symphony concerts. The urban environment of Richmond was an arena of diversity.[5]

Streams of overhead wires attached to poles flowed throughout the city, calling attention to the fact that Richmond, like other urban areas, was a powerhouse of machinery and technology. The city was laced with miles of electric streetcar lines. Other innovations which were at first primarily tools of businesses soon found their way into households. In 1900 Richmond had only 2,000 telephones in service, but by the mid-1920s, residents had grown so accustomed to using their telephones that they made more than 250,000 telephone calls daily. Whereas less than 5 percent of Virginia farmhouses had gas or electricity, most Richmond houses used electricity. Electricity also powered thousands of city streetlights and local factories. Though most famous for its tobacco plants, Richmond was an industrial city containing iron, locomotive, stove, flour, chemical, paper, and furniture factories. Filled with machinery, some individual industries boasted of their technological prowess. One stationery firm ballyhooed its ability to print 12,000 envelopes an hour and its "unique" automatic ruler, which ruled paper on both sides, in four colors, and "crosswise at one operation." With mechanization a local bakery produced 30,000 loaves of bread daily. For thrills, people rode a roller coaster at a local amusement park. The technology of the late 1920s drew Richmond closer to the outside world. The city opened an airport and became one of the first communities in the country to have a Dow-Jones ticker. Richmond also became the home of two radio stations, including WRVA, which soon joined the National Broadcasting Corporation. Technology did not always yield attractive results. When horns and signaling devices became required equipment on cars, one commentator deplored the results. "Every variety of siren, moan, screech, howl, and scream that mechanical ingenuity can contrive and human inconsiderateness can produce," he complained, could be "heard all over the city at all hours of the day and night." Indeed, in the city the signs of technology were omnipresent.[6]

In contrast to the rural South's poverty, twentieth-century Richmond prospered. Richmond ranked among the nation's leading cities in per capita wealth and reported per capita real estate and property values that were twice the average for the state. The city's selection as the site for a Federal Reserve District Bank in 1914 strengthened its already substantial constellation of banking firms. The chamber of commerce boasted that local banks held 140,000 savings accounts. In 1924 almost one-fourth of all Virginia income tax returns paid into the federal treasury came from metropolitan Richmond. Chicago's Dartnell Corporation estimated the metropolitan area's buying power to be more than twice the average for the entire state. And Richmond citizens could spend their money to enjoy the goods offered by the many local retail firms. A shopper could purchase merchandise at downtown stores offering their specialties: clothing, stationery, furniture, musical instruments, jewelry, confections, cigars, coffee, trunks, shoes, groceries, china, bicycles, and carriages. By the 1920s the city's two major department stores, Thalhimers and Miller & Rhoads, became favored shopping spots, with Miller & Rhoads arranging 361,980 square feet of floor space to display its wide variety of wares. In explaining the significance of department stores for cities, Alan Trachtenberg refers to them as "lavishly designed palaces of consumption," and Gunther Barth argues that in many ways they "reflected the culture of the modern city." Even Richmond's poorest residents played Victrolas and visited movie houses. The city's many hospitals supplied medical care, and Richmond's ratio of doctors and dentists to the population was one of the best in the South. The community's wealth was, of course, not evenly distributed. Elegant West End mansions stood in contrast to rickety hovels along Bragg Street, Shockoe Valley, or Locust Alley. Still, unlike Virginia's rural areas, Richmond's wealth was substantial, visible, and sufficiently accessible to offer a high standard of living for city residents.[7]

Richmonders, unlike many other Virginians, relied on an active local government to provide services which enhanced their lives. By the late nineteenth century, America's largest cities, argues urban historian Jon Teaford, achieved an "unheralded triumph" as their governments supplied the costly services required to meet their growing needs. From the city dock to Oakwood Cemetery, Richmond's government faced a range of demands and duties. During one year, officials proudly cited the planting of more than four thousand trees in the community. Law enforcement, fire protection, public education, poor relief, public health, and city parks formed major items on the agenda of the city's government. And citizens expected delivery of such services. Between 1898 and 1901, according to one scholar of Richmond's city government, "many miles of sidewalk, sewer, and street had been laid, yet there were still complaints." In 1905, as the owner of the local gasworks, the city had to appropriate a large sum to upgrade it, and in 1924 the city began operating a new water filtration plant which cost half a million dollars. As Richmond added territory and population, the demands and costs of city government soared. A city budget of $1.6 million in 1900 climbed to more than $8 million in 1929, and the city's bonded debt skyrocketed. Richmond offered its children longer school terms, provided white teachers with higher salaries, and paid more per capita for education than did all but two Virginia counties. Whether as the beneficiaries of clean water, attractive parks, good schools, or municipal jobs, Richmonders regularly relied on local government in a way uncommon in rural areas.[8]

As a city, Richmond also fostered specialization and organization. The city's mass demands created the financial opportunities for specializations of jobs and products. Architects, bacteriologists, certified public accountants, interior decorators, and private detectives stayed busy. So, too, did an advertiser whose primary talent was developing window displays. Twentieth-century demands for stenographers, typists, nurses, and social workers added to the ranks of those with specialized training and enhanced the importance of local business schools and a new school of social work and public health. Urban citizens also patronized businesses supplying specific services ranging from dry cleaning to automobile batteries. One Richmond firm devoted itself to producing ice cream dishes and ice cream spoons. Organizations, like specializations, proliferated in Richmond. Labor unions, fraternal societies, civic organizations, ethnic associations, country clubs, the Woman's Club, and church groups reflected a community in which formal structuring, not informal gatherings, paid social dividends, just as local factories, stores, and government agencies created an organized working world.[9]

A Virginian leaving Richmond would travel some distance before reaching another major urban area. The state's second largest city, Norfolk, was situated more than one hundred miles to the southeast across the James River, where it flowed into the Chesapeake Bay. With an overland trip of more than one hundred miles, a person who headed north could reach Washington, D.C. After a westward journey through the Piedmont, a traveler would climb the Blue Ridge mountains and enter the Shenandoah Valley. Only the towns of Lynchburg and Roanoke interrupted an otherwise relentlessly rural trek. To the south of Richmond lay tobacco country. Aside from mill towns, no concentrations of populations existed between Richmond and Atlanta to the southwest or between Richmond and Charleston to the south.

Like Richmond, the South's other major cities developed an urban culture that set them apart from their rural counterparts, and the differing lifestyles provoked critics and earned champions. In *I'll Take My Stand,* the celebrated 1930 collection of essays defending a traditional South, one author, John Crowe Ransom, repudiated the urban South, "with its heavy importation of regular American ways and regular American citizens." A horrified Ransom correctly associated wealth, industry, ambition, "the gospel of Progress," and "the gospel of Service" with southern cities. On the other hand, George and Broadus Mitchell, scholars with Richmond roots, celebrated urban conditions. In *The Industrial Revolution in the South,* they declared that "cities mean variety of work, keenness of competition, sharpening of wits, relief in amusements. . . . They have left behind the headless, slimy ponds of the back country." Comparing data in *Rural and Urban Living Standards in Virginia,* two sociologists avoided taking sides but agreed that "rural and urban life in many ways are fundamentally different."[10]

Yet anyone wishing to generalize about southern cities of the late nineteenth and early twentieth centuries faces a bedeviling task. Differences in the economies, the sizes, the geographies, and the cultural backgrounds of southern cities, observes urban historian Blaine Brownell, "precluded the existence of a 'solid' urban South. In some ways Birmingham more closely resembled Youngstown, Ohio than New Orleans in the early twentieth century." For all the talk about a single New South, southern cities presented an assortment of images to the rest of the nation. Atlanta's vigorous commercial boosters, Charleston's tradition-bound patricians, Birmingham's innovative coal and iron barons, Richmond's established tobacco manufacturers, Houston's young oil boomers, Nashville's wholesalers and academicians, and New Orleans's Creoles and jazzmen reflected distinctive community cultures.[11]

These dissimilarities notwithstanding, southern cities shared a key characteristic: growth. The period between 1880 and 1920 brought impressive population gains to most major southern cities. Despite the handicap of an antebellum economy dedicated to rural agriculture, in the twentieth century the South began to urbanize at a rate matching other parts of the country. In doing so the South began to overcome a historic tendency to "lag" behind the rest of the nation in the urbanization process. To be sure, not all southern cities were dynamic. As Don Doyle has documented, Charleston and Mobile lacked city leaders with energy and enthusiasm for change, and those cities languished. More often, though, southern cities flourished and displayed an urban environment distinct from rural cadences.[12]

In a sweeping classic, *The Mind of the South,* W. J. Cash observed that in the early twentieth century, "new churches were building in Dixie almost as fast as new factories." But those churches have gained only limited attention from historians. Despite an outpouring of scholarship about southern religion in recent decades, the region's urban religious setting has remained largely unmapped. In a 1967 essay, Samuel S. Hill cited the South's urban religious experiences in an agenda of essential research awaiting historians. In 1977 historians Blaine Brownell and David Goldfield called upon historians to study the role of churches in the South's "urbanization process." Only to a limited extent has that call been heeded. Writing about the antebellum South, E. Brooks Holifield depicted cities and towns as centers of religion. In a history of Nashville, Don Doyle incorporated accounts of the activities of religious groups. Wayne Flynt recounted the social activism of some Birmingham church leaders in the early twentieth century. In a richly informative book, Elizabeth Hayes Turner detailed the manifold reform activities of religious women of Galveston, Texas. Still, no larger portrayal exists of the multifaceted ideas and deeds of religious leaders and institutions in the South's major urban arenas in the twentieth century. That omission is a serious one because organized religion thrived in the urban South in the early twentieth century.[13]

The success of southern urban religion was notable in a nation in which religious leaders expressed fears about the ability of churches to address urban conditions during the century's first three decades. In a famous 1907 volume, minister Josiah Strong cataloged urban problems and admonished that "the city is the challenge to the Church today, and we have a generation instead of a century in which to meet it." Others joined Strong in his conviction that growing American cities constituted a special challenge to organized religion. The physical expansion of American cities seemed to dwarf their religious institutions and to imply a decline in their significance. By the early 1930s, a writer for the President's Research Committee on Recent Social Trends reported that had an American returned to this country after an absence of twenty years, he would perceive that "in our great cities at least, church buildings now appear trivial and unimportant in contrast with the enormous skyscrapers of commerce and finance."[14]

Richmond's white Protestants also expressed apprehensions about the prospects for religious institutions in their own growing, industrial city. In 1901 the editor of the *Central Presbyterian* noted that a "new and vigorous life has come to the city of Richmond. Its industries have grown, its commercial life has expanded, and its population has become more varied and heterogeneous." Still, other changes seemed to threaten the city's spiritual welfare. A few years later the same religious newspaper declared that churches had difficulty gaining the attention of people in the city, where "there is rush, absorption in work and gain and the pursuit of pleasure," not to mention a multiplication of "temptations and vices." One Episcopalian fretted that on Sundays young people now slept late, missed church, and treated the Sabbath as a day for amusement and recreation. City Baptists repeatedly expressed anxiety about their ability to create an effective urban ministry. In 1900 a local laywoman maintained that Baptists constituted a declining proportion of the city population because they were preoccupied with their individual congregations, exhibited a "low state of religion," and had given up "all systematic endeavor" to engage in activities reaching out to the general community. A Baptist minister cited past denominational successes in poorer, rural areas but asked, "Have we a gospel with which we can go up to the great business, social, industrial, and educational centers and make them become servants of our king? The city is weighing us in the balances. Shall we be found wanting?" In a 1912 statement, the Baptist Council of Richmond tried to alert their rural associates to the need for focusing special attention on urban areas. The council warned that "unless churches are vigilant, active, [and] aggressive" and "unless they keep their grip upon the growing city, ere long the city, like a child improperly controlled, will be far beyond the influence of the churches." Only somewhat jokingly, a Methodist minister and editor admitted that "there are many things about city life I just can't work out, for I was raised in the country and haven't gotten over it." If not constantly perplexed by urban behavior, Richmond's Protestant leaders did worry about the ability of their denominations to respond to the city's changing population and lifestyle.[15]

In addressing the contemporary challenges posed by urban conditions, Richmond Protestants built on a firm foundation which existed in 1900. Most of Richmond's white church members belonged to one of six major Protestant denominations. Southern Baptists and Methodists boasted the largest church memberships in Richmond, as they did elsewhere throughout the South. Episcopalians, Presbyterians, the Disciples of Christ, and Lutherans ranked behind the larger white Protestant denominations. These six groups collectively dominated white religious life in Richmond. Leaders of these groups frequently interacted and to some extent engaged in a form of cultural self-definition by their membership in the Richmond Ministerial Union. The city was the home of five statewide denominational weekly newspapers. Presbyterians and Methodists maintained publishing houses there, Southern Baptists directed their Foreign Mission Board, and Episcopalians maintained the headquarters of the Diocese of Virginia. The Methodist Virginia Conference Orphanage and three denominational homes for women constituted important traditional charitable institutions. The city had the potential to serve as a center of religious education. Baptists supported Richmond College and the Woman's College of Richmond, and Presbyterians celebrated the recent shift of their Union Theological Seminary from Hampden-Sydney, Virginia, to Richmond's Ginter Park suburb. At nearby Ashland, Methodists offered higher education at Randolph-Macon College.

In early-twentieth-century Richmond, Protestants created an urban religious culture notable for seven characteristics that serve as interpretive themes for this book. These characteristics constituted avenues of faith which Richmond Protestants traveled as they related their religion to their community. First, they and their city fostered religious diversity. Although Baptists, Methodists, Episcopalians, Presbyterians, Disciples of Christ, and Lutherans identified themselves as evangelicals and held much in common, they differed among themselves and within their own denominations over matters ranging from theology to public policy. Second, despite such differences, church leaders promoted interdenominational cooperation and participated in an impressive array of interdenominational activities. Third, as urban conditions multiplied the demands made on ministers, churches developed specialized facilities and specialized roles for leaders, a change which opened positions of leadership to women. Fourth, city Protestants depended on careful planning and organization. That systematic work brought visible results in evangelism as Protestants substantially increased the number of churches and church members and made the city a religious stronghold. Fifth, although congregations counted on clergymen to provide leadership, laywomen and laymen assumed significant responsibilities as well. Sixth, faced with changing urban conditions, church leaders adapted old practices, adopted innovations, and expanded the scope of their religious endeavors. Seventh, to deal with urban problems and to confront injustices, clergymen and laypersons practiced as well as preached social Christianity. As points of departure for each of these avenues of faith, Protestants relied on individual religious commitment and corporate worship.

Using a topical format, subsequent chapters will examine the ideas, the actions, the major leaders, and the institutions of Richmond's white Protestant community of the early twentieth century. Chapter 2 depicts and analyzes Richmond's often dynamic urban environment. Adapting to a changing community, congregations and pastors modified some of their patterns of worship, as chapter 3 explains. Chapter 4 identifies methods and mechanisms of urban evangelism and explores the reasons for their success. Chapter 5 considers efforts to sustain traditional religious practices deemed vital to individual and collective spiritual well-being. When saloon liquor, civic corruption, and sexual immorality seemed to imperil the community's moral welfare, church leaders tried to disarm such dangers, as chapter 6 details. Believing that "the kingdom of God" called for attention to temporal needs as well as to eternal salvation, Richmond clergymen and laypersons embraced social Christianity. With words, deeds, and programs, these religious leaders transformed Richmond and Virginia in important ways, as chapters 7 and 8 document. Yet calls for social justice had limits. As chapter 9 reveals, Richmond white Protestants only partially accepted Jews, Catholics, and African Americans. Chapter 10 details the Protestant community's expanding concerns about international conditions as well as its struggle to deal with World War I and its implications. Chapter 11 recounts the roles of prominent Richmond Protestant leaders in the fundamentalist controversy of the 1920s and assesses why Fundamentalism failed in Richmond.

To tell this substantial story it has been necessary to limit this book's focus to the city's major mainline white Protestant denominations: Southern Baptists, Methodists, Presbyterians, Episcopalians, Disciples of Christ, and Lutherans. Collectively constituting the largest religious affiliations, sharing many theological views, and often collaborating in activities, they also engaged in forms of self-definition by their formation and membership in such local organizations as the Richmond Ministerial Union. These mainline denominations so dominated the city's religious landscape that other white Protestant churches, including holiness, Pentecostal, and independent congregations, accounted for fewer than a score of congregations and only a few hundred members in the late 1920s. The choice of these major denominational groups thus seemed appropriate as well as necessary. Still, it is important to understand that a significant number of white Richmonders affirmed other religious beliefs. For example, Roman Catholics outnumbered Episcopalians; Jews outnumbered Presbyterians. This book devotes only limited attention to these groups, largely considering their relationships to city Protestants. Likewise, this book does not attempt to address the rich religious culture of Richmond's African Americans. All of these groups correctly claim important places in Richmond's religious heritage, and in some cases historians have already written excellent accounts of those experiences.[16]

In the late afternoon of 25 May 1929, mourners assembled in downtown Richmond for the funeral of H. D. C. Maclachlan, pastor of Seventh Street Christian Church. Pallbearers from the congregation transported the casket between two lines of honorary pallbearers. At the head of the latter group were Rabbi Edward N. Calisch of Temple Beth Ahabah and the Very Reverend Felix F. Kaup, vicar general of the Roman Catholic Diocese of Richmond. In addition to Maclachlan's fellow Disciples of Christ ministers, prominent Baptist, Methodist, Presbyterian, Episcopal, Lutheran, and Unitarian clergymen attended. The presidents of the Baptist University of Richmond and the Methodist Randolph-Macon College led a group of educators including professors from the University of Richmond and the director of a local Episcopal boys school. The rector of St. Paul's Episcopal Church delivered the eulogy and characterized Maclachlan as a "man of rare culture and an eloquent preacher," as well as a "prophet of social righteousness" whose "ministry overflowed into the life of the community." Echoing that testimonial, an obituary concluded that "his Christian work in the field made him Richmond's pastor as well as the Seventh-Street Church's pastor." A local newspaper editorialized that it would "be difficult to find a successor to one who has meant so much" to Richmond and Virginia as well as to his church and family.[17]

During his twenty-one-year ministry, Hugh David Cathcart Maclachlan had indeed left his imprint on Richmond. Born in Scotland in 1869, he had earned a master's degree at the University of Glasgow before coming to the United States at the age of twenty-four. After several years as a Texas cowboy and as a journalist, Maclachlan studied at Transylvania College and the University of Chicago and then was ordained and married in 1904. Following a brief tenure at a Shelbyville, Kentucky, church, he accepted the pastorate at Seventh Street Christian. During his first ten months in Richmond, he delivered eighty-two sermons, presented twelve addresses to other groups, and made 560 personal visits. Under his leadership his congregation grew in size, embraced innovations, became "famous for its hospitality to ministers of other denominations," and acted as a center for city social service activities. As another writer noted, Maclachlan always had "time for warm friendship, and for wise counsel with the hundreds who brought him their problems." As a denominational leader, he served as president of the Virginia Christian Missionary Society, delivered a lecture series at the University of Chicago, and published articles in the *Christian Century*.[18]

Yet Richmond remembered Maclachlan because "he was forever preaching active Christianity as against the Christianity of traditional ceremonies and hollow forms." He played major roles in the creation of the city and state juvenile court systems as well as in the founding of the Richmond School of Social Work and Public Health. Celebrated for his breadth of knowledge, his skill as a conversationalist, "his enthusiasm, his tact, and his command of logic," Maclachlan brought together three hundred Protestants, Catholics, and

Jews for a goodwill dinner in 1928. Disturbed by the apparent intolerance of some fundamentalists of the 1920s, he deplored those who "would burn a man at the stake for questioning their theological creed, yet who in their daily lives prove themselves guilty of the worst heresy of all—the heresy of narrow, unsympathetic self-seeking behavior." Often preaching about social justice, Maclachlan signed the 1927 "Appeal to the Industrial Leaders of the South" and supported U.S. participation in the international peace movement after World War I.[19]

The year that Maclachlan died, 1929, signaled the beginning of the Great Depression and thus has served to mark the end of a period in national history. In a different sense, 1929 also signified the end of an era for Richmond Protestants. During the late 1920s, other prominent local religious leaders died, retired or left the area after notable careers in the community. The Richmond that all of these people left was vastly different from what it had been when they arrived and so, too, were the city's religious organizations. In a March 1927 sermon, Maclachlan had urged his congregation to be alert to "those new sermons on the Mount," which Jesus taught in every age, as well as to "those quiet whisperings of his love as he walks and talks with us even in the crowded thoroughfares of our twentieth-century cities." Maclachlan embodied that vision. To meet the challenge of the twentieth-century city, other Richmond Protestants joined him in recasting traditions, revitalizing forms of worship, launching new denominational endeavors, initiating civic programs, embracing new ideas, and expanding their definitions of what it meant to be a clergyman or layperson. In doing so, they created new avenues of faith in their historic southern city.[20]

2

Restless Richmond

In 1900 a Richmond journalist lamented the loss of the city's minor league baseball team and traced the cause to falling attendance during the previous three years. "The fact is," he explained, "that people are too busy to lose one or two afternoons a week, even to devote themselves to the exhilaration that comes with a good game of ball." "There is," he added, "too much business going on to allow time to go to a ball game." In 1913 an editorial writer rendered another assessment of the city: "All in all, Richmond is in the exact condition of an old town suddenly growing very vast. Many things demand improvement." Taken together the two commentaries revealed the direction of early-twentieth-century Richmond. The community achieved three decades of steady economic growth and counted a population in 1930 that was more than double the number tallied in 1900. With this success came problems energetic reformers tried to remedy. Though not always agreeing about solutions, these Richmond progressives did fan a progressive breeze that reshaped a city better known for its history.[1]

In the early twentieth century, a visitor to Richmond could have easily concluded that the city was still preoccupied with its past. Richmond surrounded guests with vestiges of bygone days. Located at the falls of the James River, the city's hilly terrain perpetuated clusters of compact neighborhoods where old houses and public buildings became sources of local pride. The Masonic Hall dated to 1785. Based on designs submitted by Thomas Jefferson, the state capitol had been completed in 1796. In the twentieth century, preservationists protected the home of U.S. Supreme Court Chief Justice John Marshall, probably antebellum Richmond's most esteemed resident. Believed to be one of the city's oldest buildings, "the Old Stone House" was converted into a museum for Edgar Allan Poe, who had grown up in Richmond. From the capitol grounds, with its statues of George Washington and Henry Clay, visitors could travel to the city's younger West End, where Monument Avenue and Hollywood Cemetery provided striking reminders of the Confederacy. To visit Richmond was to enter a landscape laden with heroic images of the past.[2]

Yet Richmond reckoned with a more complex history that revolved around its role as a center of trade, government, and industry. In the 1640s English colonists built a fort near the falls of the James River. In the 1670s William Byrd I established a trading post, and William Byrd II created the town of Richmond, incorporated in 1742. During the American Revolution, a prudent Virginia assembly shifted the state capital to Richmond from the more militarily vulnerable Williamsburg. Functioning both as a seat of government and as a military storehouse, Richmond thrived.[3]

After the Revolution, Richmond began a process of erratic but substantial economic growth. By the 1830s transportation improvements placed Richmond in a position of regional commercial dominance. Arriving shipments of tobacco, iron ore, and wheat fueled Richmond's growing industries. With fifty cigar and tobacco factories in 1860, Richmond manufactured more tobacco than any other city in the world. The most prominent of the city's seven flour mills, the Gallego mill was the second largest in the world. Tredegar Iron and Belle Isle formed the foundation for the city's iron industry and contributed to a diversified manufacturing sector. German and Irish immigrants, as well as free people of color, comprised a significant portion of the population, as did slaves, who provided an important source of skilled and unskilled labor. Richmond's educational institutions included more than a score of private schools, Richmond College, the Medical College of Virginia, and the Richmond Female Institute. In 1860 four newspapers were published in the city, as was the *Southern Literary Messenger.*[4]

The Civil War earned Richmond a permanent place in American history but did so at the cost of chaos, carnage, and economic catastrophe. As the Confederate capital, Richmond saw its population swollen with strangers—rowdy regiments from the Deep South, refugees from Union-controlled territory, Confederate officials and civil servants, Union prisoners, wounded soldiers, prostitutes, gamblers, and criminals. Overwhelmed municipal officials struggled to provide adequate city services. Shortages of food, housing, and medical supplies plagued the community, leading to privation for many and inflation for all. Doctors ministered to suffering at the fifty city hospitals, and battles produced avalanches of corpses. The climactic tragedy occurred 3 April 1865, when retreating Confederate soldiers ignored the protests of the city's mayor and ignited the stocks of tobacco in city warehouses. A strong wind spread the fire throughout the downtown, destroying an estimated nine-tenths of the business district and more than nine hundred buildings. Arriving Union troops finally brought the fire under control, but it left a stark scene of charred rubble.[5]

During the next three decades, Richmond failed to regain its antebellum economic vitality. With damage extending beyond the "Burnt District," the city's wartime casualties included banks, factories, shops, government buildings, restaurants, residences, railroad depots, and bridges. Visitors noted a lingering mood of gloom. As late as 1900, a Richmond girl told a national writer that Civil War memorabilia represented "tears, desolate homes, and poverty . . . deep, lasting poverty." But as historian Michael Chesson has concluded, the greatest problem lay with the city's business and political leaders. Conservative politicians focused their energies on combating aspiring political and social groups, including African Americans. With deteriorating transportation facilities, Richmond began to lose its regional commercial dominance. The city languished as a rail center, and its industries did not keep pace with new competitors in other cities.[6]

Meanwhile, Civil War memories enshrouded Richmond. The crucible of war had bonded Richmond with the Confederacy. In the striking imagery of scholar Emory Thomas, "the city had prayed with Jackson, danced with Stuart, and sought to emulate the nobility of Lee. Spiritually, most of all, Richmond and the Confederacy were one." But Richmond's ties were often sadder. During the 1860s dying Confederates began to stake their enduring claims on the city's landscape. Between May and August of 1862, thousands of corpses had arrived from the nearby battlefields of the Peninsula Campaign. One Richmond woman later recalled the daily "wailing dirge of military bands preceding a soldier's funeral." In peacetime more funerals followed the familiar paths between churches and cemeteries. Somber crowds gathered to watch regiments of Confederate veterans march in processions for former comrades, including the first of the dead recovered from Gettysburg for reinterment in Hollywood Cemetery. The burials of former Confederate generals drew huge crowds, but no other moment matched the 1893 funeral for former Confederate President Jefferson Davis.[7]

Like the funerals, Memorial Days became important to Richmonders. Each May after 1865, thousands of people walked to cemeteries located throughout the city and decorated the graves of former Confederates. The major destinations were Oakwood Cemetery, which eventually held the remains of approximately 16,000 Confederates, and Hollywood Cemetery, which held more than 18,000. Beginning with Gen. Jeb Stuart's burial in 1864, Hollywood gained the distinction as the final resting place of famous Confederates, including Jefferson Davis and twenty-two Civil War generals. With the recurrent cycle of funerals and Memorial Days, grieving for loved ones and grieving for the Confederacy seemed inseparable. Reminiscing about childhood in Richmond of the 1890s, an Episcopal rector recalled how his grandmother had revered her Civil War veteran husband. His memory and "the memory of everything he represented became the sovereign fact" in her life. "To her, as to many in Richmond, the past was sacred. . . . To decorate the graves of the Confederate dead in Hollywood on memorial days, and to preserve the inherited traditions like flames burning on an altar, was a continuing religion." The sense of loss extended beyond widows, children, and siblings. As newspaperman Douglas Southall Freeman discerned, the war had killed young men who would have otherwise married a generation of young women. In the 1920s Freeman depicted "Mother Virginia" as still recovering from the mourning process. Women as well as men were mourned. In 1916, when nurse-heroine Capt. Sally Tompkins died, a local newspaper cited her as an example of women who "gave their all to the Confederacy" and whose "memories will remain forever enshrined among the holiest memories of a day that is gone."[8]

Some "Lost Cause" commemorations took on an almost festive air. Richmond hosted huge crowds for the unveiling of Civil War monuments. The 1875 extravaganza for the Stonewall Jackson monument was followed by others for monuments to Robert E. Lee, Jefferson Davis, and Jeb Stuart. In 1898, 1907, 1915, and 1922, thousands of members of the United Confederate Veterans came to Richmond for weeklong national conventions. They paraded in their uniforms and swapped stories about the war. A number of veterans assumed prominent social and political positions and wrote books and essays celebrating southern wartime heroism. Joseph Bryan, an industrialist and owner of the *Richmond Times-Dispatch* had served under cavalry leader Col. John Singleton Mosby. In the words of his son, he made the Bryan home "a bivouac for survivors of that famous command," and his newspaper featured the series "Our Confederate Column."[9]

By the early twentieth century, Richmond had begun to resemble a shrine to the Confederacy. In addition to cemeteries, statues, and nearby battlefields, guests could visit the former "White House" of the Confederacy and, after 1921, the Confederate Memorial Institute, Battle Abbey. A trip to Richmond could become a sort of pilgrimage to the "holy city" of the Confederacy. Indeed, the Lost Cause observances constituted behavior which historian Charles Reagan Wilson has identified as a form of "civil religion." Religious language was invoked to justify the war and explain its meaning. Joseph Bryan's *Times-Dispatch* firmly declared that "we have never doubted the righteousness of the Confederate cause any more than we have doubted the Christian religion." Even though publisher Bryan was a New South industrialist, he was buried in his Confederate uniform in 1907. Indeed, with columns of veterans, funerals for former Confederates were religious rituals. Memorial activities crossed religious boundaries. In May 1903 the pastor of First Baptist Church conducted services in Hebrew Cemetery, the choir of Temple Beth

Ahabah sang, and city dignitaries attended in large numbers. Hollywood Cemetery, with its many dead, became a sacred place of the Confederacy, as did St. Paul's Episcopal Church, where Robert E. Lee and Jefferson Davis had worshiped. In the 1890s St. Paul's memorialized both men with windows of Tiffany glass. Alluding to Lee's loyalty to the South, the Lee window portrayed Moses leaving Pharaoh's court and included an inscription from Exodus. The Davis window depicted Paul standing before Herod Agrippa II and also quoted scripture: "This man doeth nothing worthy of death or of bonds." Certain southern heroes were elevated to a status approaching sainthood. Robert E. Lee's birthday evoked religious discourses about his model character. According to recent scholars, such groups as the United Daughters of the Confederacy exerted pressure to ensure that only a southern interpretation of the Civil War was presented in schools, thereby transmitting a type of civil doctrine to succeeding generations. By 1929 only thirty Confederate veterans assembled for Memorial Day services, but the *Richmond News Leader* continued to remind readers that the dead "were in a very special sacred sense, the defenders of the city."[10]

Still, it would be easy to overstate the impact and oversimplify the meaning of Lost Cause occasions for twentieth-century Richmond. If united in affection for the Confederacy, different Richmond groups held a variety of goals, ranging from mourning to socializing to educating. Personal differences among leaders and disputes between organizations interrupted some commemorative plans. At times leaders had to overcome the community's seeming apathy and inability to raise funds. A secular, not a religious, pulse pounded at some veterans' encampments, not to mention at political rallies and at business meetings where shrewd entrepreneurs decided to wrap their products in Confederate images.[11]

The passing of generations eventually weakened ties to bygone days. Young Richmonders did not always view the southern cause with the same reverence as had their parents. Writer James Branch Cabell later described his childhood reaction to adults who romanticized the Confederacy: "It was confusing, the way in which your elders talked about things which no great while before you were born had happened in Richmond.—Because you lived in Richmond and Richmond was not like Camelot. Richmond was a modern city with sidewalks and plumbing and gas lights and horsecars." Furthermore, the ranks of the city's older citizens steadily diminished, as each Confederate reunion revealed. Indeed, as novelist Ellen Glasgow observed, before World War I the "lament for the dead was already succeeded by the regimental bands of the living." In 1907 a delighted journalist estimated that the Confederate reunion drew approximately 80,000 visitors and calculated that each spent an average of fifty-five dollars. Richmond boosters used the 1915 United Confederate Veterans reunion to celebrate local progress as much as southern history. Convention souvenir booklets and city guidebooks devoted more space to Richmond's industry and commerce than to the Civil War. The president of the Richmond chapter of the United Daughters of the Confederacy, Janet Henderson Randolph, remarked that it was well to look back, but better to look forward. She welcomed northern visitors and told them to bring their money.[12]

Indeed, Mrs. Randolph characterized Richmond in 1915 as "a strong fortress of industry, progress, culture, and wealth," and, as the owner of a paper company, she was in a position to know. The city's chamber of commerce proclaimed that "Richmond is today something besides the Old Capital of the Confederacy, the graveyard of the 'Lost Cause.'" While respecting the past, "the Richmond of today has turned aside from mourning over past glories to the winning of new worlds in trade." Other commentators provided similar refrains. In 1900 a journalist for a national magazine reported that "the commercial growth of Richmond is phenomenal. New plants for manufacturing purposes are constantly being established." Richmond newspaperman Henry Sydnor Harrison's 1911 novel *Queed* included a character who testified to changes in Richmond: "My own eyes have seen from these windows a broken town, stagnant in trade and population and rich only in memories, transform itself into the splendid thriving city you see before you. Our faces, too long turned backward, are set at last toward the future." Not everyone was pleased by the changes. In *The Sheltered Life* Ellen Glasgow conveyed the dismay of conservative residents about downtown Richmond of the 1920s. It had become a "world in which factories boomed, steam whistles blew, bad smells sprang up on the wind, and the new red touring cars buzzed through the streets."[13]

Richmond's physical changes did signal a new era. With businessmen often in the vanguard, city leaders engaged in a series of successful campaigns to annex adjacent areas. As a result, Richmond increased its incorporated jurisdiction from five and one-half square miles to twenty-four square miles. The new pieces of the city map included suburban communities to the east, north, and west, as well as the industrial town of Manchester lying to the south across the James. By 1930 the U.S. census counted 182,929 Richmonders, more than double the 85,050 tabulated in 1900. Births, annexations, and migration swelled the population. To accommodate that growth, builders constructed more than 19,000 new dwellings. Erected in 1904, the nine-story American National Bank building heralded Richmond's entry into the skyscraper age and began the process of transforming the city's skyline.[14]

Changes continued on the ground as well. In 1900 Richmond remained largely a "walking city" where many businessmen, professionals, and workers lived in proximity to their stores, offices, and factories. Horse-drawn carriages and wagons were familiar sights. With increasingly dispersed housing patterns, electric streetcars became more important forms of transportation. When the first motor vehicle arrived in 1900, no one could have imagined that 16,667 cars would be in operation in 1923. Motorists faced an eight-mile-per-hour speed limit in 1905, but motorists of the 1920s complained about a speed limit of thirty-five miles per hour. Other complaints about street noises, automobile horns, and congestion merely confirmed that Richmond had changed markedly since 1900. The dispersal of population was accompanied by a pattern often identified by urban scholars, greater specialization of space for specific purposes and functions such as retailing and wholesaling.[15]

Much of the city's bustle could be traced to economic growth. Members of Richmond's business community sometimes literally led parades for change. When the city held a weeklong street carnival in May 1900, organizers devoted the first day to a parade of floats exhibiting local products. The city began to advertise its products, and a once-moribund chamber of commerce awakened to spearhead annexation campaigns, support community improvements, and promote the area with its monthly *Richmond* magazine. In 1911 and 1912 city boosters gathered for three-day railroad trips to Virginia and North Carolina towns. In 1921 businessmen organized a "Made in Richmond" exposition to encourage local consumers to patronize hometown products. At the anniversary of the 1865 evacuation fire, the *Richmond News Leader* of 1915 provided the headline: "Smoke of Industry Rises Where Conflagration Raged."[16]

Indeed, so much smoke of industry rose that residents and visitors remarked about it. And Richmond's economic growth was driven by a revival of industry and commerce. For 1900 the city and its soon-to-be annexed neighbor, Manchester, reported a combined $30,646,808 of manufactured goods. In 1929 the metropolitan Richmond area reported $234,619,094 of industrial production. A 1906 newspaper article proclaimed that "tobacco is king." During the next decades, tobacco continued its reign but changed some of its raiment and shared some of its economic authority. In the late nineteenth century, Richmond's tobacco ascendancy had been challenged by North Carolina competitors. The scores of locally owned tobacco factories gradually became part of national corporations such as American Tobacco Company, American Cigar Company, P. Lorillard, Liggett and Myers, and Philip Morris. Still, tobacco played an imposing role in Richmond's industrial order. Producing chewing tobacco, pipe tobacco, cigars, cheroots, and cigarettes, Richmond factories at times accounted for as much as one-quarter of the value of the industrial goods made in the city. During the 1920s, tobacco companies expanded older plants, built new ones, and hired more hands.[17]

A 1912 article in *Harper's Weekly* reported, "So diverse are the manufactures of Richmond that the city is saved from those periods of depression that invariably come to a community that is dominated by a single industry." Indeed, Richmond's industrial success did rely on a variety of industries. With foundries, machine shops, and agricultural implements factories, the city's metal industries claimed a second place ranking to tobacco. In addition to Tredegar Iron, Old Dominion Iron and Nail, and Virginia Pipe and Foundry, Richmond housed a number of stove factories. Even after the American Locomotive Company purchased locally owned Richmond Locomotive Company, it thrived. The Virginia-Carolina Chemical Company headed the list of local companies producing chemicals, fertilizer, cement, and lime. In 1929 the DuPont Company opened a rayon factory near the city. Claiming national and international markets, Richmond flour mills reflected the importance of the city's food processing plants.[18]

Several other tiers of industrial operations contributed to Richmond's increasing economic diversity. A number of businesses provided wood products —lumber, boxes, and barrels. Occupying fourteen acres and calling itself "the largest of its kind in the world," Richmond Cedar Works often employed more than fifteen hundred people to produce such household goods as tubs, kegs, pails, churns, and clothespins. Three Richmond companies claimed to fill 65 percent of the national market for blotting paper, and more than a dozen other paper companies vied for regional and national markets. As a regional source for books, newspapers, government documents, and other publications and periodicals, Richmond's publishing industry flourished. Shoe manufacturers enjoyed notable success, as did the makers of such leather goods as harnesses and saddles. Before the 1930s Richmond housed successful car factories and earned profits from the production of drugs and medicine. In 1921 newspaper columnist Cally Ryland alluded to Henry Grady's earlier complaint that everything a southerner wore and owned was made in the North. By contrast she triumphantly depicted the daily routine of a hypothetical Richmond couple who spent their entire day using only products made in Richmond.[19]

Writing in the 1905 volume *The Rise of the New South,* Virginian Philip Alexander Bruce attributed much of Richmond's prosperity to its success as one of the chief points in the South for the wholesale distribution of merchandise. Bruce's assertion proved to be both a fact and a prediction. In subsequent years business transactions spiraled. At the dawn of the twentieth century, Richmond claimed annual wholesale activity amounting to approximately

$35.5 million, but by the late 1920s that figure usually exceeded $200 million. In 1912 five hundred traveling salesmen who represented local jobbing firms met at a hotel and plotted strategy. Such ventures were blessed with success. By 1920 the Spotless Company claimed to be "the largest mail order house of the entire South." Baughman Stationery Company developed, manufactured, and sold special bookkeeping forms for "several of the large railway systems of the country." While many firms combined manufacturing and wholesaling, others combined wholesaling and retailing. And Richmond's retail district flourished as it expanded on to Grace Street, which a city newspaper audaciously compared to New York's Fifth Avenue. No economic achievement evoked more local pride than Richmond's 1915 selection as the site for a Federal Reserve district bank. Richmond soon gained the reputation as a regional headquarters for both banking and insurance companies.[20]

With the James River and six railroads providing potential shipping routes to and from the city, Richmond appeared poised for economic growth. These transportation sources proved troublesome, however. Bouts of local complacency, occasional floods, and the geology of the river itself had often left the James inadequately dredged for navigation by modern vessels. And a failure to develop locally owned steamship companies left Richmond vulnerable to competition from traditional rival Norfolk. Yet Richmond succeeded as an entrepôt by relying on railroads and later on highways. In 1900 the city opened a new terminal for the Seaboard Airline and in 1901 opened new Main Street Station for the Chesapeake and Ohio Railroad. To serve the Richmond, Fredericksburg, and Potomac Railroad with its vital northbound traffic, commodious and handsome Broad Street Station began operations in 1919. By 1917 eighty passenger trains arrived daily in the city. In 1928 the chamber of commerce asserted that 5.5 million tons of freight arrived and left Richmond annually. Some of it arrived over the newly inaugurated Richmond-Washington highway, and by the late 1920s hard surface roads reached from the capital city to Petersburg, Norfolk, and the Shenandoah Valley.[21]

Motor vehicles and trains brought not only goods but guests to Richmond, which gained status as a convention city. An estimated 350,000 visitors arrived annually. The clientele included such professional groups as the National Education Association and the American Historical Association, as well as such business groups as the American Cotton Manufacturers and the American Banking Association. Religious gatherings included the 1907 Triennial Meeting of the Protestant Episcopal Church and a couple of annual meetings of the Southern Baptist Convention. Richmond also served as the site for state and regional meetings. By opening the regal Mosque in 1927, the city boasted a spectacular new auditorium and rolled out the carpet for even larger conventions. By the 1930s the Richmond area reported more than one thousand persons who held licenses for tourist homes.[22]

Richmond's economic success was achieved by a growing and changing labor force. According to the U.S. census, the number of Richmonders employed rose from 37,392 in 1900 to 83,794 in 1930. The greatest increase occurred in the manufacturing sector, which added more than sixteen thousand employees. Still the largest industry in town, cigar, cigarette, and tobacco companies employed more than six thousand workers in 1930. Another five hundred hands worked at the new nearby DuPont rayon plant. For such skilled workers as carpenters and joiners, machinists, iron and steel workers, painters, and printers, the century's first three decades brought hundreds of new positions. The number of electricians soared from 79 in 1900 to 501 in 1930.[23]

Notable changes affected other occupations. In 1900 more than one thousand men served as teamsters, draymen, or hackmen, but by 1930 those roles gave way to almost two thousand men who were employed as truck drivers and chauffeurs. The number of telegraph operators doubled in that time span, and by 1930, 606 women served as telephone operators, a job category not listed in 1900. Living in a railroad center, Richmond's rail labor force more than tripled by 1930. Making use of rails and highways, 838 traveling salesmen lived in the state capital in 1930, in contrast to the 263 living there in 1900. The number of merchants and dealers had doubled by 1930, and they hired a growing army of salespersons, clerks, and cashiers. This surge was matched by a dramatic increase in the number of white-collar jobs that supported all types of businesses—bookkeepers, clerks, copyists, stenographers, and typists. In 1900 approximately 2,600 people held such positions, but by 1930 almost 11,000 worked at such jobs. Richmond's community of professionals climbed from 1,888 in 1900 to almost 6,500 three decades later. Hundreds of new engineers, doctors, lawyers, and teachers helped account for this increase, as did 1,100 trained nurses.[24]

Even in an era of dynamic changes, gender and race shaped the city's occupational structure. In Ellen Glasgow's fictional Richmond of the 1890s, spunky Gabriella Carr horrified friends and family with her decision to work as a salesperson in a dry goods store. At the turn of the century, the U.S. census found approximately four hundred saleswomen in Richmond, but by 1930 the number of saleswomen and clerks in stores reached 1,635. This change reflected a pattern of increased white-collar occupational opportunities for white women. In 1900 women comprised only a tiny portion of the city's clerical workforce. In 1930 more than 5,500 white women worked as bookkeepers, accountants, stenographers, and typists. White and African American women gained many positions as teachers, trained nurses, and social workers. Still, women remained largely excluded from the skilled crafts and from professional roles as lawyers, physicians, and engineers. None of the city's more than 1,000 insurance agents was female, and only 176 female merchants conducted business.[25]

By 1930 9,000 more African Americans held jobs than had done so in 1900, but they still encountered barriers to certain occupations. In 1930 more than 1,000 Richmonders were factory owners, managers, and officials, but only 6 African Americans held such positions. By 1930 about 300 African Americans were among the 11,000 people holding clerical positions, and only 148 African Americans were employed in the more than 5,200 retail sales positions. Only 5 black men joined the city's small army of traveling salesmen. The growth of city government created hundreds of new public jobs, but no blacks held positions as firemen and policemen. Though comprising more than one-quarter of the city's male labor force, only a few hundred African Americans gained employment in the skilled crafts. The primary jobs available to blacks were positions as unskilled laborers, servants, waiters, waitresses, and laundresses. Some changes did occur. The number of Richmond African Americans in the professional ranks rose from 315 in 1900 to 938 in 1930. These successes indicated a sturdy and slowly emerging African American middle class within a society offering greater occupational opportunities for whites.[26]

At times when the city's pattern of steady growth was interrupted, plants halted production and laid off workers. The city's worst experience occurred in 1921. Such major firms as American Locomotive Works, Tredegar Iron Company, Richmond Cedar Works, and Old Dominion Iron and Nail Company temporarily shut down. Awaiting orders for new shipments, these companies stayed closed for months and left almost one-fourth of the city's labor force unemployed.[27]

Attentive to the problems of workers, organized labor surged forward as a force in the first decades of the twentieth century. Though estimates varied, unions probably counted more than 5,000 members in the early 1900s, and organizers tallied more than 12,000 members at the beginning of the 1920s. Machinists Lodge Number 10 claimed to be the area's largest union, with more than 750 members in 1916. Male-dominated trade unions like the International Typographical Union formed especially strong locals. Organizing, however, extended to office workers, and the Baking Powder Union formed the only all-female labor organization in the city. The Central Trades and Labor Council coordinated local activity; a labor weekly, *The Square Deal*, rallied readers to labor causes; and tens of thousands gathered for citywide Labor Day festivities.[28]

Rebounding from defeats during the Knights of Labor era of the 1880s, organized labor maintained a potent political presence. Spearheading activity, the Central Trades and Labor Council staked out political positions, endorsed candidates, urged workers to vote, and at times arranged payment of poll taxes. In 1904 labor favorite "Honest Dick" Taylor suffered a narrow defeat in his bid for a fifth term as city mayor, but close to one-third of the city council still relied on working-class votes. Responsive to some labor reform proposals, city government instituted a nine-hour day for municipal employees and later created a public employment bureau. In 1912, when Richmond experimented with a new form of municipal government called the Administrative Board, it provided a city government temporarily dominated by labor supporters, including John Hirschberg, a man whose political star rose rapidly. Hirschberg suffered a narrow defeat in the mayoralty race of 1920 but lost support in the 1928 mayoralty race, an ominous sign for organized labor.[29]

Indeed, the 1920s proved to be a difficult decade for organized labor in Richmond, just as it was for unions throughout the United States. An unsuccessful 1922 streetcar workers strike betokened bad times for local unions. In the past cautious Richmond unions had rarely resorted to work stoppages. The major exception to this pattern had been a 1903 streetcar strike that lasted sixty-nine days. That strike featured strikebreakers, mob violence, the occupation of Richmond by the state militia, and destruction of the union. Involving a different streetcar company and a different union, the 1922 strike avoided the overt conflicts of the 1903 confrontation, but the result was the same—the union was defeated.[30]

Richmond worked, but Richmond also played. The preferred forms of relaxation often depended on a person's social status, gender, or age, and the choices of diversions changed across time. Well-to-do adult males joined private organizations like the Richmond Club, the Westmoreland Club, and Country Club of Virginia or later the Hermitage Club. Working-class men socialized at saloons until statewide prohibition took effect in 1916. Men often joined fraternal organizations or civic clubs. Boys formed neighborhood gangs, which engaged in pranks as well as rock fights with other gangs. From debutante balls to fancy parties, the city's elite maintained a busy year-round social season, which often included the Richmond German Club, an exclusive society devoted to formal dancing. Before World War I, new dances like the turkey trot gained popularity and intruded into the stiffer traditional atmosphere. With the 1920s, Charleston contests as well as dance marathons signaled the direction of popular tastes. Members of the city's elite left Richmond for summer resort areas like White Sulphur Springs, and groups of other people arranged railroad excursions to coastal beaches.[31]

Other forms of entertainment beckoned. Despite a brief absence, professional baseball returned to Richmond and quickly regained its popularity. In 1908 the Richmond "Lawmakers" drew an estimated 400,000 men and women to the ball yard on Broad Street and thereby eclipsed the attendance of several major league baseball teams. In 1912 fan support made Richmond the only successful franchise in the short-lived United States Baseball League. During summers, families enjoyed both public and private parks. By the late 1920s, the city owned 975 park acres, and adults and children relaxed at baseball diamonds, playgrounds, and a municipal lake. In the fall thousands attended the annual state fair hosted by the city. In the early 1900s, penny arcades and vaudeville attracted customers, but the new century also brought Victrolas, radio broadcasts, automobile drives, and moving pictures.[32]

Richmond remained a regional cultural center. The Academy of Music and the Wednesday Club hosted concerts frequently featuring distinguished artists. The Richmond Philharmonic and opera performances formed essential parts of the local music community, and other musicians—ranging from John Philip Sousa to Paul Whiteman to Sergei Rachmaninoff—made guest appearances in the city. A diverse procession of out-of-town lecturers often drew large audiences. Judge B. B. Lindsey, Julia Lathrop, and Samuel Gompers championed reforms; Booker T. Washington and W. E. B. DuBois spoke as educators. Carl Sandburg read poetry, Will Rogers told jokes, but probably no other speaker moved an audience as profoundly as did Helen Keller.[33]

Richmond boasted its own intellectual community, and several of its members gained national reputations. Writers Kate Langley Bosher and Emily Clark received mostly local attention. Initially celebrated for writing historical fiction, Mary Johnston used one of her novels, *Hagar,* to promote woman's suffrage, and she became a leader in the Equal Suffrage League of Virginia. Richmond's most acclaimed novelists of this era were James Branch Cabell and Ellen Glasgow. Both writers drew heavily on Richmond as the locale for their stories, and both authors portrayed the tensions of people struggling with changing conditions. During the 1920s, Emily Clark briefly succeeded in making *The Reviewer* a literary journal notable for its famous national authors.[34]

Women were often at the center of Richmond's commitment to culture, and no organization was more important than the Woman's Club. Organized in 1894, the club hosted distinguished national speakers, musical events, literary discussion groups, and teas. Securing an antebellum house on East Franklin Street in 1900, the club renovated it and added a spacious auditorium in 1916. With more than two hundred members, the Woman's Club gradually extended its programs to include classes in such subjects as history and French. One of the founders of the Woman's Club was Mary-Cooke Branch Munford, an Episcopal laywoman. As president in 1901, she advocated a new direction, the promotion of social reforms in the community. With some members already active in local educational and health campaigns, the club soon also backed conservation and prison reform measures as well as laws in behalf of working women.[35]

The activists at the Woman's Club formed an essential cadre within an emerging corps of city progressive reformers. A diverse lot who championed a variety of causes, these people shared a perception that Richmond's success still left a host of matters that needed attention. At the beginning of the twentieth century, though, a timid city council remained preoccupied with reducing the city's bonded debt and with extending such basic services as roads and sidewalks. Persistent reformers nonetheless launched campaigns for more significant changes in the next two decades. In the mid-1920s, new state laws placed the city in a revenue squeeze, and voters elected conservative Fulmer Bright as mayor. But until that period, reformers fanned a progressive breeze which relied on an interplay of civic groups and city government. They could claim the greatest improvements in the city's public education and its public health.[36]

Mary-Cooke Branch Munford was the most restless member of the Woman's Club and one of the most restless people in the city. Born into the prestigious Branch family, she was only three years old when her father died in an accident. Bound by tradition, Mary-Cooke's mother schooled her in the Lost Cause but blocked her ambition to attend college. After a seven-year courtship, she married lawyer Beverley Munford, a man who shared her affinities for music, books, and social reforms. The couple was delighted by the birth of two children but devastated by a diagnosis that Beverley was terminally ill with tuberculosis and could expect to live less than a year. During a determined ten-year struggle to exceed that dire prediction, husband and wife played major roles in community reforms. A member of St. Paul's Episcopal Church, Mary-Cooke counseled her nephew as he attended seminary: "pray more, work more, and live outside self-seeking, and God's spirit will come upon you in power, I believe." She later suggested to him that "humanity halted and hungered" for thoughtful, courageous leaders "around which to gather and reform, and so lift the world to a new level of understanding and work." Writing as her biographer, the same nephew concluded that "God had been a reality in her life from the beginning," but that "religion had never been associated for her with rest." Mary-Cooke would attain distinction as the driving force behind educational reforms, and one of her first challenges was close at hand, the Richmond public school system.[37]

The weakness of Richmond's schools in 1900 could not be disguised. A northern journalist called the major public school a "disgrace" and criticized the curricula, the books, the methods, and the administration. Comparing Richmond to twenty-four other American cities, a local newspaper disclosed that only Atlanta spent less money per student per year. Reformers soon changed that situation. Already at work were the Conference for Education in the South and the Southern Education Board, which united northern businessmen and educators with southern reformers. Richmond's participants included Richmond College professor Samuel Chiles Mitchell, Beverley and Mary-Cooke Munford, and B. B. Valentine and his wife, Lila Meade Valentine, of Monumental Episcopal Church. Mary-Cooke later characterized her involvement in this movement as one of "the major interests of my life." After the Richmond Education Association (REA) was chartered in 1900, Mary-Cooke served as treasurer and then succeeded Lila Meade Valentine as president between 1904 and 1911. To promote better schools, the REA lobbied the city council, conducted public meetings, distributed pamphlets, and participated in the 1905 statewide "May Campaign" to improve Virginia schools. Mary-Cooke moved from the REA to head the statewide Cooperative Education Association and became the first female member of the Richmond school board, serving between 1920 and 1931.[38]

The campaigns for educational improvements yielded a steadily expanding list of new courses and new services to students. The school system added kindergartens in 1903, evening classes as well as courses in manual training and cooking courses in 1905, physical education in 1909, and classes for the deaf and nearsighted in 1926. In November 1914, exercising a peculiar Virginia local option law for education, Richmond voters passed a compulsory education ordinance for the city. Students used free textbooks after 1912, participated in testing programs after 1917, and ate cafeteria lunches after 1918. The school board provided classes for retarded children, free dental work, and annual medical examinations. Average daily attendance of public schools rose from 9,659 in 1900 to 28,453 in 1929. Between 1900 and 1930, the city doubled the number of its public schools, and the value of its school property increased from $442,500 in 1900 to $9,582,397 in 1930. Teachers' salaries tripled, and the ratio of teachers to students rose. In a 1935 letter to Mary-Cooke Branch Munford, S. C. Mitchell suggested that John Marshall High School, "the most important building in Richmond," served as a monument to her. Her statewide work meant that "millions of children who do not know your name have profited in life by what you have done for them."[39]

At the beginning of the twentieth century, no graver problem confronted Richmond than the community's health. Business leaders had long expressed concerns about the city's unhealthy reputation, and some reports listed Richmond among America's deadliest cities. Between 1900 and 1907, twice as many city residents died as were born, and the local press issued a barrage of editorials demanding wide-ranging reforms. In 1906 beleaguered members of the city health board pointed out that its annual appropriation was a mere $9,000, compared to Atlanta's health board, which received $20,000. In July 1906 the board of health was reorganized and placed under the direction of Dr. E. C. Levy. Already well known for his work as city bacteriologist, E. C. Levy began an eighteen-year tenure in which he rallied public and private resources to fight communicable diseases.[40]

Levy's public health campaign relied on education, expanded services, regulation, and support from civic organizations. Levy and his assistants took a number of steps to disseminate information about disease prevention. They talked to community groups, arranged public exhibits, made a film, and distributed thousands of pamphlets. They instructed residents about proper methods of milk storage, the importance of trash removal, and the health hazards posed by flies and rats. Levy began sending nurses to homes of newborn babies to teach their mothers how to care for them and how to practice proper hygiene. In 1913 the city set aside two weeks for a massive cleanup campaign, distributed 50,000 circulars, and involved civic groups and schoolchildren. A local housing expert testified that mountains of ashes, garbage and other filth had been removed and everyone appeared to be enthusiastic about the result.[41]

City officials increased funding of the board of health and expanded health services. Levy established three infant welfare clinics staffed by volunteer physicians and instituted the use of Behring diphtheria antitoxin. The health officers provided free small pox and typhoid fever vaccinations and occasionally instituted quarantines. The city subsidized and then acquired Pine Camp, a tubercular sanatorium and provided tuberculosis tests at locations throughout the city. Beginning in 1902, the city council funded a series of improvements to expand Richmond's water system and purify the water, and in 1924 a new $800,000 water filtration plant began operation. The city continued to extend sewerage lines to more houses and, with the aid of a 1925 bond issue, reduced the number of homes without sewerage connections from 3,000 in 1921 to 211 in 1928. Health officers distributed copies of sanitation laws, prosecuted homeowners who failed to clean up their yards, and won a strict local ordinance regulating garbage disposal. Some efforts encountered opposition. For example, only after several heated confrontations with milk producers did Levy succeed in implementing a carefully graded dairy farm inspection program that included testing of cows for tuberculosis.[42]

Private organizations served as constant allies in the health reform campaigns. Even prior to Levy's leadership, nurses from the Instructive Visiting Nurses Association (IVNA) had begun providing health care and information to the city's poorest neighborhoods. In 1905 alone the nurses had made visits to approximately 6,000 households, a number which would increase to almost 54,000 in 1927. Organized in 1905, an Anti-Tuberculosis Association sponsored free checkups. In 1909 and 1910 an African American Anti-Tuberculosis Association held rallies and arranged to distribute information through local school teachers and preachers. Richmond newspapers boosted health department policies and provided information about disease prevention. In an attempt to involve and educate children, the *Times-Dispatch* sponsored a "Swat the Fly Contest," furnished swatters, awarded Sarah Johnson a twenty-five-dollar prize, and calculated that 4.5 million flies had perished during the two-week hunt. New sanitary markets and privately donated public baths reduced other sources of communicable disease. Dairymen voluntarily pasteurized most of Richmond's milk. Local physicians and nurses played major roles in community organizations, as did the faculty members of Richmond's two medical schools, the Medical College of Virginia and the University College of Medicine.[43]

The community reaped large benefits from these combined efforts. The mortality rate of residents dropped from 23.68 per 1,000 in 1900 to 12.78 in 1930. The mortality rate from tuberculosis was cut in half between 1907 and 1923, as was the infant mortality rate. Unlike the 1890s, when between forty-five and fifty children died annually of diphtheria, only twelve died in 1923 though the city's population had doubled. In 1928 Richmond was the only southern city to record no deaths from typhoid, a feat matched by only six other U.S. cities.[44]

If public health was Richmond's gravest problem at the turn of the century, fires were its most glaring menace. The city that "rose from the ashes" seemed far too tolerant of flames, which devoured every type of structure: factories, warehouses, amusement parks, department stores, churches, college buildings, and private residences. A 1901 fire that incinerated most of the elegant Jefferson Hotel tarnished community pride, but 1902 visits by representatives of insurance companies brought potent threats. Observing that several companies had suffered millions of dollars in Richmond losses during recent years, the agents warned that changes must be made or else rates would soar or companies would withdraw coverage entirely. Richmond authorities needed no local campaign to motivate them. The city's new water system, a tougher building code, and improved fire protection equipment helped cut Richmond's fire losses by more than one-half. By 1924 the fire underwriters praised the Richmond fire department, and a 1929 survey in *American City* magazine showed Richmond's record to be superior to most other urban areas.[45]

The successful progressive recipe frequently required a combination of ingredients used in the education and public health campaigns: devoted local leaders, robust community organizations, persuasive outside experts, and a dose of persistence. Sometimes the visiting experts provided essential boosts. When local reformers advocated the creation of a juvenile court, they utilized participants at the 1908 meeting of the National Conference of Charities and Corrections held in the city. One speaker, the famous "children's judge" B. B. Lindsey of Denver, returned in 1909 and helped launch Richmond's Juvenile Protective Society, which did win support for the state's first juvenile court. In 1912 Rowland Haynes, field secretary of the Playground and Recreational Association of America, investigated Richmond's recreational facilities. His arrival was welcomed by reformers who had long favored better facilities for children. He reported that 70 percent of the children who played outdoors played in the streets. The next year the Playground and Recreational Association of America met in Richmond. By then city government was busy creating a model playground, hiring a staff, developing playgrounds at schools, installing lights at some playgrounds, and offering sessions in "scientific recreation" at John Marshall High School. Municipal authorities continued to acquire new recreational facilities and expanded the city's park system.[46]

On the other hand, the strange, protracted campaign to establish a public library demonstrated the importance of persistence for progressives. In March 1901 the board of aldermen passed a proposal to accept the money and the terms of philanthropist Andrew Carnegie to finance the construction of a public library. The proposal was derailed in the city's common council, thanks largely to a tight-fisted finance committee and to opponents who generated a list of divisive questions about its importance, its location, and its potential patrons. Even the support of the Richmond Education Association and local professional groups failed to overcome the objections, and by 1906 the proposal was dead. Renewed efforts between 1911 and 1915 also failed. Finally, in 1922, with Carnegie's contribution no longer available, the REA, the Richmond Public Library Association, and other civic groups persuaded the city council to finance the library. The Richmond Public Library Association probably gained the victory by enlisting ten thousand members. In October 1924 the Richmond Public Library opened, and in 1925 a much smaller branch library opened to serve the city's African American community. In 1929 approximately thirty thousand patrons borrowed almost five hundred thousand books from the libraries, and in 1930—thanks to a large bequest from the Dooley family—a new main library building welcomed book lovers.[47]

The progressive breeze that blew through Richmond even carried across the Capitol grounds occupied by state legislators and governors. A conservative bastion, the rural-dominated Virginia General Assembly usually hewed to the direction set by the state's political machine headed by Thomas S. Martin. With purposeful pragmatism the Martin machine resisted changes, then accommodated some reforms, and proceeded either to isolate or to woo successful independents. Between 1905 and 1920, the Martin machine's calculated flexibility permitted the progressive breeze to reach into state government. Albeit reluctantly, legislators addressed such issues as public education and social welfare reform. Richmond clergymen and laypersons often played key roles in advancing these reforms. Frustrated by the 1922 assembly's failure to act on compulsory education or road bond proposals, H. D. C. Maclachlan denounced the members as "reactionaries." That session offered a glimpse of Virginia's political future. Elected governor in 1925, Harry Byrd adopted an austere approach to government finances, gained control of the state machine, and stilled the state's progressive breeze for years to come.[48]

A different script led to similar results in the city of Richmond itself. In 1907 some reformers turned their attention to the city's government, an institution with several apparent flaws. The city council's ponderous committee structure had invariably delayed adoption of improvements. Critics charged that the ward system of electing members to the city's bicameral legislative body prompted politicians to practice costly logrolling to ensure services for their own constituents. In circumspect Richmond, occasional revelations of corruption and reports of unwisely spent funds created alarm. Some local reformers wanted to improve the quality and quantity of municipal services by restructuring city government. Little did they know that their experiment would boomerang, delivering economy but stifling reform.[49]

In January 1913 Richmond inaugurated a new form of city government, its administrative board. That five-member body was elected from the city at large. Reduced in size, the city council retained its power to make laws, but the administrative board assumed duties previously exercised by the council's committees and supervised city departments. As historian Christopher Silver has concluded, the new board functioned more "as a body of city managers" than as a commission. In some respects the board operated very well. Elections produced a board dominated by men with backing from organized labor and middle-class reformers. The new system proved more responsive to constituents and to proposals for city improvements. The board quickly addressed educational and recreational needs, expanded city services, and resisted attempts of private companies to achieve monopolies over local utilities and public transportation. Critics, however, charged that city government still operated awkwardly, hired incompetents, and tolerated unnecessary expenses.[50]

Unhappy about organized labor's large role in governance, Richmond businessmen began a counteroffensive by recruiting outside experts to evaluate the board. In 1917 the New York–based Bureau of Municipal Research assessed the system, concluded it was complex and ineffective, and recommended a more centralized approach. The administrative board revised its procedures but could not survive a deluge of negative publicity. In the August 1918 municipal election, Richmond citizens overwhelmingly voted to replace the board with a system based on a strong mayor. The result for progressives was disastrous. When competing factions within the existing labor–middle class reform coalition could not reconcile differences in 1924, physician Fulmer Bright was elected mayor on a platform of government retrenchment. Reelected in 1928, Bright ran a government bereft of progressive ventures.[51]

Richmond's progressives stalled before they addressed the disadvantages suffered by the city's African Americans, a group who comprised 29 percent of the community in 1930. African Americans claimed their own distinctive local heritage. Before the Civil War, slaves and free blacks worked as artisans and skilled craftsmen in a complex industrial labor system that provided an unusual level of autonomy for blacks. Beyond the world of work, blacks exercised further autonomy through their families and their churches. Citing property ownership as evidence, one scholar has concluded that between 1830 and 1860 Richmond free blacks "prospered."[52]

The aftermath of the Civil War offered new opportunities. African Americans became extensively involved in local politics and formed secret societies for collective self-improvement and mutual assistance. As the president of the Independent Order of St. Luke's, Maggie Walker became a legendary local businesswoman whose successes involved a bank, a department store, and a weekly newspaper. In a 1908 book, national journalist Ray Stannard Baker recited numerous other business achievements of Richmond blacks and counted a number of African American professionals as well. Not the least of them was John Mitchell, who headed the Mechanics Bank as well as owned and edited the *Richmond Planet*. Just as the *Planet* gained national attention, so, too, did Virginia Union University and nearby Hartshorn Memorial College for Women. In 1915 local African Americans hosted a "Negro Historical and Industrial Exposition" at the state fairgrounds, and black schools and colleges across the nation contributed exhibits. Booker T. Washington, W. E. B. DuBois, and Marcus Garvey spoke in Richmond, and national African American conventions also met in the city. The energy and excitement among the community's African Americans made them very much a part of the city's restless mood. Yet they invariably experienced frustration as they encountered boundaries set by race.[53]

In 1900 a Richmond newspaper editorialized that "God Almighty drew that color line and it cannot be obliterated." But white men drew that line, and they kept redrawing it to the disadvantage of blacks. As soon as blacks had gained the right to vote, unhappy whites initiated steps to stop them. To circumscribe the influence of black voters, whites created a new gerrymandered political district, Jackson Ward. In the 1870s, thugs and policemen tried to discourage black voters. Later a state law prescribed elaborate procedures for balloting and thereby enabled officials to invalidate black votes. Virginia's 1902 constitutional convention delivered a decisive political blow to blacks by enacting a poll tax and by establishing a registration process that amounted to a literacy test. Designed to remove ignorant voters of both races, these measures lowered white voter participation but virtually eliminated black voter participation. In 1900 a total of 6,427 Richmond African Americans had been registered voters, but in 1902 only 760 met the new requirements and registered.[54]

Social perimeters also constricted in twentieth-century Richmond. In the antebellum period, the inconvenient practice of residential segregation had been uncommon, but by 1891 the vast majority of whites and blacks lived in segregated areas. During the early twentieth century, African Americans inhabited seven major areas as well as seven smaller locations. Almost one-half of them lived in Jackson Ward in the north part of the city. Restrictive covenants and real estate agents promoted segregation by ensuring that blacks did not move into new areas. Yet some blacks and whites continued to share blocks. In 1911 the city council passed a law prohibiting blacks from moving into blocks with white majorities and whites from moving into blocks with black majorities. A U.S. Supreme Court decision, however, soon rendered that ordinance unconstitutional.[55]

Local customs made the color line pervasive. Blacks persevered in a verbal world replete with racist epithets, phrases, comments, and jokes. Annual "community" Christmas festivities featured a night for whites and a night for "colored." Most public occasions were segregated, from the state fair to schoolchildren's spelling bees. Since hospitals with segregated wards did not permit black physicians, African Americans established their own hospital facilities. In 1900 a state law provided for segregated railroads, and in 1904 city laws codified the practice of streetcar segregation. Lacking any political power to influence city government, blacks endured neighborhoods where city services were meager. Living in inferior and overcrowded housing, blacks suffered higher rates of disease and mortality. With limited educational facilities and a segregated occupational structure, only a small percentage of blacks ascended the mythical ladder of social and economic mobility.[56]

The progressive breeze did float through black Richmond, but its impact was limited. Recognizing the plight of African Americans, some white reformers repeatedly advocated improvements but rarely succeeded in gaining support. Operating through civic organizations and in collaboration with whites, blacks did secure some benefits. In 1915 more blacks attended high school in Richmond than in any other city of the former Confederacy. The city opened new Armstrong High School in 1922, but it was too small to accommodate all of the black students who wanted to attend. The total number of city school buildings devoted to black students increased, as did the percentage of young blacks attending schools. Improvements in public health lowered the mortality rate for blacks from 31.1 per thousand in 1907 to 21.34 per thousand in 1930. The incidence of infant mortality and disease among blacks also fell dramatically. Nine playgrounds served black youngsters, and Virginia Union students ran a recreational area that included a swimming pool. Still, the services provided blacks never matched those of whites, nor did blacks receive services proportionate to their fraction of the city's population. During the 1920s a few whites and blacks formed state and local interracial committees which tried to address some of the needs of African Americans.[57]

One member of Virginia's state interracial committee, Douglas Southall Freeman, embodied the spirit of early-twentieth-century Richmond. Freeman was a man deeply enamored with the past but energetically engaged in the present. Born in Lynchburg, Virginia, in May 1886, he moved with his family to Richmond five years later. Educated at a private school in the city, he attended Richmond College, where he fell under the influence of history professor, Baptist layman, and reformer Samuel Chiles Mitchell. Freeman caught the attention of the college's president, who wrote his father that "Douglas overflows with energy and seems destined for a large work. I pray that the Lord may bless and direct him to wide usefulness." Although the undergraduate Freeman flirted with an acting career, he earned his Ph.D. in history from Johns Hopkins University in 1908. His enthusiasm for history could be traced both to Mitchell and to his own father, who had been wounded at the Battle of Seven Pines and who had become a leader in the United Confederate Veterans. Following his graduation from Johns Hopkins, Freeman returned to Richmond and served a stint as the secretary of the state tax commission. A leader in the Anti-Tuberculosis Association, Freeman gave the major address, "The Social Needs of Richmond," when thousands assembled for a 1913 meeting of Richmond's Social Service Federation. In 1914 he married Inez Goddin.[58]

The next year Freeman began to weave together his noteworthy career as the editor of the *Richmond News Leader* and his calling as a historian. In 1915 he concluded his first major historical publication, an edited and annotated volume, *Lee's Dispatches to Jefferson Davis, 1862–1865*. That achievement won him an invitation to write a biography of General Lee, a project that occupied him until 1935, when the Pulitzer Prize–winning, four-volume *R. E. Lee* appeared. Freeman garnered national fame as a biographer, but he made his mark locally as a newspaper editor. His effectiveness in that role was based on a special relationship with the primary owner of the *News Leader,* John Stewart Bryan. Reminding Freeman that "your friendship and companionship mean a great deal to me," Bryan wrote to him about the need to "be ready for the fight against ignorance, prejudice, lethargy, and inertia." Clearly agreeing, Freeman editorialized, calling for a "sane liberalism." "In government, in industrial relations, in all the queer involvements of urban life, there must be the open, the experimental, the tolerant, the liberal mind," he maintained. As editor, he readily articulated the need for reforms.[59]

Probably no one else was as restless in Richmond as was Douglas Freeman, his unhurried demeanor notwithstanding. To perform his dual duties as editor and historian, Freeman developed a legendary work regime that began at 2:30 each morning. On one occasion, he declared that very few would "agree with me that when we waste time we sin." Still, within his busy schedule, he reserved time daily to read parts of the New Testament in Greek and to serve as an active layman at Second Baptist Church. Though reared in a devout home and educated at a Baptist college, Freeman had plunged into religious doubts during his graduate school years. With his faith rejuvenated through observation, thought, study, and experiences, he taught a men's Bible class, which became so popular that loudspeakers were installed in order for his words to reach overflow crowds standing outside. In a series titled "Parables of City Streets," he suggested that if Jesus were on earth, he would take his parables "from business, from automobiles, from the life we lead. I am sure if he walked in his graciousness down the business thoroughfares of any American city, he would give us a parable of the shop window." Freeman's Richmond pulsated with the rhythms of economic and social changes. Like Freeman, other Richmond religious leaders pondered the meaning of their faith for the life of the city throbbing about them. And, like Freeman, they would combine the old and the new, supply thoughtful but restless energy, and fan the city's progressive breeze.[60]

3
City Sounds and Joyful Noises

In 1914 the vestry of St. Paul's Episcopal Church expressed concerns about "sundry disturbing noises" around the church during services. The vestrymen asked the manager of the nearby Richmond Hotel to suspend playing music during Sunday evening worship services or to relocate such entertainment "to a more remote place from this church during that time." The gentlemen also sent one of their members to check with the Virginia Railway and Power Company "to see if something could not be done to abate the constant nuisance of the noise of the streetcars." These efforts were apparently successful, and the issues disappeared from future discussions. That same year, though, a former downtown congregation, St. James's Episcopal Church, opened its new building in the city's more residential West End. In listing the reasons for relocating, a vestry committee explained that, because stores were filling the old neighborhood, "all of the surroundings are most unattractive, even on Sunday, and during the week are positively repulsive." Furthermore, a new streetcar line then under construction would mean "noise disturbing the services." In fact, the streetcars would pose a danger to children crossing the street to attend Sunday school, the vestry concluded. In wrestling with changes surrounding their houses of worship, both St. Paul's and St. James's demonstrated a recurrent theme of religious life in the early twentieth century. Whether churches stayed in their old locations or shifted to new ones, they adjusted their traditional patterns of worship in response to the changing urban environment of Richmond.[1]

At first glance, however, Richmond churches appeared to be so deeply rooted in history that they might resist innovations. In 1900 the church newspaper *Monumental Messenger* rejoiced that "our city has been wonderfully blessed with a long line of able, faithful and godly men in the various pulpits of the city." It proceeded to cite a list of past Baptist, Presbyterian, Methodist, and Episcopal leaders "whose lingering radiance" "has blessed our city." Invoking the names of a pantheon of Richmond's religious heroes, Baptist preacher James B. Hawthorne characterized them as part of a celestial "cloud of witnesses" who sympathetically observed the deeds of contemporary Christians. These past saints, he emphasized, "bequeathed their works and duty to us" and "exhort us to do our part as they did theirs." And each major Protestant denomination transmitted a distinctive religious heritage to a new generation.[2]

The city's venerable Episcopal churches claimed a lengthy legacy matched by no other denomination. The structure eventually named St. John's was built in 1741. At that site in March and July 1775, conventions assembled with such delegates as George Washington, Thomas Jefferson, and Patrick Henry to determine Virginia's direction in the colonial crisis with England. From 1789 to 1814, worship services were held irregularly at St. John's, and its rector, John Buchanan, alternated with Presbyterian minister John Blair in conducting services in the hall of the House of Delegates in the state capitol. Stories about the friendship of the affable "two parsons" became local legends, and their relationship served as a precedent for later interdenominational activities. Following Richmond's great theater fire of 26 December 1811, the community interred the remains of the seventy-two people killed on the site and erected a church on the spot of the tragedy. As a commemoration to the victims, the church was named Monumental and sheltered a marble monument listing the names of those buried beneath the church. By a vote of those contributing funds to construct the building, it became an Episcopal church. Added to Monumental's haunting past was the fact that as a foster child young Edgar Allan Poe had worshiped there, as had such dignitaries as John Marshall and the Marquis de Lafayette. Organized in 1835, St. James's Episcopal Church became associated with popular Confederate Gen. Jeb Stuart, who worshiped there. As rector of St. James's for thirty-seven years, Joshua Peterkin left a large imprint on the city, as did one of his successors, William Meade Clark.[3]

Consecrated in 1845, St. Paul's Episcopal quickly gained attention with its 225-foot steeple, which dominated the city's skyline, and with its rector of thirty-three years, Charles Minnegrode. During the Civil War, Confederate President Jefferson Davis, Gen. Robert E. Lee, and a number of other Confederate leaders worshiped there. On the long-remembered Sunday of 2 April 1865, the church sexton interrupted Davis in his pew and handed him a message from Lee warning him of the need to evacuate Richmond. Davis quietly left the church, as did military officers, who were summoned to their commands. Thereafter, St. Paul's proved that a respect for history could be united with contemporary concerns. After one rector suggested that the church itself might serve as a memorial to former communicants, members financed improvements in memory of family members. The memorial funds paid for stained glass windows, communion linen, a communion rail, a baptismal bowl, marble flooring, new lighting system, and a substantial interior redecoration.

Other members donated numerous commemorative plaques and tablets. In surrounding its congregation with history, St. Paul's also enhanced its setting for worship. At the dawn of the twentieth century, Richmond's Episcopal churches were located at the heart of the city historically as well as geographically.[4]

Presbyterians honored a heritage notable for the long tenures of remarkable ministers. Beginning in the 1790s, "Parson" John Blair alternated with Episcopalian "Parson" Buchanan in conducting Sunday services at the state capitol. Blair also presided over a regular gathering of Presbyterians who delayed formally organizing their Shockoe Hill Presbyterian Church until 1821. Renamed United Presbyterian following a merger, that congregation suffered the complete destruction of its church building during the Civil War. After relocating and erecting a new structure, the congregation adopted the name Grace Street Presbyterian. In 1812 minister John Holt Rice organized First Presbyterian Church in the heavily settled Rocketts section of town near the James River. Rice was studious, sober, and cerebral. After he left to become a seminary professor, his successors followed his model and published extensively, particularly in the state's denominational press. To meet the needs of the residents in the city's western section, First Presbyterian organized Second Presbyterian in 1845. To outsiders, Second Presbyterian was famous because Gen. Stonewall Jackson worshiped there during the Civil War. In Richmond, though, Second Presbyterian would be forever linked to the incomparable fifty-four-year tenure of its first minister, Moses Drury Hoge, and often thereafter it was known simply as "Dr. Hoge's Church." Second Presbyterian's initial success could be traced to a man who sacrificed his salary for the church building, who traveled widely, and whose oratory reached not only his own congregation but audiences at a mission in the city's poorer district.[5]

Local Baptists traced their roots to a meeting conducted in a private household in 1780. At that time, according to historian W. Asbury Christian, "Richmond was not a congenial place for churches." From that service emerged the congregation which eventually adopted the name First Baptist Church. A biracial congregation until 1841, First Baptist served as the parent to many other local churches, including Second Baptist, formed in 1820. Also initially biracial, Second Baptist was the church from which Richmond College was launched, at which the first meeting of the Baptist General Association of Virginia was convened, and at which the *Religious Herald* was founded. Before the Civil War, Baptists also established churches which sooner or later took the name of their locations: Grace Street, Leigh Street, Pine Street, and Bainbridge Street. The Baptist constellation of heroes included Jeremiah Jeter, who served a total of thirty-one years as pastor at First Baptist and Grace Street, who edited the *Religious Herald,* and who served as the first president of the Southern Baptist Foreign Mission Board. Baptists also revered the longtime president of Richmond College, Robert Ryland, and J. L. M. Curry, a professor at Richmond College. When Baptists celebrated their local past, they emphasized their educators and their educational institutions, including the Woman's College of Richmond.[6]

Richmond was initially a mere stop for Methodist preachers riding a circuit. In 1786, at a private house in old Manchester on the south side of the James River, area Methodists formed a congregation which endured as Central Methodist Church. In Richmond itself, Methodists first met in the county courthouse and in a refurbished stable before erecting a church in 1799. That congregation, Trinity Methodist, proudly retained its title as the "Mother Church of Richmond Methodism." In 1810 Methodists also established Shockoe Hill Church. In 1839, the centennial year of Methodism, that congregation raised funds to construct a new building west of the capitol, where they adopted a new name, Centenary Methodist.[7]

Despite advocating an end to denominational divisions, the Disciples of Christ were a group born into controversy in Richmond, as in the rest of the country. In the early 1800s, the followers of Thomas and Alexander Campbell called for a restoration of New Testament forms of Christianity. Favoring immersion and rejecting creeds, the "Campbellites" initially emerged in Richmond as members of First Baptist Church. Though perceiving themselves as only reformers, Campbell's supporters deeply troubled the pastor and other members at First Baptist. Citing differences in doctrine and church government, the minister asked them to withdraw and form a separate fellowship based on their own beliefs. The new congregation built its own Sycamore Church in 1822 and moved west in 1872. At the new location, the congregation adopted the name Seventh Street Christian Church and became the mother church for a series of Disciples of Christ congregations created in the late nineteenth and early twentieth centuries. The leaders of the Disciples consistently reiterated their historic theme of Protestant unity and served as catalysts for interdenominational cooperation throughout Richmond.[8]

Richmond's German population served as the constituency for three other churches. In 1843 a German congregation, St. John's, convened as a Lutheran church and many decades later joined the Evangelical Synod of North America. Dissatisfied with that church's failure to affiliate with a Lutheran organization, some of its former members helped found Bethlehem Lutheran in 1852. Due to difficulties in securing a German pastor from the Virginia Synod, that congregation shifted its membership to the Missouri Synod. After several unsuccessful ventures in Richmond, the Lutheran Evangelical Synod of Virginia established a church there in 1869, and that congregation adopted the name First English Evangelical Lutheran in 1876. Constituting a sturdy ethnic and religious minority, these Protestant churches usually joined those of larger denominations in community activities. While they occasionally collaborated, these three congregations remained aligned with different national denominations.[9]

In the twentieth century, Richmond churches joined in interdenominational activities but did so despite differences. Just as each of the city's major denominations claimed a distinct niche in the city's history, each major Protestant group adhered to its own ecclesiastical structure, theology, and forms of worship. In 1900 only city Episcopalians were part of a truly national denomination, the Protestant Episcopal Church. In October 1907 Richmond welcomed Episcopalians from across the country as it hosted the national Triennial meeting, a two-week extravaganza climaxed by a sermon delivered at the state capitol by the bishop of London. That same year the Southern Baptist Convention held its annual meeting in Richmond. Like the Baptists, city Methodists and Presbyterians were part of denominations that had separated from their northern counterparts prior to the Civil War. The Methodist Episcopal Church, South, considered proposals for national reunification, and the Presbyterian Church of the United States also debated unification. In each case Richmond leaders were divided over the issue, and in each case the proposed reunification failed. Dividing regionally only at the time of the Civil War, Lutherans achieved a reunited organization in 1918, and First English Lutheran hosted the biennial meeting of the United Lutheran Church in America in 1926. Technically belonging to a national denomination, churches of the Disciples of Christ tended to be clustered in the center of the country, especially the Midwest.[10]

These denominations also differed in their internal structures. Episcopalians and Methodists featured hierarchies in which ecclesiastical officials such as bishops exercised some governing power over local churches. In contrast, Baptists and Disciples staunchly exercised congregational autonomy. In some decisions such differences had a significant impact. For example, Methodist bishops appointed preachers generally for two-year terms at individual churches. Churches of other denominations invited or "called" their ministers, and their length of service was not regulated. Canon law bound local Episcopal churches, but resolutions passed at annual meetings of the Southern Baptist Convention lacked similar power over individual congregations. When the Women's Christian Temperance Union requested Episcopal rector W. E. Evans to substitute grape juice for wine in communion services, he responded pointedly. "Some people have a notion that a clergyman can make well-nigh any change in the order of service that he has a mind to or that they suggest." On the contrary, Evans declared, "I have no authority nor disposition to depart from the ancient order of the church," and he proceeded to cite a list of resolutions passed by Episcopal conferences and conventions. Viewing a similar request as reasonable, a Baptist minister responded that the board of deacons in his congregation would need to make that decision. When the local Dover Baptist Association directed its member churches to withdraw fellowship from members who sold alcoholic beverages, First Baptist responded with a polite but firm rebuff that asserted its prerogative as a congregation over matters of church discipline. The Dover Association almost humbly acknowledged that it was "the creature, not the creator of churches in its membership."[11]

The denominations also differed over matters of theology and doctrine. As definitions of faith, Presbyterians affirmed the Westminster Confession, and Episcopalians and Lutherans proclaimed the Apostles Creed and the Nicene Creed. But Baptists and Disciples rejoiced in being "creedless" churches, with the Bible alone serving as their source of religious authority. Unlike the other Protestants who practiced infant baptism, Baptists and Disciples immersed adults who affirmed their faith. Still propounding a version of Calvinism, Presbyterians offered the narrowest range of theological interpretation. Organized with an ecumenical purpose, the Disciples of Christ willingly listened to a variety of religious views.[12]

The different denominations maintained distinct styles of worship. Episcopalians and Lutherans participated in liturgical services. *The Book of Common Prayer* prescribed the order for services in Episcopal churches, and congregations observed special holy days as designated by an ecclesiastical calendar. The only boundaries on Presbyterian worship were set forth in the *Directory of Worship*, a historic document revised in 1893. As interpreted by southern Presbyterians, the *Directory* repudiated liturgical services for simple forms of worship. Titles and trappings of religious authority, such as clerical clothing, were unheard of among Presbyterians, Baptists, and Disciples. One popular Presbyterian minister defied convention by wearing his Geneva gown while preaching but eventually found it necessary to justify his aberrant behavior. Observing that ordination for Baptists conferred "no rank" or privilege, the editor of the *Religious Herald* declared that it merely commended a man to his brethren as fit for service. "Anything beyond this takes us straight in the direction of Romanism with its priesthood and priestcraft," the writer warned. Unlike the Episcopalians and Lutherans, who viewed communion as a sacrament in which Christ's presence was real, the Presbyterians, Baptists, Methodists, and Disciples observed the Lord's Supper as a commemorative ordinance.

Presbyterian, Baptist, and Methodist congregations might conduct services with the Lord's Supper four or five times annually, but the Disciples did so weekly. Such differences, though, did not prevent a major departure of the twentieth century: interdenominational cooperation.[13]

On Sunday afternoon, 24 June 1900, hundreds of Richmonders assembled at the Academy of Music for the second annual Festival of Christian Unity. A program of hymns, prayers, and presentations by Protestant ministers stressed the theme that "denominational differences were of minor importance." That meeting symbolized the future. Discounting denominational distinctions, Richmond clergymen thereafter reiterated the message of cooperation. Baptist J. B. Hutson deplored those who would "unChristianize" persons of other denominations, and he celebrated "the universal, invisible church." After Baptists heard a talk by a Disciples of Christ preacher, the editor of the *Religious Herald* concluded that the two denominations were not "widely or deeply separated" and predicted a greater "mutual respect and deepening of fellowship" between the two denominations. The minister of First Presbyterian Church declared that Presbyterians believed that "the church of God consists of all Christians" and "did not condemn those who differ from us." The city's denominational newspapers issued similar pronouncements. In 1910, at the behest of the Episcopal Diocese of Virginia, representatives from the city's major Protestant churches met and issued a statement. They called upon the governing bodies of evangelical denominations to aid in steps for "closer union and Christian fellowship." In a lengthy 1914 discourse about Christian unity, the minister of Second Presbyterian Church invoked the historic example of Richmond's "two parsons" and envisioned a possible future union of Episcopalians and Presbyterians. At Seventh Street Christian Church, H. D. C. Maclachlan tersely remarked in 1919 that the day was coming when "denominationalism" would be viewed as a sin.[14]

During the early twentieth century, Richmond Protestant leaders steadily accelerated their cooperation in ways small and large. In 1900 twelve clergymen of four denominations created the Duodeciom Club, a social and literary organization with monthly meetings. On each occasion dinner followed a book review and a paper presented about "just about anything." The Richmond Ministerial Union met weekly, included all the clergy of the major white Protestant denominations, often listened to guest speakers, and discussed any matter of religious concern to the city. The laity of churches enjoyed recreational activities like the Church Hill baseball league, composed of teams from congregations in that area of town. Union services among churches in particular neighborhoods grew in popularity, especially during summers, when heat and vacations threatened to shrink Sunday attendance at individual churches. To support conservation measures during the winter months of World War I, churches also held union services. Ministers of nearby churches of different denominations began to exchange pulpits. In 1907 the Episcopal General Convention slightly facilitated such activity by amending a canon that had required a person officiating at a service to be ordained as an Episcopal minister. The amendment applied only to special occasions, still required approval of a bishop, and left the Episcopalians as the most restricted group of clergymen. When any denominational gathering such as a state or national convention brought visiting ministers to Richmond, they served as guest speakers in most Protestant churches.[15]

Building on past cooperative ventures such as the Virginia Bible Society, religious leaders embarked on a series of new collaborative endeavors. In 1903 ministers formed an interdenominational group to try to mediate the city's streetcar strike. To deal with legal matters such as saloon regulation or Sunday observance laws, religious leaders readily joined forces. Churches joined in organizing annual Sunday school teacher training programs. Beginning in 1909, the major denominations acted collectively to sponsor a series of six citywide revivals. Protestant denominations acted in concert to conduct religious surveys of individual neighborhoods as well as one massive citywide religious census in 1912. Between 1908 and World War I, Richmond served as a regional center for the interdenominational Laymen's Missionary Movement. By the 1920s Richmond laywomen had also organized an interdenominational missionary union. When Presbyterians initiated a factory mission program, they recruited leaders of other Protestant groups to participate. In 1920 an Interdenominational Board of Religious Activities in State Institutions funded and appointed a director of religious work for the Virginia state penitentiary. In 1923, with H. D. C. Maclachlan heading the effort, the leaders of all the evangelical churches in the city formed the Richmond Council of Churches.[16]

On rare occasions collective activity extended to other religious groups besides the major white Protestant denominations. At times of crisis, such as the assassination of President William McKinley, citywide prayer services included Rabbi Edward Calisch. The pastor of First Baptist as well as a few other Protestants ministers spoke at Calisch's Temple Beth Ahabah. St. Paul's Episcopal Church held joint services with St. Constantine, a Greek Orthodox church. The rector of St. Paul's won the support of the Episcopal Diocese of Virginia for a national "pact of reconciliation" drafted by leaders of fifteen denominations. A center for religious diversity, Seventh Street Christian hosted a 1923 "better acquaintance" speaking program featuring religious leaders of most faiths, including Rabbi Calisch and Quaker judge J. Hoge Ricks. In 1928 Seventh Street's Maclachlan arranged a goodwill dinner that brought together

Richmond Protestants, Catholics, and Jews. Though not matching Seventh Street for promoting interfaith programs, most churches joined in a variety of interdenominational activities.[17]

Meanwhile, church members embraced other innovations by redesigning the settings and forms of worship. For many congregations the most significant change was a decision to relocate and to construct a new building. Even at the beginning of the twentieth century, city population shifts gained the attention of religious leaders. In 1902 C. S. Gardner, the pastor of Grace Street Baptist Church, declared that the members of large downtown churches were scattered across the city. He speculated that less than one-fifth of a typical congregation's members lived in its immediate neighborhood. Gardner's fears were premature. By 1925, though, a study done for Second Presbyterian Church documented the trend. In 1907, 65 percent of its members had lived within a mile of the church, but by 1925 that figure fell to 20 percent. In 1911 Episcopalians began expressing concerns about Monumental Church, and those concerns were warranted. Monumental's directories of communicants reveal that in 1900 approximately 69 percent of its 444 members lived within a mile of the church. By 1919 only 39 percent of its 439 members lived within such easy walking distance. Furthermore, members who relied on streetcar transportation could encounter problems. In 1915 the Virginia Railway and Power Company suspended service pending a new franchise from the city. Monumental's vestry sent letters of protest to the company and to the city council. That same year the church felt compelled to raise money to purchase an adjacent lot, lest a property owner fulfill his threat of constructing a tenement on it to house twenty black families. Worshiping in one of the city's uniquely historical sites, members of Monumental did not entertain the idea of moving.[18]

But other congregations did relocate. The 1900 Richmond city directory listed sixty-one churches belonging to one of the major white Protestant denominations. By 1930 only thirty-one of them remained at their former locations. Alert to the shifting population, such denominational organizations as the Baptist Council of Richmond and the Presbyterian League decided to facilitate the dispersal of churches. Concluding that the past pattern of centralization would no longer suffice, the newsletter of the Presbyterian League endorsed the "planting of churches in every part of the city." City Episcopalians similarly created a special committee to develop plans for locating future churches. Still, churches in newer parts of town had to cope with neighborhood residents who maintained their old downtown affiliations. For example, in 1921 five Protestant churches of Barton Heights conducted a survey and learned that approximately 45 percent of the 3,315 people listing themselves members of those denominations remained members of churches outside that neighborhood.[19]

Many churches moved to new sites on the city's growing West End. Several congregations relocated in advance of residential construction. In 1909, when the pastor of First Lutheran proposed constructing a new building on Monument Avenue, he had to overcome fears of members who were understandably anxious about the sparse population of the area. While First English acted, the pastor of First Baptist confidently told his downtown congregation that "Providence has favored our church. The city grows in every direction and we are at its centre. The population does not move away from us, but rather revolves around us in ever widening circles." Yet within a decade, a gift of a large tract of land enticed the pastor and members of First Baptist to reconsider and erect a larger church in the West End.[20]

At a new location a congregation generally constructed a handsome, modern, and larger church building. When First English Lutheran consecrated its building on May 1911, it proudly pointed to its gothic style architecture of "James River granite," pews of mahoganized birch, a new organ, carpets and glass windows purchased from Richmond firms, an auditorium seating five hundred people, and "probably the most commodious chancel in the South." When First Baptist held its first service in its new home, it welcomed visitors to an auditorium seating 1,350, and it offered a guided tour of its more than 130 rooms. Already located on the city's West End, the Presbyterian Church of the Covenant opened its new building in 1907. A journalist extolled its large sanctuary, new organ, excellent acoustics, outstanding system of electrical lights, and beautiful stained glass windows. When Grace Street Presbyterian Church united with the Church of the Covenant in 1915, the new Grace Covenant Church reflected another trend among Richmond churches: downtown churches moving and merging with other congregations on the city's periphery.[21]

Financing new facilities could be difficult. At times construction was delayed as churches engaged in fund-raising campaigns, and some churches struggled to pay off debts incurred from ambitious building programs. One church saw its indebtedness rise from approximately $3,000 in 1909 to more than $39,500 in 1929, a year in which its annual receipts totaled barely more than $47,600. Like the Church of the Covenant and First Baptist, other churches benefited from donations of land and several sizeable individual contributions for buildings and furnishings. By 1930 Richmond's array of new brick and stone churches made the few remaining wooden frame buildings seem like quaint relics of a bygone era.[22]

Churches that did not relocate also transformed their settings for worship by remodeling their structures and erecting new buildings on adjoining property. Some changes came involuntarily. In 1911 city inspectors discovered that the wooden frames of the steeples of a number of downtown churches had deteriorated, leaving the steeples precariously perched. Prudent congregations removed them and often replaced them with shorter, sturdier towers. To enhance worship services, churches remodeled sanctuaries. As a historian of Presbyterian worship once observed, beginning in the late nineteenth century Americans discovered beauty, and they carried their newfound impulse for aesthetics into their churches. Thanks to a generous member, Centenary Methodist installed cathedral glass windows as well as electric lighting in 1909. Seventh Street Christian also added stained glass windows. Other churches engaged in wholesale redecoration. In 1912 Park Place Methodist installed electric lights, refurnished its auditorium with mahogany woodwork and cream painted walls, and added a new Kimball organ. That same year Leigh Street Baptist described its newly paneled, white auditorium, including new mahoganized pews, carpets, a new balcony, baptistery, communion table, and lectern.[23]

Like other churches, Leigh Street took special pride in its new organ. Produced by the Kimball company, the organ stood thirty-two feet wide by seventeen feet high, was finished in mahogany, and featured two thousand speaking pipes finished in gold. Describing this "splendid instrument," a church member reported that the organ had three manuals, thirteen adjustable combination pistons, and double action with all the pistons. By adding powerful and elaborate organs, churches sought to foster a mood of reverence in services. Surrounding worshipers with deep, rich sounds that reverberated throughout the sanctuaries, the new organs created a dignified, somewhat formal atmosphere for services. The availability of electricity and technological innovations permitted the development of orchestral organs. By the 1920s these newer organs expanded the range of auditory experiences by using imitative orchestral stops to simulate the sounds of such instruments as French horns, clarinets, oboes, and chimes.[24]

Organs and other new equipment enriched worship services with a symphony of beautiful musical sounds, but they did so at a cost. Only a $1,000 gift from Andrew Carnegie enabled one Disciples of Christ congregation to purchase a new organ. As an individual congregation announced its purchase of a new organ, it frequently identified a prestigious company as the firm producing the exquisite instrument. Indeed, churches often seemed to compete for the honor of owning the most impressive organ in the community. In announcing the purchase of a Hook and Hastings organ in 1900, one church boasted that the tubular organ was "the most powerful made" and cost $7,000.

By 1926 St. Paul's Episcopal Church reported that it insured its organ for $20,000. By comparison, the church budgeted $13,300 for salaries for six persons the following year. Thanks to a gift, St. James's Episcopal transformed the sounds of worship even more extensively in 1926. A massive set of chimes quickly became a distinctive symbol of the church as their peeling reached a distance of several miles. Earlier Seventh Street Christian had added equipment to aid those with limited hearing. The Ladies Aid Society bought an acoustican with six ear pieces, and ushers were instructed to conduct those who were deaf to pews furnished with that device.[25]

Attempting to reach out to individuals who were not already church members, several congregations remodeled their buildings or built new "institutional churches," designed to involve people in a variety of ways in addition to worship services. St. Andrew's Episcopal Church followed this course in a striking manner, as chapter 7 will detail. After World War I, Richmond Methodist leaders decided to renovate sixty-year-old Broad Street Church at a time when most of the church's former members had moved to the suburbs. A demographer, A. C. Zumbrunnen, conducted a social survey of Broad Street's neighborhood and identified groups of people who remained unaffiliated with any church. He cited thousands of visiting students, hospital patients, hotel guests, and people who worked in the area throughout the week. City Methodists marshaled their resources and reorganized the church to attract those people. The pastor, Frederick Chenault, explained that the new Broad Street Church tried "to reach the needs of the whole man." Operating seven days a week, its facilities included a community house with a kitchen, a social hall, reading rooms, a library, a day nursery, a gymnasium, tennis courts, and a roof garden. Chenault helped men find employment, and he acted as a guardian for wards of the juvenile court. In addition to religious programs, Broad Street Methodist Church sponsored night classes and a community recreation program.[26]

Other congregations constructed additions to their main buildings and experimented with new equipment. In 1911 seven Baptist churches occupied or began erecting new Sunday school buildings. Later Pine Street Baptist opened a new Sunday school building with its seventy-two rooms. Like the construction at new sites, the additions could prove costly. To open a new Sunday school building in 1929, Third Presbyterian had to spend more than $52,000, the largest expense it had ever incurred. After 1915, when First Presbyterian acquired a movie projector, other churches did so as well, and some added slide projectors. In 1922 Seventh Street Christian began showing films each Sunday night in an attempt to show Richmond "how movies may be made to serve the Lord during the hot summer Sundays." The church's newsletter praised the moral value of such movies as "Pollyanna" and "Black Beauty." The most significant innovation occurred at Grace Covenant Presbyterian Church, which created its own radio station, WBBL, and began broadcasting in 1924. The broadcasts were well received, particularly by invalids, and in 1927 ten local church choirs broadcast hymns over the station during a weeklong citywide revival. Radio proved to be one of the most far-reaching examples of how innovation served as an avenue of faith. By 1929 listeners hundreds of miles from Richmond heard sermons broadcast on WBBL, and Monumental Episcopal began to broadcast, too.[27]

Another change occurred as churches made participation more accessible. A vestige of the past, pew rents were slowly phased out by congregations still using them. In 1905 First Baptist Church and Grace Street Presbyterian eliminated them, and in 1918 Second Presbyterian did too. Only in the 1920s did several of the historic Episcopal Churches remove pew rents. In 1925 the vestry of St. Paul's Episcopal Church noted that the change was hardly novel and that it would help attendance. The rector concurred, praising the change for removing the appearance of rights based on money and for reflecting a human's "equal footing in the House of God." In an attempt to expand the number of contributors, congregations adopted the use of duplex envelopes—and some church leaders praised the results.[28]

In 1901 the editor of the *Central Presbyterian* led the chorus of opposition to one innovation that sparked controversy, the introduction of individual communion cups. In 1902 an outraged editor of the Episcopal *Southern Churchman* denounced individual cups as a "heretical" idea which would destroy the integrity and "the entire character of the sacrament." The rector of All Saints Episcopal Church shared that view, calling the cups a blow to the spirit of brotherhood in the Lord's Supper and arguing that the alleged dangers of spreading germs from a common cup were exaggerated. Nonetheless, between 1908 and 1914 Baptist, Methodist, Presbyterian, and Disciples congregations purchased new sets of individual cups for communion, and a number of churches implemented a request of prohibitionists to serve grape juice rather than wine.[29]

In the use of music, Richmond churches also departed from tradition. As a local journalist discerned in September 1901, "the tendency is towards the chorus instead of the quartette," "which is a change from former years." The shift would be gradual because of lingering congregational pride in their quartets. As one music historian has noted, the mixed quartets and individual solos were "probably the best-established performance tradition in the urban denominational church in 1900." The 1901 newspaper account captured congregational pride and competition for musicians as it outlined the plans of celebrated, paid singers and organists either to remain at their current churches or to accept invitations from others. One organist left Monumental Episcopal Church for a Presbyterian church, thereby creating an opportunity for teenage prodigy John Powell Jr., a future internationally acclaimed pianist. A female soloist who had formerly sung at First Baptist forsook it for an Episcopal church. St. James's Episcopal had reportedly pursued Norman Call, "whose superb bass voice was first heard last session at St. Paul's Church." But "Mr. Call has not yet decided with what church he will identify himself for the winter." Beautiful music mattered mightily, especially to city Episcopalians, who were most inclined to pay musicians, but the practice could cause difficulties. On several occasions a worried vestry of St. John's Episcopal Church raised fees paid to singers. Nonetheless, it lost a tenor when it failed to match the salary offered by another church. Only reluctantly did some churches replace quartets with chorus choirs. In 1927 Barton Heights Baptist Church finally made that change. Throughout the early twentieth century, churches gradually adopted robed or vested choirs, an often controversial decision. Only after a petition from the choir and a unanimous vote of the vestry did a reluctant rector of St. John's Episcopal Church finally bow to that preference. He warned them, however, that even with renovations, the church was not suitable for processing and recessing, "which I do not admire." By the 1920s Centenary Methodist and Seventh Street Christian had adopted vested choirs, but Pine Street Baptist resisted the trend until 1939.[30]

Congregational singing also involved changes and controversies. Instead of using weekly hymn slips, First Baptist placed copies of the *Baptist Hymnal* in pew racks after 1905. When Episcopalians adopted a new hymnal in 1916, no one voiced complaints. In 1907 the *Central Presbyterian* praised the new *Standard Songs* hymnal for combining older standards with modern hymns. After 1927 churches began to use the new *Presbyterian Hymnal.* Still, some Presbyterians did express displeasure about trends in church music. At a midwinter's course open to the community, a Union Theological Seminary professor condemned "various abuses in evidence" and "made a strong plea for the great hymns of the ages as against the doggerel songs and ragtime tunes so much in vogue." Only in 1916 did First Presbyterian direct the congregation to stand to sing all hymns and to end each one with "amen."[31]

Some innovations affected mostly members of an individual congregation or of a single denomination. Seeking a reverent atmosphere for worship, a new minister at Centenary Methodist requested that all people kneel in silent prayer upon entering the sanctuary and that the congregation kneel together for a few moments following the benediction. Beginning in 1922, Second Presbyterian added a violinist to accompany the organ during Sunday services. One Episcopal church organized the only boy choir in the city, and at another church the congregation and the choir sang the entire liturgy. Despite some protests from Richmond ministers, Episcopalians adopted a revised version of the *Book of Common Prayer* in 1928.[32]

At times a single change in the worship setting signaled others. In 1924 Seventh Street Christian purchased an expensive Austin organ, which received attention in *The Diapason,* a publication of the National Association of Organists and the Organ Builders Association of America. Nationally renowned organist Edwin H. Lemare also arrived to give a recital before an audience that reportedly filled pews, crowded into aisles, and spilled over onto the church steps. Admittedly a "nonliturgical people," Seventh Street Christian nonetheless sought to provide "a dignified, orderly, worshipful service." To that end the worship committee adopted a new order of service, used the weekly church newspaper to instruct members about features of the service, and requested that questions and criticisms be delayed until after each facet had been described. At the very least the new order of worship meant more elaborate services. Before the service the recently vested choir bowed in prayer with the minister. To the resonant sounds of the Austin organ, the choir processed and recessed, and during the service the congregation chanted the Lord's Prayer in unison.[33]

A few commentators feared that the most important part of worship services, the sermon, was changing and was diminishing in quality and significance. In a 1901 essay, "The Decline of the Pulpit," Union Seminary professor Thomas English recited a litany of concerns. Relying on new attractions such as beautiful music to draw people into churches, modern ministers had lost their sense of independence and authority, he asserted. They had forsaken messages of conviction and spiritual power for discourses on politics, sociology, and literature, English complained. Other conservative critics charged that some ministers deserted their area of expertise, biblical truth, for secular topics about which they were ill-informed. In a 1916 letter to a denominational newspaper, one Richmonder pointed to sermon topics listed in the local press, criticized their emphasis on contemporary issues, and bemoaned the neglect of "preaching to the impenitent." As late as the 1920s, a local Baptist minister joined those who were distressed about "the modern tendency to turn the pulpit into a rostrum for the discussion of industrial and political problems."[34]

Contrary to such fears, Richmond pulpits exhibited both vitality and change. Individual ministers relied on a variety of personal sermon styles. For example, at Second Presbyterian Church, Russell Cecil embodied a traditional approach to preaching. Kentucky born and Princeton educated, he believed that a preacher should craft a sermon with a direct purpose: instruction in doctrine, consolation of the bereaving, or conversion of the ungodly. Appropriate language would be direct, logical, "picturesque and luminous," but not cluttered with platitudes, oratorical flourishes, and anecdotes. Cecil's own sermons followed that script. In contrast, Grove Avenue Baptist's James B. Hawthorne was an unrivaled pulpiteer. As a young Alabamian, he had studied law but later embarked on a lengthy ministerial career. In 1899 the sixty-two-year-old minister returned to Richmond for his second pastorate in the city. Standing six feet four inches, Hawthorne had a robust appearance and spoke with energy and eloquence. With a voice notable for its range, resonance, and sweetness, he gradually accelerated his speaking cadence, raising and lowering his voice for emphasis. Hawthorne spoke passionately, but lyrically, and laced his presentations with literary allusions.[35]

Senior and often cerebral, Hawthorne also broke from tradition. He ruffled conservatives by departing from "the simple Gospel" and preached about topics ranging from vice to political corruption. Responding to criticism, Hawthorne declared that "Christianity in its entirety covers all human relations, ills, problems, and needs." In holding this view, Hawthorne was hardly by himself in Richmond. Even at the beginning of the twentieth century, other ministers spoke about social issues, and younger clergymen later joined in addressing matters ranging from equal suffrage to international peace. One rector acknowledged that such attempts to "bring the motives of God into the midst of everyday life" placed a heavy responsibility on preachers to be thoughtful, informed, and aware of human needs. First Baptist's George W. McDaniel emphasized the importance of study "to freshly interpret the Gospel" and "better preach the changeless Christ to a changing age."[36]

When delivering sermons, city ministers faced demanding listeners. McDaniel's wife later commented that the presence of three female authors in his congregation spurred him intellectually. That reaction was fortunate. After listening to some of young McDaniel's early sermons, one member wrote her mother and confessed her disappointment. Admitting that McDaniel drew large crowds and was an energetic and effective speaker, she still despaired that "all he says is obvious as a b c. . . . Doubtless he will improve." Early in a career at Ginter Park Presbyterian Church, pastor John A. MacLean warned that a city congregation was "composed of highly educated people, naturally critical." In order to hold that audience, a minister had "to measure up to the intellectual demands of a public none too tolerant," he declared.[37]

One group merited special attention. Soon after Walter Russell Bowie arrived at St. Paul's Episcopal Church in 1909, he began conducting children's sermons as a part of the worship service. Noting that children did not respond to vague generalizations, he later reported that preparation for those sermons forced him to be alert all week. He tried to find "something that would kindle the children's imagination and draw its own quick lesson." By stimulating him "to think pictorially," he believed, the preparation for a children's message impelled him to use more vivid language in his other sermons. Infatuated with the children's sermons, Bowie began publishing collections of them. Other Richmond ministers began to add children's sermons to their services, too.[38]

The men who delivered new types of sermons during Sunday services stayed busy coping with their changing roles as congregational ministers. In 1911 the *Union Seminary Magazine* characterized city pastors as "hardworking martyrs." A city parson was interrupted "by every grieved, puzzled person of the great throngs," including many who did not even know him but still sought "the solutions of every imagined trial." Pine Street Baptist's Joshua B. Hutson provided evidence to support this assessment. In 1904, when the *Richmond Times-Dispatch* conducted a contest to determine the state's most popular minister, Hutson won easily, receiving more votes than the rest of the field combined. When he had been queried earlier about the secret of his success, he responded, "hard work." Before retiring after a forty-two-year career at Pine Street, he saw the scope of his duties expand. His congregation of 167 in 1872 grew to more than 1,800 members. As they built a new church, they developed an array of programs from Sunday schools and vacation Bible schools to special activities like summer excursions to tidewater beaches. As Hutson guided these ventures, he also served as president of the Southern Baptist Foreign Mission Board and as president of the state mission board. Yet next to preaching, he ranked visiting as his most important duty. He visited every family in his congregation twice a year in addition to trips during such crises as illnesses and deaths. By the time of his retirement, he had made 49,294 visits, as well as conducted 1,459 weddings and 2,084 funerals. According to Hutson, a minister needed to learn to take shortcuts and tolerate "incursions of the unexpected." He voiced only one regret—that he lacked time for reading and studying. His career illustrated that city ministers risked being overcome by their expanding roles as pastors and as administrators.[39]

Even preaching seemed a less important duty than pastoring in Richmond. In honoring a local minister who had retired, left town, or died, a eulogy invariably praised his pastoral work. The rector of a large Episcopal church was characterized as the tireless "shepherd to his flock." No "individual case of distress among the members of his congregation ever escaped his notice." Comforting the sick, rich, or poor, he prayed with them and turned their attention to God. One Baptist explained that a preacher should live "in the life of his people"—visiting with them, praying with them, joking with them, and working with them.[40]

Such noble intentions, though, required effort to implement. A writer for

Richmond's *Presbyterian of the South* seemed almost to exude a sigh, asserting that "few people have any idea of the nervous strain of pastoral visiting." Regardless of how pleasant one encounter might be, a series of them "will produce great fatigue." Moving from home to home, a minister had to adjust to the psychological needs of each family. "There are very few people that do not pour their troubles into the ear of their pastor and so lay their burden upon his heart." The same writer added than an effective minister was "continually studying the condition of each member of the church" in an attempt to nurture his or her faith. Other commentators explained how pastoral duties had grown more difficult. Not only did individual churches have more members, those people were scattered across greater distances. One minister observed that scheduling visits had become more problematic because busy men were seldom at home except in the evenings and even then they might be drawn away by business or civic meetings. Another minister drew a different conclusion. With so many church gatherings held in the evenings, it was necessary, he decided, to make visits in the afternoons. Human needs also extended beyond the membership of a minister's congregation. One Episcopalian was lauded as a counselor for "an influential body of businessmen" as well as "a friend to those in trouble and sorrow." Hanover Avenue Christian Church's George W. Kemper was remembered as an unofficial pastor of Broad Street baseball park and of the streetcar barns.[41]

In fulfilling the enlarged role of pastor, First English Lutheran's John J. Scherer Jr. earned a reputation probably unmatched by any other city minister. A graduate of Roanoke College and Gettysburg Seminary, Scherer was called from West Virginia to serve First Lutheran in 1906. Prior to his arrival in Richmond, he had requested a list of the names and addresses of elderly and infirm members in order that he might visit them and administer the Lord's Supper before his inaugural worship service. The request was an indication of the young man's future. When the church moved to its new Stuart Circle location, Scherer quickly reached beyond his own congregation and spent much time at nearby hospitals. Physicians praised his efforts. "With common sense and with an understanding heart," remarked one prominent doctor, Scherer "seeks and finds the opportunity to help those who are broken, those who are weak." Another physician maintained that local doctors and social workers "owe him a debt which can never be repaid." "No situation is so distressful, no suffering is so great, no crime is so atrocious that a consultation does not bring all concerned the three great blessings of faith, hope, and charity." Scherer accepted an unusually heavy set of pastoral duties. Yet, like him, other ministers attended to the needs of both their own members and others in the community.[42]

Growing congregations, larger facilities, and new programs increased ministers' administrative tasks. For example, during George W. McDaniel's twenty-year tenure at First Baptist Church, the membership increased from 923 to 2,041 and the church budget increased from $12,093 to $73,467. A Richmond Presbyterian minister maintained that "the needs of a modern city have revolutionized the program of the local church, and the burden ever grows heavier on the pastor." Another writer explained that a city pastor now operated as an executive who headed a great institution. He had to plan, organize, and inspire, as well as resolve controversies. While pushing forward laggards and holding back the impetuous, he had to patiently entertain the theories of "every visionary" and endure the criticisms and complaints of members who felt "neglected and aggrieved." Yet as long as the laity remained active in new programs, churches benefited. But whenever their enthusiasm waned, the responsibility for the added programs devolved to "the already overburdened shoulders of the regular ministry," as one pastor ruefully remarked.[43]

Aid for busy city ministers arrived in the forms of delegation, innovation, and specialization. In 1904 Richmond Episcopalians formed the Laymen's Church League to train lay readers who could conduct services when needed. These men assumed their duties after being accredited by their own congregations and licensed by their bishop. By the 1920s some downtown churches added assistant pastors. Generally young men, they assumed some pulpit responsibilities, often conducted Sunday night services, and held services at missions established by their congregations. Some assistants devoted their energies to religious education programs, including Sunday schools and young people's groups. Thus, specialization accompanied delegation. A committee of one church conducted a survey of twenty area churches and determined that eight congregations employed youth workers, individuals properly trained and devoted exclusively to that type of work.[44]

A woman often served in that capacity. As later chapters will detail, even though women remained excluded from church pulpits, they steadily gained leadership roles in church activities. Early in the twentieth century, several Episcopal churches employed deaconesses who directed mission programs and visited members of their congregations. In 1899 a deaconess at St. Andrew's Church made 1,450 visits. A 1911 study by the Young Women's Christian Association reported that at least one Baptist church and two Presbyterian churches also employed "paid visitors." Fresh from a three-year training program, Sister Ruth Wagner began her career as a deaconess at First Evangelical Lutheran Church in 1919. In that role she teamed with pastor Scherer in making visits, organizing church programs, and attending to administrative details. At First Baptist Church, Miss Emmie Day was hired for a position which combined the tasks of treasurer, executive secretary, and church missionary. After a short stay at Seventh Street Christian, Jessie Spencer moved to Hanover Avenue Christian Church, where she won praise for handling the dual duties of financial secretary and director of religious education for elementary grades. As president of the Presbyterian General Assembly Training School for Layworkers, Walter L. Lingle actively promoted the employment of women to assist pastors throughout the South. Supported by Richmond's Presbyterian League in 1927, a young female graduate of that school visited the homes of the poor and the sick as well as hospitals, factories, and jails.[45]

Specialization was further evident when Episcopalians, Methodists, and periodically Baptists employed an individual to fill a position designated as city missionary. The Episcopal city missionary traveled widely, visiting the sick, aiding the needy, distributing Bibles and food, and holding religious services. In addition to hospitals, jails, factories, the Confederate Home, and the state penitentiary, he stopped at individual houses. When the partially blind and deaf Cary Montague assumed this position in 1918, he added a special dimension. Hired to assist him as a secretary and chauffeur, a young Episcopalian, Maria Williams, later recalled each day as an "adventure." But "after all, just getting across the street had an element of uncertainty" for Montague. According to Williams, the red-headed Montague combined naïveté and sophistication. Well-educated and racially liberal, he joyously interacted with disadvantaged people. Accompanying Montague, Williams reported, she lost "any feeling I might have had of the church as a pedestrian routine or as abracadabra or as bread pills on the medicine shelf 'to be taken on Sundays for the soul.'" Instead, a pervasive religious spirit seemed to touch the grimmest situations. Montague's trips took him to the Pine Camp Tuberculosis Sanatorium, where, he noted, "many are dying," to a girl's reformatory, and to the city almshouse. At the city jail the men responded to the popular song "Life Is Like a Mountain Railroad." An impressed Maria Williams reported, "In that dismal jail cell, Mr. Montague often sounded inspired and Jesus of Nazareth seemed very near."[46]

Cary Montague and other religious leaders experimented with unusual locations and innovations in worship. In 1926 Montague held interdenominational services in Richmond's huge, new Colonial Theater. By that date, a willingness to experiment with worship was not new. In the early 1900s Baptists, Presbyterians, and Methodists secured a large tent in which they held summer outdoor meetings on the city's East End. The Episcopalians soon embraced the same idea and reported heavy attendance. By 1916 the Presbyterian-sponsored factory mission program brought weekly luncheon services into many local plants, including the terminal of the Virginia Railway and Power

Company, where a streetcar served as the chapel. City religious leaders found that these unconventional worship locations well served two of their major goals, evangelism and social service.[47]

In 1897 the congregation of Fulton Baptist Church began worshiping in its new sanctuary. Living in a working-class neighborhood, members had done much of the work on the new building themselves. One member who owned a brickyard had contributed bricks, another member assumed responsibility for the church's oak ceiling, and others had done the carpentry. Later congregational historians proudly asserted that the building's simplicity created an environment "conducive to worship" and contrasted it with the "elaborate and ornate" edifices of other churches. Similarly, in 1900 an anxious editor of the *Central Presbyterian* denounced the increasing "elaboration of musical service" in churches, deploring such departures as "imitations and poor imitations of worship of the liturgical churches." Instead, the writer called for a continued simplicity of worship services that created an atmosphere of "strength and dignity." In early-twentieth-century Richmond, the story of Fulton Baptist was rarely repeated, and the advice of the *Central Presbyterian* was rarely heeded.[48]

Instead, Richmond's major Protestant denominations created places of worship and styles of worship notable for their increasing intricacy, not their simplicity. A generation of young Protestants who reached maturity in the 1920s participated in different patterns of worship than had their parents. Arriving at a remodeled church or at a new edifice on the city's periphery, a person entered a sanctuary where new furnishings reflected attention to the aesthetics of worship. Pew rents no longer restricted where a person could sit. Gazing at an impressive stained glass window, a church member might be moved by the mighty resonance of a new organ majestically sounding the chords of a new hymn as the vested choir entered the auditorium. Choral anthems, responsive readings, and the minister's sermon combined familiar messages of faith with modern themes. Not only did the preacher feel free to address contemporary issues, he and the congregation participated in interdenominational worship services and activities. And even those new technological devices, the movies and the radios, were employed to serve as a means of worship. At times weary from mounting administrative and pastoral duties, many ministers gained the aid of paid assistants, including women. Thus, as Richmond changed, so did its churches and the worship services they conducted. And as Richmond grew, those churches with their commitment to evangelism organized and grew dramatically, too.

4
Mighty Engines of Evangelism

In 1911 Baptist minister James W. Durham suggested that some congregations expected to attract new members merely by offering "the vocal gymnastics of an operatic choir and the homiletic pyrotechnics of a sky-scraping preacher." By contrast he praised members of other churches, who "are pulling off their coats, rolling up their sleeves, adapting themselves to changed conditions, and are succeeding handsomely." The actions to which Durham referred often occurred in a rather reserved manner. On 7 March 1916, a local newspaper portrayed a scene from the previous evening. "Groups of people moved quietly up the avenues and over the cross-streets . . . into private homes. By 8:30 Richmond was on her knees and her prayers were rising from a hundred simple altars. It was unusual. It was heart stirring. No one class and no one denomination prayed." The account described people involved in cottage prayer meetings at which many small groups of church members assembled in preparation for a citywide revival. The occasion, though striking, constituted just one moment in a larger pattern of activities. As evangelicals, Richmond Protestants cared deeply about converting people to Christianity, about uniting professed Christians with churches, and about rearing devout children. In the early twentieth century, however, Protestant leaders feared that they were not succeeding at these tasks in Richmond. They soon determined that citywide revivals, Sunday schools, and denominational educational institutions could operate as mighty engines of evangelism.[1]

As Richmond's population more than doubled between 1900 and 1930, ministers and laypersons warned that local churches were failing to match that growth. In 1903 Baptist layman John Garland Pollard recited statistics from the past several decades and glumly concluded that "the growth of Richmond Baptists . . . has not been encouraging." Even with later successes, Baptists remained anxious. In 1916 the editor of the Baptist *Religious Herald* rejoiced that "Richmond is coming to be one of the great cities of the land" but cautioned that "Baptists have not been notably successful in great cities." In 1904 a Methodist minister observed that church attendance had been falling in Richmond. A few years later, a presiding elder regretted that Methodists ranked second numerically and financially in the capital city and failed to wield "the influence in affairs that a great denomination should." In 1910 the weekly *Presbyterian of the South* editorialized that "the provision for evangelizing the masses in the city is far short of that in the country." Later the same publication portrayed the rapid growth of southern cities, including Richmond, and argued that the denomination should invest more money in reaching out to "the countless multitudes of people moving into these communities." Proud of recent congregational growth, Richmond Episcopalians alone seemed relaxed in the early 1900s. Even among them, there were exceptions. In 1910 a special committee of Episcopal ministers designated Richmond's westward population growth as a problem and concluded that "the condition so far as our church is concerned is steadily growing worse."[2]

Such bleak assessments dared not be ignored by Richmond's white Protestants, who believed that evangelism was the most important single task of their churches. A Presbyterian editor affirmed that "the church's greatest business is to witness for Christ and to preach the Gospel and to bring men to that attitude toward spiritual things which will induce them to seek regeneration of their souls." In sermons clergymen urged listeners to embrace Christianity and to join churches. In a typical plea for individuals to receive "salvation," Baptist James B. Hawthorne urged people to acknowledge they were lost sinners, submit to God, look to Christ as Savior, and try to live pure lives. The Methodist *Baltimore and Richmond Christian Advocate* declared that any church activity which did not assist in "bringing souls to Christ" or "building up souls in Christ" was "not a proper form of church activity." In 1925 Christ Episcopal Church proclaimed in its church newspaper, the *Trumpet:* "In accordance with Scripture, we believe that the supreme work of the church is to win souls for Christ and we give first place to evangelism."[3]

Richmond Protestants found that large citywide revivals could be a powerful means of evangelism. It was a surprising discovery. Ministers repeatedly voiced their misgivings about such mass revivals, and between 1894 and 1909, Richmond did not host a single citywide revival campaign. Several denominations did occasionally conduct weeklong "simultaneous meetings" at their churches. But in 1903, when a few preachers suggested that the Richmond Ministerial Union sponsor "interdenominational evangelical services," the proposal aroused so much opposition that the clergymen abandoned it.[4]

Richmond clergymen opposed mass revivals because they objected to the type of professional evangelist who frequently conducted such meetings. Ministers charged that evangelists often used crude language, even when they preached about sacred matters. For example, the editor of the Baptist *Religious*

Herald criticized renowned evangelist Billy Sunday for employing "the language of coarseness and blackguardism" when he spoke about "matters so high, so serious, so tremendously important." Other ministers complained that evangelists presented their own preconversion sins in such lurid detail that audiences received an education in how to sin. Furthermore, how could listeners receive much spiritual benefit from sermons so "unscriptural" and "intellectually shallow"? And religious leaders feared that church work would actually be hindered by visiting evangelists, who made extravagant statements in order to attract large crowds. Thereafter, as one religious editor observed, churchgoers could become so fond of "sensational preaching" that they had "no relish for the plain, simple substantial rations which pious and devoted pastors are in the habit of furnishing."[5]

The 1909 Chapman-Alexander revival changed Richmond's attitude about citywide revivals. Early in 1908 the Richmond Ministerial Union invited Presbyterian evangelist Wilbur Chapman to conduct a two-and-one-half week revival in the city. After Chapman and his musician associate Charles Alexander agreed to come, an interdenominational committee headed by Episcopal rector Thomas Semmes went to work. Local ministers and laypersons began systematic preparations for the meetings that would occur between 6 and 21 January in 1909. During that period they scheduled "simultaneous meetings" at churches throughout the rest of the city while Chapman preached at the city auditorium. Churches raised funds to pay for the expenses of hosting Chapman and his twenty-one-member staff, and the city government used the occasion to finance improvements for the auditorium. An interdenominational force of eighteen hundred voices was organized into six choirs. Twenty-five hundred personal workers divided into sixty-five squads, which attended services and visited with converts. Advertisements on streetcars, on billboards, and in parlor windows publicized the meetings. Newspapers offered subscriptions at discount rates to enable people to read about meetings they missed. An impressed Methodist editor concluded that "everything is organized and everything is business-like." In December 1908 local congregations held a week of prayer meetings in anticipation of the January services.[6]

Even snow did not stop huge crowds from attending the Chapman-Alexander meetings. Local ministers praised Chapman for his dignified manner and his plain, practical preaching. They also commended Alexander's tasteful use of worshipful music. Audiences filled the seats, spilled into the aisles, and stood outside the city auditorium. Chapman conducted special services for such specific groups as men, mothers, and the aged. For a service for the infirm and "shut-ins," a volunteer force assembled carriages and automobiles to provide transportation. A graduate of Lane Seminary and a former pastor, Chapman used a talk to students at Union Theological Seminary to emphasize the importance of a seminary education. Meanwhile, two of Chapman's associates, William Asher and his wife, held a sequence of meetings at the Tuxedo Pool Room, the Police Court, Murphy's Hotel, McKeel's Bar, Katy Howard's Saloon, machine shops, the city prison, and a reformatory.[7]

Local religious leaders enthusiastically labeled the Chapman-Alexander meetings a success. By one estimate, the services brought more than three thousand conversions. At the end of January, students from Richmond's Union Theological Seminary decided to sustain the religious fervor of the meetings and began holding services throughout the city. After the revival, local Presbyterian ministers wrote Chapman a letter of appreciation. They gave thanks that during the revival "the church of God was mightily presented before the community and greatly strengthened." A Baptist editor applauded the extensive fellowship and interdenominational cooperation the meetings fostered.[8]

The Chapman-Alexander campaign served as a model for citywide interdenominational revivals in 1916, 1919, 1921, 1923, and 1927. Each time, the major white Protestant churches organized services throughout Richmond for special meetings that occurred over a period of one to six weeks. Cottage prayer meetings preceded the well-advertised services held either in churches or in the city auditorium. In 1916 local ministers conducted the services and African American churches participated. After the rector of Monumental Episcopal Church suggested that laymen lead services in 1921, the idea was quickly adopted. Laymen and laywomen also conducted afternoon meetings at the YWCA, the YMCA, factories, shops, and sometimes even on the "principal thoroughfares of the city." In 1927 laymen again led the revival meetings, and ten local church choirs broadcast hymns from radio station WBBL during the weeklong evangelistic campaign.[9]

The most elaborate revival occurred in early 1919 when evangelist Billy Sunday held a six-week campaign in Richmond. That event relied on the now familiar tools of community organization. In December 1918 an advance man for Sunday arrived to begin coordinating plans for the meetings scheduled to start the following January. A local committee divided Richmond into eight districts in which twice-weekly prayer meetings were held before Sunday arrived. Almost 3,750 people attended the 273 prayer meetings, and two choirs of 750 voices prepared to perform. Laymen assembled 300 volunteers to serve as doorkeepers, ushers, and secretaries. The latter group was especially important because they handled the duties of securing the names, addresses, and possible church preferences of persons making professions of faith at the conclusion of each program. A businesswomen's committee encouraged working women to attend services. One major planning problem did handicap the meetings. With World War I conservation measures in place, the government refused to approve the use of lumber and labor to construct a large "tabernacle," which Billy Sunday customarily required. An unhappy Sunday used the slightly renovated city auditorium, which rarely accommodated the large crowds in attendance.[10]

Billy Sunday's appearance dominated Richmond news between January and March 1919. He delivered four sermons on Sundays and two each day of the rest of the week except Monday. Conservative in theology and flamboyant in style, Sunday delivered loosely structured presentations that lasted between forty-five minutes and an hour. He emphasized the need for listeners to become Christians, but he peppered his messages with attacks on social sins, including corporate greed, individual extravagance, divorce, the use of alcoholic beverages, and lewd entertainment. With blunt language and colorful phrases, he blasted perceived foes of God's work: "weasel-eyed, peanut grafting politicians," backsliding church members, Bolsheviks, liberals, and Germans. Sunday made trips to the campuses of Union Theological Seminary, Randolph-Macon College, and Westhampton College, then serving as a war hospital. By delivering five sermons one Sabbath, Sunday preached before more than 25,000 people.[11]

At times the dramatic Sunday visit seemed like a mixed blessing. An ungracious Sunday grouched about the inadequacies of the city auditorium. African Americans protested that no accommodations had been made for them. A defensive local arrangements committee rejoined that they had offered blacks segregated seating but that black ministers had refused tickets offered to them. Other critics deplored the cost of supporting Sunday's visit, which occurred just as most of the major Protestant denominations were launching massive, national fund-raising campaigns. A few ministers reiterated earlier objections that Sunday used crude language and anecdotes and dealt with religion in a superficial manner. Even the mild-mannered pastor of Second Presbyterian Church, Russell Cecil, criticized Sunday for his distracting stories and "gesticulations" and called some of his "expositions of the scriptures" "indefensible."[12]

Yet Sunday's revival also pleased area church leaders. As Russell Cecil observed, the evangelist used a simple and direct speaking style that listeners readily understood. Others commended Sunday for his earnest, sincere presentations that attracted people who were not church members. Sunday made a point to praise ministers and to urge converts to join churches. Local congregations did, in fact, report a surge of new members during the first months of 1919. A past critic of Sunday, R. H. Pitt, the editor of the *Religious Herald,* acknowledged that Sunday's campaign had been beneficial to the city. Pitt added, however, that "a tribe of Billy Sundays would be an affliction, not a blessing."[13]

Three years later "Cyclone Mack" McLendon demonstrated why local religious leaders were apprehensive about inviting evangelists to the city. With only the support of several churches, he conducted a two-week revival on the city's Southside, a blue-collar neighborhood. Cyclone Mack condemned preachers for "perfunctory, mechanical, stereotyped preaching that deals out soothing syrup on a spoon." He told one audience that religion "means being on the square and doing right, not going to church." In another sermon he referred to church members as "pharisees" and "religious pachyderms" "who are so crooked that they have to screw their shoes on every morning." McLendon was the very type of evangelist Richmond ministers renounced. He could draw big crowds. But he was not likely to win new converts who would join churches, and he might weaken the allegiance of people who were already church members.[14]

More often, city revivals were characterized by a quieter mood, and Richmond's Protestant leaders invariably expressed happiness with the results. Referring to services at Hanover Avenue Christian Church during the 1921 citywide revival, the *Chesapeake Christian* furnished an apt description of the prevailing religious atmosphere. "There was no sensationalism," the writer reported. "For three weeks the word of God was quietly and beautifully unfolded, the speaker rarely going outside the Bible for an illustration." Clergy and laity believed that the collective experiences of the revivals led to greater goodwill and cooperation among the city's different denominations. Ministers concluded that church members received spiritual inspiration and that nonmembers joined churches. At times congregations tried to count the number of new memberships that could be attributed to revival services. The numbers were impressive. Local churches claimed that there were 4,500 conversions in the 1916 revival. The Dover Baptist Association reported 2,200 additions to Baptist churches alone due to the Billy Sunday meetings in 1919. The week-long revivals in 1921 brought 700 additions to Richmond churches. City congregations reported 3,085 new members during the 1927 revival.[15]

Even during years when no interdenominational, citywide revivals were held, individual denominations sometimes conducted simultaneous meetings in their own churches. As a result of the 1914 and 1915 revivals, hundreds of people joined Baptist and Methodist churches. By 1930 Richmond's Protestant leaders had taken a new direction in reaching out to the city's unchurched citizens. Ministers and laypersons had not only experimented with revivals, they had mastered the organizational skills that made citywide, interdenominational meetings expansive participatory occasions that drew nonmembers into churches. Even as city Protestants began to harness the power of mass revivals as a means of evangelism, they ignited yet another engine, Sunday schools.[16]

No phenomenon of religious life in Richmond was more striking than the emergence of a strong Sunday school movement. Like churches of other communities, many Richmond congregations had established Sunday schools before the Civil War. At the beginning of the twentieth century, though, Protestant leaders concluded that their programs were weak. The editor of the *Southern Churchman* repeatedly criticized the quality of existing Sunday school instruction in Episcopal churches. Too much teaching, the journal complained, was done in a "haphazard and unintelligent fashion." The *Religious Herald* asserted that Baptists had made fewer improvements in their Sunday schools than in any other branch of their denominational work. The *Herald* noted that many Sunday school students lacked Bibles and that many programs used only "cheap hymn books." Southern Presbyterians were sufficiently concerned about their programs that they appointed A. L. Phillips as the first general superintendent of Sabbath schools and young people's work, and he moved to Richmond to begin his work. In 1906 the Episcopal Diocese of Virginia created a Sunday School Commission.[17]

To infuse new vitality into Sunday schools, local religious leaders turned to innovations, most notably the use of Sunday school institutes. Some institutes were conducted as interdenominational gatherings; others were held by individual denominations. All the institutes, though, generally shared certain characteristics. Initially involving a couple of days of meetings, they soon developed into elaborate weeklong programs, often called Sunday-school training schools. Beginning on a Sunday, an institute offered evening classes lasting two and a half hours. A person would devote the entire period to the study of a particular subject. The topics of courses ranged from Sunday school administration to biblical scholarship to teaching methods. Experts, frequently from out of town, served as instructors. Participants used textbooks or other printed material and completed projects. At the end of the week, anyone who had attended all sessions and finished assigned work received a certificate. In an era when relatively few people had access to higher education, the instruction offered at the institutes was prized. As a Methodist editor observed, "Not all of us have had the advantage of a college education, but all can take these courses."[18]

In 1903 Presbyterians initiated the first area institute, and seventy-five "delegates" from nineteen Sunday schools attended. The following year, local Presbyterians provided another boost by hosting the third annual meeting of the Sunday School Editorial Association of the United States and Canada. The visiting experts spoke at a mass meeting of Richmond Sunday school workers at Grace Street Baptist Church. In 1908 Baptists conducted an institute that attracted 618 people, 158 of whom earned diplomas. Local Presbyterians, Methodists, and Disciples of Christ regularly collaborated in organizing annual institutes. After arranging to use John Marshall High School for their 1920 institute, leaders were excited when more than six hundred people participated. In 1921 the instructors included an Emory University professor, a professor from the Disciples' Bethany College, the dean of a state normal college, and two professors from Richmond's Union Theological Seminary. Denominational Sunday school leaders such as A. L. Phillips directed some courses. By the 1920s those courses became more specialized, addressing such subjects as adolescent psychology and techniques of storytelling. In response to requests, the 1921 institute arranged to conduct follow-up programs at the high school for six weeks.[19]

Eager Sunday school teachers found other local resources. Richmond served as the headquarters for southern Presbyterian Sunday school work, and the Presbyterian Committee of Publication was located there. The staff of the committee wrote, edited, and published the denomination's Sunday school literature. In 1904 the committee moved to a large new building in downtown Richmond, and during the next thirty years it expanded its series of Sunday school periodicals from seven to twenty-eight. In 1918 Union Theological Seminary established an endowed professorship in Sunday school work, and in 1919 it became the first southern Presbyterian seminary to establish a separate department for Sunday school work. Union President Walter W. Moore announced that the new department would be devoted to the "scientific study of all phases of Sunday school organization, equipment, and management, paidology, pedagogy, and teacher training field extension." To implement that program, the seminary opened new Schauffler Hall in 1921. When the Presbyterians inaugurated their General Assembly Training School for Layworkers, it, too, provided coursework in Sunday school programs. In 1912 leaders of the city's major Protestant denominations organized a Sunday school association to exchange information about organizational methods. Both the *Religious Herald* and the *Baltimore and Richmond Christian Advocate* established weekly columns carrying news about Sunday schools.[20]

Experts agreed that successful Sunday schools relied on enthusiastic, well-prepared teachers under the direction of attentive superintendents. Up-to-date equipment and educational materials were also essential. Since each class needed its own room, churches constructed Sunday school buildings. Experts also agreed that Sunday schools, like public schools, should be graded—

organized by age groups. As a Presbyterian Sunday school manual explained, such an organization permitted teachers to "adapt the instruction to the age and capacity of the pupil."[21]

Children, of course, were expected to be the primary clients of Sunday schools. A Methodist minister declared that a Sunday school "evangelizes the child before he goes astray." The editor of a local newspaper similarly argued that it was far easier to teach children "in the right way than to bring into the way those who have gone astray." Emphasizing the importance of religious education, a Presbyterian writer asserted that "from the earliest period" "the great doctrines of the Bible should be instilled into a child's mind . . . in the form of a story, or picture, or complete statement." Religious leaders believed that a child who attended Sunday school was more likely to grow up as a Christian and that his parents would be more likely to attend church as well. At Sunday school institutes, instructors provided courses addressing the learning abilities of children of different age groups and demonstrated appropriate teaching techniques for specific groups. Youngsters also enjoyed annual Sunday school picnics, which became popular. Monumental and All Saints Episcopal churches began conducting daylong Sunday school excursions to a Virginia beach in the summer. Soon the beach excursion developed into a lively, annual, citywide Episcopalian custom.[22]

The Sunday school movement elevated women into positions of religious leadership. The Presbyterian Committee of Publication employed women to write, edit, and illustrate Sunday school quarterlies, weekly newspapers, and books. The daughter of two Richmond educators, Anna Binford was hired in 1909 to edit a weekly paper for adolescents. Binford, who wrote a number of Sunday school books and pamphlets, later recalled that her work required much Bible study and changed constantly. She "loved the job and found it engrossingly challenging to the best I had." As demands for contacts with individual congregations increased, Binford split her time between writing and fieldwork, including personal visits. As her supervisor R. E. Magill recalled, "She rendered a service of inestimable value, and at a time when the churches were strongly opposed to women speaking in public before mixed audiences." Magill savored the fact that Binford's presentations were so effective that even meetings intended for women alone attracted men, too. Another laywoman, Elizabeth Shields, created a series of graded songbooks for children. As a proud Magill noted, "The books have been adopted by two of the largest denominations in the United States, and they are widely used in other churches." At Sunday school institutes women drew on their professional training and experiences to present specialized courses. The *Presbyterian of the South* emphatically commended one institute conducted mostly by females. "These women are all experts in their lines," the editor declared, and those "privileged to attend greatly benefitted." Not only did women serve as Sunday school teachers, some assumed professional positions as directors of religious education. In that role at Seventh Street Christian Church and later at Hanover Avenue Christian, Jessie P. Spencer earned praise. At Seventh Street, H. D. C. Maclachlan called her an "ideal educational director" who "did a world of good." He added that "in some departments the results were revolutionary in the best sense; in all they were real and tangible."[23]

Not to be outdone by children or women, Richmond males marshaled impressive brigades of men's Bible classes. On Sunday afternoon, 21 November 1909, approximately four thousand men, assembled four abreast, formed a procession extending several blocks and paraded through the principal downtown streets. The recently created interdenominational Richmond and Manchester Men's Federation of Bible Classes organized the march, which halted at the city auditorium. There the men listened to a choir, a prayer, a scripture reading, and a presentation by Baptist state Sunday school secretary Joseph T. Watts. After a University of Pennsylvania psychology professor spoke about the Bible and character building, Gov. Claude Swanson concluded with a patriotic and "manly presentation." The parade was more than a gesture. It signified the real, burgeoning strength of men's Bible classes in the city.[24]

As specific classes demonstrated, they were as formidable individually as they were collectively. Organized in 1896, the Bates Bible Class at Union Station Methodist Church increased in size from thirty-five members to more than three hundred members in 1919. The class stayed busy. Members visited the sick and "the destitute." They engaged in evangelism at the "homes of the unsaved" as well as at hospitals, asylums, and prisons. The men conducted prayer meetings, helped members find employment, and financially supported an orphan, a seminary student, and a missionary. And they honored their "beloved teacher," Frank T. Bates, for his inspirational leadership and his example as "a typical Methodist Christian citizen." Though a bit smaller, the Men's Bible Class of First English Lutheran was similar to the Bates class. At its peak the class counted ninety-eight members. They subdivided their tasks by committees that enlisted prospective members, contacted absentees, developed devotional programs, visited the sick, arranged for socials, and helped men find employment. For a few years the executive committee of the class generated suggestions for improvements in the church and forwarded the ideas to the church council.[25]

The Businessmen's Bible Class of Second Baptist Church became famous for its teachers. With Richmond College English professor J. C. Metcalf serving as teacher, the class's size swelled to more than 200 members. In the 1920s, after Douglas Southall Freeman succeeded Metcalf, the membership rose to more than 650. When overflow crowds came to Second Baptist to listen to Freeman, the church set up loudspeakers so that people outside could hear him. One May Sunday morning in 1925, Freeman had an audience of 1,159 men, including the governor and his staff, a delegation from the Rotary Club, and students from the University of Richmond and the Medical College of Virginia. When Freeman began making radio broadcasts, he reached an even larger audience. Other men's classes made their distinctive marks in other ways. For example, the thirty musicians who formed the orchestra of the Ragland Bible Class at Barton Heights Baptist became so acclaimed that they gave performances throughout the city.[26]

The Richmond Sunday schools of the early twentieth century did prove to be mighty engines of evangelism. In 1913 the *Richmond Times-Dispatch* referred to local Sunday schools as the churches' "greatest recruiting ground." There could be little doubt that the carefully organized Sunday school work brought results. For example, in 1910 Baptists reported an increase of 1,000 Sunday school members over the previous year. J. T. Watts, the director of Richmond Baptist Sunday school work, proclaimed that "no city in the country of the same size can boast of as many large Sunday schools as Richmond." Union Station Methodist Church boasted the largest Methodist Sunday school in the state. In 1925, when Tabernacle Baptist Church celebrated its thirty-fifth anniversary, 1,934 people literally paraded up Grove Avenue and then attended Sunday school. During the 1920s other Sunday schools also continued to increase their memberships. In January 1923 the *Richmond News Leader* reported attendance of more than 900 people in nine different local Sunday schools. According to the U.S. census, Sunday school enrollment in Richmond's major white Protestant churches increased from 17,355 in 1906 to 51,365 in 1926. Baptist churches devoted special attention to improving their Sunday schools, and their Sunday school enrollment increased from 4,215 in 1906 to 23,789 in 1926. Sunday schools had proved their evangelizing power.[27]

As mass revivals and Sunday schools delivered more members into Richmond churches, religious leaders recognized the need for improving another vehicle of evangelism, institutions of religious education. In 1908 the pastor of Second Baptist Church, W. R. L. Smith, told the Dover Baptist Association that denominational colleges were "an invaluable evangelical factor." Other Richmond ministers emphasized that denominationally supported schools, colleges, and seminaries could be important instruments of evangelism. Each of Richmond's largest Protestant denominations tried to expand local opportunities for religious education.[28]

Protestant educators maintained that Christian educational institutions promoted evangelism in two important ways. First, church-supported schools trained future ministers and church members in skills necessary for winning converts and maintaining churches. Union Seminary's Walter W. Moore asserted that the Protestant ministers made their religious appeals primarily to people's minds. To make such appeals effectively, he emphasized, those preachers needed college and seminary preparation. Baptist Frederic W. Boatwright, president of Richmond College, declared that converts and Christian young people were potential leaders who needed to receive sound educations to embark upon lives of service. Methodist R. E. Blackwell, president of Randolph-Macon College, likewise contended that educated laymen were also vital to evangelistic work. In the United States, he claimed, "intelligence rules." Therefore, "the church that has the largest number of educated and cultured, godly members is going to be the ruling church and the one that will prove most attractive to cultivated Christians." According to Protestant educators, religious schools not only trained future church leaders, those institutions could also buttress the faith of other Christian young people. The *Central Presbyterian* warned that an education based strictly upon secular ideas would result in "the enfeeblement of the spiritual nature and the dwarfing of spiritual life." Ministers praised denominational colleges, where students were subject to the influence of Christian teachers. Students could take courses in biblical history and Christian beliefs. Bolstered by the religious influence of denominational schools, young people would become devout and dedicated church members.[29]

Relying on Sunday schools to educate younger children, city Protestants organized only a few elementary or high school programs. On Oregon Hill, St. Andrew's Episcopal Church developed an extensive educational program that included a parochial school composed of a kindergarten and an elementary school. Children began each day with prayer and devotional periods, received regular, graded religious instruction, and gathered for a Friday afternoon worship service to which their parents were invited. Teachers and the rector of St. Andrew's visited the homes of the school's students. Bethlehem Lutheran Church also maintained a parochial school. In 1922 the Presbyterian League of Richmond purchased the Collegiate School for Girls. Not officially affiliated with Presbyterianism, the school did offer a religious environment for education.[30]

In 1920 the Episcopal Diocese of Virginia announced the purchase of two local boarding schools as part of a large statewide educational program initiated by Bishop William Cabell Brown. Renamed St. Catherine's and St. Christopher's—for girls and boys, respectively—the schools provided college preparatory courses, religious instruction, and a moral atmosphere for their young pupils. Intending to apply religious ideals to modern life, St. Catherine's affirmed its mission to develop "a noble type of Christian womanhood . . . in body, mind, and spirit for gracious service in home, church, and nation." Calling "continuous and systematic training in religion" "an integral part" of the school's education, St. Catherine's provided for daily devotional periods as well as for instruction in religious studies. In establishing St. Catherine's, city Episcopalians deliberately acquired not only the facilities of an existing school but the esteemed reputation achieved by its principal, Virginia Randolph Ellett. A woman who devoted seven summers to studies at Harvard, "Miss Jennie," as she was affectionately known, had begun her small, elite school in 1890. In the early twentieth century she gained distinction for placing her students at Bryn Mawr. Within Richmond "Miss Jennie's girls" were known for their keen minds and their polish. A leader in the Richmond Education Association, she introduced Montessori classes at her school. After three moves, the Virginia Randolph Ellett School obtained a seven-and-one-half-acre site in Westhampton in the city's West End. Though conducting a nondenominational school, Miss Jennie worshiped at St. Paul's Episcopal Church and clearly exerted a religious influence on her students. One of them, a Baptist, characterized her as "an unusually devout person." When she sold her school to the Diocese of Virginia, she remained as associate principal and as an English and history teacher. The school and its students took pride in sustaining the reputation earned by Virginia Randolph Ellett and her past graduates.[31]

In establishing St. Christopher's School, the Virginia Diocese followed a similar path. It acquired a boys school directed by Dr. Churchill Gibson Chamberlayne. An Episcopal priest as well as a scholar trained in Germany, Chamberlayne opened his school in 1911. Like the Ellett school, it had relocated in Westhampton. Like Miss Jennie, Chamberlayne remained with the school after he sold it in 1920. Like St. Catherine's, St. Christopher's included religious instruction and devotional services. Continuing as headmaster, Chamberlayne explained that the aim of the school was to impress on its pupils the importance of service. "The best way to serve God," he declared, was "to be of service to one's fellow man." He emphasized that "a true Christian" acted upon such principles as honesty, obedience, self-denial, diligence, fearlessness, and benevolence. Chamberlayne championed the cause of church-supported schools. Not only did they improve the standard of education in the state and "the level of religion and morality in the community," they recruited potential ministers and laypersons "interested in the work of the Church and spreading the Kingdom." Both St. Catherine's and St. Christopher's flourished. To meet the demands of increasing enrollments, city Episcopalians engaged in an extensive fund-raising campaign in 1926. During the 1929–1930 academic year, St. Catherine's enrollment reached 291 students, and St. Christopher's enrollment reached 254 students.[32]

A concerned group of local Baptists concentrated upon improving Richmond College, the denomination's foremost educational institution in Virginia. City Baptists feared that their young people could not afford to pay for higher education. In 1900 the Education Board of the Dover Baptist Association concluded that "either the Lord of the harvest calls too many poor boys to labor in his harvest, or Baptists give too little money for their help." Three years later, another committee of the association warned that because Baptists were not providing more money for education "much of their best material is annually going to waste." Other leaders claimed that Baptists who could afford higher education did not attend Richmond College.[33]

At the turn of the century, the college's administrators wrestled with significant problems. Founded in 1830, named Virginia Baptist Seminary in 1832, and chartered as Richmond College in 1840, the institution had closed during the Civil War. In the late nineteenth century, the college succeeded in repairing its damaged and neglected buildings and in recruiting a notable faculty. But other difficulties remained. The school itself was small. In 1895 only 185 students had attended classes at the college's twelve-and-one-half-acre city campus. For many years Richmond College offered a limited curriculum of strictly classical courses. The school faced the twin handicaps of a small endowment and an awkward system of handling finances. In 1895 a group of prestigious professors resigned when the board of trustees reorganized the college and transferred administrative power from the faculty to the newly created position of college president. A 1906 report for the Baptist General Association of Virginia characterized the school as "rich in spiritual possessions" but lacking material equipment and an adequate endowment.[34]

Changes were under way, however, and the major force propelling those changes was Frederic W. Boatwright. When he became president of Richmond College in 1895, the twenty-seven-year-old Boatwright brought a precocious presence to the new position. The son of a Baptist minister, Boatwright grew up in several small towns in rural western Virginia. Surviving a seemingly fatal childhood accident, he attended both private and public schools. Following his father's example, he graduated from Richmond College and earned a master's degree. His alma mater hired him almost immediately to teach Greek. But Boatwright secured leaves of absence and spent almost two years studying in Germany and France. Returning to Richmond College as a professor of modern languages, he arrived with an appreciation for the flexible and innovative pedagogical methods he had encountered in Europe.[35]

During Boatwright's administrative career, Richmond College was transformed. It broadened its curriculum and moved to a new campus, which it shared with its new companion, Westhampton College for women. The new president had carefully studied other educational institutions in the United States and Europe. Drawing upon this experience, Boatwright initiated many changes. He won approval for a restructured curriculum as well as for the addition of new courses. Calling education "the poor man's opportunity," Boatwright maintained that poverty should not bar talented young people from college. To that end he successfully sought funds for scholarships and modern laboratories and recruited talented faculty members. In 1895 nine professors served Richmond College; by 1920 forty-six professors taught courses. Boatwright took an important symbolic stance in behalf of academic freedom by hiring controversial William Heth Whitsitt, who had been pressured to resign as a professor from Southern Baptist Theological Seminary in Louisville. National organizations recognized the enhanced quality of higher education offered in Richmond. By 1910 Richmond College met the accreditation standards of the Southern Association of Colleges and Secondary Schools. Rechartered as the University of Richmond in 1920, the institution met the requirements for a Phi Beta Kappa chapter in 1928. In 1929 the American Bar Association added the college's law school to its list of approved institutions.[36]

To achieve improvements at Richmond College, city Baptist leaders participated in several exhaustive fund-raising campaigns. In 1901 Boatwright contacted John D. Rockefeller through the American Baptist Education Society. Rockefeller agreed to donate $25,000 if the college raised $75,000. After an intensive fund-raising campaign, the college met the goal, and the total of $100,000 was set aside as an endowment. In 1906 Boatwright and several other local Baptists met with representatives of the General Education Board (GEB), a Rockefeller-backed philanthropic organization committed to improving southern education. The board offered to contribute $150,000 if the school could raise $350,000 in subscriptions and cash. By agreement the college would allocate $100,000 of this sum for building a separate division for women. In addition to Boatwright, other Baptist educators, ministers, and laymen worked vigorously to raise the funds. They contacted alumni, and they urged churches to release ministers so that they could devote their attention to fund-raising. The editor of the *Religious Herald,* R. H. Pitt, filled that state newspaper with appeals for funds. Still, these leaders had difficulty raising the money. Only after the GEB granted Boatwright and his coworkers several extensions did they raise enough money and subscriptions. Finally, in 1914 the total sum was collected.[37]

Boatwright tapped other sources to secure needed financial resources. In 1902 he gained a $25,000 settlement from the Federal government for property destruction of Richmond College by Union soldiers during the Civil War. Between 1917 and 1919 he launched another campaign to raise a million dollars for new buildings and scholarships. In 1927 he directed a drive to raise more than two million dollars. Boatwright garnered additional funds from the General Education Board, including $100,000 to replace a science building destroyed by a fire in 1925.[38]

Baptist educators overcame several problems during these fund-raising drives. First, most Virginia Baptists had modest incomes. At the conclusion of the 1906–1908 campaign, the *Religious Herald* claimed that nine-tenths of the money came from people of modest means or people who were "positively poor in the world's goods, though rich in faith." The *Herald* later applauded Richmond's Grace Street Church for raising $12,000, despite the fact that it did not have a single member of "very large means." Second, the national economic depression of 1907 had a potent impact in Richmond and delayed contributions from local congregations. Third, according to historian Reuben Alley, the Baptist General Association of Virginia actually adopted policies which hindered fund-raising. The association decreed that the college's representatives could not directly solicit contributions from congregations. For several years the association refused to elect non-Baptists to the board of trustees, and this policy apparently alienated some potential donors. Furthermore, a clash between Boatwright and the pastor of First Baptist Church limited support from some Richmond area Baptists.[39]

Despite these problems, Boatwright and his supporters acquired funds to improve Richmond College, and the new resources permitted dramatic changes. The fund-raising campaigns brought to fruition a long-entertained goal, facilities for educating women. Since 1854 Baptists had provided education to young women at the Richmond Female Institute and its successor, the Woman's College of Richmond. When the Boatwright era began in 1895, professor S. C. Mitchell opened his new history course to local residents, including some women. Boatwright, who had earlier advocated admission of women to Richmond College, gained the support of the board of trustees, and a few women began taking classes in 1898. With Richmond serving as a base for a statewide public education movement and with women still denied access to state universities, the moment seemed auspicious for a major change.[40]

R. H. Pitt led the local campaign for women's education. After labeling the lack of college facilities for Baptist women "a shameful neglect," he posed the question: "Is the education of women less important than that of men?" In sharply rhetorical phrases, he wondered why Virginia Baptists invested much money in a college for men, but gave "practically *nothing* for the education of women?" (Pitt's emphasis). Pitt and others believed that Baptists needed to match the educational opportunities that state Methodists had created when they had established Randolph-Macon Woman's College in 1893. Second Baptist's W. R. L. Smith called for a women's college equal in quality to that provided for men. Spurred by a funding requirement of the General Education Board, Virginia Baptists chose an approach promoted by Boatwright and Mitchell. A new college, eventually named Westhampton College, was created as part of the larger Richmond College. This coordinate college method meant that male and female students would share some campus facilities but would remain segregated by gender most of the time. As an initial step, the Woman's College of Richmond united with Richmond College, but the new coordinate structure seemed to necessitate more space than available in the vicinity of the existing campus of Richmond College.[41]

The shift to coordination thus accelerated another change, movement to a new location. In 1910 the board of trustees decided to purchase a site in the city's West End. On approximately 290 acres of rolling and wooded hills, a new campus began to take shape. Separated by a lake, Richmond College for men and Westhampton College for women slowly emerged in a distinctive brick collegiate gothic style of architecture. Dormitories, dining halls, an administrative building, a gymnasium, a stadium, a science building, a chapel, and a power plant were constructed. In 1920 two Baptist laywomen were elected to the board of trustees, and the first female student was admitted to the university's law school.[42]

In 1932, when the University of Richmond belatedly celebrated its one hundredth anniversary, it clearly had changed since Boatwright became president. The university offered a more diverse curriculum, had gained national recognition, and welcomed women to Westhampton College. In 1895 there had been nine faculty members; in 1931 there were sixty-one. In 1895, 183 students attended classes; in 1931, 1,350 students enrolled. Now on a spacious campus, the value of university property had risen from $300,000 in 1895 to more than $2.5 million. The school's endowment of $400,000 in 1895 now exceeded $2.6 million.[43]

Throughout the decades of change, the university remained committed to both Baptists and the city of Richmond. Faculty members were usually Baptists, and students regularly attended chapel services. The faculty taught religion courses, as well as a course in Sunday school pedagogy, and in 1929 the university began conducting a special summer school for ministers. At times Baptist ministers held revivals on campus. In February 1920, for example, the college closed classes for two hours daily as the pastor of Second Baptist Church conducted a revival. For one hour each day he met privately with students to talk with them about their religion. Speaking to the board of trustees,

Boatwright affirmed the institution's purpose of educating preachers and missionaries but added that its other major mission was to provide the best possible higher education to the young people of Richmond and of Virginia. Much of the school's impact on the city of Richmond came from its students and faculty. Faculty members were often active laypersons and spoke in Richmond churches. Some professors like S. C. Mitchell and Rolvix Harlan earned respect as dynamic community leaders.[44]

Other Protestant denominations also encouraged church members to send their children to denominational colleges and to contribute money to support these schools. Methodist leaders promoted their two major schools in Virginia, Randolph-Macon Woman's College in Lynchburg and Randolph-Macon College, located less than twenty miles from Richmond in Ashland. In 1901 John P. Branch, a Richmond banker, layman, and philanthropist, established a $100,000 endowment for Randolph-Macon's use. The *Richmond News Leader* praised Randolph-Macon College's "atmosphere of intellectual honesty" as well as its "thoughtfulness in education." The newspaper urged Richmonders to contribute to the school whose graduates constituted "an honor roll of public servants."[45]

As a source of religious education, no institution in Virginia rivaled Richmond's Union Theological Seminary. In 1916 Union reported that it furnished three-fourths of the Presbyterian ministers in the Synod of Virginia and three-fifths of the Presbyterian ministers in the Synod of North Carolina. With students from twenty-seven states and nations in 1926, Union's influence extended far beyond its immediate region. Founded in 1812 in rural Hampden-Sydney, Virginia, Union had a distinguished history. But in 1898 it completed its move to Ginter Park, then a Richmond suburb. Union Seminary of the twentieth century bore the remarkable imprint of Dr. Walter W. Moore, the first man to hold the newly created position of seminary president.[46]

Walter Moore's route to Richmond had been a demanding one. Born in Charlotte, North Carolina, in 1857, he endured his father's death from tuberculosis in 1863. His mother taught school to provide for her three children, and bookish Walter held a series of part-time jobs to help support the family. With funds from summer jobs and with financial assistance from his mother and older brother, he studied at a rigorous private high school and then entered Davidson College in 1874. After graduating from Union Theological Seminary, he was ordained as a Presbyterian minister and spent the next two years in western North Carolina. As a mountain missionary, he rode his horse hundreds of miles each month to deliver sermons at widely separated locations. After serving at a Kentucky church, he accepted an invitation to return to Union, where he became a professor of Hebrew.[47]

At Union Seminary in Hampden-Sydney, Moore became a leader. He quickly distinguished himself as a skillful teacher as well as a founder and a contributor to the *Union Seminary Magazine*. On several occasions he assumed the responsibility of raising funds for Union. He soon concluded that the only way for the seminary to thrive and grow was for it to relocate to a major city. As he later recalled, "The need was to put the institution into more effectual contact with the great throbbing heart of the Church and with all the varied lines of her world-wide work." As a forceful proponent of the controversial idea of relocation, Moore galvanized supporters, persuaded opponents, consummated negotiations, and arranged for the move to Richmond. In these often arduous endeavors, Moore benefited from the assistance of ministers and laypersons of Richmond's major Presbyterian congregations.[48]

In Walter W. Moore's 1905 inaugural address as president of Union, he began to articulate his vision for the seminary. He asserted that its primary purpose was not to make learned theologians but "to make effective preachers of the cross." This simple statement hardly conveyed the scope of Moore's aspirations. In a 1911 letter to a future Union professor, Walter L. Lingle, Moore expressed his conviction that the seminary should bring together "evangelical faith, real scholarship and practical efficiency" so that a young man could receive as good an education "as can be found anywhere in the world." Even such a famous seminary as Princeton did not always succeed. In another letter to Lingle, Moore described Princeton as being "far more out of touch with anything practical and vital in the work of the church today than perhaps any other theological seminary whatsoever." In his 1905 address, Moore explained that the "church is largely what her authorized teachers are, and that her teachers are chiefly what their theological training makes them." Himself a dedicated teacher, Moore understood that the seminary needed modern facilities, skillful faculty members, and innovative programs.[49]

Moore used his distinctive combination of talents to make Union the leading Presbyterian seminary in the South. The tall, mustached Moore engaged listeners with his calm, pleasant, dignified demeanor and elicited generous responses from donors. With direct appeals he gained the respect and won the confidence of several philanthropists who repeatedly made substantial gifts to the seminary. Speaking to a mass meeting held at Richmond's First Presbyterian, Moore emphasized the Presbyterian tradition of an educated clergy and carefully explained the courses of study followed by current seminarians. In canvassing other Presbyterians, he relied on a gentle, but sometimes subtle style. In a Lynchburg church in 1926, he delivered a sermon about the prophet Elijah and made only an allusion to the need to aid modern "prophets" so that they could receive necessary training. Moore closed the service without mentioning money, but the church contributed $10,000 in cash and made subscriptions for additional amounts.[50]

Moore also succeeded because he worked very hard. Making scores of out-of-town presentations each year, he traveled to churches from San Antonio and New Orleans to Kansas City and Chicago. Still serving as a classroom professor, he rarely had the assistance of a replacement instructor or of an additional financial agent. In one letter he noted that the "strenuous work" of one fund-raising campaign necessitated "shortened nights, much railroading, much canvassing, much speaking." As a devoted husband and father, Moore did reserve time for his family. At times Moore expressed his frustration that administrative tasks left too little time for his teaching and his scholarship. Yet he repeatedly refused calls to prestigious churches, such as Fifth Avenue Presbyterian Church in New York City, and to other seminaries, such as McCormick Theological Seminary in Chicago. Slowed by heart problems after 1923, Moore struggled to resume his old duties but retired in April 1926 and died on his birthday a few months later.[51]

But Moore's efforts had yielded impressive results. The seminary acquired additional land, built a refractory, and constructed a special building to house a new Sunday school department with model Sunday school facilities. Relying on the financial backing of women's mission societies, Moore opened a special complex, Mission Court, to house missionaries on furlough. Union also established a lectureship for visiting scholars, endowed several faculty chairs, diversified its curriculum, added a graduate department, and developed an annual midwinter course for ministers. At the beginning of Moore's presidency, Union Theological Seminary included six buildings and grounds valued at $80,000. By the end of his tenure, there were eighteen buildings and grounds valued at $651,781. The faculty had increased from four professors to nine professors, who offered a substantially more diverse curriculum. The seminary's endowment had increased from $252,575 to $1,218,672.[52]

When Moore began his work, Union Theological Seminary was a struggling rural seminary with a declining enrollment and a doubtful future. By 1927 the seminary's student body had increased to 158 men, making it the largest southern Presbyterian seminary. Moore admitted that he preferred a seminary that was conservative in theology but progressive in method. First a student and later a professor at Union, religious historian Ernest Trice Thompson at times criticized Union's theological conservatism. But he acknowledged that during Moore's lifetime, Union "pioneered" in areas of theological education and that other southern Presbyterian seminaries followed its example. By the end of Moore's presidency, younger faculty members like Thompson and Walter Lingle brought new theological ideas into Union as well. They did so with Moore's blessing. Moore's penchant for practicality and innovation made him an important figure in creating another educational resource, the Presbyterian General Assembly Training School for Layworkers.[53]

When Richmond Presbyterians launched the General Assembly Training School, they opened the doors of religious leadership to women. In 1907 a local woman who had been appointed as a foreign missionary was granted permission to attend lectures at Union Seminary. After a Union committee approved the creation of a summer school for layworkers and missionaries, fourteen women enrolled in 1909. For the next four years Union professors offered courses for layworkers. With the support of Moore, A. L. Phillips, the general superintendent for Sunday schools of the Presbyterian Church in the United States, successfully championed the cause of a layworkers school. In a series of actions between 1911 and 1913, the denomination's general assembly approved the establishment of a school and selected Richmond as its site. To its Richmond promoters, the need for the school was clear. As W. W. Moore later recalled, Presbyterians provided extensive training for their ministers. But "at the very time when the activities of our laymen and women were coming to their maximum, we had in connection with our church no provision whatever for training them for their work." Graduates of the program would serve as foreign missionaries, home missionaries, Sunday school leaders, teachers in schools and colleges, and assistants to city pastors.[54]

Still, the school had to survive a start which Moore described as "precarious." Opened in November 1914, the General Assembly School for Layworkers held its initial year of classes in downtown Richmond in the building housing the Presbyterian Committee of Publication. With Moore and a Union professor directing fund-raising, the Richmond Presbyterian League financed the school for its first three years and acquired property and buildings near Union, where courses were taught between 1915 and 1917. With only one paid, full-time faculty member, the school relied on Union faculty, Sunday school administrators, Richmond ministers, and laypersons who donated their services as instructors. In 1917 the school's dean expressed his dismay over the failure of the Presbyterian General Assembly to provide sufficient funds to maintain the school, which became known by the abbreviation ATS.[55]

The eventual success of ATS can be traced to one of its early presidents, Walter L. Lingle. In private correspondence, W. W. Moore declared that Lingle "saved the life" of ATS and "set it on the highway to the largest success." Lingle's leadership of the school was part of a larger life of denominational service. A graduate of Davidson College and Union Seminary, he arrived in Richmond after serving several pastorates in South Carolina and Georgia. From 1911 to 1924 he was a professor at Union Seminary, and for most of that period he was editor of the *Union Seminary Review.* Except for one year between 1918 and 1924, he served as acting president of the ATS, and between 1924 and 1929 he was the school's full-time president. Meanwhile, he accepted other duties. From 1911 to 1925, he was chairman of the program committee and platform manager for the southern Presbyterians' extensive summer conferences at Montreat, North Carolina. In 1920 he became moderator of the General Assembly of the Presbyterian Church in the United States. Thereafter, he chaired one committee that revised the Book of Church Order and another that created a new hymnal. He also served on the board of directors of the Federal Council of Churches. President of the board of trustees of Davidson College between 1906 and 1929, he accepted a call to become president of Davidson in 1929. Lingle articulated a vision of a southern Presbyterian church attentive to social problems, willing to consider unification with the Presbyterian Church in the United States of America, and ready for expanded roles for women.[56]

A busy Walter Lingle nonetheless led a life that revolved around his family. Born in North Carolina in 1868, he revered his farm parents who worked hard to provide for their seven children, their one adopted daughter, and one of his grandmothers. His mother had taken care of the family during her husband's Civil War military service and earned a reputation for helping others. Lingle admired his father as a "progressive," "public spirited" man deeply concerned about his children's education. A teenager when his father died, Walter assumed responsibility for running the farm. As an adult, Lingle maintained close ties to family members, including many nieces and nephews. He wrote often to older brother Will, a missionary in China, and younger brother Tom, a professor at Davidson. In 1900 Walter married Merle Dupuy. In a letter to a family member, Lingle later counseled that good marriages were based on "team work. You ought to work together in everything." Apparently Merle and he succeeded. When she stumbled upon some of their old letters, almost two decades old, she reflected on the intervening years. "They made me love you better than ever," she wrote her husband.[57]

The Lingles devoted much of their attention to their children, a priority Walter W. Moore understood well. Attempting to entice Lingle to join the Union faculty, Moore had assured him that the salary would be sufficient to support the family and that the neighborhood around Union was "a paradise for children," with its "wide spaces, green yards," and an excellent school. Writing a friend in China, Lingle effused that "a man could talk about his wife and children all day long" and recited their activities from academic achievements to musical feats to Boy Scout outings. The family read aloud to each other and spent much of each summer together at Montreat in the mountains of North Carolina. When attending schools and colleges away from home, the young Lingles eagerly shared news of their studies, friends, extracurricular activities, and problems—and complained if Lingle lagged in responding. Merle remained at the center of the family's round of activities. In "my dear sweetheart" letters sent from Montreat, she provided kind but candid assessments of the children's behavior. She also described joint ventures, including sewing with one daughter, reading with another, looking for a lost cat, and making ice cream, washing clothes, and packing possessions for shipment to Richmond.[58]

The Assembly Training School united Lingle's roles as a denominational leader and a family man. The faculty and students became, in effect, surrogate members of Lingle's extended family. One graduate of ATS, Louise McComb, later described Lingle as the "beloved father figure with personal concern" for students' welfare. During one academic year when enrollment exceeded available housing, seven students boarded with the Lingles. Walter Jr. later testified that the training school "became an integral part of our family." "Every decision in connection with the school tended to be a topic of conversation within our house, which was next door." According to one account, his father checked the furnaces in the residences, "fired them if necessary," and shoveled snow when weather required it. Lingle raised funds, taught courses, hired instructors, organized the curriculum, located jobs for his graduates, and often continued to serve as a counselor to them after they attained professional positions or pursued graduate school degrees. Many graduates sent letters of appreciation reflecting their respect and affection for him.[59]

Yet even this paternal role could create stress and could require Lingle's ample diplomatic skills. Writing to W. W. Moore in the summer of 1923, Lingle admitted he was suffering from "nervous indigestion," apparently caused by "a situation for the past ten days that has literally made me sick and almost sent me to be bed." During a women's conference at Montreat, Lingle had attempted to solicit financial support for ATS, only to discover that many of the participants had doubts about the commitment of some ATS and Union faculty members to women's work in the denomination. A stunned Lingle reported that "they had every man and wife on our campus rated somewhat as Bradstreet would rate mercantile firms." Their concerns had merit. As members of Ginter Park Presbyterian Church, several of Union's conservative faculty members and their wives had once opposed the formation of the Presbyterians' woman's auxiliary. As a member of that church, Lingle had written a lengthy appeal against such a course warning of "its unwisdom, its injustice, and the possibilities of serious injury" for the church as well as "its influence for harm far beyond the bounds of our congregation." In 1923 Lingle did succeed in establishing that the ATS and the Union faculty supported the

Woman's Auxiliary, and the Woman's Auxiliary raised essential funds for constructing school buildings.[60]

Indeed, in the 1920s, the Assembly Training School thrived. It acquired a twelve-acre site adjacent to Union Seminary. With the support of the city's Presbyterian League, Lingle raised additional funds. The school soon constructed a dormitory, a dining hall, and houses for the president and the full-time professors. ATS continued to utilize Union's faculty, library, chapel, and classrooms. Students completed a two-year curriculum that included courses in theology, church history, missions, music, psychology, sociology, and physical education. The Virginia Board of Education recognized these studies as college level courses. Students participated in the Presbyterian League's factory mission program each week as well as in its Seventeenth Street Mission for African Americans. In 1928 more than two hundred women took courses at ATS. With Lingle encouraging southern Presbyterian leaders to employ them, graduates began careers in church work as well as in home and foreign missions.[61]

Busy organizing and supporting revivals, Sunday schools, and educational institutions, Richmond congregations reached out to local residents by other means such as visiting the homes of prospective members. Even in these activities, though, they experimented with new methods that frequently featured interdenominational cooperation. In 1912, 7,000 church workers conducted a religious census of Richmond and its suburbs, and the workers recorded information about approximately 160,000 people. Canvassers ascertained the religious preference of these residents and notified neighborhood ministers from appropriate denominations. At several meetings in 1916, representatives from churches considered the merits of using advertising to draw more people into church services. Initially reluctant, ministers and laity soon approved the use of tasteful publicity, as subsequent church budgets and advertisements in local newspapers demonstrated.[62]

To coordinate some citywide evangelistic endeavors, Baptists formed the Baptist Council of Richmond and Manchester, and the Presbyterians organized the Presbyterian League. Each group was composed of ministers and laypersons. The Baptist Council assisted in creating two Baptist settlement houses. It also organized new churches and provided financial support for them. Formed in 1911, the Presbyterian League developed a more multifaceted agenda. It, too, raised funds to assist newly created churches, and it purchased land for future building sites. The league provided financial support for the General Assembly Training School during its early years and sponsored the Seventeenth Street Mission for African Americans. Laywomen inaugurated a factory mission program which conducted weekly, noon prayer meetings in Richmond industrial plants, and clergy and laity from other Protestant churches assisted.[63]

The white Protestant religious community included industrial workers as well as the city's growing middle class and its well-to-do citizens. The working class neighborhoods of Fulton, Fairmount, Oregon Hill, and Manchester all supported large churches of the major denominations. Several local labor leaders led men's Bible classes. Episcopal city missionary, R. Cary Montague, praised the large Baptist men's Bible classes for "bringing men of all walks of life into closer social touch" and letting "men of all professions and occupations" share experiences "on a basis of perfect social equality." To facilitate access to churches, Methodists and Disciples particularly rejected the concept of a large central church in favor of numerous smaller congregations scattered in different neighborhoods throughout the city.[64]

In 1920 an editor of the *Presbyterian of the South* pondered the status of urban evangelism. He observed that "it seems harder for the Church to reach those outside of her fellowship when they are crowded all about her doors than it is to reach the destitute in some far off mountain section." Responding to the challenge of urban evangelism, Richmond ministers and laypersons used organized and innovative measures which brought results. Between 1906 and 1926, membership in Richmond's white Protestant churches increased from 33,030 to 60,864. During that same twenty-year period, local Protestants established thirty-two new churches. Data for individual congregations provided further evidence of significant growth. Still, statistics alone hardly measured the impact of evangelistic efforts. Hundreds of graduates of Union Seminary served as ministers and missionaries; hundreds of graduates of the General Assembly Training School served in churches and in mission fields. The young men and women who attended St. Andrew's school, Bethlehem Lutheran's school, St. Catherine's, St. Christopher's, Richmond College, and Westhampton College approached adulthood with religious training which sensitized them to the opportunities for Christian service as laypersons. Relying on careful, systematic organization, Richmond Protestants had transformed revivals, Sunday schools, and denominational schools into mighty engines of evangelism.[65]

5
Paths of Grace

In 1909 a Methodist layman lamented, "It is a struggle in the city to keep from moral and spiritual bankruptcy." For Richmond Protestants that struggle was important. As local churches added members through evangelistic activities, ministers emphasized that becoming a Christian meant more than subscribing to a set of beliefs—it meant leading a transformed life. God's grace saved individuals, Baptist James B. Hawthorne affirmed, but God also wanted each person to grow into spiritual adulthood, a process often requiring "patient, persistent and arduous effort." Protestant leaders encouraged church members to follow four paths to maintain a sense of spiritual direction. Each individual needed to practice personal devotions, including participation in worship services. Each family should nurture the spiritual welfare of its members. Each Christian should observe Sunday as a sacred occasion. And each person could foster a pious community by respecting organized government, by demanding honest leaders, and by insisting on the separation of church and state. These paths of grace first led inward into the religious consciousness of a believer but then led inexorably outward to face an evolving urban arena.[1]

A devout Christian needed to give daily attention to his or her spiritual welfare, local ministers advised. A welcoming God, Hawthorne assured, had "left an inviolable zone of life for exclusive transactions between himself and the individual soul." With a "sweet trust in God which brings peace, we walk with him; we feel that we are overshadowed by his presence and that nothing can separate us from his love." Christians encountered this sense of God's spiritual presence by engaging in daily devotions, by praying regularly, and by attending church services. Hawthorne counseled that each person needed daily "spiritual food," which could be received only through private moments of contemplation and prayer. According to Methodist minister Edward Pell, Christians should develop regular habits which "will keep the channels of our spiritual nature open to life—to the spirit of Christ who is our life." Pell cautioned that it was "folly to hope that you can spend the day with God if you are not willing to begin it with him." Pell recommended setting aside one-half hour each morning to read the Bible and pray, and he suggested designating a specific place for the exclusive purpose of devotions in order to avoid interruptions.[2]

The *Presbyterian of the South* encouraged readers to "practice spirituality. Cultivate spiritual habits. Live in the realm of the unseen. Educate the imperishable faculties of the soul." Such an education meant reading the Bible. As Union Seminary President Walter W. Moore stated simply in his volume *The Indispensable Book,* "The Bible is necessary to our spiritual life." Methodist Pell favored placing a Bible on a table near one's bed. Devotional reading included various types of religious publications. As weekly denominational newspapers, the *Southern Churchman,* the *Religious Herald,* the *Richmond Christian Advocate,* the *Presbyterian of the South,* and the *Chesapeake Christian* delivered articles about a wide range of religious topics and presented columns for differing interests and age groups. Operating in Richmond, the Presbyterian Committee of Publication printed the weekly papers *Junior Life, Story Hour,* and *Onward* for children of different ages. The Methodists maintained a publishing house in Richmond, and the Nashville-based Southern Baptist Sunday School Board published a variety of materials, including collections of sermons.[3]

During daily devotions, a Christian should not only read, he or she should think as well. Observing that "the habit and grace of meditation" had "almost perished" "in our age of rush and hurry," the *Southern Churchman* recommended moments of "spiritual stocktaking" and self-examination. Then "in the privacy of our own communion" with God, church members could assess their own attitudes and behavior. Similarly unhappy that the apparent "slogan of the age" was "not think but act," James B. Hawthorne cited the results: "feeble and superficial thought." He asserted that "very few men, comparatively, purpose to do wrong." Yet they yielded to temptations because "they have no time to think calmly about distinctions between right and wrong." By contrast, devout Christians should set aside time for private contemplation. "The good and great things we do," Hawthorne maintained, "we do by a power which comes from God in our quiet hours of introspection and prayer." Episcopal rector Walter Russell Bowie advised that private worship and prayer helped keep people ready for times "when the Master appears to us in daily life in business or other activities."[4]

And Richmond ministers emphasized the importance of prayer. In a collection of children's sermons, Bowie taught that people "cannot do good by themselves." They needed to pray for God's help. If we would fly to heights, instructed Bowie, "we must ask God to let us fly with His wings." Hawthorne described prayer as "commerce between earth and heaven" in which the soul climbed up to God. Second Presbyterian's pastor, Russell Cecil, characterized prayer as "an expenditure of soul energy," "a going out of all the powers of the soul in a desperate effort to find God." These preachers did not refer to philosopher and psychologist William James and his path-breaking 1902 volume, *The Varieties of Religious Experience.* Still, they would have concurred with his interpretation of prayer as "intercourse with God" and as "the very soul and essence of religion."[5]

Prayer meant spiritual communion with a loving God who would answer a person's petitions—though not always at the time or in the manner sought. The "availing prayer" should be fervent, reasonable, and submissive to God's will. Furthermore, as one Presbyterian pastor explained, the very individual who offered a prayer should request that God use him or her as the means of answering that prayer. Baptist George W. McDaniel suggested that in answering prayers, God would place responsibility in the hands of a believer who became a partner with God. A Christian should also pray for others and give thanks for blessings received. And as Cecil assured, God revealed himself to those who prayed and guided them each day.[6]

In addition to daily prayers, Christians turned to God in times of such crises as illnesses, accidents, or death. Referring to prayer, Edward Pell pitied the person who in "hours of helplessness has no Heavenly Father's eyes into which he may look." In making pastoral visits, a minister invariably prayed with his hosts. Describing one local rector, an Episcopal laywoman reported that "he met every crisis in the life of each parishioner with a prayer." Even at night he telephoned those who were invalids and prayed with them. In eulogizing H. D. C. Maclachlan, a writer recounted a poignant pastoral visit when a child was deathly ill. Kneeling with the parents, Maclachlan offered a deeply importuning prayer, then rose, and correctly predicted the child's recovery. Sunday school teacher Douglas Freeman also shared an example of what he called the "treasure" of "answered prayer." He recalled an incident in 1920 when physicians had diagnosed his daughter as having contracted spinal meningitis and had advised him that even if she survived, she would "live in utter misery with her mind gone." A stunned Freeman had gone "to the Cross," and following his earnest prayer she had recovered. He concluded that "I have access to my Father, and so long as I have access to Him, then from Him every need of life will be assured." Other religious leaders reported episodes of medical recoveries in response to their prayers. Following intensive pastoral casework at hospitals and consultations with doctors, Lutheran minister John J. Scherer wrote several articles about the relationship between religion and disease. While advocating the use of all available human medical procedures, including psychotherapy, he emphasized the importance of prayer in healing. Years earlier, William James had similarly concluded that it was a "medical fact" that in "certain environments," prayers might contribute to recoveries from illnesses.[7]

Devout Protestants prayed not only individually but collectively. An Episcopalian contrasted individual prayer, which "often seems futile," with corporate prayer, which strengthened one's purpose and overcame a person's sense of loneliness. Ministers urged parents to pray with their families daily. In addition to prayers at Sunday worship services, many churches held Wednesday night prayer meetings. An especially devout layperson might be eulogized as "a Wednesday evening Christian." Each year during the Lenten season, Episcopal and Lutheran churches conducted prayer meetings. For a number of years Protestants assembled for an interdenominational week of prayer for Christian unity. Prior to citywide revivals, church members hosted neighborhood cottage prayer meetings. At times of national or international crises, Richmonders gathered for prayer. In 1901, when President William McKinley was assassinated, citizens converged upon Centenary Methodist Church for a prayer service. During one extended drought, church leaders prayed for rain. During World War I, churches held special prayer services. At most church gatherings, from Sunday schools to meetings of men's and women's organizations, church members paused to pray. In 1926, when the *Richmond News Leader* conducted a survey of religion, 93 percent of the 1,120 people answering a question about prayer affirmed their belief in prayer as a means of a personal relationship with God. This figure compared to a national response of 84 percent. For Richmonders, prayer apparently formed an essential part of the devotional path of grace.[8]

Protestant leaders also reminded Christians to sustain their spiritual wellbeing by attending church services. To enter a church was to enter "God's house" or, in the words of anthropologist Mircea Eliade, "sacred space"—a location where religious people could transcend the "profane" conditions of the world outside. Before conducting regular worship services in a building, church leaders consecrated it or dedicated it to God. At First Baptist Church, George W. McDaniel explained that worshiping in church brought men and women into the presence of God. There, according to McDaniel, people could have their "souls fed" and their spiritual strength renewed. Even in an empty church, a person could kneel and engage in silent worship, observed one Episcopal rector. There "we feel a sensation of God's sacred presence," and "this feeling of nearness to God is an awe and inspiration which the devout nature will wish to cherish." At church people could put aside secular interests to concentrate on God. Ministers cautioned that those who failed to attend church might find their faith languishing when confronted by the pressures of the secular world.[9]

At church, too, people engaged in corporate worship as well as participated in sacred occasions such as communion, baptisms, christenings, weddings, and funerals. Churches were focal points for such holy days as Christmas, Palm Sunday, and Easter. By beautifying sanctuaries and offering majestic music, congregations sought to create a reverent mood for worship services. Diligent pastors scrutinized proposed innovations, lest they diminish rather than enhance a sense of reverence. One Presbyterian leader suggested that churches furnish their own hand fans rather than use those supplied by local businesses. The latter fans, he feared, could deflect minds from worship services to "some good bargains that may be purchased at some well-known store on Monday." Another Richmond minister cautioned against a national tendency to make church "a place of entertainment and a rival to theaters, vaudevilles, concerts, and the like." Richmond churches did not fall prey to that temptation. On the front page of the Sunday church program, Hanover Avenue Christian Church used an unattributed quotation to guide those in attendance: "Whosoever thou art that worships in this church, enter it not without the spirit of reverence and leave it not without a prayer to God for thyself, for those who minister, and for those who worship." Of the 1,081 people who responded to the 1926 *Richmond News Leader* religion survey, 88 percent claimed that they attended services regularly. That figure compared favorably to that of a national survey in which approximately 70 percent of the respondents claimed to attend services regularly.[10]

In private devotions and church services, Protestants encountered three recurring messages about their spiritual status: God loved humans; each individual soul was valuable; and Christians should love others. Indeed, ministers characterized love as "the essence" of God, Jesus, and Christianity. Russell Cecil portrayed God as a caring father whose love for humans was readily available, inexhaustible, and active in the world. A Baptist minister declared that from the beginning men and women had been the objects of God's love and that love constantly guided God's hand. Ministers focused on manifestations of God's love. He had sent His son Jesus as the divine incarnation. The ministry of Jesus, his sacrificial, atoning death, and God's forgiveness of human sinfulness testified to God's love, according to the ministers. As the parable of the Prodigal Son showed, God loved even those who lost their way. In the Old Testament, as H. D. C. Maclachlan explained, a righteous God heard the cries of "the humblest citizen" and protected him. In the New Testament Jesus taught that the basis of His kingdom was love and went about healing people. Richmond preachers invoked affectionate images of God and Jesus as hosts, companions, partners, and lovers.[11]

A loving God, the ministers assured, responded to people's needs and blessed them. On one hand, God had prepared heavenly mansions for Christians—a consoling conviction in times of adversity. On the other hand, God's caring presence could be experienced in this world. According to Maclachlan, a healing Jesus remained close to believers, bearing their burdens, comforting them in sorrow, warning them away from temptations, and revealing his will to them. Maclachlan referred to experiences of personal crisis and tragedy that he had witnessed and testified that he had been amazed by the sense of God's presence which shone in the faces of those who were suffering. Emphasizing Jesus' presence in everyday lives, Walter Russell Bowie advised: "If we will look for Him, He will be there." Episcopal laywoman Margaret Prescott Montague celebrated the joy of a Christian life "in the presence of the Great Companion who is the inspiration for it all" and who understood each individual as no human could. The pastor of Grace Street Baptist, W. W. Weeks, rejoiced about "an unseen presence" which "watches over every step that we take and guards us more tenderly than ever a mother guarded her babe."[12]

God's love pointed to another truth: the worth of each person. In Bowie's words, God has "set upon every human soul a divine and immortal worth." Though marred by sinfulness, "human nature is essentially great," affirmed James B. Hawthorne. He added that, unlike people, God saw beneath superficial appearances and recognized the value of individuals living seemingly ordinary lives or surviving in poverty or infirmity. Jesus had told people they were worthwhile and that they had immortal spirits, an unusual message for his era, Edward Pell observed. Calling attention to the fact that Jesus always saw the best in people, McDaniel titled a collection of sermons, *Seeing the Best.* In touching individual lives, Baptist W. W. Weeks believed, "God always makes beautiful souls."[13]

Sermons and devotional readings coupled the themes of God's love and individual worth with an injunction that Christians should love others. With a continuous consciousness of God's love, Christians should lead "love filled lives," W. W. Weeks declared. Preachers pointed to such biblical lessons as the Golden Rule, the Sermon on the Mount, the parable of the Good Samaritan, and the apostle Paul's description of love in I Corinthians 13. A Christian should avoid selfishness, jealousy, and greed. Instead, he or she should act with kindness, grant forgiveness, and make peace with any enemies. Just as Jesus ministered to others and symbolically washed his disciples' feet, so, too, should Christians engage in acts of service. To comprehend God's love of other humans meant understanding that "they are worthy of all you can do for the betterment of their present and eternal welfare," Hawthorne exhorted. God ultimately would consider "our everyday lives for little deeds of kindness and little acts of compassion" as true indications that Christians loved him and served him, instructed Edward Pell. Thus, in traveling the path of personal devotions, a Christian encountered a loving God, whose presence affirmed individual worth and who beckoned his followers to serve others. These devotions constituted a form of "sacred time," a concept developed by Mircea Eliade to designate occasions in which people interrupt secular time to recover the religious dimension of life.[14]

To secure this spiritual direction, each Christian should rely on a devout family as a vital path of grace. In nineteenth-century America, according to historian Colleen McDannell, "good Christians" saw a "natural and inseparable" connection between religion and the home. In early twentieth-century Richmond, religious leaders continued to laud families as sources of spiritual nurturing. One minister characterized the Christian home as a "religious shrine . . . dedicated to service and humanity." Presbyterian educator Walter L. Lingle identified the family as "the one social organization that is of divine origin." According to ministers, marriages were sacred, lifetime contracts that required selfless, even sacrificial behavior.[15]

God's ideal for the family, according to Lingle, was for it "to raise up godly seed." An Episcopal leader called religious education "one of the greatest responsibilities God has laid upon parents." That task required parents to serve as good role models. Children, James B. Hawthorne reminded, learned to love goodness "by seeing it in you" and by imitating their elders. Parents should teach children to love and obey God, should instruct them in the Bible, should pray with them, and should bring them to church for worship services. The Richmond Ministerial Union endorsed "exhorting and admonishing parents of the God-imposed obligation of seeing that their children are at church worship." Mothers and fathers should teach children to respect them but should also exercise patience and restraint as well as avoid harsh punishments. Ministers reminded parents of the importance of spending time with their children. Shifting the focus of one children's sermon to parents, Walter Russell Bowie applauded the example of former President Theodore Roosevelt as a father who delighted in playing with boys and girls.[16]

Ministers maintained that women, particularly mothers, played crucial roles as spiritual guides and guardians of their families. Protestant leaders, including laywomen, endorsed the proposition that women were naturally more religious than men. Declaring that God gave women a special faculty for religion, George W. McDaniel praised them for leading men to fear and serve God. Unlike men who were slow to respond, said McDaniel, women invariably assumed the initiative in church work and provided important financial support. As Walter Lingle noted, women accounted for a substantial majority of church members and Sunday school teachers. A Methodist editor praised women for refraining from the "gross vices to which men were addicted." Ministers reasoned that by spending most of their time outside the home, men became preoccupied with worldly concerns and neglected spiritual matters. The pastor of First Presbyterian Church, Robert P. Kerr, repeated a commonly expressed view that women were men's equals but occupied a "divinely appointed" separate sphere. "In the struggles of life," a man should act as a woman's protector and his wife should remain in the background as a "custodian of virtue."[17]

According to Kerr, woman's "proper sphere of usefulness" was the "quiet sanctities of home." In a typical paean to motherhood, W. W. Weeks proclaimed that the best thing a woman could do for society was to raise her children to be "men and women of high ideals and Christ-like conduct." Claiming that fathers lacked their wives' ability to guide children, Edward Pell prized mothers for their roles as moral guides and guardians. At the beginning of the twentieth century, Kerr described a child's first school as at a "mother's knee," where "we learn to pray." More than twenty-five years later, Episcopal laywoman and child welfare specialist Dr. Mary Evelyn Brydon invoked the same image as she advised, "God cannot help but hear the prayer of a little child and his mother kneeling together." Devout parents, particularly mothers, provided essential examples and guidance, a religious foundation for children throughout their lives.[18]

Walter Lingle acknowledged that throughout history the real conditions of family life had often departed from "God's ideal." The modern American family, Lingle concluded, faced its own set of tests. Other Richmond ministers identified problems which seemed to endanger the idealized, spiritually directed Christian family. At times, preachers denounced "the divorce evil" as a mounting challenge to the sacred bonds of marriage and to the religious education of children. Speaking before local Presbyterian ministers in 1905, the former president of Hampden-Sydney College calmly reviewed divorce laws and characterized divorce as a necessary evil. Reciting statistics, he noted a national divorce rate of 1 per 380 inhabitants, a state rate of 1 per 717 habitants, and a Richmond rate of 1 per 608 inhabitants. With Virginia holding the second lowest divorce rate in the nation, the situation hardly seemed grave. But after World War I, Richmond experienced a surge in divorces. A few worried clergymen forcefully reiterated that divorces should be granted only in cases of adultery and that preachers should refuse to remarry any divorcee unless that person had been victimized by a former spouse's adultery. Still, Richmond was not Reno. With the divorce menace hovering beyond the city's gates, religious leaders had little need to take significant action.[19]

Other problems, though, did come close to home. As the years passed, family members spent less time together than had once been the custom. By 1916 newspaper columnist Cally Ryland lamented that Richmond had become a "city of houses, not of homes." According to her, contemporary families were disrupted by a myriad of outside activities. Because each person's interests lay outside the home, families broke up after every meal. Ministers echoed Ryland's assessment. They added that busy lives, irregular hours, public schools, traveling time, and crowded conditions kept parents separated from children and limited individual household privacy. A Methodist clergyman grieved that the family altar was being supplanted by the family auto. Edward Pell indicted the "ever-increasing demands of our modern material civilization" for "driving a wedge between husbands and wives," who no longer found time for "the quiet hour of spiritual comradeship." Lutheran pastor John J. Scherer grew particularly concerned about the implications for children. Citing his experience as an associate justice of the juvenile court, Scherer asserted that too many parents were in a mad rush to attend meetings when their children needed care.[20]

To dramatize the point, Scherer halted a Wednesday night prayer meeting and sent his congregation home to worship with their families. With this gesture he joined other ministers in stressing the importance of a "family altar," a time set aside for every member of the household to gather for prayer, Bible reading, and conversations about religion and morals. In 1918, after a deadly flu epidemic closed churches for weeks, one minister concluded that the episode produced one blessing, the rediscovery of family altars where members could engage in a "daily communion with God." Walter Lingle encouraged parents to include hymn singing and to experiment with using the Victrola as accompaniment. In 1927 Dr. Mary Evelyn Brydon, the director of Virginia's Bureau of Child Welfare, wrote five articles for the *Southern Churchman* in which she emphasized the parental duties of religious training and spiritual guidance of children. The recurrent calls for the use of family altars apparently had limited impact. In answering questions for the 1926 *News Leader* religion poll, only 43 percent of 969 respondents claimed that they "regularly have family worship" at home, an insignificant 3 percent above the average reported for a national survey.[21]

Ministers perceived another threat to family religion: many young women had begun to hold jobs. George W. McDaniel warned that a woman who became busy in commerce and industry could have her "higher sensibilities" stifled. One preacher warned that a young woman who was "crowded into streetcars, elevators, jitneys, and behind counters" could easily lose her sense of "personal propriety and sanctity of her body." Indeed, the changing status of women in many facets of life seemed to challenge the traditional family ideal. At the beginning of the twentieth century, commentators deemed the outgoing "new woman" to be a sharp departure from reserved female piety. The boisterous youth of "the Jazz Age" fueled fears that women were abandoning their roles as family moral guardians. A few ministers condemned woman's suffrage for taking women away from their proper sphere and for thereby reducing their moral influence. Other religious leaders, however, applauded such changes. Responding to disparaging remarks about women made by a Medical College of Virginia professor, the pastor of Grace Street Baptist Church delivered a sermon in which he emphasized women's intellectual prowess and professional accomplishments. In contrast to conditions of an earlier era, he observed, modern women occupied a "large and honorable place in the modern business world," including thousands of lawyers, architects, ministers, physicians, and surgeons. In the 1920s the Methodist *Richmond Christian Advocate* similarly rejoiced that a woman "can do most anything now and we are not sorry these doors are open to her." Notwithstanding changing roles and behavior within families, Richmond Protestant leaders continued to identify the devout family as a sacred path which nurtured its members' spiritual well-being.[22]

Sundays also formed an important path of grace. Preachers pronounced that the Sabbath was a divine institution since, according to the Bible, God had created and sanctified one day in seven. Pastors reminded their congregations of the Fourth Commandment: "remember the Sabbath day, to keep it holy." Christians celebrated Sunday as a commemoration of the Resurrection. Religious leaders envisioned Sunday as a time for collective worship and as an occasion for personal communion with God. A Methodist writer depicted God as calling men "away from material and transient" affairs to things "spiritual and eternal." A Presbyterian editor explained that a "man's soul needs a time when it can get away from business, the cares, the worries, the temptations of the world and hold communion with its God." As the writer concluded, Sunday offered that time when a person could "let God speak" "fully through his written and preached word." Putting aside secular cares and pleasures, devout Protestants attended church services, studied the Bible, participated in Sunday schools, spent time with their families, and relaxed. The *Southern Churchman* suggested that no other "outward gauge . . . more accurately indicates a man's religious standing and quality than his manner of keeping Sunday and his estimate of the day as a spiritual value."[23]

Religious leaders assailed activities that threatened to undermine traditional Sabbath observance. Some businessmen pursued profits, even on Sunday. In March 1900 an upset Presbyterian minister described an earlier crosstown trip to preach at a Methodist church. Along the route he had counted forty-four stores open for business. Clergymen contended that greed drove businessmen to open saloons, stores, and recreational facilities on Sunday. Merchants also plied their trade in Sunday newspaper advertisements. Even worse, retailers arranged display windows to attract the attention of people en route to church. In 1913, speaking for the Methodist Richmond District Conference, one preacher deplored the "merciless wheel of an industrial system" for breaking the Sabbath and giving employees no day of rest. The *Southern Churchman* attacked the "great God" business as a "veritable Frankenstein" treading over laws and social conventions "with a mechanical indifference."[24]

Urban entertainment presented subtle and persistent challenges to traditional observances of Sunday. By offering enticing escapes from a week of work, new recreational forms threatened to transform Sunday from a holy day into a holiday. A Presbyterian editor warned that Sunday play was merely the first step toward Sunday work. According to ministers, seemingly innocent forms of recreation could distract people's attention from religious thoughts. Although Sunday band concerts might feature sacred music, they still destroyed the quiet and allegedly created an irreverent holiday atmosphere. Ministers objected to amateur baseball games and discouraged members from taking excursions and reading secular books. Religious leaders viewed the Sunday press as a menace. Even a devout person could be tempted to spend Sunday mornings with a newspaper rather than a Bible. As a result, an individual's mind could be turned away from God to "low grade actresses and professional athletes and murderers and thieves and degenerates of all kinds." Protestants especially indicted comic sections for polluting the minds of impressionable children. Likewise, if people went to horse races, band concerts, movies, playgrounds, or amusement parks, they concentrated on personal pleasure rather than on spiritual contemplation. The Richmond Ministerial Union surmised that increasing numbers of city residents were placing recreation before meditation, and secular observers agreed.[25]

In countering assaults upon a quiet, reverent Sunday, ministers acted with an important ally, Sabbath observance laws. Dating to the colonial era, state and local statutes prohibited most forms of commerce and labor on Sunday. Preachers asserted that these laws were primarily protective rather than religious. The clergymen referred to research indicating that workers needed a day of rest each week. Without Sabbath laws, the ministers charged, some greedy businessmen would require seven days of work for six days of wages. Since Christians accounted for the vast majority of the community's population, it merely made sense for that one day of rest to coincide with the day they designated for religious observance. On one hand, Baptists and Presbyterians stressed that Sunday laws were civil, not religious, devices. On the other hand, when businesses seemed to disturb the religious atmosphere of Sunday, ministers called for rigorous enforcement of the laws. In 1921 First Baptist's George W. McDaniel asserted that the operation of stores and movie houses "on the streets along which people walk to worship" as well as near churches constituted "an invasion of the rights of the people to enjoy quietly and without disturbance their religious liberty."[26]

Religious leaders relied largely upon exhortations of the public to observe the Sabbath, but they episodically organized campaigns calling for enforcement of Sunday closing laws. In 1900 clergymen and laymen organized a Sabbath Observance League to secure enforcement of existing laws. Members sent letters to local shop owners reminding them of city laws against conducting business on Sundays. Concluding that many Richmonders lacked interest in the matter, the league recruited an outside expert, the Rev. Dr. Edward Thompson of the Sunday League of America. In 1901 Thompson spent two and one-half weeks in town and delivered more than twenty lectures designed to inform the public and win support for action. Horrified that virtually all of the city's three hundred barrooms operated on Sunday, the league initiated legal proceedings against ten saloon owners. In 1901 a judge fined them and warned them that any additional violation would result in the revocation of their licenses. Convicted again eighteen months later, Andrew Giorlami did lose his license. To placate protests in 1902, owners of a local race track agreed to limit Sunday performances to a horse show. In 1906 and 1907, the proprietor and employees of Idlewood Amusement Park incurred fines for opening the facility and working on Sundays.[27]

Yet the Sunday observance laws proved to be unreliable allies. In 1901 a frustrated city police chief called the laws "antiquated" and complained that "in attempting to enforce them my men are ridiculed to the limit of endurance." Even ministers acknowledged that people should be permitted to engage in certain "works of necessity." Religious leaders, however, disagreed with secular leaders as to which activities were truly critical to the city's welfare. For years Richmond newspapers did not publish Monday editions, which would have required labor on Sunday, but in 1905 the *Richmond Times-Dispatch* began Sunday printing. The *Richmond News Leader* maintained that the changing conditions of urban life had increased the number of specialized services which citizens needed. The paper's editors argued that thousands of people depended upon others for such necessities as transportation, telephones, newspapers, ice service, and baked goods. In 1916 Mayor George Ainslie and Judge

John J. Crutchfield tried to make the same point. They instructed local policemen to make no exceptions when enforcing blue laws. Officers arrested workers, such as florists and organists, who primarily assisted churchgoers. Some denominational leaders recognized the merit of this argument, but most ministers did not readily reinterpret "works of necessity." During World War I, Protestant clergymen objected when the national government failed to suspend war-related activities on the Sabbath.[28]

The 1920s brought a slight but significant shift in attitudes about Sabbath behavior. Between 1920 and 1924, clergymen helped to thwart a blue law repeal campaign, which they traced to such entertainment interests as movie theater owners. Other religious leaders, however, favored a less restrictive approach to Sabbath observance. Arguing that what amounted to Sabbath desecration for one man did not do so for another, Episcopal city missionary Cary Montague advocated leaving the matter to individual consciences. The pastor of Leigh Street Baptist Church took a similar position. He suggested that Sunday recreational activities served the goals of resting and refreshing people's minds and bodies. *The Southern Churchman* and the *Chesapeake Christian* also called for more flexible views of appropriate Sunday conduct. Richmond's labor newspaper, the *Square Deal*, scolded clergymen for holding narrow views which would deprive working people of fun during their one free day.[29]

In the late 1920s, Richmonders engaged in several debates about Sunday observance laws. In 1926 the *Richmond News Leader* printed a series of letters from readers who volunteered their views about Sunday closing laws. Most of the correspondents, including a Sunday school teacher, opposed the laws as unreasonable and as likely to alienate people from churches. Between 1926 and 1929, the Richmond ministers debated how to respond to the opening of municipal parks, playgrounds, and a lake for swimming on summer Sundays. In 1926 the Richmond Ministerial Union opposed the opening of city playgrounds on Sundays. But in 1929 the Union voted against requesting the mayor to close the lake on Sundays or even on Sunday mornings. The majority of ministers concluded that as Protestants they had no right to promote a policy which would deny access to the lake to Jews and Catholics, who might have already attended religious services. Furthermore, the ministers wanted to avoid the impression that they opposed "innocent amusement." Nonetheless, the mayor responded to a petition from sixty-six people and closed the lake from nine to noon on Sundays.[30]

Richmond took pride in being a "churchgoing city," and the citizens preserved that reputation by their generally scrupulous observance of the Sabbath. Historian Arthur Schlesinger once concluded that by the late nineteenth century, most northern cities experienced a "growing secularization of the Sabbath," and their officials no longer enforced Sabbath observance laws. Not so Richmond. Writing to the *Richmond News Leader* in 1926, a local merchant remarked about his experiences as well as those of tourists and travelers in the capital city. Richmond, he assured other readers, "is the one town in the United States, whose Sunday is totally and impressively dull." Yet in preserving reverent Sundays, many religious leaders adjusted their views to accommodate the changing urban conditions. With a slightly altered appearance, Sabbath observance remained an important path of grace in Richmond's religious culture.[31]

Although devotions, family altars, and Sabbath observance provided sacred paths in a secular city, Richmond Protestant leaders counseled special respect for one secular institution, organized government. To foster the spiritual welfare of individuals and the community, church leaders stressed both participation and separation. On one hand, church members should participate in government by fulfilling their duties as citizens and civic leaders. On the other hand, ministers should protect their churches' spiritual agenda from the distractions of secular politics. Facing urban social issues, local religious leaders struggled to maintain this somewhat compartmentalized approach to the relationship between church and state.

Portraying government itself as a divine creation, ministers urged Christians to respect the state and its laws. As the *Southern Churchman* advised, "Reverence for law and obedience to law is akin to reverence and obedience for God." Any evidence of lawlessness led churchmen to condemn the offenders, including lynchers, corrupt politicians, capitalists, labor unions, bootleggers, social activists, or felons. According to this viewpoint, good Christians should not only obey laws, they should also participate in civic affairs as stewards of God. Acting as informed citizens, they should vote and elect good and righteous men to office. Lest politics be left to those who sought only personal gain, preachers further advised, a Christian should be prepared to serve in a political position. Ministers expected officials to be honest, able, prayerful, God-fearing men who worked for the public good, not their own selfish purposes. The clergy also wanted civic leaders to enact laws which would be, in the words of a Methodist minister, "consistent with the requirements of the gospel of Jesus Christ." In tones bordering on sanctimonious self-congratulation, Richmonders periodically praised their own city for its record as a law-abiding domicile of decent people. In 1910, for example, a local newspaper editorialized that "we do not believe there is a more orderly, God-fearing, well-behaved community than Richmond anywhere in the world." Though extravagant, this assessment did reflect the community's often expressed ideal of responsible citizens and honest leaders.[32]

While calling for a righteous government, church leaders opposed direct ecclesiastical involvement in such efforts and championed the principle of separation of church and state. Preachers rarely addressed political issues from their pulpits. Neither they nor church groups officially endorsed political candidates or promoted partisan political issues. Weekly denominational newspapers adhered to an editorial policy of excluding political issues. In 1920 the Episcopal *Southern Churchman* referred to its tradition of avoiding "any manifestation of political partisanship on the part of its editors or contributors." As Baptist editor R. H. Pitt explained, church members, as private citizens, might demand reforms, but churches themselves should not "attempt to control through their organized action *the legal method of accomplishing these reforms*" (Pitt's emphasis).[33]

Religious leaders maintained that the separation of religious and political matters protected individuals and churches from harm. As evangelical Protestants, local ministers contended that religion itself was necessarily a matter of personal choice involving the relationship between a believer and God. R. H. Pitt called this "freedom of choice" a "hallmark of man's nobility." Believing that all souls had the right to direct access to God, Protestant leaders viewed any attempt to control or govern a person's religious expression as a form of spiritual tyranny. Since the "Kingdom of God" was spiritual, according to Baptist James B. Hawthorne, it could have "no organic connection with external government." To compromise this position meant opening the door to government interference with a person's religious practices.[34]

Indeed, some Richmonders invoked the phrase that when "the church gets into politics, politics will get into the church." That expression implied several potential problems. Church members who disagreed about a political issue might create divisions within a congregation and distract it from its more valued spiritual mission. As a Presbyterian editor cautioned, if churches dabbled in politics, they immediately squandered their religious and moral influence with most people. Furthermore, if clergymen entered the political arena, they might misuse the power of government to discriminate against those of other faiths. To illustrate this peril, Protestants cited episodes of religious oppression in other countries as well as their local historical examples.[35]

Baptists and Presbyterians traced their commitment to the principle of separation of church and state to historical experiences. In colonial Virginia the Church of England had operated as a state-supported institution, funded by the government and taxpayers. Anglican vestries filled quasi-governmental functions, such as administering poor relief, and only Anglican ministers had authority to perform marriages. By law all other religious groups could hold meetings only after obtaining licenses from the colonial assembly. Believing that no secular authority should determine how individuals worshiped, most Baptists refused to apply for licenses, and more than a score of them were imprisoned. Some Presbyterians and Baptists endured social pressure and physical abuse, often meted out by local political figures such as county sheriffs. During and after the American Revolution, Baptist and Presbyterians petitioned the Virginia legislature to cease support of the Anglican church and adopt measures providing for religious freedom, actions eventually taken. Quoting the arguments of Virginia's Revolutionary-era leaders, twentieth-century Baptists urged diligence in upholding the separate religious role of churches from the political functions of states. Baptists passionately recited a potent history lesson: when the government and religious groups intermixed, individuals could lose their freedom to practice religion according to their personal beliefs and consciences.[36]

Also viewing the colonial experiences as a cautionary story, Presbyterians added a chapter. In the antebellum period, southern Presbyterian leaders grew unhappy with the national antislavery crusade and its eventual entry into politics. In 1861, when the Presbyterian Church in the Confederate States of America organized, its general assembly passed a resolution committing the denomination to an exclusively spiritual mission. After the Civil War the renamed Presbyterian Church in the United States determinedly perpetuated this "spirituality of the church" doctrine and carefully detached the denomination and its leaders from matters likely to have political implications. In 1901, for example, the Richmond Presbyterian Ministers Association considered whether the group should endorse the Anti-Saloon League and its program. The ministers demurred lest they attach themselves to a movement other than that "to which the Church of Christ by its scriptural authority" was "commissioned." In 1905 the Virginia Synod cited the denomination's historic stance, favored members striving for righteousness laws, but reaffirmed that "ecclesiastical bodies, as such," should not attempt to "influence the agencies of the state for promotion of moral or spiritual ends."[37]

Though less categorical than the Baptists and the Presbyterians, the city's other Protestants largely subscribed to the belief that religious institutions and political institutions should operate in distinct spheres that should rarely overlap. A minister who attempted to respect this view of politics sometimes faced an unpleasant dilemma. In a 1915 letter to the president of the Equal Suffrage League of Virginia, Walter Russell Bowie declined an invitation to speak before a rally at the state Capitol. Though a supporter of woman's suffrage, he wrote that the time was "not quite ripe" for him to "take a pronounced part in partisan propaganda in meetings and by addresses." He could not ignore "the particularly legitimate prejudice against a minister's 'taking the stump'" on a controversial issue. By speaking, he believed, he would diminish rather than increase his influence for the cause of equal suffrage.[38]

Like Bowie, other Richmond ministers pondered what to do about social and political issues. Despite sharing a commitment to the separation of church and state, religious leaders increasingly disagreed about the precise boundaries and occasions for applying the principle. Much to the irritation of others, Baptists usually interpreted the principle very strictly. For example, Baptists joined Jews in protesting the use of the word "Christian" in the Virginia Constitution of 1901. Baptists also opposed the federal government's hiring chaplains for the armed forces and the state government's employing a chaplain at the penitentiary. Local Baptists and Methodists criticized state and city financial aid to sectarian charities. In 1910 Second Baptist Church concluded that the Anti-Saloon League was a political organization and refused its requests to hold a field day and to raise funds.[39]

The strict Baptist stance on separation of church and state led to a conflict with other Richmond Protestants who advocated compulsory Bible reading in public schools. These ministers argued that the state had an obligation to teach moral values as well as academic skills. In 1904 an Episcopal rector, Robert Strange, claimed that the state had the right to use every necessary means to teach morality. Strange, like some other clergymen, believed that the Bible was the best available guide to moral conduct. In *The Indispensable Book*, published several years later, Walter W. Moore expanded this argument. He maintained that Bible reading was "essential" for the "best mental culture of our children" and for "the making of the best type of moral character, which is the real end and aim of all true education." Moore and others also submitted that the Bible's literary value alone made it essential reading for a well-educated person. To exclude the Bible from schools, Moore heatedly declared, would be "to perpetrate fraud upon the intellects of the rising generation." Protestant ministers who favored Bible reading in schools asserted that the policy could be implemented without violating the principles of individual liberty. Strange claimed that no sectarian doctrines would be taught, only the "fundamental truths of the Christian religion, on which all the churches or societies are founded." Strange's list of "fundamental truths," however, included the Lord's Prayer, the Apostles Creed, and the Ten Commandments, as well as the Bible. Proponents of Bible reading suggested that if parents of Jewish children objected to the plan, they could keep the children at home one-half hour later than usual.[40]

Richmond Baptists steadfastly opposed compulsory Bible reading in public schools. Following a 1904 discussion by the Richmond Ministerial Union, Episcopalians, Methodists, and Presbyterians endorsed compulsory Bible reading. But city Baptist ministers adamantly opposed the proposal. The pastor of Leigh Street Baptist Church declared that the city's Protestant majority had no right to force their ideas upon religious minorities. Other Baptists also charged that compulsory Bible reading would violate the principle of separation of church and state set down in the Bill of Rights. The *Religious Herald* editorialized that teachers would inevitably interpret the Bible, thus becoming instructors in religious matters. Faced with this opposition, proponents of Bible reading dropped the matter. One Methodist minister complained that opposition to the idea came only from atheists, Roman Catholics, and "a few excellent Baptists who are alarmed over the ghost of an issue dead and buried a century and a quarter ago."[41]

In 1913 the Richmond city school board issued instructions to teachers to open public schools with the reading of the Bible. Richmond Episcopal and Methodist ministers passed resolutions endorsing this decision, but once again, Baptists protested. The Baptist Ministers Conference formally opposed the policy, and several ministers addressed the school board in an effort to have the new policy rescinded. Baptists joined Jews and Unitarians in maintaining that religion had no place in public schools. Noting that the school board had only "requested" the use of biblical selections, R. H. Pitt concluded that many people had construed that request "as equivalent to command."[42]

George W. McDaniel, pastor of First Baptist Church, emerged as the most prominent Protestant opponent of Bible reading in public schools. Calling the policy "unAmerican" and "unconstitutional," he spoke passionately and repeatedly against the measure. In personal letters Rabbi Edward Calisch thanked him for raising his "powerful" voice "in the cause of justice and freedom of conscience." No doubt McDaniel seemed a somewhat unlikely opponent of Bible reading. Throughout his career he articulated fairly conservative theological views. A native of rural Texas, he had been only thirty years old in 1905, when he assumed leadership of the Richmond's oldest Baptist church. Fond of horseback riding and hunting, he delighted in his dogs and frequently punctuated his sermons with dog stories. If McDaniel retained some rustic edges, he was hardly a rube. As an undergraduate at Baylor, he had excelled as a debater; at Louisville seminary he had earned the president's respect as "a brilliant student in theology." Before leaving Texas, he married Martha Douglass Scarborough, a member of Baylor's modern language department. Following brief pastorates in Texas, McDaniel began a twenty-two-year tenure in Richmond, where he distinguished himself as a preacher, a pastor, and a skillful administrator. Rabbi Calisch correctly identified McDaniel as a person with a powerful voice, and in the 1920s he used that voice as the president of the Southern Baptist Convention. But in 1913, the city school board did not heed it and refused to rescind its instructions.[43]

In 1916 the Virginia State Board of Education approved a policy of giving optional high school credit for one unit of Bible study at home or at a religious institution. The interdenominational committee which recommended this plan included Baptists and Catholics. Nonetheless, between 1924 and 1926, proponents of compulsory Bible reading lobbied for a state law to require Bible reading in public schools. Opposing the measure, the Richmond Baptist Ministers Conference insisted that, "according to our conception, the State should not function in religion." Comprised mostly of Richmond churches, the Dover Baptist Association adopted a resolution objecting to compulsory Bible reading as a violation of religious liberty. McDaniel, now president of the Southern Baptist Convention, and R. H. Pitt forcefully condemned the proposal. Emphasizing that families and churches should accept the responsibility for a child's religious education, Pitt deplored "the whole business" as "mischievous and menacing."[44]

In 1926 Pitt authored "A Memorial Address by the Baptist General Association of Virginia to the General Assembly of Virginia, 1926, against the Compulsory Reading of the Bible in Public Schools." He repeated arguments made previously by Baptists. He maintained that the Bible was a distinctly religious book and that the very selection of a version of the Bible was a sectarian act. He noted that according to the Virginia Statute of Religious Liberty, religion was supposed to be voluntary, not compulsory. He added that even if students from different denominations were excused during Bible reading, they would suffer embarrassment and might be the objects of "reproach and perhaps of insult." The work of Pitt and other Baptists led to the defeat of the compulsory Bible reading legislation.[45]

The debates about compulsory Bible reading, like the discussion about Sabbath observance laws, underscored a dilemma which Richmond Protestants increasingly confronted as urban residents. They valued the principle of separation of church and state. Yet government bodies invariably rendered decisions with moral, religious, and even sectarian implications. Local churches and denominational organizations generally refused to enunciate political positions. Still, when an individual clergyman announced his personal support for a certain cause such as prohibition, it required some subtle logic to separate the man's role as citizen from his role as a religious leader. Presbyterian Walter Lingle concluded that at a time of "a great moral emergency . . . it may become the duty of ministers to lead the moral forces of the community." But what constituted "a great moral emergency" might depend on individual vantage points.[46]

Furthermore, throughout the twentieth century, ministers increasingly advised church members to broaden their interpretation of the word *spiritual* so as to apply it to all the activities of their lives. H. D. C. Maclachlan explained that to be spiritual meant "to practice the presence of God in everything one does." He added that the gospel had even more to do with "getting heaven into people" than it did with getting people into heaven. That perspective included social issues, sometimes requiring government action. Believing that "all of life belongs to Christ," R. H. Pitt proclaimed that "the wide-awake denominational journal now takes" a greater interest in public issues and no longer hesitates to take positions about issues which "profoundly affect the moral welfare of our people." An unmatched champion of separation of church and state, Pitt still concluded that spirituality had to include feeding the hungry, clothing the naked, sheltering the homeless, nursing the sick, visiting the prisoner, and doing "anything and everything within our ability to bless and brighten the world." In following a traditional path which regulated the relationship between religion and government, devout Protestants found the route to be expanding and leading to closer ties between the two formerly separate institutions.[47]

James B. Hawthorne advised that "the life which walks in the humblest path and does the humblest work can be made by God's grace as perfect, beautiful, and divine as that of the canonized saint whose fame has filled the world." Individual devotions, church worship, Sabbath observance, devout families, and moral but nonsectarian political institutions could enable a Christian to point his or her life in a sacred direction. In a changing urban environment, Protestants cherished these paths but adjusted their contours. Furthermore, ministers increasingly urged church members to extend those paths of grace into a secular world and transform the conditions on earth to be more like the Kingdom of God. Those efforts would touch Richmond in many ways.[48]

6
Disarming Dangers

On 1 March 1901, eight Baptist, Methodist, and Presbyterian ministers gathered to create the Richmond Anti-Saloon League. Following another meeting in the home of a Methodist pastor, the group organized the Virginia Anti-Saloon League at a session held in the basement of Second Baptist Church. In January 1902 more than two hundred delegates assembled at Grace Street Baptist for the first annual convention of the Virginia Anti-Saloon League. According to news accounts, many women and local clergymen attended. Addressing this audience, Baptist preacher James B. Hawthorne condemned the liquor traffic as sinful, emphasized the moral purpose of the new organization, and pointedly proclaimed, "We are not a political party." "What is our demand?" asked Hawthorne. "It is that the state shall not legalize but prohibit the saloon." In organizing against saloon liquor, Richmond Protestants embarked on the first of a sequence of moral crusades. During the next three decades, they also launched campaigns against civic corruption, prostitution, and new, sexually suggestive forms of youthful behavior. In each case the religious leaders perceived a danger to the morality of individuals and the community. In each case the clergy and laity initially promoted simple solutions to disarm a threat. In each case local Protestants partially succeeded in disarming that perceived danger. Yet they achieved victories only after discovering that the dangers and solutions involved issues of greater complexity than they had once imagined.[1]

In summoning church members to act against saloons, the founders of the Virginia Anti-Saloon League targeted an institution that many citizens already regarded as a moral abomination. In memoirs written in the 1940s, an early opponent of saloons, Richmond College professor Samuel Chiles Mitchell, admitted that "it is hard now, especially for young people, to realize what a running sore on the social body the saloon of that day was." In the early twentieth century, Mitchell and others furnished detailed explanations about how saloons imperiled individuals and the community. Religious leaders began by indicting the saloons for serving liquor, which, they argued, destroyed human beings. Citing the findings of scientists, doctors, government officials, and insurance spokesmen, ministers maintained that drinkers incurred greater risks of disease as well as higher mortality rates. A drinker could completely lose his or her reason and mental health. With this impaired judgment, a person would lose any sense of morality, would become a brute dominated by a maddening appetite for alcohol, and would become more likely to commit crime. Robbed of reason, self-respect, and moral perception, that person permitted his or her soul to be guided by liquor rather than by God. Thus, Protestant leaders admonished, a person who drank liquor not only harmed the body but jeopardized the soul.[2]

Ministers further censured the saloon as an antagonist of the Christian Sabbath. Saloon owners flagrantly violated Sunday closing laws. In 1901 the Richmond chief of police reported that nearly every city barroom operated on Sunday. Incensed, an interdenominational group of preachers and laymen formed the Sunday Observance League and successfully pressured authorities to enforce Sabbath laws. Local judges dispensed stiff fines, but saloon owners persisted. Many of them attempted to circumvent the law by forming fake social clubs. Preachers denounced the subterfuge and identified the offenders for officials. Only when threatened with license forfeiture did saloon owners yield. By 1909 newspapers reported that Sunday liquor sales had ceased. Still, such battles reinforced the impression that saloon keepers lacked respect not only for the Sabbath but for churches as well.[3]

Ministers particularly condemned the saloon as an enemy of that sacred institution, the family. They accused the saloon of harming families in four ways. First, it deterred husbands from fulfilling their duty to be breadwinners because they squandered their wages on alcohol. Men who drank on the job were subject to discharge, and men who drank liquor were more likely to incur disease, accidents, or death. These men would leave their families without financial support. City missionaries, who aided poor people, testified that saloons siphoned money away from workingmen's families. The normally even-tempered Methodist preacher J. T. Mastin erupted in rage as he recounted one experience with a husband whose drinking habit had impoverished his family, had "made beggars and worse of his daughters just coming into womanhood," and had caused the starvation death of his infant child.[4]

Raising a second issue, preachers charged that intoxicated men physically abused wives and children. Baptist George W. McDaniel once grimly recalled that he had seen the "liquor traffic . . . enter the cottage of the poor and in a moment of madness curse and beat the wife whom the husband had vowed to protect. I have seen it turn a father into a savagery lower than the beast and slay his own offspring." And saloon alcohol, warned the ministers, contaminated not only drinkers but also their offspring. Describing alcoholism as a disease, Methodist preacher W. A. Cooper traced childhood idiocy, imbecility, epilepsy, insanity, and mortality to parental drinking. McDaniel's wife attributed much of his prohibition ardor to a conviction that drinking caused both prenatal and postnatal injury to children.[5]

Ministers lamented a third injury that liquor inflicted on families: it caused men to act disrespectfully to women and to engage in immoral sexual behavior. After consuming liquor at a saloon with its "lewd pictures" and vulgar music, men emerged swearing, cursing, and using obscene language. In fact, because of such conduct by customers, saloons along the north side of Richmond's major commercial artery had gained a particularly bad reputation. No decent woman would walk on the "wrong side of Broad" Street. And with many saloons located near the city's red-light district, ministers warned that after leaving saloons, husbands might succumb to adultery. Indeed, by serving as doors to brothels, saloons also ruined virtuous women, the clergymen warned. Saloon owners did little to allay those fears. Bartenders ignored laws against serving drinks to women and minors. Episcopal rector Thomas Semmes charged that several so-called social clubs existed "for the sole purpose of ruining young women." Committed to families as spiritually nurturing institutions, horrified ministers perceived saloons as dangerous adversaries destroying families financially, physically, emotionally, and, of course, morally.[6]

Furthermore, warned ministers, saloons fomented lawlessness. City officials and newspapers joined Anti-Saloon League leaders in characterizing saloons as hangouts for lawbreakers. The *Times-Dispatch* lambasted the "all night dive," which "starts the brawls, unlooses the passions, and harbors the criminals that menace the whole community." The editor of the *Southern Churchman* wrote ominously that "when a type of utterly brutish negro with no conception of moral standards or restraints combines with whiskey, bad things can occur." Saloon owners themselves exhibited a criminal bent by violating Sunday closing laws as well as laws forbidding liquor sales to women and children.[7]

To garner favorable treatment from city government, liquor dealers supported political candidates, lobbied members of the city council and state legislature, and thereby fueled fears of a government dominated by their interest group. Baptist editor R. H. Pitt asserted that no dry candidate could be elected to represent Richmond in the state's general assembly. In 1904 the Liquor Dealers Association openly endorsed the incumbent mayor. Four years later, an Anti-Saloon League leader reprinted letters distributed by dealers to raise funds for legislative campaigns. The ministers attributed defeats of local liquor restrictions to the political influence of saloon interests and charged that "wet" politicians adulterated all regulations, rendering them unenforceable. Ministers estimated that saloon interests controlled as many as 4,500 city voters. According to churchmen, when politics were "hatched out" in barrooms, municipal leaders formed a government "of saloons, by saloons, for saloons." Thus, Protestant leaders concluded that liquor dealers contemptuously corrupted the legal process to profit at the expense of individuals, families, and churches.[8]

Faced with the morally offensive conduct of saloon owners, many Richmond Protestants rallied behind the Anti-Saloon League. Still, to succeed, the leaders of the Virginia Anti-Saloon League had to allay some misgivings. Though deeply upset about saloons, Baptist leaders wanted to act within their tradition of noninvolvement in politics and preferred to use education to persuade people of the evils of alcohol. Respecting the "spirituality of the church" doctrine, Presbyterian ministers expressed sympathy for the anti-saloon cause but at first rarely participated in the league. The Virginia Anti-Saloon League ultimately united leaders of most major white Protestant denominations by stressing three key features of the organization. First, the Anti-Saloon League defined itself as "the church in action against the saloon." By emphasizing this claim, leaders in essence inducted every church member into their organization. Second, the league made public education, not political action, its first priority and thereby placated some wary local Baptists. Third, the league harped on its primary goal with the slogan "The Saloon Must Go." With this telling phrase, the Anti-Saloon League recruited people with a wide range of views about the use of alcoholic beverages, including citizens who drank but objected to the unsavory conditions fostered by the saloons. "The majority of the people" in most communities would vote to abolish saloons, averred James B. Hawthorne, if saloon opponents did not insist upon prohibition or intrude into existing political relations.[9]

Protestant clergymen and laypersons directed and supported state and local anti-saloon campaigns. Methodist, Baptist, and Disciples of Christ ministers served as officers in the Virginia Anti-Saloon League. Prominent Protestant ministers of all denominations denounced saloons. Local Methodist and Baptist organizations endorsed the league's activities and created temperance committees. Churches supplied buildings for league meetings, and they provided members for the organization. League representatives lectured congregations during worship services and collected offerings on "field days" held at churches. Baptist and Methodist journals appealed for donations to sustain the league's work, and Presbyterian and Episcopal weekly newspapers joined in calling for regulation of alcoholic beverages. Some churches distributed Sunday school literature stressing the harms of drinking.[10]

Believing that enlightened citizens would refrain from the use of alcohol and would demand laws restricting saloons, ministers initially concentrated on "agitation" or education rather than political activity. The clergymen understood that the only route to long-term success lay in convincing most citizens that liquor was truly destructive. In 1900 the Richmond Ministerial Union endorsed a proposed law that would require school lectures about the harms of alcoholic beverages. Several local preachers testified before the state legislature, which enacted the law. Preachers, women's groups, Sunday school teachers, social service commissions, and denominational journals spread messages about the dangers of alcohol.[11]

Within a few years of its founding, the Virginia Anti-Saloon League deftly began to shift its emphasis from education to legislation and eventually modified its stated goal from annihilation of saloons to prohibition. With these changes the league increasingly engaged in political activity. In 1905 the Methodist Richmond District Conference openly backed the election of temperance advocates. The Anti-Saloon League began to poll candidates about their prohibition sentiments, and some Protestant leaders urged voters to elect dry candidates. The religious press encouraged citizens to write state and national legislators in behalf of anti-liquor legislation. Local Protestant leaders generally supported this shift in tactics. Acting as a single-issue pressure group, the Anti-Saloon League claimed to be nonpartisan and "omnipartisan," a stance that satisfied some ministers who otherwise had qualms about political activity. Not all churches accommodated the change in the Anti-Saloon League tactics. In 1910, concluding that the league had become a political organization, Second Baptist Church, a past supporter, refused to conduct a field day and to collect an offering for the league.[12]

Methodist minister James Cannon Jr. commanded the Virginia Anti-Saloon League as it changed its direction. From the league's headquarters in the capital city, Cannon initiated plans, coordinated activities, rallied supporters, supervised staff, formulated strategy and tactics, and drafted and maneuvered laws through the state legislature. Neither a native Virginian nor a Richmond resident, Cannon succeeded despite attributes and an agenda that clashed with the religious culture of Richmond. To a city that thrived on civility, Cannon brought a combative personality. To Protestant denominations devoted to separation of church and state, Cannon presented an expanding list of political targets. Praised by some Richmond Protestants who admired his relentless assault on alcoholic beverages, Cannon showed himself to be an energetic, determined, and thorough leader. Though bearded, bespectacled, and thin, Cannon proved to be a fierce warrior. Stern, austere, and legalistic, he issued scathing and verbose statements. Critics characterized him as self-righteous, shrewd, manipulative, pragmatic, and hypocritical. Perceived by critics as arranging a deal with Virginia's established political machine, Cannon made unpredictable political endorsements that mystified even his allies. By 1918 he had risen from the role of country parson to become a bishop in the Methodist Episcopal Church, South, and for more than a decade he achieved national and international stature, primarily as a prohibition leader.[13]

Cannon began his ascent from an advantageous background. Born in 1864, he grew up in Salisbury, Maryland, where his father was a merchant. Both his parents were active laymembers in the local Methodist church. An excellent student and an avid reader, James aspired to become a lawyer and a member of the Supreme Court of the United States. During a revival at Randolph-Macon College, however, he professed his religious faith, decided to become a preacher, and subsequently received a license to preach from the Methodist Virginia Annual Conference. After earning a master's degree from Princeton College and a divinity degree from Princeton Seminary, Cannon returned to Virginia. There he served both rural and urban congregations. In 1894 Cannon reluctantly accepted a plea to become the principal of the fledgling Methodist Blackstone Female Institute. Located more than fifty miles from Richmond, Blackstone became the home for Cannon, his wife, and seven children. As the head of Blackstone, Cannon used his resourcefulness, his own financial assets, and his managerial talents to make the school a success. In 1904 he became part owner and editor of the *Baltimore and Richmond Christian Advocate,* which he sold to the Methodist Virginia Annual Conference in 1918. In 1911 Cannon assumed duties as superintendent for the new Southern Assembly at Lake Junaluska. Cannon later reported that during much of this time he worked sixteen- to eighteen-hour days, and critics portrayed him as a man who worked feverishly, like a person driven.[14]

Nothing drove Cannon more than the scourge of alcoholic beverages. Throughout his life he had endured personal experiences that testified to the damage caused by intoxication. As a youngster, he had accompanied his mother when she donated food and clothing to needy families. Cannon witnessed searing scenes of destitution that he traced to drunken husbands and fathers. A beloved uncle died from improper medical treatment following an attack by a vicious dog that had not been restrained by his drunken owner. Cannon later candidly admitted that he had "always charged" that tragic death "up as a debt in the balance sheet with the saloon." At Randolph-Macon College, Cannon rescued and subdued drunken classmates whose rowdy behavior might have otherwise led to disciplinary action. While at Princeton Seminary, he spent some weekends at city missions in New York City's Bowery. At a Newport News church, Cannon once ministered to the suffering of a family whose alcoholic father impoverished them. While inebriated, the same man accidentally killed an infant son and then stole the child's burial clothes to pay for liquor. Like many Richmond ministers, when Cannon denounced the ravages of the saloon, he could readily invoke firsthand experiences.[15]

With Cannon supplying forceful leadership, the Virginia Anti-Saloon League won many victories in the first decade of the twentieth century. Using press credentials to gain access to the floor of the Virginia General Assembly, Cannon helped draft and pass the Mann law of 1903 and the Byrd law of 1908. The Mann law installed a complicated and expensive licensing procedure for anyone wishing to maintain a saloon in a rural area or in a small town. Exempting only summer resorts, the Byrd law prohibited the sale of liquor in any town with a population of fewer than five hundred people. The same law prohibited saloons from employing women or minors, added licensing restrictions and fees for distilleries and social clubs, and prohibited the sale of liquor on passenger trains. A subsequent law forbade saloons from selling alcoholic beverages to women and minors. Taken together these laws essentially prescribed prohibition for rural Virginia. In response to Anti-Saloon League efforts, a number of Virginia cities also adopted prohibition in local option elections. The number of saloons in Virginia declined from 1,795 in 1901 to 671 in 1910. By that date approximately 70 percent of Virginia's population lived in areas which were legally dry.[16]

The Anti-Saloon League claimed significant successes in Richmond, too. In 1902 the city council raised licensing fees for saloons. Fearful of even higher fees in the future, liquor dealers organized to support candidates in the 1904 municipal elections. But the Anti-Saloon League also organized and dealt the dealers a major defeat. In 1906 the city council passed an ordinance requiring saloons to close between midnight and 6 A.M. Despite the appearance of seventy-five saloon owners at a city council meeting in 1907, the council eventually adopted a measure which doubled saloon licensing fees to $500, restricted saloons to nonresidential areas, and limited the number of saloons to 150. As a result of the new ordinance, approximately one hundred saloons closed. In reviewing license applications, judges refused to authorize saloons located at streetcar transfer points, where intoxicated patrons might annoy the public, particularly women. The Richmond Ministerial Union and the Anti-Saloon League backed these steps, but support was widespread. Though opposed to prohibition, the *Richmond Times-Dispatch* repeatedly published articles and editorials that depicted many unregulated saloons as sources of promiscuity, crime, and political corruption.[17]

By 1909 the major state and local legal victories of the anti-saloon leaders seemed to have mitigated the worst features of saloons. Confined to nonresidential areas, Richmond saloons did not operate late at night or on Sunday, could not employ or serve women or minors, and faced licensing fees and procedures designed to eliminate cheap and disorderly establishments. Many Richmonders appeared to be satisfied with these achievements. In an April 1909 editorial, the *Richmond Times-Dispatch* portrayed the city as a "peaceful, happy, and prosperous town." Asserting that there was "nothing in its civic life" which justified "interference with existing conditions," the newspaper pleaded "Richmond Asks to Be Let Alone."[18]

Not sharing that assessment, James Cannon promptly replied: "No gentlemen, we are not going to let Richmond alone. We are going to battle against the *appetite* and *covetousness* of some of her citizens till the capital of the great state is redeemed" (Cannon's emphasis). Anti-Saloon League members enumerated a host of harms still perpetrated in Richmond. Operating for only a few weeks each year, the Virginia state fair served as a vivid symbolic target around which to rally anti-saloon forces. After attending the fair at its north Richmond site in 1908, Methodist ministers protested that liquor was served to minors. In subsequent years, too, visiting preachers complained that bars served alcoholic beverages to women and children and that drunken males used indecent language. Cannon castigated the fair for debauching "the country people and the school children of Richmond." Neither a petition campaign nor a boycott supported by local Methodist and Baptist leaders moved directors of the fair to modify their policies of serving alcohol.[19]

Located next to the state fair grounds, a brewery operated and represented another grievance against Richmond. The very success of state anti-saloon laws had ironically solidified Richmond's status as a wet enclave in a dry state. Like the brewery, a number of other businesses profited from the sale of alcoholic beverages, and critics charged that their profits increased with their nearly monopolistic status. In 1914 the Baptist *Religious Herald* listed the most obvious Richmond businesses benefiting from the sale of alcoholic beverages: the one brewery, one distillery, twelve social clubs, ten wholesale dealers, thirty-four retailers and shippers, six firms that rectified liquor, and 150 saloons. Raising the cry of "city nullification," opponents of liquor charged that by serving as shipping and distribution centers, urban areas contaminated the dry countryside. Irate prohibitionists accused cities of setting "sensual and devilish traps" to rob visitors of "their money and their good name and their character."[20]

Some anti-saloon leaders identified another urban menace, city newspapers. Though favoring local option and saloon regulation, Richmond newspapers editorially opposed prohibition, criticized Cannon, and occasionally printed articles slanted against the Anti-Saloon League. After 1908 Cannon engaged in a running battle with the Richmond press—a battle that quickly degenerated into a blood feud lasting for decades. An unhappy Cannon issued vitriolic personal denunciations of editors, reporters, and owners. Claiming that he could not receive fair treatment in the Richmond dailies, he established his own newspaper, the *Richmond Virginian* in 1910. Cannon charged that through selling advertising, the Richmond newspapers, like the saloons, profited from the vile liquor trade.[21]

Seemingly frustrated by a failure to gain greater support in Richmond, Cannon and other Anti-Saloon leaders blamed the city's "fashionable society," which, they alleged, dominated local churches as well as business and politics. With a bittersweet article, "Alas Poor Richmond!," written in 1914, Cannon praised the city as "beautiful," "interesting," historical, and "teeming with the life of a new age." Yet, concluded Cannon, although it was, in many respects, "the pride of all Virginians," it retained the reputation of a saloon stronghold, spewing out thousands of criminals, drunkards, and victims.[22]

That same year, 1914, the Anti-Saloon League finally achieved an important goal, a popular referendum for statewide prohibition. In 1910 the league had announced its intention to replace its strategy of relying on education and local option elections with a campaign for a statewide prohibition law. Charging that urban liquor dealers continued to ship alcohol into the dry countryside, Anti-Saloon leaders justified the change in goals as essential to protect rural residents from the intrusion of alcohol. The league organized systematically and thoroughly, and it received substantial support from Protestant religious leaders. During the months before that election, the editors of Baptist and Methodist state newspapers printed scores of articles backing prohibition. In expressing "Our Position," the *Presbyterian of the South* called the liquor traffic "the source of the major part of the ignorance, poverty, pauperism, disease, insanity, dishonesty, vice and crime in our land." A few churches actually granted leave to pastors so they could devote their time to soliciting votes. In the weeks before the election, a number of Baptist and Methodist preachers delivered sermons supporting prohibition. Unable to attend a prohibition rally in downtown Richmond, Union Seminary's Walter W. Moore sent a letter of support that was read to the audience and was thereafter highly publicized. He expressed his hope that "fully informed" and "thoroughly aroused" citizens would vote for the statewide proposition and would "forever roll away the reproach of Richmond." The Episcopal *Southern Churchman* gave strong support to the campaign. Acknowledging that people might differ over the appropriate means, the Episcopal Diocesan Council urged "Christian men" to give their "influence and activity" to efforts to reduce the consumption and sale of liquor "with the goal of the annihilation of traffic in intoxicating liquors."[23]

Having organized at Leigh Street Baptist in 1910, the Woman's Prohibition League of America (WPLA) formed an important column in the statewide crusade. By 1915 the WPLA had established 110 chapters throughout the state and tallied a membership of more than seven thousand. The women held weekly prayer meetings, distributed literature at the state fair, and enlisted children to sign pledges of total abstinence. During 1914 they employed full-time fieldworkers, printed a special sixteen-page booklet, and conducted massive mailings of literature to every qualified Richmond voter. For two weeks preceding the election, the women held nightly open-air meetings at a downtown lot. On election day they conducted prayer meetings in many of the city's Methodist and Baptist churches.[24]

But Richmond trade unions, the chamber of commerce, and the daily newspapers had long opposed prohibition. Based in Richmond, the Local Self-Government Association championed local option as a continued alternative and engaged in a modest public campaign. Calling the proposal unnecessary and coercive, the members of this group argued that such a law would be unenforceable, would damage the state's economy, and would substantially reduce the state's tax revenues. Even some prominent Protestants opposed the statewide measure. One Methodist minister expressed horror when several local Methodist and Baptist laymen signed a public petition against the referendum. On election day the referendum won decisively. But Richmonders reversed the statewide pattern, casting 6,239 ballots against it and only 4,054 for it. In many of the city's twenty-two precincts, the vote was close, but the referendum won favor in only three. The strongest support for statewide prohibition in Richmond occurred in old Manchester, a working-class area, and in Jefferson Ward, the political stronghold of organized labor's favorite city candidate, John Hirschberg.[25]

The successful statewide prohibition referendum heralded a new era for Virginians, who saw prohibition gradually implemented. On 31 October 1916, a large temperance audience gathered at Grace Street Baptist Church and sang hymns as the new state law took effect at midnight. The next day a local newspaper carried the headline: "In Good Humor, Richmond Greets Prohibition Era, No Outbreak of Disorder." In carrying out the voters' mandate, state legislators produced a law that may have contributed to such good humor. This new law permitted each household to acquire one-fourth gallon of liquor, or one gallon of wine, or three gallons of beer each month. After 1914, as the head of the national Anti-Saloon League's legislative committee, James Cannon spent most of his time in Washington, D.C., where he and other opponents of alcoholic beverages forged forward with a campaign for national prohibition. Seizing upon the need for wartime food conservation measures, the Anti-Saloon League secured a series of national wartime prohibition laws. Ratified in 1919, the Eighteenth Amendment to the Constitution of the United States prohibited the manufacture, sale, or transportation of "intoxicating liquors." To implement the amendment, Congress then passed the Volstead Act, a stern law which defined intoxicating liquors very broadly and which required collaboration between federal and state enforcement agencies.[26]

Within Richmond, prohibition received mixed reviews. Pointing to an immediate steep drop in arrests for drunkenness, Baptist R. H. Pitt lauded Richmond as a "transformed city." Praising conditions in 1923, Presbyterian Walter L. Lingle contrasted the absence of liquor in the city with an earlier period when saloons and liquor abounded. The *Southern Churchman* concluded that prohibition "has brought immeasurable benefit to America, as thoughtful and unselfish citizens everywhere recognize." In 1925, however, newspaper columnist Cally Ryland asserted that "the best people" in Richmond and Virginia broke the prohibition law "every day." Following an initial decline in arrests for drunkenness in Richmond, those statistics rose steadily as the city's population increased. Deploring the continued, alleged lawlessness of the liquor industry, some Richmond clergymen resumed the crusade against alcoholic beverages. Declaring that there was abundant evidence of organized efforts to relax, repeal, and evade prohibition laws, they denounced any perceived lapse in enforcement. Closely monitoring the state and local scene, Baptist George W. McDaniel criticized Richmond authorities whenever he thought they dispensed light sentences for prohibition offenses. When Virginia Gov. Westmoreland Davis reduced funds for prohibition enforcement and pardoned convicted bootleggers, local Anti-Saloon leaders condemned him. Stung by the sharp criticism, the governor angrily counterattacked with charges of "clerical Kaiserism."[27]

Harsh and polemical, Davis's epithet nonetheless pointed to a significant change. The price of prohibition included a fee that most local religious leaders had been loath to pay: political activity. Discarding the early advice of Baptists and Presbyterians, the Anti-Saloon League had carried some church leaders into divisive political activity. At first the league had politely relied on education and political persuasion. Under the leadership of Cannon, though, the league began to quiz candidates for state office about their stance on liquor legislation, to publicize those positions, and finally to target opponents for defeat. Cannon himself moved beyond lobbying for laws to drafting them and to announcing his preferences in gubernatorial and presidential races. After statewide prohibition became law, Methodist minister J. Sidney Peters, a Virginia Anti-Saloon League leader, served as the state's first prohibition commissioner, and critics soon charged him with misusing his office for partisan purposes.[28]

The political activity of local religious leaders reached a climax over the presidential candidacy of New York Gov. Al Smith. In 1923 Smith supported and approved a proposal to eliminate the prohibition enforcement agency in his state. For the next five years, Smith served as a symbolic villain representing any person or group who wished to adjust the Volstead Act even slightly. Virginia prohibitionists inveighed against Smith as a hapless tool of corrupt, liquor-dominated, Tammany Hall machine politicians. The *Religious Herald* instructed readers that Smith had voted for "the liquor interests" twenty-five times in his political career. With Smith as the Democratic presidential candidate in 1928, some Richmond ministers even used their pulpits, state and local organizations, and the religious press for partisan purposes. Protestant weekly newspapers repeatedly cited Al Smith's anti-prohibition statements and actions. Smith lost and failed to carry Richmond, normally a strongly Democratic city. Somewhat defensively, R. H. Pitt claimed that of the more than five hundred Virginia Baptist ministers, no more than five had delivered sermons or public addresses stating their presidential political preference. Meanwhile, a series of scandals involving James Cannon shook local supporters and emboldened old adversaries. As Cannon fended off charges of gambling on the stock market, hoarding food during World War I, engaging in land speculation, and committing adultery, critics loudly denounced him as an immoral hypocrite. During the 1928 presidential campaign, local Protestant leaders had contended that the key issue was, in the words of a Methodist editor, "whether we shall lose all we have won by returning liquor people to power." In 1928 they had not lost. Dating from the beginning of the century, the moral crusade against saloons had been won, and the campaign for prohibition had achieved a temporary victory. But those successes had involved some unexpected costs.[29]

In contrast to the three-decade assault against saloon liquor, Richmond religious leaders waged short but intense campaigns to defend the community against government corruption in 1902, 1915, and 1918. In the early twentieth century, America's city governments gained notoriety for the illegal behavior of their officials. Although Richmonders rarely confronted municipal misconduct, several episodes of police corruption created furors in the community. In 1902, already upset about lax enforcement of Sunday closing laws, ministers voiced outrage about three other matters. A grand jury indicted a former alderman who, while in office, had allegedly accepted a bribe from a paving contractor. Although the man was convicted, fined, and sentenced to a year in jail, the affair shook the confidence of some religious leaders in the righteousness of local public officials and alerted them to other possible wrongdoings.[30]

Ministers merged the bribery incident with another scandal involving the failure of city policemen to enforce laws against gambling. Preachers deplored gambling as an immoral activity equivalent to theft because a gambler sought gratification "at the expense and even of the ruin of one's fellow man." And gambling was illegal. In July 1902 a patrolman charged his captain, James Angle, with interfering with gambling enforcement. After conducting a hearing, the Board of Police Commissioners exonerated the captain. Upset clergymen, though, urged a further investigation. The *Religious Herald* suggested that if such "flagrant" gambling violations could occur undetected by the police, then that negligence shattered "the confidence of the community in their vigilance and trustworthiness." Seven gamblers who were subsequently convicted paid fines but were incarcerated for only five hours, during which they enjoyed a special meal complete with wine. The *Religious Herald*'s editor termed this episode "a roaring farce," and other religious leaders joined him in condemning officials. A nervous police board then suspended Captain Angle, who resigned to avoid a further investigation.[31]

In October 1902 James B. Hawthorne created a sensation by charging that the police had failed to enforce laws against prostitution. Hawthorne asserted that 450 brothels operated within the city. The city's chief of police admitted the existence of one hundred such houses but publicly defended his policy of closing only disorderly bordellos. Were the vice laws strictly enforced, he maintained, prostitutes would disperse throughout the city. As he asked one rector, "If I drive these people from there, how do I know they will not rent a house right by you?" Instead, the chief argued, policemen could easily supervise houses concentrated in one area. Hawthorne categorically rejected this policy of discretionary enforcement and urged Christians to demand the enforcement of all laws. After a hearing the city council concluded that no investigation was warranted. At least one other clergyman criticized Hawthorne for using outdated information and defended the policy of discretionary enforcement. In the wake of the gambling and vice controversies, the police chief resigned, but his successor made no announced changes in how the department dealt with prostitution.[32]

In fact, the Board of Police Commissioners continued to accept prostitution as inevitable and quietly established a segregated vice district in 1905. They required "inmates" of the houses to furnish photographs and descriptions and to submit to medical examinations. The premise of the policy was to confine the illicit behavior to one area of the city where it could be supervised.

As the chief of police later explained, "I did not think it was a proper place for that kind of houses to be in the lady's shopping district." In 1912 officials informed several clergymen about the district, and they relayed the facts to the Richmond Ministerial Union. Accepting the segregation policy as a temporary necessity, the ministers urged vigilant police enforcement to prevent the operation of other houses of assignation. Writing on behalf of the ministerial union, a committee expressed its "unalterable opposition to immoral houses and its hope of finding a satisfactory solution." Yet, as Richmond's population increased, policemen had difficulty controlling, much less eliminating, prostitution. Between 1910 and 1915, the number of arrests for "red-light crimes" more than doubled.[33]

In January 1914 the Richmond Ministerial Union called for a renewed attack on vice, and Mayor George Ainslie, running for reelection, appointed a commission to study the problem. The fifteen-member commission radiated morality. Six Protestant ministers, including Joseph T. Mastin, the secretary of the State Board of Charities and Corrections, participated. Rabbi Edward Calisch, the president of the Ladies Hebrew Benevolent Association, the president of the McGill Catholic Union, juvenile court officer Sarah Roller, the president of the Richmond Chamber of Commerce, the president of the Central Trades and Labor Council, and a local attorney also served. Handicapped by a limited budget, the commission still obtained the assistance of investigators from the American Social Hygiene Association, conducted extensive research, produced a five-hundred-page report, and rendered twenty conclusions and recommendations which shook Richmond. The commission's first conclusion was devastating: the policy of segregation had failed so badly that more than four hundred prostitutes operated outside the segregated district compared to approximately two hundred living within it.[34]

The revelation of extensive prostitution beyond the segregated district triggered calls for another probe into possible police corruption. Upset that the violations had occurred even though the city had "stomached" the "noisome, sinning district," the *Richmond News Leader* advocated an official inquiry. Even the Board of Police Commissioners favored an investigation. Lacking legal power to investigate the police, the vice commission had avoided commenting about them and had thereby opened the door to speculation about police misconduct. After quickly closing the segregated district, Mayor Ainslie asked the vice commission for any information that implicated the police. Always guarded about its material, the commission sent Ainslie a five-page summary and cooperated with the city council, which did conduct an investigation. During those hearings, policemen and prostitutes testified that several police board members had prevented vice arrests and had patronized brothels. The executive committee of the Richmond Ministerial Union warned of a possible whitewash, a fear seemingly validated when no disciplinary actions were taken against the accused police board members and none resigned. The board, however, did dismiss a patrolman who testified against them.[35]

The patrolman's firing inflamed many preachers who denounced the Board of Police Commissioners. Speaking from pulpits and at large public meetings, even clergymen who normally avoided political controversies played prominent roles. Methodist Bishop Collins Denny attacked the commissioners for slack law enforcement and personal impropriety and asserted that it was "our duty" as citizens "to force them out of office." Faced with this public reaction, the mayor intervened to reinstate the patrolman, and two commissioners resigned. Ainslie complained that the decentralized city government limited his control of the police department. Agreeing with him, the city council dissolved the police board and gave the mayor greater power over the department.[36]

Nonetheless, in 1918, with citizens preoccupied with World War I, another police scandal jolted Richmond. Mayor Ainslie replaced one police chief because of allegations that he had ignored liquor offenses, and a grand jury indicted nine policemen for trafficking in illegal liquor. The jury further concluded that city morality had reached a low ebb, recommended dismissal of the new police chief, and censured the mayor for weak leadership. At the same time, Richmonders learned that the police had continued to disregard vice violations. In May, nearby Camp Lee reported more new cases of venereal disease than did any other U.S. Army base. The camp's commander traced many infections to Richmond, and military authorities threatened to place the city off limits to soldiers.[37]

Incensed by news of the two scandals, citizens concluded that the police and possibly the mayor had again failed to uphold the law. Demanding that "Richmond Shall Not Be Disgraced," *News Leader* editors declared: "A city of churches, a city of Christians, a city of decency, Richmond will not permit her face to be blackened by a forced alliance with the prostitute, the gambler and the panderer and the bootlegger. . . . Richmond shall be clean." Affirming a "deep and sincere attachment for Richmond," the editor of the *Religious Herald* then voiced his "sense of shame and humiliation" over the news reports and called for "such a housecleaning as we have never had." With similar passion, other ministers insisted upon an investigation. In an unprecedented declaration, the Richmond Ministerial Union resolved that if the mayor could not or would not enforce the laws, citizens should find someone who would. Juries acquitted the policemen, but Mayor Ainslie initiated a separate investigation, which led to the resignation of two officers. By passing a city charter reform, voters gave the mayor direct control over all municipal agencies, including the police department, and this change carried the prospect of holding the mayor politically accountable for any future malfeasance. As the confrontations with the mayor and the police demonstrated, religious leaders were increasingly willing to use political pressure to ensure that municipal leaders respected the law.[38]

The three campaigns against police corruption restored a prized sense of civic virtue, but those same episodes addressed another danger—prostitution. Just as lawless officials jeopardized the community's legal integrity, prostitutes threatened the sexual purity that ministers deemed essential to righteous lives and pious families. Indeed, Protestant leaders viewed a prostitute as the antithesis of the ideal Christian woman, whose moral qualities influenced her entire family. The 1915 Richmond vice commission reported that most prostitutes drank liquor, smoked cigarettes, and used habit-forming drugs. As a social worker asked rhetorically, "Can parents inculcate high moral standards when across the street or down the block are houses of the red-light district?" A prostitute could lure husbands into adultery, and even worse, she might transmit a "loathsome disease" that could injure innocent family members. This concern gained new urgency as medical research revealed the severe consequences of venereal diseases and as studies linked the spread of them to prostitution. Thus, a prostitute departed so far from morally acceptable behavior that few people believed that she could be rehabilitated. Social reformer Arthur W. James later recalled that "many respectable people who gave generously to charities and who supported other social reforms turned away in disgust from the young prostitute." According to him, a prostitute "was considered incorrigible, an outcast, a pariah. Once fallen, it was assumed she would remain a disreputable character for the rest of her life and that efforts at reform or restraint would be of no avail." When the vice commission reported that hundreds of prostitutes lived in residential areas, including the fashionable West End, the news unnerved citizens, who no longer felt protected from such moral menaces.[39]

Richmond Protestant leaders took several types of action to deter prostitution. They used the legal system for some direct solutions. In 1915 ministers served on the vice commission, and clergymen led a public outcry resulting in the closing of the segregated district. A second ministerial-led public clamor compelled authorities to enforce laws against prostitution in 1918. Throughout the 1920s city arrests for the crimes of operating a house of ill-repute and of streetwalking declined, probably indicating that the practices had diminished in the city. Serving as secretary of the State Board of Charities and Corrections, Richmond Methodist preacher Joseph T. Mastin secured the passage of five state laws similar to anti-prostitution laws enacted elsewhere in the nation. One law raised the age of consent to fifteen years. A second law required the hiring of a policewoman in cities larger than 15,000 people. A third law provided that anyone who sent a woman to a house of ill-repute could be convicted of a felony, and another made it unlawful to reside in or to visit a brothel or bawdy house. A fifth law designated such houses of ill-repute to be public nuisances, making them subject to closing with a court injunction that ordered the owner to vacate persons engaged in immoral conduct.[40]

As part of the legal approach to dealing with prostitution, reformers tried to deflect young girls from becoming involved in vice. Beginning in 1912, Richmond's Juvenile Protective Society supported an early version of the city's juvenile court. The president of that society, H. D. C. Maclachlan, reported that "a very important aspect" of the court "has been the care of young girls who have been guilty of offenses against morality." The court soon employed probation officer Sarah Roller, particularly to deal with "the young girl problem." In justifying continued financial support for the court from the city council, Maclachlan included the need to "save from lives of shame young girls who, unless cared for, will inevitably lead such lives." During most of the first decade of the twentieth century, young women convicted of violating laws were incarcerated in jails, subjected to influence by older, "hardened" criminals, some of whom were prostitutes. This situation was remedied only through the efforts of J. T. Mastin, Richmond Baptist ministers James Buchanan and George W. McDaniel, Methodist layman John P. Branch, and Judge John J. Crutchfield. Thwarted several times, these men led a successful 1909 campaign to finance the building of a correctional institute for girls. In 1914 the private board of managers transferred this Virginia Home and Industrial School for Girls to the state of Virginia, which assumed administrative responsibilities for it. Using the legal system, city religious leaders promoted sterner enforcement of existing laws, new laws to deter prostitution, and a juvenile justice system designed to intervene in the seemingly vulnerable lives of girl delinquents.[41]

Fearing that desperate, stigmatized, unwed mothers might resort to prostitution, city church women tried to help those girls in the Spring Street Home. Established in 1874, the home operated under the supervision of an interdenominational board of lady managers and relied heavily on the committed leadership of Lucy Ambler Mason, wife of Landon R. Mason, rector of Grace Episcopal Church. According to Mrs. Mason, these "often homeless and perfectly desperate" "fallen girls" had frequently been "turned adrift by their enraged and deeply mortified families." Without the home, many of the young women could have found "no other refuge except some horrible den of infamy," where they would have been "hardened into abandoned wretches." In one annual appeal for funds, Mrs. Mason suggested that while "the world" might gossip, jest, or smirk about the plight of these young people, "only God has sufficient sympathy and love for fallen men and women." In attempting to aid a North Carolina father anxious about his pregnant daughter, Walter Lingle endorsed the Spring Street Home. He described it as "a Christian institution" where "they try to save the girl from becoming an outcast and a loose woman." Lingle reported that "the girls who go there are as a rule from the humbler walks of life as far as I can judge." Each young woman was expected to keep her child and stay at the facility for at least a year. Mrs. Mason praised a female superintendent for her "tactful, motherly treatment of her charges," who engaged in various domestic tasks to maintain the house. Operating with an endowment, the home counted on annual campaigns directed by Mrs. Mason to gain funds and garner contributions of linen, furniture, household goods, and provisions. Each year the Spring Street Home cared for between twenty-four and forty girls and several dozen infants. Some young women returned to their parents, and others obtained employment. In 1908 Mrs. Mason noted that many of the women had been able to "marry well after a full confession of their previous lives."[42]

Although the legal system and rehabilitation measures could lessen the prospects of prostitution, religious leaders favored preventive steps, too. Social reformers still worried about the vulnerability of the city's thousands of young female workers. As George W. McDaniel observed, when "unsuspecting country girls" arrived in the city, they faced "manifold temptations," especially as they encountered "evil minded men in offices and factories." A study done by the Southern Woman's Educational Alliance echoed that fear. A rural girl arriving in Richmond, it concluded, might quickly fall under "disintegrating moral influences," change her entire outlook, and "degrade her standards for all the future." Even more experienced working women could grow weary and lonely because of separation from their friends and families. As layman Douglas Freeman complained in 1913, some local factories paid very low wages. Some female operatives, he asserted, drifted near starvation, and with their economic hardship they faced enormous "temptation."[43]

To protect young females, religious groups took several steps. Protestant women tried to help young women as they arrived in Richmond. In 1910 the Young Women's Christian Association (YWCA) created a Travelers Aid program to meet trains carrying rural women into the city. Assisted by many volunteers, the staff of four persons greeted twenty-four trains daily. In 1913 the association met more than 1,947 women. In 1914 the Travelers Aid program separated itself from the YWCA to affiliate with the national Travelers Aid

Society and continued to provide personnel to meet new arrivals. The YWCA also provided low-income housing, including a rooming hotel for businesswomen and a residential building for "younger girls." The two residences held 119 beds, which served a total of 2,029 women, both permanent and transient, in 1925. Using its own registry in 1926, the Richmond YWCA helped 2,833 women locate housing. Also concerned that new "working girls" might board in cheap houses under a "bad environment and subjected to very degrading influences," city Methodists established the Wilson Inn in 1912. The facility offered inexpensive, temporary room and board to young women who moved to Richmond. By staying at the inn, a young woman had a chance to begin earning income and locate a suitable, long-term residence. A deaconess supervised the inn, which provided some recreational rooms where the young women could play games, listen to a Victrola, play a piano, and entertain male friends. In 1926 the one hundred women who resided there for varying lengths of time included business college students, stenographers, telephone operators, sales ladies, and tobacco workers.[44]

Churches also provided some solutions to loneliness. Working women could find companionship through participation in church social activities. Yet, as laywomen conceded, following a six-day work week, factory women wanted an entire day of rest. In 1916, under the aegis of the Presbyterian League, Richmond Protestants began a concentrated program to reach employed women. Aiming to bring "life into dull and dreary lives," ministers and laity held lunchtime devotional services at factories. These meetings also included health talks, music, and singing. In addition, Baptist women sponsored summer trips for working women to a rural camp. Although the program was modest, an ebullient director claimed that "many eyes dulled by toil and strain of factory life, by insufficient food, illness and broken homes have had their eyes brightened and their hearts made glad." The Methodist Institute, St. Andrew's Episcopal Church, and the Baptist Neighborhood House offered such resources as libraries, playgrounds, and homemaking classes. Later, Broad Street Methodist Church and the Baptist House of Happiness provided additional social and recreational opportunities.[45]

Still, no organization rivaled the YWCA's opportunities for socializing. Formed in 1887, the Richmond YWCA claimed to be the oldest in the South. In the early twentieth century, much of the Y's success could be traced to the energetic leadership of two young laywomen, Katherine Hawes of Second Presbyterian Church and Lucy Randolph Mason, daughter of Lucy Ambler Mason. An interdenominational organization with impressive vitality, the Richmond Y developed an assortment of programs. In addition to special lectures, the organization offered courses in topics ranging from history and mathematics to sewing and cooking. Equipped with its own swimming pool and gymnasium, the Y taught swimming, hosted dances, organized a glee club, and sponsored plays. It operated two cafeterias that served more than 200,000 meals in 1926, and it owned a summer camp which 220 women enjoyed that same year. In completing an annual report, Lucy Randolph Mason placed supplying "social recreation for young industrial and business girls" at the top of her lists of "peculiar" responsibilities that the association addressed in behalf of the community.[46]

In dealing with the problem of low wages, church leaders largely relied on moral suasion and repeatedly called attention to the need to pay workers adequately. These appeals were supported by the 1915 vice commission, the local press, and organized labor, all of whom agreed that some women resorted to prostitution to supplement low wages. George W. McDaniel angrily charged that some women earning four dollars a week had to pay five dollars a week for board. Episcopal city missionary R. Cary Montague called upon churches to ascertain what constituted a living wage and then "require" employers to pay it. Lucy Randolph Mason repeatedly spoke and wrote in behalf of higher wages for working women.[47]

In attempting to protect the city from prostitution and trying to protect young women from becoming prostitutes, Richmond's religious leaders confronted an even larger and more intricate moral danger—the apparently increasing sexual immorality of young people. Novelist F. Scott Fitzgerald popularized the 1920s as "the jazz age," and journalist Frederick Lewis Allen argued that a "revolution in morals and manners" occurred during that same decade. Historians have since concluded that young people began to deviate from traditional behavior before World War I. In a sense, events in Richmond support both sets of conclusions. Before World War I Richmond Protestants detected distressing changes in youthful behavior, but only after the war did they perceive such activity to have become so disturbing that it required a series of reactions.[48]

To deal with youthful sexual morality, religious leaders had to overcome the major obstacle of traditional sexual etiquette. Like much of the nation, Richmond adhered to a sexual etiquette designed to protect women from impure and profane influences, and that etiquette prohibited public discussions of sexuality. At the beginning of the twentieth century, men, not women, shopped at public markets on Saturdays. As Col. John Cutchins later recalled, "The appearance of a young woman on Main Street, unless accompanied by a member of her family or a very old friend or her fiancee, was indeed a rare sight." In 1905 Mayor Carlton McCarthy ordered the removal of "indecent" posters advertising a play and insisted that retailers fully clothe mannequins in their shop windows. In 1912 when South Carolina Sen. Cole Blease used profanity in a speech at the Jefferson Hotel, women left the audience. Young men called on young women at their residences, and chaperoned young people attended parties and dances. In 1910 a young male employee of a movie theater was arrested for flirting with a female patron and required by the judge to post a bond of $1,000 to ensure his good behavior for the next twelve months. From time to time clusters of male mashers defied the city's code of sexual etiquette. In 1913 and 1914, for example, a newspaper reported about two groups of mashers who congregated at different locations. In an editorial the *Richmond News Leader* declared that it had received complaints from female readers who had found it necessary to avoid those areas "to escape the stares of these parasites." An indignant editorialist proclaimed that "Richmond fathers and husbands will not permit their daughters and wives to be the target of insults, or even of impertinent stares." Noting that local merchants risked the loss of "valued customers," the writer urged the police to enforce a local "move-on" ordinance.[49]

Even talking about sexuality violated community rules of sexual etiquette. In the early 1900s, ministers used vaguely worded sermons to promote sexual ideals of chastity and marital fidelity. Clergymen instructed young men to exercise "self-control," lest they yield to the passions of their "lower natures." During the 1902 vice controversy, the *Richmond Times* criticized the investigation as a public parade of an ugly subject before "the young and the innocent who had no business to know." The 1915 vice commission held closed hearings and left no public transcript. In an Ellen Glasgow novel set in Richmond, one character scolded her female cousin for asking intimate questions about marriage. Even liberal minister H. D. C. Maclachlan refused to talk about sexual matters before mixed audiences of men and women. Richmonders thus adhered to what one scholar has described as the "rule of euphemism and silence" about sexuality prevalent in America in the early twentieth century.[50]

Religious leaders began to urge direct public discussions of sexuality as well as of sexual morality. In 1914 Methodist pastor John W. Shackford expressed regret that the church itself had hindered sex education by casting a "veil of impurity" over this "most holy sanctuary." He reasoned that for many people, since "there is nothing holy about it, there can be no perversion that is very unholy." He called upon churches and families to break their silence about sexuality. They should, Shackford contended, teach each child about reproduction, "lest untaught or wrongly taught, he desecrate and defile the sanctuary." Later, Episcopal Bishop William Cabell Brown urged women to meet with girls to discuss sexual conduct intelligently and sympathetically. Seventh Street Christian Church laity opened a class "in physical culture and hygiene" designed to aid children from lower income families. In 1926 Dr. Roy Flannagan of the State Board of Health spoke to the Richmond Ministerial Union about social hygiene and encouraged "preventive education." During the 1929 Sprunt Lectures at Union Seminary, Walter Lingle called on the church to "find a way" to teach young people about "the mystery of life" and admitted such teaching was "one of the most delicate and difficult of all the tasks which lie before Christian fathers and mothers."[51]

The new earnestness about addressing sexuality stemmed from Richmond's changing conditions and from new information. As medical research revealed the harmful consequences and communicability of venereal diseases, ministers directed much of their attention at men. During World War I, clergymen became especially distressed about the "moral and spiritual weakness" of soldiers and "young sports." The Richmond Ministerial Union denounced the "double standard of morals" as "false to the kingdom of God which governs social life." Baptist and Episcopal leaders endorsed a plan whereby ministers would marry only those males who presented medical certificates showing them to be free of venereal disease.[52]

During the war the vice commission traced youthful immorality to dance halls, modern fashions, and movie theaters. In the early 1920s some Protestants rallied against all three such forms of entertainment. In 1919 the editor of the *Religious Herald* ruefully recalled that Americans had been engaged in a dance craze before World War I. Although some religious leaders objected to almost any form of dancing, those new styles had seemed especially offensive. Compared to the two-step and the waltz, the tango, the bunny hug, and the turkey trot involved greater body contact between partners as well as far more vigorous body movements. According to ministerial critics, these dances—as well as their successors of the 1920s, the Charleston and the black bottom—were lewd, incited lusty thoughts, and encouraged sexual immorality. In 1912 and 1913 several Richmond Methodist preachers charged that such immodest dances contributed to juvenile delinquency and vice. The city's denominational weekly newspapers joined in criticizing the dances as voluptuous and indecent.[53]

The renewed dance craze after World War I provoked an even sharper set of commentaries. Ministers characterized the new dance styles with phrases ranging from "hugging set to music" to "vile and licentious" to "a viper that destroys." Clergymen warned that dancers compromised their modesty and sometimes their morality. Hinting at where such conduct led, a Methodist editor advised that "when a normal young man with the red blood of youth, holds in close bodily contact the throbbing form of a normal young woman with the red blood of youth, in a warm evening and both in motion, they are not thinking astronomy or metaphysics or literature or art." One flamboyant local minister even claimed that dancing led to the downfall of 350,000 young women annually.[54]

Although Richmond parents might discount such an extravagant claim, they could not dismiss so easily an appeal by Ennion G. Williams, the health commissioner of Virginia. Already revered as a pioneer in Virginia's public health movement, Williams was also a Richmond Episcopal layman. In a calm, five-minute presentation before the Richmond Ministerial Union in 1921, he ascribed modern problems with moral delinquency to contemporary dance and fashion styles and urged the clergymen to combat such moral degeneracy. As one listener reported, statements coming from such an expert carried "great weight." Two days later Williams reiterated his call for action as he spoke to a large audience at Monumental Episcopal Church. And Richmond's chief of police concurred with Williams's assessment. Speaking to the ministerial union, he designated modern dance, fashions, and automobiles as "the greatest agencies contributing to moral delinquency."[55]

Williams's testimony ignited a small crusade against dancing. After his talk to the ministerial union, the Methodist *Richmond Christian Advocate* reported, "The preachers have been dealing with the modern dance in no uncertain manner." Indeed, many Protestant ministers did deliver sermons condemning dancing. One Baptist pastor declared that members who attended dances or hosted them at their houses should be expelled. Another suspended a popular young woman from the church choir because she attended a high school graduation dance hosted by the governor. Rather than "repent," she left the church. A third Baptist congregation expelled five members for dancing. Lecturing approximately three thousand women and girls, visiting public health expert Dr. Rachelle Yarros spoke about "social hygiene" and included warnings about the evils of modern dance and dress. Officials of Randolph-Macon College and of the University of Richmond reserved the right to prohibit women from attending dances elsewhere. In 1921 coeds at Westhampton College organized an anti-dancing society, and hundreds of coeds across the South joined. In 1922 a Lutheran layman serving as a member of the city council proposed an ordinance which would have required any girl attending a dance to be accompanied by a parent or guardian. Despite the endorsement of Richmond Methodist preachers, the measure did not pass.[56]

The 1921 moral crusaders perceived a moral threat not only in contemporary dancing styles but also in the immodest fashions worn by many young women. With low necklines, high hemlines, and clinging fabric, dresses of the 1920s had already become the target of local criticism. The editor of the *Southern Churchman* had complained of "a pandering to the sensuous so gross that it can hardly be unconscious." Following Dr. Ennion G. Williams's request, ministers escalated their condemnations of the "immodesty" of new fashions. Liberal rector Walter Russell Bowie deplored a "gross ugliness in dance and dress" and counseled that even an innocent carelessness among young women and young men was "fraught with danger." Warning how such fashions affected men, Baptist minister John J. Wicker claimed that a man could not keep "pure thoughts" while walking down Broad Street. Imploring young women to help men live good lives, he suggested that women could do so by rejecting "styles designed by the lowest class Parisians." Like Wicker, other preachers assumed that young people had innocently gone astray. Seemingly confident that young women would return to more tasteful apparel, moral reformers shifted their attention to movies.[57]

Even before World War I, some ministers had warned that movie theaters posed a threat to youthful morality. One clergyman worried that young people had too much opportunity for contact in a darkened room, "where the lower nature" had already been aroused by suggestive scenes. And, according to preachers, after the shows, adolescents roamed the city with its nightlife temptations, including illegal saloons, gambling dens, and brothels. Serving as a juvenile court officer, H. D. C. Maclachlan reported that following picture shows, girls flirted with mashers, initiated conversations with strangers, and committed "other acts of indiscretion." He advised parents that "the future of many homes depends upon preventive work done at an opportune time." At first religious leaders largely relied upon parental censorship and urged Christians to patronize only moral movies. In 1910, though, an irate Presbyterian editor complained that movies depicted scenes "which decent people would blush to describe" and called for movie censorship. The 1915 vice commission added to fears with its conclusion that current moving picture shows tended to promote vice.[58]

Postwar films heightened the anxieties of moralists. Moviemakers increasingly used risqué titles, themes, and advertising. Episcopalian Cary Montague concluded that "clean" movies were rare. More often, he charged, movies put immoral ideas into the heads of young women "whose means of subsistence are already too precarious." According to a Methodist editor, "Modesty, purity and reverence are being outraged on the screen every day in our Commonwealth." By 1922 many local clergymen had concluded that government regulation was necessary. Several prominent Baptist, Episcopal, and Methodist preachers testified in support of a state censorship bill, and the Richmond Ministerial Union endorsed the same legislation. The measure empowered a three-member board to censor movies that were "obscene, indecent, sacrilegious or tended to corrupt the morals of youth." Despite the opposition of novelist Thomas Dixon, Rabbi Calisch, and Maclachlan, the legislature enacted the law. Later, religious leaders applauded the censors' work. In 1923 the Richmond-dominated Dover Baptist Association praised a report indicating that the censors had required the editing of more than one thousand films and had rejected seven others.[59]

At times the campaign against entertainment took on the trappings of a campaign against young people as well. Rejecting that assessment, preachers like Second Presbyterian's Russell Cecil defended young people as the moral equals of earlier generations. In an article for the *Christian Century,* Maclachlan celebrated youthful energy, freedom, adventurousness, and frankness. Contending that even "youthful follies" aided in character development, he counseled that young people had to take their own risks, and he warned against damming the energy of youthful revolt. In a sermon, Maclachlan characterized modern young men as kinder, "cleaner," and more honorable than older generations. Serving as an associate judge of the city's juvenile court, Lutheran pastor John J. Scherer still marveled "to see how fine our young people really are." An Episcopal rector likewise affirmed the importance of open-mindedness and urged churches to adopt a "sympathetic attitude towards youth." In 1927 an exasperated Methodist editor and preacher Joseph M. Rowland proclaimed that he was tired of hearing adults blame young people for everything and concluded that despite "manifold temptations," "youth is not going to the dogs." Still, Rowland recommended greater social outlets for young people.[60]

In fact, Richmond churches had been steadily expanding their constellation of programs and activities for young people. Some individual congregations took special pride in their distinctive organizations. At Second Presbyterian Katherine Hawes had organized a group of young men called the Covenanters in the late 1890s. During the ensuing years, the ever-expanding group combined an athletic program, a choir, a fife and drum corps, and projects devoted to service and foreign missions. The Covenanter program served as a model for scores of other southern Presbyterian churches, but in 1916 Second Presbyterian Church discontinued it in favor of forming a Boy Scout troop. By the 1920s a number of other Richmond churches had begun to sponsor chapters of the Boy Scouts, Girls Scouts, and Camp Fire Girls. Between 1910 and 1920, Richmond's Methodist churches boasted a soaring enrollment in their Epworth Leagues. In 1913, adapting an effective device from their Sunday school programs, city Baptists began to hold training institutes for their Baptist Young People's Union. In 1914 an interdenominational group of Protestant clergy and laity inaugurated the city's first Vacation Bible School with month-long programs held at Seventh Street Christian Church and at the Methodist

Institute. Young people also participated in groups ranging from choirs to baseball and basketball teams. By the 1920s several churches housed athletic facilities, including gymnasiums and courts for basketball, tennis, and volleyball. In the 1920s many churches began to employ specially trained youth directors to coordinate their expanding programs. The Young Men's Christian Association and the YWCA offered an assortment of recreational programs, and both organizations offered access to swimming pools and gymnasiums. Through congregational, denominational, and interdenominational programs, religious leaders ensured that young people had social opportunities aside from the less wholesome secular attractions.[61]

In 1926 the editor of the Methodist *Richmond Christian Advocate* welcomed a report from "some expert" who claimed that jazz was dying. The editor wryly added, "May the funeral not long be delayed." Noting the fad of placing the word *jazz* in front of every contemporary form of activity, the clergymen suggested that it would be "a sweet relief" when people could stop "some of this plunkety plunk, blippty blip and flippty flip. Then we will not have to dress like we are crazy, walk and ride like we are on the way to the bug house, and carry on all our social life like rabbits eating turnips." By the end of "the Jazz Age," Richmond ministers had fought a successful series of battles to protect the community's morality. The capital city no longer tolerated saloons, a segregated district, or police corruption. The dance craze had subsided, and a state board now censored movies. Yet defending traditional morals had been a complex process that involved unanticipated political activism, necessitated departures from traditional sexual etiquette, and left somewhat unresolved how churches could channel the zest for recreation that seemed to preoccupy a younger generation. In addressing the moral dangers, though, city church leaders had affirmed their conviction that clergy and laity should apply religious beliefs to conditions in their urban environment. In the meantime, a similar sense of religious purpose had guided many clergymen and laypersons in deeds of social service.[62]

Looking west from Broad and Tenth Streets, this panoramic view of Richmond, circa 1895, reveals a skyline dominated by church steeples. Among the churches visible are, from left to right, St. Paul's Episcopal, Second Presbyterian, St. Peter's Catholic, Seventh Street Christian, Centenary Methodist, Grace Street Presbyterian, and St. James's Episcopal. *(Courtesy of the Valentine Museum, Richmond, Virginia)*

Downtown Richmond boasted a busy retail, commercial, and hotel district along Broad Street. This scene, circa 1913, looks east from Seventh Street to Ninth Street. *(Courtesy of the Cook Collection, Valentine Museum, Richmond, Virginia)*

The Richmond Locomotive Works contributed to Richmond's diversified industrial base, which produced tobacco, iron, paper, and food products. *(Courtesy of the Cook Collection, Valentine Museum, Richmond, Virginia)*

Like many congregations, Leigh Street Baptist Church was proud of its powerful new organ. *(Courtesy of the Cook Collection, Valentine Museum, Richmond, Virginia)*

By the 1920s Broad Street Methodist had become an institutional church. The community house to the right of the church building featured an auditorium, a reading room, a social hall, a kitchen, a day nursery, and a library as well as a gymnasium, showers, and courts for tennis, basketball, and volleyball on the roof. *(Courtesy of the Cook Collection, Valentine Museum, Richmond, Virginia)*

Many congregations erected handsome new church buildings often located on the city's growing periphery. Among them was First English Evangelical Lutheran Church, which moved to Monument Avenue at Lombardy Street. *(Courtesy of the Foster Collection, Virginia Historical Society, Richmond, Virginia)*

In 1907 Richmond hosted the General Convention of the Protestant Episcopal Church. This biracial procession of Episcopal bishops at Grace and Holy Trinity Episcopal Church represented one of the rare departures from segregated worship in the city. *(Courtesy of the Cook Collection, Valentine Museum, Richmond, Virginia)*

The men's Bible class of Tabernacle Baptist Church celebrated its thirty-fifth anniversary on 19 April 1925 and formed one of many large Bible classes for men in a city where churches created strong Sunday school programs. *(Courtesy of The Library of Virginia, Richmond, Virginia)*

At the beginning of the twentieth century, Union Theological Seminary had just begun to fill its campus with new buildings. *(Courtesy of the Cook Collection, Valentine Museum, Richmond, Virginia)*

The quiet countenance of laywoman Mary-Cooke Branch Munford hid a restless energy that made her a leading reformer, particularly in education. *(Courtesy of the Virginia Historical Society, Richmond, Virginia)*

Attending class at St. Andrew's School in 1908, these children as well as others in the Oregon Hill neighborhood benefited from a host of social service activities sponsored by St. Andrew's Episcopal Church. *(Courtesy of the Virginia Historical Society, Richmond, Virginia)*

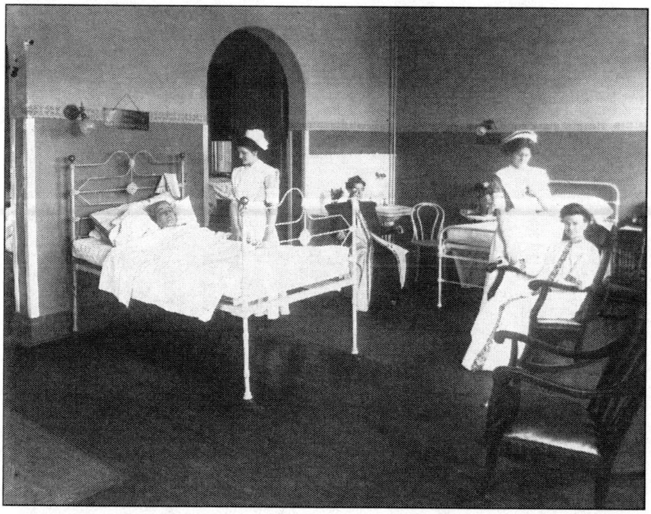

Founded and directed by churchwomen, Sheltering Arms Hospital provided free medical care and reflected the commitment of local Protestants to improve the community's health. *(Courtesy of the Virginia Historical Society, Richmond, Virginia)*

CAPTAIN W. RUSSELL BOWIE, Chaplain.

By 30 January 1918 Captain Walter Russell Bowie had returned to Richmond after the sobering experience of serving as a chaplain for a hospital unit in France. As rector of St. Paul's Episcopal Church, he joined other Richmond clergymen who championed the cause of international peace agreements in the 1920s. *(Courtesy of The Library of Virginia, Richmond, Virginia)*

Always one of the city's most innovative congregations, by 1921 Seventh Street Christian Church had added an electric sign to the front of its building. *(Courtesy of the Valentine Museum, Richmond, Virginia)*

7
"A New Pentecost"

At the annual meeting of the Virginia Conference of Charities and Correction in December 1913, Richmond's H. D. C. Maclachlan addressed the gathering about "the church at work in social service." With striking phrases he advised his listeners "that the Church of the twentieth century stands at the crossroads of a new Pentecost and is already learning to speak with other tongues—the tongues of social justice and brotherly love." Maclachlan was correct. For decades as Protestants throughout the United States had wrestled with the problems of an increasingly urbanized and industrialized society, many of them had espoused "the Social Gospel," a theology committed to transforming this world so that God's will might be done "on earth as it is in heaven." Disinclined to use the term *Social Gospel,* Maclachlan and many other Richmond Protestant leaders nonetheless affirmed their commitment to social service and social justice, phrases with comparable meaning. And the words and deeds of Christian social service radiated through early-twentieth-century Richmond.[1]

In Maclachlan's address, he explained the purpose and agenda of Christian social service. He did affirm that individual conversions and spiritual experiences remained the "supreme business" of the church. And churches, he allowed, should avoid divisive involvement in partisan politics. Still, while believing "in the same divine-human facts and forces as our fathers . . . we believe them in a different way," a way which gives them a "new significance for our age." "Spirituality" no longer consisted of merely "pious and mystical experiences" and of a heavenly afterlife. Rather, "spirituality" now entailed an effort to make earth more like heaven "through every-day service to humanity." According to Maclachlan, "The sacraments of modern life" were concrete endeavors such as housing commissions, social settlements, and child labor committees. Citing the Sermon on the Mount, Jesus' miracles of healing, and "His acts of poor benevolence," Maclachlan characterized Jesus as "the greatest of all social servants." Social service was not something added on to Christianity, but "Christianity itself, functioning at its highest power in the kingdom of God on earth." Yet, since "the present world-order is not in harmony with the spirit of Jesus," "we cannot be satisfied with things as they are." Lest the strong continue to exploit the weak, the church must act as "a force for social righteousness."[2]

Maclachlan identified specific actions which individual churches should take to foster social service and social justice. Religious leaders should preach and teach "the social conception of salvation." In contrast to a former emphasis on individual salvation, this new view stressed "community redemption" through the "re-adjustment" of individuals to the social order. Through "systematic instruction" and through organized activities, churches should train children that social service was as integral to religious life as were confession and baptism. Churches should unite to solve community problems. Through institutional programs, certain churches could operate as community centers, providing recreational and educational opportunities. To aid the impoverished, churches needed to join in programs of "scientific" charity. Organized Christianity further needed to free itself "from all suspicion" of an allegiance with "predatory wealth" and earnestly face "the mighty task of Christianizing the industrial order of the world." At the time Maclachlan spoke, Richmond Protestants had begun to implement the very agenda he articulated.[3]

Congregations throughout Richmond heard sermons preached in the language of the "new Pentecost," the phrases of social Christianity. At Marshall Street Christian Church on Church Hill, B. H. Melton described God's "standard of greatness" as "real service" rendered to humanity. At nearby Leigh Street Baptist Church, M. Ashby Jones maintained that the church must teach people to replace the "principle of competition for gain" with the principle of competition for service. W. A. Cooper, pastor of Central Methodist across the James River in Manchester, regularly advocated reforms to implement social service goals. At downtown Centenary Methodist in Richmond, W. J. Young advised that "true manliness" could be achieved only in a "strenuous life in the service of others." At Grace Street Baptist, C. S. Gardner cited "a vast body of Jesus Christ's social principles" and called upon ministers to teach those principles until members applied them to "the totality of their lives." Often a speaker in city pulpits, Richmond College professor S. C. Mitchell characterized the church as a "federation of human forces at war with man made sorrow."[4]

Richmonders encountered messages about social Christianity in a variety of media. City newspapers reported several sermons each week, thereby enabling a preacher to reach an audience larger than his own congregation. Denominational weeklies also featured articles about social service. Long attentive to social issues, the Episcopal *Southern Churchman* added a column titled

"Christianity and Community," which focused on social causes. Walter Russell Bowie wove Social Gospel ideas into his children's sermons, recounting the selfless deeds of heroic figures and urging youngsters to aid the poor and improve conditions in city slums.[5]

Church groups began to confront social issues. In 1912 Bowie organized a Social Service Commission for the Episcopal Diocese of Virginia. Other local and state denominational groups created such commissions and used them to consider social problems. The Diocese of Virginia offered scores of Social Gospel books at a "social service lending library," which it established at St. Paul's. Women's circles and adult Bible classes discussed social issues and initiated community service projects. For example, the women of Seventh Street Christian Church issued the first directory of social agencies for the city of Richmond. Several Richmond churches devoted Lenten services and special conferences to social problems. Some of these groups not only talked, they acted. When a committee of the Richmond city council scheduled hearings about appropriating money for city playgrounds, Seventh Street Christian's Sunday school classes and the Social Service Circle made plans to attend.[6]

To be sure, not all local Protestants quickly endorsed the cause of social service. Remaining true to the tradition of "the spirituality of the church," Richmond Presbyterians initially approached social Christianity cautiously. But they, too, began to speak its language, and the most important instruction in it occurred at Union Theological Seminary, where conservative professors had resisted such an innovation. When Walter L. Lingle joined the faculty in 1911, he assumed responsibility for teaching a course in Christian sociology. As Lingle later quipped, it seemed more important to know "something about the housing conditions of Richmondites than to be intimately acquainted with the family life of the Hittites; the Richmondites being still alive, and the Hittites having been a long time dead." Lingle assigned his students classic works by Social Gospel authors, and he reviewed new books in the *Union Seminary Magazine.* Lingle's students at the General Assembly Training School also took a course in Christian sociology and engaged in fieldwork at such locations as Richmond's juvenile court. Lingle was not alone. As an author at the Presbyterian Committee of Publication, Anna Binford wrote a book for young people, *Some Social Teachings of the Bible.* When new Union Seminary graduates such as Walter L. Carson and John MacLean occupied Richmond pulpits, they, too, conveyed social messages.[7]

In a fitting climax to his Richmond career, Lingle delivered the 1929 Sprunt Lectures at Union and spoke about social Christianity. Published as *The Bible and Social Problems,* that volume repeated, refined, and expanded views he had taught for years and had expressed in the *Presbyterian of the South.* Remarking that the Bible was "full of social service," Lingle referred to Jesus feeding the multitude and healing the sick, as well as to the Sermon on the Mount and the parable of the Good Samaritan. Liberally quoting Social Gospel theologian Walter Rauschenbusch, Lingle emphasized the idea that the kingdom of God "shall come as fully on earth as it has already come in heaven and that the will of God shall be done as perfectly on earth as it is done in heaven." To illustrate valuable forms of social service, Lingle listed "feeding the hungry, clothing the naked, ministering to the sick." He also criticized America's excessive individualism for creating social problems, and he called upon church members to attack the causes of poverty and to implement Jesus' social principles. Adapting a phrase from the Presbyterian Book of Church Order, he declared that "it is the business of the church to *proclaim,* to *administer,* and to *enforce* these great principles" (Lingle's emphasis).[8]

In a variety of settings across the city, Protestants transformed the vision of social service into deeds. Atop Oregon Hill, long a working-class neighborhood, St. Andrew's Episcopal Church functioned as the religious center for a complex of social services. In January 1904 Bishop Robert A. Gibson consecrated the new church building, an exquisite edifice. Constructed of granite and adorned in English gothic architecture, the new building ascended heavenward with a 115-foot square tower at its front. To enter the church, a person passed beneath a triple-arched porch with its inscription, "Come unto Me, all ye that labor and are heavy laden, and I will give you rest." Within the interior with its vaulted ceiling, worshipers might gaze at the extensive ornamental woodwork as well as at more than thirty stained glass windows, including several rose windows. From a transept at the south of the chancel, an organist played chords on a powerful new pipe organ. In providing seating for more than 700 people, the new interior might have seemed unnecessarily spacious for a church counting only 181 communicants in 1901. Indeed, though magnificent, the new church building reflected the fact that St. Andrew's was still taking shape, and some of its most impressive features lay outside the church doors.[9]

St. Andrew's owed its grand new existence to Richmond heiress Grace Arents. Born in New York City in 1848, she and her mother, one brother, and two sisters came to Richmond following the death of her father. In their new location, the family resided with a maternal uncle, Lewis Ginter, who accumulated wealth as a co-owner of Allen and Ginter Cigarette Manufacturers. Living downtown, she became a member of St. Paul's Episcopal Church and in the 1870s assisted in establishing the Oregon Hill mission, which eventually became St. Andrew's. In 1895 she moved with her uncle to a handsome West End mansion close to St. Andrew's and lived there for the next twenty-two years. Shy and afflicted with bad eyesight, Miss Grace was described by a contemporary reporter as "serious," "keenly intellectual," petite, and skillful at avoiding publicity. Upon her uncle's death in 1897, she inherited a fortune. Before her own death in 1926, she became an almost legendary benefactress whose donations supported countless projects to enhance Richmond. Nowhere else were her contributions of talent and money more significant than on Oregon Hill and in support of St. Andrew's. In 1897 she purchased a house to serve as the church's rectory, and in 1903 she donated another building to replace it. She contributed a large sum of money for the new church building, and she assumed financial administration when problems arose with construction. She established an endowment that financed some of the church's operating expenses. In 1904 the church opened a new parish hall, which she funded and which included a gymnasium to be used by parishioners and students at St. Andrew's School.[10]

St. Andrew's School evolved into an elaborate educational enterprise. Begun as a sewing class in 1894, the school quickly augmented its curriculum and its staff. By 1901 the school had inaugurated the first kindergarten in Richmond, provided primary courses for children, and offered manual training classes in drawing, woodworking, and sewing. Emphasizing reading, grammar, arithmetic, spelling, history, literature, and science, the school developed a class in physical education using the parish gymnasium and nearby playgrounds purchased by Grace Arents. Each class day began with devotions, and each school week concluded with chapel services on Friday. St. Andrew's night school attracted students from the entire city. Since they often arrived after working and without having eaten, the school began to furnish soup suppers. Throughout the week the school offered music classes in the afternoons, and on Saturdays it continued to conduct its sewing school. For a time Grace Arents served as principal of St. Andrew's School and financed a new school building, which opened in 1901. Having already started a library near the school, she made the library free to the public in 1899. In 1908 Arents furnished a new library building and reportedly selected each one of the more than ten thousand volumes in the Grace Arents Free Library.[11]

By offering educational opportunities to the working-class families of Oregon Hill, St. Andrew's provided a precious resource. In 1904, as the Richmond Education Association (REA) campaigned to improve public schools, its president reported that "a number of our schools" remained "dark, dingy, and overcrowded, with playgrounds totally inadequate for their purpose." As a member of the board of directors of the REA, Grace Arents well knew the limitations of the public school system. Thanks to her, St. Andrew's furnished a tuition-free private school, complete with a new building, small classes, and a gymnasium. St. Andrew's provided the Oregon Hill neighborhood a kindergarten, night classes, and vocational training before the public schools included them. While wrangles over the Andrew Carnegie offer left the city without a public library until the 1920s, the Grace Arents Free Library served eager readers. When the improved public school system failed to construct an elementary facility near Oregon Hill, Grace Arents gave the city a lot and contributed $5,000 for the fittingly named Grace Arents school built in 1912.[12]

St. Andrew's School constituted the church's foremost social service program but not the only one. St. Andrew's defined itself as an institutional church, a term used to designate a church that provided religious and social services to its community seven days a week. In addition to customary groups for men, women, and children, St. Andrew's created others. For example, the music director enrolled one hundred members in a "Chapter of Praise," which rehearsed weekly, occasionally supported or replaced the church choir, and gave special performances which included secular music. After 1918 the Episcopal Diocese of Virginia employed Mrs. R. L. Chiles to use St. Andrew's as a base for a ministry to deaf men and women. About six blocks down the hill from St. Andrew's, between the Virginia penitentiary and the James River, the church maintained a mission. Under the direction of deaconess Mary Davison, the mission featured a parish school which, like St. Andrew's School, offered daily classes as well as classes in home nursing and sewing. The deaconess took special pleasure in the Thursday mothers' meetings, which gave "worn out" women a respite from their daily tasks as wives and mothers. Indeed, the immediate area was one of poverty and "incessant drudgery seven days in the week." At this Belvidere mission, visiting nurses and later the city public health department provided free tests for tuberculosis. Next to the mission Grace Arents built and St. Andrew's managed the city's first public baths. St. Andrew's loaned, then leased, and finally sold some of its property to the Instructive Visiting Nurse Association. The Nurses' Settlement provided health care in the neighborhood and throughout much of the city.[13]

St. Andrew's relied on others in addition to Grace Arents. In launching St. Andrew's various programs between 1897 and 1919, rector Thomas Semmes played a major role. When he left St. Andrew's, an interdenominational group of ministers and laymen honored him with a farewell luncheon and praised him for his involvement in "many movements for social, civic, and religious betterment of the city" despite the many responsibilities of his large church. Arriving in Richmond in 1898, deaconess Mary Eltinge Davison dedicated the rest of her life to serving God, St. Andrew's, and Oregon Hill. Born in 1850, the deaconess had completed Deaconess Training School in Philadelphia and had served in that city for five years. Dressed in a deaconess habit, Davison became a familiar figure on Oregon Hill, teaching school, running the mission, supervising the women's public baths, and acting as a neighborhood agent for the Associated Charities. With a broadly drawn charter, St. Andrew's Association acted as a board of directors to manage the church's projects and finances, and Grace Arents served as a member of the board. Although the clergy and laity of St. Andrew's handled most of the programs, members of other Protestant churches sometimes assisted.[14]

As St. Andrew's extended educational services on Oregon Hill, Methodists in the heart of old Richmond attended to more immediate human needs. In 1895, at the behest of pastor Joseph T. Mastin, Trinity Methodist began providing temporary shelter for indigent and transient men. After 1899 city missionary George Wiley expanded that program and created the Methodist Institute. All of the city's Methodist churches supplied financial assistance and all participated in the organization's board of directors. The institute, according to Wiley, aided "men of roving disposition" struggling with economic misfortune. Many of them, he observed, were smart, educated, products of Christian homes, and skilled workers. Wiley's successor explained that the institute tried to give a man "'who is down' . . . an opportunity to get back on his feet." Few of the men, he noted, arrived there with any "money, friends or even decent clothing." The directors of the institute consistently avowed two goals deemed to be complementary: ministering to bodies and ministering to souls. Though a veteran evangelist, Wiley announced that "for the glory of God . . . Richmond's mission field" needed "baths more than we need Bibles," children's clubs more than prayer meetings, and nutrition instruction more than tracts.[15]

The Methodist Institute developed an expanding, multifaceted program. After purchasing the old United States Hotel, the institute refurbished its twenty-five rooms to provide inexpensive accommodations. In 1902 seven hundred men lodged a total of 1,500 nights. Anyone unable to pay a small boarding fee chopped wood, which was sold to defray expenses. When Sunday breakfasts proved popular, the institute established a coffee house and began serving thousands of low-cost lunches. Local physicians volunteered to staff an infirmary, and the institute acquired a set of baths. For diversions the institute provided a reading room, a small library, and a playground. Worried about the welfare of homeless boys, Wiley set aside one room for a boys club. Female volunteers and a deaconess started clubs for girls and women, too. Beginning with a night school, which offered basic educational instruction, the institute added classes in sewing, domestic service, and such trades as carpentry. Operating a job placement service, Wiley secured jobs for several hundred men annually. A female board of visitors distributed food, clothing, and medicine to needy neighborhood families. Each year the lady board of managers prepared an elaborate Christmas dinner. The institute conducted weekly worship services and Sunday school classes, held other religious services on Tuesday and Friday, and hosted a temperance meeting on Saturday. Praising Wiley's work, a local newspaper maintained that he showed "how Christianity is reduced to practice."[16]

Hitting its stride in the century's first decade, the Methodist Institute subsequently coped with some difficult transitions. After a fire damaged its building, the institute relocated twice but reestablished its former programs, added a kindergarten, and boasted a staff of seven "thoroughly trained workers." In 1923 the Methodist Virginia Conference implemented a plan to transform Trinity Methodist into an institutional church by placing all city missions under it. Trinity assumed oversight for the Methodist Institute, the Wilson Inn, and the recently inaugurated Goodwill Industries. Thereafter the Methodist Institute functioned primarily as a community center. Collecting and renovating old clothing and furniture, Goodwill provided work and sold its products to two stores, where its inexpensive prices made the goods accessible to patrons with low incomes. Under the direction of a deaconess, Goodwill employed workers, organized clubs for men, women, and children, offered vocational classes, and opened a summer camp for children. Trinity and Goodwill collaborated to sustain the earlier vision of attending to a person's physical needs and his or her spiritual welfare.[17]

Between 1904 and 1906, city Baptists operated a facility comparable to the Methodist Institute. After the Baptist Council of Richmond and Manchester decided to create a downtown mission, they made an even more momentous decision—they chose James Buchanan of Brooklyn, New York, to direct it. A stout, genial, forty-year-old native of Scotland, Buchanan quickly earned respect in Richmond for his knowledge, diligence, and resourcefulness. At his suggestion the Baptist Council rented a few rooms in the old Ballard Hotel and then rented the entire building to house their new Central Neighborhood House. As one writer later noted, the council intended to reach the "homeless wanderers and social outcasts" of the city. Buchanan had certainly selected the appropriate neighborhood. A local journalist reported that the area had fallen into "disrepute with all classes" because of the "depravity, squalor," and immoral behavior of its residents. With the red-light district nearby, "obscene alleys radiated in all directions." The once grand Ballard Hotel had entertained celebrities in the nineteenth century, but it had become a deserted hulk except for a gang of thieves who lived in its cellar, vandalized the building, and stole and sold its pipes and furnishings.[18]

With the aid of his wife, Abbie, Buchanan proceeded to convert the dilapidated five-story building into useful space. Each of the top three floors contained twenty-two large bedrooms as well as a toilet and bath. The lower floors provided an office, a dining room, a social hall, a chapel, and a library. The Baptist Council had originally intended their new program to aid only men, but Baptist women's groups also wanted to employ a female city missionary. They chose Mrs. Buchanan, who opened a "Women's Industrial Home" on the building's second floor. In a separate building behind the hotel, Mrs. Buchanan and volunteers started a kindergarten, which functioned largely as a nursery for working mothers. The Neighborhood House offered low-cost room and board as well as clothing and medicine. Some men chopped wood, which was either used or sold. Other residents cooked, cleaned, and renovated the building. Intending to minister to both body and soul, the Buchanans conducted religious services with the aim of converting listeners to Christianity. As James Buchanan noted, a "considerable" portion of the Neighborhood House's services were devoted to workers who had become displaced by changes occurring in industries. A busy world easily lost sight of such people and, he observed, society "feels that 'those who are down deserve to be down.'"[19]

Buchanan's combination of skills as a social worker and an administrator quickly impressed others in the community. During 1905, a group of citizens gathered to consider ways of coordinating and consolidating charitable activities within the city. In 1906 they chose Buchanan to head the new Associated Charities. At first the Baptists shared both Buchanan and the Neighborhood House with the infant organization. But the dual set of duties proved taxing for Buchanan. The Executive Committee of the Baptist Council of Richmond and Manchester acknowledged that they had taken up this "civic business only because there was an urgent need for someone to do it properly." By late 1906 the council rejoiced that "the principles of our social work for the poor have been established, the public has been aroused." Turning their attention to other matters, the council surrendered the Ballard House to a career of service for Richmond's Associated Charities.[20]

After a brief hiatus, though, area Baptists renewed their city mission program when they opened the House of Happiness in 1914. Using the name of a book by a local author, members of the city's Woman's Missionary Union (WMU) established a community center in a neighborhood populated with eastern European immigrants. The new facility operated much like a Baptist settlement house in Louisville, Kentucky—itself modeled after the famous Hull House of Chicago. Representatives from twenty-one churches organized committees to raise money and donate furnishings. A member of Grove Avenue Baptist Church and a recent graduate of the WMU's Louisville Training

School, young Nannie West directed the House of Happiness during its first decade. In 1924 the House of Happiness settled into a new brick structure, where it remained for almost six decades. The handsome three-story building included a lecture room, an assembly hall, a gymnasium, and showers. During 1924 almost 25,000 people participated in House of Happiness activities.[21]

Nannie West, her successors, several paid staff members, and scores of volunteers arranged a variety of activities, many for children. Much of the program was devoted to education with classes in sewing, cooking, millinery, music, shorthand, basketry, woodworking, English, and health and social hygiene. Young and old used the library and the playground. An active boys club engaged in team sports and went camping. A chapter of the Camp Fire Girls also used the summer campsite, which the House rented and then purchased. Volunteers visited homes in the neighborhood, distributed food, clothing, and medicine to the needy. They also aided immigrants in obtaining medical care, in dealing with the courts, and in locating jobs, particularly for teenagers. In 1924, a man who should have known, Methodist minister and reformer Joseph T. Mastin, called the House of Happiness "the best piece of Christian social work in the state."[22]

In 1905 a group of religious and civic leaders organized the city's Associated Charities and later selected James Buchanan to direct the organization. As the massive number of clients at the Methodist Institute and the Baptist Neighborhood House demonstrated, Richmond lacked an adequate means of helping people with economic problems. To assist needy people, twentieth-century industrial Richmond relied on a combination of mechanisms inherited from the nineteenth century. Funded by the municipal government, the City Home offered shelter to truly destitute individuals and could accommodate approximately 250 people. In the course of a year, the home provided shelter to a total of approximately 1,400 people, particularly the elderly, the ill, and the insane. According to state officials who began to regulate such facilities in this period, the City Home generally operated well compared to similar institutions elsewhere in Virginia and in the rest of the nation. In 1907 and 1908, though, one investigation labeled conditions there a "disgrace" to the city, and another indicted it for its inexperienced medical personnel, careless supervision of medicine, an inefficient staff, inadequate records, and insufficient budget. The superintendent repeatedly pleaded with the city council for a larger appropriation to remedy the home's weaknesses. Much of the home's budget was allocated to outdoor relief: food, medicine, shoes, clothing, and fuel dispensed to the needy. Two private organizations assisted the home in outdoor relief and added their own resources. The Citizens Relief Association and the City Mission, an interdenominational women's group, extended assistance through a geographically organized system of districts. Individual churches and synagogues, as well a number of private charities such as an ice and milk mission, also aided those in need. The city government provided some of these charities with small subsidies.[23]

The interdenominational group, which assembled in 1905, hoped to devise a more effective private charity system "to meet the growing needs" of the city. A subcommittee visited New York, Baltimore, Philadelphia, and Washington to consult the leaders of charity organizations in those cities. The plan adopted for Richmond's Associated Charities entailed consolidation of several charities and cooperation among the remainder. The Associated Charities integrated the City Mission, the Citizens Relief Association, and the Baptist Neighborhood House into its new structure. The Baptists donated space in and then sold their cavernous Neighborhood House to serve as the headquarters for the Associated Charities. The Baptists also supplied the leadership for the new organization. Between 1906 and 1919, minister James Buchanan served as the general secretary of the Associated Charities. One of the founders of Virginia's Juvenile Protective Society, Buchanan used the Associated Charities facilities to place homeless children in families. Later acting as a probation officer for Richmond's fledgling juvenile court, he used the Associated Charities building as a temporary detention center for juveniles—a vastly superior alternative to the city's overcrowded and mismanaged jail. Abbie Buchanan acted as an associate in running the Associated Charities.[24]

The Buchanans endeavored to implement a highly organized, systematic, scientific form of charity. At its central office the Associated Charities operated a homeless department providing temporary food and shelter. Dividing Richmond into twenty-nine geographical districts, volunteer visitors delivered food, fuel, and clothing to the needy of specific neighborhoods. In one month in 1908 the organization provided 990 pints of milk to tuberculosis patients. Operating an employment bureau, the Associated Charities secured jobs for hundreds of people each year. Attempting to aid the truly needy, the new organization also tried to exclude chronic beggars, an increasingly large group according to some local critics. By using a casework approach, James Buchanan assembled information that would permit assistance appropriate to an individual's specific needs. As a result, the Buchanans' tasks varied from person to person—obtaining medical care for a sick person, securing a pension for a widow, renting and furnishing a house for an abandoned wife and children, financing transportation to another town for a displaced worker. Thus, the Associated Charities sought to solve long-term problems as well as supply immediate aid.[25]

The Associated Charities proved a success but not a panacea. Dedicated to the concept of scientific charity, Buchanan endured criticism from several people for neglecting to evangelize his clients. A man who ran a local nondenominational mission for the homeless complained that by offering charity without religion Buchanan provided nothing to "uplift" the poor. Some applicants apparently objected to an interview as a condition of assistance. With the program devised to aid whites, not African Americans, a surprised Buchanan suddenly faced hundreds of blacks seeking assistance during the winter of 1914–15. Sadly noting that many African Americans had walked several miles and waited in line for hours for aid, Buchanan began dealing with their problems on a case-by-case basis, too. In one Associated Charities publication, he identified a problem of large scope. Many dependent families his organization aided were rural migrants with "a rural aptitude and country appetites" that made them "economic misfits" in the city. Without mechanical skills or an education, many of them could earn a good living in the country, but not in the city. Buchanan and his successor, Charlotte Whiting, also wrestled with sudden, sharp economic shifts that closed factories, creating mass needs for assistance among workers. The most dramatic surge of applicants occurred during a 1921 recession that followed a World War I economic boom. The many needy exhausted the organization's resources, and Associated Charities closed temporarily.[26]

In 1919 James Buchanan retired as general secretary but continued to serve on the board of directors. Throughout his tenure and that of Whiting, the organization increasingly devoted much of its assistance to women and children. Widows, victims of desertion and nonsupport, and neglected children constituted expanding groups in the lists of casework. In annual reports the organization counted the families that it had thereby held together. In 1925, reflecting the organization's changing identity, it adopted the name Family Services and has continued to serve Richmond since then. Operating in an age of transition for charitable organizations in American cities, Richmond's Associated Charities displayed institutional attributes common to that era. Volunteer workers assisted Buchanan, a paid director. Early in the organization's existence, those friendly visitors tried to foster middle-class habits of work and efficiency, and Buchanan expected many of those receiving shelter to work as compensation. Investigations served, as historian Robert Bremner has observed, to thwart fraud but also to provide intelligent solutions to individual economic problems. In the process of providing aid, local charity workers increasingly emphasized that people suffered economic difficulties because of external environmental conditions beyond their control, not because of defects of individual character.[27]

While local clergy and laity played pivotal roles in reorganizing the city's public charities, one Richmond Methodist minister developed the public welfare system for the entire state of Virginia. In February 1908 the State Board of Charities and Corrections met to choose a secretary, a person responsible for directing the daily activities of that newly created agency. Much to the surprise of the public and, no doubt, to the seventeen applicants for the job, the board unanimously selected a nonapplicant, Richmond minister Joseph T. Mastin, a man whose subsequent accomplishments fully vindicated the board's decision. Lean and tall, J. T. Mastin wore a thick brown mustache and a serious countenance, which did not hide a gentle demeanor. He arrived at his new office with significant credentials: experience with personal hardship, firsthand knowledge of the state, proven administrative ability, and a deep devotion to Christian social service.[28]

Born in Northern Virginia in May 1855, Joseph T. Mastin suffered the death of his father in 1859. Mastin's mother lost a small inheritance in a family estate squabble but used resources left by her husband to send Joseph to a preparatory school and to Randolph-Macon College. A bank failure, however, cost Mastin the money he needed to complete his undergraduate education. Having decided to become a Methodist minister, he served a series of rural circuits, where he lived simply and traveled extensively. In 1879 he married Fanny Cowles Nottingham, and they adopted a daughter several years later. Sent to the booming railroad town of Crewe, Mastin began to wrestle with social problems, a process he continued at his next assignment, a church in the port city of Norfolk. There he assisted unwed mothers and developed a concern about the difficulties some young women faced. While at his rural congregations, Mastin directed campaigns to build new churches, and in Norfolk he led a successful campaign to reduce his congregation's debt. In 1896 Mastin arrived in Richmond, and at Trinity Methodist he launched the project that evolved into the Methodist Institute. Serving as financial agent and then superintendent of the Virginia Conference Orphanage, he raised funds to eliminate the institution's indebtedness, supervised the construction of the new buildings, and then managed the new facility.[29]

In the course of his career, Mastin developed an extensive knowledge about human suffering in Virginia. During the early twentieth century, he and several other ministers joined reformers who campaigned for a state board to supervise Virginia's public and private charities and correctional institutions. As a member of the Virginia Conference of Charities and Correction, he marshaled evidence to demonstrate the need for such a government agency. At the 1906 meeting of the conference, he provided a detailed report about conditions in Virginia's almshouses and jails, denounced the existence of almshouses, and called upon the state to "care for its aged and infirm citizens."

Mastin's impatience with these harsh social conditions and with others that he encountered was based on his religious convictions. In later reflecting about his career, he pointedly observed that Jesus worked among the lowly, described the Gospel of Luke as "the best thing" ever written "about the story of social work," and expressed the hope that all social workers would be guided by its spirit of "tender human-heartedness."[30]

During Mastin's sixteen years in his new position, he initiated a transformation in how Virginia's public and private institutions responded to a host of human needs. During that period, as his two successors testified, Mastin "was the Board so far as performance may be concerned." He skillfully used the power given to the State Board of Charities and Corrections to supervise state and private charitable and penal institutions. Operating with a small staff and a limited budget, he personally visited those facilities, directed studies of social problems, proposed laws to remedy them, administered new programs, and helped organize community social workers.[31]

As head of the State Board of Charities and Corrections, Mastin began taking steps to reform Virginia's patchwork system of city and county almshouses. In his first year in office, he visited 108 almshouses. He documented unsanitary conditions, inadequate care of physically and mentally handicapped inmates, inadequate fire protection, and the general absence of programs for education and recreation. Local governments administered almshouses, and they indiscriminately placed all persons deemed social misfits together in almshouses. People who were poor, old, blind, crippled, insane, or epileptic, as well as unmarried mothers, were housed together, and none of these groups received any attention for their specific problems. The failure of local officials to coordinate their aid caused inadequate care. Responding to Mastin's recommendation, the state legislature enacted a law establishing county and city boards of poor commissioners, who would coordinate services offered at almshouses with other so-called outdoor relief. Convinced that larger, district almshouses could provide better living conditions than the small, scattered, local almshouses, Mastin and his successors at the state board advocated consolidation. They persuaded the directors of some almshouses to arrange for inmates to board in other county almshouses or at old-age homes, where they could receive better care. As a result, thirty-three almshouses soon closed. After 1918 that process accelerated when the state legislature enacted a law permitting county almshouses to consolidate into district houses. By 1926 only thirty-four of the almshouses remained.[32]

Some reform efforts yielded mixed results. In 1910 the state legislature established a separate facility for white epileptics and thereby helped relieve overcrowding at the four state hospitals for the insane. By housing patients in these hospitals, the board rescued them from horrid conditions that they endured in local almshouses and jails and the state penitentiary. Other related decisions, though, created hardships. Relying on widely accepted social theories and research, Mastin concluded that insanity, mental retardation, and epilepsy were inheritable conditions. With the advent of intelligence tests, social reformers tried to identify individuals who were mentally retarded or "feeble-minded" and care for them. Hoping to prevent the birth of children with such problems, Mastin endorsed laws prohibiting the marriage of epileptics, the insane, and mentally retarded individuals. He also favored a policy of sterilization of people who had been confined in state institutions and who had these conditions. Based on faulty science and implemented in a somewhat capricious manner in Virginia, these measures, it is now clear, operated at odds with Mastin's larger vision of making the state a protector of helpless individuals.[33]

Mastin devoted much of his attention to aiding needy women and children. He used his authority to inspect and license maternity homes to check unethical operators who attempted to exploit patrons and who neglected children. He closely supervised child-caring institutions such as orphanages and all child-placing agencies and foster homes. One new law required that child-placing agencies visit an adopted child once every six months to ensure that the new family was providing proper care. In 1918 he obtained state legislation permitting localities to pay monthly allowances to widows with dependent children. Mastin also won legislative approval of a law requiring parents to support children until they reached the age of sixteen. Following another recommendation, the state legislature passed a law authorizing judges to grant probation to men convicted of nonsupport of their families. With the men at work, rather than in jail, a probation officer collected their wages and ensured that their families received money that they needed. By 1920 Richmond probation officers were collecting almost $100,000 each year.[34]

Throughout his tenure in office, Mastin continued to champion the cause of dependent children. When he investigated the status of crippled children, he learned that a large portion of them could be cured if they received prompt, appropriate medical care. By persistently lobbying the state legislature, he secured some funds to support the treatment of destitute crippled children at seven hospitals, and in 1918 the legislature funded a crippled children's hospital. Granted new authority in 1914, the state board proceeded to place destitute and delinquent children in state institutions or foster homes. In 1911 Mastin assembled the first child welfare conference held in the South. Forty-two experts in child care visited Richmond to discuss such problems as infant mortality, education, child labor, illegitimacy, delinquency, and sex education. Mastin also laid the groundwork for the Virginia Children's Code Commission of

1921. Appointed by the governor, the commission recommended twenty-six new laws to protect and help children. The state's general assembly immediately passed twenty-two of those laws. That legislation established a Children's Bureau, which supervised and aided children who were mentally defective, dependent, delinquent, or neglected. With the State Board of Charities and Corrections reorganized in 1922, Mastin became Virginia's first commissioner of public welfare. His successor in that position termed this system of aid for children "Dr. Mastin's greatest bequest to Public Welfare in Virginia."[35]

Other Richmond Protestants shared Mastin's concern about children. In the western outskirts of the city, Methodists opened their Virginia Conference Orphanage in 1902. Having heard "the cry of the children," declared one writer, Methodists wanted to feed, clothe, house, and educate "the homeless children in our midst." Not limited to Methodist children, the institution welcomed "every little one within our reach who needs food and a home." An ambitious building program soon placed the orphanage in financial jeopardy, but it secured Mastin to serve as its financial agent. Traveling throughout Virginia, he raised cash and subscriptions and eliminated the orphanage's debt. Hired as superintendent, he further economized by initially accepting no salary. During Mastin's tenure and that of his successor, the orphanage cared for hundreds of children and expanded its services. In 1903, 51 children resided in the orphanage; in 1928, 70 boys and 130 girls lived in five cottages. Employing five teachers, the orphanage provided classes through tenth grade, and older children attended vocational classes.[36]

Another Methodist minister, William J. Maybee, also heard the cry of the children. As he later recalled, after fourteen years as a preacher, "a call came to me as clearly to take up the ministry of the homeless and neglected children as when I was called to the regular pastorate." In January 1900 the Children's Home Society of Virginia was incorporated. An interdenominational board of directors, which often included Rabbi Calisch and a Catholic priest, guided the organization. That board tended to be dominated by Richmond area clergymen and laymen, and Baptist layman and future Virginia governor John Garland Pollard served as the board's president for twenty years. From a "receiving home and central office" in the East End of Richmond, Maybee directed the agency for almost three decades. In celebrating the organization's twenty-fifth anniversary, he began by expressing "humble gratitude" for "the conscious blessing and help of our Heavenly Father" throughout the period, "for without His approval and aid our efforts would have failed."[37]

Maybee and the Children's Home Society stayed busy. The society's avowed goal was to save orphans, as well as homeless, neglected, and abused children. It temporarily provided the youngsters food, clothing, and training at its own facility but endeavored to place them in approved family homes. Forcefully declaring that it stood for the "rights of children," the society maintained that every child was "entitled to a pure home and good training." Indeed, with court approval the organization could legally remove children "from grossly cruel and immoral parents." To publicize its program, the society initially relied on articles in local newspapers and in religious weeklies. It then printed pamphlets and, in the 1920s, a newspaper, the *Virginia Children's Home Finder.* Those publications featured endorsements by civic and religious leaders, fetching photographs of children, stories about youngsters successfully placed in homes, and solicitations for contributions. The organization clearly stated its rules. Adoptive parents had to be "moral, sabbath-observing and church-going." A trial placement occurred for ninety days or more. If the society and the new family agreed that the adoption was satisfactory, it would be completed. If either party objected, the child had to return to the custody of the organization, not any other party. By 1913 the society had placed almost 1,300 children in new homes and 640 in houses under its supervision. For the year 1916, Maybee reported that 210 children had been placed, 850 foster homes had been visited, and temporary aid had been supplied to 200 families. In 1924 Maybee was elected president of the Children's Home Society of the United States. By the late 1920s, the society had moved to a new facility in Richmond's Highland Park suburb, had increased its staff, and gained access to greater medical care. Contemporary social worker Arthur W. James characterized the Children's Home Society as "efficiently managed" and as the "most important" adoption placement agency in the state.[38]

Some Richmond Protestants championed the cause of public education as a form of social service. In 1902 layman B. B. Valentine invoked a phrase of Thomas Jefferson, "preach against ignorance," as the text for a poem in which he celebrated education's benefits to all people, including the "outcast." Valentine issued a challenge to "Preach the crusade! and preach it now, make unto heaven a patriot's vow; That henceforth none shall wander blind, But all serve God with lightened mind. . . . Preach the crusade, preach the crusade." A member of Monumental Episcopal Church, Valentine and his wife, Lila Meade Valentine, had already joined other reformers to organize the Richmond Education Association, which served as a lightning rod for educational change in the city and the state.[39]

When Benjamin B. Valentine wed Lila Hardaway Meade in October 1886, he must have known she was an extraordinary person. Although she would be best remembered as the leader of the Virginia woman's suffrage movement, Lila Valentine moved near the center of most major reform activities in early-twentieth-century Richmond. As the University of Richmond's S. C. Mitchell testified, "There was no aspect in the life of this city into which her sympathies and influence did not go." Her keen mind and her social consciousness refused to let her rest comfortably in a life of sheltered wealth. Born in Richmond on 4 February 1865, she was one of five children of Kate and Richard Meade. With old Virginia roots, her father, a wholesale druggist, ensured that his daughter received an appropriate education from private tutors and at a private school. Her thirst for knowledge exceeded a conventional education for ladies, and both her father and her husband supported and encouraged her. An avid reader, she developed special interests in art, music, sculpture, and literature, and she spoke several foreign languages. A tall brunette, Lila was a gracious hostess who enjoyed entertaining at dinner parties and delighted in ballroom dancing. Her husband shared her cultural enthusiasms as well as her commitment to social reform. Surgery performed in the aftermath of a stillbirth in 1888 impaired her health and left the couple childless. Revitalized during an extended visit to England in 1892, she gradually became an important force in her native city. Upon her death in 1921, her rector characterized her as "a deeply religious woman" who "took her religion with her into all her manifold activities." A former rector wrote her sister praising "the Christian character and spirit," which sustained "all her public service and beneficent activities."[40]

In 1900 Lila Meade Valentine hosted a meeting at her house, where she, Mary-Cooke Branch Munford, and three other people formed the Richmond Education Association (REA). Chartered in May 1900, the REA announced its intention "to create and foster an interest in the education of children." This modest language set the stage for the REA to become a formidable civic organization that persistently and successfully exerted pressure on city government to improve public schools. Between 1901 and 1904, Lila Meade Valentine served as REA president, and between 1904 and 1911, Mary-Cooke Branch Munford led the organization. To succeed, the REA recruited additional members. By 1902 it counted 372 members; by 1915 it listed 587. In 1901 the REA created its own Kindergarten Training School, hired out-of-town experts to teach in the program, and used the kindergarten at St. Andrew's Parish School—an arrangement no doubt facilitated by Grace Arents, who served on the REA's board of directors. The REA lobbied the city council to establish a kindergarten program in the public schools and then lobbied to expand that program. When the first kindergarten opened in 1903, the school board voted to name it the Valentine Kindergarten "in honor of Lila Valentine . . . to whose influence the kindergarten movement is much indebted." By 1914 the city school board operated fifteen kindergartens, and the REA finally achieved another long-sought goal, a kindergarten for African American children.[41]

As Valentine outlined in her presidential address of 1904, the REA had many goals, and it lobbied to change the face of Richmond public education. She called the city high school "a disgrace," and S. C. Mitchell later recounted some of the tactics used to gain support for a new one. When a group of women meeting with Valentine praised the existing structure, Valentine suggested inviting reporters to accompany them on a visit to the school, which proved to be "a fire-trap and a rat trap." Assembling a group of men at city hall, Munford gave each one a petition supporting the new building, instructed them to distribute the petitions in a specific area, and announced that she expected each man to return with between 100 and 150 signatures to be presented to the city council. Richmond did build John Marshall High School, which became a source of community pride and the first of many new school buildings constructed in the next several decades. Responding to an REA proposal, the school board added manual training classes for white children and authorized such programs for black children, too—provided that no additional funds were required. A determined Munford raised that money from private sources and two national organizations in order to acquire the necessary equipment.[42]

Often prompted and supported by the REA, city officials expanded the number and quality of local schools. An REA committee hung artwork at schools, and the schools added music classes, physical education courses, and night classes. In advance of the rest of the state, Richmond provided free textbooks and implemented compulsory education. In less than twenty years, average daily attendance in schools quadrupled, and the city raised teachers' salaries and built a normal school. REA leaders not only lobbied the city council, they lobbied state legislators. In doing so they operated as the nucleus for an important state organization, the Cooperative Education Association. Valentine, Munford, and Mitchell played pivotal roles.[43]

Writing in the *Religious Herald* in March 1902, Samuel Chiles Mitchell applauded "Virginia's Educational Revival." But that revival had only begun, and Mitchell was an appropriate evangelist. An irrepressible southern progressive, he vigorously championed every cause that promised to better his city, his state, his region, his nation, and the world. An ordained Baptist minister, Mitchell served as an associate editor for the *Religious Herald* and wrote extensive essays for it. In one of them, he emphasized God's love and immanence and celebrated the age's spirit of progress, "working everywhere toward the same divine ends." A dedicated history professor, Mitchell earned the respect of his students. One of them, Richmonder John A. Cutchins, lauded Mitchell for inspiring students, for following their careers, and for becoming "almost a part of the life of every boy who ever came under his influence." For most of the period between 1908 and 1920, Mitchell held positions outside

Richmond as president of the University of South Carolina and then as president of Delaware College. While in Richmond, though, he contributed substantially to the cause of public education.[44]

To become a leading southern educator, Mitchell needed some good fortune. Born in Mississippi during the Civil War, Mitchell moved often during his childhood as his father sought to overcome economic setbacks. Throughout the many moves, Samuel garnered only a smattering of formal schooling and relied heavily on his own reading skills to gain an education. He later recalled that "during all those years, I yearned for more training." "It would be long to recount my private efforts to overcome this handicap." Mitchell's desire for an education impressed an employer whose business Mitchell saved by an alert action while the man was out of town. With financial assistance from that merchant, Mitchell attended Georgetown Academy and then Georgetown College in Kentucky. When the sudden death of his benefactor jeopardized Mitchell's academic aspirations, the widow of the former college president supplied him with room and board, permitting him to complete his undergraduate degree. Mitchell then earned a master's degree, taught at Mississippi College, and returned to teach at Georgetown College. In Kentucky he met and married Alice Broadus, the daughter of the president of Southern Baptist Theological Seminary. After joining the faculty at Richmond College, Mitchell arranged a leave of absence to earn his Ph.D. in history at the University of Chicago.[45]

Having struggled to acquire an education, Mitchell wanted others to gain schooling more readily. According to his vision, public schools would liberate the masses from ignorance, empower them to participate in a truly democratic society, and enable them to solve social problems. In one essay he declared that "confidence in the common man is the creed of this crusade." Educated people, Mitchell believed, would forsake prejudice for reason and replace self-interest with a concern for humanity. "To accomplish these things," he argued, "is the specific mission of the school in the South. It is to enforce the Golden Rule and to embody the spirit of the Good Samaritan." Clearly church leaders had a religious duty to fulfill that mission. In one address Mitchell characterized Jesus as "an extremely busy man," recited his many deeds of sacrificial healing, and concluded that the Bible was a dead and meaningless book unless it aroused his followers to do likewise. In another presentation Mitchell described Jesus as emphasizing the worth of each human and refusing to recognize conventional distinctions and privileges. Similarly, "the school must be the solvent of all artificial distinctions existing among men." In several 1902 articles for the *Religious Herald,* Mitchell explained the elements of the so-called Ogden movement for education. Each year the Conference for Education in the South brought together people from across the nation who shared an interest in promoting public education. The Southern Education Board (SEB), headed by businessman Robert Ogden, gathered and distributed information about education in the South. Supported by John D. Rockefeller, the General Education Board (GEB) financed programs to improve education in the South.[46]

Mitchell, Valentine, and Munford helped to strengthen ties between the Ogden movement, Richmond, and Virginia. Several other Virginia educators, particularly Hollis Frissell of Hampton Institute, had been deeply involved with the movement from its origins, and Frissell invited REA leaders to attend meetings of the Conference for Education in the South (CES) in 1902. Valentine and Munford promoted the idea of hosting the next CES convention in Richmond, and Virginia Governor Montague, an active REA member, issued the invitation. As REA president, Valentine went to work to ensure the meeting would be a success. Mitchell recalled that she "set about the task with her usual energy and tact, holding committee meetings in her home." For three days in April 1903, Richmond hosted the CES with its national dignitaries, some of whom delivered addresses at the Academy of Music. A local journalist reported that Robert Ogden was so excited about the conference that "he was willing to talk about it almost any length of time." The CES gathering stirred some souls in Richmond. Rabbi Edward Calisch wrote Lila Valentine that she deserved the thanks of the entire community for her instrumental role in bringing the CES to Richmond and for "having so skillfully and thoroughly perfected the arrangements." "Every lover of our city and of culture and humanity should thank you," declared Calisch, "and, I for one, do so most heartily and earnestly."[47]

After conferring with Mitchell, Frissell, and two other educators, Governor Montague summoned a larger group who formed the Cooperative Education Association of Virginia and elected Mitchell president. Prior to the meeting Mitchell had enumerated four objectives for education in Virginia. Listening to a wide range of views expressed over several days, Mitchell and his wife "pecked out on the typewriter" eight principles about which the group agreed. These principles became, in Mitchell's words, "the commandments of the movement," and they included the four goals he had earlier designated. The CEA set as its goals a nine-month school term, high schools within proximity of every child, better-trained teachers, agricultural and industrial training, efficient supervision of schools, school libraries, proper education for handicapped and destitute children, and the creation of citizens organizations in all counties and cities. By mobilizing public support behind the movement for public schools, the CEA persuaded state and local political leaders to modernize Virginia's educational system. Mitchell, Lila Valentine, and another member wrote the organization's constitution. Between 1904 and 1908, S. C. Mitchell headed the CEA; between 1910 and 1924, Mary-Cooke Branch Munford served as the president.[48]

The CEA's first major success was the "May Campaign" of 1905, an idea apparently originating with Mitchell. Already discussing possible courses of action with agents of the Southern Education Board, CEA members gathered in Norfolk, where the tactic of the May Campaign was broached, embraced, and initiated. In an earlier letter to Hollis Frissell, Mitchell had advocated "hammering away" on a "clear-cut line" of ideas. The May Campaign promised to accomplish that feat with proponents of public education devoting an entire month to holding meetings and rallies across the state. The May Campaign exceeded expectations in its scope and impact. Politicians delivered speeches, ministers preached special sermons, newspapers reported stories, and the CEA distributed hundreds of thousands of pamphlets. The Richmond College Board of Trustees and the college's alumni association proclaimed their support for the movement, and Richmond's denominational newspapers featured articles supporting the campaign, too. As the Methodist *Baltimore and Richmond Christian Advocate* observed, the Cooperative Education Association "found a corps of workers in each of the churches who had been plowing and planting for a quarter of a century or more."[49]

Impressed politicians promptly attended to educational issues. In 1906 the Virginia General Assembly responded to the campaign by passing five major education bills that increased funding for public schools. According to a committee of the Richmond Education Association, that legislature passed a total of fifty-two bills to aid children and education. The REA committee happily noted the building of 168 high schools in the state, which had formerly claimed fewer than 20. The committee further reported the construction of a total of 236 new school buildings, as well as 70 others that had been improved or enlarged. Between 1900 and 1910, total school revenue doubled in Virginia, and school attendance rose dramatically. The number of high schools increased, as did the length of school terms, teacher salaries, and the number of educational associations. As evidence of grassroots support, Mitchell proudly noted that within a five-year period localities quadrupled their spending on schools. A sponsor of the 1906 state law to finance the construction of high schools, Gov. William Hodges Mann announced that in 1913 Virginia operated 491 high schools.[50]

After the May Campaign, reformers continued to work for educational improvements, and clergymen remained active. The Committee of General Education of the Baptist General Association of Virginia made its sentiments clear: "The key to the educational situation in Virginia is largely in the hands of the ministry. We come into close, constant touch with the people. They look to our leadership. Let us not fail to lead them into a growing interest in education. Nothing that makes for higher life and larger service should be foreign to the pastor." The REA and the CEA sustained successful, long-term campaigns for educational improvements, and Protestant groups continued to promote public schools, higher teacher salaries, educational associations, and higher education. Citing Virginia's "great progress" in public education during the first decades of the twentieth century, one historian has assigned "much of the credit" to the CEA. The most thorough historian of the CEA, William Bowden, concluded that for more than a decade the organization's history was "largely the story" of Mary-Cooke Branch Munford. Ministers J. T. Mastin and H. D. C. Maclachlan were outspoken advocates of compulsory education, one reform which Richmond implemented but which state legislators did not soon adopt. Even in Richmond, reformers did not always win speedy victories. Between 1905 and 1922, Protestant clergymen and laypersons participated in repeated campaigns to establish a city public library. In promoting that cause, S. C. Mitchell emphasized its value to the city's working people. The Richmond Ministerial Union urged the city council to appropriate funds for a library. Finally, in 1922 the city government financed the project.[51]

During World War I, church leaders participated in the founding of another educational institution, the Richmond School of Social Economy. Citing "the need for more trained social workers in the South," the school offered instruction under "trained teachers" who would examine social problems "in light of scientific knowledge of the day." Representatives from all of the city's major white religious groups and many of its civic groups filled positions on the school's initial organizing committee and on its board of directors. That list included ministers James Buchanan, H. D. C. Maclachlan, J. T. Mastin, and John J. Scherer, as well as laypersons Mary-Cooke Branch Munford, Katherine Hawes, and later Douglas Freeman. At a time when only a dozen colleges offered social work degrees, the new school advertised itself as the first school of social work in the South. In an article in the *Baltimore and Richmond Christian Advocate* in 1918, J. T. Mastin and the school's new president, Henry Hibbs, described the school and delineated the "advantages" of social work as a profession. Social work, they affirmed, required "the missionary spirit" and "a belief and fervent exposition of the teachings of Christ."[52]

During the school's first decade, local churches aided it. No doubt new director Hibbs welcomed such help. An experienced social worker, he had earned a Ph.D. at Columbia University and had held teaching positions in Illinois and Tennessee. When he arrived in Richmond to direct the school, the

Presbyterian Publishing House furnished him office space. J. T. Mastin, local health officers, and professors from Richmond College taught courses until the new school secured a regular faculty. Between 1919 and 1924, Monumental Episcopal Church provided a three-story building rent free to the renamed Richmond School of Social Work and Public Health. Students gained direct experience in social work by assisting at such facilities as the Baptist House of Happiness. In 1919 the school became affiliated with the College of William and Mary, enabling it to participate in a four-year curriculum through which students could earn a bachelor's degree. In 1925 the school relocated to Richmond's West End and became more tightly connected to William and Mary as its Richmond Division. In 1939 the growing, changing college was renamed the Richmond Professional Institute (RPI). The Medical College of Virginia and RPI merged in 1968 to form Virginia Commonwealth University. Lutheran pastor John J. Scherer remained an important figure in the school from its origins until his death in 1956. A friend and consultant of Hibbs, Scherer chaired the board of directors for virtually the entire period. A pastor devoted to personal counseling, Scherer increasingly concentrated on the relationship between health and religion. For him and other Richmond Protestants, social service meant aiding the sick and improving the community's public health.[53]

Addressing the first graduating class of the Richmond School of Social Work and Public Health, H. D. C. Maclachlan described medicine as the "regular channel through which God works in the cure of disease." You, he told the graduates, "are only fellow workers with a Higher Power." Maclachlan's presentation reflected a prevailing attitude in Richmond—by combating disease, Christians engaged in an important form of social service. When Baptist layman Douglas Freeman delivered the presidential speech to the Virginia Conference of Charities and Correction in 1913, he illustrated the connection between churches and public health. As the executive secretary of the Virginia Anti-Tuberculosis Association and the director of publicity for the state board of health, Freeman recalled a time when "the preacher frowned on the health officer and his pretention." By contrast, he declared, today the minister "welcomes the officer into his pulpit and rejoices to think that Jesus Christ was the physician to men's bodies not less than to their spirits."[54]

In fact, Richmond churches proved to be logical allies for officials promoting public health. Like Freeman, a number of other health professionals moved simultaneously in medical and religious circles. For example, Episcopal layman Dr. Ennion G. Williams distinguished himself in a twenty-two-year career as Virginia's first state health commissioner. On at least one occasion, Williams spoke to students at Richmond's Union Theological Seminary about the opportunities which they would have in their future ministries to aid the cause of public health. Enlisting in that cause, Richmond ministers portrayed Jesus as a healer and encouraged their members to prevent the spread of disease and to minister to the victims of illnesses. At times ministers spoke bluntly. Declaring that "cleanliness is essential to Godliness," one preacher recited a lengthy list of all the refuse in his congregation's neighborhood.[55]

Laywomen also engaged in public health efforts. As Sadie Heath Cabaniss and Nannie J. Minor organized the Nurses' Settlement, they turned to the churches for support. Following a presentation at the Woman's Club, Lila Meade Valentine hosted a gathering at her house, where the Instructive Visiting Nurses Association (IVNA) was organized. With an interdenominational board of directors that included Protestants, Catholics, and Jews, the IVNA secured financial assistance from church groups, particularly the Episcopal women's Daughters of the King. Between 1911 and 1914, Grace Arents provided a rent free building near St. Andrew's for the settlement.[56]

Religious leaders helped to check the spread of one deadly communicable disease, tuberculosis. Distressed that the city council had budgeted no money to combat tuberculosis in 1906, Richmond Methodist preachers pointed to the 275 residents who had died from the disease that year. The ministers urged the council to take some "decided action" against tuberculosis, a timely request as the city's new board of health initiated a campaign against TB. And churches supplied forums for health officials. For example, the head of the city's board of health, Dr. E. C. Levy, delivered a lecture at Pine Street Baptist Church. Debunking myths about the causes and cures of tuberculosis, he described the appropriate "scientific treatment" and enumerated steps to prevent the spread of the "dreaded disease." On "Tuberculosis Sunday" the pastor of Centenary Methodist spoke before members of the International Typographical Union and praised the organization's national effort against the disease. From city pulpits and in denominational weeklies, religious leaders publicized the prevention programs of the city's public health department. When city officials began to offer free tuberculosis checkups, some churches, the Methodist Institute, the House of Happiness, and St. Andrew's Mission furnished space for the stations. For a brief period the Methodist Institute provided rent-free housing to the Richmond Tuberculosis Institute, which treated a small number of patients. Acting on behalf of Sheltering Arms Hospital, Episcopal laywoman Frances Branch Scott discovered that the Richmond area had no major facility except the City Home which even pretended to care for tuberculosis patients. In a series of meetings with Dr. Levy, local nurses, and some private citizens, she launched a campaign that eventually led to the construction of Pine Camp Hospital just north of Richmond. That achievement required effort. As she later recalled, she had to "interview" every member of the finance committee of the city council and almost all of the other members, too. She also supervised the design and construction of the new facility.[57]

Sheltering Arms did even more than originate Pine Camp. By providing free medical care for people unable to pay, Sheltering Arms Hospital delivered a unique service in the city and state. In February 1889 Rebekah Peterkin, daughter of the rector of St. James's Episcopal Church, founded the institution. She did so, according to a later hospital newsletter, because of her experiences working among the poor. After her death in 1891, her mother directed the organization until 1910. Rebekah Peterkin, though, remained an abiding symbol of Sheltering Arms. In the words of one hospital pamphlet, "The whole of this Christ-like charity sprang from the head and brain of one noble Christian woman." Nonetheless, many others helped Peterkin and her successors. Circles of the Episcopal Daughters of the King raised money as well as collected and made linen, blankets, and bedding. Churches contributed funds to this nondenominational facility, and physicians donated services. As the hospital expanded, the Richmond city council gradually increased the amount it appropriated to support Sheltering Arms. The hospital established a training school for nurses and pioneered in aiding crippled children. In 1900 the hospital treated 125 patients. In 1928 it treated 1,236 patients—an increasing portion of whom were women and children. Still, financial restraints compelled Sheltering Arms to turn away approximately fifty people a month. The hospital's president, Frances "Boxie" Scott wrote a letter in 1926 to the governor and pleaded for state financial support. She emphasized that the hospital served the entire state as well as the city and reported that in the past year it had aided more than 400 patients from outside Richmond.[58]

Frances Scott had inherited the mantle of leadership from the Peterkins, and she wore it well. With the support of an interdenominational board of directors and her brother, who served as the institution's treasurer, Frances Scott managed Sheltering Arms with a spirit consistent with its founder. Upon leaving the board, one member wrote that Scott's "high ideals" and "gracious manner" would always be "an inspiration in my life to try day by day to live nearer the Master." The writer concluded by invoking a blessing that "for ages to come" God would make the hospital a means of "spiritual uplift" as well as a source of "bodily restoration." At the time of Frances Scott's death in 1937, the city's Daughters of the King eulogized her "exemplary life of Christian service." In the same statement the Daughters declared, "Her aim was ever to do God's work in the world and her labors were richly blessed." No doubt many former patients of Sheltering Arms would have concurred.[59]

Two wealthy laypersons aided the cause of public health by supplying Richmond with public bathhouses. In 1904 Grace Arents furnished the Oregon Hill area with low-cost bath facilities and gave them to the city government to manage in 1920. In January 1905 a group of men began a subscription campaign to construct additional baths in the downtown area. They stressed the need for the facility since "it is a known fact that not one in twenty of the houses occupied by our working people and poorer classes" had baths. One of Richmond's wealthiest citizens, Methodist layman John P. Branch, offered to construct the baths and donate them to the city if the city council would pledge to maintain them. After some delays, in 1909 the new Branch public baths opened. The first floor of the bathhouse included a laundry, and the second floor featured seventeen showers for men, as well as two tubs and five showers for women. Adult bathers paid a five-cent charge, children paid three cents, but anyone unable to pay bathed for free. During one week in July 1909 almost 1,700 men used the new bathhouse but only slightly more than 100 women. Costing more than $25,000, the bathhouse was the most expensive gift that had ever been given to the city by a single individual. In addition to that bathhouse, which was located in downtown Richmond, Branch funded a $45,000 bathhouse erected further west in 1914. Each year during the ensuing decades, thousands of people used the two Branch bathhouses and the baths built by Grace Arents. In 1921 alone the three public bath facilities provided almost 90,000 baths.[60]

Church leaders gave the city public health movement another boost when they created the Society for the Betterment of Housing and Living Conditions in Richmond. In 1908 the new director of the Methodist Institute, J. W. Dixon, had perceived a problem with overcrowding in parts of the city and called for an investigation. As studies in other cities had shown, congested living conditions contributed to high levels of communicable disease. In June 1912 members of St. Paul's Episcopal Church organized the Society for the Betterment of Housing and Living Conditions in Richmond. The group assembled an interdenominational board of directors, which included Methodist Dixon and Catholic priest Father Charles Hannigan. Mary-Cooke Branch Munford and Grace Arents as well as African American educator Webster Davis also served on the board. After consultation with a national organization, the society employed Gustavus Weber to serve as secretary and to direct a study of living conditions in parts of the city. Between February and April 1913, Weber's brother and a group of volunteers visited 682 dwellings in low-income sections of Richmond. Integrating the data from their fieldwork, statistics from government agencies, and an analysis of local laws, Weber wrote a final report. The eighty-page document included maps, charts, photographs, and comparisons with other cities. The data showed that Richmond had above-average mortality rates from tuberculosis, cerebral hemorrhages, Bright's disease, and whooping cough.[61]

The Weber report offered reassurances and a bundle of recommendations. "Housing and living conditions of the people in the neglected sections of Richmond are not so bad as to cause any alarm," Weber concluded. Despite the city's high mortality rate in 1911, data since then showed a "remarkable reduction." Although overcrowding existed in some individual houses, that situation could be easily remedied because the city had a great deal of unused land within its boundaries and immediately beyond them. On the other hand, the city needed to install water in every household, get rid of dumps and rubbish, convert Shockhoe Creek into an underground sewer, clean city streets, encourage the building of more houses for working-class residents, and arouse civic pride to keep streets, alleys, and exposed places free from rubbish. Weber also enumerated potential problems with the city's building code.[62]

The Weber report had an immediate impact on the community. Responding to one of its primary recommendations, the city government sponsored a two-week clean-up campaign in May 1913. The Society for the Betterment of Housing and Living Conditions conducted public meetings and distributed notices. City public health officials issued instructional pamphlets and policemen distributed them. Schools, churches, businesses, and labor organizations disseminated information. The Superintendent of Street Cleaning provided personnel and targeted specific areas of town on certain days. Given a school holiday as an incentive to help, more than ten thousand children enthusiastically pitched in to remove rubbish. Weber himself was pleased. Before the campaign, the litter, trash, and refuse cluttering Richmond's streets, alleys, and vacant land had constituted a problem as bad as "can be found in any city of its size in the country," he asserted. After the campaign he concluded that the effort had been "thorough," that almost every yard had been cleaned up, and that "mountains of ashes, garbage, and other filth have been removed." In November 1913, the city council further responded to the report's recommendations by passing a lengthy ordinance. Filling a previous legal gap, the law prohibited a wide variety of forms of littering and regulated the methods of disposing of rubbish. Health officials enforced the new law. The city eventually implemented a number of other recommendations from the Weber report, including placing municipal trash cans on sidewalks, collecting garbage frequently, and providing almost every household in the city with water, garbage, and sewerage service. Housing shortages for working-class citizens remained a largely unresolved problem for the city. The Weber report, though, did spur the city's public health movement and did provide a blueprint for action.[63]

Churches collaborated with the IVNA to deal with a major health crisis, the Spanish influenza epidemic of 1918. When the outbreak of the disease occurred in October, officials closed churches, schools, and theaters in order to prevent the spread of germs, and that ban remained in effect for a month. Some Richmonders wore gauze masks over their noses and throats as they walked about town. Still, the disease spread rapidly. Newspapers reported 10,000 cases by the end of the first week in October. Seven years later a journalist observed that "even today one can hardly find a home in Richmond where the mention of 'Spanish flu' will not sober the most laughing countenance." Soon after the disease was detected, IVNA leaders suggested to the city's board of health that they open soup kitchens in churches throughout the city. Beginning promptly at St. James's Episcopal Church, they eventually operated forty-three soup kitchens from which they served an estimated 1,700 to 1,800 people daily. Church members, including Methodist Bishop Collins Denny, worked in the soup kitchens. The kitchens were valuable because entire families had been temporarily disabled, and no one remained healthy enough to prepare meals. Not only did the kitchens prepare food, ministers and members also delivered it to some households. Students of Union Theological Seminary worked round-the-clock shifts helping victims housed at John Marshall High School, which served as a temporary hospital. Pastor John J. Scherer gained local acclaim for his efforts to mobilize people to aid victims. More than 11,000 city residents contracted the disease. Including all influenza deaths in 1918 and 1919, city officials reported a total of 786 fatalities. A local health official termed the church soup lines "indispensable" in halting the epidemic.[64]

The flu epidemic demonstrated that medical tragedies could not always be averted. But church members joined in taking steps to prevent and to minimize those sad occasions. They no doubt agreed with H. D. C. Maclachlan that good health was an invaluable gift from God. Maclachlan affirmed that "the church of today" believes that "God cares for the bodies as well as for the souls of men; that he is the enemy of all needless pain, disaster, and disease." Richmond church members endorsed Maclachlan's statement with their deeds.[65]

In 1928 Episcopal city missionary R. Cary Montague explained that social service could be defined simply as "Christianity in action." In short, he wrote, "any helpful thing voluntarily done for anybody in the name of Jesus Christ is Christian Social Service." Montague then enumerated a list of twenty-five specific activities, including teaching someone to read, serving as a volunteer at a social agency, adopting an orphan, helping an unemployed person secure a job, and assisting someone who was ill. As Montague's list suggests, people could and did engage in a wide range of social service activities and often did them informally or privately—thereby easily escaping the attention of historians. Still, these actions had an impact on the community. For example, on Richmond's West End, Protestant women built new facilities to care for elderly women of their respective denominations. Created in 1875, the Protestant Episcopal Church Home for Ladies moved into new quarters in 1905. Founded in 1881, the Baptist Home for Aged Women resided in a spacious new three-story building in 1913. When the female board of managers had proposed the new project in 1910, they had encountered opposition from the male board of trustees. Undeterred, the fifty-two women representing Richmond Baptist churches appointed a building committee, which raised the necessary funds and selected plans submitted by the local architectural firm of Carneal & Johnson. The *Religious Herald* complimented the new facility for its attractive lawn, large shade trees, gracious reception room with "home-like fireplaces," and large dining room. A majestic, wide porch surrounded the home on three sides. The building provided thirty-two "large, airy and bright bedrooms." In 1914 Methodist and Presbyterian women combined their resources to open the Richmond Home for Ladies, which accommodated fifty women. Each of the three homes required an initial entry fee but thereafter charged little or nothing for room and board.[66]

In December 1913, when H. D. C. Maclachlan spoke to the Virginia Conference of Charities and Correction, he titled his presentation "the Church at Work in Social Service." Indeed, Richmond churches had been at work in social service, and their multifaceted activities merited Maclachlan's strong metaphor of speaking in a new language, much like the disciples after Pentecost. The words and deeds of Richmond's religious leaders testified to a vibrant version of social Christianity in the American South, an important reality once overlooked but now increasingly documented by scholars.[67]

Less than a month after Maclachlan addressed the Virginia gathering, *The Survey,* the nation's leading social work periodical, published a collection of hymns. Responding to popular demand, the journal reprinted them in a separate volume, *Social Hymns of Brotherhood and Aspiration.* A jury of critics selected the music for this interdenominational collection and chose some famous older hymns as well as the works of renowned poets. The hymnal contained Washington Gladden's "O Master, Let Me Walk with Thee" and Frank Mason North's "Where Cross the Crowded Ways of Life," social gospel hymns of lasting significance. The first song in the new hymnal had been written by a Richmond's Walter Russell Bowie. Although Bowie contributed three hymns to the volume, his most enduring one was titled "O Holy City Seen of John." Laden with urban imagery, the song included a fourth stanza:

"Give us, O God, the strength to build the City that hath stood, Too long a dream, whose laws are love, whose ways are brotherhood, And where the sun that shineth is God's grace for human good." Such words for many Richmond Protestants represented an aspiration which they had been actively pursuing. In an earlier stanza, Bowie also emphasized the importance of social justice. Throughout the early twentieth century, some Richmond Protestant leaders engaged in a quest for social justice that often proved more elusive than the work of social service.[68]

8

A "Divine Discontent"

In a 1913 pamphlet *The Divine Discontent,* Episcopal laywoman Lucy Randolph Mason described discontent as "a real and purifying influence" in religion and referred to "conscientious and deeply spiritual ministers" who called for social reforms. In another pamphlet she expounded on a "spiritual awakening" that impelled people to be dissatisfied with mere "passive goodness" and to engage in "active, aggressive warfare with the forces of evil." St. Paul's Walter Russell Bowie sounded the same theme in his hymn "O Holy City Seen of John": "O Shame to us who rest content, While lust and greed for gain, In street and shop and tenement, Wring gold from human pain, And bitter lips in blind despair Cry—'Christ hath died in vain!'" Warning against routine worship and empty ceremonies, the Baptist *Religious Herald* reminded Christians that it was "their duty and privilege to hasten . . . the bringing of the Kingdom of Jesus *on earth*" (emphasis in original). Driven by a religious discontent, some Richmond Protestants called for social justice and worked for it as well.[1]

From pulpits, at civic gatherings, and in publications, Richmond's religious leaders repeatedly issued calls for social justice. Speaking to the Virginia Conference of Charities and Correction, the pastor of Central Methodist Church, W. A. Cooper, portrayed Jesus as coming "to create here in this world a 'Kingdom of God' or social order in which the righteousness of God or social justice shall prevail and brotherly love shall bind men together in bonds of spiritual kinship." H. D. C. Maclachlan applauded evidence of Christian charity but advised that "justice is a more fundamental and necessary virtue than charity."[2]

In advocating social justice, Protestant leaders expounded on four themes. They maintained that Christ had provided his followers with definite standards of right and wrong. The pastor of Grace Street Baptist Church pointed to the "vast body of Jesus Christ's social principles" and called on ministers to preach them. In fact, ministers did focus on the Sermon on the Mount, the parable of the Good Samaritan, and the Golden Rule as guides for Christian behavior. And as John W. Shackford, the future pastor of Broad Street Methodist, explained, churches must "help men see the conflict of existing conditions with the standards of the Kingdom." Writing in the *Religious Herald*, R. H. Pitt claimed that Christians could not, "without denying their Lord and Master, align themselves with the cruel, the indifferent, the heartless, the corrupt elements in society." Yet, as these same clergymen charged in a second theme, certain existing attitudes and practices were morally wrong when judged by these Christian standards. The ideal of the Kingdom of God on earth could not be achieved, Shackford asserted, so long as individuals remained selfish and disregarded the common good. Preachers warned their congregations that selfishness was as sinful as breaking biblical commandments and advised church members that selfish persons destroyed their own spiritual health in addition to harming others. Religious leaders feared that many people had become so greedy that they disregarded the destructive results of their selfish actions. Condemning the negligence of the owners of New York City's Triangle Shirtwaist Factory, R. H. Pitt contended that their "brutal selfishness" and "fiendish lust for gain" had caused them to imperil the lives of their workers, hundreds of whom perished in a fire.[3]

As a third theme, church leaders condemned people and organizations who abused their political and economic power to exploit society's weaker citizens. For instance, professor Thomas R. English of Union Theological Seminary denounced business and commercial combinations for using all their resources "unscrupulously to crush the needy and grind the poor." Maclachlan stated simply that Christ could not have "intended the weak should be exploited by the strong." A number of Richmond clergymen and laypersons called for an end to specific injustices committed against prisoners, children, laborers, women, and African Americans. Those Protestants subscribed to a fourth social justice theme articulated by Maclachlan. He believed that "the Church itself must be held up before the people as a force for social righteousness" rather than as "an ark of safety" for its own members. Social justice, instructed W. A. Cooper, must be "proclaimed from our pulpits and platforms and through our press until all the people hear and are aroused to right the wrongs of our day and establish social and economic justice among men." Cooper further insisted that where ethical pressure proved insufficient to curb greed, churches must "demand the enactment of laws that will make it criminal for the strong to exploit the weak." The *Southern Churchman* pronounced that the church must "go out into the struggle of life everywhere to take sides openly and vigorously for the right and against the wrong." Some Richmond Protestants certainly tried to do so. The divine discontent for social justice led Lucy Mason to address the injustices faced by women and industrial workers, and it led others to reform the state and local criminal justice system.[4]

In an article for the *Southern Churchman* in 1900, Lucy Randolph Mason's mother, Lucy Ambler Mason, scolded local Christians for neglecting their religious duty to visit prisoners. Because Christ had issued a "solemn command" to do so, such visits were a "binding . . . test" on whether a person took his or her faith seriously. In fact Richmond Protestants demonstrated a substantial concern about prisoners. Clergymen and laypersons led attempts to improve facilities in the state penitentiary in Richmond, to mitigate harsh conditions in jails, and to institute more humane procedures for dealing with juvenile offenders.[5]

In her article Mrs. Mason denounced the state penitentiary as an overcrowded, unventilated pesthouse in which inmates were compelled to live like brutes. She expressed her "mortification as a Virginian" when outside experts visited the site and designated it as one of the worst they had ever seen. Mason needed no such testimony herself because she frequently visited the penitentiary, conducted Bible classes there, and housed former inmates while they tried to find employment. Mason with her husband, Landon R. Mason, rector of Grace Episcopal Church, several other ministers, and a few friends began a campaign to publicize the horrid conditions in the penitentiary. The governor of Virginia authorized a committee of ministers to investigate the situation, and their report confirmed the grim assessment.[6]

Between 1900 and 1902, Richmond ministers and journalists repeatedly condemned conditions in the penitentiary and castigated the Virginia legislature's failure to provide a remedy. The *Central Presbyterian* urged its readers to contact legislators to correct this "great wrong" and remove "the great shame it brings on the name of Virginia." The Presbyterian weekly depicted the nature of that shame. More than one hundred years old, the penitentiary at times housed 1,400 people in a facility designed to hold 300. In one case twenty-nine men shared a single room. Inhabiting poorly ventilated cells, prisoners had no access to modern toilet facilities, and "vermin, disease, and filth" were "locked up with these unhappy men." After a tour of the penitentiary, a committee of Baptist ministers delivered a similarly devastating portrayal. Noting that an average cell contained six men, the ministers cited scientific calculations about the air needed per person and concluded that no man had even one-fourth that amount. Declaring that "the horrors of the place are beyond description," they called it "a menace to health," "a disgrace to the city," and appointed a committee to speak to the legislature about the penitentiary. The *Richmond Christian Advocate* similarly urged Methodists to sign petitions requesting the general assembly to enact reforms. Dr. Charles V. Carrington, who served as surgeon for the penitentiary, joined in the reform campaign and enumerated the harsh conditions. Emphasizing the threat of disease among the prisoners, he deplored the overcrowding, the insufficient ventilation, the inadequate heating, the absence of sewerage facilities, and the lack of cleanliness in the penitentiary. In old dungeons and corridors beneath the prison, he reported, rats and vermin "breed in millions innumerable." Labeling the cells "death traps," he observed that although no young people or elderly were incarcerated, the mortality rate was still high. Alluding to "rights born of humanity," he urged the state to act with justice in dealing with the prisoners.[7]

Citing concerns about a smallpox outbreak in Norfolk, officials closed the prison to visitors, but local Episcopalians continued to raise a ruckus. The *Southern Churchman* had already sarcastically proposed that judges should issue capital sentences rather than subjecting men to slow death at the penitentiary. In March 1902 the rector of St. Paul's Episcopal Church designated the penitentiary an "earthly Hell," warned state legislators that each one of them was "accountable to God" for the conditions, instructed them to visit the prison, and told them to vote and use their influence to change the situation. Finally goaded into action, the legislature responded to a recommendation from Gov. Andrew Jackson Montague and appropriated funds for a new cell building. Opened in 1904, the new building significantly alleviated the overcrowding by adding 336 cells. By 1909 the average number of persons per cell had fallen to two. The new building provided modern plumbing, electric lights, and shower baths.[8]

Methodist preacher J. T. Mastin also had the opportunity to improve the penitentiary as he served as the secretary of Virginia's State Board of Charities and Corrections. State law granted Mastin the authority to inspect the facility and formulate recommendations, but the penitentiary board and the penitentiary superintendent retained the powers of setting policies and making decisions. Nonetheless, as Virginia corrections historian Paul W. Keve has noted, "Mastin was actively involved" and apparently worked well with several superintendents who tried to manage the institution more humanely. Disgusted that the institution forced prisoners to "take their food in buckets and in their hands" to eat in their cells, Mastin called on the legislature "in simple justice" to appropriate funds for an adequate kitchen and a new dining room. When the legislature refused to do so, a cooperative penitentiary superintendent permitted prisoners themselves to modify an existing building to accommodate a new kitchen and dining hall. Beginning in 1910, a new superintendent sharply curtailed the use of flogging and paid prisoners money for their overtime work. Mastin applauded innovations such as recreational programs and a reward system for good behavior. On the penitentiary grounds, convicts worked on a contract basis for a succession of manufacturers. The prisoners earned money for the state, but, Mastin concluded, the contractors sometimes overworked the convicts. Responding to recommendations, the legislature enacted a law that regulated the penitentiary's contract labor and gave Mastin power of approval over contracts awarded.[9]

Gov. Westmoreland Davis proved to be an especially determined ally of Mastin and other prison reformers. When Davis advocated a list of penal reforms to the state legislature, Walter Russell Bowie testified in behalf of them. When the legislature refused to act, Davis appointed a new state prison board that independently initiated a series of improvements. The new board acted on one of Mastin's greatest concerns by arranging for improved medical services. The prison board abolished striped clothing and curtailed the policy of leasing prisoners to private industry. In 1920 the penitentiary abandoned contracts with private industry and shifted to its own internal work program. Officials developed an industrial department where inmates completed printing, woodworking, tailoring, and shoe projects for the state government, and prisoners received pay for their work. The penitentiary initiated a new program of instruction which included elementary education and manual training.[10]

The new educational programs addressed a goal local religious leaders had long advocated, rehabilitation of prisoners. In 1908 Baptist George W. McDaniel spoke to the annual convention of the National Congress of Prisons meeting in Richmond. Using the biblical text "He hath sent me to proclaim release to the captives," McDaniel emphasized that "the mission of the prison" is "the reclamation and restoration of the delinquent." He assured that "Underneath the prison garb" was "the marred image of deity," and officials, church members, and citizens should seek to "better the moral and spiritual condition of the prisoners" and ex-convicts. Yet prison authorities provided no job-training programs, and ex-convicts were, in the words of Episcopal city missionary R. Cary Montague, "turned loose under circumstances that almost compel a repetition of crime." In 1920 the editor of the *Richmond Christian Advocate* criticized officials for holding an outdated notion that prisons existed only to punish criminals. The Methodist weekly condemned the "pagan attitude" that would place people in prisons with no thought "of their redemption and recovery."[11]

Church leaders tried to compensate for the state's failure to assist in convict rehabilitation. As early as 1906, Methodist preacher George Wiley began an Ex-Prisoner's Aid Society. This voluntary organization counseled inmates and tried to help them solve any problems they faced immediately upon leaving prison. It also aided them in finding jobs and locating a place to live. In 1915 the society aided 150 convicts. In 1920 Mastin helped organize an Interdenominational Board of Religious Activities in State Institutions. This group employed minister R. V. Lancaster to serve as both a chaplain and as a teacher.

For his new program, Lancaster soon secured the donation of 3,800 volumes for a prison library, and he directed vocational and recreational activities. The prison board appointed by Governor Davis was so impressed with Lancaster’s work that it decided to expand the program. Dr. K. J. Hoke of the College of William and Mary assumed direction of this larger educational program which placed a special emphasis on teaching job skills to inmates.[12]

Mrs. Nannie Eddington of Pace Memorial Methodist Church remained dissatisfied about the lack of a vocational training program for women inmates. For thirty-nine years she taught religious classes at the penitentiary on Sundays, and for years she appealed to Virginia governors to establish such a program. Finally, in 1924 she launched her own limited program. She solicited contributions and established a 200-book library. Using donated equipment, she taught reading, writing, cooking, sewing, and typewriting classes. She also guided inmates in making rugs, lampshades, slippers, and aprons, which they sold. Still, in the campaign to reform penitentiary conditions, female prisoners, who comprised only a small part of the penitentiary population, received the least attention. According to a Virginia Crime and Penal Affairs Commission Report in 1929, the penitentiary’s building that housed women remained “antiquated and entirely inadequate.”[13]

Thus, some clergy and laity took the biblical injunction to visit prisoners very seriously, and one of those visits took a dramatic turn. When summoned to the penitentiary in November 1912, Baptist George W. McDaniel and Lutheran John J. Scherer encountered an especially difficult situation. They came to serve as spiritual counselors for Floyd Allen and Claude Allen, who awaited execution. On 14 March 1912, in Carroll County in western Virginia, the Allens had engaged in a courtroom shootout that quickly became known as “the Hillsville tragedy.” A judge and four other people died after a brief, violent, disputed sequence of events. Floyd Allen and his family members fled the scene but were later captured. Across the state, newspapers used lurid phrases to characterize the Allens as outlaws who had cold-bloodedly conspired to use violence to defy justice. When trials occurred, some juries had difficulty in sorting out the truth amidst the barrage of allegations and rumors. With different juries reaching various conclusions, the courts handed down disparate sentences. Three family members received lengthy prison sentences. But Floyd Allen was convicted of killing a commonwealth’s attorney and was sentenced to death, as was his son, young Claude. Scherer and McDaniel began meeting with the Allens within a week after the doomed men had been moved to the state penitentiary, where the electrocutions were to take place.[14]

The preachers concluded that the two men had not received fair trials and should have their sentences commuted. Scherer pointed to the lighter sentences meted out to men charged with committing the same crimes as Floyd and Claude. Granted a leave by his church, Scherer investigated the case himself. He discovered that witnesses had changed their testimony and that former jurors declared that they would not have voted for conviction had they seen evidence subsequently developed. McDaniel made detailed, direct, public defenses of the two men. He argued that because of the "inflamed character" of opinion in their area, they had not received fair trials. The Allens, he maintained, had not engaged in a premeditated conspiracy, had been provoked by personal enemies, and had reacted violently only as a means of self-defense when the shooting commenced in the courtroom. Citing the testimony of witnesses, McDaniel claimed that others, rather than the Allens, had fired the first shots. The Allens, he concluded, had been convicted only because "a hastily formed public sentiment" demanded harsh punishment for someone connected with the tragedy. If the state of Virginia electrocuted the Allens, it would commit "judicial murder." McDaniel vowed to pursue every possible means of redress "no matter how futile or unpopular the effort." Some others in Richmond agreed with McDaniel. The governor twice agreed to delays in execution to permit appeals to be filed. But the appeals failed, the Supreme Court of the United States refused to review the case, and the governor refused to commute the sentences. The Allens continued to proclaim innocence until their executions, and both left letters forgiving those who had falsely testified against them. Throughout the ordeal, Scherer and McDaniel counseled and prayed with the men, accompanied them to the death chamber, and witnessed their executions. According to one New York news account, a shaken McDaniel had to be lifted into his automobile afterwards.[15]

Troubled by the apparent injustices in the Allen trials, R. H. Pitt proceeded to place capital punishment itself on trial in the pages of the *Religious Herald.* He minced no words. The inequities of the Allen case challenged the notion of "the majesty of the law." Pitt admonished that the social order was as much endangered by unjust executions as it was by any guilty parties escaping punishment. Furthermore, the elaborate legal processes and procedures permitted ordinary citizens to dodge responsibility for the executions. "We might as well face the awful fact. We have actually killed a human being, the most priceless thing in all the universe of God with which we have to do." On several occasions Pitt reviewed data indicating that capital punishment did not deter people from committing murder and that showed lower homicide rates for places that had abolished the death penalty. He concluded that the only reason for the death penalty was "the lust for blood," which demanded an act of vengeance. He reiterated the religious theme of the sacredness of individual human life. Despite criticism from some readers of the *Herald,* Pitt continued to raise the issue periodically. In 1925, twelve years after the Allens's executions, he reviewed a variety of arguments and evidence about capital punishment. He concluded "surely the time has come when the quiet barbarous business of hanging, electrocuting, and suffocating human beings ought not to have the sanction of law in any civilized state." Pitt was not alone. As the Allen controversy raged, another Baptist preacher, John J. Wicker, declared that the electric chair "belonged to the dark ages." He told his Leigh Street congregation that the government did not "exalt justice by committing murder." Only when the state began to treat a criminal as an "unfortunate brother," Wicker concluded, would it "go far toward changing the hearts of bad men."[16]

Wicker's wish to change the hearts of criminals reiterated the persistent theme of religious leaders who advocated rehabilitation. During the uproar about the state penitentiary, the *Southern Churchman* reminded readers that God demanded forgiveness, and the *Central Presbyterian* denounced harsh conditions that engendered hatred for the law, not moral reformation. A strong proponent of probation, Mastin argued that "the confirmed criminal, the vilest of the inmates of the jail is a fallen man and should be dealt with as God deals with us." Mastin added, "Let him know that society believes he can do better, hopes he will, and is ready to help him." In 1915 the *Religious Herald* condemned the state corrections system for causing "unnecessary injury to self-respect, unnecessary barriers in the way of recovery of character, and unnecessary physical hardship and suffering." To restore criminals, these religious leaders believed, the state had to incarcerate them in a decent environment and adopt new policies.[17]

As secretary of the State Board of Charities and Corrections, Mastin endeavored to improve the lot of prisoners living in facilities throughout Virginia, but he rarely succeeded. The state farm for felons did construct new buildings and thereby alleviated its overcrowding and provided such basic needs as modern plumbing. But neither Mastin nor his immediate successors found a way to improve conditions in city and county jails. In 1904 Mastin had tried to obtain information about conditions in jails throughout the state. When some localities failed to respond to his inquiries, he inferred that they were trying to hide their inadequate facilities. In 1908 he personally inspected 115 city and county jails and began cataloging their abusive features. Many prisoners received inadequate food and medical care, and in many places they were not segregated by sex. Many jails confined children, citizens awaiting trials, and insane inmates together "with vicious or degenerate adults" convicted of felonies. Some localities still used chain gangs and corporeal punishment. Mastin especially deplored the fact that people unable to pay fines for misdemeanors were incarcerated in such a horrid atmosphere.[18]

Neither Mastin's initial report nor his later ones had much impact. Mastin's successor observed that the majority of Virginia jails lacked adequate provision of air, light, and water. The state legislature refused to grant the Board of Charities and Corrections any supervisory power over local jails and insisted on keeping the so-called fee system, which provided an incentive to incarcerate as many people as possible. Rather than relying on a salary, local officials received a per diem fee from the state of Virginia to feed and clothe each inmate. This arrangement permitted sheriffs to provide cheap care and to keep any surplus money they received from the state. As one critic later observed, under the fee law "it is advantageous to do a good jail business all the time." In 1918 the legislature did pass a probation and parole law that Mastin had promoted. Still, this legislation was only permissive, and most counties refused to implement it.[19]

Even in Richmond efforts to improve the city jail produced only a fiasco. After years of neglect, delay, and criticism, the city council in 1901 finally voted to replace the ancient, dilapidated city jail. The mismanaged project, though, remained incomplete for years, featured shoddy construction, and saddled the city with expensive repairs. Annually appropriating thousands of dollars to repair a new building, the city council admitted it had purchased "a gold brick" from the company that had constructed it. Others rendered harsher verdicts. Delegates to the American Prison Association meeting in Richmond in 1908 criticized the jail's lack of cleanliness and the modest budget for taking care of prisoners.[20]

Writing in the *Religious Herald,* R. H. Pitt supplied one of the more thoughtful and comprehensive critiques of the jail. Like Mastin and other critics, he deplored the jail's location in the worst part of town—near stables, the city incinerator, and bordellos. By surrounding prisoners with such a squalid environment, he asserted, the community merely reinforced the degrading influences that had led them to commit crimes. Furthermore, he charged, the jail was overcrowded, sometimes to the point of suffocation. People awaiting trials, witnesses, and individuals unable to pay fines shared cells with "habitual criminals, with the vilest of the vile." Men and women were not adequately separated. At times children between the ages of ten and fifteen years old were still locked up with convicted criminals. Pitt concluded that it was "simply impossible in such physical conditions as these to preserve all the decencies of civilized life." Despite such criticism, the city did not improve the jail. In 1927 an interdenominational women's church group termed the jail conditions "abominable." Seventy-five ministers visited the jail, criticized conditions, and agreed that a new facility was needed. The State Department of Public Welfare reported that the overcrowded jail sometimes housed more than 500 prisoners in a space designed to hold a maximum of 350 people. In 1915 an indignant R. H. Pitt had excoriated the "Commonwealth of Virginia" for its "wretched method of dealing with prisoners." Calling it "belated, deplorable, inexcusable," Pitt urged some "sound-hearted, clear-headed man" among Virginia's legislators to dedicate himself to reforming the state's jail system. But none appeared, and the problems with local jails persisted through the 1930s. Arthur W. James, who succeeded J. T. Mastin, designated jail reform as "the stumbling block of public welfare progress in Virginia."[21]

In 1909, when Mastin submitted his first report as secretary of the State Board of Charities and Corrections, he advocated that the Virginia legislature pass juvenile court laws. "The children," he implored, "are not getting their full measure of justice when we confine them in jails for however short a time." That same year at the annual meeting of the Virginia Conference of Charities and Correction, a Richmond editor also spoke about the need for juvenile courts. At one point as he emphasized the importance of a wholesome childhood environment he maintained that occasionally the state had "to step in and take upon its own shoulders the future of the little mite of humanity" and place it "where the divine, the Christ within it, would be brought out and the devil buried so deep that his very existence would be forgotten." Concerned that the existing judicial system harmed children and doomed some to lives as criminals, a number of Protestant clergy and laity denounced it as unjust and led a movement to replace it with more humane juvenile courts.[22]

Indeed, as Richmond's juvenile court movement evolved through a series of stages, city religious leaders played significant roles. In June 1908 a group of citizens organized the Juvenile Protective Society of Virginia. As Richmond College professor and Second Baptist Church layman J. C. Metcalf reported, it was a movement "long contemplated." Still, outside experts provided the impetus for action, particularly during a 1908 meeting of the National Conference of Charities and Corrections in Richmond. Attending the conference, the famous children's judge B. B. Lindsey addressed the Richmond Education Association, and reformers Julia Lathrop and Hastings Hart spoke to another community group about child welfare and juvenile courts. The next month the new Juvenile Protective Society elected officers and created an interdenominational board of directors. It also developed an expansive set of goals. It aimed to protect and train delinquent children, create charitable organizations to educate them, establish juvenile courts, and promote laws removing juveniles from adult courts.[23]

The Juvenile Protective Society (JPS) relied heavily at first on the talents of Baptist minister James Buchanan. Involved from the organization's founding, H. D. C. Maclachlan designated Buchanan "the one individual, more than any other, responsible for the beginning of the Association." Already directing the community's Associated Charities, Buchanan served the JPS as its unpaid probation officer. In his overlapping roles, Buchanan tried to fulfill several of the JPS's goals by supplying food to children and placing neglected children in new homes. The Associated Charities' old Ballard Hotel building furnished rooms that served as a juvenile detention area, thus affording separation of young people from adults in the city jail. In April 1909 the JPS appointed a committee to draft bills to propose to the Virginia legislature. The Virginia Conference of Charities and Correction endorsed the passage of juvenile court laws and appointed a committee to "communicate with all probable candidates for the next legislature." That five-member committee included Mary-Cooke Branch Munford and James Buchanan. In January 1910 Buchanan addressed the Virginia House of Delegates in support of the juvenile laws, and J. T. Mastin consistently promoted the legislation, too.[24]

In 1910 the Virginia legislature did pass a law requiring separate, private hearings for children less than seventeen years old. The law stated that courts should not incarcerate children with adults, and it authorized courts to grant probation. The statute further empowered the State Board of Charities and Corrections to approve probation officers and to supervise organizations that received custody of children. Delegates to a 1911 child welfare conference in Richmond urged localities to implement the new law. Richmond's city council passed an ordinance creating a juvenile division of the police court, and Judge John Crutchfield convened the first session on 2 April 1912. Claiming he lacked the proper training and experience to be a juvenile justice, he enlisted the help of five prominent church leaders who were members of the Juvenile Protective Society. These men, H. D. C. Maclachlan, James Buchanan, Douglas Southall Freeman, Ryland Knight, and Father Charles Hannigan, formed a special "steering committee." They heard cases with Crutchfield, advised him, worked for public support of the court, and solicited funds to finance the court. A young lawyer, J. Hoge Ricks, assumed the duties of clerk and probation officer. To ensure a female presence, the Instructive Visiting Nurses Association donated the services of Sarah Roller to act as a probation officer.[25]

At the end of the first year of the court's operation, the president of the Juvenile Protective Society, H. D. C. Maclachlan, sought continued city council support for it, and he reviewed the reasons why it was needed. He explained that the procedures of the juvenile court aimed at preventing youngsters from leading lives of crime. Unlike the public prosecutions in adult courts, the private proceedings of a juvenile session prevented a child from becoming permanently stigmatized and usually ostracized by his or her former companions.

Rather than sending a youngster to jail, the probation system offered a chance for an individual to change his or her behavior. To aid a child in mending his or her erring ways, a probation officer enlisted the support of parents, teachers, and employers "to exert every possible influence for good." If investigations revealed a child needed to be "removed from the environment which made them delinquent," the young person was placed in a carefully selected home. Keeping delinquent children at the Detention Home in the Ballard Hotel avoided "the vicious influence of the hardened criminal" at the city jail, which housed "men and women of the most depraved type." "The children of to-day are the citizens of tomorrow," Maclachlan instructed. Still in the formative period of their lives, "they will be precisely what we make them and will show the effects in maturity of the treatment they receive now." "Mercy will be rewarded with manhood," he counseled, but "injustice" would result in crime. Statistics for the court's first nine months demonstrated its commitment to reforming children rather than punishing them. The court rendered 521 decisions, and in 78 percent of them, it granted probation, discharged the child with a warning, released the youngster to the parents' custody, assigned punishment for the parents to perform, or dismissed the charges.[26]

The council did maintain the juvenile court, and the Richmond court functioned as a state laboratory for dealing with juvenile offenders. Officers investigated the causes of individual delinquencies by visiting homes and by talking with families, neighbors, employers, and physicians. A child who was granted probation received a list of rules to keep. He or she was instructed to shun bad company, attend religious services, work or attend school daily, and report to a probation officer once each week. During the court's first year, the probation procedure proved successful in over 80 percent of the cases in which it was applied, and the court successfully placed children in private homes. In addition to the detention facilities for white children, it arranged for African American wards to stay in a private home.[27]

The Richmond experiment was so successful that J. Hoge Ricks and Maclachlan drafted a juvenile court proposal that the state legislature enacted in 1914. This new Juvenile and Domestic Relations Court law broadened the court's jurisdiction to include juveniles under eighteen years of age, men charged with neglect and abuse of wives and children, persons who contributed to the delinquency of a juvenile, and destitute children. The Domestic Relations Division was designed to handle all offenses of one family member against another, excepting manslaughter and murder. Promoting the new law, the Juvenile Protective Society offered to send speakers throughout the state. The city of Richmond established its Juvenile and Domestic Relations Court in 1916. J. Hoge Ricks served as the first justice, and John J. Scherer Jr. was the first associate justice. The new institution aimed to assist families economically and to protect them physically. In 1916 alone the court collected more than $25,000 from men on probation for nonsupport, and in 1925 the court collected more than $132,500 to help the families of such men. In 1925 the Richmond court prosecuted 651 men for nonsupport and 307 men for abusing or beating their wives.[28]

As the city began construction on a new juvenile court building in the 1920s, some Richmonders reflected on the impact of the court. Almost shuddering, one newspaper editor referred to the correctional arrangements for juveniles in 1905 as amounting to "the harshest medievalism." During the court's brief existence, the writer suggested, it had carried Richmond through a "revolution" in the methods of dealing with juveniles. At the fifteenth anniversary of the court, Maclachlan recounted its history, alluded to his own participation, and affirmed that "there is nothing of which I am prouder in my eighteen years of residence in Richmond." Speaking to a group of church women in October 1929, a probation officer characterized the local juvenile court movement as "a child of the churches." Indeed, this plea for social justice had received strong community support. Richmond's juvenile court achievement proved exceptional because it was not matched elsewhere in the state. In 1928 seven city jails and fifty-seven county jails still did not separate juveniles from adults, and those facilities incarcerated almost one thousand children under the age of sixteen during that year. Thus, in calling for justice for prisoners, religious leaders counted both victories and some defeats.[29]

Lucy Ambler Mason took a stand for social justice in campaigning for penitentiary reforms. Her daughter, Lucy Randolph Mason, took a stand for social justice by campaigning for woman's suffrage and for better conditions for industrial workers. In a letter to Lila Meade Valentine, the president of the Equal Suffrage League of Virginia, Miss Mason asked to be enrolled in the league and explained her compelling motivation as "a moral conviction." "When the ballot for women is presented to me as a potent agency in the divine plan for the growth and perfection of humanity on this earth," she wrote, "I feel that I have no right to let less important considerations make me reject what I believe to be for the best and highest interests of our future, here and hereafter." Just as a divine discontent impelled Lucy Mason, it drove others to seek justice for women in churches, politics, and education.[30]

As women engaged in church work in the early twentieth century, they could easily experience discontent, divine or otherwise. They found themselves negotiating an arena rife with contradictions about their status and roles. On one hand, ministers portrayed women as the moral and spiritual superiors of men. On the other hand, men retained control of decision-making bodies within congregations, state and local organizations, and national denominations. Though numerically dominant, women deferred to men, who as a group lagged behind them in doing church work. Often impressively skillful in raising funds, women generally relied on the governing males to spend the money wisely.

These contradictions slowly gave way to changes that enabled Protestant women to gain larger roles in churches. Even cloaks of conservative rhetoric could not hide the transformation. Sexually segregated women's organizations often charted their own directions and defied rather than deferred. Indeed, excluded from official leadership positions, Episcopal women throughout the country, according to historian Joan Gundersen, had in essence created "a parallel church" in which they organized and directed their own programs. Individual Richmond women made their presence felt. Grace Arents acted decisively and exercised influence over religious and social institutions matched by few men in Richmond. Barred from pulpits, women in some denominations held the newly created position of deaconess, which often placed them in pastoral roles. As educational directors in some churches, women also began to initiate and guide programs. As some Richmond young women grew up, they attended denominational colleges and training schools, and some became foreign and home missionaries. Twentieth-century women attained new niches in their denominations, but they encountered notable resistance.[31]

In 1899 Presbyterians erected a formidable line of defense against any changes when the Synod of Virginia approved a lengthy "Report on Women in the Church." Frequently referring to scriptures and biblical episodes, the report's male authors declared that women were not inferior to men but did occupy a divinely decreed position of subordination to them. In the "divinely authorized" roles of wife and mother, a "divinely prepared" "true woman" could exert her greatest influence particularly by behaving discreetly, modestly, meekly, quietly, privately, and purely. In churches, the statement instructed, women must not hold offices, exercise authority over men, or preach, exhort, or pray in a public assembly. According to the paper, women could teach but not publicly. They fulfilled such criteria in missionary societies and Sunday schools, where women acted under the authority of churches and in sexually segregated situations. At the outset the document alluded to the "rapid and alarming development of the woman's movement." Throughout the statement, the authors dismissed or attempted to refute alternative interpretations of scripture and biblical history. For example, to those who noted the existence of female prophets, the writers countered that the prophets acted in an extraordinary capacity that differed substantially from preaching. The report confidently concluded that it conveyed "a law of God" that was "explicit," "universal," and "abiding." The pastor of Richmond's First Presbyterian Church, Robert P. Kerr, made statements much like those contained in the synod report. Comparing the separate spheres of a man and a woman, Kerr pronounced that "in the struggle of life he is in the foreground, she is in the background. . . . This is the divinely appointed order of society and of the church."[32]

Without officially abandoning this position, Richmond Presbyterians engaged in a slow but significant retreat from it. Endorsing the synod report, Richmond's *Central Presbyterian* chose to emphasize that its limited scope did not extend into the realms of education, literature, work, or marriage. Acting within approved boundaries, the Woman's Missionary Union (WMU) began an unprecedented organizational campaign that relied on creating structures within each synod. Avis Stewart, the wife of the pastor of Grace Street Presbyterian Church, served as president of the WMU of the Richmond-based East Hanover Presbytery. At a 1905 meeting she explained the need for more systematic organization and distribution of information. Anticipating that the new arrangement would "raise the old objections of fear of women attaining too much authority or power," she denied any aspirations of creating a "'board' since that seems to be a term of offense to most of our Presbyterian brothers and governing boards." Reassuring the men of an intent to continue the work along "womanly lines," she claimed only a desire to "increase our usefulness in our Master's service." That type of motivation did not always lead to acquiescence to male decisions. When the Virginia Synod rejected the idea of establishing a facility to house furloughed missionaries, the East Hanover Presbytery WMU persisted and ultimately helped found Mission Court. Within Richmond men joined in the assault on gender boundaries. At the Presbyterian Committee of Publication, R. E. Magill proudly employed female writers and editors whose fieldwork and participation in Sunday school institutes placed them in public positions of leadership. When Richmond's Presbyterian League initiated its factory mission work, laywomen participated in managing the program, and women conducted lunchtime prayer meetings at more than a score of locations.[33]

Presbyterian educator Walter L. Lingle later designated as "the most marked change" during his life a new "attitude of our church concerning the position and work of women in the church." Those changes became evident in a series of interactions between Presbyterian women and the General Assembly of the Presbyterian Church in the United States (PCUS). In 1911 a group of women led by Hallie Paxson Winsborough of Kansas City launched a campaign to unite all the disconnected women's work within the PCUS. They chose the device of the "Woman's Auxiliary" to consolidate women's groups in support of all church enterprises rather than accept the existing fragmentation in which different women's groups supported different types of church work. The women organized, petitioned the general assembly, and expressed surprise when the all-male body approved the plan without any apparent opposition. Winsborough proudly affirmed that "the Woman's Auxiliary was formulated entirely by the women themselves. No conservative restrictions were superimposed upon them." The general assembly had also given its approval for the Assembly Training School for Layworkers. Located in Richmond, that new institution educated men and women for denominational service. But an early description of the school indicated its importance for women: "the organized woman's work and the office of pastor's assistant have had the effect of opening up large possibilities to woman, and she is beginning to see there is a legitimate work for her in the extension of Christ's Kingdom."[34]

In 1915 the general assembly tried to address the status of women in the denomination, but a divided five-member committee submitted three separate reports. The general assembly then adopted a limited statement that labeled as "the settled doctrine of our church" the position that women were excluded from being licensed and ordained as ministers. Decisions about the other appropriate roles for women, though, the assembly left to the discretion of individual congregations and to "the enlightened consciences of our Christian women themselves." Women continued to speak at the summer programs at Montreat, North Carolina. When some critics complained that the women addressed mixed audiences of men and women, the general manager of the program, Walter Lingle, remarked that men caused the problem by attending gatherings intended for women. Lingle also issued a critique of scriptures used to justify limiting women's roles and contended that the New Testament accorded "larger liberties than some of my brethren would allow." Apparently others agreed with Lingle, and more changes occurred. In 1917 the general assembly chose two women to serve as trustees for the Assembly Training School, and in 1923 it placed women on four executive committees. Thereafter, women began to serve as trustees of denominational colleges and orphanages. In congregations women began to participate in searches for pastors. By the late 1920s, Lingle observed that "the whole church seems to be agreed that we will never have any women preachers or elders, but beyond that there is a variety of opinions as to what women may or may not do in church work." Although women had not gained equality, they had moved far beyond the constraints of 1899.[35]

Women in Methodist churches gained lay rights but only after a decade of conflict within their denomination. In a meeting at Centenary Methodist

Church on 18 April 1910, members of the Woman's Home Mission Society listened to their president speak about "Why Women Ask the Rights of the Laity." They then discussed the topic and signed a petition to be sent to the General Conference of the Methodist Episcopal Church, South. Women at Broad Street Methodist Church also signed a copy of the "Memorial," which requested that the general conference grant women lay rights. Presumably women in other Richmond congregations did likewise. Reporting these meetings, a writer for the *Baltimore and Richmond Christian Advocate* claimed that southern Methodist women "have less authority in their own church than the women of any Protestant church in America." The author supported that statement by pointing to Episcopal women, who could vote for local officers and vote in calls for pastors, and Baptist women, who could vote in similar situations as well as for the admission of new members to a congregation. Another article quoted Walter Lingle, who noted that Presbyterian women could vote in all of their churches' legal proceedings.[36]

Male Methodist leaders had precipitated the controversy about lay rights. In 1906 the Methodist General Conference had begun to assert administrative authority over the largely autonomous women's home and foreign mission societies. Alerted that the female Methodist societies had become vulnerable to male domination and intervention, the president of the Woman's Home Mission Society, Belle Bennett, initiated the campaign for full lay rights for women. As the coauthor of a 1909 article in the *Baltimore and Richmond Christian Advocate,* she reviewed the history and accomplishments of southern Methodist women. After describing their financial support for denominational projects, she noted that some women now served as deaconesses, teachers, and home and foreign missionaries. Granted the exceptional privilege as a woman of addressing the general conference, Bennett made an eloquent case for lay rights, but the conference voted against the proposal in 1910. Despite an energetic, well-organized campaign prior to the next meeting of the general conference in 1914, the delegates again rejected the proposal.[37]

In Richmond several Methodist leaders championed women's lay rights. In 1913 and 1914, layman Samuel Whybrew repeatedly challenged opponents of the movement. On one occasion he fumed that he was simply "out of patience with men who search the Bible with a microscope to find little passages and texts that seem to favor their views of the limited rights and privileges of women of the present century." He criticized those who would deny women lay rights despite their "magnificent work" on behalf of the church. Maintaining that the apostle Paul's writings about the status of women were meant to apply only to a specific time, place, and situation, Whybrew emphasized the "heroic women" whose deeds filled the Bible and history. Wondering if the church intended to stand still as the "world marches on," he advocated full equality for women. One preacher facetiously suggested that such male bastions as saloons, prisons, and secret societies showed the value of sexual segregation. He added that he had searched diligently for reasons to support his prejudices for male leadership but had failed to find any. Not content to support only lay rights, the eighty-year-old layman of Centenary Methodist, John P. Branch, supported a petition to the general conference permitting women to preach. Remarking that women excelled at some things more than men, Branch expressed confidence that they would "beat" some men as preachers.[38]

In 1918 the general conference approved lay rights for women, thereby making them eligible for membership and offices in a number of denominational agencies from which they had previously been excluded. At the congregational level, women could now serve on the governing board of stewards. According to the pastor of Union Station Methodist Church, in 1920 women from his congregation became the first women in Richmond to be elected to that position and the first to attend the Virginia Annual Conference. Still, in 1927 the editor of the *Richmond Christian Advocate* expressed impatience with male church members and urged them to elect more women as lay delegates to the Virginia Annual Conference and to the district conference. He chided the men for not "showing the fair and brotherly spirit they should toward the sisters." No longer institutionally barred from leadership, women still had to overcome some traditional prejudices against occupying new roles.[39]

Baptist women also gained greater rights within their denomination. In 1916 an upset R. H. Pitt criticized the Southern Baptist Convention for relegating women to "being hewers of the wood and drawers of the water for our denominational work." He protested the customs of excluding women from administrative positions in the denomination and of prohibiting them from addressing mixed audiences. Some Baptist men had complained when two women presented statements before the annual meeting of the Southern Baptist Convention. Livid about that reaction, Pitt noted that no one objected to men attending meetings of women's groups where women made addresses. Calling the situation "silly," he declared that it demonstrated the "continuing injustice and folly which characterize the treatment of our women in our religious life and activities." Pitt advocated that church women share in the management of "our common work" and hold official positions on committees, boards, conventions, and associations. In 1917 and 1918 messengers to the Southern Baptist Convention voted to admit women, and hundreds of women attended the 1919 annual meeting as messengers. In 1922 the Southern Baptist Convention began appointing women to committees and boards.

Though significant, these victories did not eradicate some significant traditional boundaries. In 1929 the *Richmond News Leader* criticized messengers to the annual meeting of the Southern Baptist Convention when they refused to permit "two brilliant women" to address them.[40]

Within Richmond itself women participated in changes. As historically self-governing bodies, Baptist congregations could make their own decisions about the roles of members. According to the constitution of Pine Street Baptist Church, white male members were to govern the congregation, but women could participate in votes concerning the calling of a pastor. In 1904 the women failed to gain the right to vote for church officers, but in 1916 women did become voting members. The changes at Pine Street reflected a pattern among local Baptist churches, many of which granted women voting privileges about the same time. Organized in 1916, Oakwood Baptist included women on its committees from the start. In 1922 the women of Leigh Street Baptist gained voting and committee privileges. In 1926, when members elected a woman to the important finance committee at Second Baptist, a local writer speculated that she might be the first Baptist woman in Virginia history to hold such a position. In the 1920s several churches experimented with deaconesses, a role unlike the full-time salaried positions of women in some other Protestant denominations. Generally aiding a congregation's male deacon board, Baptist deaconesses mostly visited church members, but the deaconesses of Grace Street Baptist also helped prepare for communion. In 1917 the Dover Baptist Association included women participants, and in 1920 the Baptist General Association of Virginia granted women the right to participate in the state convention.[41]

The Protestant Episcopal Church extended few new opportunities to women. In 1919 delegates to the Episcopal General Convention defeated a proposal that would have granted women the status as deputies to that body. According to historian Mary S. Donovan, that vote "crushed" the hopes of changes for women and left men to make "the decisions women were expected to help carry out." In the early 1920s, the diocese of Virginia appointed a seven-member committee to make recommendations about the possible representation of women in various church organizations. Favoring no changes, a majority report of the committee justified that stance by noting that women were already more active in church activities than men, by warning that a change might prompt a decline in the participation of laymen, and by claiming that women themselves had made no request for such an action. In a minority report, Walter Russell Bowie joined with another member to advocate female eligibility for service on diocese boards overseeing church schools as well as on boards and commissions dealing with missions, social service, and religious education. The minority report further called for a commission to assess the merits of female membership on vestries and the diocesan council. The minority called attention to "the tendency of our time," which placed a larger importance on women participating "in all those forces of life which they share with men." With secular organizations seeking the services of talented women, the church risked "grievous loss" of its "ablest women." If it remained indifferent, it could "lose those who might serve her greatly." In a city where prominent Episcopal laywomen did invest their energies in civic organizations, the minority arguments should have carried weight, but they did not carry the day. As Bowie later observed, his recommendations were not implemented for almost fifty years.[42]

In 1922 the Episcopal House of Deputies authorized the licensing of women lay readers. In the *Southern Churchman* R. Cary Montague tried to explain this "startling" news to "conservative Church people" and termed the decision "in line with modern developments." With mounting enthusiasm throughout his account, he traced the roles of six Old Testament women and culminated with Deborah. Not only a prophetess, Deborah governed through "the sheer force of her character in competition with men" and did so without upsetting the households of her own era. Deborah, Montague predicted, represented the future in this country, and he anticipated a female governor in some American state within the next decade. Montague, though, did acknowledge that the decision to license women lay readers remained in the hands of individual bishops. And implicitly any initiative to license them had to originate in individual congregations. By 1931 none of Richmond's Episcopal churches listed female lay readers. Deborah apparently was not yet welcomed in the parishes, and, thus, calls for justice for women within their churches were only partially answered.[43]

Suffering from the heart disease that would end his life, Episcopalian Benjamin B. Valentine wrote Lila Meade Valentine a deeply affectionate letter in which he lauded her as "the very best wife a man could have." After expressing his delight in their marriage of a quarter of a century, he added, "I hope that you will keep your work." "I believe," he continued, "that in advocating suffrage for women you are not only advocating a righteous cause but one which will aid in the relief of the weary and the heavy laden, promote patriotism in the highest sense, and advance the cause of peace among the peoples." Less than six months later, Lila Meade made her annual address as president of the Equal Suffrage League of Virginia (ESLV). She rejoiced that "our great fight for justice has been blessed by God and I look confidently to its ultimate victory." "It is," she said, "the cause for the right and therefore must prevail." In crusading for woman's suffrage, B. B. Valentine and Lila Meade Valentine, like a number of other local Protestants, believed that they campaigned for social justice.[44]

On 6 February 1911, novelist Mary Johnston, until recently a member of First Baptist Church, addressed Richmond Baptist ministers about the Equal Suffrage League. Drawn to Eastern religions, Johnston had quietly left her former congregation eleven months earlier. Observing that last year she had paid more than one thousand dollars of taxes to the city and the state, she added, "I earned every penny of that money." Viewed by the state as a person and as a citizen on taxpayer's day, "I was neither . . . when it came to deciding between stationary comets on Broad Street or schoolhouses that could seat the children." After reviewing the list of distinguished local women who had joined the Equal Suffrage League, she noted that more than thirty men, including H. D. C. Maclachlan, had also joined the league. A local reporter wrote that the meeting was well attended, the audience was attentive, and that a number of ministers complimented her on her presentation and expressed sympathy with the cause.[45]

Some ministers had already endorsed the equal suffrage cause. The week before Johnston spoke to the Baptist preachers, Maclachlan had delivered a sermon, "Women in Democracy," at Seventh Street Christian Church. Anticipating that critics would tell him that "woman's suffrage is not a fit theme for the pulpit," he countered that "the gospel has to do with human life in its whole extent." Dismissing many of the arguments against suffrage as based on prejudice, he maintained that few people were well informed about the history or accomplishments of the suffrage movement. "For centuries," Maclachlan asserted, men had been "bungling municipal and state duties" and asking women to help clean up the mess. Unlike men, who were preoccupied with property interests, women were "more human, more sensitive to the higher values of life." Using a popular metaphor of the era, he described women as municipal housekeepers who cared about public services and who would not tolerate "the exploitation of the weak and defenseless for the sake of any phantom 'prosperity.'" Moreover, Virginia's male political leaders had enacted a "large number" of laws that treated women unjustly. Husbands controlled their wives' property, widows coped with unfair inheritance laws, and all women lacked eligibility for positions of civic leadership such as service on school boards. The major opponents of equal suffrage, Maclachlan claimed, included a number of ignoble vested interests groups, such as corrupt politicians, saloon keepers, and businessmen who relied on child labor. To cultural critics of woman's suffrage, he rejoined that no one could detect damaged families or diminished femininity in states where women already voted.[46]

A handful of the city's Protestant ministers openly enlisted in the equal suffrage cause. The Equal Suffrage League of Virginia counted Monumental Episcopal's James W. Morris and Laurel Street Methodist's Joseph R. Rowland as members. A consistent champion of women's rights, Grace Street Baptist's David M. Ramsey proclaimed that "there are times when agitation is indispensable" and predicted that women would ultimately triumph in the suffrage campaign. In 1914 Central Methodist's W. A. Cooper spoke at a suffrage rally at John Marshall High School. In 1916 Leigh Street Baptist's John J. Wicker spoke in behalf of woman's suffrage to a joint committee of the state legislature. Depicting Christian civilization as an enlightened one in which women had steadily gained rights, Wicker criticized a policy of withholding equal suffrage as a "relic of barbarism," which denied women the justice they deserved.[47]

Only a very few ministers announced their opposition to woman's suffrage. Questioning the wisdom of enfranchising women, Broad Street Methodist preacher S. C. Hatcher heaped so much praise on female citizens that he may have defeated his avowed purpose. Often a reformer himself, Hatcher admitted that suffrage leaders were intelligent and unselfish individuals who sought the ballot to correct injustices, particularly ones affecting children and women. Still, Hatcher did not perceive exclusion from voting as an injustice. As his scripture for the sermon, he invoked an epistle of the apostle Paul in which he instructed that women should be discreet, chaste, obedient to their husbands, and keepers of the home. But Hatcher's stance relied more on chivalry than theology. He argued that men and women differed physically and mentally, and each group occupied distinct spheres for which they were peculiarly suited. As men's moral superiors, women diminished their own influence by entering the contentious, worldly realm of politics. Instead they should rely on men whose "glory" it was to represent the fairer sex. "True manhood, prompted by love for womanhood, goes out and fights her battles, bringing back his laurels, laying them at her feet." Hatcher then challenged local manhood to promote "all of those good reforms that true women have a right to expect you to accomplish." With a social gospel vision of "the city beautiful," he called for shorter work days, playgrounds for children, paving of streets, and an end to barrooms and brothels. Anyone hoping to hear a good, old-fashioned defense of the status quo must have been frustrated by his performance.[48]

Though supported by some men, women constituted the heart of the Equal Suffrage League of Virginia. As president of the league between 1909 and 1919, Lila Meade Valentine proved to be an impressive leader. In December 1912 she spoke "as a church woman" before Richmond's Episcopal clergy and expressed "the religious aspect of this movement." Regaling the ministers with reasons, facts, and moral appeals, she emphasized the justice of the cause. Since voting gave citizens a voice in the conditions under which they must live, she argued, the only valid reason to deny women participation would be moral incompetency. But women filled churches, and men composed most of the prison population. Women who worked in factories, schools, shops, and businesses owned property and paid taxes but could not vote. Suffrage brought with it freedom "to mould the environment in which we bring up our children," freedom to "stand side by side with man in his effort to bring about the Kingdom of God on Earth." "We desire citizenship," she told the ministers, "because as Christians we know we are our brother's keeper." Without political power, she advised, "we can do but little towards measuring up to that responsibility." Valentine matched her eloquence as a speaker with organizational skills. While lobbying legislators, she and other leaders devoted much of their efforts to informing the public about the movement and recruiting members.[49]

Though important, Valentine was not, as one historian reminds us, a "one-woman movement." Many of the other members of the ESLV shared her religious convictions. In a letter published in the *Religious Herald,* Valentine declared that "a very large proportion" of the ESLV members were not only church members but "prominent workers in the various societies of the church and in civic betterment organizations of all kinds." Among them Lucy Randolph Mason consistently made the strongest religious argument for equal suffrage. In talks, newspaper articles, and pamphlets published by the ESLV, she forcefully articulated views much like those of Valentine. Mason believed that "Christ's salvation was meant for all men and must be worked out by each individual giving his or her best to the general good." She complained that women could not make their best contribution to society unless they were permitted to vote. She maintained that they were denied the opportunity to improve social conditions because they could not influence political decisions. On one occasion she called the movement "a product of that true democracy the foundations of which were laid in the teachings of our Lord Jesus Christ."[50]

The appeal for social justice resonated with ministers such as Maclachlan, Cooper, and Wicker, but it was not so compelling in the Capitol. The divine discontent of Lucy Mason, Lila Valentine, and other ESLV members did not prove powerful enough to move Virginia's culturally conservative legislators. During the suffrage campaign, Richmond's denominational weeklies avoided the controversial issue. Still, the *Southern Churchman* celebrated the ratification of the Nineteenth Amendment, calling it a "thrilling," "great experiment." "It is the spirit of Christ," wrote the editor, as he confidently predicted that devout women would bring their spiritual values into the political arena.[51]

Active in the ESLV, Mary-Cooke Branch Munford invested much of her energy in a campaign to end another injustice, the lack of a state-supported institution of higher learning for women. Herself deprived of a coveted chance to attend college, Munford brought an intense commitment to this crusade. As her nephew and biographer Walter Russell Bowie explained, "Her early longing for education had widened out into an imaginative sympathy for all young people, and especially young girls who had the same ambition." Yet a new generation of Virginia women faced the prospect that their aspirations for learning would be ignored. In 1910 Munford and her husband hosted a gathering and organized what became known as the Co-ordinate College League. They proposed that the state legislature create a women's college near the University of Virginia in Charlottesville. The school would have its own organization as well as separate social, residence, and instruction halls. The coordinate college would, however, share libraries, laboratories, and faculty with the University of Virginia.[52]

Munford and her cohorts marshaled a list of compelling reasons to establish the coordinate college. Calling for fairness, they maintained that "our women need a college equal in quality and prestige to that offered by the state university to our men." With the development of the state's public education system, more girls were graduating from high schools than in the past. But many of these women lacked the financial resources to attend private colleges, and they had difficulty entering denominational colleges, which had become crowded. In the twentieth century, women were increasingly joining men as wage earners, the coordinate college proponents explained, and the state suffered when its citizens and workers lacked sufficient education. For example, women accounted for 75 percent of all high school teachers, yet the state made no provision for them to earn the appropriate bachelor's degree. Moreover, as taxpayers, women deserved access to a state-funded institution of higher education. With its existing physical plant, laboratories, library, museum, and faculty, the University of Virginia was "uniquely qualified" to meet these educational needs. By creating a coordinate college, the state could avoid the cost of establishing a separate institution for women. This approach had already proved successful for such schools as Radcliffe, Barnard College, Newcomb College at Tulane University, and the Women's College of Brown University.[53]

Munford had to do more than make an impressively rational case for the coordinate college. She and her friends had to rally support for the idea as well. That effort required countless conversations and extensive correspondence. The league distributed pamphlets, met with legislators, and called on governors. When the legislature convened, Munford lobbied, organized speakers to appear at education committee hearings, and made presentations herself. She secured letters of support from President Woodrow Wilson, presidents of nationally prestigious colleges, and the president of the University of Virginia, as well as endorsements from a number of educational, civic, and labor organizations. The Co-ordinate College League won the support of notable local clergymen and laymen, including J. T. Mastin, Collins Denny, Churchill Gibson Chamberlayne, and Dr. Ennion G. Williams. In the *Religious Herald,* R. H. Pitt called the existing situation a "manifest and outrageous injustice." While the state had made a "large provision over the years" for the education of men, he observed, it had done nothing for women but establish normal schools that aided only future teachers. Other young women were left "utterly without any recognition from the state in the way of provision of their higher intellectual culture and training." Citing the success of the coordinate college idea at the University of Richmond, where Westhampton College coeds shared campus facilities with their male counterparts, he endorsed the coordinate college for the University of Virginia.[54]

Though armed with reasons and endorsements, the coordinate college proponents did not prevail against their determined opponents, generally influential University of Virginia alumni. Led by businessmen and lawyers living in Richmond, the opponents organized their own meetings to exert political pressure against the proposal. Sometimes suggesting that a separate college should be created for women or arguing that limited state funds would have to be diverted from primary education, the opponents seemed to share a belief that the traditional university experience of males would be marred by the proximity of young women. At each session of the legislature for almost a decade, the proponents and opponents of the coordinate college rallied their forces. Having gradually gained support in the Virginia Senate, the proposal failed by a margin of only two votes in the House of Delegates in 1916. Calling the close vote "a very real victory for our cause," Munford attributed defeat to the influence of Methodist clergyman James Cannon, "an aggressive opponent of the bill." By the next session of the legislature in 1918, the state of Virginia had acquired the College of William and Mary, and the legislature voted to open it to women on the same conditions that applied to men. The general assembly also voted to admit women to the University of Virginia graduate schools except in the programs of law and engineering. The Virginia Senate again voted to approve the coordinate college, but the House of Delegates failed to even consider the proposal. To some the long campaign may have seemed to be a failure.[55]

Still, Mary-Cooke Branch Munford's campaign yielded important results. Women did gain admission to a state-supported institution of higher education, and, in the fall of 1920, the University of Virginia began admitting females as candidates for "vocational B.S." degrees as well as for graduate and professional degrees. Munford served as the first female member of the board of visitors of William and Mary and in 1926 began serving as a member of the board of visitors of the University of Virginia. That same year the university president, Edwin A. Alderman, reported to her statistics about the university's women. In the six years since women had gained admission to the university, 351 had enrolled and 105 had already earned degrees, including forty-three master's degrees and two doctorates. If Munford had not won a coordinate college, she and the other members of her organization had opened the state doors of higher education to young women and gained a measure of social justice. In the late 1920s, Munford spoke to women students at the University of Virginia. In reporting the episode to her nephew, she wrote, "It was like a dream come true to see the girls *really there*" (Munford's emphasis). Thus, the coordinate college campaign achieved a partial measure of justice, but the full measure remained elusive. Munford subsequently joined other Co-ordinate College League members in a renewed campaign for a women's institution at Charlottesville, but only in 1969 did the University of Virginia's board of visitors vote to admit women on the same basis as men.[56]

While seeking justice for women and prisoners, some Richmond Protestants also called for industrial justice. Discontented with the nation's economic system, they charged that greedy businessmen ignored Christian principles by seeking only profits. Such selfishness discounted the needs and worth of other human beings, the preachers contended. Citing the practices of the oil, paper, railroad, insurance, and fruit trusts, ministers and denominational newspapers indicted them for using unscrupulous methods to cheat the public. Walter Russell Bowie condemned such companies for securing "special privilege" laws, which betrayed the public good and permitted "the sordid interests of a few" to outweigh the rights of other citizens.[57]

Ministers also criticized some employers for treating their workers as mere machinery to make money. James B. Hawthorne warned that a manufacturer had no more right to run a factory "solely for his own benefit than Jesus Christ had to work miracles for his own profit." George W. McDaniel decried businessmen for "devouring their fellows in unrequited toil, unjust hours of work and child labor." Bowie censured cities that boasted about their factories, mills, dividends, bank accounts, and trade while ignoring "the broken lives on which these things are built." Appalled by New York's Triangle Shirtwaist fire in 1911, R. H. Pitt grieved for the "poor and unknown" victims and declared that the government should have protected them from being "sent as human sacrifices to appease the fiendish lust for gain." Referring to the Fifth Chapter of James in the New Testament, Walter Lingle argued that ministers should urge employers to pay their workers a "just wage."[58]

At times Richmond clergymen issued extensive critiques of America's economic system. In March 1912 Pitt began a twelve-part series, "Men or Things," in the *Religious Herald.* He expressed outrage about an economic system that exalted material goods over the welfare of humans. He accused the legal system, specific laws, courts, and legislators of elevating property rights while discounting personal rights and fostering concentrations of wealth in corporations controlled by small groups. Praising labor unions, Pitt deplored industrial abuses such as child labor, long working days, and unsafe mines and factories, which showed that "nothing is quite so cheap as human flesh and blood."[59]

An early critic of child labor, H. D. C. Maclachlan steadily broadened his critique of the economic system. He noted that business achievements tended to blind society to "industrial sins" and that businessmen rationalized their behavior, attributing any harmful results to "Providence" or Darwinism. In fact, the "survival of the fittest" outlook, Maclachlan reasoned, drove people into ruthless competition that conflicted with the goal of Christian brotherhood. He wondered, "How can we love our neighbor as ourselves when six days in the week we engage in a fierce competitive struggle with him for the necessities of life?" He repudiated this "principle of unlimited competition," which "pushes the weakest to the wall and puts a premium on self-assertion and economic brutality." The quest for profits led to sharp business practices such as underpaying workers and neglecting overcrowded, disease-breeding tenements.[60]

After World War I Walter Russell Bowie assumed editorship of the *Southern Churchman* and filled the paper with articles probing the nation's business ethics. Editing the "Christ and Community" column, R. Cary Montague took the same stance. With Americans valuing property more than people, Bowie concluded, the economic system had become based on "inequalities and injustices." Worried that churches relied too much on the rich, he urged ministers to bring the Gospel to bear on "the raw materialism" of "our everyday world." In that world, he found businesses based on selfish competition and factories with harmful working conditions. Featuring articles from the Federal Council of Churches and the Church League for Industrial Democracy, Bowie deplored child labor, high unemployment, low wages, lack of industrial safety, and the twelve-hour day. Concurring, R. Cary Montague described the weary existence of the twelve-hour laborer and referred to Moses as the "first advocate of improved working conditions." When the American steel industry dismissed the critical findings of the detailed investigation by the Interchurch World Movement, Bowie heatedly responded with an editorial "Shall Life Be Fed to the Furnace?" Bowie lamented that "Christ stands outside the barred gates of much of our economic system. He stands there in the great hunger of the underprivileged multitude for wholesomeness of life." "He stands there in the modern demand for justice," Bowie warned, and "when he enters, there will be readjustment."[61]

Only a few readjustments occurred in early-twentieth-century Virginia. Proponents of restricting child labor did wage a slow, quiet, persistent, incremental, and successful campaign. Clergymen and laypersons played key roles in those efforts. With no major local industry heavily reliant upon child labor, Richmonders seemed almost detached from the practice. One Episcopal laywoman, Kate Pleasants Minor, however, testified before a state Senate committee considering revision of child labor laws in 1903. That legislature passed a law forbidding children under twelve years of age from working in factories, mines, or mechanical establishments. Speaking to Richmond Methodist preachers in 1907, Bishop John Granberry recited the harms of child labor, condemned the "unrighteous, inhumanitarian" working conditions, identified weaknesses in Virginia's laws, and criticized parents and employers for acting selfishly. The Methodist ministers passed a resolution endorsing stronger legislation. A few months later, child labor leader Alexander McKelway arrived in the city to organize a Virginia branch of the National Child Labor Committee. James Buchanan served as secretary, and several other local clergymen joined him as members of the organization's executive committee. Within a month Buchanan swung into action and summoned members to the state Capitol, where the legislature considered and then passed another law. The new statute generally forbade children under the age of fourteen from working. According to the major historian of child labor laws in the South, widespread support in Virginia for tougher laws led to a 1912 act that removed old loopholes and limited the workday of children under sixteen years to ten hours daily. The legislature passed additional laws in 1918, 1920, and 1922. The latter measure limited the work of children under sixteen years to forty-four hours a week.[62]

Local religious leaders supported the campaigns for more restrictive child labor laws. Once prone to exonerate Virginia industrialists from charges of misusing young workers, the *Central Presbyterian* shifted its position and endorsed more stringent laws. Backing the agenda of the National Child Labor Committee, the *Southern Churchman* condemned child labor as "destructive and murderous." In the *Religious Herald* Pitt not only denounced child labor but also called upon Christian leaders to inform themselves and to "give their influence openly and steadily" to remedying those conditions. The ranks of those who did so publicly included Baptists George W. McDaniel, S. C. Mitchell, and Rolvix Harlan. Methodists J. T. Mastin, W. A. Cooper, F. T. McFaden, and W. J. Maybee as well as Episcopalians Montague, Bowie, and Mary-Cooke Branch Munford backed more restrictive laws. In one passionate protest against child labor, Maclachlan somberly remonstrated that "He who called the little ones to Himself and blessed them cannot have intended that industry should be so organized as to make grist for the money mill out of the souls and bodies of 'ragged children with bare feet.'"[63]

Some commentaries against child labor appeared as part of larger critiques of the cotton textile industry located in towns south of Richmond. In 1906 the *Baltimore and Richmond Christian Advocate* published a speech by H. W. Dunkley. A former pastor in Danville, Virginia, Dunkley provided grim personal testimony about unsafe working conditions as well as about impoverished, overcrowded living conditions. In 1908 the *Religious Herald* charged that mill towns created an atmosphere closer to feudalism than democracy and that mill hands lost their self-reliance and independence and lived in poverty. In 1927 forty-two southern church leaders issued an "Appeal to the Industrial Leaders of the South," which secular and religious newspapers published. The Appeal expressed concern about low wages, the employment of women and children under the age of sixteen, long working weeks that sometimes reached sixty hours, and living conditions in mill towns. With companies in charge, those towns did not foster education, religion, or a sense of community among residents. Emphasizing that laborers were humans, not commodities, the appeal urged industrialists to involve workers in improving conditions. If the owners did so, predicted the appeal, they could avoid wasteful, bitter industrial conflicts with the workers. Richmond's Maclachlan, Walter Lingle, Rolvix Harlan, and Episcopal Bishop H. St. George Tucker signed the appeal, as did former Richmonders M. Ashby Jones and James Cannon.[64]

When mill owners angrily rejected the appeal as unwarranted interference in their business, local ministers bristled. Responding privately to one critic, Walter Lingle recounted how he had repeatedly studied the document before signing it. He had concluded that it was "a real attempt to apply the teachings of Christ to every-day life and especially to the industrial world." Certain that "Jesus means for us to apply his teachings to every relationship of life," "I felt that nothing but sheer cowardice would keep me from signing it." Nor were the signers of the appeal ignorant of conditions in factories and mill towns, rebutted Lingle. For nine years he had lived in proximity to mill towns, and for four years "worked in the heart of a mill village. I knew more about it than any official connected with it. I went into every home, I knew every family personally." When his critic objected that the work days in the mills were not too long, Lingle did not retreat. "Bless your heart, nobody can tell me anything about work," responded Lingle, who recited his own difficult childhood experiences. While "I believe in the gospel of work," "nevertheless, it is true that in some industries the hours are still too long." A disgusted Maclachlan dismissed the assertion that the appeal's signatories knew little about the subject as a "ridiculous" and "false" accusation. What constituted truly deplorable ignorance, he rejoined, was the failure to understand that the Bible directed ministers to fill a prophetic responsibility to go beyond "pious platitudes" and call for "social righteousness." When strife erupted during union organizing efforts in 1929, the *Richmond News Leader* urged textile owners to reread the appeal and reconsider it. The *Richmond Christian Advocate* repeated the call for fair wages and good living conditions. The Methodist editor suggested that if the employers would follow the Golden Rule, "they will not be satisfied to live in palaces and see their workers living in hovels."[65]

On other occasions local ministers also sharply attacked the inequitable distribution of society's wealth. A number of ministers attributed that situation to greedy businessmen who caused poverty by exploiting wage earners. Maclachlan described grinding poverty that resulted from "the huge fortunes that are built on the exploitation of man by man." Yet religious leaders made little headway in suggesting specific solutions to the problem of want amidst plenty. Local ministers typically endorsed the proposition of paying workers a "living wage." Few of the clergymen, however, agreed about what workers should do to reach that goal. R. H. Pitt endorsed unions as "the only orderly, sustained, and serious protest against the enslaving influence of vast combinations of property." Other ministers and editors of the denominational newspapers praised union activity but objected to strikes. Believing that Christ had taught his followers to use cooperation, not coercion, the religious leaders groped for a way to implement that principle.[66]

The confusion within clerical ranks was apparent during Richmond's two greatest wage disputes. In 1903 and 1922 the entire community was paralyzed by protracted strikes of streetcar workers. During the summer of 1903, members of the Amalgamated Association of Streetcar Employees began a strike against the Virginia Passenger and Power Company, which controlled streetcars in Richmond. The union sought recognition, reduction of a twelve-hour day to a nine-hour day, grievance arbitration, and a slight pay increase. The company refused to negotiate. The ensuing strike lasted sixty-nine days and featured strikebreakers, mob violence, a dynamite incident, Pinkertons, two deaths, and the occupation of Richmond by state militia. Several ministers supported the strike. An outspoken champion of unions, the pastor of Randolph Street Baptist Church addressed the strikers at a rally. From his pulpit he declared that according to the Bible, workers had a right not only to a living wage but also to income sufficient to educate their children. Without explicitly backing the strike, the *Religious Herald* expressed sympathy for strikers and their families, who "must miss their scanty salaries." Attempting to mediate the dispute, a committee of ministers first proposed a compromise settlement and later offered to arbitrate the dispute. The company ignored both offers. When the union exhausted its limited financial resources, the traction company won the strike and destroyed the union. The strike, however, proved costly to the company, which went bankrupt the following year.[67]

By the 1920s another company had acquired the streetcar system. In January 1922 that company slashed the wages of workers between 15 and 33 percent. Once again streetcar workers went out on strike. One Baptist minister charged that even before the cut the wages had been low and the best-paid worker had received only fifty dollars a month for a ten-hour day. Several clergymen castigated the company for causing privation and accused it of union busting. The *Richmond Christian Advocate* censured the company for not paying streetcar employees enough money "to live as men should live and raise their children as true men ought." Again the traction company ignored these protests and won the dispute. Although the city's clergymen had attempted to resolve the 1903 strike, they remained divided over labor issues. Some ministers demonstrated little sympathy for unions, and others adhered to a belief that they should confine themselves to spiritual matters and avoid secular issues. Richmond ministers who favored higher wage scales could not agree upon what to do. As a result, they failed to exercise enough influence to help workers.[68]

Neither the clergy nor the laity succeeded in alleviating another local injustice—the low wages paid to women workers. In 1911 the wife of the director of the Methodist Institute reported that eight tobacco factories employed 1,788 women at an average wage of six dollars for a fifty-six-hour week. Columnist Cally Ryland reported that in 1916 the average weekly wage of women in city department stores was five dollars. Several clergymen became outspoken critics of the wage scales, and the vice investigation convinced others that desperate women workers resorted to prostitution to supplement their small incomes. In 1915 the *Presbyterian of the South* expressed concern about the young urban women working in stores and factories and "getting very small wages." In 1921 the executive secretary of the Baptist Council of Richmond favored starting a boardinghouse for young women "working in our factories and other places" without sufficient income.[69]

Lucy Randolph Mason championed the cause of female workers. In 1882

Mason had been born to parents with distinguished ancestry and with a commitment to social Christianity. Her father, Landon R. Mason, the rector of Grace Episcopal Church, once listed his reading interests as "religious sociology." Her mother's participation in the prison reform campaign and work for the Spring Street Home reflected a larger pattern of community caring. Praising both parents for aiding the needy, daughter Lucy recalled that "they knew they served God as they cared for His children." "From Miss Lucy's earliest years," records biographer John Salmond, "God was central to every aspect of her existence." Once hoping to become a missionary, Lucy soon concluded that "religion can be put to work right in one's own community." With that outlook she remained in Richmond much of her life. Educated at a private school, she taught herself to type and to take shorthand. A stenographer in a corporate law firm for eight years, she discovered that the victims of grisly industrial accidents received only tiny sums of compensation for injuries that impaired them for life. Teaching a Sunday school class that included women who worked in tobacco factories, she observed that the long ten-hour days not only harmed workers but also "disrupted family life." In 1914 Lucy accepted a job as the secretary for the Richmond Young Women's Christian Association (YWCA) and later as its general secretary. Meanwhile, she served as president of the Richmond chapter of the Equal Suffrage League of Virginia and its successor, the League of Women Voters.[70]

Lucy Mason lectured, published pamphlets, and organized a conference on the eight-hour day at Broad Street Methodist Church. She repeatedly charged that industrialists harmed families by paying wages that were so low that both men and women were forced "into a life-consuming fight for a less than living wage." With the backing of the Virginia League of Women Voters, she published a twenty-six-page plea, *The Shorter Day and Women Workers.* In it she combined reasons and statistics with portrayals of the drudgery of the ten-hour day. Believing that "the souls of individuals" should not be "bound down by unremitting toil," American churches had endorsed the eight-hour day for men and women, she wrote. Noting that a majority of Virginia women already worked for employers who had voluntarily adopted the nine-hour day, she called upon the state of Virginia to lead the South by legislating a shorter day. Religious weeklies excerpted her pamphlet, Mason testified before the legislature, but Virginia did not lead the way.[71]

And by 1929 women's wages had not improved either. The retiring president of the Retail Merchants Association complained that the low salaries of tobacco workers depressed the entire local economy. He added that Richmond could not prosper so long as "a large element of its population is in bondage to the grocer and the landlord." The *News Leader* produced a survey to show that conditions were not so bad and called tobacco workers' salaries a "saving wage," not a "subsistence wage." Letters to the editor and to a city labor newspaper disputed that conclusion. A study titled *Occupations for Women,* conducted by the Southern Woman's Educational Alliance, cited low salaries for Richmond secretaries, sales clerks, and stenographers.[72]

The appeal for higher wages for women underscored a harsh reality: the calls for social justice had limitations. First, some religious leaders remained committed to the notion that churches should not become involved in secular issues. For example, Presbyterian Russell Cecil cautioned that Christianity "is not a gospel of social reform." Divided, the clergy did not organize to exert their influence on behalf of workers. Without such organization, Lucy Randolph Mason concluded, the ministers who acted individually or together in small groups could accomplish little. Second, believing that adversarial methods contradicted the spirit of Christian love, most Richmond ministers advocated moral suasion rather than confrontation. Even Maclachlan concluded that justice belonged to "a realm which compulsion cannot reach. . . . it is not helped by strong arm methods on one side or the other." Though well respected by Richmond's labor leaders, he believed that the church itself should not take sides in labor disputes. Instead, he said, religious leaders should "teach those principles of social justice which will guide the people to a conscientious and fair-minded decision in all labor disputes."[73]

Yet, when faced by vested interests, this approach proved ineffective. Walter Lingle declared that "Christian businessmen" had told him that the Golden Rule was impractical and that they "do not try to keep it." Maclachlan remarked that he had argued for hours "with Christian businessmen in a vain endeavor to convince them" that certain business practices were un-Christian. Recognizing this limitation, the ministers seemed to rely on persistence. In 1912 R. H. Pitt noted that "the path of justice and humanity will not wind through flowery meads and along gentle gradients. It will be found, as it has always been found, steep and rocky. Entrenched power and privilege will not yield at first demand."[74]

Thus, a divine discontent did drive Richmond Protestant leaders to call for social justice. When they combined such calls with persuasion, lobbying, and action, they achieved notable successes. Officials improved conditions at the state penitentiary, the city established a juvenile court, women gained greater roles in churches and access to higher education, and children received protection from labor. But the calls for social justice had limits. Few localities improved their horrendous jails or created juvenile courts, women did not gain equality in education or in religious organizations, and many workers still encountered long work days and low wages. Lucy Randolph Mason did not accept the prevailing belief that Christians must avoid adversarial relations. Still consumed with a divine discontent for social justice, she left Richmond in the 1930s to become an effective organizer for the Congress of Industrial Organizations.[75]

9
Not Brothers or Sisters

Speaking to the women's missionary societies of two large Baptist churches, a laywoman active in the Equal Suffrage League described "the spiritual motive for social service." "The only lasting reforms must come through religion," she declared, "a religion which feels that enthusiasm for humanity which makes of us all brothers and sisters of one common fatherhead." That statement located the limits of Richmond's social Christianity. White evangelical Protestants often interacted with other religious groups in the city, shared some experiences with them, and extended assistance to them. Still, white Protestants found it difficult to treat members of some other faiths and races as true brothers and sisters.[1]

Richmond Protestants generally maintained cordial relations with local Jews. During the early twentieth century, Jews comprised a significant but diverse part of the city's population. Numbering approximately eight thousand in the 1920s, they accounted for a larger segment of the community than did Presbyterians, Disciples of Christ, or Lutherans. Organized by Sephardic Jews in 1789, the congregation of Beth Shalome merged in 1898 with Temple Beth Ahabah, the area's largest congregation. Founded by Germans in 1841, Beth Ahabah developed into a center for Reform Judaism. On Church Hill, Jews of eastern European ancestry worshiped in the orthodox Keneseth Israel congregation. In downtown Richmond, Russian Jews observed the Sabbath at Sir Moses Montefiore Synagogue. From the eighteenth century, Jews had occupied important positions in the city, and by rendering service to the Confederacy, they ensured the continued respect of Richmond's Gentiles. In twentieth-century Richmond, Jews distinguished themselves as leaders in business, politics, education, and civic affairs.[2]

Beth Ahabah's Rabbi Edward N. Calisch deserved much of the credit for the goodwill between Protestants and Jews. Born to immigrant parents in 1865, Calisch spent most of his childhood in Chicago, Toledo, and Cleveland. To prepare for the rabbinate, he completed studies under the distinguished Reform faculty of Hebrew Union College in Cincinnati. After serving a congregation in Peoria, Illinois, he came to Richmond in 1891. At the age of twenty-six, he began his lengthy career at Beth Ahabah, then a small, conservative, downtown congregation. By 1908 Calisch had added a master's degree and a Ph.D. to his accomplishments. Having written a thesis titled "The Jew in English Literature," he subsequently wrote several books. Meanwhile, Beth Ahabah moved to the West End, added members, and subtracted customs. With the urbane and articulate Calisch as rabbi, the increasingly progressive synagogue discontinued twenty-eight Jewish traditions. Some changes he made reluctantly. With the rest of the city conducting business on Saturday, attendance at worship services declined. Fearing that "Jewish spirituality is dying," Calisch added a Sunday service in 1924. Acknowledging that the Reform movement had brought radical changes to American synagogues, he urged his members to emphasize "character not catechism" and toleration not proselytizing. He challenged them to match material success with progress "in honor, in conduct, in morality, in kindness, in neighborliness, in citizenship, in public, in spirit, in private integrity."[3]

Thus, though flexible about traditions, Calisch remained firm in his religious convictions. In one sermon about justice, he decried moral standards that still traveled "at an ox-cart pace" in a faster, more complex age. As a result, society condemned a poor man for stealing bread but smiled at a rich man for stealing railroads. Calisch censured food adulterers, industrialists who neglected the safety of workers, and corrupt bank officials "as morally guilty as murderers and highwaymen." He also acted as a community cultural commentator. When a Baptist minister categorically attacked theatrical performances, Calisch rejoined that the theater had survived because it answered an inherent human need for recreation and amusement. Admitting an "obscene trend" in some productions, he advised improving the theater, not destroying it. Praising drama as a source of education, he applauded a New York opera for showing that "it is not creed but conscience, not doctrine but deed that makes a moral hero." In one well-attended lecture, he traced the origins of Shakespeare's *The Merchant of Venice* and criticized the playwright for changing a traditional Christian creditor into a Jew. With his Shylock figure, Shakespeare spread an incorrect stereotype of a Jew as a "hard-hearted and vengeful usurer." Troubled lest a moral mania sweep the city, Calisch steadfastly opposed the passage of a state movie censorship law in the 1920s.[4]

Viewed by some Jews as a controversial proponent of change, Calisch gained status and respect within Richmond. He often spoke at significant public occasions. In 1901, when city religious leaders conducted a prayer service for assassinated President William McKinley, Calisch played a prominent role. In 1907, when the Triennial Convention of the Protestant Episcopal Church met in Richmond, Calisch delivered a sermon—a very singular honor. Among his civic duties, Calisch served on the city's vice commission and supported the campaign for a woman's coordinate college at the University of Virginia. In a 1913 article in the *Presbyterian of the South,* the editor alluded to Calisch as a "learned Jewish rabbi with whom we have had frequent and happy intercourse." Calling him "one of the most spiritually-minded men we have ever met," the editor lauded him as one "whose very soul seems to be aflame with a desire to see all his people thoroughly religious."[5]

Other Jewish citizens also gained the respect and affection of Protestants. For example, the *Religious Herald* commended educator Henry Hutzler for devoting so much time to visiting orphans as well as the aged and the infirm throughout the city. Residents of the Baptist Home for Aged Women particularly expressed their gratitude for his visits. First Baptist's George W. McDaniel emphasized the need for more interaction between Jews and Protestants. According to him, Jews of the first century "eschewed Gentiles," but "we eschew Jews. They were wrong and so are we." Noting Jewish benevolence and patriotism, Methodist preacher Edward L. Pell observed that the world treated Jews badly, but they still excelled at whatever they did.[6]

On several occasions Richmond Protestants and Jews assisted one another and tried to foster greater understanding between Christians and Jews. In 1900, when Grove Avenue Baptist Church burned down, pastor James B. Hawthorne accepted Calisch's offer to join Temple Beth Ahabah in union Thanksgiving Day services. In 1903 Richmond Protestant leaders participated in several mass meetings to protest the treatment of Russian Jews. City Baptists attacked compulsory school Bible reading as discriminatory against Jews as well as a violation of the principle of separation of church and state. George W. McDaniel and Lutheran minister John J. Scherer spoke at Beth Ahabah. In 1922 H. D. C. Maclachlan invited Calisch and the members of Beth Ahabah to join Seventh Street Christian Church in several union services. At one service Maclachlan preached about "My Friends, the Jews," and at another Calisch spoke about "What Do the Jews Believe?" Throughout the 1920s Maclachlan and Calisch continued to hold annual union services. In 1927 St. Paul's Episcopal Church joined them. After attending the 1927 services, the editor of the *Chesapeake Christian* wrote that "we must admit that Dr. Calisch clearly reveals the purpose and value of God's word."[7]

Civilities and gestures of goodwill, however, did not stop bouts of friction and doses of anti-Semitism. Often aligned with Baptists, Jews objected to legal measures supported by other religious groups. At the 1901–2 state constitutional convention, Jews and Baptists vigorously protested a clause using the word *Christian* in the new document. Both groups repeatedly opposed compulsory Bible reading in public schools. The Baptist commitment to separation of church and state did not extend to Sunday closing laws, but an exemption based on religion limited their impact on Jews. Protestant preferences for Sunday observances did precipitate occasional quarrels. For example, some preachers antagonized Jews in 1920 with complaints about the Young Men's Hebrew Association playing baseball on Sundays. The Young Men's Christian Association (YMCA) paradoxically accepted Jewish members and Jewish contributions but refused Jewish lodgers. Upset about that policy, McDaniel publicly denounced the directors, urged the YMCA to serve Jew and Gentile, and recalled that neither Jesus nor St. Paul drew a "line against men who held differing beliefs."[8]

In describing the city's anti-Semitism, writer James Branch Cabell observed that Richmonders often characterized Jews as wonderful people but refused to socialize with them. After business hours, according to him, Richmond Jews led socially segregated lives. In 1910 Calisch found it necessary to speak about "Christian prejudice." Referring to the pain of being unwanted in certain hotels, apartment houses, social organizations, schools, and public offices, he traced the discrimination to churches which inaccurately taught that Jews had killed Jesus. Local ministers sometimes used harsh language in portraying Jews. During the 1920s, some clergymen faulted Jewish movie theater proprietors for wishing to show films on Sundays. One Presbyterian pastor condemned "the money grabbing Jews who control the moving picture industry." Even George W. McDaniel deplored pogroms against Jews but asserted that Jews had provoked them. McDaniel faulted "the Jew" for "isolating and egotistical traits which have made him socially *persona non grata.*" Often friendly and rarely viciously anti-Semitic, Richmond Protestants apparently could not quite accept local Jews as true brothers and sisters.[9]

The Church of Jesus Christ of Latter Day Saints maintained only one Richmond church, with approximately one hundred members. Still, leaders of the city's major white Protestant denominations regarded the Mormons as a menace. Criticism of the Mormons took several forms. Appealing for support for the Baptist Home Mission Board, a speaker at First Baptist Church declared that "Mormonism and polygamy are synonymous and the poison thereof is seriously threatening our moral and spiritual health." One Baptist minister charged that Mormon polygamy made a woman "simply a man's tool and places her at the mercy of his debased will." Opposed to the seating of a Mormon in the U.S. House of Representatives, a Presbyterian editor warned that any congressman who voted approval would deny "the sanctity and obligation of marriage and had best not return home." In 1907, when the U.S. Senate did admit a Mormon, a Richmond Methodist editor voiced a second fear, the threat of Mormon political power. Hostile to religious liberty, Mormons, their critics asserted, rejected the principle of separation of church and state—a concept revered by local Protestants. Instead, Mormons had created their own earthly "kingdom" that virtually controlled the electorate of some states. Protestants expressed a third anxiety: through aggressive missionary work, the Mormons skillfully duped innocent citizens into becoming converts. In 1911 the faculty and students of Union Theological Seminary protested a local concert by the Mormon Tabernacle Choir and urged Richmonders not to attend it. The Presbyterians called attention "to the obnoxious moral elements of Mormon belief" and warned that the choir's tour had an "ingratiating purpose," which presumably included obscuring such matters. In 1920 the Richmond Ministerial Union endorsed a campaign denouncing Mormonism. Perceived by other Protestants as holding radically wrong beliefs, Mormons remained outside the circle of religious fellowship.[10]

While not embracing Jews and repudiating Mormons, Richmond Protestants generally radiated hostility to the Roman Catholic Church. And Catholicism had a significant presence in the city. In 1906 five Catholic churches served 8,313 members and reported church property valued at more than that of any other religious body in the city. Since 1834 the city's oldest Catholic church, St. Peter's, had occupied a site on Grace Street close to the Capitol grounds. Initially serving Irish and German immigrants, St. Peter's later counted among its worshipers Confederate leaders such as Gen. P. G. T. Beauregard. Established in 1843, St. Mary's Church welcomed a German population, which grew in the nineteenth century but declined in the twentieth century. On Church Hill, St. Patrick's dated its history to 1859; in Jackson Ward, African American St. Joseph's originated in 1885. When Catholics built the handsome, brick Sacred Heart Church in 1887, they already anticipated a grander edifice in the West End. New York financier Thomas Fortune Ryan, a native of Virginia, made that dream possible with a gift of approximately $250,000. Prelates and parishioners converged at the Monroe Park location for the consecration of the Cathedral of the Sacred Heart on Thanksgiving 1907. Stories about the impressive cathedral filled city newspapers, and it quickly took its place as a source of local pride. Catholics also supported parochial schools, a convent, an orphanage, and several other charitable societies and organizations.[11]

An optimist might have seen harbingers of harmonious relations between Protestants and Catholics. Some Catholic leaders gained citywide popularity. When longtime bishop Rev. A. Van De Vyer submitted his resignation in 1908, citizens assembled in a mass meeting at the Bijou Theatre and persuaded him to withdraw it. A priest at St. Joseph's Catholic Church, Father Charles

Hannigan played an active role in local social reforms and earned the respect and affection of many in the community. Occasionally Catholics and Protestants joined forces. In 1911 some businessmen planned to erect a vaudeville theater at Eighth and Grace Streets near St. Peter's and St. Paul's Episcopal Church. Bishop Van De Vyer consulted with members of St. Paul's, and the two churches united to oppose the issuance of a building permit. Other city churches rallied to their cause, and the prospective owners selected a different site. During the ordeal of the Spanish flu epidemic in 1918, members of St. Peter's made bread, and those of St. Paul's furnished soup in a collaborative effort. According to Episcopalian Cary Montague, that grim experience brought the two congregations closer than ever. At the end of World War I, Protestants, Catholics, and Jews gathered for a Memorial Day service, and Catholic Bishop O'Connell proclaimed that Richmond had "united in one common bond of love."[12]

Such bonds were rare. Catholic leaders generally remained outside the circle of organized community religious activities. They did not participate in the annual festivals of Christian unity in the first years of the twentieth century. Catholic priests did not belong to the Richmond Ministerial Union or to the Richmond Council of Churches formed in the 1920s. When individual neighborhoods conducted union services, Catholic churches did not participate. Some Catholic leaders fostered separation with statements and actions that offended Protestants. At the ceremonies for the laying of the cornerstone of the Cathedral of the Sacred Heart, several priests made comments which, according to the *Religious Herald*, showed their contempt for Protestantism. Calling one of the priests a "religious fanatic," Baptist James B. Hawthorne declared that if this Father Pardow were correct, "all the great Protestant religious leaders are in Hell." "I cannot believe that Father Pardow represents the belief and spirit of all Richmond Catholics," moaned Hawthorne. As strong champions of public schools, city Baptists also took exception to the Catholic church's preference for parochial schools.[13]

For some Richmond Protestants, misgivings about Catholics merged with anxiety about immigrants from southern and eastern Europe. At a time when millions of the so-called new immigrants swelled the population of many American cities, only a small number arrived in Richmond. Nonetheless, local Protestants anticipated that more would soon come. A leading Baptist laywoman reacted hopefully. "Their coming is in accordance with divine purpose," she declared. Indeed, "this new land is God's, not ours, and He means it to be the home for the oppressed of every nation. He has opened the gates, and we dare not close them." She called for greater efforts to evangelize these foreigners, and local Baptists did successfully organize several ministries for eastern Europeans who moved into northeast Richmond. Another laywoman urged Baptists to greet the stranger "at the nation's gate with a friendly hand." Even these women, though, portrayed the new immigrants as potentially dangerous.[14]

Other Protestants viewed these immigrants as truly defective. Clergymen and laypersons branded the eastern and southern Europeans as poor, lazy, ignorant, irreligious, and immoral. In 1902 an Episcopal editor advised that "few of us realize what hordes of illiterate, ignorant, degraded degenerates are being poured into the country each year." As their numbers grew, Protestants expressed doubts about whether the new masses could be assimilated into the nation's existing culture. Within Richmond immigrants raised doubts about their willingness to conform. They seemed disinclined to adhere to the strict Protestant observance of the Sabbath, and Italian names appeared prominently in the lists of arrests for violating Sunday closing laws. In 1901 even a priest at St. Peter's strongly denounced some members of his congregation for operating "low-class" saloons on Sundays. Such behavior fed fears expressed in a Home Mission Board Report to the Baptist General Association of Virginia in 1904. In advocating evangelism the report warned of "the tide of immigration" bringing "the scum" of eastern Europe to "muddy" "Southern civilization." These backward people could be easily manipulated by corrupt urban politicians as well as by Catholic leaders, whose goals included a political agenda. Cities like New York and New Orleans reflected the results. In Catholic-dominated New Orleans, the famed French Quarter appeared as "a dull, dingy, and dilapidated section with decaying commerce," asserted a writer for the *Religious Herald.* By the 1920s the *Herald* as well as the *Presbyterian of the South* endorsed restrictive immigration laws.[15]

Fed by nativism, local anti-Catholic attitudes had roots in basic religious differences between Catholics and Protestants. Like their Reformation ancestors, Richmond Protestants preferred simplicity in worship and faulted Catholics for elaborate rituals. Stressing the accessibility of God to individual believers, Protestants objected to priests acting as essential intermediaries between God and humans. Protestants favored greater congregational participation in church governance than had traditionally existed within the Roman Catholic church. Few ideas disturbed Protestants more than the claim of "papal infallibility." The Bible, not the organized church or its leaders, they believed, served as the real authority for Christians. In 1901 a Richmond Methodist editor protested a papal proclamation providing for the forgiveness of sins. No ecclesiastical authority, the writer argued, had the right "to usurp the place of God and undertake to forgive sin." Prominent Protestant leaders such as George W. McDaniel and Walter Lingle described the Catholic belief of transubstantiation as a form of pagan superstition and idolatry. When reciting differences with Catholics, Protestant leaders usually condemned the Catholic church. A Presbyterian editor advised that "titles, pomp, ceremony, dress and everything else connected with the outward administration and service of the Roman Catholic church are opposed to republican simplicity and the principle that one man is as good as another man." Attributing a list of historical horrors to the Roman Catholic church, James B. Hawthorne called it "a church with a degraded ethical standard." In the past, he alleged, the church had condoned immoral, cruel, and corrupt priests, and "such a church has no power to constitute a valid gospel ministry."[16]

A greater fear stalked Protestants than their anxieties about immigrants and Catholic religious practices. The Roman Catholic church, local Protestants believed, sought to combine political and religious power. When it gained such power, warned preachers, it persecuted other religious groups. In an early-twentieth-century sermon, James B. Hawthorne charged that the Catholic church "has stained all Europe with the blood of Protestants." In 1912 George W. McDaniel labeled the Catholic church "the most dangerous influence in America today . . . a subtle force, an insidious foe, and nothing short of a vast political religious machine." Speaking to the Richmond Baptist Pastors Conference in 1914, J. J. Parsons characterized Catholicism as a "paganized political system having a religious covering." Beginning with a historical interpretation that highlighted episodes such as the Inquisition, Parsons alluded to "Protestant blood" flowing "like rivers through the streets" of Europe. The Catholic church pursued only "money and power," and, he cautioned, it opposed "free speech, free press, and free assembly." Seeking the union of church and state, the Catholic church had "laid plans for the complete subversion of our American institutions" to gain more money and power. In tones only slightly more restrained, denominational weeklies carried stories about contemporary Protestants who suffered abuses in predominantly Catholic countries. Additional testimony came from Juan Orts Gonzalez, a former Franciscan monk in Spain and the United States. As a student at Union Theological Seminary, the converted Gonzales made presentations in which he portrayed "Rome" as "muzzling" the American press and as using the Knights of Columbus to achieve political power. In 1921 the Methodist *Richmond Christian Advocate* cited statements made by a New York politician as evidence that Catholics wanted political control of the country. "They are working continuously, quietly, and secretly, perhaps, but adroitly as well, to secure political power, and when that power is assured, liberty becomes a lost treasure," it warned.[17]

The presidential candidacy of New York Gov. Alfred E. Smith unleashed anti-Catholic feeling in Richmond. Within the city some Protestant clergymen and much of the denominational press opposed Smith because of his stance on prohibition. Convinced that the Eighteenth Amendment and the Volstead Act were unenforceable, Smith advocated their repeal or modification. After accepting the Democratic Party's presidential nomination in 1928, he reaffirmed his intention to rollback prohibition, notwithstanding the party platform's promise to enforce it. To serve as chairman of the Democratic Party, he chose wealthy businessman John J. Raskob, a Catholic Republican and an ardent foe of prohibition. According to historian David Burner, Smith magnified his own weaknesses as a candidate. He stubbornly rejected advice, failed to assuage the misgivings of critics, and thereby squandered any chance of being a truly national candidate—or of being a successful one. Smith needed no additional handicaps. As a product of New York City's Tammany Hall political machine, he already carried the stigma of an organization which had a reputation for political corruption.[18]

Already perceiving prohibition to be under attack, its Virginia defenders responded forcefully to the prospect of a Smith presidency. Presumably hoping to thwart his nomination, some ministers began sounding the alarm before the 1924 Democratic Convention, where he did not succeed. After Smith's 1928 nomination, much-traveled Methodist Bishop James Cannon convened a meeting in North Carolina to organize anti-Smith Democrats and then orchestrated a southern campaign against Smith from Richmond. In addition to dispensing campaign literature, the tireless Cannon stumped the state and visited others, too. Richmond's Baptist, Methodist, and Presbyterian weeklies filled their pages with articles critical of Smith. Editors explicitly attributed their opposition to the governor's past anti-prohibition record and his present repeal stance. The *Religious Herald* maintained that any modification of existing laws would constitute a wedge that would open the door to the revival of the immoral saloons. Among the few preachers to make a public statement, Baptist John W. Storer said that he could not take a dry position on Sunday and vote wet on election day. While pillorying Smith over prohibition, several clergymen disavowed anti-Catholic motivations. Both Cannon and McDaniel had previously stated that they could support Montana Sen. Thomas Walsh, a dry Catholic. In public and private statements, Walter Lingle denied prejudice against Catholics and noted that he had once voted for a Catholic in a mayoral race rather than for a member of the church he served as a pastor. Separating prohibition from anti-Catholicism, however, required clergymen to make deft distinctions, and some did not even try. Bishop Cannon remarked that "the highest officials of the Roman Church who have spoken" opposed prohibition. Smith, Cannon claimed, "is likely to be tremendously influenced by the views of the Pope and Romish cardinals on the subject of prohibition."[19]

Indeed, lurking beneath the surface, anti-Catholic rhetoric also drove the campaign against Smith. With Smith's efforts to gain the Democratic presidential nomination in 1924, Richmond ministers began their cries of alarm. Broad Street Methodist Church hosted a program titled "Religious Liberty versus Religious Autocracy." A representative from the Federal Council of Churches made a presentation, but Cannon dominated the occasion as he recited reports of Catholic abuses of freedom of speech and religion in Latin America and Africa. Several months later in an article for the *Presbyterian of the South,* Lingle asserted that wherever "Roman Catholicism has predominated, religious liberty has perished from the land." Though providing a short list of examples, he declared that it would take "volumes to tell what Protestants have suffered in Catholic countries because they would not conform to the Catholic church." "With a Romanist in the White House," a Methodist editor wrote, "Americans believe the Vatican at Rome will be the dictator of American affairs." In 1926 McDaniel described repression of Protestants in Mussolini's Italy. "The Pope could remedy these wrongs in a day, if he would, but he is silent," maintained McDaniel.[20]

The New York governor reinforced his critics' fears. As historian Burner notes, Smith "embraced his church, simply and deeply." He therefore displayed his faith in a manner which troubled Protestants. For example, in the Governor's Mansion he hung an autographed portrait of the pope. Perhaps he committed his most grievous political indiscretion in 1926 when he hosted eight Catholic cardinals en route to an international congress in Chicago. Smith knelt before two of them and kissed the ring of Cardinal Banzano, the papal legate. Protesting this genuflection of a U.S. governor to the representative of the Vatican, the *Religious Herald* reminded readers that, unlike some other nations, the U.S. government had never recognized the pope as a temporal sovereign. The *Herald* also objected to the same ceremony for its display of the stars and stripes with the papal flag. Reacting to the episode, McDaniel imagined a similar scene in the U.S. Senate chamber with Smith as president subordinating himself to "a foreign power."[21]

By 1928 Lingle felt constrained to respond to critics who charged Protestants with intolerance. In an article which was soon reprinted as a tract, Lingle used extracts from *A Manual of Christian Doctrine,* a text attributed to a Catholic seminary professor. Lingle focused on statements suggesting that Protestants were heretics and that heads of state had a duty to proscribe heresy. He quoted an excerpt from the same text that rejected the principle of separation of church and state. If the Roman Catholic Church "would denounce any claims to civil and political power . . . the problem would be solved," argued Lingle. In a less academic presentation, one Richmond Methodist preacher devoted an hour at a Sunday evening service to explaining why he would vote against Smith. The minister proclaimed that "no first-class Catholic can be a first-class American."[22]

Other Protestant leaders resisted the political stampede sparked by anti-Catholic and prohibition fears. In fact, most local clergymen adhered to a tradition of silence about partisan politics. A Richmond newspaper estimated that no more than half a dozen ministers publicly announced their political preferences. And several ministers and laymen repudiated the political involvement of religious leaders. As a long-time champion of separation of church and state, Baptist layman John Garland Pollard—an avowedly dry politician himself—attacked Cannon for engaging in clerical politics. The *Richmond News Leader* conducted a daily forum in its editorial section about religious intolerance, and at least one prominent Baptist layman contributed a letter criticizing anti-Catholic prejudices. Believing that ministers had a special responsibility to be "separated unto the Gospel of God," Methodist Bishop Collins Denny renounced partisan political activity. Another minister crisply remarked that too many people were headed to Hell to leave time for him to deal with politics. H. D. C. Maclachlan condemned the denominational press for attacking Al Smith as a Catholic but ignoring the scandals of the previous Republican administrations. In February 1928 Maclachlan took a different tact to dissipate the climate of sectarian fear. He arranged for three hundred Protestants, Catholics, and Jews to gather at the Jefferson Hotel for a Goodwill Dinner, where they discussed social and religious issues. But the 1928 presidential campaign provided fresh evidence that there were still limits to the goodwill some local Protestants would extend to Catholics.[23]

African Americans made up a substantially larger segment of Richmond's population than did Mormons, Catholics, or Jews, but blacks also remained largely apart from white Protestants. Whether considering the spiritual welfare or the material needs of local African Americans, white clergy and laity often reacted timidly and ineffectively. Though avowed evangelicals, the city's white Protestants devoted little attention to African Americans. Given the number and size of the city's African American congregations, that minimal effort no doubt seemed appropriate. Richmond blacks worshiped at thirty-eight churches in 1900 and eighty-three churches in 1930. A number of these churches boasted rich histories, famous preachers, and substantial programs. In 1926 the city's approximately 23,500 black Baptists roughly equaled the number of the city's white Baptists. The community's earliest Baptist congregations had worshiped biracially, had begun to separate racially before the Civil War, and had organized distinct state associations after the war. Thereafter the custom of social segregation impaired interaction among members of white and black Baptist churches. From time to time, a few white Baptists advocated evangelism among African Americans, but those suggestions never won favor. In 1904 Grove Avenue's James B. Hawthorne complained that the Southern Baptist Convention had pushed aside such a proposal, which had originated with Richmond Baptist ministers and had been endorsed by the Baptist General Association of Virginia.[24]

Richmond's white Presbyterians developed Seventeenth Street Mission into their major ministry to African Americans. Founded in November 1911 by Union Seminary student Murray Grey, the mission promised to be a precarious venture. Initially using a vacant store, Grey and other students later moved the mission into another old building where they continued to improvise, using a sewing machine as a pulpit. Lamenting the indifference, ignorance, and laziness of local residents, the seminarians attributed these shortcomings to an unwholesome environment which, they suspected, would have precluded almost anyone from living virtuously. The area surrounding the mission did present a grim scene. By locating the mission in the Shockoe Bottom, Grey had placed it in the midst of one of Richmond's worst neighborhoods. The impoverished residents lived in overcrowded, dilapidated houses. Neglected by white politicians, the area suffered from inadequate sewerage facilities, unpaved streets, and periodic flooding, as well as from air and water pollution from nearby factories. Unruly saloon patrons and busy criminals furnished additional reasons to avoid this part of town, which had gained the nickname "Hell's Bottom." But Grey persevered. When the East Hanover Presbytery created an oversight committee for the mission, members reported that from 6 A.M. to 11 P.M. Grey devoted all his time and energy to the mission. The committee arranged for Grey to receive a modest salary but determined that they would have to "caution him to slow down a little."[25]

With the backing of the Presbyterian League, Seventeenth Street Mission gradually featured a substantial program. Students from Union Seminary and the General Assembly Training School aided a succession of on-site superintendents. Young people from Richmond churches also served at the mission. In addition to worship services, the Presbyterians conducted Sunday school classes and weekly prayer meetings. The mission added a playground and a small library. Volunteers taught vocational training classes as well as held special Friday afternoon gatherings for small children. When hundreds of African Americans began attending services, the decrepit old building could not accommodate them. The Presbyterian League purchased a lot and constructed a modern Sunday school building that allowed more space for games and physical recreation. One Saturday afternoon each summer adults and children boarded a string of streetcars and traveled to Bryan Park for a picnic. During the week, the mission's workers engaged in house-to-house visitation and at times dispersed badly needed food, medicine, and clothing. Although attendance at the mission fluctuated, the Sunday school attracted more than six hundred people on at least one occasion.[26]

Viewed as a success by white Presbyterians, Seventeenth Street Mission also delivered a sobering reminder of the limits of Christian love in a racially structured society. In 1928 the superintendent of the mission, Robert Wray, wrote a statement about his vision of the mission's program and met with the mission committee. "After much observation, study, thought, and prayer," he concluded that all people "black or white" "are my brothers and sisters." Believing that "my colored brother" was equally precious in God's sight, Wray wrote that he could not participate in any system designed to subordinate blacks. According to his interpretation of the Golden Rule as well as his Christian convictions, he should not engage in customs that accepted blacks as workers but excluded them as household guests or as neighbors. "Furthermore, I do not believe that the fear of intermarriage should serve as a cause for social discrimination against the colored people." Since the goal of mission work was to persuade people to follow God's will, Wray believed he needed to interact closely with members of the mission. By experiencing "the struggles, the temptations, the limitations of their lives," he could approach them on a "common ground of understanding." To do so, he needed to deal with them as any other pastor would "his own people," including meeting with them in his home. Wray recognized that his views ran "quite counter to the established policy of the Southern Presbyterian Church." He also predicted that if he implemented his convictions, he would incur criticism, churches would withhold support from the mission, and area blacks would face ill-will from whites. Wishing the mission to prosper and believing that he alone should face the consequences of his actions, Wray resigned.[27]

The *Southern Churchman* repeatedly bemoaned the meager Episcopalian support for any ministry to African Americans. Richmond, though, did boast St. Philip's Episcopal Church, a black congregation of almost three hundred communicants in 1910. Observing its fifty-fifth anniversary in 1919, St. Philip's honored its previous black ministers and extended a special invitation to "our good white friends to be present with us on this occasion." In 1903 St. John's Episcopal Church established the Chapel of the Good Shepherd in downtown Richmond and developed a Sunday school program there with the aid of black and white teachers. On the city's north side, Emmanuel Episcopal also provided Sunday school classes for African American children. The editor of the *Southern Churchman* and rector of St. James's Episcopal, William Meade Clark believed that a larger ministry to African Americans required black leaders acting without white supervision. Therefore he favored a separate black ecclesiastical jurisdiction and African American bishops. Since undoing segregation appeared to be "the hopeless dream of an uninformed visionary," blacks deserved the right to their own bishops, who could interact with them closely on the basis of "absolute social equality." By taking this approach, the denomination would show that it respected its black clergymen as much as it did "their white brethren" and would place whites and blacks on "the same footing." By this policy, the church would "give the Negro a square deal" whether or not anyone else did so. To do otherwise, he argued, was to treat blacks as "an alien and inferior race of people."[28]

Such discussions about the role of blacks affected the structure of two denominations. At the 1907 Triennial Meeting held in Richmond, Episcopal leaders debated and rejected several proposals similar to those made by Clark. A majority of the Episcopalians feared that such an ecclesiastical structure would replicate and validate Jim Crow segregation. At least one African American bishop who attended the meeting shared that assessment. In 1910 the Protestant Episcopal Church created the office of suffragan bishop, which amounted to an assistant status. Some backers of the new position believed that it would foster black leadership in the South, and several southern African Americans subsequently did fill those offices.[29]

Between 1919 and 1926, southern Methodists engaged in extensive study, negotiation, and discussion about reuniting with the Methodist Episcopal Church—or the northern Methodists, as southerners called them. Proponents of reunification attempted to resolve objections to a series of plans, but the discussion escalated into a polarizing debate among southern Methodist leaders. Some opponents of unification worried about the theological views of northerners, as well as the threat of northern domination of the new organization. The most recurring issue in the intricate, tangled controversy, though, remained the status of blacks. In 1919 a Richmond Methodist editor asserted that "except for the negro[,] . . . unification could be reached speedily." Believing that blacks and northern Methodists ultimately wanted blacks to be treated as social equals, some southern Methodists eyed any new scheme with suspicion. The Methodist Richmond Preachers Meeting adopted a resolution opposing any plan of unification that would place blacks on a level of equality with whites "in a white conference." Although a majority at the Virginia Annual Conference voted to support reunification, Richmond leaders divided over the issue with Bishop Collins Denny of Richmond acting as a leading opponent. In an elaborate argument, he objected to the unification plan because it could not ensure segregation and admitted blacks to the meetings of the General Conference. According to him, the proposal thus violated southern customs and southern laws. The Methodist Episcopal Church, South, temporarily abandoned the reunification effort after 1926.[30]

Whites and blacks occasionally met in Richmond churches. In 1901, when renowned black preacher John Jasper died, Sixth Mount Zion Baptist Church set aside a section for whites at the heavily attended funeral. In 1927, when George W. McDaniel died, W. T. Johnson, pastor of First African Baptist Church, delivered a eulogy at his funeral, but did so from a gallery area reserved for McDaniel's black friends. Having resided on the outskirts of the city, McDaniel had performed weddings of African Americans in his living room. When out-of-town speakers such as missionaries made presentations, some host churches relaxed the color line. A number of white congregations relied on black men who served as church sextons. In that capacity those black men greeted visitors, supervised church facilities, assisted leaders of church programs ranging from Sunday schools to women's societies, and prepared communion. Praised for their devotion and reliable work, some sextons gained a kinshiplike status during their lengthy and successful tenures. In 1886, at the age of sixteen, Joshua Kinney began a more than fifty-year career as sexton of Second Presbyterian Church. Later testifying to Kinney's importance, the pastor of the church stated firmly, "We depend upon his judgment."[31]

In some instances, black and white ministers acted together. In 1900 a couple of African American clergymen attended the Presbyterian Ministers Association of Richmond. African American preachers episodically visited with the Methodist Richmond Preachers Meeting. In 1911 and 1914, several black religious leaders complained about saloons in black residential neighborhoods. The Methodist preachers formed a committee to aid blacks in expelling the saloons and passed a resolution calling on the city to remove them. Thereafter the city refused to grant licenses to fourteen bars in those areas. Commending the Colored Methodist Episcopal Church in Richmond, white Methodist preachers urged their own members to assist the black congregations financially. Four white Southern Baptist clergymen and laymen served on the board of trustees of Virginia Union University, an African American institution maintained by the Northern Baptist Convention. In the 1920s the Executive Committee of the Richmond Ministerial Union (RMU) began holding joint meetings with a committee of black ministers. Following recommendations from that group, the RMU passed resolutions calling for improvements in black neighborhoods and also created an interracial committee in the 1920s.[32]

Given the tenor of the times, even these modest interactions between blacks and whites were noteworthy. During the last decade of the nineteenth century and the first decade of the twentieth century, southern culture reverberated with the ideas and policies of aggressive racists. The South's "capitulation to racism"—to use historian C. Vann Woodward's memorable phrase—meant a new constellation of injustices for African Americans. Southern states concocted a series of legal devices to deprive most blacks of the right to vote. Beginning with transportation facilities, white politicians steadily enacted statutes that prescribed racial separation in public places and private neighborhoods. Rarely did the U.S. Supreme Court uphold the rights of African Americans. Racist demagogues like Georgia's Tom Watson, Mississippi's James K. Vardaman, and South Carolina's Cole Blease used the specter of black domination to retain political power. Popular writers and journalists also relied on racist rhetoric and images. Historian I. A. Newby describes a "sudden outpouring" of "anti-Negro" literature in this period, with Thomas Dixon's *The Leopard's Spots* and *The Clansman* leading the way. Cloaked in intellectual trappings, so-called scientific racists formed an important contingent in a larger group historian Joel Williamson designates as "racial radicals," a group that "profoundly altered public and private institutions to effect real reductions in the quality of life for black people." Racial radicals argued that African Americans had retrograded since emancipation. But whites, not blacks, exhibited some of the most retrograde behavior with new rounds of lynchings and race riots. Between the lethal Atlanta riot of 1906 and World War I, the toxic tone of race relations abated slightly. During the war, however, race riots in many American cities and a rejuvenated Ku Klux Klan signaled new woes for African Americans.[33]

Conforming to the regional pattern, Virginians of the early twentieth century steadily added laws that restricted African Americans. In 1900 the state legislature passed laws requiring separate coaches for white and black railroad passengers and separate accommodations on steamboats. Meeting in 1901 and 1902, the state constitutional convention adopted a provision requiring the segregation of public schools. The constitutional convention had another mission, the disfranchisement of blacks, which it achieved with a series of devices, including a poll tax, a property qualification, and a literacy requirement. In 1904 Richmond segregated seating on its city streetcars, and in 1911 the city passed a residential segregation law.[34]

The laws reflected a racist atmosphere apparent in other facets of local culture. The daily press repeatedly portrayed blacks in derogatory terms. A *Times-Dispatch* editor described most blacks as "too shiftless and indifferent even to acquire property" assessed for school taxation. Newspapers highlighted black crimes and black failures. Readers of city newspapers could learn little about "colored people" except that a large number of them were evidently drunks, streetwalkers, gamblers, cocaine addicts, thieves, and rapists. The press especially inveighed against young blacks. Growing up without the civilizing instruction of plantation owners, these "Bad Negroes . . . let their passions run wild. Savage by nature, their savage instincts run wild and their moral nature is stunted." A Virginia Commonwealth's Attorney called them "the most lawless class in the community." Some whites laughed at the racist quips of eccentric Richmond Police Court Justice John J. Crutchfield, but blacks found only pain in such remarks and in the local legal system. Convicted in a purse snatching incident, one black man received a prison sentence of twelve years. Some racist rhetoric prompted rebuttals. In 1900 the editor of the *Southern Churchman* protested the "wild statements" of Dr. Paul Barringer, a University of Virginia professor who gained fame for his presentations about "scientific racism." Criticizing Barringer for suggesting that every young black was "a liar, a thief, a robber, a gambler, perhaps a murderer or a highwayman," the Episcopal editor denounced him for "narrow and bitter race prejudice that can only lead to harm."[35]

Still, some white Richmond Protestants dispensed a brand of racism as virulent as that of Barringer's. John J. Lafferty edited the *Baltimore and Richmond Christian Advocate* in the early twentieth century, and he used the Methodist weekly to deliver disparaging portraits of African Americans. A sixty-six-year-old Virginian, Lafferty had grown up on a plantation and idealized the racial order of a bygone era. Terming slavery "the great school in the cotton fields," he asserted that whites had rescued blacks from a harsh existence in their native land. "Official data and the books of travellers agree in representing the African as a brute, pure and simple, barely above the gorilla, and so he has been from the earliest record," declared Lafferty. Indeed, "for centuries and millenniums [*sic*], these ebon savages wallowed in their pig sties and weltered in filth, ignorance, and pools of moral pus. They in native woods are below the big baboons in courage and cleanliness," Lafferty postulated. In America, though, blacks had ascended. Within slavery, they had learned "habits of industry" and "self-control," but "this race cannot stand alone" and had begun to "retrograde" since the Civil War and emancipation. A new generation of blacks, he warned, was "growing more lazy, immoral and violent," and "provokes extermination." And educated blacks, he admonished, had proved to be especially prone to commit crimes. Repeatedly alluding to the threat of rape, Lafferty implied that modern blacks reverted to cannibalism and voodoo, which he attributed to their ancestors.[36]

Outraged over Lafferty's denunciation of blacks and his tendency to inflame "old prejudices," the *Religious Herald* called for a spirit of Christian love in race relations. A few other Protestants, though, expressed little more respect for blacks than had Lafferty. Union Seminary professor Thomas Cary Johnson also called slavery a "blessed school" for blacks. That school, however, had terminated before it had succeeded in overcoming "the ingrained habits of indolence and worthlessness, of theft, robbery, murder, rapine and lust," which had been instilled in blacks for centuries. Another Union Seminary professor, D. Clay Lilly, characterized "the Negro" as "perhaps the weakest of all races" mentally and morally. A Baptist laywoman advocated home mission work among blacks, "even if the Negro does seem to us at times the least worthy of all God's creatures." She urged fellow Christians to help uplift "a race given to immorality and steeped in vice."[37]

Other white Richmond Protestants abhorred such extreme racism and called for kindness and justice in race relations. In 1903 Richmond College's S. C. Mitchell advocated that the Southern Baptist Convention create a commission to aid African Americans and to express in "an unmistakable way" sympathetic feelings for "the wellbeing of our black brother[s]." The Richmond Baptist Ministers Association endorsed the idea and appointed a committee to promote it. Joining Mitchell as committee members, Grove Avenue's James B. Hawthorne, Leigh Street's M. Ashby Jones, Second Baptist's W. R. L. Smith, and Grace Street's C. S. Gardner constituted a cadre of pastors who advocated social Christianity and racial liberalism. With Baptist editor R. H. Pitt, they presented a racial outlook that had substantial support among other Protestant clergymen and laypersons. Accepting some prevalent racial attitudes and policies, these preachers disavowed any goal of social equality for blacks and acquiesced in disfranchisement of blacks as a political necessity. Still, as historian George Fredrickson has concluded, such moderate liberals of the early twentieth century did espouse an approach that seemed substantially different from that of the extreme racists of the era.[38]

The Baptist ministers did not hesitate to emphasize such differences. Referring to southern politicians who favored repressive racial policies, S. C. Mitchell declared: "They have confidence in might; we have confidence in right. They trust to coercion; we trust in growth." Alluding to another distinction, Mitchell concluded that "in essence, they deny not so much that they are their brother's keeper as that they are their brother's brother." By contrast Mitchell and his associates affirmed their shared humanity with African Americans. Renouncing disparaging racist rhetoric, W. R. L. Smith called it "an intolerable defamation, a coarsely ignorant blasphemy." A person with a truly Christian spirit, Smith instructed, had faith in the "manhood" and moral capacities of African Americans. To illustrate the success of blacks since emancipation, Smith cited the value of the property they had accumulated. R. H. Pitt noted the substantial number of black professionals in Richmond, and Pitt and Mitchell applauded black educational accomplishments. Believing that all humans could improve, Baptist ministers tended to view public education as a panacea. On one hand, these racial liberals revealed their own latent racism by asserting that whites had a duty as the stronger race to aid blacks. On the other hand, by recurrently invoking the principles of cooperation, fairness, and justice, the clergymen tried to chart a direction in race relations that held the prospect of healing, not hurting, everyone in the community.[39]

Yet when politicians proposed laws to disfranchise and segregate blacks, white clergymen provided little public opposition, and a few of them endorsed those policies. In supporting disfranchisement, one Methodist minister expressed his resentment that blacks had been "enfranchised through the power of bayonets." J. J. Lafferty justified disfranchisement as a means of "self-preservation" for whites to guard against "the dominacy of an inferior race." Several city religious journals endorsed suffrage restriction as necessary to eliminate political corruption and maintained that the literacy provisions should be used as a racially impartial test of citizenship. Registering a dissenting view, the Home Mission Committee of the Dover Baptist Association maintained that blacks should be educated and evangelized, not disfranchised.[40]

In 1900, when the Virginia General Assembly passed a law requiring railroads to furnish separate coaches for whites and blacks, J. J. Lafferty's *Richmond Christian Advocate* backed the legislation because "the loud, cursing odorous African seems to take pleasure in making himself a nuisance to ladies." Only one Baptist minister, M. Ashby Jones, and the *Religious Herald* protested the law. In speaking out, Jones acted in character. As pastor of Leigh Street Baptist Church between 1898 and 1908, he articulated a vision of social Christianity that included racial justice. After leaving Richmond for other southern cities, he played an active role in the Commission on Interracial Cooperation and signed the "Appeal to the Industrial Leaders of the South."[41]

Jones protested not only segregation of transportation facilities but also a proposal to base appropriations for black public schools exclusively on revenue collected from black taxpayers. White Christians had a duty, he maintained, to assist blacks in improving their minds and morals and should support public education of African Americans. Others joined Jones in this protest. James B. Hawthorne spoke about the duty of white Christians to help blacks become "a wiser, better, stronger, happier people." Believing that public education offered both whites and blacks an opportunity for advancement, S. C. Mitchell praised the use of public funds for black education as money wisely spent. Deploring the proposal to segregate funds, R. H. Pitt called it a "policy of degradation," "a policy of murder," which would stifle hopes and ambitions and would dwarf "the faculties of mind and heart and soul." The *Southern Churchman* called it a "vicious . . . unjust, unkind, reactionary and disastrous piece of legislation" that "contravenes directly in every way, every precept of the Christian religion." Local clergymen remarked that future laws might discriminate between whites of different classes or religions. The state legislature did not enact a segregated school financing law, but Virginia cities and counties found other ways of discriminating against black children. Although the Richmond Education Association consistently advocated improvements of black schools, the city spent one-half the amount per student on facilities for black education that it spent for white children. Church leaders who wanted better public education for blacks achieved only a partial victory.[42]

In condemning racial violence, however, Richmond clergymen spoke to a more receptive audience. In a community that loathed lawlessness and mobs, ministers stood in the forefront of opposition to lynching, as an episode in 1900 demonstrated. A black prisoner facing execution for murder escaped from a Portsmouth, Virginia, jail and killed two deputy sheriffs before being apprehended and jailed in Emporia, Virginia. In response to a request from a local sheriff, the governor sent troops to protect him and a white man alleged to be his accomplice. Intimidated by an angry mob, the sheriff telegraphed the governor asking him to withdraw the troops. The governor complied despite a warning from the militia colonel that violence would result. That prediction proved accurate. A biracial mob invaded the jail and lynched first the black prisoner and then the white prisoner. When S. C. Mitchell read the account in the Sunday newspaper, it "made my blood boil." Speaking at Second Baptist Church that same evening, Mitchell used the scripture "the Governor took water and washed his hands saying, 'I am innocent of the blood of this just man.'" Censuring both the mob's violence and the governor's cowardice, Mitchell called on citizens to elect leaders committed to enforcing the law. Other Richmond preachers joined Mitchell in denouncing lynching.[43]

More than a momentary outburst, Mitchell's 1900 sermon served as the first installment of a personal campaign against racial violence. In the ensuing years, he repeatedly denounced lynch mobs and those responsible for fanning racial fears and hatreds. In 1904 he formulated an extensive "Protest Against Lynching" and read it before the Richmond ministers conference, which endorsed it and recommended that the Baptist General Association of Virginia do likewise. Combining moral outrage and cold logic, Mitchell condemned lynching as "wrong" and as ineffective in deterring crime. Lynching, he warned, brutalized communities. Mobs inevitably widened the scope of their activities, executed people for a variety of alleged crimes, and tortured as well as killed their victims. Compounding such barbarity, mobs confused innocent parties with guilty ones. Furthermore, mobs undercut an essential protection for all citizens, the legal system. Civilized communities, he insisted, relied on that "sacred" system with its lengthy heritage and its embodiment of "the wisdom of mankind." Unlike mob violence, which was "chaotic and spasmodic," the law never slept. Thus, an attitude of respect for law provided the surest safety against wrongdoing, and it protected whites from potential violence by blacks. Lynching also prejudiced "the world" against the South as newspapers abroad reported such "fiendish acts" to the exclusion of southern accomplishments. As a result, frightened immigrants and investors turned elsewhere. And lynching would provoke the intervention of the federal government, which had a duty to protect its citizens. Lynching also intensified racial bitterness. By permitting lynching, white southerners shirked a responsibility. Having been denied the opportunity to vote and to select officials, each black deserved "full justice and protection." "We deny him equality; we must therefore guarantee him equity." The statement called upon preachers, teachers, lawyers, and journalists to direct the "moral sentiment of the state" against "the spirit of lynching." The *Central Presbyterian* endorsed the statement, and the Methodist Virginia Annual Conference also adopted a resolution condemning lynching.[44]

Mitchell believed that the persistent public outcry following the Emporia incident brought a virtual end to lynching in Virginia. In his memoirs, he contended that fear of political repercussions spurred subsequent governors to respond immediately to threats of mob violence. Though perhaps too sweeping, Mitchell's conclusion points to several truths. In the decades that followed, clergymen, denominational weeklies, and the daily press joined in a clamor about lynchings in Virginia and elsewhere. Horrified by the Atlanta race riot of 1906, an Episcopal editor wondered "how can a civilized, Christian community relapse so suddenly and so completely into a reign of lawlessness?" Mitchell insightfully placed much of the responsibility for that brutal episode on the shoulders of the press and politicians. Soberly observing that those killed were not criminals or suspected criminals but "were murdered simply because they were blacks," he reiterated his theme that "lynch law leads to race war." Thus, in Richmond the moral authority of the religious leaders fed a cultural and political mood that disapproved of lynching. And lynching did decline in Virginia. Historian W. Fitzhugh Brundage observes that by 1910 lynchings occurred as rarely in Virginia as they did in Illinois or Arizona. On several occasions Richmond itself avoided racial violence in the wake of alleged assaults by white and black males on females of the other race. Eschewing hysteria, community leaders and citizens of both races reacted with restraint. For example, in 1914 a white woman accused a young black man of rape, a jury acquitted him, and one observer called the verdict a popular one.

In 1928 the Virginia legislature passed an antilynching law that provided for the apprehension and punishment of lynchers.[45]

The record of racial peace did seem imperiled by the revival of the Ku Klux Klan after World War I. Nervous Richmond ministers worried that the Klan would recruit whites "antagonized by what they view as black assertiveness." Wielding fiery invective, the Klan received a frosty reception in Richmond. The Klan of the 1920s continued to parade under the banner of racial intolerance, wrapped itself in patriotism, and elevated Catholics and Jews on its list of targets. Using the cross as a symbol, Klansmen trumpeted their allegiance to traditional sexual morality, ostentatiously invaded some churches, and engaged in public displays of benevolence. In such states as Oklahoma and Indiana, Klansmen gained political clout, and the Klan of the 1920s claimed many an American city as a stronghold. But not Richmond. The so-called second Klan of the twentieth century proclaimed that its concerns extended beyond racial matters. Historians have determined that Klansmen acted with multifaceted goals and motivations. In Richmond, though, Klan critics perceived racial hostility as the central component in an agenda of intolerance, which local ministers repudiated.[46]

In November 1920 the Richmond Klan publicized its presence with an advertisement in the *News Leader.* Seeking recruits, the Klan identified itself as "a real bunch of Americans who love law and order" and who pledged to protect "pure womanhood" and the Constitution. Any "100% American" who believed in "doing things" was invited to join. As part of an apparent membership drive, the Klan later held a rally at the city auditorium and welcomed Imperial Wizard William J. Simmons. Less than a year later, Klansmen paraded in downtown Richmond. The local campaign held prospects for success. The national organization had begun an elaborate public relations effort that boosted membership across the country. In the aftermath of World War I, Richmond suffered from many of the unsettling conditions that spurred Klan growth elsewhere—an economic recession, labor disputes, and ethnic and racial tensions heightened during the war.[47]

The Klan's appearances provoked an immediate reaction from Richmond clergymen. The Sunday following the publication of the *News Leader* advertisement, a number of ministers delivered sermons about the importance of good race relations. From the pulpit of St. Paul's Episcopal Church, Walter Russell Bowie began a protracted, personal counteroffensive against the Klan. In sermons and in articles for the *Southern Churchman,* he denounced the organization. The world war, he maintained, had incited people to hate and had unleashed "old, savage instincts." Antagonized by signs of black assertiveness, some whites now turned to the Klan "with the apparent purpose to terrorize the blacks." Spreading "the poison of mob lawlessness," the Klan constituted "an insult" to orderly government. Citing the Klan's record of violence, Bowie condemned it for fueling hostility to Catholics and Jews as well as African Americans. Noting that the veiled faces carried a "veiled threat to colored people," the Episcopal rector called for a law prohibiting disguises as well as a prohibition of future Klan parades. "Any band of men who operate without daring to show their faces," he warned, formed a danger to the community. When Bowie accepted a call to Grace Church in New York City in 1923, the African American newspaper *St. Luke's Herald* lauded him as "colored Richmond's friend," praised his courage for denouncing the Klan, and credited him with putting it "out of commission" in Richmond. That credit proved slightly premature. Bowie's successor as rector of St. Paul's, Beverley Tucker, continued to denounce the Klan. So did Episcopal city missionary R. Cary Montague, who, like Bowie, used columns in the *Southern Churchman* to catalog the Klan's misdeeds. Montague further characterized the Klan as an economic menace because its lawlessness discredited the South and frightened away investors.[48]

Urging Christians to oppose the Klan, Montague believed that white ministers could do much to reduce racial animosity. Some preachers who agreed denounced the Klan. Seeing no need for the Klan, the pastor of Laurel Street Methodist Church believed that blacks should be permitted to develop "as God intended," "not as prejudicial whites" insisted. A former pastor of Laurel Street, Joseph M. Rowland had become editor of the *Richmond Christian Advocate.* He laced the newspaper with blunt, pithy, and sarcastic barbs aimed at the Klan. Announcing that he opposed "your name, your aims, and your methods," he designated the group as a menace because it wanted "strife between the races" and a breach between the North and South. If the Klan really did believe in Christian principles, it should be ashamed of how little Christians had done to aid blacks spiritually or politically. If Klansmen opposed Catholics, challenged Rowland, they should do so "the manly way," in the open, not behind masks. If Klansmen really wanted to help the South, they should "shut-up and work." At times ridiculing them as "spooks," he furnished his address "should they care to make a midnight visit."[49]

In Richmond few Klansmen stood ready to make visits. On two different occasions the organization mustered merely six hundred members for parades—a puny showing compared to the thousands who marched in processions of labor unions and men's Bible classes. Only fifty Klansmen arranged to attend a worship service at an Apostolic church. In a study of urban Klans of the 1920s, historian Kenneth Jackson estimated the size of the Richmond Klan to be one of the smallest in the South and to be comparable to those in Scranton, Pennsylvania, and Worcester, Massachusetts. In October 1922 the imperial wizard suspended the Richmond Klan and its members for failure to make proper financial reports and for withholding funds from headquarters in Georgia. The Richmond Klan renounced the national organization, which then won a court injunction requiring the local to return equipment, paraphernalia, and funds to the Georgia office. The parties apparently resolved the dispute, and the Richmond Klan remained active if unimpressive. With the national organization racked with scandal and controversy, a Richmond newspaper celebrated "the Klan's decline" in 1924. Having never achieved great heights, the Richmond Klan had little distance to fall. According to historian Nancy MacLean, throughout the South the Klan used clergymen to "sanctify its methods." In Richmond, though, only two Protestant ministers publicly endorsed the Klan, and one of them soon left his church to establish an independent congregation. Instead, some prominent ministers and editors of religious weeklies forcefully denounced the Klan and continued to condemn mob lawlessness.[50]

Coinciding with the ominous rebirth of the Klan, the birth of the Commission on Interracial Cooperation (CIC) brought hope for improved race relations throughout the nation. Organized in 1919 and 1920, the Atlanta-based CIC relied on the leadership of former Methodist minister Will Alexander. Under the aegis of the CIC, hundreds of state and local committees tried to reduce racial tensions and address injustices. In October 1920 the CIC sponsored a southwide women's conference in Memphis. Six weeks later, the Women's Section of the Virginia State Interracial Committee gathered at Seventh Street Christian Church. The interdenominational group included Jews and Catholics and representatives from the entire state. Richmond Protestant laywomen accounted for the majority of delegates, however. The women issued a lengthy statement published in most of the state denominational newspapers. Impressed that southerners faced a "new period of adjustment," the women believed that "righteousness, justice, peace and good will can be established between races of different colors." Citing the Golden Rule, the women deplored any conditions that would tend to "widen the breach between peoples." Believing that changes in public opinion could bring progress and convinced that women played major roles in shaping such "public sentiment," the delegates framed four suggestions. First, schools and churches should serve as forums to educate whites about the "condition of our negro neighbors." Second, individual communities should supply better health, educational, recreational, and welfare services to African Americans and should improve their "general living conditions." Third, newspapers should devote more attention to black achievements and less attention to "delinquencies."

Fourth, lawlessness "by self-constituted bodies" should not be tolerated. After issuing this substantial document, the women's section receded from public sight, but several of its members did take steps to implement the recommendations.[51]

The women's male counterparts moved forward quietly. S. C. Mitchell, J. T. Mastin, and Douglas Freeman served as members of the state interracial committee, and Randolph-Macon President R. E. Blackwell acted as chairman. In 1924, meeting at Seventh Street Christian Church, the committee called for an effective housing law, better equipment for Richmond's African American Virginia Union University, better library facilities for the city's black citizens, and African American probation officers for juvenile courts. From the mid-1920s, Beverley Tucker hosted quarterly meetings in St. Paul's parish house, and he emerged as a consistent champion of racial justice. One participant, S. C. Mitchell, commended the biracial committee for its "frank" discussion of problems.[52]

Meanwhile a new group of racists created more trouble than had the Ku Klux Klan. Propounding some of the popular racist theories of the era, a small group of Virginia zealots organized the Anglo-Saxon Clubs of America. Reviving past fears about miscegenation, the leaders hysterically warned that "racial amalgamation" threatened the existence of white civilization. Though never a large organization, the Anglo-Saxon Clubs succeeded in lobbying for the adoption of a sequence of state "racial integrity" laws. In 1924 the legislature passed an antimiscegenation measure that forbade any white person from marrying anyone of another race and defined as white any person without a trace of blood other than Caucasian. The Anglo-Saxon clubs promoted a 1926 proposal to require segregated seating at public gatherings. Although a few local clergymen endorsed the 1926 segregation bill, the Richmond Ministerial Union opposed it. The Methodist Richmond Preachers Meeting requested that the legislature postpone action until the issue could be examined more carefully. The Methodists admonished that the proposed statute would "seriously disturb the friendly and harmonious relations now existing between the races in our state." Beverley Tucker and other members of the Richmond interracial committee testified against the measure, but the legislature passed it.[53]

In 1929 Richmond racists seized upon the 1924 racial integrity law as a device to reinstitute residential segregation. In 1917 the U.S. Supreme Court had ruled Louisville's residential segregation law to be unconstitutional. Concluding that Richmond's six-year-old residential segregation ordinance was virtually identical to Louisville's, Judge John Crutchfield determined that the local statute was also "unconstitutional and void" and that all cases brought before him should be dismissed. For decades most Richmond blacks had resided in a cluster of seven largely segregated neighborhoods, but some whites still feared the possibility of black incursions into previously all-white areas. In 1929 the city council considered a scheme to circumvent the language of the 1917 ruling. Restructuring the city's old segregation ordinance, proponents changed the criterion for separation from a person's race to a person's ineligibility for marriage under Virginia's racial integrity act of 1924. Protesting the proposal at a large public meeting, Richmond African Americans expressed their frustration and anger. Richmond blacks, they stated, "have borne wrongs and injustices at the hands of the government of Richmond with only an occasional protest hoping that the conscience of Richmond would finally awake and that right and justice would unseat race prejudice and intolerance."[54]

The conscience of some white Richmonders was awake, and African Americans did not stand alone in opposing the new ordinance. Lucy Randolph Mason and interracial committee leaders Mary-Cooke Branch Munford and Richard W. Carrington spoke out against the proposal. Carrington, a white lawyer, addressed a thousand people at Hood Temple, African Methodist Episcopal Zion Church. At St. Paul's, Beverley Tucker called on Richmond to be just. The Richmond Ministerial Union, the Central Trades and Labor Council, the Chamber of Commerce, the Richmond Bar Association, the Real Estate Exchange, and the interracial committee urged the city council to study the issue further before voting on it. City newspapers labeled the measure unjust and advocated greater interracial cooperation. Calling the segregation ordinance "the counsel of hate or the counsel of despair," the *News Leader* deprecated both as unworthy of Richmond. For the seventh annual observance of Race Relations Sunday, Beverley Tucker and R. W. Carrington spoke at Leigh Street Colored Methodist Episcopal Church. Two days later, the Richmond board of aldermen unanimously approved the segregation ordinance. In less than a year, a federal circuit court declared the law to be unconstitutional.[55]

During the controversy, opponents of the segregation ordinance tried to prick the conscience of white Richmond. In an extended editorial, the *Richmond Christian Advocate* represented the essential issue as "not racial equality, but what is the duty of Christians to blacks." Praising black Virginians for making "a real contribution to the state," Methodist editor Joseph M. Rowland criticized whites for trying to confine them to "uncomfortable and unsanitary" slums, where they paid high rents and received few services for their taxes. Calling on whites to apply the Golden Rule, he counseled that "we must apply the Gospel we preach on Sunday to these issues on Monday if we carry out the program of Jesus." Objecting to the efforts to limit blacks to neglected neighborhoods, Lucy Randolph Mason also demanded that the city provide better services to those parts of the city. Local newspaper columnist Cally

Ryland as well as interracial committee leaders Tucker and Carrington hammered at the injustice of the horrid living conditions in black neighborhoods. These statements did not qualify as revelations. For years black and white reformers, including clergymen, had criticized the city's inattention to its black neighborhoods. But in 1929 reformers anticipated definite recommendations for action from the Negro Welfare Survey Committee of the Richmond Council of Social Agencies.[56]

In the fall of 1928 the Negro Welfare Survey Committee had begun its work thanks to financial support from St. Andrew's Association. During the next year, the committee gathered information upon which to initiate a "practical, city-wide social program" to address the needs of African Americans. The project relied on a twelve-member general committee, which included judges, educators, physicians, and Lucy Randolph Mason. Seventy citizens, including layman Rolvix Harlan and laywomen Frances Scott and Katherine Hawes, composed five subcommittees focusing on particular subjects. Selected as director, June Purcell Guild gathered and collated much of the data and prepared reports. She and subcommittee members delved into documents produced by national, state, and local government agencies and by a host of private organizations, including labor unions, insurance companies, and health associations. The committee personally conferred with nine outside consultants who visited Richmond and secured written advice from others. More information came from questionnaires distributed to schoolchildren, employers, physicians, and judges. By making more than 1,100 house-to-house visits, fieldworkers also interviewed residents of two African American neighborhoods.[57]

The survey committee summarized its findings in a 136-page report. Although Richmonders already recognized that "in every division of human welfare the position of the Negro was immensely disadvantageous," the survey furnished facts not "commonly known." Suffering higher mortality rates than whites, African Americans experienced a much greater incidence of infant mortality and tuberculosis. Inadequate access to health services magnified the harm produced by overcrowded housing in neighborhoods with poor sanitation. Unlike white areas, black neighborhoods lacked any public baths and public swimming pools. A high illiteracy rate among African Americans coincided with a city school system that spent twice as much per capita for white schoolchildren as it did for black schoolchildren. Only one kindergarten served black children, and black school teachers taught classes substantially larger than those in white schools. Excluded from some occupations, blacks received lower incomes than whites for the same jobs and faced more frequent bouts of unemployment. With many black married women forced to work, the city's almost nonexistent nursery facilities for blacks left many African American children without needed attention.[58]

In a conclusion the survey committee combined overall recommendations with those of its subcommittees. The committee advocated the appointment of a new, permanent council to continue studying the problems of local blacks and to do "everything possible to carry out the recommendations" of the survey committee. Consistently expressing concern about children, the committee urged an expansion of recreational facilities and programs as well as additional, better equipped black public schools. The committee advocated a stronger health education program, particularly aimed at prenatal instruction and early diagnosis and treatment of tuberculosis. To provide better medical care, the city should use more trained black nurses and physicians. Each of the subcommittees focused on additional needs ranging from elevating wages to paving, cleaning, lighting, and policing streets in black neighborhoods. Black schoolchildren deserved a wider curriculum, more kindergartens, and better paid teachers, concluded the education subcommittee. Noting that "the needs are so many, so diverse, and so complicated," the committee considered its own comprehensive document a necessary resource for anyone attempting to "make an actual start" toward remedying those conditions.[59]

Issued in December 1929, the survey committee's report might have easily vanished amidst the financial turmoil of the Great Depression. But Richmond did create a new biracial Negro Welfare Council, and it sustained the direction charted by the committee. The young rector of Grace and Holy Trinity Episcopal Church, Charles Sheerin, served as the council's chairman. His wife, a native Richmonder, later recalled that "constructive discussion of the race question was difficult." Still, with the council's prompting, the city did take some steps. A private campaign garnered funds for a gymnasium and recreation building in Jackson Ward, the largest African American neighborhood. The city opened a well-equipped playground for black children, created a new branch library for African Americans, expanded kindergarten programs, and built a summer camp for black youth. The city also hired African Americans as principals for black schools and included blacks in Richmond jury panels. In retrospect Lucy Randolph Mason concluded that the survey committee's report and findings proved "useful for years to come." In 1934 director June Purcell Guild identified a combination of forces, including the survey, that "have revolutionized the status of the Richmond Negro." She noted "that tolerance is increasing and tolerance is outstandingly needed." She remarked about a growing tendency of whites to deal courteously with African Americans. Purcell, however, knew that the modest progress left much that still shouted for attention. In a national magazine article, she characterized Richmond as "amazing in constant references to the Living Savior of men and willingness to let His faithful followers suffer neglect."[60]

In 1926 Episcopalian R. Cary Montague wrote that it "is the duty of all Christian white people to strive to procure justice for the Negroes." Designating housing and recreational facilities as priorities, Montague joined the Richmond Urban League, an organization destined soon to play a major role in addressing the needs of the city's African Americans. An exceptional person, Montague shook hands with blacks and violated white southern racial etiquette by addressing them with the titles of Mr., Mrs., and Miss. He and a few other white Protestant leaders did reach out to people of other faiths and races. By their words and actions, they helped minimize harmful actions against Jews, Catholics, and African Americans. Yet those leaders had only a little success in enhancing the lives of members of other faiths and races and thus did not achieve a larger goal. As young Presbyterian Robert Wray discerned at the Seventeenth Street Mission, the city's white Protestants had not expanded the boundaries of their good intentions to treat others as true brothers and sisters of a shared heavenly creator.[61]

10

"A World Made New"

Ten days after the United States entered World War I, Walter Russell Bowie spoke from the pulpit at St. Paul's Episcopal Church, where Robert E. Lee and Jefferson Davis had worshiped during the Civil War. In a prescient and hopeful sermon titled "A World Made New," Bowie warned his congregation of the wartime perils of spiritual despair and mob lawlessness. Still, he proposed, the war could signal the death of an old order and thereby create the opportunity to shape "on earth conditions under which all may live in honor, in happiness, and in self-respect." Within months Bowie donned a chaplain's uniform, joined a local hospital unit, and shipped out to France. By Armistice Day, 1925, Bowie had only slightly altered his earlier vision. He told a Richmond audience that "the soul of America" must vindicate the dead by faithfully embracing the future and "looking forward to a world living in peace." Bowie's words and deeds signified a larger transformation among Richmond Protestants in the early twentieth century. Increasingly attentive to conditions overseas before 1914, they were profoundly affected by World War I. Wartime experiences, though, did not so much disillusion as educate the city's church leaders, who thereafter strongly championed the cause of international peace. Thus, the war accelerated their extension of avenues of faith beyond Richmond into the arena of international relations.[1]

Prior to 1914, Richmond Protestants related to other lands primarily through mission endeavors. Union Theological Seminary trained students as missionaries, maintained a Society for Mission Inquiry, which fostered mission interests, and proudly counted alumni who served overseas. Missionaries on furlough often stayed in the city and spoke at local churches. Denominational newspapers featured stories about mission fields, particularly during times of crisis such as the Boxer Rebellion or the recurrent famines in China and India. After 1911 Presbyterians published their monthly *Missionary Survey* in Richmond.[2]

Southern Baptists maintained the headquarters of their Foreign Mission Board in the city. The board's tireless and skillful corresponding secretary,

Robert Josiah Willingham, presided over an organization with limited resources and substantial responsibilities. Not only did the board interview missionary candidates, coordinate missionary assignments, and raise and allocate funds, it published tracts and a monthly magazine. It also supervised the operations of hospitals, schools, colleges, seminaries, and publishing houses overseas. Willingham accomplished these tasks with the aid of a tiny staff. As a recent historian of the board concludes, much of the board's work was done by "able and dedicated" Richmond clergymen and laymen. As Willingham's daughter recounted, her mother stayed as busy as her father, offering counsel as well as lodging and meals to both returning missionaries and candidates.[3]

Congregations of all the major denominations stayed in touch with their own members who served as missionaries and with other missionaries whom they supported financially. Bessie Farrar of Seventh Street Christian Church became a missionary after her congregation and Third Christian helped to pay for her education. Grace Street Baptist counted four missionary members in the century's first three decades. At Union Station Methodist in 1908, Sallie Smith announced her decision to prepare to serve overseas. Bainbridge Street Baptist Church paid the salary of an associate minister who served in Japan, and Calvary Baptist supported a minister serving in China. When Grace Street Presbyterian and the Church of the Covenant merged in 1915, they supported three missionaries. Presbyterians and Episcopalians tended to head the Huguenot Society, an interdenominational organization composed of descendants of early Virginia Huguenots. That group held annual meetings, contributed funds to a Protestant missionary in France, and relied on laywoman Fannie E. Halyburton for leadership.[4]

Indeed, church women provided the early local impetus for foreign missions. Richmond Baptist women traced their organized support of missionaries to 1813 and inherited a tradition of hard-earned autonomy from male control. The Virginia Disciples of Christ created their Christian Woman's Board of Missions in 1876 at a meeting held at Seventh Street Christian Church. In the nineteenth century, women within other denominations organized missionary societies at the state, local, and congregational levels. Those groups continued to grow steadily in the early 1900s. A woman's missionary society of a particular church often raised funds to support a specific missionary whom they sponsored overseas.[5]

Area women's missionary societies gathered in annual denominational meetings, where they worshiped together, discussed work of the past year, reported amounts of money raised, and considered plans for united activity. For example, in 1904 the Woman's Foreign Missionary Union of East Hanover Presbytery decided to raise funds for a library to be carried by a Union Seminary graduate as he returned to his native Persia as a missionary. The longtime president of the group, Avis B. Stewart, also proposed to collect money to build a house for furloughed missionaries. Despite raising thousands of dollars by 1916, the women faced a veto from the male leaders of the Virginia Synod. The women voted not to "fall in line" with the synod, but instead "hold the money in trust, hoping to build a Virginia home some day." Union Theological Seminary President Walter W. Moore soon emerged as a valuable ally of the women. In a letter to a member of a committee reviewing the decision, Moore advised that "nothing would afford as much needed relief and help to our wearied and straitened missionaries" as such a facility. "Some day" came in 1920, when the first of two "Mission Court" buildings was completed at the new General Assembly Training School (ATS) across the street from Union Seminary. Opened in 1914, ATS itself offered a two-year curriculum that prepared unordained workers for a variety of roles, including service as foreign missionaries. The inspiration for the school dated to 1907, when a young Richmond woman successfully requested Moore's assistance in taking seminary courses to prepare her as a missionary.[6]

At meetings of the women's societies, visiting missionaries often spoke. In 1905 the women of First Presbyterian invited a distinguished black missionary to address them about his work in the Congo, and African Americans joined them, albeit in the church's gallery. In 1914 Richmond women created an Interdenominational Missionary Union, primarily to involve young people. In a highly organized two-week effort, the ladies utilized committees, circulars, letters, and rallies to enlist 1,147 youngsters. Led by Lucy Ambler Mason, the Richmond branch of the international, nondenominational Mission to Lepers met annually at city churches and raised funds for asylums throughout the world.[7]

Beginning in 1907, the Laymen's Missionary Movement (LMM) challenged Richmond males to add their minds and financial muscle to foreign mission programs. The New York–based LMM announced as its goal the preaching of the Gospel to the entire world during the lives of the current generation, a plan the Baptist *Religious Herald* politely labeled as "too ambitious." To accomplish that task, the LMM utilized familiar avenues: organization, lay participation, specialized leadership, and interdenominational cooperation. In 1907 Richmond delegates attended a national LMM convention and returned with enthusiastic endorsements of the organization's program. At a subsequent December banquet in the Jefferson Hotel, J. Campbell White, general-secretary of the LMM, enlisted prominent laymen by regaling them with reasons and statistics. He asserted that Christians had a duty to preach to those currently alive, and, he concluded, "if we will, the world could be conquered for Christ in this generation." This LMM venture was a practical plan, not a quixotic dream, he argued. White introduced calculations about the costs of maintaining missionaries in the field, estimated the number of additional workers needed to reach the 675 million "heathen people," and projected the total expense of sending those missionaries overseas. According to his tabulations, Christians needed to quadruple the number of missionaries sent abroad, an endeavor requiring an additional $80 million during the next twenty-five years. Turning his attention to area churches, he used a chart to display annual contributions to foreign missions. Since Richmond already raised $25,000 annually for missions by relying mostly on "women, children, and preachers," he asked, what could be achieved if local "manhood" joined a continent-wide campaign? Following presentations by other LMM proponents, local lay leaders endorsed the program, and the group created a committee to organize later meetings.[8]

An October 1909 regional convention transformed Richmond into an LMM center. Prior to that meeting, local clergy and laity wrote and visited churches across the state. Almost one thousand men from approximately three hundred churches throughout Virginia registered for the gathering. For four days thirty experts made presentations. The foremost speakers were LMM leader J. Campbell White, a missionary to Japan, and R. J. Willingham, who, having returned from a trip to Asia, made passionate appeals for support. Despite stormy weather, five hundred laymen attended the opening banquet on Saturday evening. After missionaries spoke at worship services on Sunday morning, White talked to between fourteen hundred and two thousand men at the city auditorium in the afternoon. Women's missionary societies simultaneously held their own interdenominational meeting at Second Baptist. The business week notwithstanding, the men assembled again on Monday morning to listen to talks and join in strategy sessions about fund-raising. On Tuesday members attended rallies held by their respective churches and denominations and then planned campaigns and set specific financial goals. Some churches hosted luncheons and distributed subscription cards to expedite fund-raising.[9]

The LMM summoned and Richmond responded. For the next seven years, the city hosted conventions, welcomed national LMM speakers, and conducted congregational fund-raising with the proceeds sent to the mission programs of respective denominations. Local committees encouraged contributions, reported results, and monitored progress in achieving goals. At St. John's Episcopal Church, the committee's chairman wrote letters to all male members who did not contribute to missions. In 1913 Richmond College gave mathematics professor R. E. Gaines a one-year leave of absence to serve as a field secretary for the LMM. By 1914 the city's six major white Protestant denominations reported 38,888 LMM members from eighty-four churches. Sums designated for foreign missions soared. Between 1908 and 1911, Seventh Street Christian Church's contributions for foreign missions tripled. Between 1909 and 1913, annual foreign mission gifts from area Baptist, Methodist, and Episcopal churches climbed from $27,132 to $44,344. These increases reflected a larger pattern apparent in reports to all state denominational bodies. To succeed, the LMM tapped the cooperational and organizational skills Richmond laymen had already mastered, and it relied on specialists whose facts impressed local laymen. In doing so it brought the international arena closer to Richmond.[10]

The substantial interest in missions was rarely matched with attention to other facets of foreign affairs. In 1904 a grumpy editorial in the *Richmond Times-Dispatch* exclaimed, "Why a preacher should turn away from the richness of the Bible to discuss Panama and Russia and automobiles is past our comprehension." That comment seemed unnecessary in Richmond, where such discussions were infrequent. Denominational weeklies rarely questioned or criticized American foreign policy. Local ministers did speak at public rallies protesting mistreatment of Jews in Russia. Faced with the carnage of the Russo-Japanese War, denominational newspapers calmly concluded that God was using the war to convince the world of the necessity of peace.[11]

Departing from a prevalent complacency about distant matters, some religious leaders took actions that presaged the strong stand of churches for international peace in the 1920s. Pine Street Baptist Church provided funds to send Richmond delegates to a peace congress in London in 1890. That same year Richmond Presbyterian minister W. A. Campbell had initiated a campaign for international arbitration treaties. Supported by other Richmond Presbyterians, he brought a lengthy petition to the General Assembly of the Presbyterian Church in the United States, which endorsed it. To carry forward the idea to a peace conference in New York, Campbell and other local religious leaders organized a national, interdenominational Ecclesiastical Branch of the Peace Arbitration Movement, headquartered in Richmond. This organization formed committees of correspondence, participated in a series of meetings in New York and Chicago, and joined a two-decade effort to garner approval of arbitration treaties by major nations. Campbell and other Richmond Protestant leaders clearly contributed to the larger arbitration movement, but as church historian E. T. Thompson observed, Campbell died in 1896 without seeing the fruits of the arbitration campaigns.[12]

Within the Richmond religious community, though, the arbitration idea remained popular. In 1904 supporters of international arbitration held a rally at the Academy of Music. In one of the presentations, S. C. Mitchell deplored the substantial costs of nations maintaining large armies and navies even during periods of peace. Citing the devastation of the Russo-Japanese War, he reviewed the past successful use of arbitration procedures to avert international conflicts. Referring to the South's suffering during the American Civil War, Mitchell suggested that the region should exert pressure on its U.S. senators to "support the principle of arbitration which means peace and good will towards men." Those assembled at the meeting adopted a series of resolutions in favor of arbitration, including a statement urging the U.S. Senate to ratify several pending arbitration treaties. In a 1906 address Mitchell traced the ascending international role of the United States and asserted that the nation had a special mission to fulfill in the world community. Representatives of the American Peace Society occasionally spoke to church groups, and some local ministers delivered "Peace Day" sermons to their congregations. Richmond Methodist preachers authored an arbitration resolution which the Virginia Annual Conference adopted. Like state Methodist and Baptist newspapers, the *Central Presbyterian* backed arbitration treaties and applauded arbitration champion William Jennings Bryan.[13]

By 1910 the U.S. government had finally tried to implement arbitration agreements. The Methodist *Baltimore and Richmond Christian Advocate* celebrated the results and outlined the prospects for peace. Arbitration, it proclaimed, was "banishing war." Five hundred disputes had already been so resolved, including 136 in 1909. The 1910 Pan-American Congress had recently adopted an agreement to arbitrate international financial claims. International law was further mitigating the prospects for war with nations accepting the neutral status of Switzerland, Belgium, Luxembourg, Norway, Honduras, the Straits of Magellan, and the Suez Canal. "Why not," asked the writer "extend this neutral ground to cover the earth?" The United States, Germany, and Great Britain should take the lead, the editorial concluded, to form a "Peace League" to outlaw war.[14]

In retrospect the optimism evoked by the American arbitration movement proved to be not only excessive but also unfounded. The arbitration process itself did hold promise as a practical diplomatic tool. In 1911 the United States negotiated treaties with England and France that were, according to historian Merle Curti, "considered as the most advanced arbitration agreements that the governments of great powers had ever sponsored." But the treaties suffered the same fate as earlier arbitration treaties. The U.S. Senate insisted on a host of amendments that, as Curti notes, "robbed" them of their special value. Apparently oblivious of the Senate's habit of mutilating such treaties, Richmond religious leaders focused instead on the achievements of the arbitration campaign.[15]

Euphoria about other international matters also seemed excessive. When France's Capt. Alfred Dreyfus was finally freed after twelve years of unjust incarceration, Centenary Methodist's W. J. Young saw evidence of God's active intervention. Perhaps justice was slow, admitted Young, but "the world we live in is a righteous world, organized on the side of justice and truth." Walter Russell Bowie later remarked that before World War I there was "an almost universal assumption that we were living in an era which would naturally continue to be prosperous and peaceful." Despite expressing support for arbitration, Richmond's clergymen apparently did not participate in any of the three prewar Protestant peace organizations. In January 1914 R. H. Pitt seemed to recognize this oversight, called for "a great concerted movement of Christendom against the brutality of the ruin of war," and lamented that organized Christianity had played "little or no part" in the movements for international peace.[16]

When war erupted in Europe in August 1914, it intruded into a Richmond enjoying the benefits of more than a decade of economic success, progressive reforms, and church growth. The *Richmond News Leader* advised: "We cannot become involved in the war. Of this we can be certain, for this we can be grateful to God. . . . We are isolated; we are secure; we are self-sustaining; we are able." At first, as the war intensified overseas, it did little to disrupt the community. In 1914 Richmond leaders celebrated the city's selection as the site for one of the Federal Reserve's regional banks. In 1915 the public health campaign reached its zenith, and a new compulsory education law increased school attendance. In February 1916, more than 1,800 delegates assembled for a Laymen's Missionary Movement convention, and in March churches conducted a lay-led, citywide revival that added thousands of converts to their congregations.[17]

Still, observant citizens paid attention to gathering storm clouds. Reporting battles on land and sea, Richmond newspapers also headlined atrocities allegedly committed by the Germans. The Richmond branch of the American Locomotive Company converted to manufacturing munitions. In October 1915 Richmond public schools began offering classes for foreign-born residents, a program aided by the U.S. Bureau of Naturalization, which supplied the names and addresses of aliens to the school board. In May 1915, after speaking to the Huguenot Society, a French minister addressed the congregations of Second Presbyterian and St. Paul's about the damaging impact of the war on church work in his country. With the leadership of Lucy Ambler Mason, a

Belgium relief committee busily solicited funds. In a letter to a friend in Scotland, Walter W. Moore reported how the local ladies "stationed everywhere on our streets for Belgium Tag Day" distributed tags marked "Belgium Sufferers," invited contributions, and quickly raised thousands of dollars. In October 1916 laypersons also sought support for Armenian refugees in Syria.[18]

At first local religious leaders had been totally stunned by the war's outbreak, coming, as the *Religious Herald* noted, on the eve of an international peace conference. A Methodist minister called the war an "awful shock" awakening Americans from the dream that the world was on the brink of abolishing war. The Episcopal *Southern Churchman* called the war a "slanderous denial of the religion" the warring nations professed. The religious press counseled the devout to pray for an end to the war and expressed faith that God might have some positive purpose in permitting the awful conflict to occur.[19]

Opponents of military preparedness spoke loudly and often. Visiting Richmond for a meeting of the Executive Committee of the Federal Council of Churches, William Jennings Bryan addressed thousands of people at the city auditorium. He warned that war preparation cultivated "suspicion and hate and hate precipitates strife." Most of the religious press rejected preparedness, charging that like European militarism, it would lead to war itself. Local Methodist leaders were particularly outspoken in their denunciations. James Cannon condemned preparedness "propaganda." At nearby Ashland, Randolph-Macon College President R. E. Blackwell repudiated college military training programs as "undemocratic and unChristian." One Richmond Methodist preacher charged the Wilson administration with a policy of "indefinite military expansion," propelled by army and navy administrators and munitions makers. When Richmond's mayor called for a preparedness parade, another Methodist minister sardonically suggested that someone should bring the "suffering, destitute, maimed, and broken people" of Europe to Richmond to demonstrate the value of preparedness.[20]

Yet others disagreed, and their ranks grew. In November 1914 Walter W. Moore wrote a friend in Glasgow, Scotland, that the "defeat of Prussian militarism is a necessity for the preservation of civilization and righteousness." R. H. Pitt voiced similar sentiments, and H. D. C. Maclachlan announced his support for preparedness. Only in 1917 did the *Southern Churchman*, a longtime opponent of preparedness, reach the same conclusion. By then most clergymen shifted their positions because of reports about German war conduct and because of their respect for Woodrow Wilson, whom they viewed as a modern Christian hero. They believed that Wilson was a moral leader who worked diligently for peace and who was not subject to political pressure. Praising Wilson's war address, James Cannon explained that "only the positive conviction that our duty absolutely demands it can reconcile the Christian to a declaration of war—with all that inevitably follows in its train."[21]

When the United States entered the war in February 1917, Richmond clergymen emphasized the nation's idealistic reasons for fighting. Bowie and T. Clagett Skinner, the pastor of Second Baptist Church, reminded their congregations that American ideals included toleration of all people, even war resisters and foreigners. The monthly church newspaper, the *Monumental Messenger,* urged prayers for "our enemies" and for deliverance from hatred and bitterness, a recurrent message in the Protestant community in early 1917. The *Southern Churchman* warned that the soul that hates "loses somewhat its own worth." Baptist Frederic W. Boatwright, president of the University of Richmond, predicted that any hatred caused by the war would perish and the way would be cleared for international brotherhood.[22]

Patriotic fervor soon produced other messages with harsher, more bellicose tones. One of the first salvos came from Methodist minister and author Edward L. Pell. In a 1917 book *What Did Jesus Really Preach About War?* he criticized the apparent lethargy of American Christians in confronting the menace overseas and tried to awaken their consciences to their moral obligation to fight. Referring to Germany's invasion of neutral Belgium, Pell contended that the United States had no right to "stand indifferently by while a tyrannical government grinds its heel in the face of a prostrate nation." Christians had a responsibility to protect the innocent, combat oppression and savagery, and fight for a peace based on a righteous order. Pell suggested that a "real man" could fight without hating. He repeatedly charged that pacifists were biblical literalists and implied that they were cowards. Pell characterized Germany as thirsting for world power. The German government, he claimed, had used that country's universities to convert its citizens into machines devoid of spiritual values. Pell's book provided an early taste of a new mixture of religion and militant patriotism.[23]

After the United States entered the war, a local newspaper admonished that "the blood of the American army will be on the head of the American people if every man and every woman does not enlist to the fullest in the army of service and of saving." There was no reason to fear lethargy in Richmond, which readily rallied to the flag. Newspapers carried such slogans as "If You Side-Step Today, You May Goose-Step Tomorrow." Each day the local press announced the names of men who had enlisted in the army, and columnists labeled those who did not as "shirkers." By 1918 so many workers had left to serve in the armed forces that only half the city's union members marched in the annual Labor Day parade. In October 1917 the city inaugurated its first Liberty Loan campaign with a spectacular parade that was eighteen blocks long. Richmonders pledged more than $69 million during four loan campaigns, and 40,000 citizens joined the Red Cross. Citizens cultivated victory gardens and observed meatless, wheatless, and porkless days as well as gasless Sundays. Local merchants equipped a "win-the-war kitchen," which demonstrated "patriotic cookery." In schools children attended patriotic rallies, bought War Savings Stamps, made garments for the Red Cross, and planted gardens.[24]

The war's darker and difficult aspects also surfaced. The head of the University of Virginia's journalism department was dismissed for allegedly making pacifist remarks. In December 1917, when young officer John A. Cutchins visited his Richmond home between military assignments, he was shocked. He later reported that he was "distressed" by the "rampant . . . spirit of chauvinism." Citizens of German ancestry faced insulting language and mistreatment. Such attitudes and behavior, Cutchins observed, were "regretfully . . . widespread." A 1918 coal shortage temporarily shut down all the city's factories, leaving approximately thirty thousand workers idle. Amidst August heat, the city food administrator announced a schedule of reductions in ice purchases. Food prices soared. Between 1913 and 1918 almost every item, including meat, milk, beans, bread, potatoes, and sugar, had more than doubled in cost. Shortages and sacrifices became less tolerable when reports confirmed that merchants had hoarded flour and sugar.[25]

The war's patriotic passions posed potential problems for evangelical churches of German heritage. In commemorating its fiftieth anniversary, Bethlehem Lutheran Church circumspectly featured such dignitaries as the field secretary of the Lutheran army and navy board, a Lutheran chaplain, and another Lutheran minister involved in religious activity at nearby Camp Lee. Although the church had introduced English language services in 1903, its anniversary program was printed in English and German. During the war, traditionally German-speaking St. John's Evangelical Church introduced English services, temporarily discontinued German language services, began to keep church council minutes in English, and appointed a committee of women to write to "the young men of the church who have been drafted to serve in the army." A congregational history later recalled that the church suffered "considerable inconvenience and heartache" during the war. Doubts about the patriotism of either church were cruelly unfair. Bethlehem ultimately counted fifty-one members in the U.S. armed forces, and St. John's reported fifty-six men in the services. Members of both congregations contributed to Liberty Loan drives, entertained visiting soldiers, and participated in Red Cross Auxiliaries, which prepared clothing and medical supplies.[26]

The war disrupted the religious life of the rest of the Protestant community in a variety of ways, large and small. During the days of diplomatic crises in early 1917, Centenary Methodist Church chimes began playing "America." Historic St. John's Episcopal Church tolled its bell in support of war bonds. Congregations often decided to display the U.S. flag inside their churches and place stars on it for members serving in the armed forces. The vestry of Grace Episcopal Church, however, voted against hanging the secular national flag in the chancel, and a divided vestry at St. Paul's Episcopal Church voted to do so over the initial objections of Bowie. To conserve fuel in the winter of 1918, churches conducted a cluster of interdenominational services in neighborhoods throughout the city. Because of a fuel scarcity, Union Seminary cut off heat to dormitories between 9 A.M. and 1 P.M., to lecture rooms after 1 P.M., and to the chapel entirely except for Sundays and Wednesdays. The seminary also coped with a scarcity of students as seminarians left to serve in the armed forces. Some, such as future church historian E. T. Thompson, interrupted their studies to serve as military chaplains. Across the city churches said goodbyes to their young servicemen, including ministers who, like Bowie, served as chaplains. In letters from France published in the *Southern Churchman,* Bowie shared a few of his poignant experiences as he cared for the sick and dying and wrote letters to their families. Some Richmond families also received bad news. In one letter, the son of Episcopal Bishop William Cabell Brown wrote his parents about a painful leg wound. But in another note, he sadly reported the death of cousin Randy Mason, brother of Lucy Randolph Mason. During the war, Walter L. Lingle endured a special torment—the sharp, principled conflict between two of his brothers. Will, a missionary to China, believed that Christianity and war were irreconcilable, heatedly criticized American involvement in the war, and wrote Lingle that his other brother had issued an ultimatum that "cuts me off from him." That other brother, Tom, a professor at Davidson College, concluded that American participation was just, enlisted in the army, and served with the conviction that the war would result in a better world.[27]

As the war continued, churches assumed expanded roles as conduits for home front patriotism. Complying with a request from the U.S. Food Administration, they served as liaisons for a voluntary conservation program. Government authorities instructed that this "simple and practical" administrative chore was "essential, a plain patriotic duty." In October 1917 city ministers delivered sermons to open "food conservation week." Churches distributed pledge cards committing members to observe meatless and wheatless days. Congregations took this task seriously. For example, Second Presbyterian Church appointed a ten-member committee to coordinate its efforts. Denominational weeklies provided detailed instructions and explanations to encourage voluntary compliance. After noting that canvassers had reported that 30 percent of Richmond homes did not have food cards in their windows, a newspaper article censoriously concluded, "Obviously many Richmond women do not attend church."[28]

At Seventh Street Christian, H. D. C. Maclachlan delivered a food conservation sermon which probably exceeded the script envisioned by the Food Administration. He did implore his congregation to make conservation efforts "part of your religion" and to follow the measures recommended by experts. But Maclachlan went much further. With the earth's abundance, he remarked, there was "no reason" for anyone to suffer, yet poverty existed due to selfishness. He warned that a church member who worked "to make it harder for many fellowmen to earn a living" actually insulted God with his prayers. Maclachlan condemned "sinister interests" for reaping wartime profits by "creating artificial prices" for necessities. He scored profiteers for "taking advantage of a world tragedy" and hoarders for hindering war work. Citing a *Wall Street Journal* report of American wastefulness, he called this nation the most extravagant one on earth and pointed to "unselfishness" and "intelligence" as keys to conservation.[29]

Richmond laywomen invested much time in patriotic activities. For example, Centenary Methodist Church created a Red Cross room, where women daily knitted, rolled bandages, and sewed hospital gowns, and Second Presbyterian did likewise. By December 1917 the women's groups in Richmond Methodist churches reported producing more than a thousand garments, more than a thousand towels, sixteen hundred pillow cases, and almost a thousand sheets. The Richmond chapter of the American Red Cross awarded badges to twenty-one women of St. Paul's Episcopal Church, each of whom had contributed more than eight hundred hours of labor. Grace Covenant Presbyterian Church offered its old downtown church building as the headquarters for city Red Cross activity. When an ammunition plant opened at nearby Seven Pines, more than twenty women of St. Paul's joined the Woman's Munition Reserve, and nine actually worked in the factory. Other women's groups stayed busy selling war bonds and savings stamps.[30]

Richmond's clergymen and laymen likewise devoted themselves to the war effort. Ministers urged audiences in Richmond to buy war bonds, and many traveled throughout the state and region bearing the same message. Richmond College students organized military units and drilled, and the new university campus served as a huge military hospital. Methodist J. T. Mastin served as chairman of a state committee on camp activities. An Episcopal men's organization, the Brotherhood of Saint Andrew, established a Soldiers, Sailors and Marines Club to meet the needs of troops who visited the city from three nearby military camps. Members of the brotherhood met soldiers at the railroad depot in South Richmond and transported them across the James River to an old residential building in downtown Richmond. In addition to furnishing lodging and food, the club offered servicemen haircuts, shoe shines, postcards, cigarettes, and use of a library and a recreation room. During the war, an estimated eight thousand men used the club, and some men were invited to dine in private homes. Members of the brotherhood also visited sick soldiers and donated a Victrola and records for the hospital ward at Camp Lee, an army installation located approximately twenty-five miles south of the city. Seventh Street Christian Church created its "Khaki Club." In the church's parish house, young women and adult chaperons staffed a reading room, where the soldiers could socialize, write letters to loved ones, or play the piano. In the parish house, members hosted parties, showed films, and gave concerts. For dances and other special occasions, the congregation "mobilized" its young women by making telephone calls from a list assembled for that purpose. Church members also visited the hospital at Camp Lee. When Maria Marchetti delivered her spaghetti to Italian-American troops, she included a prayer written in Italian.[31]

But these steps apparently did not meet all the needs of servicemen. In 1917 W. W. Moore and a group of Richmond's Protestant, Catholic, and Jewish leaders who were members of the Virginia Social Hygiene Association tried unsuccessfully to convene representatives from state social organizations for a campaign to encourage sexual morality among soldiers and sailors. In 1918 Richmond clergymen learned that a 1915 anti-vice campaign notwithstanding, the city police had continued to ignore prostitution violations. During one week in May, Camp Lee led thirty-five U.S. military camps with a report of 804 new cases of venereal disease, and federal authorities traced the problem to soldiers' visits to Richmond. Still upset about revelations of the earlier investigation, the Richmond Ministerial Union took an unprecedented action. It passed a resolution declaring that if the mayor could not or would not enforce the laws, citizens should find someone who would. Vice was not the only enemy commanding attention at home. The 1918 influenza epidemic sickened thousands, killed hundreds, and stopped worship services for more than a month. Churches responded heroically by operating soup kitchens and sending out members with food and medicine for those lying debilitated at home. Even with home front activities and problems, most of Richmond's attention remained focused "over there."[32]

As the war continued, both secular and religious leaders actually incited hatred of America's enemies. Local newspapers headlined stories about atrocities allegedly committed by German soldiers. A *News Leader* editorial called for vengeful destruction. Alarmed columnist Cally Ryland charged that the war was making it too easy for people to hate one another. Such hatred she called "a slow poison" capable of corroding "every good and kind and generous impulse we ever knew." Richmond Protestant leaders contributed to this atmosphere of fear and anger. Clergymen repeated frightful stories about Germans. For example, in a speech for the War Savings Stamps campaign, Presbyterian Russell Cecil told listeners that if Germany could land an army in America, the troops "would not hesitate to kill and destroy like barbarians." Such language was especially potent coming from Cecil, whose devotional sermons were notable for their caring tone and their emphasis on Christian love. Swept up in patriotism, other pastors subjected their congregations to impassioned rhetoric. Baptist minister John J. Wicker recounted "Hun" atrocities, and Findley F. Gibson proclaimed "the Righteousness of the Allies' Cause." In 1918, after long discounting atrocity stories, the *Southern Churchman* concluded that they were true and printed several accounts. A few weeks later the same paper drew upon a *New York Times* article and furnished a stack of statistics showing that between 1897 and 1907, Germans had committed one hundred times the number of violent crimes that British citizens had committed in the same period.[33]

Baptist George White McDaniel toured Virginia and North Carolina on behalf of the War Savings Stamps campaign. In speeches he vividly depicted scenes of German brutality. He charged that German troops had maimed children, killed and "outraged" women, and mutilated the wounded and the dead. He condemned German soldiers for using poisonous gas and for bombing cities. He portrayed Germans as laughing "in hellish glee while women and children went down to watery graves." According to him, "the Huns" had also induced "the Turks" to wage a holy war and massacre all the Christians in their territory. Speaking to the Dover Baptist Association, McDaniel proudly referred to the 165 servicemen from his church, including his own son. Arguing that they fought to prevent future wars, McDaniel labeled as "traitorous" any outcome short of "complete victory, of unconditional surrender." Printed with the title *Our Boys in France,* McDaniel's address was distributed by Virginia Baptists.[34]

Like McDaniel, as the war neared a conclusion, other prominent ministers condemned the Germans and called for harsh peace terms. James Cannon disclaimed any spirit of revenge but wanted Germans to be punished for their evil deeds. He charged that the German "nation as a whole" had stood behind the Kaiser and "rejoiced" in the devastation and looting of other countries. The *Religious Herald* contended that the "great body of the German people are filled with the same indecent lust and hate and savagery" that caused their leaders to orchestrate a program of militarism and commit atrocities. Episcopal city missionary R. Cary Montague even suggested that in order to obliterate the attitude of "might makes right," it might be necessary to annihilate those persons who held it.[35]

A few concerned religious leaders chided their associates for permitting the war atmosphere to overwhelm their commitment to Christian love. In a May 1919 letter to the *Southern Churchman,* Episcopal layman Berkeley Minor grieved about secular and religious leaders who had been teaching the next generation to hate. One Baptist wrote a letter criticizing the *Religious Herald* for "lending its influence to engender blind hate against all Germans." Reacting to a sermon "preached by a popular preacher of another denomination," the *Presbyterian of the South* rejected calls for harsh punishment of Germany and reminded readers that Christians should forgive those who had wronged them. The editor added, "We have no right to cherish hatred in our hearts."[36]

In the following years, Richmond ministers increasingly found merit in those earlier warnings, as they grimly assessed the war's impact. Walter Russell Bowie claimed that the war's worst tragedy was not the injuries to a million bodies, but the "maiming of a million souls." Protestant leaders concluded that Americans had been unable to restrain their feelings of animosity and had become so consumed with hostility that they lost their sense of morality. The preachers blamed the war for unleashing men's primal instincts of greed, lawlessness, intolerance, and sexual immorality. The editor of the *Richmond Christian Advocate* wrote that people could not "engage in wholesale killing of our fellows without brutalizing all our standards and instincts" and emerging with "coarsened souls."[37]

Richmond Protestant leaders sadly admitted that in backing war measures even churches had directed members away from the Christian ideal of brotherhood. Episcopal layman John Stewart Bryan confessed that "we fought for the love of God, and we allowed our motives to be distorted into hatred of Germany." Bowie charged that unsubstantiated rumors of enemy atrocities had been officially circulated as facts and that the war had been based on the deliberate and wholesale creation of hate. He did not specifically indict local clergymen who had recited those stories but did condemn "the passionate orators" who had "fuel[ed] the fires of revenge." The *Richmond Christian Advocate* issued a harsher critique, alleging that churches had been "recruiting stations" for the war. Walter Lingle called upon Protestants to insist that "our churches shall never again be used for war propaganda." In 1924 the Methodist Virginia Annual Conference passed a resolution declaring that any future endorsement or "use of the church's name, influence or facilities for the promotion of war must be counted as disloyal to Jesus Christ, to His ideals and to His Kingdom."[38]

In acknowledging the role of Richmond churches in World War I, local leaders identified a set of experiences shared by many American communities. In 1933 University of Pennsylvania sociologist Ray Abrams authored a critical study of American churches in the Great War. In *Preachers Present Arms,* Abrams accused religious organizations of becoming tools of the state. His detailed and gloomy assessment served, he believed, as a warning about the potency of nationalism in wartime. Abrams, however, discounted the reactions of church leaders in the 1920s and therefore missed a major implication of the episode he explored. In 1958 historian Robert Moats Miller insightfully argued that memories of the Great War haunted church leaders, and a "powerful anti-war sentiment" swept through the churches in the post-Versailles years. Indeed, exhibiting a heightened awareness of international conditions, Richmond clergy and laity persistently supported measures for international peace.[39]

Since "God's ideal" is "a warless world," Walter Lingle proclaimed, "then His people should work with might and main to make it a warless world." Throughout the 1920s, other Richmond ministers and laymen joined him in expressing the conviction that Christians must work to render another war impossible. The *Chesapeake Christian* appealed to ministers to teach Americans that they had a personal responsibility for the way their leaders conducted international relations. Episcopalian Margaret Prescott Montague charged that too many people found it easy to act like "dumb driven cattle" and to blame fate for the results. She challenged church members to use their "God-given faculties" to achieve peace. She warned "if peace again breaks down it will be our own faults." In the 1920s Lingle forcefully and repeatedly urged church leaders to preach about peace, to condemn the causes of war, and to support international organizations committed to outlawing war. "If a minister wants to preach on peace and against war, he should have no trouble in finding plenty of good texts," Lingle suggested.[40]

Lingle urged churchmen to quit glorifying war, and other ministers voiced the same plea. They maintained that civilians had developed an erroneous impression of war. Several preachers concluded that Americans had been overwhelmed by patriotic oratory and military glamour and pageantry. Lingle complained that when people saw soldiers in their fresh uniforms, listened to military bands, and watched waving flags, the thrilled civilians easily ignored the realities of war. Only soldiers themselves faced the "muck, the mire, the blood, the death, the anguish" of the battlefield. H. D. C. Maclachlan urged Christians to face the realities of war: "the horror, the insincerity, the lust, the greed, the wrong, the hate."[41]

Richmond ministers confronted their congregations with the horrible consequences of war. After visits in three countries to the graves of their "unknowns," an angry Methodist minister denounced the monuments as efforts to "bluff and blind parents to the wickedness of war." What consolation could parents gain from those anonymous tombs? he wondered. "Is this what civilization promises you when you do your best to raise your boys to manhood?" Describing war as "hell triple distilled," Maclachlan cited the use of poisonous gas, flame throwers, mutilation, and torture, as well as the prevalence of disease and famine during World War I. Writing a review of Kirby Page's *War, Its Cause, Consequences and Cure,* Lingle enumerated the victims of recent war: millions of dead and wounded soldiers, widows, orphans, and refugees. Methodist Frederick Chenault warned that in the next war, bombs dropped by airplanes would destroy whole cities and kill millions of people in a single encounter. The *Southern Churchman* reminded readers that war was "destructive of all values which Christians are striving for. It fills the world with hate and bitterness. It creates an atmosphere which stifles the ideals of the Kingdom of God."[42]

No minister was better prepared to testify about the tragedy of war than Walter Russell Bowie. As chaplain for a busy base hospital, he had comforted the wounded and sick, written letters to loved ones, and conducted religious services for the living, the dying, and the dead. In one period of three days, he had helped bury eighty men. Bowie later recalled that he had been especially shaken by the appearance of one deserted French town his unit had entered. It was a scene of devastation: streets with shell holes, buildings breached by bullets, broken windows, damaged doors, debris ranging from a torn flag to a busted doll, as well as an "unnatural stillness." At that moment Bowie comprehended that war was "an uncanny dehumanizing thing before which existence might become a desert. It was as though the skeleton of the world stood there in ghastly semblance of completeness, while the life of it had gone." Back in Richmond, Bowie repeatedly shared his experiences. At a memorial service for six men whose bodies had been returned to Richmond, he offered a vivid description of the regiments of men lying in the rain, charging over the parapets in the face of machine gun fire, and hanging lifeless on the barbed wire. The "endless line of ambulances" carried "still figures" to hospitals, where they were lifted from stretchers and placed in "long wards of agony where nurses and doctors battled all night with death. . . . Graves in the fields and gardens, long lines of graves dug new continually for men who would come back to them presently from the battles—that too was war, and its grim and tragic waste."[43]

Immediately after World War I, Richmond Protestant leaders embraced the League of Nations as a means to prevent future wars. In supporting the league, local Protestants were inspired and guided by President Woodrow Wilson, whom they respected and revered. Richmond honored him as a native Virginian who had arrived in the national spotlight with the qualities of a hero. With his achievements as an academician and a reformer, he embodied the best of the contemporary South. And Wilson's religion mattered. With a family tree laden with Presbyterian ministers, he had served as an elder in the church. Counting the president a personal friend, Russell Cecil testified to Wilson's religious convictions. Local ministers praised Wilson for carrying his faith into the political arena and for behaving with the decency and dignity befitting a Christian statesman. The crushing disappointment of the Versailles negotiations and Wilson's unsuccessful domestic campaign for the League of Nations only elevated him in the esteem of Richmond Protestants. While acknowledging that Wilson occasionally erred, local religious leaders viewed him as a moral and intellectual giant hindered by self-serving midgets at home and abroad. Felled by a stroke while campaigning for the League of Nations, Wilson left disciples for peace who viewed him and his beliefs with an adoration that was nothing less than a form of civil religion.[44]

In life Wilson articulated a vision of international relations that Richmond Protestant leaders found compelling. In death Wilson and that vision were sanctified in symbols and services. The cover of the *Presbyterian of the South* featured a drawing of Wilson with an inscription beneath it: "He gave his life for the world." In the accompanying eulogy, the paper proclaimed that "no greater man has ever passed across the stage of America's history" and that "all the world will eventually rise up to call him blessed." Wishing "the nation and the world . . . to remember and ponder the estimate this great man put on the Bible," the *Richmond Christian Advocate* devoted its cover to "Woodrow Wilson's Tribute to the Bible." Calling him "a scholar and not a schemer," "an apostle and not an apostate," the Methodist paper depicted his enemies as "hanging their heads in shame because their sins were finding them out." The editorial concluded that "the only hope of the world is his ideals for they were the ideals of the gospel of brotherhood and of God." The *Religious Herald* declared that his causes and ideals would not be defeated, but rather by his death would be "sanctified and ennobled and vitalized." S. C. Mitchell predicted that Wilson would be ranked with George Washington as the nation's two great presidents. Mitchell did admonish that "it is impotent for us to mourn [President Wilson] if we do not work for his ideal of international cooperation."[45]

Richmond mourned and worked. At noon on Wednesday, 6 February 1924, mourners filled St. Paul's Episcopal Church for an interdenominational memorial service for Wilson. Processing to "How Firm a Foundation," the governor of Virginia, the mayor of Richmond, members of Virginia's General Assembly, a delegation from the American Legion, and the ministers of the city's churches marched to the front of the interior. The church's service flag covered the altar; the U.S. flag stood at half-mast. Episcopal Bishop William Cabell Brown read the creed and the prayers. Methodist Bishop Collins Denny led a responsive reading of Psalms 39 and 40. Russell Cecil delivered a memorial address, and S. C. Mitchell spoke about "Mr. Wilson's Contribution to World Peace." St. Paul's Beverley Tucker and H. D. C. Maclachlan also participated in the service. In another service several weeks later at Second Presbyterian, pastor Cecil eulogized Wilson as a president who tried "to fulfill the will of God." Cecil described Wilson's knowledge of scriptures, service as a Presbyterian elder, his regular church attendance, and his custom of beginning cabinet meetings with prayer. Cecil characterized Wilson "as much a victim of war as any soldier on the battlefield." Just as Wilson "lay down his life" for the League of Nations, Cecil instructed, "we should do our part" to establish and maintain peace.[46]

For many Richmond religious leaders the first step to that goal was U.S. entry into the League of Nations, which offered the only real hope for basing international relations on Christian principles. In 1919 Richmond Episcopal clergymen passed a resolution endorsing the principles of the league and sent a copy to their congressman and both U.S. senators. Local Presbyterian, Methodist, and Episcopal newspapers endorsed the league, and the Baptist weekly supported it, though wishing some modifications in its structure. When the *Religious Herald* published an advertisement by the *Manufacturers Record* opposing the league, editor R. H. Pitt received so many irate letters that he responded with a defensive article about the importance of free debate in a democratic society. As part of an intercollegiate referendum on the Versailles Treaty, students at Union Seminary almost unanimously backed the league. Richmond Protestant leaders criticized the U.S. Senate for its refusal to approve American entry into the league. Disappointed layman John Stewart Bryan indicted the United States for setting back "the hands of progress" three years, or even three centuries, by refusing to join the league.[47]

Even after the Senate rejected the Treaty of Versailles, local ministers continued to hope that the United States would eventually join the League of Nations. The congregation of Leigh Street Baptist Church wanted the Southern Baptist Convention to declare its opposition to the "entire war system" and to call upon the U.S. government to "cooperate with other nations in some form of organization" devoted to permanent world peace. In 1923 the Baptist General Association of Virginia sent a letter to the U.S. Senate. Bearing the signatures of four prominent Richmond Baptists, including S. C. Mitchell and R. H. Pitt, the letter declared that a policy of isolation was foolish, and it charged that America's "moral prestige" had never been lower. The Virginia Baptists urged the Senate to support U.S. participation in the League of Nations and concluded with an admonition that "The Day of Retribution Is Bound to Come."[48]

In 1924 S. C. Mitchell employed a different tactic. He attempted to organize a national "Friends of the League" society. Mitchell noted that the League of Nations had begun humanitarian projects to improve public health and agriculture as well as to suppress traffic in drugs and white slavery. He asserted that the league had been forced to curtail this work because the United States had not joined and had not contributed an expected $400,000 to the organization. Mitchell wanted 400,000 Americans to contribute one dollar each to replace those funds. By obtaining small contributions from "the rank and file of our citizens," Mitchell proposed not only to aid the league but also to demonstrate mass support for it and prompt politicians to vote for U.S. entry into the organization. Mitchell won local support for his idea but failed to gain national backing. He hoped to persuade leaders of the League of Nations Association, an affluent pro-league group, to embrace his idea and expand its membership to include citizens of modest means. But the leaders of that association rejected Mitchell's plan. Labor leader Samuel Gompers also rebuffed Mitchell. Refusing to publish an article about Mitchell's proposal in the *American Federationist,* Gompers wrote to Mitchell explaining that there were too many other "pressing demands" upon the "good will and finances of our people." Having already collected approximately $1,500 for the Friends plan, Mitchell sent the money to the league, which used some of it to aid orphans in the Middle East.[49]

Although support for the league bore little fruit, other efforts fared better. In 1921 Richmond church leaders joined in a nationwide call for a disarmament conference. The *Southern Churchmen* urged Christians to write national leaders and let them know that people expected "results," not just talk. Expressing the belief that world peace could be promoted by arms limitations, the vestry of St. Paul's passed a resolution endorsing such a conference and sent a copy of the statement to the president and their U.S. senators and congressmen. In October 1921 the Richmond Ministerial Union organized a mass meeting at the city auditorium to express support for the Washington Peace

Conference. Ministers led prayer services during that conference, and Richmond's religious press rejoiced about the results of the Washington meetings. Protestant leaders cited the conference as proof that American Christians could exert influence upon politicians to work for peace.[50]

Throughout the 1920s, Richmond ministers continued to promote measures for international peace. Some preachers endorsed U.S. participation in the World Court. Others criticized plans for a national mobilization day. Several Protestant leaders condemned compulsory military training programs in church-related schools. Denominational weeklies printed articles about national peace conferences and organizations. In 1923 the Richmond YWCA and the Virginia League of Women Voters sponsored a conference on "International Understanding and World Friendship" at St. Paul's Episcopal Church. There local ministers and laymen delivered addresses about the World Court, the League of Nations, the British Commonwealth, international economics, and open diplomacy.[51]

During the late 1920s, ministers condemned U.S. plans for increasing naval armaments. In a 1928 editorial, "Christ or Cruisers," the *Presbyterian of the South* protested that Christian enterprises languished for lack of funds while national leaders continued to spend money on unnecessary armaments. Reciting citizen complaints about high postal rates and insufficient funds for highways, education, and law enforcement, the editorial detailed the projected seventy-one warships that were part of a $2.5 billion program and compared it to the German naval buildup before 1914. In 1928 Richmond Methodist preachers passed a resolution declaring that a "big navy" policy would provoke war, not prevent it. The preachers criticized Republicans and Democrats for including naval expansion planks in their party platforms. The ministers called upon Virginia leaders to use their influence against such proposals and later passed a resolution commending President Hoover when he suspended the naval building program. The Richmond Ministerial Union also passed a resolution opposing a "big navy" program and sent letters to Virginia senators and representatives.[52]

This criticism and opposition to the naval building program constituted a sharp break with prewar complacency about government policies and decisions. And religious leaders extended this critical mentality to challenge such policies as the failure of the United States to reduce or forgive massive wartime debts incurred by the country's allies. Struggling with a life-ending illness, H. D. C. Maclachlan still managed to skewer U.S. foreign policy in Latin America for supporting financial interests rather than upholding the rights of the people.[53]

Local religious leaders did celebrate the adoption of the Kellogg-Briand

Pact. They conceded that the agreement was weak because it lacked enforcement provisions. Nonetheless, they believed that the treaty would lead to a reduction in international conflict. The *Religious Herald* called the day when the pact was signed "perhaps the greatest day in the history of civilized nations." The *Virginia Churchman,* an Episcopal newspaper, argued that if the agreements remained in force for a few years, they might acquire great prestige.[54]

Neither World War I nor its aftermath diminished local enthusiasm for foreign missions. Systematic canvassing for missions continued during the war. Pine Street Baptist increased its donations to missions from $1,932 in 1918 to $14,252 in 1921, an impressive feat given the postwar recession in Richmond. Second Baptist's Elizabeth Ellyson and Union Station Methodist's Verna Miller were among the church members who embarked upon missionary careers. In the 1920s Third Presbyterian and First English Lutheran joined the list of congregations designating funds to support specific foreign missionaries. In May 1927 Tabernacle Baptist Church hosted a three-day mission study institute attended by 452 people.[55]

Events in the early twentieth century catapulted Richmond Protestants toward a new panorama of the world and a new orientation to affairs beyond the oceans. In the first decade of the twentieth century, churches devoted only limited and episodic attention to conditions beyond the national shoreline. Awash in idealism and patriotism, however, churches became heavily enmeshed in the country's World War I efforts. Emerging shaken and reflective, city religious leaders became dedicated proponents of measures for international peace. By 1930 Richmond clergy and laity evidenced a religious perspective of international affairs that differed in three notable ways from the dominant outlook of 1900. First, they capped three decades of escalating commitment to foreign missions. Second, they lived with a harsh legacy from the Great War. It taught them the searing lessons that patriotism could lead churches into a desecrating alliance with the state and that nationalism could unleash hatred, which threatened to suffocate Christian love. Third, with the world undeniably closer to their doors, religious leaders committed themselves in an unprecedented way to movements for international peace. If the world itself had not been made new, Richmond Protestants now approached it in a new manner. And by the end of the decade, Richmond clergymen believed that much of their work had been successful. In 1929 Walter Lingle wrote that "one of the most hopeful things on the horizon at the beginning of this New Year is the growing horror which multitudes of people have for war and the earnest effort which they are making to outlaw war."[56]

II

The Wrong Place for a Row

In 1924 Douglas Southall Freeman told a group of laymen that "the Baptists of the South have no Fundamentalist-Modernist row. And the first man who tries to start one ought to be run North of the Potomac River and kept there." Freeman's hope proved in vain. Even while Richmond Protestant leaders championed the cause of international peace, they could not escape the domestic theological conflicts of the 1920s. Prominent Richmond Protestants engaged in a series of strenuous struggles with Fundamentalism, and those rows significantly affected religious life in the capital city, in the state, and in individual denominations. The city, though, proved to be an unreceptive environment for Fundamentalism. Richmond revealed a southern religious culture that respected theological diversity, valued evangelism and denominational programs more than religious tests, and thrived on a civility incompatible with the adversarial tone assumed by fundamentalists.[1]

By the time Douglas Freeman spoke, fundamentalists had achieved a potent presence throughout the nation. Objecting to contemporary biblical scholarship propounded from many pulpits as well as to scientific ideas taught in many schools, fundamentalists had launched vigorous campaigns to reclaim the nation for their version of Christianity. After World War I, they had formed organizations such as the World's Christian Fundamentals Association and the Baptist Bible Union. Between 1920 and 1922 they had attempted to dominate the Northern Baptist Convention, and after 1923 they sought to enforce doctrinal statements within the largely northern Presbyterian Church in the United States of America. Such dynamic leaders as New York's John Roach Straton, Toronto's T. T. Shields, Minneapolis's William Bell Riley, and Fort Worth's J. Frank Norris boasted the support of large urban congregations. By the early 1920s, fundamentalists had established scores of Bible schools, including the Bible Institute of Los Angeles, Moody Bible Institute in Chicago, and Boston Bible Training School. Thus, Freeman discerned an essential truth about Fundamentalism: its origins lay outside the American South, as a recent generation of historians has documented.[2]

For fundamentalists the chief villains were "modernists," a label adopted by a number of American Protestant scholars and ministers in the late nineteenth and early twentieth centuries. These religious leaders stressed that God was actively present in human affairs, and they tried to reconcile the Christian message with new knowledge and contemporary ways of living. They sought to interpret the Bible in terms that were consistent with scientific discoveries in such fields as biology, sociology, psychology, archaeology, and philology. Modernists viewed the Bible as a source of divine revelation, but they did not accept the Bible as literally accurate. Many of them based their interpretations of the Scriptures on a form of scholarship called "higher criticism." Scholars who used this method analyzed the literary composition of biblical texts and tried to ascertain the authorship, the literary history, and the historical context of those passages. On the basis of such work, modernists reached conclusions that startled orthodox Christians. For example, some modernists concluded that Moses did not write the first five books of the Bible. Modernists also suggested that the apostle John did not write the Gospel of John and that the same gospel was historically inaccurate. Often uneasy about episodes attributed to supernatural action, some modernists denied the accuracy of biblical miracle stories, including the Virgin Birth of Christ.[3]

Thus, by the 1920s fundamentalists perceived plenty of issues warranting religious combat and an increasing number of targets meriting attacks. Fundamentalists suspected that mainline churches, mission programs, colleges, seminaries, and public schools taught ideas incompatible with true Christianity and resolved to stop such heresy. If united in purpose, though, fundamentalists could not claim uniform religious ancestry. According to scholars, the leaders who fashioned Fundamentalism into a national religious movement drew upon a complex and diverse theological heritage. Their ideational roots ranged from the Scottish Common Sense Realism prevalent at Princeton Seminary to the intricate prophetic calculations of John Nelson Darby's dispensational premillenialism. Many fundamentalists reflected the influence of "holiness" experiences fanned in such disparate locations as Keswick, England, and Azusa Street in Los Angeles. In *Fundamentalism and American Culture*, George Marsden has aptly characterized Fundamentalism as "a mosaic of divergent and sometimes contradictory traditions and tendencies that could never be totally integrated." Fundamentalists formed, in his words, "a loose, diverse, and changing federation of co-belligerents united by their fierce opposition to modernist attempts to bring Christianity into line with modern thought."[4]

Fundamentalists were not merely theological conservatives who objected to the new ideas of modernists and scientists. Operating across denominational and regional boundaries, fundamentalists shared characteristics which, taken in combination, set them apart from other Christians. First, they were committed to a literal interpretation of the Bible. Second, they adamantly demanded support of creeds or other exclusive statements of belief. Southern historian Willard Gatewood has characterized Modernism as "a fluid theology with ever-changing emphases which could scarcely be contained in creedal statements." By contrast, for southern fundamentalists, as religious historian Samuel S. Hill has argued, not only was "correct belief" "possible and necessary," so too was "testing the orthodoxy of others." Third, fundamentalists were militantly opposed to modernist scholarship and preaching. Fervently committed to their own ideas, they challenged and fought others who held differing views. Historians have found ample evidence to support Professor Marsden's conclusion that "militant opposition to modernism was what most clearly set off fundamentalism from a number of closely related traditions." Fourth, fundamentalists often espoused a premillennial interpretation of the Bible. Even as the massive destructiveness of World War I had seemed to puncture the optimism of religious liberals, it had combined with other international events to provide evidence for a prophetic script of crisis followed by Christ's Second Coming.[5]

At Richmond's Seventh Street Christian Church, H. D. C. Maclachlan was an outspoken foe of fundamentalists. Early in his ministry, he announced that he would not rely on literal biblical interpretations, nor would he assail higher criticism. Maclachlan said that he would "rather run the risk of disagreement" than try to "lead people in intellectual darkness." With sermons, essays, and special programs notable for their intellectual breadth, he won respect and popularity throughout the community. On one occasion he urged listeners to "turn the Bible loose. Set it free from the binding chains of tradition." In another sermon in which he called creedal statements "useful and necessary as crutches of faith," Maclachlan declared that people could give thanks that the essentials of Christianity did not depend on "any theological or historical definition whatsoever." Referring to fundamentalists, he asserted that "it is nothing short of treason to the Divine Spirit to limit his teachings to the dead words of a book" while keeping an ear "closed to those new sermons on the Mount which he is preaching to his people in every age." Not only did Maclachlan express dismay over the attitudes of fundamentalists, he denounced their tactics. In a sermon "False Prophets," he charged that fundamentalists would "brand," "persecute," and "ex-communicate" "all who differ from them." Other local Disciples ministers were neither as outspoken nor as theologically liberal as Maclachlan, but they showed no attraction to fundamentalist views and campaigns. In a classic account of Fundamentalism, Norman Furniss concluded that only "Northern Presbyterians" were "more shaken" by the controversies of the 1920s than were the Disciples of Christ, but such was not the case in Richmond.[6]

Preoccupied with evangelism, moral crusades, and social reform, Richmond Methodists rarely fretted about theological issues. Holding to a theological middle ground, Methodist leaders expressed some misgivings about contemporary biblical scholarship but also rejected a literal approach to biblical interpretation. As one pastor declared in 1907, "Within the range of the great essentials there is room for many differences of opinion or at least inquiry." In a book published during World War I, Methodist minister Edward L. Pell emphasized that many of Jesus' teachings should be read figuratively, not literally. In *Why I Believe in Jesus,* published in 1926, Pell eschewed attacks on modernists for condemnations of America's materialism.[7]

In the 1920s Joseph Rowland, the editor of the Methodist *Richmond Christian Advocate,* expressed disapproval of evolution and higher criticism. Rowland, however, mostly resented a patronizing attitude he attributed to pastors who promoted Modernism. He welcomed new scholarship, believing that if traditional religion could not "stand the glare of new thought, it deserves to fail." Observing that he knew of no Virginia Methodist who had joined the World's Christian Fundamentals Association, he concluded that the organization overstressed creed and understressed conduct. In one editorial he asked, "Are we not making things worse by heresy hunting and charging that orthodoxy is one of the gravest problems of the day?"[8]

As Richmond's most conservative major Protestant group, Presbyterians might have seemed likely recruits for fundamentalists. In the early 1900s, the editor of the state Presbyterian weekly, James Power Smith, periodically attacked Modernism and criticized northern Presbyterians for ordaining ministers who had expressed reservations about some church doctrines. At the beginning of the twentieth century, Union Theological Seminary was a bulwark of Presbyterian orthodoxy. Prof. Thomas Cary Johnson propounded a stern brand of Calvinism, emphasizing human depravity, judgment, predestination, and the spirituality of the church. Recalling student experiences at Union, church historian Ernest Trice Thompson later described Johnson as a "powerful figure" and a "very conservative man" who "did not teach us anything about any theological developments after the Westminster Confession and the scholastic theologians." Thompson complained that Johnson "just drilled us" with the theology of nineteenth-century Virginian Robert Lewis Dabney and discouraged student questions. With a thirty-nine-year tenure at Union and an eighteen-year pastorate at Ginter Park Presbyterian Church, Johnson wielded theological influence matched by few other local Presbyterian leaders.[9]

Several faculty colleagues joined Johnson in making Union a conservative bastion. During the 1901 academic year, Givens Brown Strickler used four issues of the *Union Seminary Magazine* to critique "the New Theology." While noting the variety of ideas articulated by contemporary scholars, a disquieted Strickler deplored some of their "unscriptural conclusions." He warned that they often denied the plenary inspiration of the Scripture, "obliterated the supernatural," and tried to "get rid of the great doctrines of the church." Prof. Edward Mack also assumed a staunchly antagonistic stance toward new biblical scholarship. In the pages of the quarterly *Union Seminary Magazine* and its successor, the *Union Seminary Review*, Mack, as well as Johnson and Strickler, reviewed new religious books, generally praised conservative authors, and often lambasted liberal writers. With their publications, their instruction of future ministers, and their sermons at local churches, Union professors spread their conclusions far beyond their campus. Union further fostered theological conservatism through its annual Sprunt Lectures, which featured visiting speakers who made addresses open to the community. Between 1919 and 1923, the lectures provided forums for such celebrated figures as G. Campbell Morgan, Francis Patton, J. Gresham Machen, and William Jennings Bryan, who carried conservative theological tunes with overtones of Fundamentalism.[10]

Richmond Presbyterians, however, held views that fit poorly with Fundamentalism. Even Thomas Cary Johnson acknowledged his belief in a form of theistic evolution, affirmed only that the "original manuscripts" of the Bible were infallible, and rejected a literal interpretation of the Bible. Likewise opposed to a literal interpretation of the Bible, Old Testament professor Edward Mack argued that "the manner and degree of the unfolding" of God's truth "changed and advanced with each age," and he called such progressive revelation "a scriptural reality, a blessed reality." In a series of talks delivered at First Presbyterian Church and subsequently published as a book, Mack faulted both liberal interpretations and extremely literal interpretations. He called the Old Testament a "book of surpassing imagery" and warned that literalists might "miss the heart of the Old Testament." Union's most theologically conservative professors selectively approved some modernist scholarship. Other faculty members praised some contemporary biblical scholarship and urged students to evaluate new ideas for themselves. Even always orthodox Union President Walter W. Moore rejected inerrancy, applauded some scholarship of higher critics, favored ministerial liberty in dealing with doctrines, and criticized opponents of modern scholarship for their "violent and abusive tone."[11]

In the wake of World War I, fundamentalists often espoused premillenialism and perceived signs of the Second Coming of Jesus. In contrast, President

Moore used a 1918 address at Union to attack premillennial theories as mere "products of times of persecution and calamity." He implied that proponents of such views forced "these arbitrary and literal interpretations onto figurative passages of Scripture" and indulged in "precarious interpretations of passing events." Likewise, Mack regretted that prophetic passages of the book of Ezekiel had been "turned to all manner of fantastic and fanatical uses" and described Armageddon as "not a single local struggle, but an age-long conflict, involving all nations" with a final consummation in "the land of Israel."[12]

By the 1920s, Union added faculty members such as Walter Lingle and E. T. Thompson, as well as President Benjamin Lacy, and they taught students more about the ideas of liberal Protestantism. Admitting that the Divinity Department at the University of Chicago was "a bit radical in spots," Lingle still recommended it to a friend. Having taken courses there himself, he declared, "I have always been glad of it," and he arranged for his daughter to study there, too. After Lingle became an editor of the *Presbyterian of the South,* he abruptly rejected an invitation to join the League for the Defense of the Bible with the comment that "the Word of God can take care of itself." At one annual meeting of the Presbyterian General Assembly, he engaged in negotiations to deflect the efforts of fundamentalists advocating a new doctrinal test of candidates for ordination. In 1924 the editors of the Philadelphia-based, fundamentalist *Sunday School Times* inquired of Lingle whether every faculty member at the General Assembly Training School for Layworkers believed and taught a list of "simple fundamentals of the Christian faith." As president of the school, Lingle vouched for the faith of his instructors but referred the *Times* to the Westminster Confession, declared that the teachers were responsible to their own presbyteries and the general assembly, and refused to submit the questions to teachers. He could not resist a parting quip: "we somehow have the feeling that the Southern Presbyterian Church is an earnest and jealous guardian of the truth." Beginning in the mid-1920s, the Sprunt Lectures featured scholars who also took a broader approach to interpreting Scriptures. In sermons and publications, local Presbyterians ministers rarely expressed the apprehensions articulated by fundamentalists. During the 1920s, a new generation of Presbyterian preachers assumed leadership in Richmond churches and, like their counterparts at Union, articulated a more liberal theology.[13]

Although city Presbyterians moved cautiously toward a more liberal theology, Richmond could not avoid dealing with the volatile issue of evolution introduced by visiting Presbyterian William Jennings Bryan. Even before the 1920s some Richmond clergymen had voiced fears about the theory of evolution. They denounced evolution as a direct assault upon Christian beliefs because it contradicted the biblical account of creation and therefore denied the reliability of the entire Bible. They also recoiled at the very idea that man could have evolved from lower animals, terming such notions as "degrading." Critics of evolution further asserted that the theory denied God's existence and portrayed a universe in which a creator God was unnecessary.[14]

Still, William Jennings Bryan's 1921 Sprunt Lectures qualified as the city's most massive assault on Darwin. After one speech attacking higher critics for undermining belief in the Bible, Bryan devoted another presentation to "the Origin of Man" and hammered at the theory of evolution. Dismissing Darwinism as "guesses strung together" rather than science, Bryan denounced it as "harmful" as well as "groundless" and "absurd." On one hand, he admitted that evolution did not deny the existence of God. But on the other hand, Bryan concluded that it placed God at such a distance from humans that they lost their reverence, indeed, their very belief in God. Furthermore, the concept of survival of the fittest denied the basic Christian belief in the efficacy of brotherhood and love. Citing Friedrich Nietzsche as a disciple of Darwin, Bryan blamed German militarism and the "bloodiest war in history," World War I, on Darwinism. Emphasizing materialism, evolution "chills the spiritual nature and quenches the fires of religious enthusiasm." By implicitly denying the supernatural as well as by creating doubts about the Bible, evolution reduced men to brutes. Bryan suggested that only true Christians—meaning those who repudiated evolution—should teach in Christian schools. On the verge of launching his antievolution law campaign, he added that taxpayers could be satisfied with "real neutrality" in public schools as long as the schools were not used "for the destruction of faith and for the teaching of materialistic doctrines."[15]

Walter W. Moore praised Bryan's lectures, and some Richmond Protestant leaders endorsed Bryan's views. One Baptist preacher inveighed against "atheistic evolutionists," called evolution a "subtle attempt to account for everything without God," and alleged that it would destroy the faith of children. Walter Lingle complained that evolution was often taught "in a crude and irreverent way, which is calculated to shock and undermine the faith of our children." In the mid-1920s, both the *Presbyterian of the South* and the Methodist *Richmond Christian Advocate* endorsed antievolution laws.[16]

Other Richmond church leaders responded that evolution did not contradict Christian beliefs. Promptly replying to Bryan's lectures, H. D. C. Maclachlan retorted that evolution did not conflict with the biblical account of creation and referred to Darwin as "God's servant." In 1922 Walter Russell Bowie claimed that the early chapters of Genesis were "poetry," not "science," and therefore could not conflict with scientific discoveries. A few years later, Beverley D. Tucker endorsed the theory of evolution and welcomed scientific knowledge as "an ever-expanding revelation of God's creative mind." Though commending Bryan's personal qualities, the Episcopal *Southern Churchman* criticized him for using "vehement denunciations" to dismiss the conclusions of scholars and warned against unleashing a "spirit of intellectual persecution."[17]

The famous Tennessee trial of John Thomas Scopes for violating the state's ban on teaching evolution in public schools did claim local headlines in 1925, but it evoked mixed reactions from the white Protestant community. As editor of the *Richmond News Leader,* Douglas Freeman presumably authored that newspaper's pointed criticisms of the celebrated trial lawyers William Jennings Bryan and Clarence Darrow. Blaming Bryan and the state of Tennessee for promoting ignorance, the *News Leader* discounted the importance of the episode. It merely showed the fragility of "the faith of those who fear that they will lose God if the way in which they were taught is proved wrong." Offended by Darrow's assault on religion and Bryan's commitment to ignorance, Richmond's denominational press tended to criticize both men. Though commending Bryan for defending religion, the *Richmond Christian Advocate* called the proceedings a "sad and distressing performance" that wasted time and energy better invested in such activities as evangelism. Calling the trial "much ado about very little," R. H. Pitt argued that the only real issue was the constitutionality of the Tennessee statute. Asserting that evolution would eventually "stand or fall according to determined facts," he wondered "what all the fuss is about." He was, however, in the process of learning what all the fuss was about. He soon joined Douglas Freeman and First Baptist's George White McDaniel in successfully opposing a proposal to ban the teaching of evolution in Virginia public schools. Rallying behind the antievolution cause, fundamentalists had begun a campaign to dictate their views in the Southern Baptist Convention, and Pitt quickly emerged as one of their most determined opponents.[18]

Writing in a December 1923 issue of the *Religious Herald,* Pitt angrily denounced "the attempt of the so-called Fundamentalists to invade the South with their peculiar propaganda." Earlier he had criticized Texan J. Frank Norris as the South's "chief apostle and prophet" of the movement and suggested that the World's Fundamentals Convention at Fort Worth should devote time to such topics as "common honesty," "simple truthfulness," and "decent manliness." Throughout the 1920s Pitt found that he had to counter Southern Baptist fundamentalists, who drew much of their support from America's Southwest. He charged that the fundamentalists threatened to divide, disrupt, and damage the Southern Baptist Convention.[19]

Born in 1853 in Tidewater Virginia, Robert Healy Pitt was destined for an impressive sixty-year career as a Baptist minister, editor, and denominational leader. The son of a rural physician, he attended Richmond College, where he distinguished himself. After more than a decade as a preacher, he became an associate editor for the *Religious Herald,* Virginia's state Baptist newspaper. In 1906 he became editor and owner of the *Herald.* He also served as president of the Baptist General Association of Virginia, as a member of the Foreign Mission Board of the Southern Baptist Convention, and as a member of the board of directors of Richmond College and its successor, the University of Richmond. As editor of the *Herald,* Pitt maintained the paper's tradition of moderate liberalism and articulated a distinctly Southern Baptist version of social Christianity. He steadfastly upheld the principle of separation of church and state, but he strongly supported campaigns for such reforms as improved public schools, higher education for women, and prohibition. In 1912 Pitt wrote a twelve-part series in which he issued a penetrating critique of America's property-conscious capitalist culture.[20]

Pitt's commentaries reflected the moderately liberal social and theological stances of a Richmond Baptist community who prized both "soul liberty" and education. Saluting the "liberalizing influence" of denominational colleges, Pitt declared in 1908 that "the spirit of Jesus is a large and liberal spirit compatible with orthodoxy and zeal for the truth." In fact, city Southern Baptist leaders often exhibited liberal leanings. Unencumbered by residual Landmarkism which characterized some Baptist fundamentalists, Richmond ministers readily participated in interdenominational activities. In the early twentieth century, they counted such socially concerned preachers as C. S. Gardner and M. Ashby Jones in their ranks. At Richmond College, President Frederic W. Boatwright invited controversial William Heth Whitsitt to join the faculty in 1901. Professors like S. C. Mitchell and Rolvix Harlan boosted both social reforms and new ideas. Emphasizing God's immanence, celebrating change, and deploring dogmatism, Mitchell promoted inquiry and praised scientific knowledge. At Second Baptist Church layman Douglas Southall Freeman voiced views similar to Pitt's. In presentations before his popular men's Bible class, Freeman rejected a literal interpretation of the Bible for progressive inspiration and depicted Jesus as "the first teacher of evolution." Uncomfortable with confessions and creeds, he reminded listeners that "the fundamental of your faith" as a Baptist "is to interpret God for yourself."[21]

Reflecting the outlook of Richmond's Baptist leadership, an alarmed R. H. Pitt decried the growing potency of fundamentalists within the Southern Baptist Convention in the 1920s. Pitt's views about four crucial matters—the Bible, evolution, religious liberty, and denominational programs—inevitably brought him into conflict with fundamentalists. Personally believing that the "original" biblical manuscripts were inerrant, he concluded that they had subsequently suffered from "transcribers, translators, printers, proofreaders," and others. "No one of any intelligence," to Pitt's knowledge, held that "the particular copy" of the Bible printed in English and sitting on "our table" is "guaranteed to us as absolutely free of error." He affirmed that the Bible, "interpreted as a whole," was authoritative on religious and ethical issues but protested its use as an infallible guide to subjects on which it touched "incidentally." Pitt saw little reason to be concerned about contemporary biblical scholarship. He maintained that the only people who used the label "higher critics" did so ignorantly or in an effort to discredit others. Pitt also differed with fundamentalists over the issue of evolution. In the *Religious Herald* he promoted the theory of theistic evolution. He argued that evolution did not "even by implication deny God" and that it aided some believers in their faith. "No blunder could be more crass and stupid," he asserted, than insisting that "the six creative 'days' of Genesis were just 24 hours long." Convinced that "real science" was an essential part of an education in Christian schools, Pitt avowed that it must not be replaced with a "patched up affair" that ignored "the verified facts of the universe."[22]

Pitt believed that Baptists had to guard "soul liberty" against fundamentalists, who threatened it by trying to impose a denomination-wide creed. No other Baptist principle was as sacred to him as "soul liberty," the right of each individual to direct spiritual access to God. Pitt urged resistance to anything that would "fetter the human spirit in its search for God." Because true religion had to be voluntary, compulsion deprived religion of its meaning. In the past, religious hierarchies and governments had violated soul liberty, but in the 1920s fundamentalists imperiled it and the Southern Baptist Convention itself. An excellent example of the individuals whom historian Bill Leonard has designated as "denominational builders," Pitt stalwartly supported the Southern Baptist Convention. The *Religious Herald* honored Baptist leaders, past and present, and praised denominational enterprises. Its pages trumpeted the value of Sunday school institutes, the Woman's Home Missionary Union, and the Foreign Mission Board and often highlighted the membership and financial accomplishments of Baptists.[23]

On each of these issues Pitt recognized that fundamentalists were at odds with him. Not only did they adopt a narrower definition of biblical authority, they sought to impose that definition on the Southern Baptist Convention. Many of them espoused premillenialism, a biblical interpretation shared by only one-fifth of Southern Baptists, according to Pitt. Rejecting evolution, fundamentalists wanted to purge Baptist colleges and seminaries of those who taught it. In "mistaken zeal" fundamentalists campaigned for Southern Baptists to adopt a doctrinal document that would have "quasi, if not actual authority" and would therefore interfere with soul freedom. Fundamentalists readily criticized Baptist leaders and, by Pitt's reckoning, provided only limited support to denominational programs. Pitt censured Norris particularly for titling his publication the *Searchlight,* thereby implying that there was "something hidden and sinister" in Baptist work. Norris, Pitt charged, "would rejoice" to see the "disintegration of the Baptist organizations in Texas" and "throughout the South."[24]

In the early 1920s, as fundamentalists attacked Baptist educators and institutions for teaching evolution, Pitt grew indignant. In February 1922 he suggested that there had been a "semi-hysterical agitation . . . in a few of our Baptist papers." He protested "in the name of simple justice and plain common sense and indeed in the name of the religion of Jesus Christ" against blanket charges of heretical teachings in Southern Baptist Convention schools. Printing letters from college presidents, he concluded there was "no teaching in science or other departments which denies or ignores God or discredits the fundamental tenets of Christianity." Pitt was horrified that "troublemakers" would "deprecate and discredit the piety" of such a man as Wake Forest College President W. L. Poteat, an "old-fashioned church-going, Bible-reading, hymn-singing, prayer-meeting and family altar Christian." Pitt objected when the 1922 Southern Baptist Convention adopted a report from its education board condemning the teaching of evolution, despite the fact that only seven of eighteen members of the board signed the report. Pitt doubted the competence of the Southern Baptist Convention to evaluate such a complicated issue as evolution. Angry at fundamentalists for their unwarranted attacks on Baptist schools, Pitt reminded them of another fundamental, "Thou shalt not bear false witness." He repeatedly criticized them as "professional agitators and disturbers of denominational unity."[25]

Pitt's defense of Baptist educators was soon subsumed by a larger task: preventing the Southern Baptist Convention (SBC) from adopting a creed. Fearful that modern biblical scholars and scientists would create doubts in pulpits and pews, fundamentalists called for the convention to adopt a statement of doctrine. At the SBC's 1924 meeting, Oklahoma fundamentalist Clarence P. Stealey made several unsuccessful proposals for doctrinal statements. In response to Stealey, a wary resolutions committee appointed a seven-member committee to assess the "advisability" of issuing a "statement of Baptist faith and message." The new committee included Stealey and Pitt, who had long opposed such a step. He believed that it was impossible to "bring the great mysteries of the Christian faith within the compass of our little two-by-four formularies. They transcend human knowledge." Nonetheless, the committee cited "the prevalence of naturalism in the modern teaching and preaching of religion" and decided to present such a document for consideration at the 1925 annual meeting. Pitt never fully reconciled himself to the endeavor. According to him, such a written document was a threat to the Baptist tradition of soul liberty and to the SBC's tradition of not supervising churches in doctrinal matters. By adhering to those traditions, the Southern Baptist Convention had thrived. Only a "serious emergency" could justify this departure, and no such emergency existed. He further maintained that any confession or creed was likely to be controversial, to create divisions among Baptists, and to divert them from their programs of evangelism.[26]

Using the structure of the 1833 New Hampshire Confession, the committee adopted and adapted much of its language. In many respects the resulting 1925 statement was fairly liberal. The document emphasized religious liberty and separation of church and state as well as added significant sections supporting education, social service, interdenominational cooperation, and the duty of Christians to seek peace. Only sentences describing the creation of man as a "special act of God" and specifically affirming the Virgin Birth and the Resurrection responded to concerns of fundamentalists. The committee attempted to address Pitt's fears about creed-making with a series of qualifying articles that formed an introduction to the statement of faith and message. The document represented itself as a "consensus of opinion" among Baptists for the purpose of instructing members. The statement was not designed to be a "complete statement of our faith" or to be final. Since the Bible was "the sole authority" for Baptists, "confessions are only guides in interpretation, having no authority over the conscience." The ideas expressed were "religious convictions" and were "not to be used to hamper freedom of thought or investigation in other realms of life."[27]

Yet, even this introduction failed to resolve Pitt's misgivings. He recognized that such a document could serve as a precedent for more restrictive declarations. He initially agreed to sign the statement, "lest in the present conditions" his refusal be misunderstood. He qualified his signature with an "assertion of my inalienable right" to change any position which might not "seem to me in strict accordance with the Word of God." He also added the caveat that the statement was "a mere expression of my own beliefs at this time" and not "a formulary to be imposed in any way upon anyone else in all the round world." At the 1925 Memphis meeting, the Southern Baptist Convention adopted the "Baptist Statement of Faith and Message," which appeared with signatures of only five committee members. Missing were the names of R. H. Pitt, whose reservations remained, and C. P. Stealey, who had wanted it to include a repudiation of evolution.[28]

Distressed by the divisive denominational controversies, Pitt identified the source of these problems: fundamentalists, particularly those based in the Southwest area of the denomination. As he observed, the SBC's system of "messengers" prevented the annual meeting from constituting a representative body of Southern Baptists. On the contrary, during the mid-1920s the locations of the annual meetings led to de facto discrimination against East Coast states, whose eligible messengers were deterred by the costs of time and travel. In 1925, Virginia, North Carolina, and Georgia were allotted a total of 4,102 messengers but mustered only 589 at Memphis. As Pitt noted, those three states could be outvoted by Arkansas and Oklahoma, states which sent their full quota of delegates but which were entitled to only one-seventh as many messengers as the former states. The comparison was no accident. Baptist leaders from Arkansas and Oklahoma joined fundamentalists from Texas as Pitt's major antagonists. In addition to implying that they packed convention meetings and imposed their doctrinal views, Pitt charged that they hypocritically refused to support the very denomination they tried to dominate. As an example, he referred to the Arkansas Baptist Convention, which required its employees to sign doctrinal statements including an antievolution plank. In 1924 Arkansas contributed less than one-half the amount to "our common work" than it had six years ago, "before we had all this agitation about doctrine." The further Arkansas went in "promulgating drastic creeds and requiring signatures," Pitt concluded, "the less they do in the way of cooperation with their brethren."[29]

The 1925 meeting left Pitt unhappy, but it left fundamentalists fuming. C. P. Stealey had tried to amend the Statement of Faith and Message to deny evolution as a means of creation, but the motion had failed. Before the 1926 SBC meeting in Houston, fundamentalists made clear their aim to adopt a similar resolution and require Southern Baptist officers and institutions to endorse it. Pitt declared that the SBC had made enough concessions to the fundamentalists. He charged that the host church for the 1926 meeting had thrown convention-wide work "overboard" and that its pastor was organizing the program to give fundamentalists a "large opportunity . . . to vent their spleen" against Baptist programs.[30]

To prevent a protracted doctrinal debate at the Houston meeting, those who agreed with Pitt enlisted the assistance of SBC President George White McDaniel. For two decades the pastor of Richmond's thriving First Baptist Church, McDaniel was a Texas native who combined a conservative theology with a commitment to Baptist traditions and denominational programs. Sharing Pitt's wariness about doctrinal statements, McDaniel believed that it was difficult to "draft a human document of finality." In his opening address at

Houston, McDaniel attempted to dissipate tensions by focusing on chapter 13 of 1 Corinthians and by stressing the unifying nature of denominational service. At the conclusion he declared: "I am happy to believe that this Convention accepts Genesis as teaching that man was the special creation of God, and rejects every theory, evolution or other, which teaches that man originated in, or came by way of, a lower animal ancestry." By prior arrangement, Louisiana's M. E. Dodd moved that McDaniel's sentence be declared "the sentiment of this body and from this point no further consideration be given to this subject." Dodd's motion was passed. Pitt and others believed that this maneuver had thwarted the fundamentalists.[31]

The fundamentalists did not quit easily. Recognizing that little had been gained by the McDaniel resolution, S. E. Tull of Arkansas introduced a resolution on the last day of the meeting. It required members of Southern Baptist boards and institutions and missionaries to give the convention assurance of their acceptance of the evolution declaration. Tull's resolution was adopted. An irritated Pitt later complained that the motion had been out of order. Renewing his argument about representation, he maintained that messengers from Texas, Arkansas, and Oklahoma had constituted a majority at the meeting.[32]

The Oklahoma Baptist Convention decided to take the Tull resolution seriously. In 1926 and 1927 the Oklahomans created a stir among Southern Baptists by withholding their contributions to some denominational programs. Perceiving the Oklahoma action as another attempt to damage the SBC, Pitt called upon the "Baptist people all over the South" to "set their faces like flint against these persistent and pestiferous interruptions of our greatest religious body in the performance of its legitimate functions." "The time is at hand," he announced, "for a show down in the Southern Baptist Convention."[33]

At the 1928 meeting, the SBC responded to the Oklahoma situation by adopting a report that emphasized the cooperative relationship between the convention and the state groups. Still, the SBC did retain its right to appeal directly to churches for financial support and did assert its right to "complete control of its own affairs." Just as the SBC had no authority to dictate about financial decisions to state conventions, "no state body has any authority to allocate funds or divert them from any object included in the Southwide budget." At the 1928 meeting, the convention also rejected a proposal from the Oklahoma Convention to create a denominational textbook commission that would secure scientists to write books "which do no violence to orthodox Baptists' conventional interpretation of the Bible." In December 1927 the board of directors of the Oklahoma Baptist General Convention had removed C. P. Stealey as editor of the *Baptist Messenger,* the state Baptist journal. In 1928 the Oklahoma Convention ceased withholding funds from Baptist programs. By then Oklahoma Baptist University professors had complied with the Tull resolution, as had the faculty at some other Baptist schools, including Baylor. Some members of the Southern Baptist Education Board and Foreign Missionary Board did so as well. Still, a majority of educators and denominational leaders such as seminary presidents Lee Scarborough and E. Y. Mullins refused to sign the statement.[34]

Historians have often portrayed fundamentalists as victorious in their attempt to dominate the Southern Baptist Convention of an earlier era. For example, historian William Ellis concluded that the 1920s witnessed "the triumph of fundamentalism" in the Southern Baptist Convention. Indeed, Southern Baptists did adopt an unprecedented document about beliefs, did repudiate evolution, and did instruct SBC leaders to renounce evolution. Other historians, however, have offered a more measured verdict. In perhaps the most perceptive analysis, church historian Bill Leonard has characterized denominational leaders as skillfully placating the insurgents with a periodic and temporary theological accommodation.[35]

These interpretations would have shocked R. H. Pitt, who was certain that the fundamentalists had "failed." That conclusion seems warranted. In fact, the fundamentalists had gained little. The evolution declarations and the 1925 Statement of Faith and Message featured a good bit of elastic phrasing that could accommodate the diversity within the SBC and would only faintly intrude on the principle of soul freedom. The Tull resolution received only brief and limited attention from Southern Baptist leaders. During the next several decades, Fundamentalism would operate more outside established Protestant denominations than within them. Pitt, who viewed the defeat of Fundamentalism as obvious, devoted a major editorial to explaining why it failed. He maintained that "doctrinal disturbances among our people are practically unknown." Yet fundamentalist leaders had tried to injure "brethren whose shoes they were unworthy to unlatch" and had disregarded the welfare of denominational programs. By failing to be honest, fair, and kind, fundamentalists had made it impossible for "quiet, decent God-fearing" Christians to follow them. The "vast majority" of Southern Baptists who gave the matter any thought viewed "the entrance into their territory of the so-called Fundamentalists (with a capital F) with all their hate and ugliness and often with the methods of the assassin, as nothing short of a calamity."[36]

In confronting fundamentalists, R. H. Pitt struggled with foes outside the community. Richmond Episcopalians, however, proved to be the only city religious group that engaged in internal theological disputes and the only group from which a significant contingent of fundamentalists emerged. Just as the highly respected Pitt forged to the center of a Baptist conflict, the popular

Walter Russell Bowie became a key figure in the Episcopalian controversy. Bowie was a child of St. Paul's. Born in Richmond in 1882, he was baptized and confirmed at St. Paul's. His father's death and family economic difficulties left young Russell for a time in the household of his aunt, Mary-Cooke Branch Munford. Her advice, her quest for spiritual well-being, and her commitment to social reform influenced Bowie throughout his life. Though rooted in Richmond, he always reached beyond. He earned his B.A. at Harvard, where he shared editorial duties on *The Crimson* with "Frank Roosevelt." He prized his theological training at Virginia Seminary in Alexandria, but he made special arrangements to attend Union Seminary in New York for one semester. Classes and interactions with Arthur C. McGiffert, William Adams Brown, and Henry Sloane Coffin introduced him to contemporary religious scholarship. But Bowie's home was Virginia. Ordained at St. Paul's, he served a rural parish near Charlottesville until Richmond beckoned him in 1912.[37]

Bowie's tenure at St. Paul's was remarkable. When he delivered his inaugural sermon there, he and the congregation began a twelve-year love feast marked by their mutual ties to tradition and by their excitement about addressing social and religious changes of the twentieth century. Whether introducing children's sermons, advocating social justice, or winning support for missions or denominational campaigns, he inspired the congregation, which doubled in size during his stay. By repeatedly rejecting calls to other large urban churches, Bowie won even greater appreciation from his communicants, who were fiercely proud of their native son. Bowie initiated efforts for a diocesan social service commission and spurred his own laymen to conduct a housing study of Richmond. Sobered by his experiences as a chaplain in the Great War, he eloquently advocated measures for international peace. Pulpit exchanges, surviving correspondence, and editorials in Richmond's religious press testify to the respect Bowie earned among other religious leaders, including Rabbi E. N. Calisch.[38]

Though popular, Bowie did become embroiled in a 1916 theological debate conducted in the columns of the *Southern Churchman.* That ruckus proved to be a precursor of a larger conflict in the 1920s. In August the *Churchman* published a letter from James W. Morris, rector of Richmond's Monumental Church. Distressed by some clerical interpretations of New Testament teachings about divorce, Morris attacked those who refused to accept the finality of scriptural statements about faith and morals. In a sweeping and somewhat ambiguous critique, he deplored scholars who questioned the infallibility of the Bible, characterized higher criticism as a "monstrous import" from Germany, and warned that such an approach to Scripture permitted people to get what they pleased from the Bible. Bowie responded with a different view. He emphasized the human fallibility of biblical writers and noted differences among well-read "earnest and sincere men" over the meaning of certain passages. Bowie argued that Jesus and the apostles had not intended to create a new legalistic moral code for future generations but rather had offered principles to be applied through the inspiration of religious experience. Expressing respect and personal affection for the older Morris, Bowie's temperately phrased letter might easily have ended the discussion.[39]

Instead, the controversy accelerated during the next three months. An unidentified Virginia clergyman sent a copy of Bowie's letter to Toronto's Dr. W. Griffith Thomas, an Anglican scholar who later helped found Evangelical Theological College, the predecessor of Dallas Theological Seminary. In a rebuttal published in the *Southern Churchman,* Griffith Thomas misquoted and misstated some of Bowie's views, incorrectly argued that Bowie had disputed the authority of the Bible, and charged that Bowie's beliefs were unfaithful to Christianity or to the Church. A surprised Bowie countered by correcting Griffith Thomas's apparent misunderstanding of his statements and by buttressing his own position by invoking a cadre of biblical scholars. Bowie claimed that he wrote only to prevent potential ministerial candidates from becoming discouraged by the rigid and literal scriptural interpretations held by some clergymen. Griffith Thomas dismissed most of Bowie's scholarly authorities either as non-Anglicans or as higher critics and apparently counted the much revered Bishop Phillips Brooks in the latter group.[40]

The *Southern Churchman*'s 1916 debate soon expanded to include other participants from Virginia as well as from more distant spots such as New Jersey, Texas, and Louisiana. In three additional commentaries, James W. Morris concluded that younger clergymen had misunderstood his initial letter. Reaffirming his commitment to inerrancy, though, he warned that modern scholars threatened to destroy the church's doctrines and "tear" the Bible "in pieces." Indeed, younger ministers had rallied behind Bowie and had presented their own reasons for a broad view of biblical interpretation. Writing from the University of Virginia, Beverley D. Tucker was among those advocating a liberal position. A Richmond layman and stockholder in the *Southern Churchman* Company, Langbourne M. Williams deplored Bowie's ideas. Assigned the task of summarizing and concluding the debate, Richmond rector Peyton Craighill took a slightly liberal stance. More significantly, with a truly Richmond attitude, he cautioned that "nothing is pleasing to Jesus Christ which is not done in a brotherly and loving spirit" and urged all to remember that those with whom they disagreed were "loyal to Christ" and "devoted to the truth." No doubt he was correct. But Morris, Bowie, Griffith Thomas, Tucker, and Williams would all have more to say in the future.[41]

In a July 1919 letter published in the *Southern Churchman*, Langbourne M. Williams denounced "this woman suffrage business" as "an inspiration of the devil" and as contrary to Christian doctrine. An indignant Lucy Randolph Mason issued a crisp reply that invoked Christian and democratic principles to support suffrage. Williams, though, had even more reasons to be upset when he read the *Southern Churchman*. In 1919 Bowie assumed substantial editorial responsibilities and became the sole editor in 1921. True to the paper's liberal past, Bowie, assisted by R. Cary Montague, condemned corporate greed, the Ku Klux Klan, and lynching as well as championed a long list of social causes and reform organizations. Favoring intellectual tolerance, the paper supported a "reverent Modernism." The *Southern Churchman*'s board of directors was so pleased with Bowie's work that its members persuaded him to remain editor after he accepted a call to New York City's Grace Church in 1923.[42]

Yet, as historian Norman Furniss later observed, 1923 proved to be a difficult year for Episcopalians in the United States. It was the year that a Fort Worth rector who questioned miracles became the object of a heresy investigation. It was also the year that Episcopal bishops asserted their authority and the authority of the creeds over the heterodoxical statements coming from some pulpits. And 1923 was the year when Bowie moved to New York, where the city's liberal rectors chafed against the rigid authority of Bishop William Manning. As Bowie relocated from South to North, controversy in his new city spread to his old one. In January 1923 Percy S. Grant, a New York rector, delivered a sermon in which he allegedly denied that Jesus had supernatural powers. Reports led many people to conclude that he had also denied Christ's divinity. Bishop Manning issued Grant an ultimatum to retract or clarify his statement of "disbelief in our Lord Jesus Christ as God and Saviour." Unless Grant complied, Manning expected him to resign. Bowie reported these events in the *Southern Churchman*. Concluding that press accounts had distorted Grant's words, Bowie called for reconciliation lest the confrontation lead to a heresy trial. After Grant clarified his theological ideas in a statement to Manning, the bishop remained dissatisfied but decided against a trial.[43]

In several editorials about the Grant-Manning affair, Bowie criticized both men but called for intellectual tolerance. Bowie believed that clergymen should have the right "to large freedom in the quest for truth," and he praised all religious leaders who engaged in "large reinterpretations of ancient formulas of the church." Bowie reprinted Grant's letter to Manning. In it Grant denied biblical miracles, disputed the existence of a literal Hell, and questioned the possibility of a physical resurrection as well as the Virgin Birth.

Emphasizing Jesus' humanity, Grant did affirm that Christ was the incarnation of God. Stating that he did not agree with all of Grant's ideas, Bowie described Grant's letter as a "temperate, careful, and very able" statement expressing "convictions essentially Christian."[44]

Grant's remarks and Bowie's apparent endorsement of them disconcerted many in Richmond. Several city ministers immediately preached sermons about Christ's divinity. The *Richmond News Leader* reported that local Episcopal clergymen had signed a petition calling for Bowie to sever his ties with the *Southern Churchman.* William E. Cox, rector of the Church of the Holy Comforter, quickly corrected that account. Although the Richmond ministers had objected to an editorial policy that appeared to support Grant and condemn the bishop, Cox asserted that they did not wish Bowie's removal as editor. But others did. Bowie's 1916 adversary, layman Langbourne M. Williams, led the campaign. In letters to other stockholders of the *Southern Churchman,* Williams condemned Bowie's acceptance of modernist theology and charged that he was acting "like a Greek horse in the Church of Virginia." Williams feared that modernist ministers were attempting to discredit his most precious beliefs. In one letter Williams wrote that he was "too much in need of a Saviour to want peace of mind at the sacrifice of my belief in the Trinity and the whole Bible as written." Williams clung to "the gospel according to St. John" and vowed to fight the "circuitous, perambulatory Unitarian evolutionary, mental gymnastics or metaphysical ambiguous diatribes of the mental wanderers."[45]

St. James's Episcopal Church emerged as the center for opposition to Bowie's position. That congregation claimed a proud past, replete with Confederate heroes, socially committed laywomen, and distinguished rectors. As a St. James's communicant, Virginia Bishop William Cabell Brown added prestige to the church. In 1923 the rector, G. Freeland Peter, joined in the criticism of Bowie's theological views. A 1916 antagonist, Toronto's W. H. Griffith Thomas, conducted Victorious Life Conferences at St. James's in March and November 1923. And Langbourne M. Williams served as a vestryman. In May 1923 the Men's Club of St. James's passed a resolution deploring the "growing tendency" of ministers "to almost, if not actually, deny the Deity of our Lord and Savior Jesus Christ, the only begotten Son of God." Several laymen delivered addresses which were subsequently reprinted and distributed. Arguing that a crisis existed in the Episcopal church, vestryman Murray McGuire deprecated clergymen who "fence with words" while questioning Christ's divinity and biblical miracles and portraying their opponents as ignorant. He condemned ministers who preached "contrary to their vows" and called for such men to resign. Like McGuire, layman Thomas Willcox focused on Jesus' divinity, but vestryman John B. Mordecai launched a wider indictment of modernists, evolutionists, and colleges and universities that undercut the faith of students.[46]

The temptation to respond to St. James's in print was more than Bowie could resist. In a July *Southern Churchman* editorial, he reminded readers that theological discussions should be conducted in "a Christian way." Furthermore, citing a recent decline in missionary offerings, he argued that such debates could distract members from the important work of the church. "Those who are most vehement in laying down their definitions about the church's faith," Bowie charged, "are not always those who are most faithful to the church's business." Alluding to an unnamed church, Bowie described laymen who zealously exhorted others to uphold traditional faith but who also encouraged members to withhold money from a nationwide missionary campaign, thereby failing to meet the goal allotted to the congregation. In a vein similar to Richmond's other evangelical leaders, Bowie suggested that less attention should be paid to other people's opinions and more to the church's kingdom work. If Bowie intended to make only a veiled reference to St. James's, the veil was too thin. By titling the editorial "Be Ye Doers of the Word," he invoked the motto of St. James's and made the church's identity obvious.[47]

Outraged, the laymen of St. James's hotly disputed the insinuation that they had discouraged contributions to the denominational campaign. Yet Bowie was at least partially correct. In 1922, unhappy about the size of the diocese quota assigned to the church, vestrymen had successfully appealed for a reduction. Nonetheless, insulted by the editorial's public portrayal of their church as stingy, the vestry and individual laymen angrily protested. A vestry resolution called the editorial "wholly unjustified" and sought an apology. None came. But the editorial dominated correspondence among the board of directors of the *Southern Churchman* as well as discussions during their December meeting. The 1923 conflict also wounded the members of St. Paul's, the largest church in the diocese and the one contributing most to denominational causes. Still fiercely proud of Bowie, irate members believed that Bishop Brown had discounted Bowie's achievements and that Virginia Seminary President Berryman Green had failed to defend Bowie during the theological disputes. The president of the *Southern Churchman* Company, Lewis C. Williams, tried unsuccessfully to soothe egos and reconcile differences.[48]

In May 1924 Bowie reluctantly resigned as editor. Earlier he had acknowledged that his New York residence made it difficult to serve in the position and had offered to relinquish it whenever the board of directors found a suitable replacement. In 1924, however, he resisted, believing that his adversaries at St. James's had deliberately overreacted to his July editorial in order to discredit him and force him out. But the *Southern Churchman*'s board of directors had grown weary of controversies, and several members finally concluded that perhaps Bowie was too theologically liberal to head the paper.[49]

The change of editors did not bring peace for the *Southern Churchman*. Bowie's successor, Joseph B. Dunn, maintained the paper's allegiance to social and theological liberalism. Calling for tolerance in religious discussions, Dunn stressed social service, discounted the importance of a literal interpretation of Scriptures, acknowledged the fallibility of the Bible, and embraced theistic evolution. Twice in February 1926, Langbourne M. Williams urged Dunn to resign because his views would "tend to shake the faith of anyone in the Bible." Dunn did resign in September, but his successor, R. Cary Montague, also antagonized Williams by articulating liberal theology. In April 1927 Williams began purchasing shares of *Southern Churchman* Company stock, gained control of a majority of them, and took charge of the paper.[50]

With Williams at the helm, the *Southern Churchman* charted a dramatically different direction and swiftly cruised toward Fundamentalism. New authors changed the paper's theological stance and used a strident tone previously foreign to the local religious press. Williams and new editors Pembroke Reed and James W. Morris were major writers. Now often critical of the Episcopal Church, the journal added articles by such national fundamentalist figures as J. Gresham Machen, William Bell Riley, and James M. Gray, as well as reprinted material from the *Christian Fundamentals Magazine* and from the Moody Bible Institute. And several churches, including St. James's, hosted Bible conferences led by fundamentalists.[51]

The new *Southern Churchman* viewed itself as defending the Bible, the creeds, and Christian doctrine against the heretical assaults of intellectuals, modernists, and other radicals. The paper's new title page proclaimed the following: "The Revelation of the Bible Is Complete. Its Doctrines Immutable. Its Truth Inviolable and Its Authority Is Absolute." Arguing that save for biblical authority humans would be "adrift with no compass," the new editors declared that "freedom from authority of the word began in Eden with Satan." Williams proudly embraced the label "Bible Belt," and other writers suggested that without the foundation of biblical authority the nation would succumb to "unbelief" and "wickedness." Replacing the paper's earlier emphasis on a Christian's earthly duties, the writers now focused on salvation, eternity, and the Second Coming. Reciting prophetic evidence, Pembroke Reed moved toward a premillennial vision. Featuring defenses of inerrancy, the Virgin Birth, miracles, the atonement, and the Resurrection, the *Southern Churchman* opposed any changes to the prayer book and supported the church's conservative bishops. Those opposing the church hierarchy were termed "social visionaries," who should "leave the church and adjourn to Moscow."[52]

Like other fundamentalists of the 1920s, the writers for the *Southern Churchman* readily identified the major threats to traditional religion: modernist preachers, scholars using higher criticism, and liberal professors. Protesting that Moses had written the Pentateuch and that Jonah's story was literally true, James W. Morris asserted that higher critics would leave it "quite uncertain what Jesus taught." Angry that such men betrayed the faith, the *Southern Churchman* denounced them harshly. Pembroke Reed charged that modern theology looked "toward Sodom, the city of destruction." Williams labeled opponents of the fundamentals, "mental funnies," "poisonous parasites," traitors, and Unitarians. He characterized them as "busy impotent apostles of despair." The *Southern Churchman* described liberal religious scholars as vain intellectuals who relied on their own subjective reasoning and their own imaginations rather than on biblical revelation. The *Southern Churchman* argued that modernist preachers and those with doubts about the creeds should leave the church. "An atheist," Williams declaimed, was better than those who "accepted the benefits of a Christian Church under false pretenses." The paper condemned modernists for robbing Christians of supernatural religion and substituting a "mangled gospel" and doubt for biblical authority.[53]

From the *Southern Churchman*'s perspective, intellectuals and educational institutions also discredited themselves. They corrupted young minds with the theory of evolution, which debased humans and discounted personal moral responsibility by placing people on a par with animals. Unlike devout Bible believers, who built government and society, intellectuals did little useful. Instead, they "shirked and sneered," obstructed progress, and sought personal rewards. Appalled when the faculty of Smith College protested the execution of Sacco and Vanzetti, Williams designated Smith and Bryn Mawr as "dangerous places." Smith, he declared, poisoned the minds of young women, encouraged atheism, infidelity, and immorality, and disregarded the duties of citizenship and "all that clean thinking Americans hold sacred."[54]

Anxious about educators, Williams soon located a closer menace: Virginia Theological Seminary in Alexandria. The trouble began when seminary president Berryman Green rejected an offer from Williams to finance the appearance of "some great learned Bible scholar." According to Williams, Green refused the opportunity lest it be seen as a reflection on his faculty. When modernist scholar Henry Sloane Coffin then visited the campus, an outraged Williams asked whether the seminary should expect truly devout people to continue to contribute to it. In March 1928 Williams launched a verbal assault on the seminary. Using both recorded and anonymous sources, he indicted two of the school's professors as modernists and asserted that two of the alumni were really Unitarians. Citing the past classroom use of Walter Rauschenbusch's *Christianity and the Social Crisis,* a "blasphemous book," Williams declared that in his "humble opinion" the school needed an "overhauling." Berryman Green only partially placated Williams by sending him a *Theological Seminary Bulletin* with underscored portions demonstrating the school's orthodoxy. This dispute did not overtly harm the seminary. But it sharpened fissures among Richmond Episcopal clergymen. After several meetings where courtesy eventually gave way to discord, fifteen of the twenty-three Richmond area ministers signed a statement expressing "complete confidence" in the seminary's faculty and teaching.[55]

At least a few readers of the *Southern Churchman* were horrified by its new version. Unhappy about its "most bigoted fundamentalist" stance, a Baltimore rector objected to its "unChristian and ungentlemanly . . . propaganda," terminated his connection with it, and declared that the Episcopal Church "would be healthier and more Christian" if others also ceased their subscriptions. A Staunton, Virginia, Episcopal paper similarly deplored the *Southern Churchman* for being "violently narrowminded and intolerant." Yet the *Southern Churchman*'s fundamentalist campaign did little to deflect the direction of Richmond's liberal Episcopalians. With Bowie's blessing, Beverley Tucker had succeeded him at St. Paul's and had maintained a commitment to liberal theology and social service. Bowie made regular visits to St. Paul's, where he was greeted by capacity audiences. Tucker assisted in the creation of an organization called Virginia Liberal Evangelicals, a group that Pembroke Reed categorically attacked as modernists. With liberal clergymen's voices excluded from the *Southern Churchman,* they gained some space in the diocesan newspaper, the *Virginia Churchman,* which R. Cary Montague began to edit. There they joined moderate leaders who reiterated their orthodoxy but expressed a wish to "adjust themselves" to "modern conditions." Thus, Williams and his fundamentalist supporters changed the direction of theological discussions in Virginia in the 1920s, but they did not overwhelm others who retained their liberal and orthodox views.[56]

After serving Grace Church, Walter Russell Bowie became a professor at New York's Union Theological Seminary and participated in the writing of *The Interpreter's Bible* and the Revised Standard Version of the Bible. Later, he returned to Virginia Theological Seminary, where he became a revered professor. In his memoirs he discounted the 1923 controversy, calling it a "misunderstanding" that "died down to nothing." In a sense, he was correct. In the 1930s, following Langbourne M. Williams's death, the *Southern Churchman* ceased to champion Fundamentalism. Its religious campaign had, in the words of Richmond journalist and historian Virginius Dabney, "made but slight headway." But for more than half a decade there had been a fundamentalist-modernist "row" in the Old Dominion's capital, and the forceful presentation of fundamentalist views had come from Episcopalians.[57]

Why did conflict erupt among city Episcopalians? Some explanations applicable elsewhere can be discarded. This fundamentalist-modernist dispute cannot be attributed to class differences since those involved tended to be personally wealthy or served as leaders of well-to-do churches. Langbourne M. Williams was a lawyer and a businessman. The men of St. James's were not the "anxious people" of the lower socioeconomic levels identified by William Trollinger in his description of First Baptist Church, Minneapolis. Similarly, the clergy and laity of the Episcopal churches came from the ranks of the well educated, not the uneducated. Unlike Richmond's Presbyterians, whose views about theology tended to coincide with age, Episcopalians could not attribute their disagreements to generational differences.[58]

Several facts do serve as keys in explaining the surge of Fundamentalism among Richmond Episcopalians in the 1920s. First, laymen played large roles. The Men's Class at St. James's served as the focal point for early expressions. In correspondence with Bowie, Murray McGuire took exception to the argument that the laity might not be qualified to assess the merits of some theological issues. He countered that laymen "compose the main body of the church," "support the church," were relied upon by ministers to provide them employment, and were therefore "entitled to be heard" and protest views they believed were contrary to church teachings. Later, while justifying his public interrogation of Virginia Seminary, Langbourne M. Williams explained how he defined his role with *Southern Churchman.* "Being merely an ordinary layman," he tried to "put into blunt words what the rank and file of the Church are thinking and asking." Such lay leadership was hardly surprising in the setting of Richmond, where male church members were conspicuous participants in most religious activities.[59]

Second, Richmond's Fundamentalism was fueled by outside controversies, outside personalities, and outside resources. The Grant-Manning dispute was an import from New York. Canada's W. Griffith Thomas intervened in the 1916 theological debate and was at St. James's during the 1923 controversy. After Langbourne Williams assumed ownership of the *Southern Churchman,* he relied heavily on authors from outside the state. Third, Richmond Episcopalians stood divided on the importance of social Christianity. The city's most conservative Episcopal leaders endorsed the post "Great Reversal" view of fundamentalists that social concerns needed to be de-emphasized. Their counterparts disagreed. In the early 1920s, some members of the board of directors of the *Southern Churchman* were especially enthusiastic about Bowie's penetrating Social Gospel editorials. But not Langbourne M. Williams. In addition to opposing woman's suffrage, he later complained to Bowie, "you stress social service and physical benefits too much." With Williams in control, the *Southern Churchman* gradually discontinued its columns devoted to social issues. In response to an Episcopalian who requested the paper's attention to Labor Sunday, Williams replied that he favored ministers "confining themselves to preaching the truth of the Bible."[60]

Fourth, unlike other major Protestant denominations, Richmond's Episcopalians had no local institution of higher learning where resident scholars personally known and respected could disarm fears about new scientific or theological ideas. Not only did the faculty of the University of Richmond serve that role for Baptists, they also hosted controversial scholars such as William L. Poteat. Even the older Presbyterian faculty at Union Theological Seminary encouraged a wide intellectual perspective, and the younger faculty tended to be moderately liberal. The proximity of Randolph-Macon College likewise influenced theological discussions among local Methodists. In February 1924 at Broad Street Methodist Church, Bishop Collins Denny defended the Virgin Birth and deity of Christ. The following week, the president of Randolph-Macon College, R. E. Blackwell told the Richmond Ministerial Union that "I do not care what a man believes about evolution and higher criticism. I am eager to work with him if he loves Christ." With Virginia Seminary located one hundred miles to the north, city Episcopalians lacked local professors who could provide reassurance.[61]

In 1928 R. H. Pitt issued a scathing critique of the fundamentalist movement and declared that fundamentalists had "failed" to gain "the general support of evangelical people." At least for Richmond's Protestants, Pitt's assessment was accurate. Although city Episcopalians weathered a fundamentalist controversy, that situation proved to be an aberration. No fundamentalist leader gained a major following, and other Protestant leaders demonstrated little affinity for the fundamentalist cause. By contrast, several theologically liberal ministers were prominent, published, and popular. Richmond's experience with Fundamentalism carries significant implications for southern history. Richmond provides additional evidence that early Fundamentalism was neither southern born nor southern bred. And Richmond serves as a staid contrast to Scopes trial caricatures portraying the South as a region inhabited by uneducated, intolerant religious zealots. But the Richmond saga is also noteworthy because it offers clues as to why Fundamentalism failed to make any major inroads in a southern city of the 1920s.[62]

Fundamentalism failed in Richmond for four reasons. First, only a few

Richmond Protestant ministers shared the fears voiced by national fundamentalist leaders. In a city where some prominent ministers embraced theological liberalism and where interdenominational activity was common, the presentation of new theological ideas rarely seemed threatening. In the early twentieth century, the *Presbyterian of the South* and professors at Union Theological Seminary did challenge new theological interpretations, but they did so selectively, not categorically. After Episcopalian Langbourne M. Williams acquired the *Southern Churchman,* several local clergymen joined him in issuing tirades against liberal theologians and scientists. But such expressions of apprehension were unusual. In the 1920s several preachers did make deliberate efforts to reiterate the basic beliefs and doctrines of their denominations. For example, in a 1923 book, *The Supernatural Jesus,* Baptist George White McDaniel robustly defended such beliefs as the Virgin Birth, the infallibility of the Bible, the Resurrection, and Christ's Second Coming. Another Baptist minister, W. W. Weeks, wrote a series of articles for the *Religious Herald* dealing with many of the same topics. The *Richmond Christian Advocate* featured a similar series about the doctrines of Methodism. Yet these ministers offered only passing criticisms of modernists or evolutionists. The ministers did not portray either group as a major threat and did not advocate any action to stifle the discussion of their ideas. On the contrary, although the conservative McDaniel disputed the theological views of some modernists, he counseled patience and sympathy for doubters, combined with "a trust that in God's own good time he will bring them his way." Indeed, McDaniel emerged as a defender of differing religious views within his denomination and within the state of Virginia. A champion of interdenominational cooperation, W. W. Weeks refused to "scold those who may differ from us in interpretations of the *New Testament.*"[63]

Second, Fundamentalism failed in Richmond because Protestant leaders rejected the fundamentalist appeal to limit the intellectual scope of Christianity. By insisting on literal interpretations of the Bible, by trying to prohibit the teaching of evolution, and by demanding rigid adherence to creeds, fundamentalists wanted to limit tightly the boundaries of acceptable beliefs. Yet Richmond Protestants were not attracted to an outlook that seemed to circumscribe thought and knowledge. The city's five denominational newspapers and one theological journal offered a variety of religious views. Serving as a center for religious education, Richmond fostered an intellectual climate that was receptive to new ideas. For example, long before the 1920s, S. C. Mitchell had celebrated "the affinities in the spirit of science and religion" and had depicted "a dogmatic mind" as "morally diseased." Arguing that "our Lord intended for his followers to progress in a knowledge of divine truth," Mitchell characterized Jesus "on the intellectual side of his being" as "progressive, tolerant and free." In commenting on one "strange interpretation" of the Bible, Union Seminary professor E. C. Caldwell wondered if his own interpretation was correct and resolved "to try to keep open-minded and active-minded towards the truth." Walter Lingle admitted that southern Presbyterians tended to be conservative, but added, "we do try to keep our minds open to the truth, no matter whether it is old or new." H. D. C. Maclachlan suggested that "we discover God and learn His ways just as we discover the facts and laws of Nature." Using hypothesis, experimentation, and experience, believers might determine that parts of creeds stood the tests while other parts did not.[64]

Other churchmen also favored a broad intellectual approach to religious faith. For example, Baptist layman A. W. Patterson aligned himself with conservative theologians, but he emphatically endorsed a belief in "progressive revelation," "which implies increasing knowledge of the truth with corresponding adaptation and custom." Episcopal rector W. E. Cox proclaimed that "the old and the new in religion are but different aspects of the truth" and that Christians should seek to relate the two to one another. In a letter to a Charlotte, North Carolina, minister, Walter W. Moore noted his own conservative views but declared that he was "'agin' the policy of trying to secure copper-plate similarity among thinking men by the terrors of presbyterial examinations." Perhaps a Baptist minister, John W. Storer, expressed the dominant reaction in Richmond to the fundamentalist restrictive view of the truth. Storer complained that there was a current theory that a person "has to shut his eyes to have an orthodox faith, and that if a man stops to think or study about it he is not a believer in God." Storer repudiated this attitude. Characterizing his faith as "more than an empty echo of an air-tight compartment," he concluded that "the more I think, the more I believe in God and believe that Christ is my Saviour."[65]

Third, fundamentalists failed in Richmond because local ministers objected to the tactics of fundamentalists. In a community which prized civility, the fiery tone of militant Fundamentalism introduced unwelcomed rancor. Maclachlan wondered if fundamentalists thought they would really serve Christianity by using the "methods of the inquisition." Walter Lingle condemned fundamentalists for their successful campaign to have a prominent professor dismissed from Princeton Theological Seminary. In a private letter, Lingle concluded that most fundamentalists he knew were "ready to burn at the stake those who differ with them. They show a certain bitterness that is beyond my understanding." Although Baptist George White McDaniel criticized modernists, he opposed requiring tests of faith that would "fetter freedom, alienate the intellectual and stop progress." Pitt denounced fundamentalists for their "reckless disregard for such fundamentals as truth, and honesty, and brotherly kindness, and justice, and fairness." Calling it neither "prudent nor Christian" to "unchurch or exile" all doubters, Richmond Methodist editor Joseph Rowland counseled that churches should "be kind and gentle, but true," and often ignore those raising questions about traditional beliefs. Rowland, who admittedly disagreed with some of the ideas expressed by liberal Methodist Bishop McConnell, defended McConnell from allegations of heresy in 1929.[66]

Fourth, Fundamentalism failed in Richmond because city ministers believed that fundamentalists did little to advance the work of churches. Religious leaders busy with denominational and interdenominational enterprises deemed theological conflict a waste of time and talent. Maclachlan maintained that any group of Christians that claimed to have a "fuller insight into the will of their Lord" than did other Christians must "justify their claim at the bar of practical results or nowhere." Maclachlan, like Bowie, argued that fundamentalists spent more time issuing tests of faith than doing church work. R. H. Pitt voiced similar criticisms. He observed that those Baptists who wanted the Southern Baptist Convention to adopt a creedal statement came from states that gave the convention the least financial support. He concluded that "it is possible to be awfully drastic and straight laced in the matter of creedal declarations and of imposing them upon other folk while we neglect the great business of promoting the Kingdom of God in the World." Walter W. Moore saw theological conflict as unnecessary and once warned a friend that southern Presbyterians should avoid it lest they "be torn into bloody pieces" and "all our work for Christ knocked out and set back indefinitely." The Methodist *Richmond Christian Advocate* warned against "contentions and factions in the family of God," suggested that fundamentalists tended to "overstress creed" and "understress conduct," and cited the world's need for conversion as "the greatest fundamental." Thus, in the 1920s, Richmond Protestants resisted both the attitudes and the agenda of fundamentalists.[67]

In short, Fundamentalism failed in Richmond because local Protestant leaders concluded that fundamentalists posed a greater threat to organized church life and to the churches' ministries than did evolutionists or modernists. Richmond clergymen were confident that Christians would not easily be led astray from their beliefs. Few ministers expressed fears that new biblical scholarship or scientific findings would damage Christianity. On the other hand, ministers found that both national and local fundamentalist leaders persistently created discord among Protestants. In 1928 R. H. Pitt seemed to express the dominant reaction in Richmond to fundamentalists: "If these self-appointed guardians of our orthodox beliefs, themselves often discredited, both in religion and morals, would let our people alone, they will find their way through the simple teaching of the New Testament and the faithful preaching and pastoral service of their chosen spiritual leaders into the very heart of the gospel of Jesus."[68]

12
Avenues of Faith

"Jesus was a city man," insisted Richmond minister John A. MacLean in November 1929. Observing that people often thought of Jesus "as a man of the country," MacLean countered that "the fact is He lived and worked largely in the city." As pastor of Ginter Park Presbyterian Church, MacLean believed that Jesus "is wanted among the bright lights as well as in the lily fields." Describing the complexity, intensity, and difficulties of urban life, MacLean called upon Presbyterians to expand their urban ministry and urged them to visualize "the Christ of the city streets." By 1929 Richmond's Protestant leaders had gained ample experience in that type of effort. In developing their urban ministries during the early twentieth century, they could claim substantial success. Ministers and laypersons had exerted a significant influence not only in their city but also in their state and in their denominations. Radiating far beyond pulpit, pew, and prayer meeting, Richmond's avenues of faith carried Protestants into their community, out to the countryside, and across the oceans.[1]

In 1907 the Baptist *Religious Herald* praised Richmond for "rapidly becoming one of our really great cities, in education, in commerce, in manufactures, in finance." Appreciating the city's "glorious and heroic past," the writer applauded its present "unconquerable and well-directed energy." Indeed, restless Richmond boasted many achievements. During the century's first three decades, the growing city more than doubled its population and quadrupled its incorporated area. While the cadres of Confederate veterans shrank, the ranks of industrial workers, urban boosters, and reformers swelled. Factories, skyscrapers, and automobiles filled the city's landscape. New commercial and retail firms employed increasing numbers of white-collar workers, including women. Mass consumption in department stores accompanied mass entertainment in grand new movie theaters and amusement parks. Reformers successfully fanned a progressive breeze that substantially altered the community with new schools, better public health programs, and more recreational facilities. At times local Protestants worried about the ability of their churches to respond to the challenge posed by the changing urban conditions. Expressions of concern, however, gave way to purposeful action. Recalling that Christianity "began as a city religion," First Baptist's George W. McDaniel affirmed that "Jesus meant for his gospel to conquer the city."[2]

As twentieth-century Richmond grew, a generation of Protestants transformed the urban landscape. In a tour of the community in the late 1920s, an automobile driver could pass scores of new churches, including some located in new neighborhoods. In Ginter Park, a once small Union Theological Seminary thrived on a campus filled with new buildings. Nearby, the General Assembly Training School and Mission Court reflected new ventures by Presbyterians. Having moved to a site in the far West End, the University of Richmond boasted more buildings, professors, and students, and it welcomed female students to its Westhampton College. Not far away, St. Christopher's and St. Catherine's likewise flourished as educational institutions. On Oregon Hill, St. Andrew's School provided educational opportunities and served as the center for neighborhood social services. The Baptist House of Happiness, the Methodist Institute and Goodwill Industries, the Wilson Inn, and the Presbyterian Seventeenth Street Mission testified to efforts to reach out to the religious and social needs of city residents. The Methodist orphanage as well as the new buildings housing the Children's Home Society and the juvenile court signified concerns about children. Public baths operated thanks to Protestant laypersons. The Richmond School of Social Work and Public Health counted religious leaders among its founders. Such facilities offered both immediate services and future benefits. At the tenth anniversary of Westhampton College, S. C. Mitchell imagined "the great host of cultured women who will throng these halls in coming centuries." And the new structures told only part of the story. In 1926 the *Presbyterian of the South* complained about a national survey of churches which focused on their physical plants. "A church ought to be equipped for its work," the writer acknowledged, "but the work is more important than the equipment." As city people, Richmond Protestants engaged in such work by developing seven notable avenues of faith responsive to their urban environment.[3]

City faith flourished along an avenue of religious diversity. Richmond defied the notion of the South as a religiously homogeneous region. Impressed by the numerous Baptists and Methodists in the South, scholars once assumed that those denominations shaped the region's religious culture. But in Richmond they shared that role. Though the largest religious groups, Baptists and Methodists together comprised less than one-half of the adult white members of churches and synagogues in 1926. In fact, Jews and Catholics outnumbered the members of every Protestant denomination except the Baptists and Methodists. Furthermore, liturgical Episcopalians and Lutherans accounted for one out of every five adult white Protestants.[4]

Numbers alone hardly captured the city's variety. Richmonders sustained a religious diversity evident in worship, church governance, ideas, and public affairs. Episcopalians, Lutherans, and Presbyterians affirmed confessions or creeds, but Baptists and Disciples of Christ adamantly resisted them. Nor did Protestants observe communion and baptism in the same manner. Individual occasions dramatized the range of religious experiences within the community. In contrast to the informal tone of tent meetings on Church Hill or gatherings organized by city missionaries, the 1907 Triennial Meeting of the Episcopal General Convention featured the bishop of London and a procession of 104 bishops in robes. Within all denominations, many congregations gradually adopted more elaborate worship services, which departed from the simple, unadorned practices still cherished in other congregations. Baptists and Disciples retained a categorically congregational form of church governance that contrasted with the more hierarchical structure of other Protestant groups. Richmond audiences listened to a variety of visiting national religious leaders. Professors at the University of Richmond and Union Theological Seminary similarly broadened the scope of religious ideas exchanged on their campuses and in the community. Only by respecting another person's beliefs, advised S. C. Mitchell, could an individual achieve "a state of mind to imbibe the truth."[5]

Richmond's own clergymen contributed to the city's variegated religious atmosphere with different styles, ideas, and positions about public policies. Men like Baptist James B. Hawthorne gained renown as forceful, eloquent pulpiteers; others, like Presbyterian Russell Cecil, earned respect for calm devotional discourses. Baptist J. B. Hutson and Lutheran John J. Scherer endeared themselves to congregations and the community through pastoral work. City ministers also felt free to champion potentially unpopular positions. For example, Scherer and McDaniel protested the execution of the Allens, and R. H. Pitt opposed capital punishment. Baptists broke ranks with other Protestants and aligned with Jews and Catholics to combat compulsory Bible reading in public schools. Theological liberals such as H. D. C. Maclachlan and Walter Russell Bowie achieved immense popularity, but Richmond also featured many orthodox leaders as well as a few fundamentalist laymen and clergymen. Leaders like R. H. Pitt resisted efforts of fundamentalists to narrow the acceptable boundaries of belief. Some Richmond ministers continued to eschew social issues, but others spoke about them and initiated reforms. In 1996 religious historian Samuel S. Hill concluded that the time was ripe to investigate the variety of religious experiences among southerners. Twentieth-century Richmond testifies to the wisdom of that position and suggests that southern cities were important locales for that diversity.[6]

Interdenominational cooperation served as another important avenue of faith for Richmond Protestants. In 1907 a Presbyterian editor welcomed the annual meeting of the Southern Baptist Convention to the city. "These are our brethren," he affirmed, and added, "may their numbers increase and their influence spread until the earth shall be filled with the glory of the one Master whom we serve." This statement reflected vastly more than polite hospitality. As Richmond religious leaders repeatedly endorsed interdenominational cooperation, they explained its purpose. S. C. Mitchell commended the "unified zeal in the Master's service," which cast aside "superficial differences" to engage in joint efforts for missions, education, and reforms. The *Southern Churchman* advised that a "divided Christendom" could not accomplish the "great work set before the Church."[7]

Richmond Protestants engaged in interdenominational cooperation frequently and zestfully. Often working within immediate neighborhoods, congregations held union services, hosted pulpit exchanges, conducted special programs, and enjoyed summer picnics together. Individual men's Bible classes paid visits to those in churches of other denominations, and the men's classes assembled for interdenominational parades and revivals. Huge, citywide revivals, Sunday school institutes, and the Laymen's Missionary Movement furnished major occasions for interdenominational activity. Presbyterians invited other Protestants to participate in their factory mission program. The Richmond Ministerial Union and the Richmond Council of Churches functioned as forums to exchange ideas and information, and, at times, staked out positions about public policy. The Associated Charities, the Spring Street Home, the Society for Improvement of Housing and Living Conditions, the Instructive Visiting Nurses Association, and the local interracial committee counted on representatives from different religious bodies. For such civic associations and for a few congregations such as Seventh Street Christian and St. Paul's Episcopal Church, the avenue of interdenominational cooperation broadened to include Jews and Catholics. Assessing urban religion in 1929, scholar H. Paul Douglass characterized interdenominational cooperation as "an inspiring field of experimentation and adventure in which most heartening progress has already been made." Richmond's experiences validated that conclusion.[8]

During the early twentieth century, Protestants made specialization another avenue of faith. In a small town, a Virginian likely would have identified preachers as the only major religious figures in the community. In a visit to Richmond, however, that same person could have discovered religious leaders occupying specialized roles and engaging in specialized tasks. City missionaries devoted their time to persons who were unchurched, invalid, or incarcerated. At the Methodist Institute, the Wilson Inn, the House of Happiness, and the Methodist orphanage, trained religious workers managed denominational facilities that provided a range of services and programs to meet the needs of specific groups. Some ministers assumed the demanding responsibilities of administering social agencies for the city and the state. Baptist James Buchanan established the city's Associated Charities; Methodist J. T. Mastin provided pioneering leadership for the State Board of Charities and Corrections; and W. J. Maybee guided the Children's Home Society of Virginia. As educators, Walter W. Moore, Walter L. Lingle, Frederic W. Boatwright, Virginia Ellett, and Churchill Gibson Chamberlayne developed institutions that enriched the community with programs and graduates. Those schools furnished talented professors who not only studied and taught but also participated in churches and in community activities. Richmond would have been a different place without the intellectual energy and civic leadership of S. C. Mitchell. In essence, Mitchell and the peripatetic James Cannon carved out a distinctive specialization as community social activists. During Cannon's extended stays in the capital city, the determined Anti-Saloon League leader established himself as an incomparable organizer and lobbyist.

Others devoted themselves to more conventional specializations. R. H. Pitt and other editors of religious weeklies gathered and distributed valuable information as well as delivered penetrating commentaries about religion and society. To launch various projects and programs, Richmond Protestants relied on resident specialists or recruited others. For example, Presbyterians A. L. Phillips, R. E. Magill, and Anna Binford provided expertise for the local Sunday school movement. Union Theological Seminary established an endowed professorship in Sunday school work and constructed a separate building designed for instruction about Sunday school programs. When Richmond turned its attention to foreign missions, it called upon R. J. Willingham, the secretary of the Southern Baptist Foreign Mission Board, which had its headquarters in the city. Individual churches also turned to specialization. As congregations grew, churches hired assistant pastors, deaconesses, and youth workers to whom ministers delegated particular facets of church work. In executing their specialized duties, these people brought a creative vitality to the city's religious institutions. In a private letter, Union's Walter W. Moore lauded A. L. Phillips's "restless, enterprising and fertile mind." Moore appreciated "the enthusiastic presentation of the ideas with which his mind bristles and many of which are really of great value." By focusing on particular tasks in the city, these religious figures made specialization an important avenue of faith for early-twentieth-century Richmond.[9]

In 1920 Episcopal city missionary Cary Montague praised local Baptist men's Bible classes as "carefully and efficiently organized" and marveled that they brought together "men of all walks of life." To bring people together in the city did require effective organization. By excelling at it, Richmond Protestants made organization another avenue of faith. Launching a synod-wide campaign for the Presbyterian Woman's Foreign Missionary Union, one Richmond laywoman explained that "this is a day of organization and cooperation in every branch of work" and the women must systematize the manner in which they spread information and gather resources. In 1924 the secretary of the Richmond Baptist Council praised Barton Heights Baptist "as the best organized church in Richmond and perhaps in the Southern Baptist Convention." That organizational skill had propelled the congregation's growth from a membership of 201 in 1910 to a membership of 1,335 in 1930. A Richmond newspaper commended Pine Street Baptist pastor J. B Hutson for his "most remarkable organization," which he exercised throughout the church but used with special effect to involve children in services and programs. And it was no accident that Sunday school memberships in white Protestant churches tripled in a twenty-year period. With careful planning, churches initiated institutes to train teachers, hosted outside experts, developed a graded class system, constructed Sunday school facilities, and held meetings with teachers throughout the year.[10]

The men's Bible classes also played major roles in citywide revivals, another example of skillful organizing. Especially when visiting evangelists Wilbur Chapman and Billy Sunday conducted lengthy meetings, individual churches raised funds to finance the meetings. Prior to the revivals, church members hosted cottage prayer meetings in their homes, organized according to neighborhoods. Congregations recruited participants for choirs and volunteers to serve as ushers and secretaries. Other people arranged publicity and transportation for those who needed it. Similarly, the success of the Laymen's Missionary Movement in Richmond relied on carefully developed organization emanating from individual churches. Protestant women's groups united in organized campaigns to construct new homes for elderly Protestant women and to create such institutions as the House of Happiness and Mission Court. The organizational skill of churches was apparent during World War I, when they served as focal points for food conservation, Red Cross work, and entertainment of servicemen. As innovations in the local religious scene, the Baptist Council of Richmond and the Presbyterian League coordinated efforts of existing churches, planned and financed new projects, and assisted in the establishment of new churches. In assessing the future of city churches in 1929, scholar H. Paul Douglass emphasized the importance of "pooled resources" and "common planning." As veteran organizers, Richmond Protestants had already learned that lesson.[11]

In 1916 the Baptist Council of Richmond welcomed the presence of laywomen. The council noted that the "ladies" had never been constitutionally excluded, that their participation was considered "desirable," and that they "constitute a very powerful and influential part of the religious life of the Baptists of Richmond." Indeed, as the council itself demonstrated, the leadership of laymen and laywomen served as another avenue of faith in Richmond. Laywork, of course, took many forms. Church choirs, Sunday schools, and youth programs relied on adult leaders, and some even achieved a bit of local fame. Douglas Freeman's men's Bible class was the most heralded in the city, and Katherine Hawes's Covenanters was one of the more celebrated youth groups. But other laity also served. In 1901, when the tin-plate department of Old Dominion Iron and Nail suspended operations, Richard Howells left town for another job in Pennsylvania. He left behind a saddened St. Andrew's Episcopal Church, where he played an important role in youth programs, led the congregation's chapter of the Brotherhood of Saint Andrew, and acted as the registrar of the vestry. Like Howells, others served on governing bodies of their congregations. Although duties and jurisdictions varied among the denominations, members of the vestry, the boards of stewards, the deacon boards, the sessions, and the church councils shouldered significant responsibilities. Laypersons also supported churches financially. Some wealthy donors like Grace Arents and Methodist John P. Branch made substantial contributions. But as the denominational press and church reports made clear, members of modest means sustained congregations as well.[12]

Laypersons contributed to the well-being of not only their own congregations but of their denominations and of the city. Lamenting the untimely death of layman Owsley Saunders in 1925, the *Presbyterian of the South* eulogized him as "the most useful member of the Presbyterian Church in Richmond." Living across the street from Union Seminary, Saunders had befriended seminarians and headed the Sunday school of his Ginter Park church. But "his most original and constructive piece of work" was the Presbyterian League, through which members of city churches had coordinated activities, supported such enterprises as the General Assembly Training School, and initiated mission work, including the factory mission program and Seventeenth Street Mission. Other laypersons supported Saunders, and laypersons guided the Baptist Council of Richmond, which operated in rather comparable fashion. Involved laity made citywide revivals and the local Laymen's Missionary Movement possible. William Ellyson distinguished himself for his long-term participation in the Southern Baptist Foreign Mission Board. Even the theological ruckus over the *Southern Churchman* in the 1920s testified to the involvement of the city's laity. In contrast to rural southern males depicted by historian Ted Ownby, Richmond men were active participants in the city's religious culture.[13]

The Richmond Baptist Council correctly characterized laywomen as "a very powerful and influential part of the religious life" of the city. Like the Galveston, Texas, women portrayed by historian Elizabeth Hayes Turner, Richmond laywomen were key participants in their churches and their community. When Maria Binford died in February 1920, the *Presbyterian of the South* issued an extended eulogy of her as a Christian, a mother, a public school teacher, and an active member in First Presbyterian. "A Wednesday evening Christian," she "loved the house and work of the Master and delighted in all that pertained to its progress." As Sunday school teachers, youth leaders, and choir members, women assumed important responsibilities in their churches. Probably no other woman could match Grace Arents in shaping the religious life of an entire church and a neighborhood. But acting through altar guilds, missionary societies, and social service associations, other laywomen touched the lives of church members and others throughout the community. Meeting regularly at Centenary Methodist, the Association of Methodist Women for Social Service listened to speakers from different denominations and acted as a forum for issues ranging from equal suffrage to race relations. Individual churchwomen reached out to the entire city. In 1927 the vestry of St. Paul's Episcopal approved the erection of a memorial tablet to honor late laywoman Kate Pleasants Minor. The proposed inscription cited her leadership in the church and the community, her "help of the heavy laden," and her "flame of passionate service, kindling all it touches." Married to Judge E. C. Minor, she reportedly had originated the idea of a state board of charities and corrections and her husband had successfully proposed it to the state constitutional convention. She had championed the causes of juvenile courts, a city public library, child labor laws, and equal suffrage. Active in her church's mission program, she had also assisted leaders of the African American YWCA.[14]

Thus, Richmond laypersons left their mark in community affairs. Organizations such as the Richmond Education Association, the Equal Suffrage League, and the YWCA benefited from the leadership of committed laypersons. As state commissioner of health, Dr. Ennion G. Williams carried his religious convictions into his professional life. Addressing Episcopal clergymen in 1928, he reminded them that "you can by preaching the Gospel put into the hearts of people the brotherly love by which they will want to protect their neighbor." Williams advocated additional public education to reduce preventable disease and mortality rates. God, he affirmed, had given humans knowledge to use, and it was their "duty to God and themselves to use that knowledge." By assuming substantial religious duties, laypersons made their participation and involvement an avenue of faith that touched churches, denominational groups, and all of Richmond.[15]

In 1911 a layman at St. John's Evangelical Church wrote a letter broaching a novel idea for this historic, predominately German-American congregation. The writer suggested that the entire church council resign and that members elect a new one composed only of women. "This would be probably something entirely new, something 'real American,'" he mused. While the proposal apparently failed to win support, the layman correctly discerned that Richmond churches thrived on "something new." Indeed, innovation constituted a major avenue of faith for Richmond Protestants of the early twentieth century. By 1930 changes had affected many facets of religious life, and some of the most striking ones had modified worship experiences. Members spent their Sunday mornings in newly constructed, beautiful, large buildings often erected in growing areas of the city. In carpeted sanctuaries with stained glass windows, the devout used individual communion cups, sang from new hymn books, and listened to vested choirs accompanied by powerful organs with imitative orchestral stops. During services, lay readers participated and ministers set aside time for special children's sermons. Preachers increasingly extended their biblical analysis to apply it to contemporary issues ranging from saloons to child labor to world peace. In doing so, clergymen moved away from traditional boundaries separating churches from social and political matters. "If the church is to inherit the future," Walter Russell Bowie maintained, "it is essential that out of the treasures of the past she should shape also the gospel which can be expressed in the new terms and answer the fresh questions of our modern age." In 1929 Baptist layman A. W. Patterson called change "the law of the universe," welcomed it, and cited changes among Baptists, including the new role of women who "can speak anywhere, even in pulpits."[16]

Innovation also meant expanding the scope of religious work. As institutional churches, St. Andrew's Episcopal Church and Broad Street Methodist Church committed themselves to providing their neighborhoods with a range of services not previously offered by area churches. Other congregations took smaller but similar steps. Leigh Street Baptist, for example, created a kindergarten, a circulating library, and a reading room open every evening of the week. Many churches built substantial new Sunday school buildings. By the

1920s churches began to broadcast services on radio stations and use movies as educational devices. Ministers relied on cars and telephones to assist in their mounting pastoral duties. Women played increasingly visible roles as deaconesses, youth directors, and Sunday school leaders. At both Westhampton College and the General Assembly Training School, women trained to serve as religious leaders. In many individual congregations, females voted, held church offices, and acted as representatives to state denominational organizations. In 1933 in the *Report of the President's Research Committee on Social Trends,* researcher C. Luther Fry observed that "within the past two decades notable changes" had occurred in American church programs. Old programs had been "significantly modified" and extended and "new elements" had been added. Richmond's experiences certainly confirmed that assessment.[17]

Such changes did not lead Richmond Protestants away from revered traditional elements of their religious lives but did mean adapting them to the contemporary scene. As evangelicals, clergymen still emphasized the importance of individual conversion and the relationship between a believer and God. But large citywide revivals, active church groups, and the impetus toward social Christianity increasingly transported individual experiences into collective situations and connected private beliefs with public behavior. Continuing to honor Sunday as a day of worship, clergymen slowly relaxed their insistence on strict community adherence to Sunday observance laws. Committed to separation of church and state, even Baptist leaders made exceptions to that tenet when they confronted compelling social causes such as saloon regulation, civic corruption, and public education. Thus, in twentieth-century Richmond, as ministers continued to discuss traditional religious beliefs, they did so in new ways. "Heaven may be our home, as the hymn tells us," advised an Episcopal editor, "but we get no good by dreaming too often of returning to it, but rather by endeavoring vigorously to bring it into the present."[18]

In a 1910 article in the Baptist *Religious Herald,* a Richmond laywoman emphasized that "the city now . . . sends up a hoarse, bitter cry, the cry of the little children, the sick, the sorrowing, the overwrought, the tempted." And, as she discussed, "there are hundreds of opportunities that come to us for ministering to the distress and suffering of the people around us." In responding to such concerns, Richmond Protestants developed social Christianity into another important avenue of faith. To describe their vision of social Christianity, religious leaders invoked two phrases, social service and social justice. The language and actions of social service pervaded Richmond in the early twentieth century. In a typical sermon on the subject, the pastor of Marshall Street Christian Church instructed his members that even the humblest person achieved the real meaning of "greatness" by serving others. Some deeds of social service were modest in scope. In 1919 women's groups at fifteen Richmond Episcopal churches sent "well-filled" gift boxes to twelve Virginia convict camps.[19]

On the other hand, a commitment to social service often motivated more systematic efforts to improve conditions in the city and the state. Baptist professor Rolvix Harlan referred to the account of Jesus feeding the five thousand and declared that "Jesus helped in collective situations and by organized or social effort." The Bible, Harlan instructed, indicated that Jesus did so "methodically by organizing the task." Local Protestants addressed major social problems by working through their congregations, their denominations, local civic organizations, and public institutions. The Methodist Institute, the Baptist Neighborhood House, the House of Happiness, and the Wilson Inn attended to the needs of the unemployed, the impoverished, immigrants, working women, and children. Under the leadership of James Buchanan, the Associated Charities ministered to the needy of the city, and under the leadership of J. T. Mastin, the State Board of Charities and Corrections tried to alleviate suffering throughout the state. Social service also translated into support and leadership for social causes. As education reformers rallied Virginians in the May Campaign of 1905, Baptist minister James B. Hawthorne exclaimed, "God bless what is known as 'the Ogden Movement.' How it electrifies our people everywhere. How mightily it is helping the South." Not only did clergymen support Virginia's educational crusade, city Protestants furnished the leadership for both the Richmond Education Association and the statewide Cooperative Education Association. In that capacity Mary-Cooke Branch Munford, Lila Meade Valentine, and S. C. Mitchell believed that they applied their religious convictions on behalf of many others.[20]

Likewise, city clergy, laity, and congregations supported the cause of public health. For a 1919 sermon, the pastor of Union Station Methodist Church pelted his audience with facts, reasons, and examples showing the importance of taking steps to prevent the spread of communicable diseases. "If we want God to bless our City with health," he instructed, "we must clean up the things that make us sick." He proceeded to offer a number of specific steps members of his congregation could take. For clergymen and laypersons, public health took the form not only of supplying information but also of providing facilities for tuberculosis clinics and soup kitchens during the 1918 flu epidemic. Public health social service inspired the creation of the Society for the Betterment of Housing and Living Conditions in Richmond, which produced the Weber report. A commitment to public health also meant support for visiting nurses, for the Richmond School of Social Work and Public Health, for Sheltering Arms Hospital, and for public baths.[21]

In traveling the avenue of social Christianity, Protestant leaders did not perceive themselves as departing from a traditional commitment to personal spirituality. On the contrary, they believed the two were complementary and inseparable. In a 1927 sermon, H. D. C. Maclachlan reiterated the importance of individual salvation. As much as he favored reforms, Maclachlan declared, "works cannot save. We must first be touched by God." For Maclachlan, salvation meant "God Himself entering into our poor, weak, erring incomplete lives and refashioning them after His own image in Jesus Christ." That salvation directed a believer not only to eternity but to the earth as well. According to Maclachlan, there could be "no heaven hereafter that is not first heaven here." That outlook meant that Jesus saved society as well as individuals. Dr. B. B. Bagby, a layman and the chief medical inspector for Richmond, expressed similar convictions. "If we are true followers of Christ, we will do all we can to improve the spiritual, the intellectual, and the physical side of our fellow men. From a Christian standpoint, the three are one and inseparable," he affirmed. One of the related premises of social Christianity was that church members should not separate their lives into religious and secular compartments. Writing to Walter Russell Bowie in 1923, a former parishioner endorsed Bowie's stance as a proponent of social Christianity. "What you teach, and what I think is most desirable, is that Christianity should be carried into business; that the difference between one's conduct on Sunday and on week days should be obliterated, and that a man should not act or feel differently in the week from what he does in the pew on Sunday." Known for efforts in behalf of penitentiary reform and the Spring Street Home, Lucy Ambler Mason declared that she wanted "to be remembered in human lives and not in stone." She apparently succeeded. She and others made social Christianity an important avenue of faith in Richmond.[22]

Yet social Christianity remained an incomplete and marred avenue, where social justice was advocated but often not achieved. To be sure, some clergymen and laypersons forcefully articulated biblical imperatives for social justice. Methodist preacher W. A. Cooper characterized the church as an instrument "by which the ideal social order, founded on right, justice and brotherhood is to be accomplished in the world." No one could question Cooper's commitment or the depth of righteous indignation expressed by the likes of H. D. C. Maclachlan, R. H. Pitt, or Walter Russell Bowie. Nor would anyone doubt the committed deeds of such people as Lucy Ambler Mason, Lucy Randolph Mason, J. T. Mastin, George White McDaniel, or Lila Meade Valentine. Some of their efforts brought important results. Prisoners benefited from better conditions in the Virginia Penitentiary. Richmond established a juvenile and domestic relations court. Women slowly gained lay rights in most denominations, and religious leaders participated in successful attempts to curb the use of child labor.[23]

Other calls for social justice, though, were only partially answered or largely unanswered. Neither in Richmond nor in the rest of the state did reformers succeed in mitigating harsh conditions in local jails. Few jurisdictions besides Richmond implemented a juvenile court system. When women gained the right to vote, they did so despite the resistance of the Virginia legislature. Women did gain access to a state institution of higher education, but most undergraduate females continued to be excluded from the University of Virginia for decades to come. Calls for industrial justice yielded few concrete results. Relying on moral suasion, city Protestant leaders sympathetic to the plight of strikers and to the needs of working women achieved little. At least a few ministers seemed exasperated by the situation. In a 1924 sermon, the pastor of First Presbyterian Church endorsed labor unions but added a pessimistic prediction. He saw no end to labor strife "so long as the capitalists are greedy, grasping, and oppressive, inconsiderate of the rights of laborers, indifferent to their interests regarding them as a mere commodity to be employed in the swelling fortunes already too large." Though thwarted, the divine discontent about social injustices remained.[24]

Nowhere were the limits of social justice more apparent than in race relations. In 1929 the editor of the Methodist *Richmond Christian Advocate* sadly cautioned that "if we are the people we ought to be, we will not forever be showing a narrow and unChristian spirit toward people because of the color of their skin." In an era notable for its virulent racism, some Protestant leaders distinguished themselves with emphatic opposition to racial abuses. Whether condemning racist ideas, rhetoric, deeds, or policies, S. C. Mitchell, M. Ashby Jones, and Beverley Tucker challenged the consciences of their community. Although white Richmonders prided themselves on harmonious race relations, such challenges were deeply needed.[25]

In August 1925 Richmond hosted a national convention of Black Elks and welcomed a reported 50,000 African American visitors. Journalist and historian Virginius Dabney later recalled that the city suspended its segregation ordinances "and the City was almost turned over to them." Gone temporarily were restrictions about streetcars, restaurants, and even private homes. The *Presbyterian of the South* remarked about the amiable mingling of whites and blacks, especially as they viewed a "marvelous" parade. The writer further applauded that "the kindly feelings" of whites and blacks "in this city have been strengthened." Yet this impressive experience apparently prompted no one to ask the obvious question: If the city operated so well without racist restrictions, why not terminate them? Instead, proponents of racial justice had to fight new battles in the late 1920s and cling to modest hopes that the Negro Welfare Survey Committee and the local interracial committee could incrementally mitigate the worst facets of racial injustice. Nor did many Protestants esteem Jews and Catholics as true brothers and sisters of a shared heavenly creator, as episodic outbursts demonstrated. In 1906 the *Central Presbyterian* had urged readers to encourage "among the white population a public sentiment that will respect [blacks] as human beings with rights and feelings that must not be trampled upon." Though the avenue of social Christianity was an important one in early twentieth-century Richmond, only a few white Richmond Protestants traveled it in the direction advocated by the *Central Presbyterian*.[26]

Returning to Richmond after living in other places, Episcopalian Maria Williams Sheerin delighted in hearing the familiar Virginia accent of parishioners as they sang hymns and recited prayers. Such distinctly local voices gave little hint of a much broader vision. In traveling avenues of faith, Richmond Protestants related their religion to people, needs, and conditions well beyond their immediate community. Some laypersons did so by furnishing leadership for statewide organizations such as the Cooperative Education Association and the Equal Suffrage League of Virginia. Minister J. T. Mastin and layman Ennion G. Williams directed statewide social agencies. Guiding the Children's Home Society of Virginia, minister W. J. Maybee touched many families throughout the state, as did laywoman Frances "Boxie" Scott in her roles with Sheltering Arms Hospital and Pine Camp. Richmond-based denominational weeklies claimed regional and national audiences, as did the authors of Sunday school publications and devotional books. Pastors George W. McDaniel and Russell Cecil were among the Richmond figures who served as denominational leaders, and resident bishops likewise affected the lives of even distant Methodists and Episcopalians. The city's growing denominational institutions of higher learning prepared their graduates to serve in faraway sites.[27]

Some laypersons felt called to Christian service far beyond Richmond. In 1907 the *Baltimore and Richmond Christian Advocate* reported that Dr. Emily C. Runyon, a practicing physician in the city, had begun her work as a medical missionary. Throughout the early twentieth century, ministers as well as laypersons developed a greater consciousness and concern about conditions beyond their own continent. Individual congregations sponsored missionaries overseas. Union Seminary and the General Assembly Training School prepared people to serve in mission fields. The Presbyterians published the *Missionary Survey* in Richmond and made Mission Court a hospitable location for furloughed missionaries. The Baptist Foreign Mission Board supervised and coordinated a substantial program for the entire denomination. With women's missionary societies already playing a large role in congregations, the Laymen's Missionary Movement succeeded in enlisting male support as well.[28]

But the participation of Richmond's churches in World War I brought the world even closer to church doors. Not only did congregations send their young men to serve, churches became major organizing points for patriotic activities ranging from food conservation measures to entertaining troops. A number of local ministers fanned out across the region to promote the financial campaigns to support the war effort. In the aftermath of the war, however, many prominent Richmond Protestants concluded that churches had been overwhelmed by war furor and had contributed to hateful attitudes toward some at home and abroad. Sobered by these experiences, Richmond ministers of the 1920s became students of international affairs and advocates of a variety of devices to resolve international disputes peacefully. Episcopalian Cary Montague explained that once an incident inflamed public opinion, it could be difficult to "stem the rising tide" favoring a military solution. Therefore, in times of peace, the church "should so firmly establish the proper name for war as wholesale murder that it will be impossible for the resort to arms to clothe itself in glory when an international quarrel arises." This consciousness of the world abroad, the active support for international organizations like the League of Nations, and the endorsement of policies and treaties to limit armed conflict constituted one of the most striking changes among churches which embraced many innovations. Thus, as Richmond Protestants met the challenge of relating their religion to the changing conditions of their immediate community, they reached far beyond it.[29]

By the 1920s Richmond Protestant leaders recognized that the real challenge for southern churches lay in the countryside, not in the city. It was not an easy lesson to master. Often reared in rural areas, Richmond ministers clung to a nostalgic vision of farm life as the wellspring of character, virtue, and religion. In doing so, they joined other Americans in subscribing to what historian Richard Hofstadter once labeled the "agrarian myth," a "complex of ideas" that emphasized the nonacquisitive attributes of farmers. Calling the country "the backbone of the Republic," George W. McDaniel asserted that America's past leaders had grown "into strong and virtuous manhood" because they had lived "close to nature and close to God." According to a Methodist editor, children who grew up in a rural world of "simplicity and spirituality" avoided the urban "glitter and glamour" which "obscure the glory of God and the life of godliness." Even cosmopolitan Walter Russell Bowie sounded the same theme. Living a simpler life, working with the soil, and relying on nature, farmers had "a more instinctive sense of God" than did urbanites, Bowie pronounced.[30]

But facts soon assaulted rural memories, reveries, and myths. Even before World War I, Protestants across the nation had begun to worry about rural churches. Working for the Home Mission Board of the Southern Baptist Convention, Victor I. Masters enumerated problems with *The Country Church in the South* in 1916. He pointed to a paucity of church programs, the prevalence of absentee pastors, the number of churches lacking ministers, and the common practice of congregations sharing preachers. An extensive survey of country churches by the Sunday School Board of the Southern Baptist Convention in 1922 further documented unpastored churches, low ministerial salaries, and the absence of Sunday schools, women's groups, and youth organizations in many communities. In the 1923 volume *The Church in the Rural South,* Edmund Brunner detailed the problems of rural congregations. Many country preachers were poorly educated and inadequately paid. Even worse, many churches lacked resident pastors. Therefore, the churches held worship services only monthly or bimonthly. Brunner deplored this situation, noting that "the common experience" of Protestants, Catholics, and Jews had "long shown that religious life can be developed and sustained only on the weekly service basis." Church programs, including Sunday schools, were often weak. Indeed, "in no other part of the United States has the country church so meager a program of church work as in the South." Brunner expressed concern about the number of very small churches as well as the number of churches that had been abandoned or become inactive. Although the proportion of Protestant church members to the total southern population was 40.4 percent, only 28.3 percent of the rural white population in his study were enrolled in churches.[31]

Not covered by Brunner's study, Virginians had steadily grown uneasy about their rural churches. In 1907 S. C. Mitchell declared that "the Lord is not at all pleased with the way we are doing things in the rural part of his kingdom." Convinced that "mere preaching" reached very few people, Mitchell deplored the lack of resident rural ministers whose pastoral care would have provided the "vital contact . . . with the life and needs" of people. Critiques such as Mitchell's, however, were rare until the mid-1920s. In May 1926 the directors of a new Department of Rural Sociology at Virginia's Agricultural Experimentation Station convened a meeting of religious leaders in Richmond and organized fifty-two clergymen and laypersons into study committees. The biracial group included S. C. Mitchell, Methodist Collins Denny, Lutheran John J. Scherer Jr., Presbyterian R. E. Magill, R. H. Pitt, and Baptist laywoman Blanche Sydnor White. During the next three years, Rolvix Harlan chaired an executive committee that created a research agenda for this Virginia Rural Church Survey. In 1927, as that group proceeded, the *Richmond Christian Advocate* published its own brief comparison of city and country Methodist churches in the state. While noting improvements in rural churches during the past decade, the *Christian Advocate* concluded that in terms of membership, country churches were "barely holding their own."[32]

In 1929 the Findings Committee of the Virginia Rural Church Survey issued a preliminary report. The committee then admitted that "many features of the rural church situation are unsatisfactory and call for concerted attention and action." According to statistics, the percentage of white rural residents belonging to churches and the percentage participating in Sunday schools fell well below that of urban residents. The report found rural churches to be disinclined to experiment with new programs and to rely heavily on annual revival meetings for evangelism and for "influencing the community." With weakly supported Sunday schools, churches seemed "only moderately successful" in efforts at religious and ethical education. Some rural churches were too small; others operated on a part-time basis. In either case those congregations failed to retain effective ministers, who might have provided valuable leadership. Issued later that year, *The Role of the Church in Rural Community Life in Virginia* provided 190 pages of details. Both documents urged greater denominational and urban support for rural churches and greater efforts by ministers to understand the distinct needs of rural residents. Many of the recommendations, though, amounted to rural applications of methods that had delivered success in cities.[33]

In the early 1930s, a consultant for the President's Research Committee on Recent Social Trends observed that "it is widely believed that country people belong to church in relatively greater numbers than city people." As the writer noted, the true situation was exactly the reverse. Yet, he admitted, had an American returned to this country after an absence of twenty years, that person would perceive that "in our great cities at least, church buildings now appear trivial and unimportant in contrast with the enormous skyscrapers of commerce and finance." In the 1927 study *The City's Church,* Protestant minister and social scientist H. Paul Douglass likewise described the physical expansion of American cities that seemed to dwarf their religious institutions and imply a decline in their significance. "May it not be," he asked, "that the contrast between the vast city and the feeble church has been unreasonably stressed?" Douglass rendered an equivocal but largely favorable assessment of the condition of urban churches. "The church," he avowed, was "deeply rooted in the city, and shows persistence and versatility in keeping up with the city's changes. But it has no assurance of a walkaway; at most it has but a fighting chance." If H. D. C. Maclachlan had reviewed Richmond's early-twentieth-century experiences, he undoubtedly would have agreed. A generation of Richmond Protestants had impressively expanded the avenues of faith within their city. Some of those routes remained incomplete, however, and the next generations would face their own set of urban challenges.[34]

Notes

Abbreviations

BRCA	*Baltimore and Richmond Christian Advocate*
CC	*Chesapeake Christian*
CP	*Central Presbyterian*
PS	*Presbyterian of the South*
RH	*Religious Herald*
RCA	*Richmond Christian Advocate*
RNL	*Richmond News Leader*
RT	*Richmond Times*
RTD	*Richmond Times-Dispatch*
SC	*Southern Churchman*
VC	*Virginia Churchman*

1. The Urban Challenge

1. Louis Rubin, "Introduction," in *A Richmond Reader, 1733–1983*, ed. Maurice Duke and Daniel P. Jordan (Chapel Hill: University of North Carolina Press, 1983), xvii–xviii.

2. *RTD*, 10 July, 1911, p. 10; U.S. Department of Commerce, Bureau of the Census, *Fifteenth Census of the United States: 1930, Population Bulletin, Second Series, Virginia* (Washington, D.C.: GPO, 1931), 69; W. T. Dabney, "Richmond's Advance from 1908 to 1928," *Richmond* 15, no. 5 (Nov. 1928): 7; Wilson Gee and John J. Corson III, *A Statistical Study of Virginia* (Charlottesville: Institute for Research in the Social Sciences, University of Virginia, 1927), 116–18; Gustavus A. Weber, *Report on Housing and Living Conditions in the Neglected Sections of Richmond, Virginia* (Richmond: Whittet & Shepperson, 1913), 10, 21–25; *RTD*, 13 Sept. 1905, p. 4; *RNL*, 3 Sept. 1929, p. 8. As one example of a crowd of thousands viewing a downtown fire, see *RTD*, 27 Mar. 1912, p. 1. In *Civic Wars: Democracy and Public Life in the American City during the Nineteenth Century* (Berkeley: University of California Press, 1997), 45–47, 70–72, 236, Mary P. Ryan interprets urban parades as integrating civic experiences which later diminished in significance. Scholars have long debated which attributes constitute essential criteria for making a community truly urban. This account roughly follows the characteristics used by H. Paul Douglass, *The City's Church* (New York: Friendship Press, 1929), 9–24.

3. *RNL*, 23 Nov. 1914, p. 2; *RH*, 9 June 1921, p. 7; Gee and Corson, *Statistical Study*, 118–22; John A. Cutchins, *Memories of Old Richmond (1881–1944)* (Verona, Va.: McClure

Press, 1973), 234–35; *RTD,* 24 Apr. 1912, p. 1; *RTD,* 19 June 1913, p. 10; *RTD,* 25 Apr. 1912, p. 3; *RNL,* 9 Dec. 1927, p. 1; *RNL,* 28 Apr. 1913, p. 4; Clarence E. Weaver, ed., *Sketches of Richmond, Virginia, U.S.A.: Who's Who and What's What* (Richmond: Central Publishing, 1924), 137.

4. Louise Fitzhugh Price, 28 June 1905 and 28 May 1905 in diary, 1904–1909, Louise Fitzhugh Price Papers, Virginia Historical Society, Richmond, Virginia; U.S. Department of Commerce and Labor, Bureau of the Census, *Census of Religious Bodies: 1906* (Washington, D.C.: GPO, 1910), 1:484–85; U.S. Department of Commerce, *Census of Religious Bodies: 1926* (Washington, D.C.: GPO, 1930), 1:523–24.

5. *BRCA,* 14 Dec. 1905, p. 2.

6. *RTD,* 23 Aug. 1916, p. 4; Weaver, *Sketches,* 74; *RNL,* 31 Dec. 1925, p. 19; Corson and Gee, *Statistical Study,* 76; "Richmond Has," *Richmond* 16, no. 5 (Nov. 1929), 44; *RNL,* 16 Apr. 1923, p. 10; *RNL,* 6 Feb. 1929, p. 8; *RNL,* 10 Nov. 1927, p. 1.

7. Alan Trachtenberg, *The Incorporation of America: Culture and Society in the Gilded Age* (New York: Hill & Wang, 1982), 131; Gunther Barth, *City People: The Rise of Modern City Culture in Nineteenth-Century America* (New York: Oxford University Press, 1980), 147; Gee and Corson, *A Statistical Study,* 29, 76, 134–35, 145–52, 193–98; Bureau of Municipal Research, New York, *County Government in Virginia* (Richmond: Davis Bottom, 1928), 93–97; *RTD,* 12 Sept. 1905, p. 1; *RTD,* 27 Feb. 1925, p. 1; U.S. Department of Commerce and Labor, Bureau of the Census, *Wealth, Debt and Taxation* (Washington, D.C.: GPO, 1907), 83; Richmond, Virginia Chamber of Commerce, *Down Where the South Begins* (n.p.: [1928]), 13–16; U.S. Department of Labor, Bureau of Labor Statistics, *Vocational Education Survey of Richmond, Virginia,* Whole No. 162, Misc. Ser. No. 7 (Washington, D.C.: GPO, 1916), 9. For the importance of being a Federal Reserve District site, see Rupert B. Vance and Sara Smith, "Metropolitan Dominance and Integration," in *The Urban South,* ed. Rupert B. Vance and Nicholas J. Demerath (Chapel Hill: University of North Carolina Press, 1954), 123–24; Cutchins, *Memories of Old Richmond,* 111–19; Weaver, *Sketches,* 94; Negro Welfare Survey Committee, *The Negro in Richmond, Virginia* (Richmond: Richmond Council of Social Agencies, 1929), 81–84; "Richmond Has," 44.

8. Jon Teaford, *The Unheralded Triumph: City Government in America, 1870–1900* (Baltimore: Johns Hopkins University Press, 1984); Carolyn Hall Leatherman, "Richmond Rejects a Library: The Carnegie Public Library Movement in Richmond, Virginia, in the Early Twentieth Century" (Ph.D. diss., Virginia Commonwealth University, 1992), 158; [John Hirschberg], "The City Government's Work," *Richmond* 2, no. 7 (June 1916): 4–5, 11–13; Richmond, Virginia, Mayor, *Annual Message and Accompanying Documents of the Mayor of Richmond to the City Council for the Year Ending December 31, 1900,* 11–13; Richmond, Virginia, Mayor, *Annual Report of the Mayor of Richmond to the City Council for the Year Ending December 31, 1929,* 44; U.S. Department of Commerce and Labor, Bureau of the Census, *Statistics of Cities Having a Population of Over 30,000: 1905* (Washington, D.C.: GPO, 1905), 302–3; U.S. Department of Commerce, Bureau of the Census, *Statistics of Cities Having a Population of Over 30,000: 1930* (Washington, D.C.: GPO, 1930), 390–91, 400–401; *RTD,* 25 Sept. 1905, p. 1; Gee and Corson, *A Statistical Study,* 145–52; "Richmond Has," *Richmond* 16, no. 5 (Nov. 1929): 44.

9. Weaver, *Sketches,* 123, 136, 183; Department of Commerce, Bureau of the Census, *Fifteenth Census of the United States, 1930: Population* (Washington, D.C.: GPO, 1930), 4:1675–78.

10. John Crowe Ransom, "Reconstructed but Unregenerate," in Twelve Southerners, *I'll*

Take My Stand: The South and the Agrarian Tradition (New York: Harper & Bros., 1930; reprint, New York: Harper Torchbooks, 1962), 20; Broadus Mitchell and George Sinclair Mitchell, *The Industrial Revolution in the South* (Baltimore: Johns Hopkins University Press, 1930), 45; Wilson Gee and William H. Stauffer, *Rural and Urban Living Standards in Virginia* (Charlottesville: Institute for Research in the Social Sciences, University of Virginia, 1929), 69.

11. Blaine A. Brownell, *The Urban Ethos in the South, 1920–1930* (Baton Rouge: Louisiana State University Press, 1975), 10–11; T. Lynn Smith, "The Emergence of Cities," in *The Urban South,* eds. Rupert B. Vance and Nicholas J. Demerath (Chapel Hill: University of North Carolina Press, 1954), 32–37. For accounts of cities in this period, see David Goldfield, *Cotton Fields and Skyscrapers: Southern City and Region, 1607–1980* (Baton Rouge: Louisiana State University Press, 1982); Lawrence H. Larsen, *The Rise of the Urban South* (Lexington: University Press of Kentucky, 1985); Blaine A. Brownell and David Goldfield, eds., *The City in Southern History: The Growth of Urban Civilization in the South* (Port Washington, N.Y.: Kennikat Press, 1977); Carl V. Harris, *Political Power in Birmingham, 1871–1921* (Knoxville: University of Tennessee Press, 1977); Marilyn M. Sibley, *The Port of Houston: A History* (Austin: University of Texas Press, 1968); David G. McComb, *Houston: The Bayou City* (Austin: University of Texas Press, 1969); Blaine A. Brownell, "Birmingham, Alabama: New South City in the 1920s," *Journal of Southern History* 38, no. 1 (Feb. 1972): 4; Joy J. Jackson, *New Orleans in the Gilded Age: Politics and Urban Progress, 1880–1896* (Baton Rouge: Louisiana State University Press, 1969).

12. One of the best explications of urban growth remains Blaine A. Brownell's "The Urban South Comes of Age, 1900–1940," in *The City in Southern History,* 123–58. See also Don Doyle, *New Men, New Cities, New South: Atlanta, Nashville, Charleston, Mobile, 1860–1910* (Chapel Hill: University of North Carolina Press, 1990); Don H. Doyle, "Urbanization and Southern Culture: Economic Elites in Four New South Cities (Atlanta, Nashville, Charleston, Mobile), c. 1865–1910," in *Toward a New South? Studies in Post-Civil War Southern Communities,* ed. Orville Vernon Burton and Robert C. McMath Jr. (Westport, Conn.: Greenwood Press, 1982), 11–36. Blaine A. Brownell, "Urbanization in the South: A Unique Experience?" *Mississippi Quarterly* 26 (spring 1973): 115; Richard J. Hopkins, "Are Southern Cities Unique? Persistence As a Clue," *Mississippi Quarterly* 26 (spring 1973): 121–41; Edd W. Parks, "Southern Towns and Cities," in *Culture in the South,* ed. W. T. Couch (Chapel Hill: University of North Carolina Press, 1935), 506; Leonard Reissman, "Urbanization in the South," in *The South in the Continuity and Change,* ed. John C. McKinney and Edgard T. Thompson (Durham, N.C.: Duke University Press, 1965), 92–96; David R. Goldfield, "The Urban South: A Regional Framework," *American Historical Review* 86, no. 5 (Dec. 1981):1009–34.

13. W. J. Cash, *The Mind of the South* (New York: Alfred A. Knopf, 1941), 227; Blaine A. Brownell and David R. Goldfield, "Southern Urban History," in *The City in Southern History,* 21; John Boles, "The Discovery of Southern Religious History," in *Interpreting Southern History: Historiographical Essays in Honor of Sanford W. Higginbotham,* ed. John B. Boles and Evelyn Thomas Nolen (Baton Rouge: Louisiana State University Press, 1987), 510–48; Samuel S. Hill Jr., "An Agenda for Research in Religion," in *Perspectives on the South: Agenda for Research,* ed. Edgar T. Thompson (Durham, N.C.: Duke University Press, 1967), 195–96; E. Brooks Holifield, *The Gentlemen Theologians: American Theology and Southern Culture, 1795–1860* (Durham, N.C.: Duke University Press, 1978); Don H. Doyle, *Nashville in the New South, 1880–1930* (Knoxville: University of Tennessee Press, 1985), especially chap. 6.

J. Wayne Flynt, "Religion in the Urban South: The Divided Mind of Birmingham, 1900–1930," *Alabama Review* 30 (Apr. 1977): 108–34; Elizabeth Hayes Turner, *Women, Culture, and Community: Religion and Reform in Galveston, 1880–1920* (New York: Oxford University Press, 1997). Indeed, early-twentieth-century urban religion remains largely uncharted for the entire nation, as noted by Jon Butler, "Protestant Success in the New American City, 1870–1920: The Anxious Secrets of Rev. Walter Laidlaw, Ph.D.," in *New Directions in American Religious History,* ed. Harry S. Stout and D. G. Hart (New York: Oxford University Press, 1997), 296–333.

14. Josiah Strong, *The Challenge of the City* (New York: Young People's Missionary Movement, 1907), 265; C. Luther Fry, "Changes in Religious Organizations," in *Recent Social Trends in the United States, Volume II,* ed. President's Research Committee on Social Trends (New York: McGraw-Hill, 1933; reprint, Westport, Conn.: Greenwood Press, 1970), 1019, 1021–22.

15. *CP,* 15 May, 1901, p. 8; *CP,* 16 Nov. 1904, p. 756; *SC,* 5 Dec. 1903, p. 8; *RH,* 15 Nov. 1900, p. 3; *RH,* 9 Jan. 1903, p. 4; *RH,* 28 Dec. 1911, pp. 4–5; *RH,* 25 Apr. 1912, p. 10; *RCA,* 15 Sept. 1927, p. 2.

16. *Hill Directory Company's Richmond Classified Business Directory* (Richmond: Hill Directory Co., 1930), 1714–1715; U.S. Department of Commerce, *Census of Religious Bodies: 1926,* 1, 523–24; Myron Berman *Richmond's Jewry, 1769–1976: Shabbat in Shockoe* (Charlottesville: University Press of Virginia, 1979). Primarily dealing with six major denominations, this book does include two others. Organized in 1843 as a Lutheran Congregation, St. John's Evangelical Church affiliated with the German Evangelical Synod of North America and then joined the Evangelical and Reformed Church. First Christian Church received its charter in 1920. Both St. John's and First Christian joined other white, evangelical Protestant groups in citywide activities.

17. Dr. Beverley D. Tucker, "The Master Is Come and Calleth for Thee," in H. D. C. Maclachlan Papers, Disciples of Christ Historical Society, Nashville, Tenn.; *RNL,* 24 May 1929, p. 1; *RTD,* 25 May 1929, p. 8; *To the Memory of H. D. C. Maclachlan, D.D.* in Maclachlan Papers.

18. *RNL,* 5 May 1929, pp. 1, 8; "Pastor's Report," 10 Jan. 1909, Minute Book, Seventh Street Christian Church Papers, Virginia Historical Society, Richmond.

19. *RNL,* p. 1; H. D. C. Maclachlan, "Chapter 4: Amos, the Prophet of Character," in "Types and Ideals of Hebrew Prophecy," p. 16, Maclachlan Papers.

20. H. D. C. Maclachlan, "The Church at School," 20 Mar. 1927, sermon collection, Maclachlan Papers.

2. Restless Richmond

1. *RT,* 14 June 1900, p. 2; *RTD,* 10 May 1913, p. 4; Christopher Silver, *Twentieth-Century Richmond: Planning, Politics, and Race* (Knoxville: University of Tennessee Press, 1984), 26. Characterizing Richmond reformers of this era as "aggressive urban boosters," historian Christopher Silver has argued that they "set out after 1900 to create nothing less than a new city." In contrast to local conservatives, Richmond progressives shared the conviction that changes were essential for the future well-being of the city and its residents. Since progressives did disagree about different proposals, their ranks were composed of a fluctuating membership, much like other political and social coalitions. At different times,

professionals, businessmen, organized labor, and neighborhood civic organizations collaborated in support of specific reforms. Thus, Richmond reformers followed a pattern perceived by Peter Filene, "An Obituary for the 'Progressive Movement,'" *American Quarterly* 22 (1970):20–34. In *The Search for Order, 1877–1920* (New York: Hill & Wang, 1967), 167–69, 176, Robert H. Wiebe distinguished between two strands of progressivism, which diverged across time: one emphasized efficiency in government; the other focused on "humanitarian" concerns such as health and education. Somewhat similarly in *Reform in Detroit: Hazen Pingree and Urban Politics* (New York: Oxford University Press, 1969), 157–81, Melvin Holli differentiated between "structural reformers" and "social reformers." George Tindall highlighted the significance of "business progressivism" for the South in *The Ethnic Southerners* (Baton Rouge: Louisiana State University Press, 1976), 142–62. Joseph Kett noted the importance of "social progressives," who tried to improve social conditions and who were committed to popular participation, education, community, and interdependence rather than individualism. See Kett, "Women and the Progressive Impulse in Southern Education," in *The Web of Southern Social Relations: Women, Family, and Education,* ed. Walter J. Fraser Jr., R. Frank Saunders Jr., and Jon L. Wakelyn (Athens: University of Georgia Press, 1985), 166–81. In *Nashville in the New South, 1880–1920* (Knoxville: University of Tennessee Press, 1985), 121–82, Don Doyle finds business progressivism and social reform coming into "direct conflict" (178). For an expansive and thorough treatment about reforms of the era, see Dewey W. Grantham, *Southern Progressivism: The Reconciliation of Progress and Tradition* (Knoxville: University of Tennessee Press, 1983).

2. Paul S. Dulaney, *The Architecture of Historic Richmond* (Charlottesville: University Press of Virginia, 1968); Mark R. Wenger, "Thomas Jefferson and the State Capitol," *Virginia Magazine of History and Biography* 101, no. 1 (Jan. 1993): 77–102. For preservation efforts in the late nineteenth and early twentieth centuries, see James M. Lindgren, "'For the Sake of Our Future': The Association for the Preservation of Virginia Antiquities and the Regeneration of Traditionalism," *Virginia Magazine of History and Biography* 97, no. 1 (Jan. 1989): 47–74, and James M. Lindgren, *Preserving the Old Dominion: Historic Preservation and Virginia Traditionalism* (Charlottesville: University Press of Virginia, 1993). For Richmond houses and neighborhoods, see Robert B. Munford Jr., *Richmond Homes and Memories* (Richmond: Garrett & Massie, 1936); Mary Wingfield Scott, *Houses of Old Richmond* (New York: Bonanza Books, 1941); and Mary Wingfield Scott, *Old Richmond Neighborhoods* (Richmond: [Whittet & Shepperson], 1950). Silver, *Twentieth-Century Richmond,* 98–99, notes the persistence of neighborhoods. Lillian Betts, "The Richmond of To-Day," *Outlook,* 25 Aug. 1900, 972–79. As an example of a heroic history by a local author, see Mary Newton Stanard, *Richmond: Its People and Its Story* (Philadelphia: Lippincott, 1923).

3. Mary Tyler-McGraw, *At the Falls: Richmond, Virginia, and Its People* (Chapel Hill: University of North Carolina Press, 1994), 9–53; Virginius Dabney, *Richmond: The Story of a City,* rev. ed. (Charlottesville: University Press of Virginia, 1990), 12–13, 21, 62–64; "'Removal of the Seat of Government': Richmond Becomes the Capital, 1779–1980," in *A Richmond Reader, 1733–1983,* ed. Maurice Duke and Daniel P. Jordan (Chapel Hill: University of North Carolina Press, 1983), 5–9. Harry M. Ward and Harold E. Greer Jr., *Richmond during the Revolution, 1775–83* (Charlottesville: University Press of Virginia, 1977), 126–42, provides a valuable account of this entire period and highlights economic growth.

4. Michael Chesson, *Richmond After the War, 1865–1890* (Richmond: Virginia State Library, 1981), 5–16; Mary H. Mitchell, *Hollywood Cemetery: The History of a Southern Shrine* (Richmond: Virginia State Library, 1985), 17–34; David R. Goldfield, *Urban Growth in the*

Age of Sectionalism: Virginia, 1847–1861 (Baton Rouge: Louisiana State University Press, 1977), 24–25, 94–98, 112, 119–29, 174–75, 187–200, 218–21; Dabney, *Richmond,* 62–69, 101–18, 133–34, 148–75; W. Asbury Christian, *Richmond: Her Past and Present* (Richmond: L. H. Jenkins, 1912), 120–83; Tyler-McGraw, *At the Falls,* 112–17.

5. Emory Thomas, *The Confederate State of Richmond: A Biography of the Capital,* (Austin: University of Texas Press, 1971), 185, 99–100, 117, 172f; Michael Chesson, "Harlots or Heroines: A New Look at the Richmond Bread Riot," *Virginia Magazine of History and Biography* 92, no. 2 (Apr. 1984): 131–75; Frank L. Byrne, "Libby Prison: A Study in Emotions," *Journal of Southern History* 24, no. 4 (Nov. 1958): 430–44. For accounts of the war in Richmond, see Thomas, *Confederate State;* Chesson, *Richmond After the War,* 25–57; Stephen W. Sears, *To the Gates of Richmond: The Peninsula Campaign* (New York: Ticknor & Fields, 1992); and Mitchell, *Hollywood,* 47–62.

6. Betts, "The Richmond of To-Day," 974; Chesson, *Richmond After the War,* 57–84, 114–68, 174–77, 185–97; Steven J. Hoffman, "Behind the Facade: The Constraining Influence on Race, Class and Power of Elites in the City-Building Process, Richmond, Virginia, 1870–1920" (Ph.D. diss., Carnegie Mellon Univ., 1993), 112–35; Nannie May Tilley, *The Bright-Tobacco Industry, 1860–1929* (Chapel Hill: University of North Carolina Press, 1948), 253–55, 281, 347; Christian, *Richmond,* 226, 236, 321–22.

7. Thomas, *Confederate State,* 191; Constance Cary Harrison, *Recollections, Grave and Gay* (New York: Charles Scribner's Sons, 1911), 84; Mitchell *Hollywood,* 83–94, 117–18, 124; Christian, *Richmond,* 337, 422, 430–31.

8. Walter Russell Bowie, *Learning to Live* (Nashville: Abingdon Press, 1969), 12–13; Douglas Southall Freeman, "Virginia: A Gentle Dominion," *Nation,* 11 July 1924, 68–71; *RTD,* 26 July 1916, p. 6; Mitchell, *Hollywood,* 57, 63–71, 118, 141–42. Ellen Glasgow provides fictional portrayals of continuing female mourning in Virginia in *The Voice of the People* (New York: Doubleday, Page & Co., 1902), 114, 172, 224. In *Ghosts of the Confederacy: Defeat, the Lost Cause, and the Emergence of the New South, 1865–1913* (New York: Oxford University Press, 1987), 36–46, Gaines Foster argues that experiences of mourning helped Southerners come to grips with the defeat of the Confederacy.

9. John Stewart Bryan, *Joseph Bryan, His Times, His Family, and His Friends* (Richmond: Whittet & Shepperson, 1935), 301–10, 381; *RTD,* 29 May–5 June 1907; *RNL,* 1–3 June 1915; Emily J. Williams, "'A Home . . . for the Old Boys,'" *Virginia Cavalcade* (summer 1979): 40–47; George L. Christian and Hunter McGuire, *The Confederate Cause and Conduct in the War between the States* (Richmond: L. H. Jenkins, 1907); *RTD,* 21 May 1903, p. 3; Thomas Cary Johnson, review of *Stonewall Jackson and the American Civil War,* by G. F. R. Henderson, in *Union Seminary Magazine* 11 (Feb.–Mar. 1900): 221–26; Thomas Cary Johnson, review of *Official Report of the History Committee of the Grand Camp of Confederate Veterans,* by George L. Christian, in *Union Seminary Magazine* 13 (Feb.–Mar. 1902): 238.

10. Charles Reagan Wilson, *Baptized in Blood: The Religion of the Lost Cause, 1865–1920* (Athens: University of Georgia Press, 1980), and Charles Reagan Wilson, "The Religion of the Lost Cause: Ritual and Organization of the Southern Civil Religion, 1865–1920," *Journal of Southern History* 46 (May 1980): 219–38; *RTD,* 2 June 1903, p. 4; *RNL,* 6 Sept. 1929, p. 8. For extended accounts about the Davis and Lee windows, see Elizabeth W. Weddell, *St. Paul's Church, Richmond, Virginia—Its Historic Years and Memorials: Volume Two* (Richmond: William Byrd Press, 1931), 373–414, 520–24. *RTD,* 21 May 1903, p. 3; *RNL,* 31 May 1929, p. 4; Fred Arthur Bailey, "Free Speech and the Lost Cause in the Old Dominion," *Virginia Magazine of History and Biography* 103, no. 2 (Apr. 1995): 237–66; Angie Parrott,

"'Love Makes Memory Eternal': The United Daughters of the Confederacy in Richmond, Virginia, 1897–1920," in *The Edge of the South: Life in Nineteenth-Century Virginia,* ed. Edward L. Ayres and John C. Willis (Charlottesville: University Press of Virginia, 1991), 219–38.

11. As historian Gaines Foster has argued, activities to commemorate the Confederacy formed a multifaceted movement which underwent several phases. For example, see Foster, *Ghosts,* 52–53, 56, 60–61, 71, 93–94, 100–103, 163, 168–79.

12. James Branch Cabell, *Let Me Lie* (New York: Farrar, Straus & Co., 1947), 146–47; Ellen Glasgow, *The Woman Within* (New York: Harcourt, Brace, 1954), 218; *RNL,* 3 Dec. 1929, p. 8; *PS,* 18 Apr. 1928, p. 1; *RNL,* 31 May 1929, p. 4; *RTD,* 5 June, 1907, p. 3; Murphy, "Looking Backward One-Half Century," *Richmond* 1, no. 10 (Apr. 1915): 9, 18–19; *United Confederate Veterans, Official Souvenir and Hand-Book, 17th Annual Reunion* (Richmond: n.p., 1907); Mary Abigail Burgess, *Richmond Guide Book: Sketches and Views of Richmond, Virginia* (Richmond: Richmond Press, 1913); Richmond, Virginia, Chamber of Commerce, *Richmond, Virginia, Yesterday and Today* (Richmond: Whittet & Shepperson, 1913); *Richmond, Virginia: A Brief Sketch of Its History, Industrial Life, Government and Educational Facilities by the 6th and 7th Year Pupils of Public Schools* (Richmond: Whittet & Shepperson, 1914).

13. Murphy, "Looking Backward One-Half Century," 9; *Richmond* (Oct. 1914): 1; Betts, "The Richmond of To-Day," 976; Henry Sydnor Harrison, *Queed: A Novel* (New York: Grosset & Dunlap, 1911), 47; Christian, *Richmond,* 470; Ellen Glasgow, *The Sheltered Life* (Garden City, N.Y.: Doubleday, Doran, & Co., 1932), 34.

14. Christopher Silver maintains that the first decades of the twentieth century represented "a new era . . . that witnessed the city's accelerated economic and physical development." Silver, *Twentieth-Century Richmond,* 17. Silver persuasively argues that annexation was a major part of the agenda of middle-class progressives who encountered resistance from the city's older, conservative elite (60–74). *RTD,* 7 Dec. 1906, p. 1; *RTD,* 11 Aug. 1907, p. D1; *RTD,* 28 June 1914, p. 4; "A Map of Richmond in 1900 and 1915," *Richmond,* Feb. 1916, cover; U.S. Bureau of the Census, *Thirteenth Census of the United States, Population: Statistics for Virginia* (Washington, D.C.: GPO, 1913), 923–25; U.S. Bureau of the Census, *Fifteenth Census of the United States, 1930: Population Bulletin, Second Series, Virginia* (Washington, D.C.: GPO, 1931), 69. According to the U.S. Department of Commerce, Bureau of Foreign and Domestic Commerce, *Real Property Inventory, 1934* (Richmond, 1934), 628, approximately 19,000 residential dwellings built since 1899 were still in use in Richmond in the 1930s—presumably others had also been constructed but did not still remain in use. Noting a statewide pattern of rural to urban migration, sociologists Wilson Gee and John J. Corson III concluded in 1929 that Richmond had gained "considerably" from rural migration. Wilson Gee and John J. Corson III, *Rural Depopulation in Certain Tidewater and Piedmont Areas of Virginia* (Charlottesville: Institute for Research in the Social Sciences, University of Virginia, 1929), 18. *RTD,* 21 June 1903, p. A4; *RTD,* 1 Jan. 1905, p. 3.

15. Bowie, *Learning to Live,* 88–89; John A. Cutchins, *Memories of Old Richmond (1881–1944)* (Verona, Va.: McClure Press, 1973), 136; *RT,* 21 May 1903, p. 1; *RT,* 5 July 1902, p. 4; *RNL,* 11 Jan. 1916, p. 1; *RT,* 27 Feb. 1900, p. 6; *RNL,* 29 Aug. 1923, p. 4; *RTD,* 19 July 1905, p. 10; *RNL,* 26 Feb. 1926, p. 1; *RNL,* 2 July 1921, p. 4; Silver, *Twentieth-Century Richmond,* 27, 29, 114; Tyler-Graw, *At the Falls,* 221–22.

16. *RNL,* 3 Apr. 1915, p. 1; Christian, *Richmond,* 471; *RTD,* 22 Sept. 1906, p. 4; 30 July 1911, p. 9; 5 Oct. 1911, p. 1; 16, 20 July 1912, p. 1; *RNL,* 21, 29 Feb. 1921; *RNL,* 2 Mar. 1923, p. 1. In "Behind the Facade," 62–126, Steven Hoffman concurs with the interpretation that the

chamber of commerce emerged as an important force in the twentieth century but dates its vitality to the late nineteenth century. The classic treatment of southern urban boosters is Blaine A. Brownell, *The Urban Ethos in the South, 1920–1930* (Baton Rouge: Louisiana State University Press, 1975).

17. *RTD,* 23 Sept. 1906, p. 1; *RT,* 23 Sept. 1902, p. 1; *RT,* 28 Feb. 1902, p. 1; U.S. Department of Commerce and Labor, Bureau of the Census, *Twelfth Census of the United States, Bulletin No. 144* (Washington, D.C.: GPO, 1902), 7; U.S. Department of Commerce, Bureau of the Census, *Fifteenth Census of the United States. Manufactures: 1929, State Series, Virginia* (Washington, D.C.: GPO, 1932), 2–3; *RT,* 1 Jan. 1902, p. 6; *RTD,* 23 Oct. 1911, p. 10; *RNL,* 21 Oct. 1926, p. 1. For the tobacco industry, see Nannie May Tilley, *The Bright-Tobacco Industry, 1860–1929,* 254–55, 259, 281, 349–53, 545, and Robert F. Durden, *The Dukes of Durham 1866–1929* (Durham, N.C.: Duke University Press, 1975), 26–82. For a sample of *News Leader* articles about tobacco industry expansion, see the issues of 1 July 1925, p. 1; 1 Sept. 1925, p. 1; 10 July 1926, p. 5; 28 July 1927, p. 1; and 12 Mar. 1929, p. 5.

18. Spencer Wolcott, "The City that Rose from a Ruin," *Harper's Weekly,* 15 June 1912, 19; Philip Alexander Bruce, *The Rise of the New South* (Philadelphia: G. Barrie & Sons, 1905), 235–37; Christian, *Richmond,* 471; *RNL,* 1 Apr. 1926, p. 4; *RNL,* 15 June 1929, p. 1; *RNL,* 3 June 1920, p. 4; *RTD,* 23 Mar. 1911, p. 6. For descriptions of some businesses, see Clarence E. Weaver, *Sketches of Richmond, Virginia, U.S.A.: Who's Who and What's What* (Richmond: Central Publishing, 1924).

19. *RNL,* 14 June 1921, p. 6; *RTD,* 10 July 1904; *RNL,* 25 Oct. 1920, p. 3; *RTD,* 29 Jan. 1913, p. 1; Weaver, *Sketches,* 73, 213; *RNL,* 12 Apr. 1928, p. 4.

20. Bruce, *New South,* 236; *RNL,* 2 Aug. 1920, p. 4; Weaver, *Sketches,* 74, 118; W. T. Dabney, "Richmond's Advance from 1908 to 1928," *Richmond* 15 no. 5 (Nov. 1928): 7; *RTD,* 29 Aug., 1910, p. 1; *RTD,* 29 Dec. 1912, p. 1; *RNL,* 24 Mar. 1924, p. 1.

21. Hoffman, "Behind the Facade," 112–35; *RNL,* 21 Oct. 1924, p. 8; *RNL,* 9 Feb. 1929, p. 1; *RTD,* 30 Oct. 1912, pp. 4, 10; *RNL,* 3 Aug. 1920, p. 4; Christian, *Richmond,* 420; Thomas E. Hale and Louis H. Manarin, *Richmond: A Pictorial History from the Valentine Museum and Dementi Collections* (Richmond: Hale, [1974]), 26, 56–57; Silver, *Twentieth-Century Richmond,* 37; *RNL,* 7 Nov. 1923, p. 1; "Richmond Has," *Richmond* 14, no. 5 (Nov. 1929): 44. Only after 1927 was the highway between Washington, D.C., and Richmond paved, as noted in Howard L. Preston, *Dirt Roads to Dixie: Accessibility and Modernization in the South, 1885–1935* (Knoxville: University of Tennessee Press, 1991), 155. *RNL,* 28 May 1927, p. 1.

22. Weaver, *Sketches,* 215; *RTD,* 20 Apr. 1908, p. 1; *RNL,* 3 June 1923, p. 4; *RNL,* 20 May 1929, p. 10; *RNL,* 28 Oct. 1927, p. 1; Preston, *Dirt Roads,* 148.

23. U.S. Department of Commerce and Labor, Bureau of the Census, *Occupations at the Twelfth Census* (Washington, D.C.: GPO, 1904), 696–98; U.S. Department of Commerce, Bureau of the Census, *Fifteenth Census of the United States, 1930: Population* (Washington, D.C.: GPO, 1930), 4:1675–78.

24. Bureau of the Census, *Occupations at the Twelfth Census,* 696–98; Bureau of the Census, *Fifteenth Census of the United States, 1930: Population,* 4:1675–78.

25. Ellen Glasgow, *Life and Gabriella* (Garden City, N.Y.: Doubleday, Page & Co., 1916), 29; Bureau of the Census, *Occupations at the Twelfth Census,* 696–98; Bureau of the Census, *Fifteenth Census of the United States, 1930: Population,* 4:1675–78. See also Elizabeth Stevens Brinson, "'Helping Others to Help Themselves': Social Advocacy and Wage-Earning Women in Richmond, Virginia, 1910–1932" (Ph.D. diss., Union Graduate School of the Union for Experimenting Colleges and Universities, 1984). Richmond's female em-

ployment patterns seem to have coincided with that of the rest of the country. William Chafe, *The Paradox of Change: American Women in the Twentieth Century* (New York: Oxford University Press, 1991), 67–72, and Alice Kessler-Harris, *Out to Work: A History of Wage-Earning Women in the United States* (New York: Oxford University Press, 1982), 116, 148–49.

26. Bureau of the Census, *Occupations at the Twelfth Census,* 696–98; Bureau of the Census, *Fifteenth Census of the United States, 1930: Population,* 4:1675–78. The twentieth-century statistics show a continuation of a pattern of working-class racial separation and discrimination documented for an earlier era by Peter Rachleff's *Black Labor in Richmond, 1865–1890* (Urbana: University of Illinois Press, 1989) and an exclusion from skilled positions noted by Leon Fink, *Workingman's Democracy: The Knights of Labor and American Politics* (Urbana: University of Illinois Press, 1983), 152.

27. *RNL,* 26 Jan. 1921, p. 1; *Labor Journal,* 8 July 1921, p. 1. Similar difficulties occurred in 1914 and 1927.

28. *RTD,* 5 June 1904, p. 10; *Square Deal,* 6 May 1921, p. 4; *Square Deal,* 15 Sept. 1916, p. 1; *RNL,* 19 Jan. 1917, p. 5; *Square Deal,* 8 Dec. 1916, p. 1; *Square Deal,* 26 Jan., 1917, p. 1; *Square Deal,* 7 Sept. 1917, p. 1; *Labor Journal,* 9 Sept. 1921, p. 1.

29. Organized labor refused to endorse a candidate in 1924, and many workers may have voted for victorious conservative candidate J. Fulmer Bright. In a three-way race in 1928, Bright retained the mayor's office by polling less than 42 percent of the citywide vote. Silver, *Twentieth-Century Richmond,* 81; *Square Deal,* 16 Nov. 1917, p. 1; *RTD,* 9 June 1911, p. 1; *RTD,* 4 Feb. 1915, p. 10; *Square Deal,* 26 May, 1916, p. 4; *Square Deal,* 2 Apr. 1920, p. 4; *Square Deal,* 9 Apr. 1920, pp. 1, 4; *RNL,* 7 Apr. 1920, p. 1; *Labor Journal,* 22 Feb. 1924, p. 4; *Square Deal,* 16 Jan. 1920, p. 1; *RNL,* 17 Aug. 1926, p. 4; *RNL,* 4 Apr. 1928, p. 1. For the Knights of Labor conflict, see Leon Fink, *Workingmen's Democracy,* 149–77, and Peter Rachleff, *Black Labor in Richmond,* chaps. 8–12.

30. *RTD,* 31 May–7 Aug, 1903; Thomas J. Headlee, "The Richmond Transit Strike of 1903" (master's thesis, University of Richmond, 1960); Christian, *Richmond,* 489–90; *RNL,* 17 Jan.–5 Apr. 1922; *Labor Journal,* Jan.–Apr. 1922. The classic account of organized labor in the 1920s is Irving Bernstein's *The Lean Years: A History of the American Worker, 1920–1933* (Boston: Houghton Mifflin, 1966).

31. Dabney, *Richmond,* 205–6, 221–22, 288; Cutchins, *Memories,* 180–83; *RNL,* 26, 30 Apr. 1923, p. 1; *RNL,* 3 Apr. 1926, p. 4; *RNL,* 5 July 1924, p. 2.

32. William S. Simpson Jr., "1908—The Year Richmond Went 'Baseball Wild,'" *Virginia Cavalcade* 26 (spring 1977): 184–92; *RNL,* 20 June 1921, p. 1; *Hill Directory Company's Richmond Classified Business Directory* (Richmond: Hill Directory Co., 1930), 11; [Hirschberg], "The City Government Works," *Richmond* 2, no. 12 (June 1916): 4–5; *RNL,* 25 Oct. 1926, p. 24.

33. *RNL,* 20 Oct. 1915, p. 4; *RTD,* 3 May 1912, p. 10; *RTD,* 11 May 1913, p. 1.

34. Marjorie Spruill Wheeler, "Mary Johnston, Suffragist," *Virginia Magazine of History and Biography* 100, no. 1 (Jan. 1992): 99–118; Anne Goodwyn Jones, *Tomorrow Is Another Day: The Woman Writer in the South, 1859–1936* (Baton Rouge: Louisiana State University Press, 1981), 183–270; Edgar MacDonald, *James Branch Cabell and Richmond-in-Virginia* (Jackson: University Press of Mississippi, 1993). Cabell concluded that particularly Richmond's upper class failed to appreciate *The Reviewer.* For his account, see Cabell, *Let Me Lie,* 201–28. In *The Advancing South: Stories of Progress and Reaction* (New York: Doubleday, Page & Co., 1926; reprint, Port Washington, N.Y.: Kennikat Press, 1969), 214–23, Edwin Mims praised Glasgow for creating characters who challenged traditions. In *The War*

Within: From Victorian to Modernist Thought in the South, 1919–1945 (Chapel Hill: University of North Carolina Press, 1982), 36, 83–110, Daniel Singal portrays Cabell and Glasgow as inwardly holding on to romantic and traditional views even as they ironically indicted the pretensions of the old order.

35. This summary relies on Sandra Gioia Treadway's superb *Women of Mark: A History of the Woman's Club of Richmond, Virginia, 1894–1994* (Richmond: Library of Virginia, 1995), 3–77; Munford quotation, 37. In *Natural Allies: Women's Associations in American History* (Urbana: University of Illinois Press, 1991), 141–58, Anne Firor Scott traces the national pattern of women's promotion of progressive reforms, particularly in cities.

36. Carolyn Hall Leatherman, "Richmond Rejects a Library: The Carnegie Public Library Movement in Richmond, Virginia in the Early Twentieth Century" (Ph.D. diss.: Virginia Commonwealth University, 1992), 147–91; *RNL*, 30 Jan. 1928, p. 8; *RNL*, 10 Dec. 1917, p. 1; *RNL*, 30 Jan. 1917, p. 4; *RTD*, 26 July 1916, p. 6; *RNL*, 4 Feb. 1919, p. 5; *RNL*, 31 Mar. 1920, p. 4; *RNL*, 3 Feb. 1923, p. 10; *RNL*, 2 Apr. 1924, p. 1. For a further explanation of progressivism in Richmond, see note 1 of this chapter. In *The Search for Order*, 213, Robert Wiebe noted that cities "contained their quotas of anxious, substantial citizens" who became "bent upon quieting reform's turmoil." Even before World War I, "the urban progressives who remained were hard pressed to defend what they still held." Richmond's progressive breeze apparently arrived later and left later than that experienced in some other American cities.

37. Walter Russell Bowie, *Sunrise in the South: The Life of Mary-Cooke Branch Munford* (Richmond: William Byrd Press, 1942), 86–87, 88, 178.

38. Betts, "The Richmond of To-Day," 975; *RT*, 13 July 1902, p. 16; *RT*, 16 May 1900, p. 5; Bowie, *Sunrise in the South*, 53–76, quotation, 68; *RTD*, 17 May 1904, p. 9; *RNL*, 2 Nov. 1914, p. 5; William A. Link, *A Hard Country and a Lonely Place: Schooling, Society, and Reform in Rural Virginia, 1870–1920* (Chapel Hill: University of North Carolina Press, 1986), 76–81. In *The Development of Public Schools in Virginia, 1607–1952* (Richmond: Commonwealth of Virginia State Board of Education, 1952), 361, J. L. Buck notes that the Virginia Constitution of 1902 and the 1908 state education law only allowed compulsory attendance statutes of localities to apply to children between the ages of eight and twelve years old. U.S. Department of Labor, Bureau of Labor Statistics, *Vocational Education Survey of Richmond, Virginia*, Whole Number 162, series no. 7 (Washington, D.C: GPO, 1916), 12; Sarah McCulloh Lemmon, "Munford, Mary Cooke Branch," in *Notable American Women 1607–1950: A Biographical Dictionary*, ed. Edward T. James, Janet Wilson James, and Paul S. Boyer (Cambridge, Mass.: Harvard University Press, 1971), 2:600–601.

39. Mitchell quoted in Bowie, *Sunrise in the South*, 173; "Richmond's Greatest and Most Important Enterprise—Its Public School System," *Richmond* 14, no. 3 (Sept. 1927): 19, 22; Rebekah R. Sharp, "A History of the Richmond Public School System, 1869–1958" (master's thesis, University of Richmond, 1958), 77, 88–92, 147; Margaret Meagher, *History of Education in Richmond* (Richmond: Works Progress Administration, 1939), 117; Richmond, Virginia, Superintendent of the Public Schools, *Thirty-First Annual Report for the Year Ending July 31, 1900* (Richmond, 1901), 7–9, 34–35; Richmond, Virginia, Superintendent of the Public Schools, *Sixty-First Annual Report for the Scholastic Year Ending June 30, 1930*, (Richmond, 1931), 14–18; *Richmond* 2, no. 8 (Feb. 1916): cover; *RNL*, 3 Nov. 1920, p. 15. For a summary of education reforms in major American cities, see Jon Teaford, *The Unheralded Triumph: City Government in America, 1870–1900* (Baltimore: Johns Hopkins University Press, 1984), 262–68.

40. Gustavus A. Weber, *Report on Housing and Living Conditions in the Neglected Sections of Richmond, Virginia* (Richmond: Whittet & Shepperson, 1913), 10. According to data in Weber, *Report,* 74–75, only Memphis had a higher mortality rate in 1911. New Orleans, Nashville, Albany, and Atlanta were close behind Richmond. Hoffman, "Behind the Facade," 173–203; *RTD,* 6 Apr. 1905, p. 8; Richmond, Virginia, Health Department, *Annual Report for the Year Ending December 31, 1910,* p. 64; *RTD,* 8 May 1906, p. 1; *RTD,* 12 Feb. 1907, p. 1; *RTD,* 22 Nov. 1906, p. 4; *RTD,* 17 July 1906, p. 1.

41. *RTD,* 13 Apr. 1907, p. 10; *RTD,* 15 May 1908, p. 10; *RTD,* 15 Dec. 1907, p. 1; *RTD,* 9 July 1907, p. 3; *RTD,* 13 July 1907, p. 10; *RNL,* 28 July 1914, p. 4; *RNL,* 12 Apr. 1920, p. 2; Hoffman, "Behind the Facade," 221; *RNL,* 22 Sept. 1923, p. 4; *RTD,* 18–21 Oct. 1909; *RTD,* 6 May, 1913, p. 1; Gustavus A. Weber, "A 'Clean-up' Campaign Which Resulted in a 'Keep-Clean' Ordinance," *American City* 10 (Jan.–June 1914): 231–34. In *Garbage in the Cities: Refuse, Reform, and the Environment: 1880–1980* (Chicago: Dorsey Press, 1981), 129–33, Martin Melosi notes the popularity and importance of cleanup days in cities throughout the country as a means of raising public consciousness about sanitation.

42. *RNL,* 22 Sept. 1924, p. 4; *RNL,* 30 Sept. 1924, p. 8; *RTD,* 18 Apr., 1910, p. 10; *RNL,* 30 Apr. 1919, p. 10; Hoffman, "Behind the Facade," 223; *RNL,* 26 June 1917, p. 16; Carolyn Hall Leatherman, "Richmond Rejects a Library," 147–51; *RNL,* 16 Aug. 1924, p. 6; *RNL,* 22 June 1921, p. 15; *RNL,* 14 May 1928, p. 6; *RTD,* 2 May 1907, p. 12; Weber, "A 'Clean-up' Campaign," 231–34; *RTD,* 30 Oct. 1908, p. 10; *RNL,* 11 and 29 July 1916, p. 1; *RTD,* 8 July 1916, p. 12; *RTD,* 24 and 29 Sept., 1907, p. 1; *RNL,* 6 Oct. 1923, p. 2. For effective accounts about the importance of milk regulation, see Judith Walzer Leavitt, *The Healthiest City: Milwaukee and the Politics of Health Reform* (Princeton: Princeton University Press, 1982), 156–89, and Stuart Galishoff, *Safeguarding the Public Health: Newark, 1895–1918* (Westport, Conn.: Greenwood Press, 1975), 81–101. On the efficacy of Behring antitoxin, see Galishoff, *Safeguarding,* 23–26.

43. *RNL,* 19 July 1921, p. 4; *RTD,* 13 Feb. 1906, p. 12; *RNL,* 19 Sept. 1928, p. 18; *RTD,* 16 Apr. 1905, p. 1; *RTD,* 12 Nov. 1909, p. 10; *RTD,* 11 Jan. 1910, p. 12; *RTD* 18 June 1912, p. 10; *RNL,* 24 July 1914, p. 1; *RTD,* 31 Jan. 1909, sec. D, p. 7; *RNL,* 29 July 1914, p. 4; Dabney, *Richmond,* 277. For discussions of antituberculosis campaigns, see Michael E. Teller, *The Tuberculosis Movement: A Public Health Campaign in the Progressive Movement* (Westport, Conn.: Greenwood Press, 1988), and Galishoff, *Safeguarding,* 120–30.

44. Hoffman, "Behind the Facade," 201; "Annual Report, Bureau of Health, Department of Public Welfare, Dec. 31, 1930," in *Annual Report of the Mayor of Richmond to the City Council for the Year Ending December 31, 1930* (Richmond, 1931), 23; *RNL,* 30 Sept. 1924, p. 8; *RNL,* 22 Sept. 1923, p. 4; *RNL,* 24 May 1928, p. 1. In many ways Richmond's public health campaign and its results were similar to those of Milwaukee, but Richmond's efforts began later and brought later declines in disease and mortality. For data, see Leavitt, *Healthiest City,* 25.

45. *Richmond Times,* 30 Mar. 1901, p. 1; *RT,* 10 Nov. 1901, p. 1; *RT,* 11, 21, and 25 Jan. 1902, p. 1; *RTD,* 26 July 1908, sec. D, p. 3; *RTD,* 12 Jan. 1910, p. 2; *RNL,* 9 May 1924, p. 4; Mabel L. Walker, "Rating Cities According to the Services Which Their Citizens Are Getting," *American City* (July 1929): 130–34.

46. *RTD,* 24 Apr. 1907, p. 1; *RTD,* 3 May 1908, p. 1; *RTD,* 29 Jan. 1909, p. 1; H. D. C. Maclachlan, *Memorial to the Honorable Council of the City of Richmond* (Richmond: Juvenile Protective Society of Virginia, 1912), 2; Arthur W. James, *Virginia's Social Awakening: The Contribution of Dr. Mastin and the Board of Charities and Corrections* (Richmond: Garrett &

Massie, 1939), 100; *RTD,* 21 Oct. 1912, p. 1; *RTD,* 28 Mar. 1913, p. 4; *RTD,* 2 May 1913, p. 10; *RTD,* 4 July 1913, p. 4; *RTD,* 8 Nov. 1913, p. 4; *RTD,* 25 Sept. 1905, p. 1; *RNL,* 20 June 1921, p. 1; *Hill Directory Company's Richmond Classified Business Directory* (1930), 11; "The City Government's Work," *Richmond* 2, no. 12 (June 1916): 4, 5. Richmond reformers held an attitude about local and outside experts that squares with Samuel Haber's statement: "For most progressives the expert was to be neither on top nor on tap. He could do less than command but more than advise," Samuel Haber, *Efficiency and Uplift: Scientific Management in the Progressive Era, 1890–1920* (Chicago: University of Chicago Press, 1964), 105.

47. For an impressively thorough treatment of the story see Leatherman, "Richmond Rejects a Library," and Carolyn H. Leatherman, "Richmond Considers a Free Public Library: Andrew Carnegie's Offer of 1901," *Virginia Magazine of History and Biography* 96, no. 2 (Apr. 1988): 181–92; *RNL,* 3 Dec. 1929, p. 11; Dabney, *Richmond,* 296–97.

48. *RTD,* 20 Mar. 1922, p. 1. The 1922 legislature did enact a new but ineffectual education law. See Buck, *Development of Public Schools in Virginia,* 361–62; The best overview of Virginia politics in this period remains Allen W. Moger, *Virginia: Bourbonism to Byrd, 1870–1925* (Charlottesville: University Press of Virginia, 1968). The machine's support for education reforms is a perfect example of its flexibility. In *Separate and Unequal: Public School Campaigns and Racism in the Southern Seaboard States, 1901–1915* (Chapel Hill: University of North Carolina Press, 1958; reprint, New York: Atheneum, 1969), 160, Louis Harlan refers to the collaboration of the machine with educational reformers as a temporary "marriage of convenience." In *Old Virginia Restored: An Interpretation of the Progressive Impulse, 1870–1930* (Charlottesville: University Press of Virginia, 1968), Raymond H. Pulley emphasizes the conservatism of much of the state's political reform efforts but admits that "Virginia no less than the other states of the Union was profoundly affected by the broader aspects of the progressive impulse," 132. William Larsen, *Montague of Virginia: The Making of a Southern Progressive* (Baton Rouge: Louisiana State University Press, 1965); Ronald L. Heinemann, *Harry Byrd of Virginia* (Charlottesville: University Press of Virginia, 1996), 1–105.

49. Leatherman, "Richmond Rejects a Library," 147–68, provides an especially effective portrait of the operations of the city government. *RTD,* 6 Nov. 1909, p. 1; *RTD,* 17 Mar. 1907, p. 4; *RTD,* 19 Sept. 1908, p. 10; *RTD,* 8 June 1909, p. 10. For a summary and analysis of the commission form of government, see Martin J. Schiesl, *The Politics of Efficiency: Municipal Administration in America, 1899–1920* (Berkeley: University of California Press, 1977), 134–48.

50. Silver, *Twentieth-Century Richmond,* 76. This account draws heavily on the excellent information and analysis of the administrative board in Silver's *Twentieth-Century Richmond,* 73–93. [John Hirschberg], "The City Government's Work," *Richmond* 2, no. 7 (June 1916): 4–5, 11–13. As examples of criticisms of the board, see *Richmond Times-Dispatch,* 22 Dec. 1912, p. 12, as well as 20 and 26 Oct. 1915, p. 4. The *Richmond News Leader* daily editorials between 10 and 23 Jan. 1917 recited perceived weaknesses in Richmond's municipal government.

51. As Silver notes, between 1924 and 1940 "Bright ruled Richmond" and "the temporary eclipse of progressivism left the reform effort incomplete." Silver, *Twentieth-Century Richmond,* 92–93; *RNL,* 7 Nov. 1917, pp. 1–2. Conducted on a day when the temperature reached 107 degrees, the vote to end the board was 6,141 to 1,864. *RNL,* 7 Aug. 1918, p. 1; *RNL,* 4 Apr. 1928, p. 1. See Schiesl, *Politics of Efficiency,* 112–24 for details about the New York Bureau of Municipal Research and its tendencies to favor centralized decision making.

52. Ira Berlin, *Slaves without Masters: The Free Negro in the Antebellum South* (New York:

Oxford University Press, 1974), 248–49, 219–20, 236–38. Berlin does note that blacks were excluded from some trades in Richmond. Howard N. Rabinowitz, *Race Relations in the Urban South* (Urbana: University of Illinois Press, 1980), 19; Writers' Program, Work Projects Administration, *The Negro in Virginia* (New York: Hastings House, 1940; reprint, Winston-Salem: John F. Blair, 1994), 24–25, 54–61, 146, 115–18; Chesson, *Richmond After the War,* 12; Rachleff, *Black Labor in Richmond,* 4–11; Richard C. Wade, *Slavery in the Cities: The South, 1820–1860* (New York: Oxford University Press, 1964), 33–36, 42–51, 64, 71–72; Robert S. Starobin, *Industrial Slavery in the Old South* (New York: Oxford University Press, 1970), 125–29. See also Midori Takagi, *"Rearing Wolves to Our Own Destruction": Slavery in Richmond, Virginia, 1782–1865* (Charlottesville: University Press of Virginia, 1999).

53. Rachleff, *Black Labor in Richmond,* 13–54; Ray Stannard Baker, *Following the Color Line: American Negro Citizenship in the Progressive Era* (New York: Doubleday, Page & Co., 1980; reprint, New York: Harper Torchbooks, 1964), 258. In *The Perils and Prospects of Southern Black Leadership: Gordon Blaine Hancock, 1884–1970* (Durham, N.C.: Duke University Press, 1977), 45–46, Raymond Gavins inspects 1921 data and argues that the number of Richmond blacks who were professionals or tradesmen was small. The saga of the Knights is well told in Rachleff, *Black Labor in Richmond,* 109–56, and in Fink, *Workingmen's Democracy,* 149–77. Rabinowitz, *Race Relations,* 83–89; Writers' Program, WPA, *Negro in Virginia,* 322–30. Hoffman, "Behind the Facade," 240–58, 298–337, argues that the city's African American community had sufficient economic vitality to expand and to cause Richmond's white "elite" city builders some major headaches.

54. *RT,* 12 Jan. 1900, p. 4; Rabinowitz, *Race Relations,* 321–22; Chesson, *Richmond After the War,* 157–56, 183–84, 190; Hoffman, "Behind the Facade," 258–67; June Purcell Guild, *Black Laws of Virginia: A Summary of the Legislative Acts of Virginia Concerning Negroes from Earliest Times to the Present* (Richmond: Whittet & Shepperson, 1936), 146–48; Beth Barton Schweiger, "Putting Politics Aside: Virginia Democrats and Voter Apathy in the Era of Disfranchisement," in Ayres and Willis, *Edge of the South,* 194–218; Andrew Buni, *The Negro in Virginia Politics, 1902–1965* (Charlottesville: University Press of Virginia, 1967), 24–25.

55. Chesson, *Richmond After the War,* 15–16. For an analysis of the steady movement toward residential segregation, see Rabinowitz, *Race Relations,* 99–115. *RNL,* 16 Oct. 1904, p. B4; *RTD,* 20 Apr. 1911, p. 1; Roger L. Rice, "Residential Segregation by Law, 1910–1917," *Journal of Southern History* 34 (May 1968): 179–99; *RNL,* 13 Dec. 1917, p. 1; Charles Louis Knight, *Negro Housing in Certain Virginia Cities* (Richmond: William Byrd Press, 1927), 36; *RTD,* 9 Jan. 1929, p. 1; *RNL,* 12 Jan. 1929, p. 16; *RNL,* 14 Jan. 1929, p. 2; *RNL,* 15 Jan. 1929, p. 8; *RNL,* 1 Feb. 1929, p. 1; *RNL,* 13 Feb. 1929, p. 8.

56. *RNL,* 26 Dec. 1916, p. 2; *RNL,* 22 Dec. 1922, pp. 1–2; Writers' Program, WPA, *The Negro in Virginia,* 352, 375; Guild, *Black Laws of Virginia,* 143–45, 148; *RT,* 1 July 1900, p. 6; Dabney, *Richmond,* 258; *RTD,* 20 Apr. 1904, p. 1; *RNL,* 18 June 1919, p. 1; Negro Welfare Survey Committee, *The Negro in Richmond, Virginia* (Richmond: Richmond Council of Social Agencies, 1929); *RTD,* 26 Jan. 1912, p. 10; Zane Miller, "Urban Blacks in the South, 1865–1920: The Richmond, Savannah, New Orleans, Louisville and Birmingham Experience," in *The New Urban History: Quantitative Explorations by American Historians,* ed. Leo Schnore (Princeton: Princeton University Press, 1975), 185–86.

57. *RNL,* 28 Jan. 1929, pp. 8, 17. Among those calling for improved services to the black community were members of the chamber of commerce; *RNL,* 17 May 1919, p. 2. James D. Anderson, *The Education of Blacks in the South, 1860–1935* (Chapel Hill: University of North Carolina Press, 1988), 194–95, 200–201; W. A. Daniel, "Part III: Schools," and Henry J.

McGuinn, "Part IV: Recreation," in *Negro Problems in Cities*, ed. Thomas J. Woofter (New York: Doubleday, Doran & Co., 1928), 208, 233; *Report of the Bureau of Health, Annual Report of the Department of Public Welfare of the City of Richmond, Virginia for the Year Ending December 31, 1930* (Richmond: [1931]), 21; *RNL*, 23 Dec. 1929, p. 1. The incidence of disease and mortality among blacks was substantially higher than among whites.

58. Frederic W. Boatwright to W. B. Freeman, 20 Feb. 1904, Douglas Southall Freeman Scrapbook, 1886–1923, Virginia Historical Society, Richmond; John L. Gignilliat, "The Thought of Douglas Southall Freeman" (Ph.D. diss., Univ. of Wisconsin-Madison, 1968); John L. Gignilliat, "Douglas Southall Freeman," *Dictionary of Literary Biography XVII: Twentieth-Century American Historians* (Detroit: Gail Research, 1983), 157–69; Cutchins, *Memories*, 101–3; *RTD*, 4 Nov. 1913, p. 1.

59. John Stewart Bryan to Douglas Southall Freeman, Christmas night, 1921, Freeman Papers, Library of Congress; *RNL*, 3 July 1922, p. 4; Gignilliat, "Douglas Southall Freeman," *Dictionary of Literary Biography*, 157–69; William Harris Bragg, "'Our Joint Labor': W. J. De Renne, Douglas Southall Freeman, and *Lee's Dispatches*, 1910–1915," *Virginia Magazine of History and Biography* 97, no. 1 (Jan. 1989): 3–32; *RNL*, 2 Jan. 1922, p. 4.

60. Quoted in John L. Gignilliat, "The Thought of Douglas Southall Freeman," 181; lecture, 23 Nov. [1925], in Freeman Papers; Dumas Malone, "'This Quiet Man, Whose Tireless Pen Traced the Marches [of] . . . Giant Captains': Douglas Southall Freeman," in Duke and Jordan, *A Richmond Reader*, 363–74.

3. City Sounds and Joyful Noises

1. St. Paul's Vestry Book, 8 June 1914, Papers of St. Paul's Episcopal Church, Virginia Historical Society, Richmond, Virginia; Minor T. Weisiger, Donald R. Traser, and E. Randolph Trice, *Not Hearers Only: A History of St. James's Episcopal Church, Richmond, Virginia, 1835–1985*, ed. Margaret T. Peters (Richmond: St. James's Episcopal Church, 1986), 43.

2. *Monumental Messenger*, Dec. 1900, p. 19; James B. Hawthorne, *The Cloud of Witnesses and Other Sermons* (Nashville: Sunday School Board of the Southern Baptist Convention, 1908), 12–21.

3. Ulrich Troubetzkoy, *Richmond, City of Churches: A Short History of Richmond's Denominations and Faiths* (Richmond: Whittet & Shepperson, 1957), 1–2, 11–15; W. Asbury Christian, *Richmond: Her Past and Present* (Richmond: L. H. Jenkins, 1912), 8–14, 79–82, 99; *RNL*, 27 May 1922, p. 2; Weisiger, Traser, and Trice, *Not Hearers Only*, 38–40.

4. Troubetzkoy, *City of Churches*, 14–15; *RNL*, 13 May 1922, p. 2; Elizabeth W. Weddell, *St. Paul's Church, Richmond, Virginia—Its Historic Years and Memorials, Volume I and Volume II* (Richmond: William Byrd Press, 1931), 29, 237–40, 373–575.

5. Jack Abernathy, *Living Monument: The Story of Grace Covenant Presbyterian Church, Richmond, Virginia, 1790–1990* (Richmond: Grace Covenant Church, 1989), 1–10; Wyndham B. Blanton, *The Making of a Downtown Church: The History of Second Presbyterian Church Richmond, Virginia, 1845–1945* (Richmond: John Knox Press, 1945), 19–93, 126–60; *PS*, 14 Dec. 1921, pp. 3–4; Troubetzkoy, *City of Churches*, 14–15; *RNL*, 17 June 1922, p. 2; *RNL*, 15 Apr. 1922, p. 2; Edwin Pleasants and William R. Hill, *The First Hundred Years, 1835–1935: Third Presbyterian Church, Richmond, Virginia* ([Richmond]: Third Presbyterian Church, [1935]), 18–23.

6. Christian, *Richmond,* 56; Blanche Sydnor White, *Richmond Baptists Working Together, 1780–1960* (Richmond: Richmond Baptist Association, [1961]), 1–33; Blanche Sydnor White, *First Baptist Church, Richmond, 1780–1955: 175 Years of Service to God and Man* (Richmond: Whittet & Shepperson, [1955]); Belle Gayle Ellyson, *The History of the Second Baptist Church, Richmond, Virginia: 1820–1970* (Richmond: Whittet & Shepperson, 1970), 3; William C. James, *Leigh Street Baptist Church 1854–1954: A Brief History of Its First One Hundred Years in the Service of Christ* (Richmond: Whittet & Shepperson, 1954), 4; Annie Florence Weeks, *Grace Baptist Church, Richmond: 1833–1955* (Richmond: [Garrett & Massie, 1958]), 1–24; *Beacon on a Hill: A Brief History of One Hundred Years of Christian Service, 1855–1955, Pine Street Baptist Church* (Richmond: Pine Street Baptist Church, 1955), 10–21; Blanche Sydnor White, *A Century of Service: A History of Bainbridge Street Baptist Church, 1857–1957* (Richmond: Whittet & Shepperson, 1957), 19–20.

7. Floyd S. Bennett, *Methodist Church on Shockoe Hill: A History of Centenary Methodist Church, Richmond, Virginia, 1810–1960* (Richmond: n. p., 1962); Frank B. Dunford, *A History of Central Methodist Church: Thirteenth and Porter Streets, Richmond, Virginia* (Richmond: W. M. Brown & Sons, 1942); Nannie P. Eddington, *Pace Memorial M. E. Church, South: History and Registry* (Richmond: Stout Printing, 1923); Sue Marmon and Dorothy Wilber Peers, *Reflections of Faith: A Bicentennial History, Trinity United Methodist Church, Founded, 1790* (Richmond: Trinity United Methodist Church, 1990); Mollie Roberson Wiltshire, *A Century of Service: The History of Union Station Methodist Church, 1843–1943* (Richmond: Whittet & Shepperson, 1943).

8. Marion B. Brinson, H. G. Haney, and G. Edwin Osborn, *A Century with Christ: A Story of the Christian Church in Richmond* (Richmond: Whittet & Shepperson, 1932), 15–80; Garnett Ryland, *The Baptists of Virginia, 1699–1926* (Richmond: Baptist Board of Missions and Education, 1955), 234–37; *RNL,* 29 Apr. 1922, p. 2; Troubetzkoy, *City of Churches,* 31–32. For typical expressions of the Disciples' commitment to interdenominational cooperation see, *Chesapeake Christian,* May 1922, p. 1, and Jan. 1923, p. 1. For a summary of the early activity of the Disciples, see J. Paul Williams, *What Americans Believe and How They Worship* (New York: Harper & Brothers, 1952), 254–55, and Samuel C. Pearson, "The Disciples of Christ," in *The Encyclopedia of Religion in the South,* ed. Samuel S. Hill (Macon, Ga.: Mercer University Press, 1984), 201–5. For a detailed account, see Winfred Ernest Garrison and Alfred T. DeGroot, *The Disciples of Christ: A History* (St. Louis: Christian Board of Publication, 1948).

9. Mary Grace Scherer Taylor, *Saints Alive!: A History of The First English Evangelical Lutheran Church, Richmond Virginia, The First Hundred Years: 1876–1976* (Richmond: First English Evangelical Lutheran Church, 1976), 7–21; William Edward Eisenberg, *The Lutheran Church in Virginia, 1717–1962* (Roanoke: Trustees of the Virginia Synod, Lutheran Church in America, 1967), 190–92, 233, 467–69; *Bethlehem Lutheran Church, Richmond, Virginia: 125th Anniversary* (South Hackensack, N.J.: Custombook, 1977), 5–9; Troubetzkoy, *Richmond: City of Churches,* 35–40; Kenneth Crumpton Jr., "The History of the Lutheran Church in Richmond, Virginia, 1843–1965" (master's thesis, Lutheran Theological Southern Seminary, 1967).

10. Ernest Trice Thompson, *Presbyterians in the South, Volume Three: 1890–1972* (Richmond: John Knox Press, 1973), 274–301; *RNL,* 15 Oct. 1925, p. 1; *RCA,* 29 Oct. 1925, p. 2; Taylor, *Saints Alive!,* 38; Garrison and DeGroot, *The Disciples of Christ,* 328–29, 411; Samuel S. Hill, *One Name but Several Faces: Variety in Popular Christian Denominations in Southern History* (Athens, Ga.: University of Georgia Press, 1996), 59–61.

11. *RT,* 2 Dec. 1900, p. 2; Dover Baptist Association, *Minutes of the One Hundred and Eighteenth Annual Session* (Richmond: J. H. Hill, 1901), 15.

12. Williams, *What Americans Believe,* 248–50; Bill J. Leonard, *God's Last and Only Hope: The Fragmentation of the Southern Baptist Convention* (Grand Rapids, Mich.: William B. Eerdmans Publishing, 1990), 76–84; Thompson, *Presbyterians in the South,* 3:215–24.

13. *RH,* 23 Mar. 1922, p. 11; Julius Melton, *Presbyterian Worship in America: Changing Patterns since 1787* (Richmond: John Knox Press, 1967), 17–27, 70, 89–92; Thompson, *Presbyterians in the South,* 3:343–45; *CP,* 20 June 1900, p. 8; *CP,* 1 Mar. 1905, p. 146, and 22 Mar. 1905, p. 196; *Directory Grace Street Presbyterian Church, Richmond, Virginia, May 1914* (Richmond: Richmond Press, 1914), 6. For summaries of worship practices, see Williams, *What Americans Believe,* 116–22, 156–60, 168–71, 250.

14. *RT,* 26 June 1900, p. 6; *RT,* 24 June 1900, p. 1; *RH,* 17 Jan. 1901, p. 3; *RH,* 27 Apr. 1905, p. 1; *CP,* 2 Apr. 1902, p. 2; *RTD,* 17 Apr. 1910, p. 10; *SC,* 23 Apr. 1910, p. 9; *PS,* 22 July 1914, p. 3; *RNL,* 8 Dec. 1919, p. 5; *BRCA,* Apr. 1900, p. 1.

15. *RT,* 1 Apr. 1900, p. 7; *RTD,* 11 Apr. 1905, p. 12; James, *Leigh Street,* p. 91; *League Record,* Jan. 1918, p. 4; *PS,* 23 Aug. 1916, p. 15; *BRCA,* 18 July 1912, p. 13; *RCA,* 21 June 1928, p. 9; *SC,* 17 July 1907, p. 15; *VC,* Oct. 1926, p. 745; James Thayer Addison, *The Episcopal Church in the United States, 1789–1931* (New York: Charles Scribner's Sons, 1951), 369–70; *RCA,* 31 Oct. 1929, p. 10; *BRCA,* 30 Nov. 1910, p. 5; *CP,* 20 Nov. 1901, p. 4.

16. *RNL,* 27 Sept. 1923, p. 1; *RTD,* 23 June 1903, p. 2; *RTD,* 12 Dec. 1903, p. 1; *SC,* 5 June 1926, p. 13; *SC,* 17 Nov. 1900, p. 3; *SC,* 10 Feb. 1907, p. 14; *League Record,* Feb. 1918, pp. 3–4; *RCA,* 15 July 1920, p. 20.

17. *RT,* 8 Sept. 1901, pp. 1–2; Douglass S. McDaniel, *George White McDaniel* (Nashville: Sunday School Board of the Southern Baptist Convention, 1928), 162; Temple Ahabah program, 15 Feb. 1923, John J. Scherer Jr. Papers, personal possession of Mary Grace Taylor, Richmond; *SC,* 8 Dec. 1923; *Friendly Church Messenger,* Jan., Feb. 1923; *Friendly Church Messenger,* 12 Feb. 1928, p. 4; *RNL,* 21 Feb. 1925, p. 4; *SC,* 7 Mar. 1925, p. 13.

18. *RT,* 2 Dec. 1902, p. 5; Blanton, *Making of a Downtown Church,* 367; Robert Hayden Bullock, "The Past Fifty Years of Presbyterianism in Richmond, Virginia" (Th.D. thesis, Union Theological Seminary, 1943), 14–16; *Monumental Messenger,* Feb. 1900, pp. 7–15; *Monumental Messenger,* Jan. 1919, pp. 9–13; *Monumental Messenger,* May 1915, 10–11; *SC,* 20 Nov. 1915, p. 7.

19. *League Record,* Nov. 1919, p. 2; *J. L. Hill Printing Company's Directory of Richmond and Manchester, Virginia, 1900* (Richmond: J. L. Hill, 1900), 1356–59; *Hill Directory Company's Richmond Classified Business Directory* (Richmond: J. L. Hill, 1930), 1714–15; *RH,* 26 Oct. 1916, p. 10; "Report of Special Committee on Church Extension to the Richmond Clericus, 7 Feb. 1910," Papers of Grace and Holy Trinity Church, Virginia Historical Society, Richmond; *RCA,* 13 Oct. 1921, p. 15. Race relations also affected population dispersal. In 1917 residential segregation ordinances were declared unconstitutional. In 1918 members of Clay Street Methodist concluded that because so many white families had left their neighborhood their location was no longer viable. They disbanded and most members joined Grace Methodist Church. See *A History of Clay Street M. E. Church (South), Richmond, Virginia: 1844–1918* (n.p., n.d.), 20, and *RNL,* 19 Aug. 1922, p. 2.

20. White, *First Baptist,* 151; Taylor, *Saints Alive!,* 23; *RH,* 15 Apr. 1920, p. 2; *RCA,* 6 May 1920, p. 2.

21. *Program of Services,* 21 May 1911, Papers of First Evangelical Lutheran Church; White, *First Baptist,* 184–85; *RNL,* 24 Feb. 1925, p. 1; *SC,* 9 Jan. 1904, p. 5; *CP,* 18 Dec. 1907,

p. 1166; *PS,* 14 Dec. 1921, pp. 3–4. In 1921 Grace Covenant moved into a new church building on Monument Avenue. Another example of the merger pattern had occurred in 1913, when Marshall Street Christian and Allen Avenue Christian united to form Hanover Avenue Christian Church, as noted in Brinson, Haney, and Osborne, *A Century with Christ,* 146–47.

22. Seventh Street Christian Minute Book, 10 Jan. 1909 and 13 Jan. 1929, Papers of Seventh Street Christian Church, Virginia Historical Society. Most Richmond Baptist Churches belonged to the Dover Baptist Association. In 1900, according to association records, six of seventeen Richmond Baptist churches were made of wood; in 1930 only three of twenty-six were made of wood. Dover Baptist Association, "Historical Table," *Minutes of the One Hundred and Seventeenth Annual Session* (Richmond, n.p.); Dover Baptist Association, *Minutes of the One Hundred and Forty-Seventh Annual Session* (Richmond: Curtis Printing), 50–51.

23. *RTD,* 27 Oct. 1911, p. 1; *RTD,* 28 Oct. 1911, p. 10; Minute Book, Seventh Street Christian Church, 17 Mar. 1912; Melton, *Presbyterian Worship in America,* 115; Bennett, *Methodist Church on Shockoe Hill,* 108; Brinson, Haney, and Osborne, *A Century with Christ,* 99; *BRCA,* 20 June 1912, pp. 10–11; *RH,* 1 Feb. 1912, pp. 4–5; Frederick Jarrard Anderson, *A People Called Northminster: The History of Barton Heights and Northminster Baptist Church, 1891–1978* (Richmond: Northminster Baptist Church, 1979), 40–41.

24. *RH,* 1 Feb. 1912, pp. 4–5; *Friendly Church Messenger,* 9 Sept. 1924, p. 2; Orpha Ochse, *The History of the Organ in the United States* (Bloomington: University of Indiana Press, 1975), 321–63. For assistance in interpreting the technical features of organs, I wish to thank Centenary College Prof. Ronald Dean, an organist, a music historian, and an organ historian.

25. *SC,* 3 Nov. 1900, p. 6; Brinson, Haney, and Osborne, *A Century with Christ,* 119; St. Paul's Vestry Book, 8 Mar. 1926, p. 164; St. Paul's Vestry Book, 16 Oct. 1926, p. 194; Weisiger, Traser, and Trice, *Not Hearers Only,* 57; *Friendly Church Messenger,* 25 June 1922.

26. Frederick R. Chenault, *The Broad Street Methodist Church, South and Community House* (Richmond: Whittet & Shepperson, 1923), 6, 17; Richmond Preachers Meeting, "Minutes of Meetings, 1900–1928," meeting of 27 July 1914, Special Collections and Archives, McGraw-Page Library, Randolph-Macon College, Ashland, Va.; *RCA,* 6 Nov. 1919, p. 16; *RCA,* 20 Nov. 1919, p. 21; *RCA,* 18 Oct. 1923, p. 13.

27. *Friendly Church Messenger,* 11, 18 June 1922, p. 1; *RH,* 7 Dec. 1911, p. 12; *RH,* 8 Apr. 1927, p. 6; Pleasants and Hill, *First Hundred Years,* 48; *PS,* 20 Oct. 1915, p. 8; Abernathy, *Living,* 89–91; *RNL,* 3 Feb. 1925, p. 8; *RNL,* 26 Mar. 1927, p. 6; *PS,* 6 Nov. 1, 1929, p. 1; *RNL,* 27 May, 1922, p. 2. On Easter Sunday in 1922, Atlanta's radio station WSB probably transmitted the first broadcast of an entire church service. Talmage W. Dean, *A Survey of Twentieth Century Protestant Church Music in America* (Nashville: Broadman Press, 1988), 142.

28. St. Paul's Vestry Book, 25 Oct. 1925, p. 25; *CP,* 1 Mar. 1905, p. 142; White, *First Baptist,* 149–51; Blanton, *Making of a Downtown Church,* 85; Weisiger, Traser, and Trice, *Not Hearers Only,* 53; *RH,* 1 Feb. 1917, p. 7; St. Paul's Vestry Book, 20 Feb. 1911, p. 17; *Beacon on a Hill,* 47; James, *Leigh Street,* 100; Pleasants and Hill, *First Hundred Years,* 40; *SC,* 4 June 1904, p. 9.

29. *SC,* 26 Apr. 1902, p. 8; *SC,* 5 Apr., 1902, p. 8; *CP,* 17 Apr. 1901, p. 8; Cutchins, *Memories of Old Richmond (1881–1944)* (Verona, Va.: McClure Press, 1973), 50–51; James, *Leigh Street,* 101; *Beacon on a Hill,* 34; Weeks, *Grace Baptist,* 58; Bennett, *Methodist Church on Shockoe Hill,* 120; *PS,* 12 May 1908, p. 23; Seventh Street Minute Book, 13 July 1910.

30. *RT,* 15 Sept. 1901, p. 16; St. John's Vestry Book, 1900–1914, 3 May 1904, 5 June, 1906 and 4 June 1907, Papers of St. John's Episcopal Church, Virginia Historical Society, Rich-

mond; Dean, *Twentieth Century Protestant Church Music,* 35; *RT,* 15 Sept. 1901, p. 1: *RH,* 22 June 1905, p. 1; Bennett, *Methodist Church on Shockoe Hill,* 127; *Beacon on a Hill,* 116–18.

31. *PS,* 21 Jan. 1920, p. 8; White, *First Baptist,* 149; *CP,* 16 Oct. 1907, p. 945; Thompson, *Presbyterianism in the South,* 3:356; *SC,* 1 Nov. 1919, p. 1; Dean, *Twentieth Century Protestant Church Music,* 112–15; Blanton, *Making of a Downtown Church,* 238.

32. Bennett, *Methodist Church on Shockoe Hill,* 102; Blanton, *Making of a Downtown Church,* 240; *SC,* 6 Oct. 1928, p. 3; *SC,* 2 Feb. 1929, p. 7; Addison, *Episcopal Church,* 305–6.

33. *Friendly Church Messenger,* 7 Oct. 1928, pp. 1–2; *Friendly Church Messenger,* 7 Sept. 1924, p. 2; *Friendly Church Messenger,* 1 Mar. 1925, p. 1; Brinson, Haney and Osborne, *A Century with Christ,* 103, 105. Without making specific reference to the Church Life Foundation, Seventh Street may have participated in this worship movement among the Disciples of Christ. Noting that the Disciples had been a rural-based group, this movement attempted to be sensitive to tastes of urban residents and advocated that worship services be beautiful, reverent, and structured. For the Church Life Foundation, see William S. Lockhart, *The Ministry of Worship: A Study of the Need, Psychology and Technique of Worship* (St. Louis: Christian Board Education, 1927).

34. Thomas R. English, "The Decline of the Pulpit," *Union Seminary Magazine* 12, no. 4 (Apr.–May 1901): 304–16; *PS,* 26 Aug. 1914, p. 5; *RH,* 10 Aug. 1922, p. 5; *SC,* 24 Nov. 1900, p. 1; *CP.* 17 Sept. 1902, p. 8; *RT,* 14 Dec. 1900, p. 4.

35. *RH,* 23 Jan. 1902, p. 2; *PS,* 1 July 1925, p. 2; Blanton, *Making of a Downtown Church,* 271; Russell Cecil, *The Religion of Love* (Richmond: Presbyterian Committee of Publication, 1925). As an example of one of Cecil's published sermons see "The Years That the Locust Hath Eaten," *Union Seminary Magazine* 18, no. 4 (Apr.-May. 1907): 314–20. "The Love of God in the Heart," 18 July 1915 is one of many such Cecil sermons in a collection at William Smith Morton Library, Union Theological Seminary/Presbyterian School of Christian Education. *RH,* 3 Mar. 1910, p. 10; *RH,* 24 Mar. 1919, p. 8; *RTD,* 25 Feb. 1910, p. 2; Edgar Estes Folk, "Introduction," in James B. Hawthorne, *An Unshaken Trust and Other Sermons* (Philadelphia: American Baptist Publication Society, 1899), 7–18; *RH,* 30 Jan. 1902, p. 4.

36. *RH,* 22 Jan. 1903, p. 2; *SC,* 8 Apr. 1922, p. 5; *RH,* 27 May 1909, p. 4.

37. Alice B. Mitchell to her mother, 20 Aug. 1905 in the Samuel Chiles Mitchell Papers #1003, Southern Historical Collection, Wilson Library, University of North Carolina at Chapel Hill; *PS,* 6 Nov. 1929, p. 5; McDaniel, *George White McDaniel,* 80.

38. Walter Russell Bowie, *Learning to Live* (Nashville: Abingdon Press, 1969), 89–93; Walter Russell Bowie, *Sunny Windows and Other Sermons for Children* (New York: Fleming H. Revell, 1921).

39. "City Pastorates," *Union Seminary Magazine* 23, no. 2 (Dec.–Jan. 1911–1912): 174–76; *RT,* 28 Oct. 1900, p. 11; *RH,* 4 Mar. 1909, p. 4; *RTD,* 20 Dec. 1904, p. 12; *RH,* 5 Nov. 1914, p. 3; *RH,* 9 Feb. 1922, p. 10.

40. *The Parish Register,* Mar. 1911, Robert Wright Forsyth Papers, Virginia Historical Society, Richmond; *RH,* 13 Feb. 1913, p. 4.

41. *PS,* 20 Sept. 1916, p. 2; *VC,* May 1925, p. 486; *SC,* 25 June 1910, pp. 3–5; *RH,* 28 June 1923, p. 14; *RNL,* 3 Oct. 1921, p. 4; *RH,* 25 Aug. 1927, p. 5.

42. A. Douglas Smith Jr., ed., *A Tribute to John Jacob Scherer, Jr. On the Occasion of His 25th Anniversary as Pastor of First English Evangelical Lutheran Church, Richmond, Virginia, Dec. 1931* (Richmond: Dietz Press, 1931), 19–20; Taylor, *Saints Alive!,* 64–65, 22; undated, untitled news clipping, summer 1920, Scherer Papers, personal possession of Mary Grace Scherer Taylor. For more about Scherer, see Donald Smith Armentrout, "John Jacob Scherer Jr.: A Type of Southern Lutheran" (Ph.D. diss., Vanderbilt University, May 1970).

43. *PS,* 6 Nov. 1929, p. 4; *RH,* 2 Nov. 1911, p. 10; H. D. C. Maclachlan, "Haggai," in "Types and Ideals of Hebrew Prophecy," p. 9, Machlachlan Papers, Disciples of Christ Historical Society, Nashville; McDaniel, *George White McDaniel,* 88–89.

44. *SC,* 23 Apr. 1904, p. 6; Blanton, *Making of a Downtown Church,* 339–42; Brinson, Haney, and Osborne, *Century with Christ,* 101–2; Grace and Holy Trinity Vestry Book, 2 May 1929, 87–93, Papers of Grace and Holy Trinity Episcopal Church, Virginia Historical Society, Richmond.

45. *(St. Andrew's) Parish Record,* Easter 1901, pp. 12–13; "Churches" in "Know Your City Survey," Young Women's Christian Association Papers, Special Collections and Archives Department, James Branch Cabell Library, Virginia Commonwealth University, Richmond; Taylor *Saints Alive!,* 29–30, 68; White, *First Baptist,* 155–56; Jessie Spencer file, Disciples of Christ Historical Society, Nashville; Walter L. Lingle to E. D. Brown, 25 June 1920, Lingle Papers, Presbyterian Historical Society, Montreat, N.C.; *PS,* 7 Dec. 1927, p. 2.

46. Maria Williams Sheerin, *The Parson Takes a Wife* (New York.: Macmillan, 1948), 5–12; *Forward,* Nov. 1921, p. 6; *SC,* 2 May 1903, p. 5.

47. *VC,* Mar. 1925, p. 452; *RCA,* 31 July 1902, p. 5; *SC,* 11 Oct. 1903, p. 6; *SC,* 8 July 1905, p. 6; *PS,* 28 Feb. 1917, p. 16.

48. Charles P. Anderson and Dorothy D. Anderson, *History of the Fulton Baptist Church, Richmond, Virginia: A Study of Baptist Work in Fulton, 1865–1944.* ([Richmond: Whittet & Shepperson, 1944]), 15–16; *CP,* 20 June 1900, p. 8.

4. Mighty Engines of Evangelism

1. *RH,* 28 Dec. 1911, p. 4; *RNL,* 7 Mar. 1916, p. 4.

2. *RH,* 7 May 1903, p. 2; *RH,* 5 Oct. 1916, p. 10; *BRCA,* 25 Mar. 1909, p. 8; *PS,* 19 Jan. 1910, p. 66; *PS,* 19 Aug. 1914, p. 9; *SC,* 5 Dec. 1903, p. 8; "Report of Special Committee on Church Extension to the Richmond Clericus," 7 Feb. 1910, Papers of Grace and Holy Trinity Church, Virginia Historical Society, Richmond.

3. *PS,* 12 Nov. 1913, p. 10; *RTD,* 16 June 1903, p. 5; *BRCA,* 12 Jan 1911, p. 1; *RNL,* 13 Jan. 1925, p. 2.

4. *RTD,* 10 Nov. 1903, p. 1; W. Asbury Christian, *Richmond: Her Past and Present* (Richmond: L. H. Jenkins, 1912), 437–515; *RTD,* 8 Dec. 1903; *RH,* 24 Nov 1903, p. 8; *RT,* 3 Mar 1901, p. 8; *RCA,* 5 Apr. 1900, pp. 8–9.

5. *RH,* 18 Feb. 1915, p. 10; *RH,* 5 Oct. 1922, p. 10; *BRCA,* 18 June 1908, p. 9; *RT,* 13 Dec. 1900, p. 4; *BRCA,* 10 Oct. 1901, p. 1; *RCA,* 20 May 1926, p. 2.

6. *BRCA,* 14 Jan. 1909, p. 20; *RTD,* 28 Apr. 1908, p. 12; *BRCA,* 4 Feb. 1909, pp. 19–20; *CP,* 10 Feb. 1909, p. 22; *CP,* 27 Jan. 1909, p. 4; *RTD,* 7 Jan. 1909, p. 1; *SC,* 4 Dec. 1909, p. 11; *SC,* 19 Dec. 1908, p. 11.

7. *RH,* 28 Jan. 1909, p. 4; *RH,* 4 Feb. 1909, p. 7; *SC,* 23 Jan. 1909, p. 13; *BRCA,* 4 Feb. 1909, p. 18; *SC,* 16 Jan. 1909, p. 1; *RTD,* 9 Jan. 1909, p. 4; *RTD,* 12 Jan. 1909, p. 2; *RTD,* 19 Jan. 1909, p. 7; *CP,* 10 Feb. 1909, p. 22.

8. Presbyterian Ministers Association of Richmond, Virginia, "Minutes of Meetings, 1900–1928," meeting of 8 Feb. 1909, William Smith Morton Library, Union Theological Seminary/ Presbyterian School of Christian Education; *RH,* 4 Feb. 1909, p. 3; *CP,* 3 Feb. 1909, pp. 4, 21; *CP,* 24 Feb. 1909, pp. 22–23; *BRCA,* 14 Feb 1909, pp. 18–20.

9. *Forward,* Apr. 1921, p. 6; *PS,* 23 Feb. 1916, p. 8; *PS,* 1 Mar. 1916, p. 8; *PS,* 8 Mar. 1916, p. 1; *PS,* 29 Mar. 1916, p. 8; *RNL,* 14 Mar. 1916, p. 1; *RNL,* 19 Mar. 1916, p. 12; *SC,* 26 Mar.

1921, p. 9; *RCA,* 22 Mar. 1923, p. 10; *RNL,* 26 Feb. 1923, p. 7; *RCA,* 7 Apr. 1927, p. 10; *RCA,* 21 Apr. 1927, p. 11.

10. *RNL,* 18 Dec. 1918, p. 1; *PS,* 1 Jan. 1919, p. 12; *RNL,* 7 Jan. 1919, p. 15; *PS,* 5 Mar. 1919, p. 9; *RNL,* 15 Jan. 1919, p. 2; *PS,* 22 Feb. 1919, p. 9. For valuable biographies and assessments of Sunday, see William G. McLoughlin, *Billy Sunday Was His Real Name* (Chicago: University of Chicago, 1955) and Lyle W. Dorsett, *Billy Sunday and the Redemption of Urban America* (Grand Rapids, Mich.: William B. Eerdmans Publishing, 1991).

11. *RNL,* 3 Mar. 1919, p. 1; The *News Leader* carried the texts of Billy Sunday's sermons from 13 Jan. to 3 Mar. 1919; *PS,* 29 Jan. 1919, pp. 8–9; *PS,* 19 Feb. 1919, p. 8.

12. Russell Cecil, "Some Lessons Which Ministers May Learn from Rev. William A. Sunday," *Union Seminary Review* 30, no. 3 (Apr. 1919): 232–39; *RNL,* 8 Feb. 1915, p. 1; *RNL,* 13 Jan. 1919, p. 1; *RNL,* 18 Feb. 1919, p. 1; *RNL,* 11 Nov. 1918, p. 4; *RCA,* 13 Mar. 1919, p. 2; McLoughlin, *Billy Sunday,* 274.

13. *RH,* 6 Mar. 1919, p. 10; *RH,* 6 Feb. 1919, p. 4; *PS,* 22 Jan. 1919, p. 2; *PS,* 2 Apr. 1919, p. 12; *RH,* 10 Apr. 1919, p 7; *RCA,* 6 Feb. 1919, p. 2.

14. *RNL,* 22 Sept. 1922, p. 1; *RNL,* 26 Sept. 1922, p. 1; *RNL,* 28 Sept. 1922, p. 4.

15. *CC,* Apr. 1921, p. 10; *BRCA,* 18 Jan. 1917, p. 1; Dover Baptist Association, *Minutes of the One Hundred and Thirty-Sixth Annual Session* (Richmond: Appeals Press, 1919), 10; *RNL,* 28 Mar 1921, p. 12; Richmond Ministerial Union, "Minutes of Meetings 1919–28," meeting of 13 June 1927, Richmond Public Library, Richmond.

16. *RNL,* 9 Nov. 1914, p. 4; *RNL,* 29 Mar. 1915, p. 7; *BRCA,* 22 Apr. 1915, p. 12; *RNL,* 28 Oct. 1914, p. 9; *RNL,* 7 Nov. 1914, p. 11.

17. *SC,* 20 May 1905, p. 8; *RH,* 24 Oct. 1907, p. 12; *SC,* 21 July 1900, p. 8; *SC,* 19 Jan. 1903, p. 8; *SC,* 18 June 1904, p. 2; *CP,* 29 Aug. 1900, p. 8; Ernest Trice Thompson, *Presbyterians in the South,* 3:141–45; *SC,* 28 July 1906, p. 6. For a history of early Sunday schools, see Anne M. Boylan, *Sunday School: The Formation of an American Institution, 1790–1880* (New Haven, Conn.: Yale University Press, 1988), and for recent developments, see Robert W. Lynn and Elliott Wright, *The Big Little School: Two Hundred Years of the Sunday School,* 2d ed. (Nashville: Broadman Press, 1980), 117–33. Focusing on children, Boylan concludes that early Sunday schools made conversion the major goal, but gradually changed their curriculum to emphasize lifelong Christian nurture. In catering to all age groups, Richmond leaders of the early twentieth century readily combined those two goals. See Boylan, *Sunday School,* 112, 133–65.

18. *RCA,* 10 Apr. 1919, p. 2.

19. *CP,* 16 Dec. 1903, p. 834; *CP,* 15 June 1904, p. 377; *RTD,* 16 May 1907, p. 2; *RH,* 10 Dec. 1908, p. 8; *PS,* 14 Jan. 1920, p. 8; *PS,* 10 Mar. 1920, p. 8; *School of Methods for Sunday School and Church Workers,* program, Feb. 20–25, 1921, Jessie P. Spencer Papers, Disciples of Christ Historical Society, Nashville; *PS,* 9 Mar. 1921, p. 12.

20. *League Record,* Aug. 1919, p. 3; Walter W. Moore, "Address at the Dedication of Schauffler Hall," Moore Papers, William Smith Morton Library, Union Theological Seminary/Presbyterian School of Christian Education, Richmond; Ernest Trice Thompson, *Presbyterians in the South,* 3:141–47; *PS,* 15 Dec. 1909, p. 2; *RTD,* 14 Mar. 1912, p. 10; *RH,* 15 Apr. 1909, p. 14; *BRCA,* 4 Jan. 1912, p. 14.

21. *Manual of the Graded Course of Instruction in Sabbath-School and Family* (Richmond: Presbyterian Committee of Publication, 1903), 3; *SC,* 21 July 1900, p. 8; *SC,* 31 Jan. 1903, p. 8; *RTD,* 25 Sept. 1906, p. 12; *RTD,* 20 Feb. 1907, p. 12; *RH,* 27 Aug. 1900, p. 9; *RH,* 12 Oct. 1916, p. 2; *RH,* 24 Nov. 1910, p. 8.

22. Richmond District Conference, Virginia Conference, Methodist Episcopal Church, South, "Forty-Eighth Session," 22–24 June 1915, p. 318, Special Collections and Archives, McGraw-Page Library, Randolph-Macon College, Ashland, Va.; *RT,* 27 Nov. 1900, p. 4; *Manual of the Graded Course of Instruction,* 6; *RH,* 18 Nov. 1915, p. 11; Frederick Jarrard Anderson, *A People Called Northminster: The History of Barton Heights and Northminster Baptist Churches, 1891–1978* (Richmond: Northminster Baptist Church, 1979), 37; *Monumental Messenger,* June 1915, pp. 12–13, and Sept. 1915, p. 7; Maria Williams Sheerin, *The Parson Takes a Wife* (New York: Macmillan, 1948), 1–2.

23. Anna B. Binford, "My Home Town and Me: Richmond Virginia, 1871–1948," 86–88, Anna Binford Papers, Virginia Historical Society, Richmond; Presbyterian Committee of Publication, Richmond, Virginia, "Appointment of Women to Official Positions," R. E. Magill Papers, Presbyterian Historical Society, Montreat, N.C.; *PS,* 16 Nov. 1927, p. 8; H. D. C. Maclachlan, letter of recommendation, 10 Apr. 1919, Jessie Spencer Papers.

24. *BRCA,* 25 Nov. 1909, p. 19; *PS,* 15 Dec. 1909, p. 2; *RH,* 2 Dec. 1909, p. 9.

25. *RCA,* 29 May 1919, p. 6; Mollie Roberson Wiltshire, *A Century of Service: The History of Union Station Methodist Church, 1843–1943* (Richmond: Whittet & Shepperson, 1943), 83–84; "Men's Bible Class of the First English Evangelical Lutheran Sunday School," Records of Minutes of Business and Executive Committees from July 9, 1917–1930, First English Evangelical Lutheran Church, Richmond.

26. *BRCA,* 12 Sept. 1912, p. 3; *RH,* 11 Feb. 1915, p. 11; *RH,* 18 May 1925, p. 10; Anderson, *A People Called Northminster,* 55.

27. *RTD,* 27 Oct. 1913, p. 10; *RH,* 21 Apr. 1910, p. 3; *RH,* 29 July 1909, p. 13; *RH,* 16 Sept. 1909, p. 11; Wiltshire, *Century of Service,* 28; *RH,* 18 May 1925, p. 10; *RNL,* 11 Jan. 1923, p. 4; U.S. Department of Commerce and Labor, Bureau of the Census, *Census of Religious Bodies: 1906* (Washington, D.C.: GPO, 1910), 1:484–85; U.S. Department of Commerce, Bureau of the Census, *Census of Religious Bodies: 1926* (Washington, D.C.: GPO, 1930), 1:523–24.

28. Dover Baptist Association, *Minutes of the One Hundred and Twenty-Fifth Annual Session* (Richmond: Walthall Printing, 1908), 20.

29. Virginia Annual Conference of the Methodist Episcopal Church, South, *Minutes of the One Hundred and Twenty-Second Session* (Richmond: Lipscomb Fergusson, 1904), 44; *CP,* 19 Feb. 1908, p. 172; Walter W. Moore, "The First Fifty Years," *Union Seminary Review* 24, no. 1 (Oct.–Nov. 1912): 14–47; *RH,* 22 Feb. 1906, p. 3; *RH,* 19 Dec. 1907, p. 13; George W. McDaniel, *Churches of the New Testament* (Nashville: Sunday School Board of the Southern Baptist Convention, 1921), 137–38; *RH,* 27 Aug. 1908, p. 5.

30. *(St. Andrew's) Parish Record,* Easter 1901, p. 16; "St. Andrew's Work: Report from September 1929 to May 1930," 2–4, Papers of St. Andrew's Episcopal Church, Virginia Historical Society, Richmond, Virginia; *Bethlehem Lutheran Church, Richmond, Virginia: 125th Anniversary* (South Hackensack, N.J.: Custombook, 1977), 20; The Collegiate Historian Society *Fifty Years of Collegiate; A History of the Collegiate Schools, 1915–1965* (Richmond: n.p., 1967), 25; *The Collegiate Schools in the City of Richmond, Golden Anniversary, 1915–1965* (Richmond: n.p., [1965]).

31. *Annual Catalogue of St. Catherine's School, 1922–1923,* 9, 11; Josephine Augusta Clarke Knight, *Symbols of the South: Education and Early Life in Richmond Under Tutorship of Miss "Jennie" Ellett* (Richmond: Garrett & Massie, 1941), 40, 54, 71; Susan L. Klaus and Mary Porter Johns Martin, *A Part of Us Forever: A Centennial History of St. Catherine's School, 1890–1990* (Richmond: St. Catherine's School, 1989), 10–30; *SC,* 22 May 1920, p. 3; *SC,* 19 June 1920, p. 11; *SC,* 22 May 1920, p. 9.

32. Churchill Gibson Chamberlayne, "On Having Principles and Acting on Them," sermon, 19 May 1929, Churchill Gibson Chamberlayne Papers, Virginia Historical Society, Richmond, Virginia; Virginius Dabney, *Richmond: The Story of a City,* rev. ed. (Charlottesville, University Press of Virginia, 1990), 280; *Forward,* Dec. 1921, p. 13; *SC,* 13 Mar. 1926, p. 26; *Journal of the One Hundred and Thirty-Fifth Annual Council of the Protestant Episcopal Church in the Diocese of Virginia* (n.p., 1930), 120, 123. DeWitt Hankins, *The First Fifty Years: A History of St. Christopher's School, 1911–1961* (Richmond: St. Christopher's School Foundation, 1961), focuses on student life, but includes some information about Churchill Gibson Chamberlayne and the purchase of the school by the Virginia Diocese in pages 1–3, 259–61.

33. Dover Baptist Association, *Minutes of the One Hundred and Seventeenth Annual Session* (Richmond: n.p., 1900), 17; Dover Baptist Association, *Minutes of the One Hundred and Twentieth Annual Session* (Richmond: J. L. Hill, 1903), 16.

34. Baptist General Association of Virginia, *Minutes of the Eighty-Third Annual Session* (Roanoke: Stone, 1906), 39; W. Harrison Daniel, "Southern Baptists and Education, 1865–1900: A Case Study," *Maryland Historical Magazine* 64 (fall 1969): 218–37; Reuben E. Alley, *Frederic W. Boatwright* (Richmond: University of Richmond, 1973), 23–45; Reuben E. Alley, *History of the University of Richmond, 1830–1971* (Charlottesville: University Press of Virginia, 1977), 8–10, 13.

35. Alley, *Boatwright,* 2–44.

36. *RH,* 19 Dec. 1907, p. 13; Baptist General Association of Virginia, *Minutes of the Ninetieth Annual Session* (n.p., 1913), 84; Alley, *Boatwright,* 28–45, 49–50, 69, 72, 80, 88, 90; W. Harrison Daniel, *History at the University of Richmond* (Richmond: W. Harrison Daniel, 1991), 56; *RH,* 18 Apr. 1929, p. 23; Alley, *University,* 90, 92, 97, 187.

37. Alley, *Boatwright,* 48–49, 58–76; Daniel, *History at Richmond,* 26–27; *RH,* 16 Aug. 1900, p. 4; *RH,* 28 Apr. 1901, p. 9; *RH,* 12 Sept. 1901, p. 5; *RH,* 5 Dec. 1901, p. 8; *RH,* 26 Dec. 1901, p. 1; *RH,* 2 Jan. 1902, p. 4; *RH,* 14 Oct. 1906, p. 19; Alley, *University,* 137; *RH,* 6 Dec. 1906, p. 12; *RH,* 30 Apr. 1908, p. 12; *RH,* 23 Jan. 1913, p. 2; *RH,* 3 Apr. 1913, p. 1; *RH,* 8 May 1913, p. 12; *RH,* 31 Oct. 1913, p. 2; *RH,* 1 Jan. 1914, p. 10; *RH,* 8 Jan. 1914, p. 10; *RH,* 12 June 1924, p. 6.

38. Daniel, *History at Richmond,* 27; Alley, *Boatwright,* 51, 79–82, 112–13; *RH,* 27 Apr. 1916, p. 2; *RNL,* 1 Feb. 1917, p. 6; *RH,* 13 Feb. 1919, p. 7; *RH,* 20 Feb. 1919, p. 7; *RH,* 6 May 1926, p. 3; *RNL,* 18 May 1927, p. 13; *RH,* 12 Jan. 1928, p. 6; *RNL,* 10 June 1929, p. 1.

39. *RH,* 23 Apr. 1908, pp. 12–13; *RH,* 12 Nov. 1908, p. 13; *RH,* 9 Apr. 1908, p. 7; *RH,* 8 Feb. 1906, p. 9; *RH,* 30 Apr. 1908, p. 12; Alley, *Boatwright,* 77–78, 86, 94, 96, 98.

40. Alley, *Boatwright,* 22, 60; Daniel, *History at Richmond,* 17, 75; Alley, *University,* 112–15, 121–24. R. H. Pitt, "The College—The University, 1895–1932," *The First Hundred Years: Brief Sketches of the History of the University of Richmond* (Richmond: Whittet & Shepperson, 1932), 71–77.

41. *RH,* 25 Dec. 1904, p. 8; *RH,* 26 Jan. 1905, p. 8; *RH,* 1 Feb.–22 Mar. 1900, p. 2; *RH,* 22 Feb. 1906, p. 3; *RH,* 8 Dec. 1904, p. 1; *RH,* 12 June 1924, pp. 6–7; Alley, *Boatwright,* 61–63; Daniel, *History at Richmond,* 75–76; 82–83; Alley, *University,* 138–42; Pitt, "The College—The University," 72–77.

42. Baptist General Association of Virginia, *Minutes of the Eighty-Ninth Annual Session* (n.p., 1912), 83; Alley, *Boatwright,* 67–68, 74; Daniel, *History at Richmond,* 76–84, 168–70; *RH,* 16 June 1910, p. 6; *RH,* 16 Jan. 1913, p. 2; Alley, *University,* 132–36, 167, 171.

43. Pitt, "The College-The University," 91.

44. Alley, *Boatwright,* 38–39, 71–74; Daniel, *History at Richmond,* 180–81; *RH,* 26 Feb. 1920, p. 6; Alley, *University,* 108, 150.

45. Virginia Annual Conference of the Methodist Episcopal Church, South, *Minutes of the One Hundred and Twentieth Session* (Richmond: Williams Printing, 1902), 57; *BRCA,* 16 June 1904, p. 1; *BRCA,* 18 Feb. 1904, p. 1; *RCA,* 6 Jan. 1921, p. 2; *RCA,* 27 Jan. 1921, p. 2; *RCA,* 10 Feb. 1921, p. 12; *RCA,* 9 June 1921, p. 10; *RNL,* 14 Jan. 1926, p. 8. For an effective account of Randolph-Macon, see James E. Scanlon, *Randolph-Macon College: A Southern History, 1825–1967* (Charlottesville: University Press of Virginia, 1983).

46. *PS,* 23 Aug. 1916, p. 4; J. Gray McAllister, *The Life and Letters of Walter W. Moore* (Richmond: Union Theological Seminary, 1939), 558; Walter W. Moore, "The First Fifty Years," *Union Seminary Magazine* 24, no. 1 (Oct.–Nov. 1912): 14–47.

47. *PS,* 23 June 1926, p. 2; McAllister, *Walter W. Moore,* 17–131.

48. McAllister, *Walter W. Moore,* 131–310, quotation, 260; *PS,* 13 Aug. 1924, p. 8; *PS,* 23 June 1926, p. 2; Thompson, *Presbyterians of the South,* 3:201–3.

49. McAllister, *Walter W. Moore,* 379; Walter W. Moore to Walter L. Lingle, 14 July 1911 and 17 May 1911, Lingle Papers, Presbyterian Historical Society, Montreat, N.C.

50. McAllister, *Walter W. Moore,* 337; *CP,* 5 Feb. 1908, p. 126; McAllister provides accounts of most of the large contributions and the *Central Presbyterian* and *Presbyterian of the South* also reported most of them.

51. McAllister, *Walter W. Moore,* 428, 405; "W. W. Moore Sermon Records," Moore Papers; *PS,* 23 June 1926, p. 2. For accounts of family life, see McAllister, *Walter W. Moore,* 297, 363–67, 533–35.

52. Thompson, *Presbyterians in the South,* 3:203–5; McAllister, *Walter W. Moore,* 558; *PS,* 23 June 1926, p. 2; Walter W. Lingle, "The Last Fifty Years," *Union Seminary Magazine* 24, no. 1 (Oct.–Nov. 1912): 48–75.

53. Thompson, *Presbyterians in the South,* 3:203–5; McAllister, *Walter W. Moore,* 210, 558.

54. McAllister, *Walter W. Moore,* 446–64, quotation, 445; Louise McComb, *Presbyterian School of Christian Education: The First Seventy Years* (Richmond: Presbyterian School of Christian Education, 1985), 3–4; "Article on the Assembly's Training School" (typewritten, ca. 1917), in folder "Schools and Colleges: General Assembly's Training School," General Information File, Presbyterian Historical Society, Montreat, N.C.

55. *PS,* 18 Oct. 1914, p. 17; McAllister, *Walter W. Moore,* 463; McComb, *Presbyterian School,* 4–10; Dean [William Megginson] to R. E. Magill, Jan. 1917, Lingle Papers; *PS,* 25 Mar. 1914, p. 17.

56. W. W. Moore to Mrs. N. F. McCormick, 9 Apr. 1919, Lingle Papers. For more about Lingle, especially his concerns about social reform, see J. Wayne Flynt, "'Feeding the Hungry and Ministering to the Broken Hearted': The Presbyterian Church in the United States and the Social Gospel, 1900–1920," in *Religion in the South,* ed. Charles Reagan Wilson (Jackson: University Press of Mississippi, 1985), 83–137 and chaps. 7 and 8 of this volume.

57. Walter L. Lingle, unpublished autobiography, 8–13, quotation, 11 in Lingle Papers; Walter L. Lingle to Lena, 9 June 1917; Merle to Walter Lingle, undated 1915; W. L. Lingle to J. E. Edgerton, 4 May 1927, Lingle Papers.

58. W. W. Moore to W. L. Lingle, 9 and 10 June, 1911; Walter L. Lingle to Lena, 9 June 1917; W. L. Lingle to Mrs. H. Kerr Taylor, 8 Sept. 1920; J. P. McCallie to W. L. Lingle, 26 May 1923; Merle Lingle to W. L. Lingle, 6 Sept. 1924 and undated letter; W. L. Lingle to Samuel A. Derieux, 1 Jan. 1923, in Lingle Papers.

59. McComb, *Presbyterian School,* 19–20, 22; W. L. Lingle to Ruth Jones, 15 Sept. 1920, Lingle Papers.

60. W. L. Lingle to W. W. Moore, 19 July 1923; Walter L. Lingle to Rev. T. C. Johnson and Owsley Sanders, L. R. Carrie, J. H. Reed and J. A. Lancaster, 5 May 1914; W. L. Lingle to Ryerson Turbull, 7 July 1923; W. W. Moore to W. L. Lingle, 23 July 1923, in Lingle Papers.

61. McComb, *Presbyterian School,* 18–23; *Year Book of the Assembly Training School for Lay Workers: Announcement 1915–1916* (n.p., n.d.); *The General Assembly Training School for Lay Workers, Richmond, Virginia, Bulletin Catalogue 1928–29* 11 (Jan.–Mar. 1929); *PS,* 4 Sept. 1929, p. 2; *PS,* 24 Oct. 1928, p. 9.

62. *RTD,* 29 May 1912, p. 1; *RNL,* 22 July 1921, p. 7; *RNL,* 30 Sept. 1924, p. 2; *RNL,* 28 Apr. 1920, p. 21; *RTD,* 30 Sept. 1916, p. 1; *RNL,* 5 Oct. 1916, p. 11; *PS,* 11 Oct. 1916, p. 806; *RCA,* 30 May 1929, p. 2.

63. *RH,* 26 Oct. 1916, p. 10; Baptist Council of Richmond and Manchester "Minutes of the Executive Committee, 1905–1929," meetings of 3 Oct. 1905 and 10 Jan. 1908, Virginia Baptist Historical Society, University of Richmond, Richmond; *PS,* 22 Nov. 1916, pp. 17, 20–21; *PS,* 9 Nov. 1927, pp. 9, 17; *League Record,* Mar. 1916, p. 4; *League Record,* Mar. 1918, pp. 3–4.

64. *SC,* 17 Apr. 1920, p. 13.

65. *PS,* 29 Sept. 1920, p. 1; Bureau of the Census, *Census of Religious Bodies: 1906,* 1: 484–85; Bureau of the Census, *Census of Religious Bodies: 1926,* 1:523–24.

5. Paths of Grace

1. *BRCA,* 3 June 1909, p. 4; James B. Hawthorne, *The Cloud of Witnesses and Other Sermons* (Nashville: Sunday School Board of the Southern Baptist Convention, 1908), 170–75; *BRCA,* 16 Nov. 1916, p. 2; Robert Pollok Kerr, *Will the World Outgrow Christianity and Other Interrogatives on Vital Themes* (Chicago: Fleming H. Revell, 1901), 145–46; William W. Weeks, *The Heart of God* (Nashville: Sunday School Board of the Southern Baptist Convention, 1924), 82–83.

2. Hawthorne, *Cloud of Witnesses,* 191, 265, 175, 118; Edward L. Pell, *Four Feet on a Fender* (New York: Dutton & Co., 1917), 63–80, quotations, 96, 70; Edward L. Pell, *Why I Believe in Jesus: A Personal Experience* (New York: Fleming H. Revell, 1926), 80.

3. *PS,* 14 Apr. 1915, p. 1; Walter W. Moore, *The Indispensable Book* (New York: Fleming H. Revell, 1910), 102; Pell, *Four Feet on a Fender,* 67.

4. *SC,* 12 Feb. 1910, p. 3; Hawthorne, *Cloud of Witnesses,* 55, 63; Walter Russell Bowie, *Road of the Star* (New York: Fleming H. Revell, 1922), 58.

5. Walter Russell Bowie, *Sunny Windows and Other Sermons for Children* (New York: Fleming H. Revell, 1921), 73; Hawthorne, *Cloud of Witnesses,* 164; Russell Cecil, "Wrestling with God," sermon 34, 1915, Cecil Papers, William Smith Morton Library, Union Theological Seminary/Presbyterian School of Christian Education, Richmond; William James, *The Varieties of Religious Experience: A Study in Human Nature* (New York: Random House, 1902), 453–54.

6. Kerr, *Will the World Outgrow Christianity,* 34–44; George W. McDaniel, *Seeing the Best: Sermons and Addresses* (Nashville: Sunday School Board of the Southern Baptist Convention, 1923), 103–6, 108–9; *CP,* 11 Sept. 1901, p. 8; *CP,* 18 Sept. 1901, p. 8; Edward L. Pell, *The Life Worth While* (Richmond: Robert Harding, 1906), 110, 142; William W. Weeks, *The*

Face of Christ (Nashville: Sunday School Board of the Southern Baptist Convention, 1927), 174; Bowie *Sunny Windows,* 97, 107; H. D. C. Maclachlan, "Our Daily Bread," undated sermon, Maclachlan Papers, Disciples of Christ Historical Society, Nashville; Russell Cecil, "Profit in Prayer," 22 Feb. 1914, Cecil Papers.

7. Pell, *Life Worth While,* 107–8; Maria Williams Sheerin, *The Parson Takes a Wife* (New York: Macmillan, 1948), 93; Douglas Freeman, lecture, 29 Mar. 1925, Freeman Papers, Library of Congress, Washington, D.C.; James, *Varieties of Religious Experience,* 454; *To the Memory of H. D. C. Maclachlan, D.D.,* ([Richmond], 1929), 19, in Maclachlan Papers; *PS,* 23 Feb. 1927, p. 2; John J. Scherer Jr., "Christianity, the Church, and Disease," [1932] and "A Report of Several Cases of Fear Complex with a Statement of the Non-Scientific and Non-Orthodox Treatment Used," [1935], Scherer Papers, personal possession of Mary Grace Scherer Taylor, Richmond. Also see Robert S. Armentrout, "John Jacob Scherer Jr.: A Type of Southern Lutheran" (Ph.D. diss., Vanderbilt University, 1970), 90–99. Walter L. Lingle to J. N. Summerell, 18 May 1925, Lingle Papers, Presbyterian Historical Society, Montreat, N.C.

8. *Forward,* May 1921, p. 3; *PS,* 19 May 1920, p. 23; *RH,* 12 Sept. 1901, p. 1; *RT,* 8 Sept. 1901, pp. 1–2; *RNL,* 11 Dec. 1926, p. 3.

9. Mircea Eliade, *The Sacred and the Profane: The Nature of Religion* (New York: Harcourt, Brace & World, 1959), 24–26, 72; *RH,* 23 Feb. 1922, p. 7; *VC,* Apr. 1925, p. 469; *CP,* 21 Oct. 1903, p. 710; *PS,* 17 Dec. 1919, p. 10; *SC,* 12 Jan. 1918, p. 4.

10. *PS,* 15 Sept. 1926, p. 2; *League Record,* May 1918, p. 1; Hanover Avenue Christian Church, printed program of worship, 12 Mar. 1922, p. 1, Jessie P. Spencer Papers, Disciples of Christ Historical Society, Nashville; *RNL,* 16 Dec. 1926, p. 1.

11. H. D. C. Maclachlan, "Chapter III: Elijah, the Prophet of Loyalty," 9–11, in "Types and Ideals of Hebrew Prophecy," Maclachlan Papers; Russell Cecil, *The Religion of Love* (Richmond: Presbyterian Committee of Publication, 1924), 25; *RTD,* 26 Oct. 1925, p. 9; *BRCA,* 19 Dec. 1912, p. 2; Russell Cecil, "Our Supply in God," sermon, 21 Feb. 1915, and "The Lord's Table," sermon 10, 1914, Cecil Papers; Weeks, *Face of Christ,* 41, 56, 57; Pell, *Why I Believe in Jesus,* 25, 86; H. D. C. Maclachlan, "Jesus," undated sermon, Maclachlan Papers; Weeks, *Heart of God,* 69–73, 148.

12. Bowie, *Road of the Star,* 96; *SC,* 9 Feb. 1924, p. 8; Weeks, *Face of Christ,* 105, 120; Weeks, *Heart of God,* 107–9; Pell, *Life Worth While,* 21–22, 146; *RCA,* 8 Sept. 1927, p. 3; H. D. C. Maclachlan, "Jesus," and "The Stiller of the Storm," undated sermons, Maclachlan Papers. Among the many other portrayals of a caring God are Hawthorne, *Cloud of Witnesses,* 222, and Russell Cecil, "The Sympathizing Saviour," sermon 43, 1915, Cecil Papers.

13. Walter Russell Bowie, "Half Life and Whole Life: An Interpretation of the End of Social Striving," Proceedings of the National Conference of Charities and Corrections, *Forty-Second Annual Meeting,* 12–19 May 1915 (Chicago: Hildman Printing, 1915), 21; Hawthorne, *Cloud of Witnesses,* 128, 129, 132–36, 145; Weeks, *Face of Christ,* 109; Russell Cecil, "The Incarnation of Christ," 20 Dec. 1914, Cecil Papers; Pell, *Why I Believe in Jesus,* 24–25; McDaniel, *Seeing the Best,* 16.

14. Weeks, *Face of Christ,* 43; Hawthorne, *Cloud of Witnesses,* 149–50, 158, 164; Eliade, *The Sacred and the Profane,* 68–72; Pell, *Four Feet on a Fender,* 158; Pell, *Life Worth While,* 48–49, 117–18; Cecil, *Religion of Love,* 51–53; Cecil, "The Love of God in Our Hearts," sermon, 18 July 1915, Cecil Papers.

15. Colleen McDannell, *The Christian Home in Victorian America, 1840–1900* (Bloom-

ington: University of Indiana Press, 1984), xiii; Walter L. Carson, "The Christian Home," 28 May 1927, Mother's Day sermon, Carson Papers, Presbyterian Historical Society, Montreat, N.C.; Walter L. Lingle, *The Bible and Social Problems* (New York: Fleming H. Revell, 1929), 68–70, 132–33, 137–38; Pell, *Why I Believe in Jesus,* 136; *PS,* 24 Aug. 1921, p. 8; *SC,* 30 Aug. 1924, p. 6. In *Subduing Satan: Religion, Recreation, and Manhood in the Rural South, 1865–1920* (Chapel Hill: University of North Carolina Press, 1990), 103–21, Ted Ownby notes the importance of family religion in rural areas.

16. Lingle, *Bible and Social Questions,* 133; *(St. Andrew's) Parish Record,* Epiphany, 1904, p. 7; Hawthorne, *Cloud of Witnesses,* 72; Richmond Ministerial Union, "Minutes of Meetings, 1919–1928," meeting of 10 Jan. 1927, p. 34, Richmond Public Library; Bowie, *Sunny Windows,* 16–17; Pell, *Four Feet on a Fender,* 125–35; *CP,* 21 Aug. 1907, p. 753; *CP,* 8 July 1908, p. 652; *BRCA,* 13 Sept. 1906, p. 2; *SC,* 5 Feb. 1927, p. 11.

17. *BRCA,* 10 Oct. 1901, p. 8; Robert Pollok Kerr, "Woman's Place in the Church and the World," *Union Seminary Magazine* 16, no. 3 (Feb.–Mar. 1905): 217–18; McDaniel, *Seeing the Best,* 60, 62; *PS,* 17 Oct. 1923, p. 2; *CP,* 23 Nov. 1904, p. 772; *CC,* Oct. 1922, p. 2.

18. Kerr, *Will the World Outgrow Christianity,* 72–73; Weeks, *Heart of God,* 117–18; *SC,* 26 Feb. 1927, p. 12; Pell, *Four Feet on a Fender,* 129–30.

19. Lingle, *Bible and Social Problems,* 135–43, 148; *CP,* 1 Mar. 1905, p. 140; *CP,* 15 Mar. 1905, p. 178; *RNL,* 15 July 1921, p. 14; *BRCA,* 27 Oct. 1904, p. 1; *SC,* 5 Nov. 1904, p. 9. For national divorce patterns, see William F. Ogburn and Clark Tibbits, "The Family and Its Functions," in *Recent Social Trends in the United States, Vol. I,* ed. President's Research Committee on Recent Social Trends (New York: McGraw-Hill, 1933; reprint, Westport, Conn.: Greenwood Press, 1970), 692–96. William O'Neill, *Divorce in the Progressive Era* (New Haven, Conn.: Yale University Press, 1967) and Elaine Tyler May, *Great Expectations: Marriage and Divorce in Post-Victorian America* (Chicago: University of Chicago Press, 1980) address changing attitudes, laws, and patterns of the period.

20. *RNL,* 18 Mar. 1916, p. 6; Pell, *Why I Believe in Jesus,* 186, 189; *RCA,* 10 May 1923, p. 2; *RTD,* 9 Dec. 1923, sec. 7, p. 2; *SC,* 12 June 1909, p. 3; *PS,* 2 June 1908, p. 4; *RCA,* 5 Apr. 1923, p. 3; Lingle, *Bible and Social Problems,* 131. The concern expressed by Richmond ministers were part of a national phenomenon. In *Domestic Revolutions: A Social History of American Family Life* (New York: Free Press, 1988), 107–31, Steven Mintz and Susan Kellogg document changes in American families of the early twentieth century and conclude that Americans suffered a "profound sense of crisis," as observers agreed that the family was "undergoing a profound transformation," 112–13.

21. *League Record,* Oct. 1918, p. 2; *RTD,* 9 Dec. 1923, sec. 7, p. 2; *RNL,* 16 Dec. 1926, pp. 1, 3; *PS,* 4 July 1928, p. 2; *SC,* 8 Jan., 22 Jan., 29 Jan., 5 Feb., 26 Feb. 1927, p. 11; W. L. Carson, "The Christian Home," 28 May 1927, Carson Papers; Lingle, *Bible and Social Questions,* 131. In the famous analysis of Muncie, Indiana, *Middletown: A Study in Modern American Culture* (New York: Harcourt, Brace & World, 1929; reprint, New York: Harvest Books, 1956), 337, Robert S. Lynd and Helen Merrell Lynd reported that in the estimation of pastors of six Protestant churches between 3 and 25 percent of their members conducted family altars. Thus, compared to residents of Muncie, Richmonders did show a greater tendency to engage in family devotions.

22. *RTD,* 27 June 1910, p. 10; *RTD,* 20 Jan. 1908, p. 2; *RCA,* 5 May 1927, p. 2; *RNL,* 27 Aug. 1923, p. 20; *BRCA,* 3 June 1909, p. 4; *RCA,* 5 May 1923, p. 3; *RTD,* 13 Apr. 1904, p. 4; Kerr, *Will the World Outgrow Christianity,* 73; Lingle, *Bible and Social Questions,* 131–32.

23. *RCA,* 3 July 1919, p. 2; *PS,* 1 Mar. 1916, p. 114; *SC,* 29 Mar. 1913, p. 3; *RH,* 10 May 1900,

p. 3; *RH,* 11 Aug. 1921, pp. 8–9; *PS,* 16 Mar. 1921, p. 2; *PS,* 1 July 1914; *BRCA,* 16 Aug. 1906, p. 6.

24. *BRCA,* 26 June 1913, p. 6; *SC,* 29 Mar. 1913, p. 3; *RT,* 16 Mar. 1900, p. 1; *RH,* 21 July 1921, p. 6; *BRCA,* 7 Feb. 1918, p. 2; *PS,* 22 Aug. 1923, p. 1; *PS,* 14 Apr. 1920, p. 1.

25. *SC,* 30 Jan. 1909, p. 3; *SC,* 6 Jan. 1900, p. 1; *CP,* 23 Sept. 1903, p. 639; *BRCA,* 18 July 1907, p. 15; *RTD,* 31 May 1906, p. 1; *CP,* 6 June 1906, p. 360; *PS,* 15 Mar. 1916, p. 2; *CP,* 7 Oct. 1901, p. 8; *PS,* 23 Mar. 1923, p. 1; *BRCA,* 9 Aug. 1906, p. 8; Richmond Ministerial Union, "Minutes of Meetings 1919–28," meeting of 10 July 1923, Richmond Public Library, Richmond.

26. *RH,* 28 July 1921, p. 6; Thomas R. English, "The Sabbath," *Union Seminary Magazine* 11, no. 4 (Apr.–May 1900): 262–73; Givens B. Strickler, "The Sabbath and Modern Civilization," *Union Seminary Magazine* 15, no. 3 (Feb.–Mar. 1904): 300–307; *RH* 10 May 1900, p. 3; *RT,* 5 Feb. 1901, p. 4; *RTD,* 8 July 1907, p. 8; *CP,* 11 Apr. 1900, p. 8; *PS,* 21 Oct. 1902, p. 1; *RT,* 24 Oct. 1902, p. 2; David N. Laband and Deborah Hendry Heinbuch, *Blue Laws: The History, Economics, and Politics of Sunday-Closing Laws* (Lexington, Mass.: Lexington Books, 1987), 29–31, 131–33; Thomas J. Buckley, *Church and State in Revolutionary Virginia, 1776–1787* (Charlottesville: University Press of Virginia, 1977), 181–82.

27. *RT,* 13 Mar. 1900, p. 7; *RT,* 16 Mar. 1900, p 1; *RT,* 30 June 1900, p. 5; *RT,* 1 Mar. 1900, p. 1; *RT,* 6 June 1901, p. 3; *RT,* 3 May 1901, p. 6; *RT,* 17 Dec. 1902, p. 2; *RTD,* 11 Aug. 1903, p. 1; *BRCA,* 9 Aug. 1906, p. 8; *BRCA,* 18 July 1907, p. 19; *RTD,* 25 July 1906, p. 1; *RTD,* 5 Aug. 1907, p. 5.

28. *RT,* 12 Jan. 1901, p. 1; *RH,* 10 May 1900, p. 3; *BRCA,* 5 Sept. 1907, p. 2; *PS,* 8 Mar. 1916, p. 2; *RH,* 11 Aug. 1921, p. 9; *RNL,* 19 June 1916, p. 4; *RTD,* 3 July 1916, p. 16; *RTD,* 4 July 1916, p. 14; *PS,* 10 Oct. 1917, p. 777; *PS,* 3 Apr. 1918, p. 2.

29. *PS,* 18 Feb. 1920, p. 1; *RH,* 21 July 1921, p. 6; *RH,* 31 Jan. 1924, p. 8; *SC,* 11 Dec. 1921, p. 13; *RH,* 21 Feb. 1921, p. 12; *SC,* 14 May 1921, p. 6; *CC,* Oct. 1923, p. 4; *Square Deal,* 16 Apr. 1920, p. 4; *RCA,* 5 Jan. 1922, p. 2.

30. *RNL,* 29 June 1929, p. 2; *RNL,* 2 July 1926, p. 8; *RNL,* 12 July 1926, p. 8, *RNL,* 16 July 1926, p. 8; Richmond Ministerial Union, "Minutes of Meetings, 1919–1928," meeting of 8 Nov. 1926, p. 6, Richmond Public Library; *RNL,* 6 July 1929, p. 1; *RNL,* 9 July 1929, p. 8.

31. Arthur Schlesinger, *The Rise of the City, 1878–1898* (New York: Macmillan, 1933), 333–36; *RNL,* 27 July 1926, p. 8.

32. *SC,* 1 June 1907, p. 1; *BRCA,* 28 Mar. 1912, p. 8; *RTD,* 27 June 1910, p. 4; Russell Cecil, "Christian Citizenship," 25 Apr. 1915 and "Nations and Their Rulers," 6 Jan. 1915, Cecil Papers; *SC,* 27 Sept. 1902, p. 8; *RT,* 5 Mar. 1901, p. 9; *RTD,* 29 Apr. 1912, p. 1; *CP,* 13 Mar. 1901, p. 3; *BRCA,* 10 July 1913, p. 12; *CP,* 13 Mar. 1901, p. 3; *PS,* 22 Oct. 1924, p. 2; Kerr, *Will the World Outgrow Christianity,* 78–83; Lingle, *Bible and Social Problems,* 72–73.

33. *SC,* 30 Oct. 1920, pp. 3–4; *RH,* 11 Nov. 1909, p. 10.

34. *RH,* 19 Nov. 1925, pp. 10–11; Hawthorne, *Cloud of Witnesses,* 75; *RH,* 14 Feb. 1901, p. 1; *PS,* 9 July 1924, p. 2; George W. McDaniel, *The People Called the Baptists* (Nashville: Sunday School Board of the Southern Baptist Convention, 1925), 34–37.

35. *RH,* 3 Sept. 1903, p. 2; *RTD,* 3 Apr. 1910, sec. C, p. 4; *PS,* 12 Nov. 1913, p. 1066; *SC,* 24 Nov. 1900, p. 1; *BRCA,* 28 Mar. 1912, p. 7; *CP,* 14 Nov. 1900, p. 1.

36. *RH,* 7 Feb. 1901, p. 1; *RH,* 6 Feb. 1919, p. 4; McDaniel, *The People Called Baptists,* 16–19, 37; Garnett Ryland, *The Baptists of Virginia, 1699–1926* (Richmond: Baptist Board of Missions and Education, 1955), 60–137. Among the historical works tracing the activities of Baptists as well as their support for these political leaders are Rhys Isaac's *The Transforma-*

tion of Virginia, 1740–1790 (Chapel Hill: University of North Carolina Press, 1982) and Richard Beeman's *The Evolution of the Southern Backcountry: A Case Study of Lunenburg County, Virginia, 1746–1832* (Philadelphia: University of Pennsylvania Press, 1984). Buckley's *Church and State in Revolutionary Virginia* remains the most comprehensive account of the subject. For a concise treatment, see Thomas J. Curry, *The First Freedoms: Church and State in America to the Passage of the First Amendment* (New York: Oxford University Press, 1986), 134–48.

37. Presbyterian Ministers Association of Richmond, Virginia, "Minutes of Meetings, 1900–1928," meeting of 28 Jan. 1901, pp. 44–45, William Smith Morton Library, Union Theological Seminary/Presbyterian School of Christian Education, Richmond; *RTD,* 31 Oct. 1905, p. 5; Thomas Cary Johnson, *Virginia Presbyterians and Religious Liberty in Colonial and Revolutionary Times* (Richmond: Presbyterian Committee of Publication, 1907); Thomas Cary Johnson, "The Presbyterian Church in the United States," *Union Seminary Magazine* 11, no. 4 (Apr.–May, 1900): 282–89. For more about the doctrine of the spirituality of the church see Ernest Trice Thompson, *Presbyterians in the South, Volume I: 1607–1861* (Richmond: John Knox Press, 1963), 530–40, *Presbyterians in the South, Volume II: 1861–1890* (Richmond: John Knox Press, 1973), 403–8, and *Presbyterians in the South, Volume III: 1890–1972* (Richmond: John Knox Press, 1973), 260–73. As Thompson notes in volume 3 (p. 297), the commitment to the "spirituality" of the church remained "the primary obstacle" to reunification during the first two decades of the twentieth century. For example, tracing the spirituality of the church doctrine to the Gardiner-Spring resolution passed in 1861, Walter L. Lingle questioned the validity of that statement, particularly as a continuing principle which divided modern Presbyterians. When he did so, however, the reaction was heated. "One would suppose that I had denied the authenticity of the Holy Scriptures," he wrote. Walter L. Lingle to W. H. Roberts, 5 Dec. 1919, Lingle Papers.

38. Walter Russell Bowie to Lila Meade Valentine, 12 Apr. 1915, Valentine Papers, Virginia Historical Society, Richmond.

39. *RT,* 18 July 1901, p. 1; *BRCA,* 25 July 1901, p. 1; *SC,* 27 July 1901, p. 6; *RH,* 4 Jan. 1900, p. 8; *RT,* 17 Feb. 1900, p. 1; *RH,* 15 Feb. 1900, p. 8; *BRCA,* 1 Aug. 1901, p. 8; *RTD,* 20 May 1910, p. 1.

40. Moore, *Indispensable Book,* 19–33, 50, 78–87; *RTD,* 31 Jan. 1904, p. 4; *RT,* 5 Nov. 1901, p. 6; *RTD,* 3 Feb. 1913, p. 1.

41. *RTD,* 2 Feb. 1904, p. 2; *RH,* 28 Jan. 1904, p. 8; *RTD,* 31 Jan. 1904, sec. A, p. 4; *RTD,* 9 Feb. 1904, p. 2.

42. *RH,* 13 Mar. 1913, p. 12; *RTD,* 1 Feb. 1913, p. 3; *RTD,* 25 Feb. 1913, p. 10; *SC,* 8 Feb. 1913, p. 13; *RH,* 6 Feb. 1913, p. 10; *BRCA,* 13 Feb. 1913, p. 8; *BRCA,* 6 Feb. 1913, p. 1; *RH,* 27 Feb. 1913, p. 10; *BRCA,* 13 Mar. 1913, p. 2.

43. *RTD,* 10 Feb. 1913, p. 1; Edward N. Calisch to George White McDaniel, 11 Feb. 1913 and 19 Sept. 1913, McDaniel Papers, Virginia Baptist Historical Society, Richmond; Douglass S. McDaniel, *George White McDaniel* (Nashville: Sunday School Board of the Southern Baptist Convention, 1928), 53; *RH,* 10 Jan. 1913, p. 1; *RH,* 25 Aug. 1927, pp. 3, 10.

44. Richmond Ministerial Union, "Minutes of Meetings, 1919–28," meeting of 14 Jan. 1924; *RH,* 13 Aug. 1925, p. 10; *RTD,* 30 Aug. 1916, p. 12; *RCA* 16 Oct. 1924, p. 2; *RH,* 20 Mar. 1924, pp. 4, 10; *RH,* 10 Dec. 1925, p. 3.

45. *RH,* 18 Feb. 1926, pp. 2–3; *RNL,* 26 Feb. 1925, p. 8; Virginius Dabney, *Liberalism in the South* (Chapel Hill: University of North Carolina Press, 1932), 305-6; *RH,* 4 Mar. 1926, p. 10; Ryland, *Baptists of Virginia,* 340–41.

46. *PS,* 25 Jan. 1928, p. 2.

47. H. D. C. Maclachlan, *Church and State* (Richmond: Richmond Press, 1910), 5; *RH,* 3 May 1906, p. 8; *RH,* 24 Apr. 1913, p. 12; *RCA,* 21 Aug. 1919, p. 2; *SC,* 29 June 1901, p. 8; *BRCA,* 17 Aug. 1905, p. 8; *SC,* 6 May 1922, p. 5; Weeks, *The Face of Christ,* 98–109; Lingle, *Bible and Social Problems,* 47; Bowie, *Road of the Star,* 42.

48. Hawthorne, *Cloud of Witnesses,* 221.

6. Disarming Dangers

1. *RT,* 17 Jan. 1902, pp. 1, 3; *RT,* 1 Mar. 1901, p. 6; Samuel Chiles Mitchell, "An Aftermath of Appamattox [*sic*]: A Memoir" (Atlanta: mimeographed, 1954), 85–87; C. C. Pearson and J. Edwin Hendricks, *Liquor and Anti-Liquor in Virginia, 1619–1919* (Durham, N.C.: Duke University Press, 1967), 224.

2. Mitchell, "An Aftermath," 85–86; *RH,* 19 Sept. 1901, p. 8; *BRCA,* 15 Nov. 1906, p. 5; *PS,* 16 Sept. 1914, p. 10; *BRCA,* 3 July 1913, p. 3; *CP,* 3 Sept. 1902, p. 8; *RH,* 10 Feb. 1921, p. 4; *RH,* 7 Aug. 1902, p. 8; *CP,* 1 Jan. 1908, p. 3; *SC,* 29 Aug. 1914, p. 3; *BRCA,* 17 Sept. 1914, p. 3. For a summary of arguments used by opponents of the liquor trade see, James H. Timberlake, *Prohibition and the Progressive Movement* (Cambridge, Mass.: Harvard University Press, 1963), 4–9 and 42–53 for a detailed account of scientific arguments. For more about the scientific arguments, see Norman H. Clark, *Deliver Us from Evil: An Interpretation of American Prohibition* (New York: W. W. Norton & Co., 1976), 121.

3. Baptist General Association of Virginia, *Minutes of the Eighty-Third Annual Session* (Roanoke: Stone, 1906), 77; *RT,* 12 Jan. 1901, p. 1; *CP,* 15 May 1901, p. 8; *RT,* 6 June 1901, p. 3; *RT,* 17 Dec. 1901, p. 2; *RT,* 16 May 1902, p. 1; *RTD,* 25 Apr. 1906, p. 1; *BRCA,* 18 Jan. 1906, p. 2; *RTD,* 3 Nov. 1906, p. 4; *RTD,* 17 Aug. 1909, p. 10.

4. Joseph T. Mastin, "Some Needs of Almshouses and Jails in Virginia," Virginia Conference of Charities and Correction, *Proceedings of the Fifth Annual Session* (Petersburg: Frank A. Owens, 1907), 59; *RH,* 15 Nov. 1906, p. 18; *RH,* 10 Feb. 1921, p. 4; *RTD,* 14 Jan. 1906, sec. A, p. 9; *CP,* 5 Feb. 1908, p. 4; *BRCA,* 21 Nov. 1901, p. 2; *BRCA,* 2 Feb. 1905, p. 1; *BRCA,* 25 Oct. 1906, p. 17; Dover Baptist Association, *Minutes of the One Hundred and Thirty-First Meeting* (Richmond: Clyde W. Saunders, 1914), 29.

5. *RH,* 10 Feb. 1921, p. 4; *BRCA,* 2 Feb. 1905, p. 1; *BRCA,* 14 Dec. 1911, p. 6; *BRCA,* 22 Jan. 1914, p. 3; Douglass S. McDaniel, *George White McDaniel* (Nashville: Sunday School Board of the Southern Baptist Convention, 1928), 143. In *Prohibition and the Progressive Movement,* 44–45, Timberlake notes that prohibitionists elsewhere in the nation cited the threat of inherited diseases as a serious problem.

6. *RTD,* 14 Jan. 1906, sec. A, p. 9; *BRCA,* 24 Oct. 1912, p. 9; *SC,* 20 Apr. 1907, p. 4; *CP,* 1 Feb. 1905, p. 12; *BRCA,* 19 Dec. 1912, p. 7; *RTD,* 6 Jan. 1903, p. 10; *RH,* 17 Sept. 1914, p. 11; *RH,* 19 June 1902, p. 8; *BRCA,* 23 Jan. 1902, p. 1; *BRCA,* 10 Oct. 1901, p. 8; John W. Shackford, "Christian Leadership and the Social Evil," *Methodist Review* 63 (Apr. 1914): 264.

7. *RTD,* 21 Oct. 1906, p. 4; *SC,* 27 Apr. 1907, p. 1; James B. Hawthorne, *The Cloud of Witnesses and Other Sermons* (Nashville: Sunday School Board of the Southern Baptist Convention, 1908), 116; *RTD,* 21 Oct. 1906, p. 4; *SC,* 22 Feb. 1908, p. 3; *RTD,* 23 Oct. 1906, p. 4; *BRCA,* 26 Feb. 1914, p. 2; *PS,* 9 Feb. 1910, p. 164; *RH,* 17 Sept. 1914, p. 11; *SC,* 13 June 1907, p. 3; *RH,* 22 Apr. 1909, p. 10.

8. *RH,* 19 June 1902, p. 8; *RH,* 9 Apr. 1914, p. 10; *RTD,* 26 Apr. 1904, p. 1; *RTD,* 27 Apr.

1904, pp. 1,4; *RH,* 5 May 1904, p. 1; *RH,* 23 Apr. 1908, p. 3; *RTD,* 5 May 1908, p. 1; *BRCA,* 17 Aug. 1905, p. 1; *BRCA,* 13 Aug. 1914, p. 3; *CP,* 5 Feb. 1902, p. 8; *RH,* 8 Oct. 1903, p. 9; *RH,* 18 Feb. 1926, p. 10. James H. Timberlake describes the liquor industry of that era as "one of the most corrupt and predatory of all economic interests" and a "prime factor in the breakdown of honest government in the cities." For details about saloon influence in city politics, see Timberlake, *Prohibition and the Progressive Movement,* 16, 108–13.

9. *RT,* 3 Mar. 1901, p. 13; Pearson and Hendricks, *Liquor and Anti-Liquor,* 210, 223, 226–27, 239; *CP,* 26 Feb. 1908, p. 197; *CP,* 3 July 1907, p. 583; Peter H. Odegard, *Pressure Politics: The Story of the Anti-Saloon League* (New York: Columbia University Press, 1928), 38; Timberlake, *Prohibition and the Progressive Movement,* 127; Jack S. Blocker Jr., *American Temperance Movements: Cycles of Reform* (Boston: Twayne, 1989), 102, 104; *RH,* 8 Sept. 1910, p. 10.

10. *RT,* 16 Jan. 1902, p. 6; *RTD,* 25 Jan. 1912, p. 10; *BRCA,* 13 Feb. 1908, p. 9; *BRCA,* 7 Mar. 1907, p. 16; *BRCA,* 22 Jan. 1903, p. 8; *BRCA,* 1 Jan. 1914, p. 1; *RH,* 8 Jan. 1914, p. 16.

11. *RCA,* 8 Nov. 1900, p. 1; *BRCA,* 17 Sept. 1903, p. 8; *RH,* 21 Jan. 1904, p. 5; *RH,* 5 May 1910, p. 1; *RT,* 10 Jan. 1900, p. 8; Pearson and Hendricks, *Liquor and Anti-Liquor,* 199; *PS,* 1 Sept. 1909, p. 4; *BRCA,* 25 Feb. 1915, p. 5; *RH,* 25 Feb. 1904, p. 1.

12. *RT,* 10 Jan. 1900, p. 8; *SC,* 22 Mar. 1902, p. 3; *BRCA,* 3 Aug. 1905, p. 1; *BRCA,* 27 July 1905, p. 8; *RH,* 25 Mar. 1905, p. 8; *BRCA,* 8 Jan. 1914, p. 2; *RH,* 1 Mar. 1906, p. 8; *RH,* 10 Feb. 1910, p. 1; *RH,* 6 Feb. 1913, p. 10; *RTD,* 20 May 1910, p. 1.

13. Robert A. Hohner, "Bishop Cannon's Apprenticeship in Temperance Politics, 1901–1918," *Journal of Southern History* 34 (Feb. 1968): 35; Virginius Dabney, *Dry Messiah: The Life of Bishop Cannon* (New York: Alfred A. Knopf, 1949; reprint, Westport, Conn.: Greenwood Press, 1970), vii, 17; Richard Watson, "Editor's Introduction," in James Cannon Jr., *Bishop Cannon's Own Story: Life As I Have Seen It,* ed. Richard L. Watson (Durham, N.C.: Duke University Press, 1955), vi–vii; Pearson and Hendricks, *Liquor and Anti-liquor,* 254–57; Robert A. Hohner, "Prohibition and Virginia Politics: William Hodges Mann Versus Henry St. George Tucker, 1909," *Virginia Magazine of History and Biography* 74 (Jan. 1966): 88–107. For a comprehensive account of Cannon's intricate life, see Robert A. Hohner, *Prohibition and Politics: The Life of Bishop James Cannon, Jr.* (Columbia: University of South Carolina Press, 1999).

14. Dabney, *Dry Messiah,* 3–24; Cannon, *Bishop Cannon's Own Life,* 15, 33, 40–57, 82–89.

15. Cannon, *Bishop Cannon's Own Story,* 16–17, 11–12, 27–28, 53, 71, 109, 146.

16. Allen W. Moger, *Virginia: Bourbonism to Byrd, 1870–1925* (Charlottesville: University Press of Virginia, 1968), 297, 301–4; Robert A. Hohner, "Prohibition and Virginia Politics, 1901–1916" (Ph.D. diss., Duke University, 1966), 34–44, 57; Pearson and Hendricks, *Liquor and Anti-Liquor,* 231–32, 257–58; Cannon, *Bishop Cannon's Own Story,* 120–25, 132; *RTD,* 2 Mar. 1908, p. 4; *RTD,* 23 Mar. 1910, p. 6. In 1902 an Anti-Saloon League backed resolution was introduced before the state constitutional convention meeting in Richmond. Although the convention did not adopt the resolution, it did approve a provision that empowered the state legislature to regulate or prohibit the sale of liquor. For an account of that episode, see Pearson and Hendricks, *Liquor and Anti-Liquor,* 227–30.

17. *RTD,* 4 Nov. 1903, p. 1; *RTD,* 28 Mar. 1903, p. 1; *RTD,* 3 Nov. 1906, p. 4; *RTD,* 4 Nov. 1902, p. 1; *RTD,* 26 Apr. 1904, p. 1; *RTD,* 28 Apr. 1904, p. 1; *RTD,* 13 Apr. 1904, p. 6; *RTD,* 17 Jan. 1904, p. A5; *RTD,* 4 Dec. 1906, p. 1; *RTD,* 13 Nov. 1907, p. 1; *RTD,* 30 Nov. 1907, p. 1; *RTD,* 13 Dec. 1907, p. 1; *RTD,* 14 May 1908, p. 8; *RTD,* 13 Nov. 1906, p. 8. For examples

of articles against saloons see, *Richmond Times-Dispatch,* 7 Jan. 1906, p. 4; 21 and 23 Oct., p. 4; and 24 Oct., p. 1.

18. *RTD,* 14 Apr. 1909, p. 6.

19. *BRCA,* 22 Apr. 1909, p. 4; *BRCA,* 19 Aug. 1901; *BRCA,* 23 July 1914, p. 2; *BRCA,* 15 Oct. 1908, p. 1; *RH,* 24 Oct. 1912, p. 17; *BRCA,* 31 July 1913, p. 2; *RTD,* 23 Sept. 1913, p. 10; *RH,* 28 Aug. 1913, p. 10.

20. *BRCA,* 2 Feb. 1911, p. 12; *RH,* 2 Apr. 1914, p. 10; *BRCA,* 27 Jan. 1910, p. 2; *RH,* 19 Mar. 1914, p. 10. The shipment of liquor from wet areas into dry territories constituted a major grievance of saloon opponents and formed an integral part of the conflict leading to national prohibition as demonstrated by Richard F. Hamm, *Shaping the Eighteenth Amendment: Temperance Reform, Legal Culture, and the Polity, 1880–1920* (Chapel Hill: University of North Carolina Press, 1995).

21. Early indications of the press war appear in the *Baltimore and Richmond Christian Advocate,* 3 Sept. 1908, p. 1, and 11 Mar. 1909, pp. 1–2. For a vehement outburst by Cannon, see the *Baltimore and Richmond Christian Advocate,* 9 Nov. 1911, p. 1. For criticisms about advertising, see examples in *Baltimore and Richmond Christian Advocate,* 24 Nov. 1910, p. 10; 6 Apr. 1911, p. 4; and 29 June 1911, p. 1. For a retrospective commentary about the origins of the hostilities, see *Bishop Cannon's Own Story,* 114–15. Journalist and biographer Virginius Dabney first noted conflict in 1910, *Dry Messiah,* 74–76.

22. *BRCA,* 11 Dec. 1913, p. 4; *BRCA,* 26 Jan. 1914, p. 2.

23. *PS,* 8 July, 1914, p. 10; *PS,* 16 Sept. 1914, p. 1; *Our Diocesan Work* 30 (June 1914): 3; *SC,* 29 Aug. 1914, p. 3; *RH,* 10 Sept. 1914, p. 3; *BRCA,* 9 Mar. 1916, p. 4; *PS,* 30 Sept. 1914, p. 9; *PS,* 22 July 1914, p. 10; *RNL,* 1910; Pearson and Hendricks, *Liquor and Anti-Liquor,* 274, 281; Robert A. Hohner, "Prohibition Comes to Virginia: The Referendum of 1914," *Virginia Magazine of History and Biography* 75 (Oct. 1967): 473–88; Dabney, *Dry Messiah,* 81–88; Cannon, *Bishop Cannon,* 154–60; *RNL,* 13 July 1914, p. 5.

24. *PS,* 22 July 1914, p. 10; Dabney, *Dry Messiah,* 87. The Women's Christian Temperance Union (WCTU) also maintained a modest presence in Richmond. According to a 1911 survey conducted by the Young Women's Christian Association, five local chapters of the WCTU included approximately one hundred members. "Know Your City Survey," Young Women's Christian Association Papers, Special Collections and Archives Department, James Branch Cabell Library, Virginia Commonwealth University, Richmond.

25. *RTD,* 14 Apr. 1909, p. 1; *BRCA,* 9 Mar. 1911, p. 3; *RNL* 15 May 1914, pp. 1, 13; *BRCA,* 28 May 1914, p. 7; *RNL,* 21 July, p. 1; Pearson and Hendricks, *Liquor and Anti-Liquor,* 276–81; *RNL,* 23 Sept. 1914, pp. 1, 11. Apparently unaware of the voting patterns within the city, Paul Boyer, in *Urban Masses and Moral Order in America, 1820–1920* (Cambridge, Mass.: Harvard University Press, 1978), 213, incorrectly infers that "a strong contingent of evangelical middle-class voters nearly carried" Richmond into the dry ranks in the referendum. Richmond Protestants appear to have been divided over the wisdom of statewide prohibition, and working-class areas gave the measure the strongest support. In "The Prohibitionists: Who Were They?" *South Atlantic Quarterly* 68 (autumn 1969): 499–500, Robert A. Hohner included a study of Virginia's Women's Christian Temperance Union members and identified 55 percent as part of a "lower middle class." Hohner suggested that these families with wage earners and skilled workers might have been attempting to escape their working-class origins.

26. *RNL,* 1 Nov. 1916, p. 1; *RH,* 9 Nov. 1916, p. 8; Cannon, *Bishop Cannon's Own Life,*

167–92; Dabney, *Dry Messiah,* 115–37; Blocker, *American Temperance Movements,* 112–24; Clark, *Deliver Us from Evil,* 130–32; Timberlake, *Prohibition and the Progressive Movement,* 180–83. In *Liquor and Anti-Liquor,* 299, Pearson and Hendricks cite the national Anti-Saloon League *Year Book* for 1924 which designated Virginia's state enforcement law as "one of the most drastic state prohibition codes" in the country.

27. *RH,* 7 Dec. 1916, p. 10; *SC,* 18 Nov. 1922, p. 5; *RNL,* 3 Oct. 1925, p. 6; *PS,* 7 Nov. 1917, p. 1; *RNL,* 27 Jan. 1921, pp. 1, 4; *RNL,* 12 Feb. 1921, p. 1; *RCA,* 10 Apr. 1919, p. 2; *RH,* 29 May 1919, p. 1; *RH,* 10 Feb. 1921, p. 4; *RH,* 17 Feb. 1921, p. 3; *PS,* 21 Nov. 1923, p. 2; *RNL,* 31 Oct. 1917, p. 1. In 1915, the year before statewide prohibition was implemented, authorities reported 2,083 arrests for the offense of drunkenness and for being drunk and disorderly. In 1928, authorities reported 2,947 arrests for comparable offenses. For data, see *Annual Report of the Chief of Police of the City of Richmond, Virginia, for the Year Ending Dec. 31, 1916* (Richmond, 1916), 19; *Eleventh Annual Report of the Department of Public Safety of the City of Richmond, Virginia for the Year Ending Dec. 31, 1929* (Richmond, 1930), 16–17. *RCA,* 10 Feb. 1921, p. 2; *RH,* 4 Mar. 1920, p. 11; *RNL,* 8 Dec. 1924, p. 12. In *The Paradox of Progressivism, 1880–1930* (Chapel Hill: University of North Carolina Press, 1992), 316–21, William A. Link argues that prohibition was a failure in Virginia. The evidence for Richmond, however, is inconclusive. Illegal drinking occurred, but gone were the complaints with public intoxication and alcohol abuse which provoked the intense reaction during the century's first decade.

28. *BRCA,* 24 July 1917, p. 3.

29. *RH,* 28 Apr. 1927, p. 10; *RCA,* 1 Dec. 1927, p. 2; *RCA,* 14 June 1923, p. 2; *RCA,* 20 Sept. 1928, p. 3; *RH,* 20 Jan. 1927, p. 10; *RNL,* 6 Nov. 1928, p. 1; *RH,* 7 Nov. 1929, p. 10. K. Austin Kerr, *Organized for Prohibition: A New History of the Anti-Saloon League* (New Haven, Conn.: Yale University Press, 1985), 266, notes the long-term reverberations among southern Democrats. For the Virginia battle, see Dabney, *Dry Messiah,* 175–95. For details about Cannon's problems see, Robert A. Hohner, "The Other Harry Golden: Harry Golden and the Cannon Scandals," *North Carolina Historical Review* 65, no. 2 (Apr. 1988): 154–72; Michael S. Patterson, "The Fall of a Bishop: James Cannon Jr., Versus Carter Glass, 1909–1934," *Journal of Southern History* 39, no. 4 (Nov. 1973): 493–518; and Dabney, *Dry Messiah,* 195–291. In 1930 Cannon faced the additional charges of embezzling contributions during the 1928 election campaign, and these allegations resulted in protracted legal proceedings which exonerated Cannon. In *Symbolic Crusade: Status Politics and the American Temperance Movement* (Urbana: University of Illinois Press, 1963), Joseph Gusfield distinguishes between two reform traditions in the American temperance movement. When culturally dominant, foes of alcoholic beverages engaged in "assimilative" reforms. As righteous humanitarians, these temperance advocates sympathized with weaker individuals and tried to persuade and convert them. By the late nineteenth century as temperance proponents no longer felt culturally secure, they resorted to "coercive" reforms and no longer viewed their opponents as victims but rather as adversaries who rejected the established culture. In attempting to apply this interpretation to Virginia and to Richmond, two facts stand out. First, although antisaloon leaders probably combined the two impulses, the "assimilative" motive seems to have been primary. Second, the "coercive" style did make a forceful appearance in the mid-1920s in the battle against Al Smith. For more about that campaign, see chapter 9.

30. *RT,* 11 Sept. 1902, p. 1. In a series of magazine articles subsequently published as *The*

Shame of the Cities in 1904, Lincoln Steffens delivered the most famous exposé of corruption in city governments.

31. *RH,* 10 Apr. 1902, p. 1; *RH,* 28 Aug. 1902, p. 8; *RH,* 25 Sept. 1902, p. 8; *RTD,* 1 Dec. 1903, p. 1; *RT,* 26 July 1902, p. 1; *RT,* 27 July 1902, p. 1; *RT,* 29 July 1902, pp. 1, 6; *RT,* 19 Aug. 1902, p. 6; *RT,* 23 Sept. 1902, p. 1; *RT,* 27 Sept. 1902, p. 1; *RT,* 17 July 1902, p. 1; *BRCA,* 28 Aug. 1902, p. 1; *SC,* 27 Sept. 1902, p. 8; *RT,* 3 Oct. 1902, p. 1.

32. *RT,* 24 Oct. 1902, p. 2; *RT,* 14 Oct. 1902, p. 12; *RT,* 24 Oct. 1902, pp. 1–2; *RTD,* 6 Feb. 1904, p. 1; undated news clipping in John J. Crutchfield Scrapbook, Crutchfield Papers, Virginia Historical Society, Richmond.

33. Richmond City Council, "Special Joint Committee, Appointed to Investigate Official Conduct of Members of the Board of Police Commissioners and Members of the Police Force of the City of Richmond," Stenographer's Transcript, Mar.–May 1915, Office of the City Clerk, Richmond (hereafter cited as Special Committee, Transcript), 59, 60–61, 67, 389, 410, 431, 436; *RNL,* 30 Sept. 1915, p. 1; *RTD,* 11 Feb. 1915, p. 1; *RNL,* 3 Feb. 1916, p. 1.

34. *RTD,* 6 Jan. 1914, p. 10; *RTD,* 18 Mar. 1914, p. 1; "Report Number 1," in Special Committee, Transcript, 33; *RNL,* 8 Jan. 1915, pp. 1,2; *RNL,* 6 Feb. 1915, p. 4; *RNL,* 2 Feb. 1915, p. 1; Arthur W. James, *Virginia's Social Awakening: The Contribution of Dr. Mastin and the Board of Charities and Corrections* (Richmond: Garrett & Massie, 1939), 114–17. This writer was unable to locate the report of the vice commission itself. City newspapers and the transcript of the subsequent police investigation contain much of the information gathered by the commission. According to Ruth Rosen, *The Lost Sisterhood, Prostitution in America, 1900–1918* (Baltimore: Johns Hopkins University Press, 1982), 14, between 1910 and 1917, forty-three American cities conducted formal investigations about prostitution.

35. *RNL,* 11 Feb. 1915, p. 4; *RNL,* 8 Feb. 1915, p. 1; *RNL,* 9 Feb. 1915, p. 1; *RNL,* 15 Feb. 1915, pp. 1, 10; *RNL,* 2 Mar. 1915, p. 1; *RNL,* 16 Mar. 1915, p. 1,2; Special Committee, Transcript, 96f, 763; *RTD,* 19 Apr. 1915, p. 1; *RNL,* 29 Mar. 1915, p. 1; *RNL,* 1 Oct. 1915, p. 1.

36. Collins Denny, notes at mass meeting, speech, 7 Oct. 1915, Papers of Bishop Collins Denny (MSS 2672), Special Collections Department, University of Virginia Library; *RTD,* 4 Oct. 1915, pp. 1, 2; *RNL,* 8 Oct. 1915, p. 10; *RTD,* 8 Oct. 1915, p. 1; *RTD,* 11 Oct. 1915, p. 10; *RNL,* 4 Oct. 1915, p. 4; *RH,* 7 Oct. 1915, p. 3; *RNL,* 7 Oct. 1915, pp. 1–2; *RNL,* 24 Nov. 1915, p. 4; *SC,* 2 Oct. 1915, p. 14; *RNL,* 1 July 1916, p. 14; Louis Bernard Cei, "Law Enforcement in Richmond: A History of Police-Community Relations, 1737–1974" (Ph.D. diss., Florida State University, 1975), 152–53.

37. *RTD,* 24 May 1918, p. 1; *RNL,* 25 June 1918, pp. 1, 4, 14; *RTD,* 25 June 1918, p. 1. *RTD,* 11 June 1918, p. 10; *RTD,* 19 June 1918, p. 1; *RNL,* 12 June 1918, p. 1; *RNL,* 14 June 1918, p. 1; *RTD,* 14 June 1918, p. 7; *RTD,* 12 June 1918, p. 1.

38. *RNL,* 12 June 1918, p. 4; *RH,* 20 June 1918, p. 10; *RNL,* 8 July 1918, p. 1; *RTD,* 9 July 1918, p. 10; *BRCA,* 11 July 1918, p. 1; *RTD,* 8 Aug. 1918, p. 1; *RTD,* 6 Aug. 1918, p. 1; *RNL,* 17 July 1918, p. 1; *RNL,* 18 July 1918, p. 1; Cei, "Law Enforcement in Richmond," chap. 8.

39. Virginia Conference of Charities and Correction, *Proceedings of the Ninth Annual Session* (Richmond: Richmond Press, 1912), 32; James, *Virginia's Social Awakening,* 89; Special Committee, Transcript, Report No. 1; *RTD,* 17 Feb. 1915, p. 6; *BRCA,* 18 Feb. 1915, p. 2; *Our Diocesan Work,* July 1914, p. 1; John W. Shackford, "Christian Leadership and the Social Evil," *Methodist Review* 63 (1914): 260, 265. For accounts of national concerns about venereal diseases and about prostitution as a source of spreading them, see Allan M. Brandt, *No Magic Bullet: A Social History of Venereal Disease in the United States since 1880* (New York:

Oxford University Press, 1985), 9–32, Mark T. Connelly, *The Response to Prostitution in the Progressive Era* (Chapel Hill: University of North Carolina Press, 1980), 67–90, and Rosen *Lost Sisterhood,* 53. In *Uneasy Virtue: The Politics of Prostitution and the American Reform Tradition* (New York: Basic Books, 1987), 166, Barbara Meil Hobson suggests that immediately before World War I, discussions about venereal disease in the United States had escalated to a nearly hysterical level.

40. The *Annual Report of the Chief of Police of the City of Richmond Virginia for the Year Ending Dec. 31, 1915* (Richmond, 1916), 16–17, and *Eleventh Annual Report of the Department of Public Safety of the City of Richmond, Virginia for the Year Ending Dec. 31, 1929* (Richmond, 1930), 16–17, each provide data for five-year periods. James, *Virginia's Social Awakening,* 113, 120. Another law apparently collapsed when a state judge ruled against requiring the physical examination of anyone arrested in a disorderly house. Brandt, *No Magic Bullet,* 120; Connelly, *Response to Prostitution,* 45–46; Mary E. Odem, *Delinquent Daughters: Protecting and Policing Adolescent Female Sexuality in the Untied States, 1885–1920* (Chapel Hill: University of North Carolina Press, 1995), 9, 14–15. In *Lost Sisterhood,* 28–29, Ruth Rosen notes that by 1917, thirty-one states had enacted some form of abatement law and that such laws were often used to warn owners who then vacated offensive tenants.

41. H. D. C. Maclachlan, *Memorial to the Honorable Council of the City of Richmond* (Richmond: Juvenile Protective Society of Virginia, 1913), 6–8; James, *Virginia's Social Awakening,* 87–91. For an example of a plea for financial support by George W. McDaniel, see *Richmond Times-Dispatch,* 24 Jan 1910, p. 2.

42. *SC,* 15 Jan. 1910, pp. 7–8; *SC,* 11 Feb. 1905, p. 2; Walter L. Lingle to Guy Weaver, 29 Feb. 1916, Lingle Papers, Presbyterian Historical Society, Montreat, N.C.; *SC,* 25 Jan. 1908, p. 12; *SC,* 19 Jan. 1907, p. 11.

43. *RTD,* 24 Jan. 1910, p. 2; Orie Latham Hatcher, *Rural Girls in the City for Work: A Study Made for the Southern Woman's Educational Alliance* (Richmond: Garrett & Massie, 1930), 72; Virginia Conference of Charities and Correction, *Proceedings of the Tenth Annual Session* (Richmond: Southern Press, 1913), 14. These concerns about young working women were common in most American cities during this era, as Connelly notes in *Response to Prostitution,* 31–47.

44. *BRCA,* 14 Nov. 1912, p. 16; Elizabeth Stevens Brinson, "'Helping Others to Help Themselves': Social Advocacy and Wage-Earning Women in Richmond, Virginia, 1910–1932" (Ph.D. diss., Union Graduate School of the Union for Experimenting Colleges and Universities, 1984), 87; Lucy R. Mason, "Annual Report to the National Board of the Young Women's Christian Associations," 1926, B-9, YWCA Papers; *BRCA,* 6 Nov. 1913, p, 15; *RCA,* 18 Feb. 1926, p. 8. For comparable reactions elsewhere, see Julia Kirk Blackwelder, *Now Hiring: The Feminization of Work in the United States, 1900–1995* (College Station: Texas A & M University Press, 1997), 24–29.

45. *League Record,* July 1916, p. 3; *League Record,* Jan. 1917, p. 1; Belle Gayle Ellyson, "Forty Years of the House of Happiness: An Historical Sketch" (typewritten, Virginia Baptist Historical Society, 1954), 4; *BRCA,* 29 Jan. 1914, p. 3; *RTD,* 13 Oct. 1904, p. 12; *SC,* 12 Mar. 1904, p. 5; *BRCA,* 13 Nov. 1913, p. 12; *RH,* 2 Nov. 1905, p. 2.

46. Lucy R. Mason, "Annual Report to the National Board of the Young Women's Christian Associations," 1926, B5-B10, YWCA Papers; Brinson, "'Helping Others to Help Themselves,'" 84–91.

47. *SC,* 1 June 1918, p. 13; *RNL,* 6 Feb. 1915, p. 4; *Square Deal,* 22 May 1915, p. 4; *RNL,* 1

Feb. 1916, p. 13; *RTD*, 27 June 1910, p. 10; Virginia Conference of Charities and Correction, *Proceedings of the Tenth Annual Session* (Richmond: Southern Printing, 1913), 14; *SC*, 7 Apr. 1923, p. 11; Lucy Randolph Mason, *The Shorter Day and Women Workers* (Richmond: Virginia League of Women Voters, 1922); Brinson, "'Helping Others to Help Themselves,'" 94–99, 117–30.

48. Frederick Lewis Allen, *Only Yesterday* (New York: Harper & Brothers, 1931; reprint, New York: Harper & Row, 1964), 73–101. Among those essentially subscribing to Allen's interpretation are William Leuchtenburg in *The Perils of Prosperity, 1914–32* (Chicago: University of Chicago Press, 1958), 158–77, and Paula S. Fass, *The Damned and the Beautiful: American Youth in the 1920s* (New York: Oxford University Press, 1977). Those dating the changes earlier include Henry F. May, *The End of American Innocence: A Study of the First Years of Our Own Time, 1912–1917* (New York: Alfred A. Knopf, 1959), 342–46, and James R. McGovern, "The American Woman's Pre-World War I Freedom in Manners and Morals," in *Our American Sisters: Women in American Life and Thought*, ed. Jean E. Friedman and William G. Shade, 3d ed. (Lexington, Mass.: D. C. Heath & Co., 1982), 479–99.

49. John A. Cutchins, *Memories of Old Richmond (1881–1944)* (Verona, Va.: McClure Press, 1973), 134, 28; *RNL*, 26 Aug. 1914, p. 4; Anna B. Binford, "My Home Town and Me: Richmond, Virginia, 1871–1948," 126, Virginia Historical Society, Richmond; *RTD*, 5 Dec. 1912, p. 1; Virginius Dabney, *Richmond: The Story of a City*, rev. ed. (Charlottesville: University Press of Virginia, 1990), 275; *BRCA*, 2 Mar. 1905, p. 1; *RTD*, 14 July, 1910, p. 10. In *From Front Porch to Back Seat: Courtship in Twentieth-Century America* (Baltimore: Johns Hopkins University Press, 1988), 19–20, Beth L. Bailey concludes that the national shift from calling at a young woman's house to dating occurred "gradually, almost imperceptibly" between 1890 to 1925. For other complaints about mashers, see *RTD*, 13 Feb. 1911, p. 1 and *RTD*, 15 Sept. 1916, p. 6.

50. *RT*, 25 Oct. 1902, p. 4; John C. Burnham, "The Progressive Era Revolution in American Attitudes toward Sex," *Journal of American History* 59 (1962): 886; Special Committee, Transcript, pp. 21, 561; *RNL*, 7 June 1921, p. 22; *PS*, 5 Nov. 1913, p. 9; *RCA*, 5 June 1924, p. 2; Ellen Glasgow, *The Romantic Comedians* (New York: Doubleday, Page & Co., 1926), 150. The novel is set in "Queenborough," Glasgow's fictional representation of Richmond.

51. Shackford, "Social Evil," 269–71; *Christian Monthly*, Apr. 1912, p. 2; Richmond Ministerial Union, "Minutes of Meetings, 1919–1928," meeting of 10 May 1926, Richmond Public Library; Walter L. Lingle, *The Bible and Social Problems* (New York: Fleming H. Revell, 1929), 149–50; *Forward*, June 1921, p. 15; Walter T. Thompson, review of *The Revolt of Modern Youth*, by Benjamin B. Lindsey, in *Union Seminary Review* 37 (July 1926): 395–96.

52. *RTD*, 16 Sept. 1912, p. 1; *BRCA*, 4 Oct. 1917, p. 1; *BRCA*, 7 Feb. 1918, p. 1; *SC*, 22 June 1918, p. 13; *RTD*, 8 July 1918, p. 2; *SC*, 1 June 1918, p. 13; *BRCA*, 11 July 1918, p. 1; *SC*, 30 Aug. 1924, p. 6; *BRCA*, 17 July 1913, p. 2; *RTD*, 24 June 1913, p. 1; *RH*, 29 May 1913, p. 11.

53. *RTD*, 23 Feb. 1913, p. 4; *RH*, 7 Aug. 1919, p. 10; *RTD*, 8 Sept. 1913, p. 10; *BRCA*, 6 Mar. 1913, p. 8; *BRCA*, 18 Sept. 1913, p. 5; *RH*, 20 Feb. 1913, p. 10; *PS*, 11 Mar. 1914, p. 10. For descriptions in the shifting dance styles see Mark Sullivan, *Our Times: The United States, 1900–1925, Volume IV: The War Begins, 1909–1914* (New York: Charles Scribner's Sons, 1932), 223–66, and Preston William Slosson, *The Great Crusade and After, 1914–1928* (New York: Macmillan, 1930), 281–82.

54. *RNL*, 23 May 1921, p. 1; *RH*, 7 Aug. 1919, p. 10; *RCA*, 6 Oct. 1921, p. 2; *RNL*, 30 May 1921, p. 15; *SC*, 18 June 1921, p. 3; *PS*, 9 Apr. 1919, p. 2.

55. *RCA,* 19 May 1921, p. 20; Richmond Ministerial Union, "Minutes of Meetings, 1919–28," meetings of 9 May 1921 and 13 June 1921; *RNL,* 10 May 1921, p. 1; *RNL,* 12 May 1921, p. 1; *RNL,* 11 May 1921, p. 1; *RCA,* 11 Dec. 1924, p. 3.

56. *RCA,* 9 June, 1921, p. 2; *RTD,* 23 May 1921, p. 5; *RNL,* 16 May 1921, p. 1; *RNL,* 10 June 1921, pp. 1–2; *RNL,* 6 June 1921, p. 13; *RNL,* 17 May 1921, p. 1; *RCA,* 28 June 1928, p. 3; *RH,* 7 Aug. 1919, p. 10; *RCA,* 9 June 1921, p. 20; Richmond Preachers Meeting, "Minutes of Meetings, 1900–1928," meeting of 7 Nov. 1922, Special Collections and Archives, McGraw-Page Library, Randolph-Macon College, Ashland, Va.

57. *SC,* 12 Feb. 1921, p. 4; *RTD,* 6 June 1921, p. 10; *RTD,* 30 May 1921, p. 10; *RH,* 4 Aug. 1921, p. 3; *PS,* 28 June 1922, p. 1.

58. *BRCA,* 18 Apr. 1912, p. 4; Maclachlan, *Memorial,* p. 2; *PS,* 12 Oct. 1910, p. 10; Special Committee, Transcript, Report No. 1; *BRCA,* 11 Aug. 1910, p. 1; *BRCA,* 25 June 1914, p. 2; *CC,* June 1921, p. 4.

59. *SC,* 4 Mar. 1922, p. 14; *RCA,* 26 Jan. 1922, p. 2; *RTD,* 28 Feb. 1922, p. 1; *RNL,* 13 Mar. 1922, p. 1; *RCA,* 16 Mar. 1922, p. 2; *RTD,* 11 Feb. 1922, p. 12; *RNL,* 14 Feb. 1922, p. 12; *RTD,* 20 Mar. 1922, p. 3; *RCA,* 14 June 1923, pp. 2–3, 6; Dover Baptist Association of Virginia, *Minutes of the One Hundred and Fortieth Annual Meeting* (Richmond: Saunders & Sons, 1923), 11. In "American Woman's Pre-World War I Freedom," 490, James McGovern notes that four states had already passed censorship laws by 1917.

60. H. D. C. Maclachlan, "Studies in Sin: The Sins of Adolescence," *Christian Century* 7 (Dec. 1922): 1515–19; *RNL,* 23 May 1921, p. 2; *RNL,* 11 Apr. 1922, p. 15; *VC,* Jan. 1928, p. 2; *RCA,* 3 Mar. 1927, p. 2; *SC,* 23 Sept. 1922, p. 12. Noting the shifting patterns of behavior of young people in the 1920s, historians John D'Emilio and Estelle B. Freedman, like some Richmond ministers, conclude that the "innovations" occurred within "certain peer-defined limits." D'Emilio and Freedman, *Intimate Matters: A History of Sexuality in America* (New York: Oxford University Press, 1988), 256–57.

61. Wyndam B. Blanton, *The Making of a Downtown Church: The History of the Second Presbyterian Church, Richmond, Virginia, 1845–1945* (Richmond: John Knox Press, 1945), 214–26; *SC,* 16 Mar. 1912, p. 9; *Virginia Conference Annual, One Hundred-Twenty-Eighth Annual Session* (Richmond: Waddey, 1910), 125; *Virginia Conference Annual, One Hundred-Thirty-Eighth Annual Session,* (Richmond: Everett Waddey, 1920), 172; *RH,* 13 Mar. 1913, p. 4; *RH,* 18 Jan. 1923, p. 14; *RNL,* 13 July 1913, p. 5; *RTD,* 5 Feb. 1907, p. 7; *RCA,* 25 May 1922, p. 4; *SC,* 28 Aug. 1920, p. 21; Francis H. McLean and Hilda K. Mills, *Survey of the Social Agencies of Richmond Virginia* (Richmond: American Association for Organizing Family and Social Work, 1923), 80.

62. *RCA,* 14 Jan. 1926, p. 3.

7. "A New Pentecost"

1. H. D. C. Maclachlan, "The Church at Work in Social Service," *Proceedings of the Eleventh Annual Session of the Virginia Conference of Charities and Correction* (Richmond: Ware & Duke, 1914), 59. In *Liberty and Justice for All: Racial Reform and the Social Gospel (1877–1925)* (New York: Harper & Row, 1990), xix–xxii, Ronald C. White Jr. uses phrases much like Maclachlan's to define the Social Gospel. White stresses the importance of social salvation, social justice, the immanence of God, and leaders committed to bringing God's kingdom into "the present world." Most of Richmond's leaders in social Christianity would

have agreed that social service must be combined with an insistence on social justice. Still, organized social service in itself represented an important, significant response to the urban and industrial environment of the United States. Using different methodologies, types of sources, and time units, the historians of the Social Gospel have understandably arrived at various conclusions about its impact. C. Howard Hopkins, *The Rise of the Social Gospel in American Protestantism, 1865–1915* (New Haven, Conn.: Yale University Press, 1940; reprint, 1967) and Aaron I. Abell, *The Urban Impact on American Protestantism, 1865–1900* (Cambridge, Mass.: Harvard University Press, 1943; reprint, Hamden, Conn.: Archon, 1962), render largely favorable assessments and remain informative accounts. Also focusing on the late nineteenth century, Henry F. May's *Protestant Churches and Industrial America* (New York: Harper & Row, 1949, Harper Torchbooks, 1967) criticizes the Social Gospel's limitations but delivers some faint praise. Observing that "a detailed investigation of such a subject by localities would hardly be practicable," May confined his research to situations that "commanded national attention" (xviii). This lacuna has generally continued to circumscribe the historical perspective of the Social Gospel. By tracing the persistence and the changes of religious and social activism after World War I, Paul A. Carter's *The Decline and Revival of the Social Gospel: Social and Political Liberalism in American Protestant Churches, 1920–1940* (Ithaca, N.Y.: Cornell University Press, 1954) and Robert Moats Miller's *American Protestantism and Social Issues, 1919–1939* (Chapel Hill: University of North Carolina Press, 1958) claim important places in the literature of American religious history. By focusing on the first two decades of the twentieth century, Ronald C. White Jr. and C. Howard Hopkins, *The Social Gospel and Reform in Changing America* (Philadelphia: Temple University Press, 1976), and Donald R. Gorrell, *The Age of Social Responsibility: The Social Gospel in the Progressive Era, 1900–1920* (Macon, Ga.: Mercer University Press, 1988), explore a number of important topics. In *A Consuming Faith: The Social Gospel and Modern American Culture* (Baltimore: Johns Hopkins University Press, 1991), Susan Curtis argues that the genuinely good deeds of Social Gospel proponents contributed to "the consolidation of new values and ideals in American culture" and paradoxically "made it easier for Protestant Americans to embrace a secular culture in which Protestantism was not prominently featured" (278). Differing with C. Howard Hopkins, who represented the Social Gospel as a distinctly American religious phenomenon, Paul T. Phillips provides *A Kingdom on Earth: Anglo-American Social Christianity, 1880–1940* (University Park: Pennsylvania State University Press, 1996). For historical interpretations of social Christianity in the South, please see note 67 in this chapter.

2. Maclachlan, "The Church at Work in Social Service," 58–70.

3. Ibid., 64–70.

4. *RTD,* 2 Oct. 1905, p. 8; *RTD,* 23 Oct. 1905, p. 8; *RH,* 3 Sept. 1903, p. 2; *RH,* 6 June 1907, pp. 12–13; *RH,* 18 Jan. 1923, p. 3; John Lee Eighmy, *Churches in Cultural Captivity: A History of the Social Attitudes of Southern Baptists* (Knoxville: University of Tennessee Press, 1972), 89–91.

5. Walter Russell Bowie, *Sunny Windows and Other Sermons for Children* (New York: Fleming H. Revell, 1921), 49, 74–75, 122, 177–90.

6. *Forward,* Dec. 1920, p. 12; *SC,* 28 Dec. 1912, p. 9; Walter Russell Bowie, *Learning to Live* (Nashville: Abingdon Press, 1969), 96; *Christian Monthly,* Dec. 1912, p. 7.

7. Walter L. Lingle, *The Bible and Social Problems* (New York: Fleming H. Revell, 1929), 11–12; Ernest Trice Thompson, *Presbyterians in the South,* 3:260–65; *PS,* 22 Dec. 1909, p. 20; Union Theological Seminary student reviews and Union Theological Seminary lec-

tures, Walter L. Lingle Papers, Presbyterian Historical Society, Montreat, N.C.; Montreat, N.C., program, 1916, Lingle Papers; *PS*, 17 Jan. 1917, p. 8; Addie Alexander to Walter L. Lingle, 20 May, 1922, Lingle Papers; Anna B. Binford, *Some Social Teachings of the Bible* (Richmond: Presbyterian Committee of Publication, [1921]); W. L. Carson, "Service as a Test of Greatness," 18 Feb. 1923, W. L. Carson Papers, Presbyterian Historical Society, Montreat, N.C. In 1909 another Union professor had experimented with a course in Christian sociology.

8. Lingle, *Bible and Social Problems*, 18, 47, 53, 188. For an example of earlier expressions of these views, see Walter L. Lingle, "The Teachings of Jesus and Modern Social Problems," *Union Seminary Review* 27, no. 3 (Apr. 1916): 191–205. Other earlier, handwritten lectures expressing such views are in the Lingle Papers.

9. *SC*, 9 Jan. 1904, pp. 4–5; William N. Glenn, *St. Andrew's Episcopal Church and Its Environs* (Richmond: Whittet & Shepperson, 1978), 42–49; *Journal of the One Hundred and Sixth Annual Council of the Protestant Episcopal Church in Virginia* (Richmond: William Ellis Jones, 1901), 165.

10. Nell R. Lee Murphy, "What One Woman Did for Richmond," *Richmond Magazine* 6, no. 2 (Dec. 1915): 4; Glenn, *St. Andrew's*, 27, 37–41, 54, 100–105; *RTD*, 26 Jan. 1902, p. 1. At her death, Arents left significant bequests to approximately a dozen Richmond area charitable and social organizations, *SC*, 3 July 1926, p. 15.

11. *(St. Andrew's) Parish Record*, Easter 1901, 16–19; *RTD*, 1 Apr. 1906, p. D1; Glenn, *St. Andrew's*, 34–45, 49–50, 101–4; *RT*, 29 Apr. 1900, p. 17; *SC*, 15 June 1901, p. 7; *SC*, 10 Jan. 1903, p. 6.

12. *RTD*, 17 May 1904, p. 9; Glenn, *St. Andrew's*, 103, 104.

13. *RTD*, 16 Dec. 1906, p. 2; *RTD*, 1 Apr. 1906, p. D1; *SC*, 1 June 1901, p. 6; *Parish Record* (Easter 1901), 10–11, 16; Glenn, *Saint Andrew's*, 58, 92–94; *SC*, 26 Jan. 1918, p. 8; W. Geiger Irwin, "St. Andrew's Work, Report from Sept. 1929 to May 1930" (typescript), 5, 8, in St. Andrew's Episcopal Church Papers, Virginia Historical Society, Richmond. In *The Urban Impact on American Protestantism*, 137–65, Aaron Abell describes the emergence of institutional churches in the 1890s in the United States, focuses largely on the urban northeast, and notes the variety among these churches. Intended particularly to reach out to working-class people, these churches usually emphasized education but also provided a number of social programs and services. Thus, St. Andrew's did function as an institutional church.

14. *BRCA*, 18 Apr. 1912, p. 3; Glenn, *St. Andrew's*, 57–58; *SC*, 10 Jan. 1903, p. 6; *RTD*, 1 Apr. 1906, p. D1; "Virginia's First Deaconess, Mary Eltinge Davison," biographical sketch, Mary Davison file, Records of the National Center for the Diaconate, the Archives of the Episcopal Church U.S.A., Austin, Texas.

15. *BRCA*, 17 Apr. 1902, p. 6; *RTD*, 25 Nov. 1906, p. G12; *RT*, 27 July 1902, p. 6; *BRCA*, 16 Jan. 1902, p. 2; *BRCA*, 7 Mar. 1912, p. 2.

16. *BRCA*, 20 Mar. 1902, p. 8; *BRCA*, 22 Jan. 1903, p. 6; *BRCA*, 14 Feb 1904, p. 8; *RTD*, 11 Dec. 1904, p. B7; *RTD*, 25 Nov. 1906, p. G12; *RT*, 27 Nov. 1901, p. 7; *BRCA*, 8 Jan. 1903, p. 13; Noreen Dunn Tatum, *A Crown of Service: A Story of Woman's Work in the Methodist Episcopal Church, South, from 1878–1940* (Nashville: Parthenon Press, 1960), 276–77.

17. *BRCA*, 14 Nov. 1912, p. 18; *BRCA*, 7 Mar. 1912; *Methodist Institute for Christian Work* (Richmond: [1917]); "Senior Pastor's Report," First Quarterly Conference, 1923–1924, Papers of Trinity Methodist Episcopal Church, Special Collections and Archives, McGraw-Page Library, Randolph-Macon College, Ashland, Va.; *RCA*, 12 Feb. 1925, p. 18; Tatum, *Crown of Service*, 277.

18. *RH,* 11 Jan. 1906, p. 11; *RH,* 12 Oct. 1905, p. 2; Blanche Sydnor White, *Richmond Baptists Working Together* (Richmond: Richmond Baptist Association, [1961]), 57–58.

19. *RH,* 6 Apr. 1905, pp. 2–3; White, *Richmond Baptists Working Together,* 58–64; *RH,* 19 Oct. 1905, pp. 2–3; *RH,* 26 Oct. 1905, pp. 2–3; *RH,* 2 Nov. 1905, pp. 2–3. Refusing any salary, Mrs. Buchanan suggested that the money be contributed to operate the city missionary program, a request which was honored.

20. White, *Richmond Baptists Working Together,* 65; Baptist Council of Richmond and Manchester, "Minutes of the Executive Committee, 1903–1929," meeting of 16 Oct. 1906, p. 129, Virginia Baptist Historical Society, Richmond.

21. *RH,* 3 May 1917, p. 14; Rees Watkins, *The House of Happiness: A Ministry of Love* (Richmond: Woman's Missionary Union of the Richmond Baptist Association, 1981), 11–20; White, *Richmond Baptists Working Together,* 68–70; Baptist Council of Richmond, "Minutes of the Executive Committee, 1903–1929," meeting of 22 Jan. 1917, pp. 15–17; *RH,* 8 Jan. 1914, p. 12; *RH,* 5 Nov. 1914, p. 12.

22. Belle Gayle Ellyson, "Forty Years of the House of Happiness: An Historical Sketch" (typewritten, Virginia Baptist Historical Society, 1954), preface; Watkins, *House of Happiness,* 11–20; White, *Richmond Baptists Working Together,* 68–70; Baptist Council of Richmond, "Minutes of the Executive Committee, 1903–1929," meeting of 22 Jan. 1917, pp. 15–17.

23. *RTD,* 16 July 1907, p. 1; *RTD,* 15 May 1908, p. 5; Virginia Conference of Charities and Correction, *Proceedings of the Fifth Annual Session* (Petersburg: Frank A. Owen, 1907), 61; *RTD,* 8 Aug. 1908, pp. 1, 2, 3, 5; *RT,* 1 Feb. 1900, pp. 4, 6; *RTD,* 21 Feb. 1911, p. 3.

24. *RTD,* 12 Feb. 1905, p. 12; *RTD,* 1 Jan. 1906, p. B3; *The Associated Charities of Richmond* (Richmond: 1906), 3–11. *RTD,* 17 Sept. 1909, p. 5; *RTD,* 19 Apr. 1909, p. 4; *RTD,* 18 Nov. 1910, p. 10; H. D. C. Maclachlan, *Memorial to the Honorable Council of the City of Richmond* (Richmond: Juvenile Protective Society of Virginia, 1913), 7; George Braxton Taylor, *Virginia Baptist Ministers, Sixth Series, 1914–1934* (Lynchburg, Va.: J. P. Bell, 1935), 365–66. For two years Buchanan continued to serve as the Baptist city missionary. Thereafter, he regularly preached in Baptist churches, and for two years he held a position of interim pastor for Woodland Heights Baptist Church.

25. *Associated Charities of Richmond* (Richmond, 1906), 12–31; *RTD,* 4 Feb. 1906, p. A9; *RTD,* 7 Dec. 1908, p. 8; *RTD,* 19 Nov. 1909, p. 10. Richmond's Associated Charities seems to have conformed to the type of organization widely used in American cities in the late nineteenth and early twentieth century. See Robert H. Bremner, *American Philanthropy,* (Chicago: University of Chicago Press, 1960), 99–104. In *The Shadow of the Poorhouse: A Social History of Welfare in America,* rev. ed. (New York: Basic Books, 1996), 68–87, Michael Katz traces the origins of scientific charity, describes some urban charitable organizations of the late nineteenth century and concludes they failed. Differing from those organizations somewhat, Richmond's Associated Charities constituted an improvement for the city, but did have significant limitations.

26. *"Now Abideth Faith, Hope, Charity, the Greatest of These Is Charity"* (Richmond: Associated Charities, 1913), 12; *RTD,* 4 June 1910, pp. 1, 2; *RTD,* 8 June 1910, pp. 1,3; *RTD,* 30 Nov. 1914, p. 5; *RTD,* 1 Jan. 1915, p. 10; *RTD,* 3 Jan. 1915, p. 13; *RNL,* 4 Jan. 1915, p. 2; *Twelve Months of Constructive Service, 17th Annual Report, Associated Charities* (Richmond: 1922), 4–7; *18th Annual Report, Associated Charities* (Richmond: 1923), 4–10.

27. *Twelve Months of Constructive Service,* 10–11; *Associated Charities, Annual Report, Nov. 1, 1923–Dec. 1924* (Richmond, 1925), 8–9: *RNL,* 12 Feb. 1926, p. 24. Robert H. Bremner, *American Philanthropy,* 95–104; Robert H. Bremner, *From the Depths: The Discovery of Pov-*

erty in the United States (New York: New York University Press, 1956), 123–39; James T. Patterson, *America's Struggle Against Poverty, 1900–1985* (Cambridge, Mass.: Harvard University Press, 1986), 23–27; Roy Lubove *The Professional Altruist: The Emergence of Social Work as a Career, 1880–1930* (Cambridge, Mass.: Harvard University Press, 1965), 1–13; Kenneth L. Kusmer, "The Functions of Organized Charity in the Progressive Era: Chicago as a Case Study," *Journal of American History* 60 (Dec. 1973): 657–70.

28. *RTD,* 31 July 1908, p. 10; Elwood Street, "The Story of the Virginia Department of Public Welfare," *Virginia Public Welfare* 21, no. 3 (Mar. 1943): 1; Frank Bane, "Joseph T. Mastin, 1855–1943," *Virginia Public Welfare* 21 no. 10 (Oct. 1943): 1–2. Mastin appears as a fictional character, the Reverend George Dayne, in Henry Sydnor Harrison, *Queed: A Novel* (New York: Grosset & Dunlap, 1911), 75, 127–28.

29. Arthur W. James, *Virginia's Social Awakening: The Contribution of Dr. Mastin and the Board of Charities and Corrections* (Richmond: Garrett & Massie, 1939), 177–88; Joseph T. Mastin, "Dr. Mastin Reminisces," *Virginia Public Welfare* 8 no. 8 (Aug. 1930): 1–4.

30. J. T. Mastin, "Some Needs of Almshouses and Jails in Virginia," *Proceedings of the Fifth Annual Session, Virginia Conference of Charities and Correction,* 52–61; "Dr. Mastin Reminisces," 1–4; James, *Virginia's Social Awakening,* 1–3; Elwood Street, "The Story of the Virginia Department of Public Welfare," 1.

31. James, *Virginia's Social Awakening,* v, ix; *RTD,* 19 Nov. 1911, p. 10; Mastin retired after serving fourteen years but resumed the position between 1924 and 1926 when his successor, Frank Bane, briefly left the state. Street, "The Story of the Virginia Department of Public Welfare," 2.

32. James, *Virginia's Social Awakening,* 10–16; "Secretary's Letter," *First Annual Report of the State Board of Charities and Corrections to the Governor of Virginia for the Year Ending September 30, 1909* (Richmond, 1909), 11; Arthur W. James, *The State Becomes a Social Worker: An Administrative Interpretation* (Richmond: Garrett & Massie, 1942), 130–48; Arthur W. James, *Back from "Over the Hill": The Disappearance of the County Almshouse in Virginia* (Richmond: Davis Bottom, Superintendent of Public Printing, 1926), passim.

33. James, *Virginia's Social Awakening,* 147–72; *RNL,* 2 Oct. 1915, p. 4; Virginia State Board of Charities and Corrections, *Mental Defectives in Virginia* (Richmond, 1915). For an extensive, haunting account of the misuse of alleged social science methods, see Steven Noll, *The Feebleminded in Our Midst: Institutions for the Mentally Retarded in the South, 1900–1940* (Chapel Hill: University of North Carolina Press, 1995). About Virginia, see particularly pages 13, 24–25, 35–39, 41, 60–63, 67–76, 112–22.

34. James, *Virginia's Social Awakening,* 34–66; Richmond Virginia, Juvenile and Domestic Relations Court, *Annual Report, 1925* (Richmond, 1925), 19.

35. *RTD,* 21 May 1911, p. 4; *RTD,* 26 May 1911, p. 1; James, *The State Becomes a Social Worker,* 8–15; James, *Virginia's Social Awakening,* 47, 63–78. A case can be made that in *Old Virginia Restored: An Interpretation of the Progressive Impulse, 1870–1930* (Charlottesville: University Press of Virginia, 1968), 147–50, Raymond H. Pulley misunderstands and underestimates Mastin. Pulley suggests that most of Mastin's accomplishments occurred in the area of penal reform and that after his early years he confined himself to "gradual systemization rather than bold innovation" (150). Rarely bold, Mastin seemed to seize opportunities as they arose with different officials, legislators, and governors. He did persist, and some of his most notable successes occurred with the cooperation of Gov. Westmoreland Davis near the end of Mastin's tenure.

36. *RCA,* 10 Jan. 1901, p. 2; *RT,* 10 Jan. 1902, p. 1; Arthur W. James, *Virginia's Social*

Awakening, 187–88; Virginia Annual Conference of the Methodist Episcopal Church, South, *Minutes of the One Hundred and Twenty-First Session* (Richmond: Lipscomb Fergusson, 1903), 53; *RCA,* 8 Mar. 1928, p. 19.

37. William J. Maybee, "The 25th Annual Report of the Children's Home Society of Virginia, April 30, 1926," *The Virginia Children's Home Finder* 7, no. 1, May 1926, 3, 5–8; *The Children's Home Society of Virginia* (Richmond: [1909]), 2–3.

38. *Children's Home Society,* 4–16; *RTD,* 12 June 1913, 3; *RTD,* 11 Dec. 1916, 10; *Virginia Children's Home Finder* 5, no. 2 (Aug. 1924): 3; *Virginia Children's Home Finder* 7, no. 1 (May 1926): 5–8.

39. News clipping, 2 May 1902, in Lila Meade Valentine Papers, Virginia Historical Society, Richmond.

40. *RTD,* 25 July 1921, p. 1; James W. Morris to Marianne Meade, 29 Aug. 1921, Lila Meade Valentine Papers; Adele Clark, "Mrs. Lila Meade Valentine," and Mary Holt W. Carlton, "Remembering Lila Meade Valentine," in *A Richmond Reader, 1773–1983,* ed. Maurice Duke and Daniel P. Jordan (Chapel Hill: University of North Carolina Press, 1983), 329–33; Lloyd C. Taylor Jr., "Lila Meade Valentine: The FFV as Reformer," *Virginia Magazine of History and Biography* 70, no. 4 (Oct. 1962): 471–87; Lloyd C. Taylor Jr., "Valentine, Lila Meade," *Notable American Women 1607–1950: A Biographical Dictionary* (Cambridge, Mass.: Harvard University Press, 1971), 3:504–5.

41. *RT,* 16 May 1900, p. 5; *RTD,* 29 May 1903; *RTD,* 11 Feb. 1908, p. 6; Walter Russell Bowie, *Sunrise in the South: The Life of Mary-Cooke Branch Munford* (Richmond: William Byrd Press, 1942), 68–70; *Third Annual Report, Richmond Education Association, 1902–1903* (Richmond, 1903), 5, 9; *Fifteenth Annual Report, Richmond Education Association, 1914–1915* (Richmond, 1915), 15–30; *Second Annual Report, Richmond Education Association, 1901–1902* (Richmond, 1902), 5–6; *Fourteenth Annual Report, Richmond Education Association, 1913–1914* (Richmond, 1914), 7. The organization held its first official meeting in the kindergarten room of St. Andrew's. William L. Bowden, "History of the Cooperative Education Association of Virginia: An Analysis of a Community Development Agency and Its Practice of Adult Education" (Ph.D. diss., Univ. of Chicago, 1957), 83.

42. *RTD,* 17 May 1904, p. 9; Samuel Chiles Mitchell, "An Aftermath of Appamattox [*sic*]: A Memoir" (Atlanta: mimeographed, 1954), 78; "Remarks of Dr. Samuel Chiles Mitchell Before the College Government Association at Westhampton College," Nov. 1938 in the Munford Family Papers, Virginia Historical Society, Richmond; William N. Glenn, *St. Andrew's,* 103–4; *Twelfth Annual Report of the Richmond Education Association, 1911–1912* (Richmond, 1912), 7; *Sixth Annual Report of the Richmond Education Association, 1905–1906* (Richmond, 1906), 16.

43. "Richmond's Greatest and Most Important Enterprise—Its Public School System," *Richmond* 14, no. 3 (Sept. 1927): 19, 22; Rebekah R. Sharp, "A History of the Richmond Public School System, 1869–1958" (master's thesis, University of Richmond, 1958), 77, 88–92, 147; Margaret Meagher, *History of Education in Richmond* (Richmond: Works Progress Administration, 1939), 117; Richmond, Virginia, Superintendent of the Public Schools, *Thirty-First Annual Report for the Year Ending July 31, 1900,* 7–9, 34–35; Richmond, Virginia, Superintendent of the Public Schools, *Sixty-First Annual Report for the Scholastic Year Ending June 30, 1930,* 14–18; *Richmond* 2, no. 8 (Feb. 1916): cover; *RNL,* 3 Nov. 1920, p. 15; Bowden, "History of the Cooperative Education Association," 122; J. L. Buck, *The Development of Public Schools in Virginia, 1607–1952* (Richmond: Commonwealth of Virginia Board of Education, 1952), 180.

44. *RH,* 20 Mar. 1902; *RH,* 3 Jan. 1901, p. 1; John A. Cutchins, *Memories of Old Richmond (1881–1944)* (Verona, Va.: McClure Press, 1973), 106. For a detailed account of Mitchell as a history professor, see W. Harrison Daniel, *History at the University of Richmond* (Richmond: W. Harrison Daniel, 1991), 15–46, 141–61. For Mitchell's career as an educator, see John Carroll Presley, "Samuel Chiles Mitchell: A Biography of a Southern Educator" (Ph.D. diss., University of Virginia, 1992).

45. Mitchell, "An Aftermath," 12, 1–42; Presley, "Samuel Chiles Mitchell," 14–53.

46. Samuel Chiles Mitchell, "Phases in the Educational Movement of the Day," *Sewanee Review* 16 (Jan. 1908): 19, 24; "The One Hundred and Eleventh Annual Commencement," *The University of North Carolina Record* 45 (June 1906): 8–10, clipping in Samuel Chiles Mitchell Papers, Library of Congress, Washington, D.C.; *RH,* 27 Sept. 1906, p. 12–13; *RH,* 8 May 1902, pp. 8–9; *RH,* 28 Apr. 1904, p. 2. For an account of the education movement in the South, see Charles William Dabney, *Universal Education in the South: Volume II* (Chapel Hill: University of North Carolina Press, 1936).

47. Mitchell, "An Aftermath," 79; *RTD,* 22 Apr. 1903, pp. 1–2; Edward N. Calisch to Lila Meade Valentine, 28 Apr. 1903, Valentine Papers, Virginia Historical Society; Bowden, "Cooperative Education Association," 124–26; Dabney, *Universal Education: Volume II,* 96–104.

48. Mitchell, "An Aftermath," 81; Bowden, "Cooperative Education Association," 133–43; Bowie, *Sunrise in the South,* 73; William Larsen, *Montague of Virginia: The Making of a Southern Progressive* (Baton Rouge: Louisiana State University Press, 1965), 164–69. At first the CEA was known as the Cooperative Education Conference. Mitchell proposed and lobbied for the word "Cooperative" in the name. Later, as CEA president, Mary Munford emphasized that word and praised Mitchell for choosing it.

49. Bowden, "History of the Cooperative Education Association," 143; *BRCA,* 7 Dec. 1905, p. 1. *RH,* 11 May 1905, p. 8; Bowie, *Sunrise in the South,* 73–75. On the May Campaign, see Bowden, "History of the Cooperative Education Association," 175–98; Mitchell, "An Aftermath," 82–85; Dabney, *Universal Education: Volume II,* 325–31; Louis R. Harlan, *Separate and Unequal: Public School Campaigns and Racism in the Southern Seaboard States, 1901–1915* (Chapel Hill: University of North Carolina Press, 1958; reprint, New York: Atheneum, 1969), 151–57; Presley, "Samuel Chiles Mitchell," 86–89; Pulley, *Old Virginia Restored,* 139–40; Allen W. Moger, *Virginia: Bourbonism to Byrd, 1870–1925* (Charlottesville: University Press of Virginia, 1968), 245–49; *BRCA,* 7 Dec. 1905, p. 1; *BRCA,* 11 May 1905, p. 1; *CP,* 17 Jan. 1906, p. 34; *RTD,* 18 Sept. 1905, p. 8; *SC,* 19 Aug. 1905, p. 1; *SC,* 11 Dec. 1905, p. 8; *RH,* 25 May 1905, p. 2.

50. Richmond Education Association, *Seventh Annual Report, 1906–1907* (Richmond: 1907), 39; F. A. Magruder, *Recent Administration in Virginia* (Baltimore: Johns Hopkins University Press, 1912), 25; Pulley, *Old Virginia Restored,* 140–44; Moger, *Virginia: Bourbonism to Byrd,* 249–54; Larsen, *Montague of Virginia,* 167; Mitchell, "Phases," 23; "Message of Hon. William Hodges Mann, Governor of Virginia to the General Assembly, January 16, 1914," in Etta Donnan Mann, *Four Years in the Governor's Mansion of Virginia, 1910–1914* (Richmond: Dietz Press, 1937), 272. In *Development of Public Schools,* 143–57, Buck furnishes excellent descriptions of some of the post–May Campaign laws and programs. Mitchell's goal of nine-month school terms was not soon achieved, as Buck notes on page 202. Historians Moger and Pulley emphasize the achievements of the May Campaign but admit that reformers did not achieve some of their goals until much later, if at all. Similarly, in *Separate but Unequal,* 135–69, Louis Harlan cites successes but stresses that racial discrimi-

nation in school spending deprived most of the state's African Americans of significant benefits. In an informative, nuanced treatment, *A Hard Country and a Lonely Place: Schooling, Society, and Reform in Rural Virginia, 1870–1920* (Chapel Hill: University of North Carolina Press, 1986), William A. Link perceives the early reform campaign giving way to a state educational bureaucracy, which brought "the erosion of community control over schools" (199).

51. Baptist General Association of Virginia, *Minutes of the Eighty-Fifth Annual Session* (Richmond: n.p., 1908), 50; Buck, *Development of Public Schools in Virginia,* 203–4, 361–62; Bowden, "History of the Cooperative Education Association," 286; *RTD,* 20 Mar. 1922, p. 1; J. T. Mastin, "The Prevention of Juvenile Dependency," in *The Call of the New South,* ed. James E. Mulloch (Nashville: Southern Sociological Congress, 1912), 44; *RTD,* 22 Feb. 1905, p. 1; *RTD,* 14 Jan. 1905, p. 1; Richmond Ministerial Union, "Minutes of Meetings, 1919–28," meeting of 8 May 1922, Richmond Public Library; *RNL,* 6 July 1923, p. 4; *RNL,* 9 Apr. 1928, p. 18. For excellent accounts of the library ordeal, see Carolyn H. Leatherman, "Richmond Considers a Free Public Library: Andrew Carnegie's Offer of 1901," *Virginia Magazine of History and Biography* 96, no. 2 (Apr. 1988): 181–92 and Carolyn Hall Leatherman, "Richmond Rejects a Library: The Carnegie Public Library Movement in Richmond, Virginia in the Early Twentieth Century" (Ph.D. diss., Virginia Commonwealth University, 1992). Richmond denominational weeklies and the daily press abound with articles reflecting support of religious leaders for educational reforms and for the public library campaign.

52. *The Richmond School of Social Economy* ([Richmond, 1917]), 1; Chairman, Finance Committee, "To the Churches, Societies, and Other Organizations Interested in the Social Progress of the City and State," [1916], John J. Scherer Jr., Papers, personal possession of Mary Grace Scherer Taylor, Richmond; *BRCA,* 12 Sept. 1918, pp. 12–13; *RTD,* 15 Dec. 1916, p. 2; Thomas Owen Carlton, *From Social Economy to Differential Practice: A History of the VCU School of Social Work* (Richmond: School of Social Work, Virginia Commonwealth University, 1987), 2–3, 8. As Carlton notes, the Richmond School became one of eleven charter member schools in the Association of Training Schools for Professional Social Work, which later became the American Association of Schools of Social Work.

53. Carlton, *From Social Economy,* 4–15; Henry H. Hibbs, *A History of the Richmond Professional Institute* (Richmond: Whittet & Shepperson, 1973), 13–35; Virginius Dabney, *Virginia Commonwealth University: A Sesquicentennial History* (Charlottesville: University Press of Virginia, 1987), 171–79; Watkins, *House of Happiness,* 18.

54. *RTD,* 3 June 1918, p. 10; Douglas S. Freeman, "President's Address: The New Social Conscience," *Proceedings of the Tenth Annual Session of the State Conference of Charities and Correction* (Richmond: Southern Printing, 1913), 1.

55. *PS,* 22 Dec. 1915, p. 8; *RNL,* 10 June 1919, p. 16. Denominational weeklies also carried articles about public health.

56. Samuel Nadler, "A History of the Instructive Visiting Nurse Association of Richmond, Virginia, 1900–1950" (master's thesis, Richmond Professional Institute of the College of William and Mary, 1951), 8, 26–33; *Nurses' Settlement of Richmond, Virginia* (Richmond, n.d.) in the Papers of the Instructive Visiting Nurses Association, Special Collections and Archives Department, Tompkins-McCaw Library, Medical College of Virginia; Sandra Goia Treadway, *Women of Mark: A History of the Woman's Club of Richmond, Virginia, 1894–1994* (Richmond: Library of Virginia, 1995), 44–45; *RT,* 9 Feb. 1902, p. 6.

57. *RTD,* 12 Feb. 1907, p. 8; *RTD,* 15 Oct. 1906, p. 5; *BRCA,* 31 Oct. 1912, p. 11; *RNL,* 27 Nov. 1916, p. 1; Frances Scott Branch to Nannie J. Minor, 4 Dec. 1926, Scott Family Papers,

Virginia Historical Society, Richmond; *BRCA,* 26 July 1906, p. 5; *RH,* 26 Dec. 1907, p. 9; *BRCA,* 25 July 1907, p. 11.

58. *The Sheltering Arms Free Hospital* (n.p., n.d.), 2, Sheltering Arms Scrapbook, Sheltering Arms Hospital Papers, Virginia Historical Society, Richmond; *Silver Cross,* 24 Dec. 1898, Sheltering Arms Scrapbook, Sheltering Arms Hospital Papers; *The Sheltering Arms Free Hospital: The First 75 Years, 1889–1964* (Richmond: Capital Printing, 1964), 3; Mary Wingfield Scott, *Houses of Old Richmond* (New York: Bonanza Books, 1941), 303–4; *RTD,* 14 Feb. 1911, p. 10; undated news clipping, [1901] Sheltering Arms Scrapbook; news clipping, Feb. 1927 and news clipping 10 Aug. 1929, Sheltering Arms Scrapbook; Frances Scott to "His Excellency, the Governor of Virginia," 11 Nov. 1926, Scott Family Papers, Virginia Historical Society.

59. Jeannie Ball to Frances Scott, 23 Jan. 1927, Scott Family Papers; Daughters of the King resolution, 1937, Sheltering Arms Scrapbook, Sheltering Arms Hospital Papers.

60. *RTD,* 12 Feb. 1905, p. 2; *RTD,* 18 Jan. 1905, p. 10; *RTD,* 31 Jan. 1909, p. D9; *RNL,* 4 Dec. 1962; *Annual Message of the Mayor the City of Richmond for the Year 1921* (Richmond: 1922), 34–35. Writing about public health in *The Urbanization of America, 1860–1915,* 14, 35, (New Brunswick, N.J.: Rutgers University Press, 1963), 154, Blake McKelvey records that public bathing facilities, long popular in European cities, finally began to grow in popularity in American cities only in the 1890s.

61. *RTD,* 20 Dec. 1908, p. 12; *RTD,* 10 May 1913, pp. 1, 8; Gustavus A. Weber, *Report on Housing and Living Conditions in the Neglected Sections of Richmond, Virginia* (Richmond: Whittet & Shepperson, 1913), 5–8, 77. For a discussion of the relationship of housing congestion and disease, see Roy Lubove, *The Progressives and the Slums: Tenement House Reform in New York City, 1890–1917* (Pittsburgh: University of Pittsburgh Press, 1962), 81–88.

62. Weber, *Report on Housing,* 10–17, passim.

63. Gustavus A. Weber, "A 'Clean-up' Campaign Which Resulted in a 'Keep-Clean' Ordinance," *American City* 10 (Jan.–June 1914): 231–34; *RTD,* 6 May 1913, p. 1; *RNL,* 17 Nov. 1914, p. 1; *RNL,* 2 Dec. 1914, p. 12; *Annual Message of the Mayor the City of Richmond for the Year 1921* (Richmond, 1922), 11; *RNL,* 22 July 1916, p. 12; *RNL,* 14 May 1928, p. 6; Weber, *Report on Housing,* 8; *RNL,* 24 Oct. 1914, p. 1; Christopher Silver, *Twentieth-Century Richmond: Planning, Politics, and Race* (Knoxville: University of Tennessee Press, 1984), 124–25. As Silver notes, the housing shortage especially affected the city's African American population. For more, see chap. 9.

64. *RNL,* 31 Dec. 1925, p. 4; *RTD,* 11 Oct. 1918, p. 1; *RNL,* 5 Oct. 1918, p. 1; *RTD,* 8 Oct. 1918, p. 1; *The Seventeenth Annual Report of the Instructive Visiting Nurse Association of the Nurses' Settlement, Richmond Virginia* (Richmond, [1918]), 10–17; *RTD,* 9–13 Oct. 1918; *RTD,* 24 Oct. 1918, p. 12; *League Record,* Oct. 1918, p. 2; *RNL,* 8 Dec. 1919, p. 4; *RTD,* 2 Nov. 1918, p. 1.

65. *RNL,* 10 June 1919, p. 16; Maclachlan, "The Church at Work in Social Service," 59. Richmond denominational weeklies criticized cigarette smoking, particularly by minors, as a menace to health. As examples, see *SC,* 19 Apr. 1902, p. 8, and *SC,* 22 Sept. 1900, p. 3.

66. R. Cary Montague, "A Parish Program—Christian Social Service," *Virginia Public Welfare* 6, no. 4 (Apr. 1928): 1–3; *RH,* 6 Nov. 1913, p. 8; W. R. L. Smith, *History of the Baptist Home for Aged Women* (Richmond: L. H. Jenkins, 1922), 5, 10–38; Drew St.J. Carneal, *Richmond's Fan District* (Richmond: Historic Richmond Foundation, 1996), 127–30; *Directory of Social Forces* (Richmond: Council of Social Agencies, 1937), 3, 50, 76. Several other examples of social service also illustrate this point. In 1902 an interdenominational group established a settlement house on Brook Road, where they provided a kindergarten, primary courses,

and night classes. Episcopalians apparently assumed direction of it in 1905, but this author has not located any documents which provide details about the settlement or what happened to it. *RT,* 23 Nov. 1902, p. 19 and *SC,* 21 Jan. 1905, p. 6. Local social service groups supported such nondenominational, community institutions as the Retreat for the Sick and the Belle Bryan Nursery, which provided care for children from low-income families.

67. An earlier generation of historians saw little evidence that church members addressed social problems. More recently scholars have begun to document the social activism of southern clergy and laity. In the classic, *Origins of the New South, 1877–1913* (Baton Rouge: Louisiana State University Press, 1951), 450–52, C. Vann Woodward reported finding few traces of social Christianity in the South, which seemed to place the South further outside the national mainstream. In "Fourteen Points on the Social Gospel in the South," *Southern Humanities Review* 1, no. 2 (summer 1967): 126–40, Robert Moats Miller offered an insightful commentary in which he grudgingly admitted a small Social Gospel influence in the South but built a lengthy case against its significance. In a pioneering work, *Southern White Protestantism in the Twentieth Century* (New York: Oxford University Press, 1964), Kenneth K. Bailey confined his attention to Baptists, Methodists, and Presbyterians, rarely inspected local activities, and portrayed southern Protestants as conservatives who eschewed social concerns. With powerful titles, two important historical treatments of Southern Baptists could be easily misinterpreted. In *At Ease in Zion: Social History of Southern Baptists, 1865–1900* (Nashville: Vanderbilt University Press, 1961), Rufus Spain concluded that "Baptists *did* develop a degree of social consciousness during the late nineteenth century" (Spain's emphasis), 211. By ending his account at the dawn of the twentieth century, Spain did not pretend to analyze an era in which Baptists expanded their expressions of social concern. Despite the title *Churches in Cultural Captivity,* John Lee Eighmy provided examples of social Christianity among Presbyterians, Methodists, and Baptists into whose "thought" and "life" "the social-gospel ideology had made definite inroads" (91).

Since the publication of Eighmy's work, scholars have more thoroughly defined the scope of southern social Christianity. More than anyone else, Wayne Flynt has redefined our understanding of southern social Christianity, especially with "Dissent in Zion: Alabama Baptists and Social Issues, 1900–1914," *Journal of Southern History* 35 (winter 1968): 523–42 and "'Feeding the Hungry and Ministering to the Broken Hearted': The Presbyterian Church in the United States and the Social Gospel, 1900–1920," *Religion in the South,* ed. Charles R. Wilson (Jackson: University Press of Mississippi, 1985), 83–117. Other important historical accounts include John Patrick McDowell's *The Social Gospel in the South: The Woman's Home Mission Movement in the Methodist Episcopal Church, South, 1886–1939* (Baton Rouge: Louisiana State University Press, 1982); John W. Storey, *Texas Baptist Leadership and Social Christianity, 1900–1980* (College Station: Texas A&M University Press, 1986) and Keith Harper's *The Quality of Mercy: Southern Baptists and Social Christianity, 1890–1920* (Tuscaloosa: University of Alabama Press, 1996).

68. Mabel Hay Barrows Mussey, ed., *Social Hymns of Brotherhood and Aspiration* (New York: A. S. Barnes, 1914), preface, vii–x, 1, 6, 42.

8. A "Divine Discontent"

1. Lucy Randolph Mason, *The Divine Discontent* (Richmond: Equal Suffrage League of Virginia, 1913), 10; Lucy Cary, *The Religious and Social Aspects of the Suffrage Movement* (Richmond: Equal Suffrage League of Virginia, 1912), unpaginated, Lucy Randolph Mason

Papers, Rare Book, Manuscript, and Special Collections Library, Duke University. Mason used the pseudonym Lucy Cary for a time to avoid upsetting her father, who did not share all her views. See John A. Salmond, *Miss Lucy of the CIO: The Life and Times of Lucy Randolph Mason, 1882–1959* (Athens: University of Georgia Press, 1988), 11. Mabel Hay Barrows Mussey, ed., *Social Hymns of Brotherhood and Aspiration* (New York: A. S. Barnes, 1914), 42; *RH,* 17 Mar. 1910, p. 10.

2. W. A. Cooper, "President's Address," *Proceedings of the Eleventh Annual Session of the Virginia Conference of Charities and Correction* (Richmond: Ware & Duke, 1914), 14; H. D. C. Maclachlan, "The Church at Work in Social Service," *Eleventh Annual Session of the Virginia Conference of Charities and Correction,* 62.

3. *RH,* 3 Sept. 1903, p. 2; *BRCA,* 28 Mar. 1912, p. 7–8; *RH,* 2 May 1912, p. 6; *RH,* 30 Mar. 1911, p. 10; *SC,* 4 Dec. 1920, p. 6; *RH,* 8 Dec. 1910, p. 8; *RCA,* 21 Nov. 1929, p. 3; *BRCA,* 2 May 1912, p. 9; Walter L. Lingle, "The Teachings of Jesus and Modern Social Problems," *Union Seminary Review* 27, no. 3 (Apr. 1916): 191–205; Maclachlan, "The Church at Work," 64; H. D. C. Maclachlan, "The Inside of the Cup," Maclachlan Papers, Disciples of Christ Historical Society, Nashville; *SC,* 5 Jan. 1920, p. 3; *RH,* 26 Mar. 1903, p. 8; *RTD,* 11 Feb. 1907, p. 8.

4. *CP,* 5 Dec. 1906, p. 868; Maclachlan, "Church at Work," 61, 66; Cooper, "President's Address," 14; *BRCA,* 20 June 1912, p. 9; *SC,* 24 Aug. 1907, p. 1; *BRCA,* 2 May 1912, p. 9; *SC,* 5 Apr. 1919, p. 7; Maclachlan, "The Inside of the Cup," Maclachlan Papers; *BRCA,* 20 June 1912, p. 9; Lingle, "The Teachings of Jesus and Modern Social Problems," 200–202.

5. *SC,* 1 Sept. 1900, p. 5. The Episcopal city missionary in May 1903 furnished one example of local concern about prisoners. In a three-month span, he made thirty public and private visits to the penitentiary, the city jail, and the county jail. *SC,* 2 May 1903, p. 5.

6. *SC,* 1 Sept. 1900, p. 5; Lucy Randolph Mason, *To Win These Rights: A Personal Story of the CIO in the South* (New York: Harper & Brothers, 1952), 3; *RT,* 27 Apr. 1900, p. 4. The 1900–1902 campaign has escaped the attention of two otherwise valuable histories, Arthur W. James, *Virginia's Social Awakening: The Contribution of Dr. Mastin and the Board of Charities and Corrections* (Richmond: Garrett & Massie, 1939), 124–27, and Paul W. Keve, *The History of Corrections in Virginia* (Charlottesville: University Press of Virginia, 1986). In *One Dies, Get Another: Convict Leasing in the American South, 1866–1928* (Columbia: University of South Carolina Press, 1996), 6–8, Matthew J. Mancini traces the limited improvements of the Virginia corrections system in the late nineteenth century and uses the state as a counterpoint to the harsher penal systems further South.

7. *CP,* 28 Nov. 1900, p. 8; *RT,* 23 Jan. 1901, p. 5; *RT,* 27 Mar. 1901, p. 1; *RCA,* 31 Jan. 1901, p. 1; *RH,* 22 Feb. 1900, p. 8; *RH,* 31 Jan. 1901, p. 1; Mason, *To Win These Rights,* 3.

8. *SC,* 8 Dec. 1900, p. 8; *RT,* 4 Mar. 1902, p. 1; *RTD,* 24 July 1904, p. C5; James, *Virginia's Social Awakening,* 127; William Larsen, *Montague of Virginia: The Making of a Southern Progressive* (Baton Rouge: Louisiana State University Press, 1965), 138–39.

9. James, *Virginia's Social Awakening,* 126–33, Mastin quotation, 27; Keve, *History of Corrections,* 130–36; *Fourth Annual Report of the State Board of Charities and Corrections to the Governor of Virginia for the Year Ending September 30, 1912* (Richmond, 1913), 10; *Annual Report of the Board of Directors of the Penitentiary, Fiscal Year Ending Sept. 30, 1921* (Richmond, 1922), 11. In "The Penal Reform Movement in the South during the Progressive Era, 1890–1917," *Journal of Southern History* 17 (Nov. 1951): 474, Jane Zimmerman also credits Mastin with initiating reforms within the penitentiary.

10. "Message of Hon. William Hodges Mann, Governor of Virginia to the General

Assembly, January 16, 1914, Session 1914," in Etta Donnan Mann, *Four Years in the Governor's Mansion of Virginia, 1910–1914* (Richmond: Dietz Press, 1937), 278–81; James, *Virginia's Social Awakening,* 134–37; Gov. Westmoreland Davis to Walter Russell Bowie, 31 Jan. 1922, Walter Russell Bowie Papers, Bishop Payne Library, Virginia Theological Seminary, Alexandria; *Annual Report of the Board of Directors of the Penitentiary, Fiscal Year Ending Sept. 30, 1920* (Richmond, 1920), 1–10; *Annual Report of the Board of Directors of the Penitentiary, Fiscal Year Ending Sept. 30, 1921* (Richmond, 1922), 11; *Public Welfare* 7, no. 7 (July 1929): 2.

11. George W. McDaniel, *Seeing the Best: Sermons and Addresses* (Nashville: Sunday School Board of the Southern Baptist Convention, 1923), 115–33, quotation, 130; *RH,* 10 Dec. 1908, p. 6; *SC,* 17 May 1919, p. 13; *RCA,* 15 July 1920, p. 3.

12. *RTD,* 25 Apr. 1906, p. 12; *RTD,* 8 Mar. 1910, p. 6; James, *Virginia's Social Awakening,* 133, 136; *SC,* 14 May 1921, p. 15; *RCA,* 15 July 1920, p. 3; *PS,* 14 July 1920, p. 8; *Thirteenth Annual Report of the Board of Corrections and Charities to the Governor of Virginia for the Year Ending Sept. 30, 1920* (Richmond, 1920), 12; *Annual Report of the Board of Directors of the Penitentiary, Fiscal Year Ending Sept. 30, 1920* (Richmond, 1921), 10; *VC,* Oct. 1924, pp. 352–53; Keve, *History of Corrections in Virginia,* 254.

13. "Virginia's Penal Institutions (Resume of Crime and Penal Affairs Commission's Report)," *Public Welfare* (Jan. 1930): 1–3; *RCA,* 5 Mar. 1925, p. 11; *RCA,* 11 June 1925, p. 22.

14. *RTD,* 2 Nov. 1912, p. 12; Elmer Jackson Cooley, ed., *The Inside Story of the World Famous Courthouse Tragedy—As Told by a Native Countryman Familiar with the Facts and Conditions Surrounding the Event That Shocked the Civilized World* (Charlottesville, Va.: [Michie, 1961]), 80–81; *RTD,* 15–19 Mar. 1912; Mann, *Four Years in the Governor's Mansion,* 302–10; *RTD,* 18 May 1912, p. 1; *RTD,* 28 July 1912, p. 1; *RTD,* 12 Sept. 1912, p. 1. One Allen family member agreed to a plea bargain and received an eighteen-year prison sentence. In the course of three trials, another Allen received a total sentence of thirty-five years for killing three people, including the judge. Pleading guilty to second-degree murder, a third person was sentenced to twenty-seven years in prison.

15. *RTD,* 2 Nov. 1912, p. 12; *RTD,* 5 Nov. 1912, p. 8; *RH,* 3 Apr. 1913, p. 13; *RH,* 14 Nov. 1912, p. 10; E. J. Cooley, *Inside Story,* 80–81, 97, 103; Douglass S. McDaniel, *George White McDaniel* (Nashville: Sunday School Board of the Southern Baptist Convention, 1928), 162–65; John J. Scherer, III, "John J. Scherer Jr.," unpublished biography, Scherer Papers, personal possession, Mary Grace Scherer Taylor, Richmond; Mann, *Four Years in the Governor's Mansion,* 308–19; Gov. William Hodges Mann to George White McDaniel, 15 Nov. 1912, McDaniel Papers, Virginia Baptist Historical Society, Richmond; *RTD,* 28 Mar. 1913, p. 1; *RTD,* 28 Mar. 1913, p. 1.

16. *RH,* 3 Apr. 1913, p. 12; *RH,* 10 Sept. 1925, p. 3; *RTD,* 17 Mar. 1913, p. 4; *RH,* 26 Dec. 1912, pp. 10–11; *RH,* 2 Jan. 1913, p. 10; *RH,* 9 Jan. 1913, p. 10; *RH,* 27 Mar. 1913, p. 12; *RH,* 23 Sept. 1915, p. 10.

17. *SC,* 8 Dec. 1900, p. 8; *Second Annual Report of the State Board of Charities and Corrections* (Richmond, 1910), 129; *RH,* 21 Jan. 1915, p. 10; *CP,* 5 Mar. 1902, p. 8.

18. *Proceedings of the Fifth Annual Session of the Virginia Conference of Charities and Correction* (Petersburg: Frank A. Owen, 1907), 52, 60–61; James, *Virginia's Social Awakening,* 19–23, 31–34; *First Annual Report of the State Board of Charities and Corrections* (Richmond: 1909), 11; Frank Bane, *Shall the Local Jail Be Abolished?* (Richmond: Davis Bottom, Superintendent of Public Printing, 1922).

19. "The Virginia Jail System with Suggestions for Improvement," *Public Welfare* 14, no. 1 (Jan. 1936): 3–4; Bane, *Shall the Local Jail Be Abolished?,* 6; James, *Virginia's Social*

Awakening, 19–31; Arthur W. James, "Virginia's Jail Problem," *Public Welfare* 9, no. 10 (Oct. 1931): 1–4.

20. *RTD,* 7 Sept. 1909, p. 10; *RT,* 15 May 1901, p. 3; *RTD,* 19 Nov. 1908, p. 12; *BRCA,* 5 Feb. 1914, p. 2; *RTD,* 1 Oct. 1911, p. 1; *First Annual Report of the State Board of Charities and Corrections* (Richmond, 1909), 152; *Fourth Annual Report of the State Board of Charities and Corrections* (Richmond, 1913), 68; *RH,* 4 Nov. 1915, p. 10. For an excellent account of much of the fumbling and blundering leading to the new jail, see Carol Hall Leatherman, "Richmond Rejects a Library: The Carnegie Public Library Movement in Richmond, Virginia in the Early Twentieth Century" (Ph.D. diss, Virginia Commonwealth University, 1992), 152–58.

21. *RH,* 4 Nov. 1915, p. 10; *RNL,* 8 Apr. 1927, p. 1; *RNL,* 26 Apr. 1927, p. 20; James, *Virginia's Social Awakening,* 34; *RTD,* 15 Oct. 1909, p. 1; *RNL,* 11 July 1929, p. 6; *RNL,* 8 Apr. 1927, p. 1; *RNL,* 26 Apr. 1927, p. 20; "State Board Makes Richmond Jail Survey," *Public Welfare* 4, no. 5 (May 1927): 4. James attributed this failure to the conservative social attitudes of Virginians, who revered their tradition of strong local government. "In Virginia, we are bound by three centuries of precedent which makes improvements slow and difficult," he concluded. James, "Virginia's Jail Problem," 4.

22. *First Annual Report of the State Board of Charities and Corrections to the Governor of Virginia* (Richmond, 1909), 220; C. B. Cooke, "The Objects and Need of a Juvenile Court Law for Virginia," *Proceedings of the Seventh Annual Session of the Virginia Conference of Charities and Correction* (Picot Printing, [1909]), 31–40.

23. *RH,* 9 July 1908, p. 9; *RTD,* 3 May, 1908, p. 1; Elwood Street, "The Story of the Juvenile and Domestic Relations Court of Virginia," *Virginia Public Welfare* 21, no. 9 (Sept. 1943): 1–2. For example, at the annual meeting of the Richmond Education Association in 1907, that organization had passed a resolution favoring the establishment of a juvenile court. *RTD,* 24 Apr. 1907, p. 1.

24. H. D. C. Maclachlan, "Address," *Annual Report, Juvenile and Domestic Relations Court* (Richmond, 1925), 4; *Seventh Annual Session of the Virginia Conference of Charities and Correction,* 40; *RTD,* 18 Nov. 1908, p. 10; *RTD,* 19 Apr. 1909, p. 10; Street, "Story of the Juvenile and Domestic Relations Court," 2; *RTD,* 28 Jan. 1910, p. 5; James, *Virginia's Social Awakening,* 99–101.

25. James, *Virginia's Social Awakening,* 31, 100–102; *RTD,* 26 May 1911, p. 1; Street, "Story of the Juvenile and Domestic Relations Court," 2; *Annual Report, Juvenile and Domestic Relations Court* (Richmond, 1925), 4.

26. H. D. C. Maclachlan, *Memorial to the Honorable Council of the City of Richmond* (Richmond: Juvenile Protective Society of Virginia, 1913), 2–8. These reasons are largely the same as invoked by most proponents of juvenile courts in the United States in this era. See Ellen Ryerson, *The Best-Laid Plans: America's Juvenile Court Experiment* (New York: Hill & Wang, 1978), 24–56.

27. *RTD,* 10 Dec. 1913, p. 3; *RTD,* 19 Apr. 1915, p. 10; *RTD,* 21 July 1910, p. 10; Street, "Story of the Juvenile and Domestic Relations Court," 3–4; James, *Virginia's Social Awakening,* 103, 106; Maclachlan, *Memorial,* 3–4.

28. James, *Virginia's Social Awakening,* 106–9; Street, "Story of the Juvenile and Domestic Relations Court," 3–4; *Annual Report Juvenile and Domestic Relations Court* (Richmond, 1925), 19, 25; *CC,* June 1929, p. 6; news clippings in John J. Crutchfield Scrapbook, Virginia Historical Society, Richmond; *SC,* 22 July 1916, p. 12; *RTD,* 15 Dec. 1915, p. 12; *RTD,* 22 Feb. 1915, p. 1; *RNL,* 30 Jan. 1923, p. 4; *RNL,* 22 Dec. 1915, p. 1.

29. *RNL,* 2 Oct. 1926, p. 8; Maclachlan, "Address," 5; *RNL,* 11 Oct. 1929, p. 34; James, *Virginia's Social Awakening,* 34. Historians have rendered some negative verdicts about the juvenile courts. For example, in *The Best-Laid Plans,* Ellen Ryerson maintains that even the early courts often failed to function as intended and that reformers themselves admitted disappointment. Furthermore, across time the courts operated unsatisfactorily because they unreasonably combined judicial and therapeutic goals, because they lacked adequate resources for the large task of modifying individual behavior, and because they violated civil liberties. In a gloomy conclusion, she argues that neither "experience nor theory has been kind" to many of the assumptions behind the juvenile courts. She notes a prevalent "belief that we do not know what to do about juvenile crime, and a fear we can collectively do nothing," 161. In a study focusing on Illinois and Chicago, *The Child Savers: The Invention of Delinquency* (Chicago: University of Chicago, [1969]), Anthony M. Platt likewise delivers a critical assessment of juvenile courts. In *Mothers of All Children: Women Reformers and the Rise of Juvenile Courts in Progressive Era America* (University Park: Penn State Press, 1998), 198, Elizabeth J. Clapp concludes that "local circumstances and the priorities of individual juvenile court judges and administrators were the most important influences on how juvenile court laws operated in practice." Examining different reformers and juvenile courts, Clapp discerningly traces strengths, weaknesses, and changes in the juvenile courts. Through the 1920s Richmonders seemed to think their juvenile court worked well. At least as an alternative to the previous methods of dealing with juveniles, the court seems to merit a favorable assessment.

30. Lucy Randolph Mason to Lila Meade Valentine, 10 Jan. 1911, Lila Meade Valentine Papers, Virginia Historical Society, Richmond.

31. Joan R. Gundersen, "Women and the Parallel Church: A View from Congregations," in *Episcopal Women: Gender, Spirituality and Commitment in an American Mainline Denomination,* ed. Catherine M. Prelinger (New York: Oxford University Press, 1992), 111–32. About Episcopal deaconesses, see Mary Sudman Donovan, *A Different Call: Women's Ministries in the Episcopal Church, 1850–1920* (Wilton, Conn.: Morehouse-Barlow, 1986), 88–122. Donovan notes that male deacons had both liturgical and educational roles but that deaconesses were confined to the latter. Still, by carefully filling educational and pastoral roles and by rooting themselves deeply in individual parishes, deaconesses developed an important female presence within the Episcopal Church. About Methodist deaconesses, see Noreen Dunn Tatum, *A Crown of Service: A Story of Woman's Work in the Methodist Episcopal Church, South from 1878–1940* (Nashville: Parthenon Press, 1960), 325–28, and John Patrick McDowell, *The Social Gospel in the South: The Woman's Home Mission Movement in the Methodist Episcopal Church, South, 1886–1939* (Baton Rouge: Louisiana State University Press, 1982), 62–64.

32. Synod of Virginia, Presbyterian Church in the United States, *One Hundred and Twelfth Annual Session* (Richmond: Whittet & Shepperson), 121–34; Robert Pollok Kerr, "Woman's Place in the Church and the World," *Union Seminary Magazine* 16, no. 3 (Feb.–Mar. 1905): 215–18; Robert Pollok Kerr, *Will the World Outgrow Christianity and Other Interrogatives on Vital Themes* (Chicago: Fleming H. Revell, 1901), 72–73.

33. Woman's Foreign Missionary Union, East Hanover Presbytery, "Seventeenth Annual Report," in "Minutes of Woman's Work in East Hanover Presbytery, Volume 2, 1889–1918," 14 Apr. 1905, p. 2, William Smith Morton Library, Union Theological Seminary/Presbyterian School of Christian Education; *CP,* 10 Jan. 1900, p. 8; Woman's Missionary Union, Presbytery of East Hanover, "Minutes of Annual Meeting," 19–21 Apr. 1916, p. 8,

"Minutes of Woman's Work in East Hanover Presbytery"; "Appointment of Women to Official Positions," R. E. Magill Papers, Presbyterian Historical Society, Montreat, N.C.; *League Record,* July 1916, p. 3; *League Record,* Mar. 1916, p. 4; *League Record,* May 1922, p. 3.

34. Walter L. Lingle, "Changes That I Have Seen," 1, typewritten, no date, Walter L. Lingle Papers, Presbyterian Historical Society, Montreat, N.C.; Hallie Paxson Winsborough, *The Woman's Auxiliary, Presbyterian Church, U.S.* (Richmond: Presbyterian Committee of Publication, 1927), 26–27; "Article on the Assembly's Training School" (typewritten ca. 1917), p. 1, in folder "Schools and Colleges: General Assembly's Training School," General Information File, Presbyterian Historical Society, Montreat, N.C.

35. Lingle, "Changes That I Have Seen," 4; Walter L. Lingle to E. D. Brown, 25 June 1920, Lingle Papers; *PS,* 8 June 1927, p. 2; Ernest Trice Thompson, *Presbyterians in the South,* 3:398–402.

36. *BRCA,* 5 May, 1910, pp. 1, 4, 5.

37. Virginia Shadron, "The Laity Rights Movement, 1906–1918: Women's Suffrage in the Methodist Episcopal Church, South," in *Women in New Worlds: Historical Perspectives on the Wesleyan Tradition,* ed. Hilma R. Thomas and Rosemary Skinner Keller (Nashville: Abingdon Press, 1981), 261–75; McDowell, *The Social Gospel in the South,* 125–40; Tatum, *A Crown of Service,* 37–41; *BRCA,* 11 Nov. 1909, p. 10; *RTD,* 20 May, 1910, p. 1; Methodist Episcopal Church, South, *Journal of the Seventeenth General Conference* (Nashville: Publishing House, Methodist Episcopal Church, South, [1914]), 215.

38. *BRCA,* 26 Mar. 1914, p. 8; *BRCA,* 26 Feb. 1914, p. 6; *BRCA,* 30 Jan. 1913, p. 6; *BRCA,* 29 May 1913, p. 7; *BRCA,* 20 Nov. 1913, p. 8; *BRCA,* 10 Apr. 1913, p. 6.

39. *RCA,* 15 Dec. 1927, p. 8; Methodist Episcopal Church, South, *Journal of the Eighteenth General Conference of the Methodist Episcopal Church, South* (Nashville: Publishing House, Methodist Episcopal Church, South [1918]), 138–40; *The Doctrines and Discipline of the Methodist Episcopal Church, South,* ed. Gross Alexander (Nashville: Publishing House, Methodist Episcopal Church, South, 1914), 31, 36, 78, 83, 94, 99, 103, 228, 241, 244; Mollie Roberson Wiltshire, *A Century of Service: The History of Union Station Methodist Church, 1843–1943* (Richmond: Whittet & Shepperson, 1943), 28, 108. At the end of the 1920s, as an unsuccessful movement to license women as Methodist preachers developed, the pastor of Richmond's Fairmount Methodist Church expressed his unhappiness about the lack of support for that reform among those attending the Virginia Annual Conference. If women were qualified, he believed men who blocked their way did not "have the highest interests of Christ's Kingdom at heart." *RCA,* 7 Nov. 1929, p. 10.

40. *RH,* 16 Mar. 1916, p. 10; *RH,* 29 June 1916, p. 10; *RNL,* 11 May 1929, p. 8; *RNL,* 16 May 1918, p. 4; Harry Leon McBeth, "The Role of Women in Southern Baptist History," *Baptist History and Heritage* 12 (Jan. 1977): 3–25; *RNL,* 18 May 1922, p. 1.

41. *Beacon on a Hill: A Brief History of One Hundred Year of Christian Service, 1855–1955; Pine Street Baptist Church, Richmond Virginia* (Richmond: Pine Street Baptist Church, 1955), 104–5; Gertrude Lee Flippen, Julia May Nicholas Gates, Virginia Nicholas Sanders, *The History and Memories of Oakwood Baptist Church, 1916–1976* (n.p., n.d.), 108–9; William C. James, *Leigh Street Baptist Church, 1854–1954: A Brief History of Its First One Hundred Years in the Service of Christ* (Richmond: Whittet & Shepperson, 1954), 102; *RNL,* 21 Jan. 1926; Annie Florence Weeks, *Grace Baptist Church, Richmond, 1833–1958* (Richmond: Garrett & Massie, 1958), 65, 77; Dover Baptist Association, *Minutes of the One Hundred and Thirty-Forth Annual Session* (Richmond: Clyde W. Sanders, 1917), 40; *RNL,* 17 Nov. 1920, p. 1. Virginia Baptists lagged behind those in a number of other states who granted female

membership to state conventions before 1900. Rufus Spain, *At Ease in Zion: Social History of Southern Baptists, 1865–1900* (Nashville: Vanderbilt University Press, 1961), 169–70.

42. Donovan, *A Different Call,* 162–65; *Majority Report to the Council of the Diocese of Virginia: Minority Report* (n.p., [1920]), Churchill Gibson Chamberlayne Papers, Virginia Historical Society, Richmond; Walter Russell Bowie, *Learning to Live* (Nashville: Abingdon Press, 1969), 135.

43. *SC,* 30 Sept. 1922, p. 5; *Journal of the One Hundred and Thirty-Sixth Annual Council of the Protestant Episcopal Church in the Diocese of Virginia* (n.p., 1931), 251–69.

44. B. B. Valentine to Lila Meade Valentine, 8 Aug. 1918, Lila Meade Valentine Papers, Virginia Historical Society, Richmond. Lila Valentine apparently treasured this particular letter which tenderly expressed love, appreciation for her as a wife, and support for suffrage. See Lloyd C. Taylor Jr., "Lila Meade Valentine: The FFV as Reformer," *Virginia Magazine of History and Biography* 70, no. 4 (Oct. 1962): 486–87. Lila Meade Valentine, "Annual Address," Jan. 1919, Lila Meade Valentine Papers, Virginia Historical Society, Richmond.

45. *RTD,* 7 Feb. 1911, p. 10. Reared as a Southern Baptist, Johnston left First Baptist in March 1910. Mary Johnston to George W. McDaniel, 24 Mar. 1910, George White McDaniel Papers, Virginia Baptist Historical Society, Richmond. On her interest in Eastern religion, see Majorie Spruill Wheeler's "Introduction," Mary Johnston, *Hagar* (Boston: Houghton Mifflin, 1913; Charlottesville: University Press of Virginia, 1994), xvii–xviii. For an excellent account of Johnston's role in the suffrage campaign, see Marjorie Spruill Wheeler, "Mary Johnston, Suffragist," *Virginia Magazine of History and Biography* 100, no. 1 (Jan. 1992): 99–118.

46. *RTD,* 30 Jan. 1911, p. 1.

47. *RTD,* 20 Dec. 1909, p. 8; *RNL,* 1 Feb. 1916, p. 13; membership list, Equal Suffrage League of Virginia, Lila Meade Valentine Papers, Virginia Historical Society, Richmond; *RNL,* 20 July 1914, p. 5.

48. *RTD,* 16 Jan. 1911, p. 1.

49. Lila Meade Valentine, speech before the Episcopal Clericus, Dec. 1912, Lila Meade Valentine Papers, Virginia Historical Society, Richmond; Taylor, "Lila Meade Valentine: The FFV as Reformer," 481–87; Marjorie Spruill Wheeler, *New Women of the New South: The Leaders of the Woman Suffrage Movement in the Southern States* (New York: Oxford University Press, 1993); Sarah Hunter Graham, "Woman Suffrage in Virginia: The Equal Suffrage League and Pressure-Group Politics, 1909–1920," *Virginia Magazine of History and Biography* 101, no. 2 (Apr. 1993): 227–50; Elna C. Green, *Southern Strategies: Southern Women and the Woman Suffrage Question* (Chapel Hill: University of North Carolina Press, 1997), 151–77.

50. Green, *Southern Strategies,* 158; *RH,* 4 Jan. 1912, p. 7; Lucy Randolph Mason, *The Divine Discontent; RTD,* 28 Apr. 1912, p. 12; *SC,* 2 Aug. 1919, p. 9; Lucy Cary, *The Religious and Social Aspect of the Suffrage Movement* (Richmond: Equal Suffrage League of Virginia, 1912); *RTD,* 28 Apr. 1912, p. 12; *RTD,* 5 May 1912, p. 4; Salmond, *Miss Lucy of the CIO,* 12–29.

51. *SC,* 28 Aug. 1920, p. 3.

52. Walter Russell Bowie, *Sunrise in the South: The Life of Mary-Cooke Branch Munford* (Richmond: William Byrd Press, 1942), 91–144, quotations, 93, 127; Walter Russell Bowie, *Learning to Live,* 97–108.

53. *The Co-ordinate College: The State's Need of It* (n.p., 1914), 3–7, quotation, 7; Mary-Cooke Branch Munford and Virginia S. McKenney, *A Plea for Co-ordination* (Charlottesville, Va.: n.p., 1914).

54. *RH,* 27 Jan. 1916, p. 10; Bowie, *Sunrise in the South,* 102–44; [Women's Committee Interested in the Establishment of a State College for Women at the University of Virginia], *The Co-ordinate College at Charlottesville Affiliated with the University of Virginia* (Charlottesville, Va.: n.p., 1913), 73, 124–25; "Delegation Received by Governor Davis," 8 Feb. 1918, Westmoreland Davis File, Mary-Cooke Branch Munford Papers, Archives Research Services, Library of Virginia; Anne Hobson Freeman, "Mary Munford's Fight for a College for Women Co-ordinate with the University of Virginia," *Virginia Magazine of History and Biography* 78 (Oct. 1970): 481–91.

55. Mary-Cooke Branch Munford, Chairman, Central Committee, to My dear friend, 14 Mar. 1916, Churchill Gibson Chamberlayne Papers, Virginia Historical Society, Richmond; Petition to legislative committee by alumni for Senate bill number 230, 13 Feb. 1918, Munford Papers, Library of Virginia; Freeman, "Mary Munford's Fight," 483–85; Bowie, *Sunrise in the South,* 98–144; Bowie, *Learning to Live,* 102–8; *RNL,* 19 Feb. 1918, p. 1; *RNL,* 4 Mar. 1918, p. 1.

56. Bowie, *Sunrise in the South,* 167; *University of Virginia Alumni News,* 7 no. 7 (Feb. 1920): 150–51; E. A. Alderman to Mary-Cooke Branch Munford, 14 June 1926, Munford Papers, Library of Virginia; Freeman, "Mary Munford's Fight," 481, 489–91. Barbara Miller Solomon's *In the Company of Educated Women* (New Haven, Conn.: Yale University Press, 1985), 53–56, reports the South's reluctance to admit women to universities, thereby limiting their educational opportunities.

57. W. Russell Bowie, "Half Live and Whole Life: An Interpretation of the End of Social Striving," *Proceedings of the Forty-Second Annual Meeting of the National Conference of Charities and Corrections* (Chicago: Hildman Printing, 1915), 17; *RH,* 28 Mar. 1912, p. 10; *BRCA,* 9 Aug. 1906, p. 8; *CP,* 11 Dec. 1907, p. 1135; *RH,* 1 Nov. 1906, p. 4; H. D. C. Maclachlan, "Studies in Sin," *Christian Century,* 19 Oct. 1922, 1291; *RTD,* 15 July 1907, p. 8; *RTD,* 11 Feb. 1907, p. 8; *SC,* 1 Sept. 1908, p. 1.

58. James B. Hawthorne, *An Unshaken Trust and Other Sermons* (Philadelphia: American Baptist Publication Society, 1899), 109; *RH,* 18 June. 1908, p. 14; Bowie, "Half Live and Whole Life," 18; Walter L. Lingle, "Synods or Councils and Social Questions," *Union Seminary Review,* 27 no. 4 (July 1916): 357–60; *RH,* 30 Mar. 1911, p. 11. For other examples of this theme, see Report of the Social Service Committee, Baptist General Association of Virginia, *Minutes of the Ninety-Seventy Annual Session* (Richmond: Richmond Press, 1921), 69; *RTD,* 11 Feb. 1907, p. 8; *SC,* 4 June 1921, p. 8; *PS,* 25 May 1921, p. 1; *BRCA,* 27 June 1912, p. 3; *RTD,* 6 Feb. 1922, p. 3.

59. *RH,* 25 Apr. 1912, p. 10; *RH,* 23 May 1912, p. 10; *RH,* 2 May 1912, p. 10. The "Men or Things" series ran from 14 March to 13 June in the *Religious Herald.*

60. H. D. C. Maclachlan, "Studies in Sin: Sinning at Long Range," *Christian Century,* 22 Mar. 1923, p. 364; H. D. C. Maclachlan, "The Church's Contacts with Socialism," *Christian Century,* 15 July 1920, p. 11; Maclachlan, "The Church at Work in Social Service," 61; H. D. C. Maclachlan, "An Old Text in a New Setting," undated sermon, Maclachlan Papers; Maclachlan, "Studies in Sin," *Christian Century,* 19 Oct. 1922, 1291. In a series of talks at Seventh Street Christian, Maclachlan characterized ancient Hebrew prophets as condemning a profligate society where leaders exploited the poor. This presentation formed part of a manuscript, "Types and Ideals of Hebrew Prophecy," which Maclachlan was preparing for publication at the time of his death. An ethical God, Maclachlan maintained, sided with the "humblest citizen whose rights were threatened." Jesus, who was poor, Maclachlan affirmed, taught that the existence of extreme wealth and extreme poverty was

a social wrong of the first magnitude. Quotation from "Types and Ideals," chap. 3, 9, Maclachlan Papers.

61. *SC,* 15 Feb. 1919, p. 4; *SC,* 4 June 1921, pp. 8–9; *SC,* 6 May 1922, p. 5; *SC,* 7 May 1921, p. 6; *SC,* 27 July 1923, p. 6; *SC,* 16 June 1923, p. 5; *SC,* 4 Aug. 1923, p. 5.

62. *BRCA,* 26 Sept. 1907, pp. 1–2; *RT,* 23 Jan. 1903, p. 1; *RTD,* 20 Dec. 1907, p. 10; James Buchanan to Samuel Chiles Mitchell, 30 Jan. 1908, S. C. Mitchell Papers, Library of Congress; Elizabeth H. Davidson, *Child Labor Legislation in the Southern Textile States* (Chapel Hill: University of North Carolina Press, 1939), 244–47. According to Davidson, the 1922 law also required physical certificates and prohibited the work of youngsters under that age from jobs designated as dangerous. Walter I. Trattner's *Crusade for the Children: A History of the National Child Labor Committee and Child Labor Reform in America* (Chicago: Quadrangle Books, 1970) surveys the widespread use of child labor in many American industries of the era and notes the increased use of child labor in the South beginning in the late nineteenth century.

63. *SC,* 6 Jan. 1906, p. 8; *RH,* 13 Feb. 1913, p. 11; Maclachlan, "Inside of the Cup," Maclachlan Papers; *CP,* 13 Aug. 1903, p. 10; *CP,* 30 Jan. 1907, p. 101.

64. *BRCA,* 28 June 1906, p. 5; *RH,* 21 May 1908, p. 12; *RH,* 19 May 1927, p. 9; *Richmond Labor Herald,* 8 Apr. 1927, p. 1. In a classic study, *Millhands and Preachers: A Study of Gastonia* (New Haven, Conn.: Yale University Press, 1942; reprint, 1965), Liston Pope portrayed ministers as often ignorant of conditions, grateful for financial support of mill owners, preoccupied with eternal salvation to the exclusion of temporal matters, and unwilling to criticize or challenge the industrialists. By contrast, the Appeal of 1927 attributed some of the destitution of mill villages to an absence of churches and religious leaders.

65. Walter L. Lingle to J. E. Edgerton, 4 May 1927, Lingle Papers; H. D. C. Maclachlan, "Types and Ideals of Hebrew Prophecy," chap. 7, 5, in the Maclachlan Papers; *RCA,* 3 May 1928, p. 7; *SC,* 30 July 1927, p. 10; *RNL,* 2 May 1927, p. 8; *RCA,* 21 Nov. 1929, p. 3; *RNL,* 6 Apr. 1929, p. 8.

66. Maclachlan, "An Old Text in a New Setting," and "The Inside of the Cup," Maclachlan Papers; *RH,* 28 Mar. 1912, p. 10; *BRCA,* 14 Jan. 1915, p. 2; *BRCA,* 27 June 1912, p. 3; H. D. C. *BRCA,* 26 Aug. 1915, p. 2; *BRCA,* 29 Jan. 1914, p. 3; *RH,* 17 July 1908, p. 9; *SC,* 15 Feb. 1919, p. 4; *CP,* 5 Dec. 1906, p. 868; Lingle, *The Bible and Social Problems,* 86; *SC,* 21 July 1923, p. 7; *RCA,* 3 June 1926, p. 3; *RTD,* 4 Nov. 1913, p. 3; *BRCA,* 3 Feb. 1910, p. 1; *CP,* 7 Aug. 1901, p. 8; *CP,* 22 July 1903, p. 480; *RCA,* 2 Oct. 1919, p. 2. As a result, several ministers seized upon the idea of profit sharing as the best way of obtaining justice and industrial harmony.

67. *RH,* 25 June 1903, p. 1; *RTD,* 24 May 1903, p. B4; *RTD,* 31 May–7 Aug. 1903; *RTD,* 24 Aug. 1903, p. 1; *RNL,* 17 Jan. 1922, pp. 1, 17; Thomas J. Headlee, "The Richmond Transit Strike of 1903" (master's thesis, University of Richmond, 1960); W. Asbury Christian, *Richmond: Her Past and Present* (Richmond: L. H. Jenkins, 1912), 489–90; *RTD,* 24 June 1903, p. 1; *RTD,* 30 June 1903, p. 1; *RTD,* 23 June 1903, pp. 2, 3; *RNL,* 17 Jan. 1922, pp. 1, 7.

68. *RCA,* 26 Jan. 1922, p. 3; *RNL,* 17 Jan.–5 Apr. 1922; *Labor Journal,* Jan.–Apr. 1922; *RTD,* 9 Jan. 1922, pp. 1, 4; *RTD,* 23 Jan. 1922, p. 3; *RTD,* 30 Jan. 1922, p. 1; *RNL,* 5 Apr. 1922, p. 4; *RNL,* 31 Aug. 1922, p. 10. Traction company officials apparently wanted to use the wage dispute as a vehicle for negotiating a more favorable franchise with the city. Despite the strike, Richmond's city council refused to renegotiate the contract. *PS,* 1 Nov. 1916, p. 2; *RCA,* 10 Oct. 1922, p. 2; *RH,* 25 June 1903, p. 1; *RH,* 2 July 1903, p. 1; *CP,* 22 July 1903, p. 480; *RH,* 10 Aug. 1922 p. 5; *RCA,* 2 Oct. 1919, p. 2.

69. *PS,* 25 Aug. 1915, p. 1; Baptist Council of Richmond, "Minutes of the Executive Committee, 1903–1929," meeting of 25 Apr. 1921, Virginia Baptist Historical Society, Richmond; *RTD,* 8 Aug. 1907, p. 10; *RTD,* 26 Apr. 1911, p. 10; *RNL,* 29 Mar. 1916, p. 6.

70. *RT,* 1 Apr. 1900, p. 7; *SC,* 26 Jan. 1918, p. 8; Lucy Randolph Mason, *To Win These Rights,* 4; Salmond, *Miss Lucy of the CIO,* 6, 7–22. During this period, Mason upset Florence Kelley by rejecting an offer to serve as general secretary of the National Consumer's League.

71. Lucy Randolph Mason, *The Shorter Day and Women Workers* (Richmond: Virginia League of Women Voters, 1922), 25; Elizabeth Stevens Brinson, "'Helping Others to Help Themselves'": Social Advocacy and Wage-Earning Women in Richmond, Virginia, 1910–1932" (Ph.D. diss., Union Graduate School of the Union for Experimenting Colleges and Universities, 1984), 97–99; *RTD,* 29 June 1910, p. 10; *RNL,* 1 Feb 1916, p. 13; *SC,* 1 June 1918, p. 13; *League Record,* July 1916, p. 3; *PS,* 25 Aug. 1915, p. 1; *SC,* 14 Apr. 1923, p. 11; *Labor Journal,* 24 Feb. 1922, p. 1.

72. *RNL,* 19 Feb. 1929, p. 8; *RNL,* 1 Mar. 1929, p. 1; Orie Latham Hatcher, *Occupations for Women: A Study Made for the Southern Woman's Educational Alliance* (Richmond: Southern Woman's Educational Alliance, 1927), 164, 211–12.

73. *PS,* 4 Mar. 1925, p. 3; H. D. C. Maclachlan, "Studies in Sin: the Sin of Duress," *Christian Century,* 14 June 1923, pp. 747–49. For similar views see, *SC,* 4 Dec. 1920, p. 2; *RCA,* 26 Aug. 1926, p. 2; *RCA,* 10 Aug. 1922, p. 2. Cecil, like most Richmond ministers, believed that the compelling spirit of Christian love would guide a devout person to take the morally correct action and that actions of force and fear carried a person away from that spirit. See Russell Cecil, *The Religion of Love* (Richmond: Presbyterian Committee of Publication, 1924), 54–60.

74. W. L. Carson, "The Only Cure for the World's Ills," sermon, First Presbyterian, 25 May 1924, Walter L. Carson Papers, Presbyterian Historical Society, Montreat, N.C.; Maclachlan "The Church at School," Maclachlan Papers; Lingle, "The Teaching of Jesus and Modern Social Problems," 200; *RH,* 16 May 1912, p. 10. Bowie, "Half Live and Whole Life," 17, makes the same argument as Maclachlan and Lingle. In memoirs, *Learning to Live,* 97, Bowie supplies an example of a local businessman's reluctance to consider matters other than profits.

75. For her career, see Mason, *To Win These Rights,* and John Salmond's biography, *Miss Lucy of the CIO.*

9. Not Brothers or Sisters

1. *RH,* 7 May 1914, p. 8.

2. U.S. Department of Commerce, Bureau of the Census, *Census of Religious Bodies: 1926* (Washington, D.C.: GPO, 1930), 1:523–24; Ulrich Troubetzkoy, *Richmond, City of Churches: A Short History of Richmond's Denominations and Faiths* (Richmond: Whittet & Shepperson, 1957), 32–34; Virginius Dabney, *Richmond: The Story of a City,* rev. ed. (Charlottesville: University Press of Virginia, 1990), 83; Myron Berman, *Richmond's Jewry, 1769–1976: Shabbat in Shockoe* (Charlottesville: University Press of Virginia, 1979).

3. *RNL,* 1 Mar. 1924, p. 4; *RTD,* 24, Sept. 1911, p. 10; Berman, *Richmond's Jewry,* 241–71.

4. *RTD,* 2 Jan. 1909, p. 1; *RTD,* 20 Feb. 1909, p. 10; *RTD,* 6 Feb. 1904, p. 3; *RTD,* 17 Mar. 1906, p. 1; *RTD,* 15 Mar. 1909, p. 10; *RTD,* 4 Mar. 1922, p. 1.

5. *PS,* 1 Jan. 1913, p. 11; *SC,* 26 Oct. 1907, p. 11; Petition of legislative committee in

support of Senate bill number 230 signed by alumni of the University of Virginia in the Mary Cooke-Branch Munford Papers, Archives Research Services, Library of Virginia, Richmond.

6. George W. McDaniel, *Churches of the New Testament* (Nashville: Sunday School Board of the Southern Baptist Convention, 1921), 72; *RH,* 2 June 1927, p. 15; *RTD,* 31 May 1903, p. A4.

7. *Friendly Church Messenger,* 22 Oct. 1922, p. 1; *Friendly Church Messenger,* 10 Dec. 1922, p. 1; *CC,* Oct. 1927, p. 4; *RT,* 30 Nov. 1900, p. 5; *RTD,* 2 June 1903, p. 8; Edward N. Calisch to George W. McDaniel, 11 Feb. 1913, McDaniel Papers, Virginia Baptist Historical Society, Richmond; *RTD,* 15 Sept. 1913, p. 1. Douglass S. McDaniel, *George White McDaniel* (Nashville: Sunday School Board of the Southern Baptist Convention, 1928), 162; *Friendly Church Messenger,* 11 May 1924, p. 1; Temple Ahabah program, 15 Feb. 1923, John J. Scherer Jr. Papers, personal possession, Mary Grace Scherer Taylor, Richmond.

8. *RTD,* 15 Sept. 1913, pp. 1, 6; Berman, *Richmond's Jewry,* 255; *RTD,* 1 Feb. 1913, p. 3; *RNL,* 18 June 1920, p. 1; *RTD,* 10 May 1910, p. 10; *RH,* 24 June 1920, p. 10.

9. W. L. Carson, "The Neighborhood's Responsibility for the Sin of the Individual," 8 July 1923 in the Walter L. Carson Papers, Presbyterian Historical Society, Montreat, N.C.; *RTD,* 12 Mar. 1910, p. 12; McDaniel, *Churches of the New Testament,* 212; Berman, *Richmond's Jewry,* 246, concludes that "overt manifestations of anti-Semitism in Richmond were minuscule when compared to many areas in the North." James Branch Cabell, *Let Me Lie* (New York: Farrar, Straus, & Co., 1947), 218. In *Antisemitism in America* (New York: Oxford University Press, 1994), 177, Leonard Dinnerstein argues that "the almost total acculturation of Jews in the South allowed them to maintain a facile cordiality with Gentiles, even though just beneath the surface lay a bed of prejudice ever ready to label Jews as Christ-killers and Shylocks." Experiences in early-twentieth-century Richmond essentially support that conclusion. Noting southern ambivalence about Jews, David Goldfield points to expressions of warmth and perpetuation of crude stereotypes. *Region, Race and Cities: Interpreting the Urban South* (Baton Rouge: Louisiana State University Press, 1997), 146–47. See also John Higham, *Strangers in the Land: Patterns of American Nativism, 1860–1925* (New Brunswick, N.J.: Rutgers University Press, 1955; reprint, New York: Atheneum, 1971), 26–27, 66–67, 92–95, 160–61, 185–86, 277–86.

10. *RH,* 24 Apr. 1902, p. 7; *RH,* 11 June 1903, p. 2; *CP,* 24 Jan. 1900, p. 8; *BRCA,* 7 Mar. 1907, p. 4; *PS,* 22 Sept. 1915, p. 1; *Union Seminary Magazine* 23, no. 2 (Dec./Jan. 1911/1912): 173; Richmond Ministerial Union, "Minutes of the Meetings, 1919–1928," meeting of 12 Jan. 1920, p. 5, Richmond Public Library; *RCA,* 7 June 1923, p. 2.

11. U.S. Department of Commerce and Labor, Bureau of the Census, *Census of Religious Bodies: 1906* (Washington, D.C.: GPO, 1910), 1:484–85; Troubetzkoy, *Richmond, City of Churches,* 24–30; Raymond H. Schmandt, "An Overview of Institutional Establishments in the Antebellum Southern Church," in *Catholics in the Old South: Essays on Church and Culture,* ed. Randall M. Miller and Jon L. Wakelyn (Macon, Ga: Mercer University Press, 1983), 60–62, and Jon L. Wakelyn, "Catholic Elites in the Slaveholding South," *Catholics in the Old South,* 220–21; John G. Zehmer, *Old Richmond Today* (Richmond: Historic Richmond Foundation, 1988), 53, 88–90; Drew St. J. Carneal, *Richmond's Fan District* (Richmond: Historic Richmond Foundation, 1996), 91–93; Dabney, *Richmond,* 273, 309; *RTD,* 28 Oct. 1906, pp. 1, 3, 10; *RTD,* 30 Nov. 1906, p. A3.

12. *RNL,* 30 June 1919, p. 4; John A. Cutchins, *Memories of Old Richmond (1881–1944)* (Verona, Va.: McClure Press, 1973), 45; *RTD,* 17 Oct. 1911, p. 4; *RTD,* 17 Aug. 1911, p. 1;

Committees of St. Peter's and St. Paul's churches to Rev. J. J. Gravatt, 11 May 1911, Papers of Grace and Holy Trinity Episcopal Church, Virginia Historical Society, Richmond; *RNL,* 30 June 1920, p. 4; *RTD,* 8 Apr. 1911, p. 4; *SC,* 14 Dec. 1918, p. 13.

13. *RTD,* 16 June 1903, p. 5; *RH,* 22 Feb. 1917, p. 14; *RH,* 11 June 1903, p. 9; *RH,* 18 Nov. 1918, p. 10; *SC,* 17 Nov. 1900, p. 1. James Cannon cited a 1928 papal encyclical as evidence that the Catholic church still viewed Protestants as heretics. James Cannon Jr., *Bishop Cannon's Own Story: Life As I Have Seen It,* ed. Richard L. Watson (Durham, N.C.: Duke University Press, 1955), 391–94.

14. *RH,* 4 Mar. 1909, p. 12; *RH,* 5 Mar. 1908, p. 10; *RH,* 9 June 1921, p. 7. In *Immigrants, Baptists, and the Protestant Mind in America* (Urbana: University of Illinois Press, 1973), Lawrence B. Davis concludes that Northern Baptists began to abandon their nativist sentiment for a more tolerant set of attitudes in the early twentieth century.

15. *SC,* 4 Oct. 1902, p. 1; *RT,* 14 May 1901, p. 6; *RTD,* 18 Nov. 1904, p. 1; *RH,* 16 May 1901, p. 5; *RH,* 10 Mar. 1921, p. 10; *PS,* 26 Feb. 1913, p. 10; *PS,* 5 Feb. 1908, p. 124.

16. *BRCA,* 28 Mar. 1901, p. 1; *PS,* 2 Apr. 1913, p. 9; James B. Hawthorne, *The Cloud of Witnesses and Other Sermons* (Nashville: Sunday School Board of the Southern Baptist Convention, 1908), 240–41; *RH,* 22 July 1926, p. 2. For other examples, see *BRCA,* 24 Apr. 1902, p. 1; *PS,* 5 Dec. 1927, p. 2; *PS,* 13 Apr. 1927, p. 2; *PS,* 21 July 1915, p. 4; *PS,* 7 July 1926, pp. 2, 3.

17. Hawthorne, *Cloud of Witnesses,* 240; *RH,* 5 Sept. 1912, p. 4; *RH,* 19 Feb. 1914, pp. 4–5; Juan Orts Gonzalez, *Why I Am a Protestant* (Richmond: Presbyterian Committee of Publication, 1913); Juan Orts Gonzalez, "Certain Phases of Protestant Mission Work among Spaniards," *Union Seminary Magazine* 21, no. 3 (Feb.–Mar. 1907): 230–40; *BRCA,* 14 Apr. 1921, p. 2; *PS,* 18 Feb. 1925, p. 2; *BRCA,* 23 Apr. 1914, p. 3; *PS,* 25 Nov. 1925, p. 2.

18. David Burner, *The Politics of Provincialism: The Democratic Party in Transition, 1918–1932* (New York: Alfred A. Knopf, 1968), 179–216. Failing in 1928, Al Smith did attract urban, Catholic immigrant voters to the Democratic Party and thereby set the stage for Franklin D. Roosevelt's presidential victory in 1932, as Samuel Lubell details in *The Future of American Politics,* 3d ed. (New York: Harper & Row, 1965), 48–63.

19. Cannon, *Bishop Cannon's Own Story,* 407. For Cannon's personal account of the campaign, see *Bishop Cannon's Own Story,* 390–447. Virginius Dabney, *Dry Messiah: The Life of Bishop Cannon* (New York: Alfred A. Knopf, 1949; reprint, Westport, Conn.: Greenwood Press, 1970), 173–89; John Stanley Hopewell, "An Outsider Looking In: John Garland Pollard and Machine Politics in Twentieth Century Virginia" (Ph.D. diss., Univ. of Virginia, 1976), 122–43. *RNL,* 28 May 1928, p. 8; Walter L. Lingle to Leon Westmoreland, 24 Sept. 1928, Lingle Papers, Presbyterian Historical Society, Montreat, N.C.

20. *RCA,* 24 Apr. 1924, p. 6; *PS,* 9 July 1924, p. 2; *RCA,* 1 Oct. 1925, p. 2; *RH,* 23 July 1926, p. 4. In *Politics of Provincialism,* 206–10, Burner argues that Smith failed to take reasonable steps to defuse Protestant fears. James H. Smylie, "The Roman Catholic Church, the State, and Al Smith," *Church History* 29 (Sept. 1960): 321–43, presents information about the basis of some Protestant fears. For additional analysis of anti-Catholic attitudes among Southern Baptists, see James J. Thompson Jr., *Tried As By Fire: Southern Baptist and the Religious Controversies of the 1920s* (Macon, Ga.: Mercer University Press, 1982), 180–94.

21. Burner, *Politics of Provincialism,* 185, 207; *RH,* 15 July 1926, pp. 4–5; *RH,* 24 June 1926, p. 10.

22. *PS,* 29 Feb. 1928, p. 2; *RNL,* 2 July 1928, p. 25; *RCA,* 23 Sept. 1926, p. 2. The basis for Lingle's concerns can be found in Seminary Professor, *Manual of Christian Doctrine,* 49th ed. (Philadelphia: J. J. McVey, 1929,), 115–18, 129–33.

23. *RNL,* 15 Aug. 1928, p. 8; Hopewell, "An Outsider Looking In," 122, 131, 139; *RNL,* 18 July 1928, p. 1; *RNL,* 25 May 1928, p. 8; *RNL,* 8 Aug. 1928, p. 8; *RCA,* 14 June 1923, p. 2; *RH,* 20 Jan. 1927, p. 10; *RH,* 26 July 1928, p. 14; *Friendly Church Messenger,* 12 Feb. 1928, p. 4; Untitled news clipping, 25 Mar. 1928, Files of Seventh Street Christian Church, Richmond.

24. *J. L. Hill Printing Company's Directory of Richmond and Manchester, Virginia, 1900* (Richmond: Hill Printing Co., 1900), 1358–59; *Hill Directory Company's Richmond Classified Business Directory* (Richmond: Hill Printing Co., 1930), 1714–15; Bureau of the Census, *Census of Religious Bodies: 1926,* 1, 523–24; Ulrich Troubetzkoy, *Richmond, City of Churches,* 17–19, 22–24, 29; Garnett Ryland, *The Baptists of Virginia, 1699–1926* (Richmond: Baptist Board of Missions and Education, 1955), 303–5, 314–16, 329–31; Writers Program, Work Project Administration, *The Negro in Virginia* (New York: Hastings House, 1940; reprint, Winston-Salem: John F. Blair. 1994), 274–78; *RTD,* 18 Nov. 1904, p. 2; *RTD,* 10 Nov. 1903, p. 12.

25. [Committee on Seventeenth Street Colored Mission] to Rev. S. L. Morris, 1 May 1914 in Lingle Papers; *PS,* 6 July 1927, p. 2; *PS,* 21 Apr. 1915, p. 9; *PS,* 26 Apr. 1915, p. 11; Cothran G. Smith, "The Seventeenth Street Mission," *Union Seminary Review* 33, no. 4 (July 1922): 317–26.

26. *PS,* 8 July 1914, p. 14; *PS,* 6 July 1927, p. 2; *PS,* 28 Apr. 1915, p. 11; *PS,* 6 June 1917, p. 8; Smith, "Seventeenth Street Mission," 317–26; "Report to East Hanover Presbytery, Spring Meeting, 1915, By Committee on Seventeenth Street Colored Mission," Lingle Papers; Robert Wray "Seventeenth Street Mission Report, July 1926," Lingle Papers; Robert Wray, "Seventeenth Street Mission, May 1928 Report," Lingle Papers.

27. Robert Wray to Walter L. Lingle, 11 June 1928, Lingle Papers.

28. *SC,* 18 Jan. 1919, p. 1; *SC,* 23 May 1914, p. 3; *SC,* 30 May 1914, p. 3; *SC,* 16 May 1914, p. 3; *SC,* 3 Oct. 1903, p. 5; *Journal of a Special Council of the Protestant Episcopal Church in the Diocese of Virginia* (Richmond: Whittet & Shepperson, printers, 1911), 240–41, 251–54.

29. James Thayer Addison, *The Episcopal Church in the United States, 1789–1931* (New York: Charles Scribner's Sons, 1951), 296–97, 344; *RTD,* 5 Oct. 1907, p. 3; *RTD,* 19 Oct. 1907, pp. 1–2. For an excellent analysis of this intricate episode, see Gardiner H. Shattuck Jr., *Episcopalians and Race: Civil War to Civil Rights* (Lexington: University Press of Kentucky, 2000), 22–26.

30. *RCA,* 24 July 1919, p. 2; Richmond Preachers Meeting, "Minutes of the Meetings, 19," meeting of 27 Oct. 1919, p. 182, Special Collections and Archives, McGraw-Page Library, Randolph-Macon College, Ashland, Va.; Robert Watson Sledge, *Hands on the Ark: The Struggle for Change in the Methodist Episcopal Church, South, 1914–1939* (Lake Junaluska, N.C.: Commission on Archives and History, United Methodist Church, 1975), 90–123; *RNL,* 5 Mar. 1920, p. 18; *RCA,* 29 Oct. 1925, p. 21; *RNL,* 15 Oct. 1925, p. 1.

31. Wyndam B. Blanton, *The Making of a Downtown Church: The History of Second Presbyterian Church, Richmond, Virginia, 1845–1945* (Richmond: John Knox Press, 1945), 310–16, quotation, 315; *RT,* 4 Apr. 1901, p. 4; Douglass S. McDaniel, *George White McDaniel,* 134–39, 221–22; *PS,* 22 Apr. 1925, p. 1.

32. Presbyterian Ministers Association of Richmond and Vicinity, "Minutes of the Meetings, 1900–1928," meetings of 22 Jan. 1900, p. 6; 5 Feb. 1900, p. 11; and 17 Dec. 1900, p. 39; William Smith Morton Library, Union Theological Seminary/Presbyterian School of Christian Education, Richmond; Richmond Preachers Meeting, "Minutes of the Meetings, 1900–1928," meeting of 6 Apr. 1914, p. 294, and undated resolution following the minutes of 10 Apr. 1911; *RTD,* 5 June 1914, p. 1; *RCA,* 21 Apr. 1927, p. 10; Baptist Council of Richmond, "Annual Report, 1925," Virginia Baptist Historical Society, Richmond; Richmond Ministe-

rial Union, "Minutes of the Meetings, 1919–1928," meetings of 16 Dec. 1920, p. 29; 11 Mar. 1921, p. 41; and 14 Mar. 1921, p. 42; Richmond Public Library.

33. C. Vann Woodward, *The Strange Career of Jim Crow,* 3d ed. (New York: Oxford University Press, 1974), 67–116; I. A. Newby, *Jim Crow's Defense: Anti-Negro Thought in America, 1900–1930* (Baton Rouge: Louisiana State University Press, 1965), 7, 19–51, 83–109; H. Shelton Smith, *In His Image, but . . . : Racism in Southern Religion, 1780–1910* (Durham, N.C.: Duke University Press, 1972), 260–305; Joel Williamson, *The Crucible of Race: Black-White Relations in the American South Since Emancipation* (New York: Oxford University Press, 1984), 6, 111–258; J. Morgan Kousser, *The Shaping of Southern Politics: Suffrage Restrictions and the Establishment of the One-Party South, 1880–1910* (New Haven, Conn.: Yale University Press, 1974); Rayford W. Logan, *The Negro in American Life and Thought: The Nadir, 1877–1901* (New York: Dial Press, 1954), 52, 97–116; George M. Fredrickson, *The Black Image in the White Mind: The Debate on Afro-American Character and Destiny, 1817–1914* (New York: Harper & Row, 1971), 256–82; C. Vann Woodward, *Origins of the New South, 1877–1913* (Baton Rouge: Louisiana State University Press, 1951), 321–68; George B. Tindall, *The Emergence of the New South, 1913–1945* (Baton Rouge: Louisiana State University Press, 1967), 143–96; Neil R. McMillen, *Dark Journey: Black Mississippians in the Age of Jim Crow* (Urbana: University of Illinois Press, 1990), 4–8, 41–70; Jack Temple Kirby, *Darkness at the Dawning: Race and Reform in the Progressive South* (Philadelphia: J. B. Lippincott, 1972), 8–24; Grace Elizabeth Hale, *Making Whiteness: The Cultures of Segregation in the South, 1890–1940* (New York: Pantheon Books, 1998). As John Hope Franklin and Alfred A. Moss Jr. write in *From Slavery to Freedom: A History of Negro Americans,* 40th anniv. ed. (New York: Alfred A. Knopf, 1988), 238, "the law, the courts, the schools, and almost every institution in the South favored whites. This was white supremacy."

34. June Purcell Guild, *Black Laws of Virginia: A Summary of the Legislative Acts of Virginia Concerning Negroes from Earliest Times to the Present* (Richmond: Whittet & Shepperson, 1936), 145–48, 181–84; Allen W. Moger, *Virginia: Bourbonism to Byrd, 1870–1925* (Charlottesville: University Press of Virginia, 1968), 188–95; Raymond H. Pulley, *Old Virginia Restored: An Interpretation of the Progressive Impulse, 1870–1930* (Charlottesville: University Press of Virginia, 1968), 66–91; Writers Program, WPA, *The Negro in Virginia,* 262–69; *RT,* 1 July 1900, p. 6.

35. *RTD,* 11 July 1903, p. 4; *RTD,* 15 Jan. 1903, p. 1; *RT,* 3 Apr. 1900, p. 4; *RT,* 8 June 1900, p. 6; *SC,* 10 Mar. 1900, p. 8; *RTD,* 7 Jan. 1911, p. 10. For an example of Crutchfield's behavior, see *Richmond Times,* 2 June 1900, p. 5. Unlike the *Southern Churchman,* the *Central Presbyterian,* 11 Mar. 1900, p. 8, praised Barringer's assessment of blacks.

36. *BRCA,* 10 Dec. 1903, p. 4; *BRCA,* 17 Dec. 1903, p. 1; *BRCA,* 18 Dec. 1902, p. 1; John J. Lafferty, *Sketches and Portraits of the Virginia Conference: Twentieth Century Edition* (Richmond: n.p., 1901), 417–21.

37. *RH,* 10 Dec. 1903, p. 8; Thomas Cary Johnson, "The Presbyterian Church in the United States," *Union Seminary Magazine* 11, no. 4 (Apr.–May 1900): 291f; D. Clay Lilly, "The Attitude of the South to the Colored People," *Union Seminary Magazine* 16, no. 3 (Feb.–Mar. 1905): 270–71; *RH,* 6 Feb. 1902, p. 7.

38. *RH,* 15 Oct. 1903, p. 8; *RTD,* 3 Nov. 1903, p. 2; *RTD,* 24 May 1904, p. 12; *RH,* 28 Feb. 1901, p. 8; *RT,* 12 Sept. 1900, p. 4; Fredrickson, *Black Image in the White Mind,* 283.

39. *RH,* 28 Apr. 1904, pp. 2–3; *RH,* 27 Nov. 1902, p. 2; *RH,* 30 Mar. 1905, p. 8; *RTD,* 13 Mar. 1906, clipping in Samuel Chiles Mitchell Papers, Library of Congress; *RH,* 25 June 1903, p. 1; *RTD,* 24 May 1904, p. 12.

40. *RTD,* 28 Apr. 1903, p. 9; *BRCA,* 26 May 1904, p. 1; *RH,* 28 Feb. 1901, p. 8; *CP,* 11 Feb. 1903, p. 88; "Home Mission Report," *Minutes of the One Hundred and Nineteenth Annual Meeting of the Dover Baptist Association* (Richmond: J. L. Hill, 1902), 22–24 July 1902.

41. Lafferty quoted in *RT,* 7 Jan. 1900, p. 4; *RT,* 12 Sept. 1900, p. 4; *RH,* 1 Apr. 1909, p. 11; *RTD,* 7 Mar. 1906, p. 3.

42. *RTD,* 24 May, 1904, p. 12; *RH,* 27 Nov. 1902, p. 2; *SC,* 3 Feb. 1906, p. 8; *RT,* 12 Sept. 1900, p. 4; *RH,* 30 Mar. 1905, p. 8; *RH,* 18 July 1901, p. 8; *RH,* 28 Feb. 1901, p. 8; *SC,* 23 Nov. 1901, p. 8. The Richmond Protestant support for black schools stands in contrast to Southern racists who feared that educated blacks would be more independent and less subservient. See Neil R. McMillen, *Dark Journey,* 90–92.

43. Samuel Chiles Mitchell, "An Aftermath of Appamattox [*sic*]: A Memoir," (Atlanta: mimeographed, 1954), 74–75; *RT,* 27 Mar. 1900, p. 1; W. Fitzhugh Brundage, *Lynching in the New South: Georgia and Virginia, 1880–1930* (Urbana: University of Illinois Press, 1993), 178–79; John Carroll Presley, "Samuel Chiles Mitchell: A Biography of a Southern Educator" (Ph.D. diss., Univ. of Virginia, 1992), 60–62; *CP,* 28 Mar. 1900, p. 8; *CP,* 6 Nov. 1901, p. 4.

44. *RH,* 3 Nov. 1904, p. 9; *BRCA,* 24 Nov. 1904, p. 6; *CP,* 2 Nov. 1904, p. 724.

45. *SC,* 6 Oct. 1906, p. 1; *RH,* 8 Nov. 1906, p. 12; Mitchell, "An Aftermath," 212; Brundage, *Lynching in the New South,* 141; *RTD,* 30 Oct. 1914, pp. 1,7; *RTD,* 31 July 1912, p. 10; *RCA,* 8 Mar. 1928, p. 3; *RH,* 25 Oct. 1921, p. 10; *RCA,* 2 Sept. 1926, p. 3; *RNL,* 12 Mar. 1921, p. 4. In the 1890s twenty-seven African Americans were lynched in Virginia. The following decade that number fell to thirteen. Between 1910 and 1919 three blacks were lynched in Virginia, and in the 1920s six were lynched. Brundage, *Lynching in the New South,* 263. Some white southerners justified lynching as an appropriate response to rape, a crime which few lynching victims had committed. For an incisive but poignant assessment of this issue, see Jacquelyn Dowd Hall, *Revolt Against Chivalry: Jessie Daniel Ames and the Women's Campaign Against Lynching* (New York: Columbia University Press, 1979), 129–57.

46. *SC,* 20 Nov. 1920, p. 3; *RNL,* 29 July 1919, p. 4. In *The Great Crusade and After, 1914–1928* (New York: Macmillan, 1930), 306–14, Preston William Slosson stresses the Klan's anti-Catholicism but argues that the Klan's "chief source" of strength was its tendency to be "all things to all men." (308). John Higham's *Strangers in the Land,* 285–99, represents the Klan as initially attempting to intimidate blacks but shifting its emphasis to anti-Catholicism. In *Hooded Americanism: The History of the Ku Klux Klan* (New York: Doubleday & Co., 1965), 110, David M. Chalmers detects an early shift from an emphasis on white supremacy to nativism. In *The Emergence of the New South,* 187–96, George B. Tindall characterizes the Klan as a "paradoxical" movement with ill-defined goals but with nativism as its priority. In *The Ku Klux Klan in the City, 1915–1930* (New York: Oxford University Press, 1967), 26, Kenneth T. Jackson also argues that "the race issue" was not the Klan's "exclusive" nor its "predominant" reason for existence in the South. In *Behind the Mask of Chivalry: The Making of the Second Ku Klux Klan* (New York: Oxford University Press, 1994), Nancy MacLean highlights Klansmen's economic and cultural concerns. After examining the Klan's membership in Athens, Georgia, she provides a striking portrait of an organization which reacted across class lines.

47. *RNL,* 13 Nov. 1920, p. 4; *RTD,* 6 Dec. 1920, p. 1; *SC,* 24 Sept. 1921, p. 3; *RNL,* 19 Sept. 1921, p. 18; Jackson, *Ku Klux Klan in the City,* 5–27; MacLean, *Behind the Mask of Chivalry,* 3–5; Tindall, *Emergence of the New South,* 188–95. The *News Leader,* 16 Nov. 1920, p. 4, apologized for accepting the Klan's advertisement, acknowledged that the organization's very name aroused apprehensions, and promised to print no more Klan advertisements.

48. *SC,* 20 Nov. 1920, p. 3; *SC,* 30 July 1921, p. 6; *SC,* 11 Dec. 1920, p. 13; *RTD,* 19 Sept. 1921, p. 1; *SC,* 22 Oct. 1921, p. 11; *St. Luke's Herald,* 6 Jan. 1923, p. 2; *RNL,* 4 Dec. 1920, p. 2; newspaper clipping, 19 Sept. [1921] in Walter Russell Bowie Papers, Bishop Payne Library, Virginia Theological Seminary, Alexandria, Virginia; *RNL,* 22 Sept. 1924, p. 1; *SC,* 5 Mar. 1921, p. 13.

49. *RCA,* 29 Sept. 1921, p. 7; *RCA,* 16 June 1921, p. 4; *RCA,* 1 Feb. 1922, p. 3; *RCA,* 26 July 1922, p. 3; *SC,* 5 Mar. 1921, p. 13; *SC,* 11 Dec. 1920, p. 13; *PS,* 22 Dec. 1920, p. 1.

50. *RNL,* 19 Aug. 1924, p. 10; MacLean, *Behind the Mask of Chivalry,* 15; *RNL,* 19 Sept. 1921, p. 18; *RNL,* 5 July 1924, p. 4; *RNL,* 17 Sept. 1923, p. 4; Jackson, *Ku Klux Klan in the City,* 239; *RNL,* 14 Oct. 1922, p. 4; *RNL,* 21 Oct. 1922, p. 1. Only the pastor of Fairmont Avenue Baptist and Joseph Harker of East End Baptist publicly defended the Klan. He later established his own "people's church." See *RNL,* 11 Feb. 1929, p. 17 and *RNL,* 6 Aug. 1921, p. 1. In "A Note on the Relationship between the Protestant Churches and the Ku Klux Klan," Robert Moats Miller *Journal of Southern History* 32 (1956): 355–68, traces opposition to the Klan and concludes that "many Protestants" "found the courage to oppose the Klan." Still, the opposition of Richmond clergymen to the Klan did stand in contrast to the Klan's favorable reception by Baptists in Birmingham, as noted in J. Wayne Flynt, *Alabama Baptists: Southern Baptists in the Heart of Dixie* (Tuscaloosa: University of Alabama Press, 1998), 355.

51. *RCA,* 22 Dec. 1921, p. 6; *SC,* 3 Dec. 1921, p. 12; *PS,* 11 Jan. 1922, pp. 7, 13; *Friendly Church Messenger,* 20 Nov. 1921, p. 3; Tindall, *Emergence of the New South,* 177–79; Hall, *Revolt Against Chivalry,* 60–65, 89–106. Hall concludes that women's groups relied on persuasion and conciliation, remained subordinate to male committees and therefore had little impact. Mitchell, "An Aftermath," 212–13; See also Wilma Dykeman and James Stokely, *Seeds of Southern Change: The Life of Will Alexander* (Chicago: University of Chicago Press, 1962).

52. *RCA,* 11 Dec. 1924, p. 12; *RH,* 25 Dec. 1924, p. 15; Mitchell, "An Aftermath," 213–14; *RNL,* 7 Nov. 1924, p. 6; The author of *In Search of the Silent South: Southern Liberals and the Race Issue* (New York: Columbia University Press, 1977), 22, Mort Sosna, concludes that the CIC "began and remained more or less an expression of sentiment rather than an official group with carefully defined policies." He also provides an overview of the CIC, 22–41.

53. *RCA,* 4 Mar. 1926, p. 8; Guild, *Black Laws of Virginia,* 35–36; Richard B. Sherman, "'The Last Stand': The Fight for Racial Integrity in Virginia in the 1920s," *Journal of Southern History* 54, no. 1 (Feb. 1988): 69–92; Walter Russell Bowie, *Sunrise in the South: The Life of Mary-Cooke Branch Munford* (Richmond: William Byrd Press, 1942); *RNL,* 9 Feb. 1926, p. 1; *RTD,* 3 Mar. 1926, p. 13. Renewing agitation in 1928 and 1930, the Anglo-Saxon Clubs eventually gained another law designating as "colored" "every person in whom there is ascertainable any Negro blood." Guild, *Black Laws of Virginia,* 36.

54. *RTD,* 9 Jan. 1929, p. 1; *RNL,* 13 Dec. 1917, p. 1; Roger L. Rice, "Residential Segregation by Law, 1910–1917," *Journal of Southern History* 34 (May 1968): 179–99; Howard N. Rabinowitz, *Race Relations in the Urban South* (Urbana: University of Illinois Press, 1980), 105–15; Charles Louis Knight, *Negro Housing in Certain Virginia Cities* (Richmond: William Byrd Press, 1927), 35–53. As Christopher Silver notes, private covenants in deeds remained an effective device to stop the expansion of the African American population into white residential areas. Christopher Silver, *Twentieth-Century Richmond: Planning, Politics, and Race* (Knoxville: University of Tennessee Press, 1984), 109–13.

55. *RNL,* 31 Jan. 1929, p. 12; John A. Salmond, *Miss Lucy of the CIO: The Life and Times*

of Lucy Randolph Mason, 1882–1959 (Athens, Ga.: University of Georgia Press, 1988), 42; *RNL*, 12 Jan. 1929, p. 16; *RNL*, 14 Jan. 1929, p. 2; *RTD*, 14 Jan. 1929, p. 9; *RNL*, 28 Jan. 1929, p. 8; *RNL*, 1 Feb. 1929, p. 1; *RTD*, 14 Jan. 1929, p. 8; *RTD*, 11 Feb. 1929, p. 9; *RTD*, 13 Feb. 1929, p. 1; *RNL*, 5 Feb. 1929, p. 8; Silver, *Twentieth-Century Richmond*, 112.

56. *RCA*, 7 Feb. 1929, p. 3; Salmond, *Miss Lucy of the CIO*, 42; *RNL*, 15 Jan. 1929, p. 20; *RNL*, 5 Feb. 1929, p. 8; *RNL*, 28 Jan. 1929, p. 17; *SC*, 2 Feb. 1929, p. 15. The Richmond press offered a similar critique. See *RTD*, 12 Jan. 1929, p. 8.

57. Negro Welfare Survey Committee, *The Negro in Richmond, Virginia* (Richmond: Richmond Council of Social Agencies, 1929), iii, 1–4, 8–15, 135–36, (quotation, 8).

58. Survey Committee, *Negro in Richmond*, 6.

59. Ibid., 103–31; quotations, 102–3.

60. Maria Williams Sheerin, *The Parson Takes a Wife* (New York: Macmillan, 1948), 98–103; quotation, 100; Lucy Randolph Mason, *To Win These Rights: A Personal Story of the CIO in the South* (New York: Harper, 1952), 8; June Purcell Guild, "Black Richmond," *Survey Graphic* (June 1934): 276–78; quotation, 276; *RNL*, 23 Dec. 1929, p. 1.

61. *SC*, 16 Oct. 1926, p. 13; *RNL*, 14 June 1929, p. 29; Sheerin, *The Parson Takes a Wife*, 6. In *American Protestantism and Social Issues, 1919–1939* (Chapel Hill: University of North Carolina Press, 1958), 10, 296–313, Robert Moats Miller suggests that in the early twentieth century, few Protestants challenged the racial status quo but some later made significant contributions to improved race relations. In *Liberty and Justice for All: Racial Reform and the Social Gospel (1877–1925)* (New York: Harper & Row, 1990), Ronald C. White Jr. emphasizes Social Gospel clergymen, including southerners, who favored better treatment of African Americans. In *The Social Gospel in Black and White, American Racial Reform, 1885–1912* (Chapel Hill: University of North Carolina Press, 1991), Ralph E. Luker admits that proponents of social Christianity held a variety of racial views at the beginning of the twentieth century. But Luker, like White, perceives the Social Gospel leaders as charting a course that largely helped African Americans. In *Redeeming the South: Religious Cultures and Racial Identities among Southern Baptists, 1865–1925* (Chapel Hill: University of North Carolina Press, 1997), 231, Paul Harvey fairly contends that racial "liberalism" among white Baptists of the South amounted to racial conservatism. Still, anyone taking that stance played a constructive role by resisting some of the reactionary currents within the region and the nation.

10. "A World Made New"

1. *SC*, 21 Apr. 1917, pp. 4, 12; *RNL*, 10 Nov. 1925, p. 13. The Great War brought an "end of innocence" to Richmond Protestants just as it did to the entire nation, according to Henry May. The war, he has argued, completed the destruction of the nation's flawed prewar sense of optimism. Henry F. May, *The End of American Innocence: A Study of the First Years of Our Own Time, 1912–1917* (New York: Alfred A. Knopf, 1959), ix–xiv, 332–34, 393–97. Somewhat submerged in Robert E. Osgood's massive *Ideals and Self-Interest in America's Foreign Relations: The Great Transformation of the Twentieth Century* (Chicago: University of Chicago Press, 1953), 322, is the observation that in the 1920s "idealism remained a strong force in the American attitude toward international relations." The Richmond experience supports that conclusion. Sources about the role of churches in World War I are limited. In *American Churches in World War I* (Athens: Ohio University Press, 1985), 1, John Piper ob-

serves that "most historians of the churches in the era of the Great War have worked around the war itself." Piper focuses on national organizations created by churches, not activities in communities. Ray H. Abrams, *Preachers Present Arms: A Study of the War-Time Attitudes and Activities of the Churches and the Clergy in the United States, 1914–1918* (New York: Round Table Press, 1933) discusses episodes throughout the nation but provides scant attention to the South. David M. Kennedy, *Over Here: The First World War and American Society* (New York: Oxford University Press, 1980), and Ronald Schaffer, *America in the Great War: The Rise of the War Welfare State* (New York: Oxford University Press, 1991) do not include churches in their otherwise excellent portrayals.

2. *PS,* 23 Jan. 1918, pp. 1–2; *PS,* 25 Mar. 1914, p. 17; *RCA,* 7 June 1900, p. 1; *BRCA,* 11 Apr. 1907, p. 2.

3. William R. Estep, *Whole Gospel—Whole World: The Foreign Mission Board of the Southern Baptist Convention, 1845–1995* (Nashville: Broadman & Holman, 1994), 159–86, 205, quotation, 178. As Estep notes, Richmond's J. B. Hutson served on the board for thirty-five years, and William Ellyson served for twenty-eight years. Elizabeth W. Willingham, *The Life of Robert Josiah Willingham* (Nashville: Sunday School Board of the Southern Baptist Convention, 1917), 216–19.

4. *Christian Monthly,* Dec. 1901, p. 12; Annie Florence Weeks, *Grace Baptist Church, Richmond, 1833–1958* (Richmond: Garrett & Massie, 1958), 116; *BRCA,* 9 July 1908, p. 17; *RH,* 1 Feb. 1912, p. 5; Blanche Sydnor White, *A Century of Service: A History of Bainbridge Street Baptist Church, 1857–1957* (Richmond: Whittet & Shepperson, 1957), 94; Jack Abernathy, *Living Monuments: The Story of Grace Covenant Presbyterian Church, Richmond, Virginia, 1790–1990* (Richmond: Grace Covenant Church, 1989), 114; *CP,* 21 Mar. 1900, p. 4; *CP,* 28 Feb. 1906, p. 129; *PS,* 16 Nov. 1927, p. 8.

5. Frederick Jarrard Anderson, *Hearts and Hands, Gathering Up the Years: An Illustrated History of Woman's Missionary Union of Virginia, 1874–1988* (Richmond: Woman's Missionary Union of Virginia, 1990), 14–24; *Christian Monthly,* Dec. 1901, p. 2; Woman's Missionary Union, Presbytery of East Hanover, "Minutes of Woman's Work in East Hanover Presbytery, Volume 2, 1889–1918," Mar. 27–29, 1912, pp. 4–8, William Smith Morton Library, Union Theological Seminary/Presbyterian School of Christian Education, Richmond; Edith Denny White, *The Elect Ladies of Centenary: The Story of the Organization and Development of Women's Work in Centenary Methodist Church, Richmond, Virginia, 1810–1960* (n.p., 1964), 41–64; William C. James, *Leigh Street Baptist Church, 1854–1954: A Brief History of Its First One Hundred Years in the Service of Christ* (Richmond: Whittet & Shepperson, [1955]), 107.

6. Woman's Mission Union, Presbytery of East Hanover, "Minutes of Woman's Work," meeting 19–21 Apr. 1916, pp. 8–9; J. Gray McAllister, *The Life and Letters of Walter W. Moore* (Richmond: Union Theological Seminary, 1939), 501–4, 444–45; Woman's Foreign Missionary Union, Presbytery of East Hanover, "Minutes of Woman's Work," meeting 5 Apr. 1905.

7. Woman's Foreign Missionary Union, East Hanover Presbytery, "Minutes of Woman's Work," meeting 4 Apr. 1905, p. 2; *RH,* 10 Dec. 1914, p. 12; *BRCA,* 14 Apr. 1907, p. 7.

8. *RH,* 5 Aug. 1909, p. 10; *CP,* 11 Dec. 1907, p. 1137; *CP,* 6 Nov. 1907, p. 1076; *CP,* 27 Feb. 1907, p. 196.

9. *BRCA,* 4 Nov. 1909, p. 4; *SC,* 30 Oct. 1909, pp. 12–13; *PS,* 22 Dec. 1909, p. 22; *RH,* 16 Dec. 1909, p. 5; Willingham, *Willingham,* 162–64, 188; "Men's Missionary Meeting" program, Sunday, 12 Dec. 1909, Papers of First English Evangelical Lutheran Church, First Lutheran, Richmond, Virginia.

10. *SC,* 9 Apr. 1910, p. 8; *BRCA,* 26 Feb. 1914, p. 14; St. John's Minute Book, 4 Jan. 1910, Papers of St. John's Episcopal Church, Virginia Historical Society; *PS,* 8 Apr. 1914, p. 14; Seventh Street Christian Church Minute Book, 10 Jan. 1909 and 14 Jan. 1912, Papers of Seventh Street Church, Virginia State Historical Society; *RH,* 17 Apr. 1913, p. 16; *SC,* 4 Feb. 1911, p. 13; *PS,* 2 Apr. 1913, p. 302; *SC,* 26 Feb. 1916, p. 8.

11. *RTD,* 27 Jan. 1904, p. 4; *RTD,* 2 June 1903, p. 8; *CP,* 15 Nov. 1905, p. 753; *BRCA,* 22 Sept. 1904, p. 1; *CP,* 28 Sept. 1904, p. 644.

12. *PS,* 9 Jan. 1929, pp. 2–4; *Beacon on a Hill: A Brief History of One Hundred Years of Christian Service, 1855–1955, Pine Street Baptist Church* (Richmond: Pine Street Baptist Church, 1955), 30; Ernest Trice Thompson, *Presbyterians in the South,* 3:243–44. For the arbitration movement, see Charles DeBenedetti, *The Peace Reform in America* (Bloomington: University of Indiana Press, 1980), 64–69, and C. Roland Marchand, *The American Peace Movement and Social Reform, 1898–1918* (Princeton, N.J.: Princeton University Press, 1972), 33–52. Some of the most useful information about the arbitration movement is sprinkled throughout the pioneering work, Merle Curti, *Peace or War: The American Struggle, 1636–1936* (New York: W. W. Norton & Co., 1936). For a concise overview of the peace movement, see the editor's introduction of Charles Chatfield, ed., *Peace Movements in America* (New York: Schocken Books, 1973), ix–xxxii.

13. *RTD,* 17 Dec. 1904, p. 1; *RH,* 29 Dec. 1904, p. 2. Still, Mitchell cautioned, in order to fulfill such a role, America would have to surmount materialism, sectional jealousies, class distinctions, and corporate power, as well as overcome racial, political, and economic injustices. *RH,* 16 Aug. 1906, p. 9; *CP,* 15 May 1907, p. 5; Presbyterian Ministers Association of Richmond, Virginia, "Minutes of Meetings, 1900–1928," meeting of 16 Mar. 1908, William Smith Morton Library, Union Theological Seminary/Presbyterian School of Christian Education, Richmond; *SC,* 5 Aug. 1911, p. 3; *RTD,* 23 Mar. 1908, p. 3; *RCA,* 11 Aug. 1907, p. 4; *CP,* 5 June 1907, p. 486.

14. *BRCA,* 25 Aug. 1910, p. 3.

15. Curti, *Peace or War,* 223–24; DeBendetti, *Peace Reform,* 88–89.

16. *BRCA,* 26 July 1906, p. 6; Walter Russell Bowie, *Learning to Live* (Nashville: Abingdon Press, 1969), 109; *RH,* 1 Jan. 1914, p. 3; DeBendetti, *Peace Reform,* 85–86. In *The American Peace Movement,* 323–80, Charles Marchand suggests that American religious leaders began to "discover" or "rediscover" the peace movement after 1910. For examples of prewar Richmond optimism, see *CP,* 28 Sept. 1904, p. 644 and *BRCA,* 11 Aug. 1910, p. 2.

17. *RNL,* 3 Aug. 1914, p. 4; *RNL,* 2 Jan. 1917, p. 4; *RNL,* 10 Apr. 1916, p. 1.

18. McAllister, *Walter W. Moore,* 473; *PS,* 18 Nov. 1916, p. 1; *SC,* 4 Dec. 1915, p. 12; *PS,* 2 June 1915, p. 17; *RNL,* 7 Nov. 1914, p. 1; *RNL,* 26 Nov. 1914, p. 10; *PS,* 18 Nov. 1916, p. 1.

19. Edward L. Pell, *What Did Jesus Really Teach About War?* (New York: Fleming H. Revell, 1917), 155; *SC,* 22 Aug. 1914, p. 3; *RH,* 3 Sept. 1914, p. 10; *BRCA,* 24 Sept. 1914, pp. 3–4. For examples of the themes of prayer and faith, see *SC,* 10 Oct. 1914, pp. 3–4; *PS,* 12 Aug. 1914, p. 11; *RH,* 17 Dec. 1914, p. 1.

20. *PS,* 16 Dec. 1914, p. 1; *BRCA,* 7 Sept. 1915, p. 4; *RNL,* 18 Nov. 1916, p. 2; *BRCA,* 11 Nov. 1915, p. 5. *BRCA,* 1 June 1916, p. 6; *SC,* 1 Jan. 1916, p. 13.

21. McAllister, *Walter W. Moore,* 472–73; *BRCA,* 5 Apr. 1917, p. 1; *RH,* 10 Aug. 1916, p. 11; *RTD,* 25 Oct. 1915, p. 3; *SC,* 17 Mar. 1917, p. 4; *PS,* 11 Nov. 1916, p. 1; *PS,* 3 May 1916, p. 2; *RH,* 6 Dec. 1915, p. 9; *SC,* 7 Aug. 1915, p. 4.

22. *Monumental Messenger,* Apr. 1917, p. 11; *SC,* 24 Aug. 1918, pp. 4–5; *RNL,* 9 July 1917, p. 4; *SC,* 21 Apr. 1917, p. 4; *RH,* 3 May 1917, p. 2.

23. Pell, *What Did Jesus Really Teach About War?*, 93, 64, 171–76, 74–78, 126–35, 41, 31.

24. *RNL*, 24 Jan. 1918, p. 4; *RNL*, 20 Apr. 1918, p. 12; *RNL*, 19 Apr. 1918, p. 1; *RNL*, 8 May 1918, p. 1; *RNL*, 2 Sept. 1918, p. 1; *RNL*, 15 Oct. 1917, p. 11; *RNL*, 21 Oct. 1918, p. 1; Arthur Kyle Davis, ed., *Virginia Communities in War Time*, Vol. 7 (Richmond: Virginia War History Commission, 1927), 267–74.

25. John A. Cutchins, *Memories of Old Richmond (1881–1944)* (Verona, Va.: McClure Press, 1973), 234–35; *RNL*, 28 Nov. 1917, p. 16; *RNL*, 2 and 4 Feb. 1918, pp. 1–2; *RNL*, 18 Jan. 1918, p. 1; *RNL*, 16 Aug. 1918, p. 1; *RNL*, 3 Dec. 1918, p. 1; *RNL*, 23 July 1918, p. 1; *RNL*, 25 July, pp. 1, 13.

26. Oscar Guthe and Arthur W. Newell, eds., *Through One Hundred Years: An Historical Booklet Published for the Centennial Anniversary of St. John's Evangelical Lutheran Church (Evangelical and Reformed), 1843–1943* (Richmond: Dietz Press, 1943), 26; *Bethlehem Lutheran Church, Richmond, Virginia: 125th Anniversary, 1977* (South Hackensack, N.J.: Custombook, 1977), 8; *Order of Services in Connection with the 50th Anniversary Celebration of the Dedication of Bethlehem Evangelical Lutheran Church, Richmond, Virginia* (Richmond: Dietz Press, 1918) and enclosed clipping *Richmond Times-Dispatch*, 27 Aug. 1918; Church Records, St. John's United Church of Christ (accession 34562 Miscellaneous Microfilm Reels 1146–48), "Protokoll Book, 1898–1920," insert following page 161 and pp. 217–18, 243, Archives Research Services, Library of Virginia, Richmond. Ulrich Troubetzkoy, *Richmond, City of Churches: A Short History of Richmond's Denominations and Faiths* (Richmond: Whittet & Shepperson, 1957), 37–39, implies that St. John's introduced English at evening services in 1907 and that Bethlehem continued to conduct some services in German until 1940. Davis, *Virginia Communities in War Time*, 7:262; Richmond church files, Virginia War History Commission, World War I, Archives Research Services, Library of Virginia, Richmond.

27. *RNL*, 14 June 1917, p. 1; *RNL*, 23 Jan. 1918, p. 1; Minutes of the Vestry, 3 Apr. 1917, Grace and Holy Trinity Vestry Book, Papers of Grace and Holy Trinity Episcopal Church, Virginia Historical Society, Richmond; St. Paul's Vestry Book, 9 Apr. 1917 and 11 June 1917, Papers of St. Paul's Episcopal Church, Virginia Historical Society, Richmond; *PS*, 30 Jan. 1918, p. 8; *PS*, 11 July 1918, p. 8; McAllister, *Walter W. Moore*, 484–86; Ernest Trice Thompson, Interview by Dr. Edgar Caldwell Mayne, 11 June 1974, transcript, William Smith Morton Library, Union Theological Seminary/Presbyterian School of Christian Education, Richmond, pp. 4–5; *SC*, 25 Jan. 1919, p. 5. According to "The Record of Union Theological Seminary, Richmond, Virginia in the War," Union students and alumni accounted for twenty-seven chaplains, eleven camp pastors, and thirty-two workers in the Young Men's Christian Association work and eleven soldiers. That information is in the Richmond files of the Virginia War History Commission, World War I, Archives Research Services, Library of Virginia, Richmond. Jack D. Brown to Ida Dorsey Brown, 15 Oct. 1918, 20 Oct. 1918, and 5 Nov. 1918, Ida Dorsey Brown Papers, Virginia Historical Society, Richmond; Will Lingle to Walter L. Lingle, 19 Aug. 1918, Walter L. Lingle Papers, Presbyterian Historical Society, Montreat, N.C.

28. *SC*, 27 Oct. 1917, p. 12; *RNL*, 30 May 1918, p. 1; *RNL*, 29 Oct. 1917, p. 7; *SC*, 11 Aug. 1917, p. 6; *RH*, 18 Oct. 1917, p. 10; Wyndham B. Blanton, *The Making of a Downtown Church: The History of the Second Presbyterian Church, Richmond, Virginia, 1845–1945* (Richmond: John Knox Press, 1945), 298.

29. H. D. C. Maclachlan, "Our Daily Bread," Maclachlan Papers, Disciples of Christ Historical Society, Nashville.

30. *RNL*, 10 Mar. 1917, p. 1; *BRCA*, 6 Dec. 1917, p. 19; Elizabeth W. Weddell, *St. Paul's*

Church, Richmond, Virginia—Its Historic Years and Memorials, Volume II (Richmond: William Byrd Press, 1931), 316–22; Davis, *Virginia Communities in War Time,* 7:328–29.

31. *SC,* 16 Mar. 1918, p. 13; *RNL,* 19 Nov. 1917, p. 2; *RNL,* 25 Apr. 1918, p. 1; *SC,* 1 Sept. 1917, p. 12; *SC,* 27 Oct. 1917, p. 12; *Monumental Messenger,* Sept. 1918, pp. 8–10; *SC,* 2 Nov. 1918, p. 12; Elizabeth W. Weddell, *St. Paul's Church, Volume II,* 324–25; *RNL,* 14 Sept. 1918, p. 12; Davis, *Virginia Communities in War Time,* 7:258–59, 354; Seventh Street Christian Church file in Papers of the Virginia War History Commission, World War I.

32. *SC,* 22 Sept. 1917, p. 12. About the vice campaign see chap. 6. About the flu epidemic, see Richmond newspapers between 5 Oct. and 11 Nov. 1919 and chap. 7.

33. *RNL,* 25 Feb. 1918, p. 6; Russell Cecil, sermon, 28 June 1918, Russell Cecil Papers, William Smith Morton Library, Union Theological Seminary/Presbyterian School of Christian Education; *RTD,* 3 June 1918, p. 6; *RTD,* 15 July 1918, p. 5; *RNL,* 9 July 1917, p. 4; *SC,* 21 Apr. 1917, p. 4; *RNL,* 7 Sept. 1917, p. 1; *SC,* 3 Aug. 1918, p. 4; *SC,* 24 Aug. 1918, p. 2. For other examples, see *BRCA,* 7 Feb. 1918, p. 8; *RH,* 27 Sept. 1917, p. 10.

34. *RH,* 15 Aug. 1918, p. 4; *RH,* 3 Oct. 1918, p. 4; George W. McDaniel, *Our Boys in France* (Richmond: Baptist State Mission Board, 1918).

35. *BRCA,* 21 Nov. 1918, p. 1; *RH,* 11 July 1918, p. 10; *SC,* 27 July 1918, p. 13; *PS,* 17 Apr. 1918, p. 1.

36. *RH,* 11 July 1918, p. 10; *PS,* 31 July 1918, p. 2; *SC,* 10 May 1919, p. 5; *SC,* 3 Aug. 1918, p. 6.

37. *RNL,* 10 Nov. 1925, p. 13; *RCA,* 20 June 1929, p. 2.

38. *SC,* 19 Nov. 1921, p. 6; *SC,* 11 Dec. 1926, p. 6; *RCA,* 20 June 1929, p. 2; *PS,* 2 Jan. 1924, p. 2; Virginia Annual Conference of the Methodist Episcopal Church, South, *Minutes of the One Hundred and Forty-Second Session* (Portsmouth: Printcraft Press, 1924), 116.

39. Abrams, *Preachers Present Arms,* 79–124; Robert Moats Miller, *American Protestantism and Social Issues, 1919–1939* (Chapel Hill: University of North Carolina Press, 1958), 317–32. Merely acknowledging that peace became an important issue for Protestant denominations of the 1920s is Charles Chatfield, *For Peace and Justice: Pacifism in America, 1914–1941* (Knoxville: University of Tennessee Press, 1971), 96. Only a brief reference to peace activity is made by Paul A. Carter, *The Decline and Revival of the Social Gospel: Social and Political Liberalism in American Protestant Churches, 1920–1940* (Ithaca, N.Y.: Cornell University Press, 1954), 133–37.

40. Lingle, *The Bible and Social Problems* (New York: Fleming H. Revell, 1929), 153–55; *SC,* 5 Nov. 1921, p. 7; *PS,* 10 Aug. 1927, p. 2.; *CC,* Sept. 1921, p. 6; *PS,* 6 Jan. 1929, p. 2; *PS,* 12 Jan. 1927, p. 2; *SC,* 12 May 1923, p. 6; *RCA,* 20 Mar. 1924, p. 7.

41. *PS,* 9 Jan. 1929, p. 2; H. D. C. Maclachlan, "Studies in Sin: The Sin of Duress," *Christian Century,* 14 June 1923, p. 747; *PS,* 6 Jan. 1926, p. 2; *PS,* 2 Jan. 1924, p. 2.

42. *RCA,* 2 May 1919, p. 3; *SC,* 14 Jan. 1922, p. 7; *SC,* 5 Nov. 1921, p. 6; *PS,* 2 Jan. 1924, p. 2; *RCA,* 8 Dec. 1921, p. 12; *RH,* 10 May 1923, p. 10. Although Richmond preachers made a variety of appeals, these sermons followed a postwar theme which Charles DeBeneditti identified as prevalent among peace proponents: that the "enormity of modern total war" meant that peace was not only "morally right and practically desirable" but also "necessary" for human survival. DeBeneditti, *Peace Reform,* 109.

43. Bowie, *Learning to Live,* 117, 122, 112–21; *SC,* 11 Dec. 1926, p. 6; Walter Russell Bowie, "The Chaplain" in *History of U.S. Army Base Hospital No. 45 in the Great War,* ed. Joseph F. Geisinger (Richmond: William Byrd Press, 1924), 195.

44. *PS,* 15 Nov. 1916, p. 1; *BRCA,* 15 Feb. 1912, p. 4; *RH,* 16 Nov. 1916, p. 10; *RCA,* 14 Feb.

1924, p. 2; *PS,* 3 Dec. 1919, p. 1; *SC,* 28 June 1919, p. 4; *SC,* 28 Jan. 1922, p. 6; William W. Weeks, *The Face of Christ* (Nashville: School Board of the Southern Baptist Convention, 1927), 158. For civil religion, see Robert Bellah, "Civil Religion in America," in *American Civil Religion,* ed. Russell Richey and Donald G. Jones (New York: Harper & Row, 1974), 21–44.

45. *PS,* 6 Feb. 1924, p. 1; *RCA,* 14 Feb. 1924, pp. 1–2; *RH,* 7 Feb. 1924, p. 10; *RH,* 14 Feb. 1924, p. 14; *CC,* Feb. 1924, p. 6.

46. *SC,* 16 Feb. 1924, p. 14; *PS,* 27 Feb. 1924, p. 12.

47. *SC,* 22 Mar. 1919, p. 10; *SC,* 15 Mar. 1919, pp. 3–4; *PS,* 3 Dec. 1919, p. 1; *RCA,* 5 Feb. 1920, p. 3; *RH,* 4 Oct. 1920, pp. 12–13; *RH,* 28 Oct. 1920, pp. 10–11; *PS,* 21 Jan. 1920, p. 8; *SC,* 28 Jan. 1922, p. 5.

48. *RH,* 8 May 1924, p. 6; *RH,* 29 Nov. 1923, p. 1. Other examples of subsequent support: *SC,* 24 Feb. 1923, p. 3; *RCA,* 8 Jan. 1920, p. 11; *CC,* 11 Nov. 1922, p. 5.

49. Samuel Gompers to Mitchell, 31 Mar. 1924, in the Samuel Chiles Mitchell Papers #1003, Southern Historical Collection, Wilson Library, University of North Carolina at Chapel Hill; *PS,* 23 Jan. 1924, pp. 1 and 4; *RH,* 17 Jan. 1924, p. 3; *RNL,* 14 Jan. 1924, p. 10; *CC,* Feb. 1924, p. 6; Samuel Chiles Mitchell, "An Aftermath of Appamattox [*sic*]: A Memoir" (Atlanta: mimeographed, 1954), 223–24; *CC,* Mar. 1924, p. 6; *PS,* 2 Apr. 1924, p. 1; *RH,* 12 Feb. 1924, p. 7. In *Keeping the Covenant: American Internationalists and the League of Nations, 1920–1939* (Kent, Ohio: Kent State University Press, 1997), 86, Warren F. Kuehl and Lynne K. Dunne note that the Friends of the League of Nations succeeded mostly in Virginia and trace part of its weakness to Mitchell's lack of time to organize a national campaign. League officials in Geneva were reluctant to accept the money because "it created the impression that the League had to beg to survive."

50. *SC,* 22 Jan. 1921, p. 3; St. Paul's Vestry Book, 14 June 1921, Papers of St. Paul's; Richmond Ministerial Union, "Minutes of Meetings, 1919–28," meeting of 19 Oct. 1921, Richmond Public Library; *SC,* 12 Nov. 1921, p. 4; *RCA,* 12 May 1921, p. 2; *CC,* Sept. 1921, p. 6; *PS,* 16 Nov. 1921, p. 1; *RH,* 15 Dec. 1921, p. 10; *SC,* 10 June 1922, p. 5; *SC,* 5 Nov. 1921, p. 6.

51. *SC,* 3 Nov. 1923, p. 5; *RH,* 29 Oct. 1925, p. 10; *PS,* 3 Sept. 1924, p. 1; *RCA,* 28 Aug. 1924, p. 2; *RCA,* 20 May 1920, p. 2; *PS,* 7 July 1926, p. 1; *RCA,* 21 Feb. 1929, p. 21; *SC,* 10 Nov. 1923, p. 5. During the 1920s, Richmond Protestant leaders did not promote the use of a war referendum, a device which was recurrently popular among peace proponents and some political leaders, as noted by Ernest C. Bolt, *Ballots Before Bullets: The War Referendum Approach to Peace in America, 1914–1941* (Charlottesville: University Press of Virginia, 1977). In *Empire without Tears: America's Foreign Relations, 1921–1933* (New York: Alfred A. Knopf, 1987), 45–62, Warren Cohen does not include religious groups in his concise and insightful account which concludes that the peace movement had a large influence on U.S. foreign policy. In *Peace or War,* 292, Merle Curti concludes that protests by church groups did lead to a "toned down" observance of mobilization day.

52. *PS,* 15 Feb 1928, p. 2; Richmond Preachers Meeting, "Minutes of Meetings, 1900–1928," meeting of 5 Feb. 1928, Special Collections and Archives, McGraw-Page Library, Randolph-Macon College, Ashland, Va.; *RCA,* 8 Aug. 1929, p. 8; Richmond Ministerial Union, "Minutes of Meetings, 1919–28," meeting of 12 Feb. 1928.

53. *PS,* 7 Oct. 1925, p. 1; *RNL,* 13 Jan. 1927, p. 8; *PS,* 7 Oct. 1923, p. 1; *PS,* 18 Aug. 1926, p. 1; *SC,* 15 Jan. 1927, p. 5.

54. *RH,* 1 Aug. 1929, p. 10; *VC,* Jan. 1929, p. 3. For other examples of support see: *RCA,* 10 Jan. 1929, p. 2; *PS,* 5 Sept. 1928, p. 1; *PS,* 28 Nov. 1928, p. 1.

55. St. John's Vestry Book, 27 Nov. 1918, St. John's Papers; *Beacon on a Hill,* 49; *RH,* 23 June 1921, p. 14; Belle Gayle Ellyson, *The History of the Second Baptist Church, Richmond, Virginia: 1820–1970* (Richmond: Whittet & Shepperson, 1970), 50–51; Mollie Roberson Wiltshire, *A Century of Service: The History of Union Station Methodist Church, 1843–1943* (Richmond: Whittet & Shepperson, 1943), 42; Edwin Pleasants and William R. Hill, *The First Hundred Years, 1835–1935: Third Presbyterian Church, Richmond, Virginia* ([Richmond]: Third Presbyterian Church, [1935]), 47; Dover Baptist Association, *Minutes of the One Hundred and Forty-Fourth Annual Meeting* (Richmond: Richmond Press, 1927), 84. Surviving bouts of financial difficulty, the Richmond-based Foreign Mission Board of the Southern Baptist Convention still boasted substantial growth and accomplishments in the 1920s, Estep, *Whole Gospel,* 187–212.

56. *PS,* 9 Jan. 1929, p. 2.

11. The Wrong Placc for a Row

1. *RH,* 22 May 1924, p. 6.

2. Robert Moats Miller, *American Protestantism and Social Issues, 1919–1939* (Chapel Hill: University of North Carolina Press, 1958), 154–65; George M. Marsden, *Fundamentalism and American Culture: The Shaping of Twentieth-Century Evangelicalism, 1870–1925* (New York: Oxford University Press, 1980); Ernest R. Sandeen, *The Roots of Fundamentalism: British and American Millenarianism* (Chicago: University of Chicago, 1970); Ferenc Morton Szaz, *The Divided Mind of Protestant America, 1880–1930* (Tuscaloosa: University of Alabama Press, 1982); George W. Dollar, *A History of Fundamentalism in America* (Greenville, S.C.: Bob Jones University Press, 1973); William Vance Trollinger Jr., *God's Empire: William Bell Riley and Midwestern Fundamentalism* (Madison: University of Wisconsin Press, 1990); Bradley J. Longfield, *The Presbyterian Controversy: Fundamentalists, Modernists, and Moderates* (New York: Oxford University Press, 1991); Allyn C. Russell, *Voices of American Fundamentalism: Seven Biographical Studies* (Philadelphia: Westminster Press, 1976); Virginia Lieson Brereton, *Training God's Army: The American Bible School, 1880–1940* (Bloomington: University of Indiana Press, 1990); Barry Hankins, *God's Rascal: J. Frank Norris and the Beginnings of Southern Fundamentalism* (Lexington: University Press of Kentucky, 1996); William Glass, "The Development of Northern Patterns of Fundamentalism in the South, 1900–1950" (Ph.D. diss., Emory University, 1991).

3. About Modernism, see William R. Hutchison, *The Modernist Impulse in American Protestantism* (Cambridge, Mass.: Harvard University Press, 1976) and Kenneth Cauthen, *The Impact of American Religious Liberalism* (New York: Harper & Row, 1962).

4. Marsden, *Fundamentalism and American Culture,* 43, 4. Often part of an intricate theology, premillennialism is a belief that at the end of the current age Jesus will return to earth and, with the aid of the resurrected righteous, defeat the Antichrist and establish a millennial reign. See Timothy P. Weber "Premillennialism and the Branches of Evangelicalism," *The Variety of American Evangelicalism,* ed. Donald W. Dayton and Robert K. Johnston (Knoxville: University of Tennessee Press, 1991), 5–21.

5. Willard Gatewood Jr., ed., *Controversy in the Twenties: Fundamentalism, Modernism, and Evolution* (Nashville: Vanderbilt University Press, 1969), 15; Samuel S. Hill, "Fundamentalism and the South," *Perspectives in Religious Studies* 13 (fall 1986): 50; Marsden, *Fundamentalism and American Culture,* 4. In *Understanding Fundamentalism and Evangelicalism*

(Grand Rapids, Mich.: William B. Eerdmans Publishing, 1991) Marsden writes that "fundamentalists are not just religious conservatives, they are conservatives who are willing to take a stand and to fight," 1–3. Endorsement of that emphasis comes from religious historian Martin E. Marty, "Fundamentalism and the Scholars," *Key Reporter* 58, no. 3 (spring 1993): 4. For another valuable summary and analysis, see Nancy Ammerman, "North American Protestant Fundamentalism," in *Fundamentalism Observed,* ed. Martin E. Marty and R. Scott Appleby (Chicago: University of Chicago Press, 1991), 1–65. About premillennialism, see Timothy P. Weber, *Living in the Shadow of the Second Coming: American Premillennialism, 1875–1982,* rev. ed. (New York: Oxford University Press, 1979; reprint, Grand Rapids, Mich.: Zondervan, 1983), especially chaps. 5–7. Paul Boyer, *When Times Shall Be No More: Prophecy Belief in Modern American Culture* (Cambridge, Mass: Harvard University Press, 1992) offers a helpful summary, particularly in chap. 3.

6. *RTD,* 23 May, 1910, p. 10; *RNL,* 25 Oct. 1921, p. 5; H. D. C. Maclachlan, "The Inside of the Cup," "The Church at School," "False Prophets," undated sermons, Maclachlan Papers, Disciples of Christ Historical Society, Nashville; Norman Furniss, *The Fundamentalist Controversy, 1918–1931* (New Haven, Conn.: Yale University Press, 1954), 12.

7. *BRCA,* 23 May 1907, p. 7; Edward L. Pell, *The Life Worth While* (Richmond: Robert Harding, 1906), 152–57; Edward L. Pell, *What Did Jesus Really Teach About War?* (New York: Fleming H. Revell, 1917), 34–41; Edward L. Pell, *Why I Believe in Jesus: A Personal Experience* (New York: Fleming H. Revell, 1926).

8. *RCA,* 14 Sept. 1922, p. 2; *RCA,* 29 July, 1926, p. 2; *RCA,* 25 Sept. 1919; *RCA,* 8 Mar. 1923, p. 3; *RCA,* 2 Aug. 1923, p. 2; "Minutes of the Richmond Preachers Meeting" and "Minutes of the Richmond District Conference" reveal no concern by Methodists about Modernism and evolution. In *Hands on the Ark: The Struggle for Change in the Methodist Episcopal Church, South, 1914–1939* (Lake Junaluska, N.C.: Commission on Archives and History, United Methodist Church, 1975), 138–64, Robert Watson Sledge reviews debates about Fundamentalism, Modernism, and Orthodoxy and notes several proposals for a formal creedal statement. Sledge observes that "as time had gone by," the Methodist Episcopal Church, South "decided that it needed no definitive statement of creed" (164).

9. Thomas Cary Johnson, "The Universal Obligation to Labor," *Union Seminary Magazine* 19, no. 3 (Feb.–Mar. 1908): 196; Ernest Trice Thompson, interview by Edgar Caldwell Mayne, 11 June 1974, transcript, William Smith Morton Library, Union Theological Seminary/Presbyterian School of Education, Richmond; Ernest Trice Thompson, *Presbyterians in the South,* 3:208; Balmer H. Kelly, "'No Ism but Bibleism': Biblical Studies at Union Theological Seminary in Virginia, 1812–1987," *Journal of Presbyterian History* 66, no. 2 (summer 1988): 110–12; Johnson, "Despise Not the Chastening of the Lord," *Union Seminary Magazine* 18, no. 1 (Oct.–Nov. 1906): 20–32.

10. Givens Brown Strickler, "The New Theology: Part I," *Union Seminary Magazine* 12, no.1 (Oct.–Nov. 1900): 1–6; Strickler, "The New Theology: Part II: The Fatherhood of God," *Union Seminary Magazine* 12, no. 2 (Dec. 1900–Jan. 1901): 89–99; Strickler, "The New Theology: Part III," *Union Seminary Magazine* 12, no. 3 (Feb.–Mar. 1901): 175–84; Strickler, "The New Theology: Part IV," *Union Seminary Magazine* 12, no. 4 (Apr.–May 1901): 268–75; Thompson, *Presbyterians in the South,* 3:210; Kelly, "No Ism but Bibleism," 111; William Jennings Bryan, *In His Image* (New York: Fleming H. Revell, 1922).

11. Thomas Cary Johnson, *God's Answer to Evolution* (Richmond: Presbyterian Committee of Publication, 1924), 7, 34; Edward Mack, *The Christ of the Old Testament: Studies in the Beginnings and Growth of Messianic Prophecy* (Richmond: Presbyterian Committee of

Publication, 1926), 180–81, 195, 33–35; Thompson, *Presbyterians in the South,* Moore quoted, 3:212, 224; Thompson, Interview by E. C. Mayne, 11 June 1974.

12. Walter W. Moore, "Memorabilia of 1917," 9 Jan. 1918, Papers of W. W. Moore, William Smith Morton Library, Union Theological Seminary/Presbyterian School of Education, Richmond; Mack, *The Christ of the Old Testament,* 36, 113–14.

13. Walter L. Lingle to M. Ryerson Turnbull, 11 June 1919 and W. L. Lingle to the Editors of the *Sunday School Times,* 20 Mar. 1924, in the Lingle Papers, Presbyterian Historical Society, Montreat, N.C.; *PS,* 17 Dec. 1924, p. 2; Thompson, *Presbyterians in the South,* 3:465, 325–26; Kelly, "'No Ism but Bibleism,'" 111–12; Russell Cecil, *The Religion of Love* (Richmond: Presbyterian Committee of Publication, 1924), 5–8, 64–67.

14. Robert P. Kerr, *Will the World Outgrow Christianity and Other Interrogatives on Vital Themes* (Chicago: Fleming H. Revell, 1901), 10; *BRCA,* 17 Nov. 1904; *PS,* 7 Oct. 1914, p. 10; *PS,* 7 June 1916, p. 1.

15. William Jennings Bryan, *In His Image,* 86–135, quotations, 94–95, 125, 11, 122. In a sympathetic treatment *Defender of the Faith: William Jennings Bryan, The Last Decade, 1915–1925* (New York: Oxford University Press, 1965), Lawrence Levine concludes that, although Bryan "had probably read the works of Darwin, he understood, or, more properly, wanted to understand, very little about Darwinian evolution" (191). About Bryan and the antievolution campaign see, Levine, *Defender of the Faith,* especially chaps. 7 and 9, and Edward J. Larson, *Trial and Error: The American Controversy Over Creation and Evolution* (New York: Oxford University Press, 1985), 28–90.

16. *RNL,* 29 May 1922, p. 2; *PS,* 4 Mar. 1925, p. 2; McAllister, *Walter W. Moore,* p. 505; *PS,* 24 June 1925, p. 1; *RCA,* 16 July 1925, p. 2.

17. *RNL,* 25 Oct. 1921, p. 5; Walter Russell Bowie, untitled newspaper clipping, 11 Dec. 1922, Bowie Papers, Bishop Payne Library, Virginia Theological Seminary, Alexandria, Va.; Beverley D. Tucker, "Christian Citizenship," *Union Seminary Review* 34 (Jan. 1928): 125–31; *SC,* 26 May, 1923, p. 5.

18. *RNL,* 30 June 1925, p. 8; *RCA,* 9 July 1925, p. 2; *RCA,* 6 Aug. 1925, pp. 2, 3; *RH,* 16 July 1925, p. 10; Virginius Dabney, *Richmond: The Story of a City,* rev. ed. (Charlottesville: University Press of Virginia, 1990), 303. Edward J. Larson's *Summer for the Gods: The Scopes Trial and America's Continuing Debate Over Science and Religion* (New York: Basic Books, 1997) provides a fresh and valuable examination of the Scopes trial and includes a review of how it has been depicted by scholars and writers in books, plays, and movies.

19. *RH,* 27 Dec. 1923, p. 10; *RH,* 12 Apr. 1923, p. 10.

20. *RH,* 22 June, 1933 and *RH,* 4 Mar. 1937 clippings in R. H. Pitt folder, Virginia Baptist Historical Society, Richmond; *RH,* 9 May, 1907, p. 10; Woodford B. Hackley, *Faces on the Wall: Brief Sketches of the Men and Women Whose Portraits and Busts were on the Campus of the University of Richmond in 1955* (Richmond: Virginia Baptist Historical Society, 1972), 73–74. Among those noting the *Herald's* earlier liberal views has been Rufus B. Spain, *At Ease in Zion: Social History of Southern Baptists, 1865–1900* (Nashville: Vanderbilt University Press, 1961), 215.

21. *RH,* 13 Aug. 1908, p. 12; Douglas Southall Freeman, "Growth" (typewritten transcript of lecture delivered May 3, 1925), Freeman Papers. For brief but effective treatments of the late-nineteenth-century movement called Landmarkism, see Bill Leonard, *God's Last and Only Hope: The Fragmentation of the Southern Baptist Convention* (Grand Rapids, Mich.: William B. Eerdmans Publishing, 1990), 34–35, and James E. Tull, "Landmark Movement," and Daniel Holcomb, "William Heth Whitsitt," in *Encyclopedia of Religion in the South,* ed.

Samuel S. Hill (Macon, Ga.: Mercer University Press, 1984), 399–401, 841–42. Among other beliefs, Landmark Baptists viewed themselves as part of an unique, unbroken, apostolic church that had always engaged in immersion as a form of baptism. They also denied participation in the Lord's Supper to those who had not been immersed, viewing other forms of baptism as illegitimate. As Bill Leonard notes, "These Baptists sought to purify the convention of all who would not conform to their dogmatic definitions regarding the nature of the church, baptism, the Lord's Supper, and salvation." John Lee Eighmy, *Churches in Cultural Captivity: A History of the Social Attitudes of Southern Baptists* (Knoxville: University of Tennessee Press, 1972), 129, notes similarities between the Landmark movement and Fundamentalism. William E. Ellis, *"A Man of Books and a Man of the People": E. Y. Mullins and the Crisis of Moderate Southern Baptist Leadership* (Macon, Ga.: Mercer University Press, 1985) consistently links Southern Baptist fundamentalists to Landmark views (41–42, 53–57, 102, 112–13). For examples of S. C. Mitchell's views, see *Religious Herald,* 30 May, 1901, p. 3; 14 Jan. 1904, p. 8; 28 Jan. 1904, p. 2; 16 Mar. 1905, p. 9. About Richmond faculty, see Reuben E. Alley, *Frederic W. Boatwright* (Richmond: University of Richmond, 1973), 49–51.

22. *RH,* 5 Jan. 1922, p. 10; *RH,* 1 Apr. 1920, p.4; *RH,* 24 Jan. 1924, p. 11; *RH,* 21 May 1925, p. 10; *RH,* 22 May 1924, p. 6; *RH,* 9 Mar. 1922, p. 6.

23. *RH,* 19 Nov. 1925, p. 10; Bill J. Leonard, *God's Last and Only Hope,* 31; *RH,* 28 July 1921, p. 11. William Wright Barnes, *The Southern Baptist Convention, 1845–1953* (Nashville: Broadman Press, 1954), correctly characterizes Pitt as a defender of Southern Baptist "nationalism," 175.

24. *RH,* 29 Mar. 1923, p. 10; *RH,* 12 Apr. 1923, p. 10; *RH,* 10 May 1923, p. 6. For Norris's activities, see Hankins, *God's Rascal* and Russell, *Voices of American Fundamentalism,* 20–78. Although Pitt identified his opponents as primarily from the Southwest, Kentucky provided strong support for Baptist fundamentalists, as William E. Ellis notes throughout *"A Man of Books and a Man of the People."* No state was totally dominated by fundamentalists, and Pitt had significant allies within Texas. In addition to Hankins's account, the Texas situation is reported in John W. Storey, *Texas Baptist Leadership and Social Christianity, 1900–1980* (College Station: Texas A&M University Press, 1986), 39–69.

25. *RH,* 9 Feb. 1922, pp. 4, 10; *RH,* 16 Feb. 1922, p. 10; *RH,* 8 June 1922, p. 10; *Annual of the Southern Baptist Convention 1922,* 33–35; *RH,* 22 June 1922, p. 10; *RH,* 7 May 1925, p. 7; *RH* 1 Oct. 1925, p. 11.

26. *Annual of the Southern Baptist Convention 1924,* 70–71, 80, 95; *RH,* 1 Apr. 1920, p. 10; *Annual of the Southern Baptist Convention 1925,* 71; *RH,* 5 May 1923, p. 10. The other members of the committee were E. Y. Mullins, L. R. Scarborough, S. M. Brown, W. J. McGlothlin, and E. C. Dargan. In *"A Man of Books and a Man of the People,"* 190–93, William Ellis depicts Stealey as a relentless force on the committee, which worried that he acted as a front for the more formidable Norris. A native of West Virginia, Stealey had served as pastor of a Richmond church between 1901 and 1905. For Pitt's views, see: *RH,* 7 Sept. 1922, p. 10; *RH,* 29 Mar. 1923, p. 10; *RH,* 28 May 1925, p. 10; *RH,* 19 Mar. 1925, p. 10.

27. *Annual of the Southern Baptist Convention, 1925,* 70–76; Herschel Hobbs, "Southern Baptists and Confessionalism: A Comparison of the Origins of the 1925 and 1963 Confessions," *Review and Expositor* 76 (winter 1979): 55–58. John Lee Eighmy, *Churches in Cultural Captivity,* 129–30, unlike some other historians, notes the liberal tone of the 1925 Statement.

28. *RH,* 5 Jan. 1922, p. 10; *RH,* 28 May 1925, p. 10; *RH,* 20 May 1926, p. 10; Ellis, *"A Man of Books and a Man of the People,"* 190–93. In 1922 the Northern Baptist Convention had

defeated a proposal by William B. Riley to adopt the New Hampshire Confession as a creed. Instead, the Woelfkin resolution was adopted: "The Northern Baptist Convention affirms that the New Testament is the all-sufficient ground of our faith and practice and we need no other statement." Robert G. Torbet, *A History of the Baptists* (Philadelphia: Judson Press, 1950), 445–46.

29. *RH,* 28 May 1925, p. 10; *RH* 5 May 1923, p. 10; *RH* 18 June 1925, p. 10.

30. Furniss, *Fundamentalist Controversy,* 123; *Annual of the Southern Baptist Convention 1925,* 76; *RH,* 9 July 1925, p. 10; *RH,* 6 May 1926, p. 10; *RH,* 29 Apr. 1926, p. 10; *RH,* 10 June 1926, p. 10.

31. George White McDaniel, *Seeing the Best: Sermons and Addresses* (Nashville: Sunday School Board of the Southern Baptist Convention, 1923), 93; George W. McDaniel, *The Supernatural Jesus* (Nashville: Sunday School Board of the Southern Baptist Convention, 1924) and *The People Called the Baptists* (Nashville: Sunday School Board of the Southern Baptist Convention, 1922); *RH,* 27 May 1976, pp. 10, 6; *Annual of the Southern Baptist Convention 1926,* 18; Barnes, *The Southern Baptist Convention,* 257.

32. *Annual of the Southern Baptist Convention 1926,* 98; Furniss, *Fundamentalist Controversy,* 123; *RH,* 3 June 1926, p. 10; *RH,* 15 July 1926, p. 10. According to William Wright Barnes, others held the same view as did Pitt about the motion being out of order. Barnes, *Southern Baptist Convention,* 258.

33. *RH,* 30 Dec. 1926, p. 10.

34. *Annual of the Southern Baptist Convention 1928,* 32–33, 27–29; Barnes, *The Southern Baptist Convention,* 258–61; Robert Baker, *The Southern Baptist Convention and Its People, 1607–1972* (Nashville: Broadman Press, 1974), 399–400; J. M. Gaskin, "Stealey, Clarence Perry," and Roger D. Hebard, "Stealey Controversy, Oklahoma," in *The Encyclopedia of Southern Baptists* (Nashville: Broadman Press, 1958), 2:1297–98; Furniss, *Fundamentalist Controversy,* 124–25; Ellis, *"A Man of Books and a Man of the People,"* 199.

35. Ellis, *"A Man of Books and a Man of the People,"* 185–208. Though less categorical than Ellis, Kenneth K. Bailey *Southern White Protestantism in the Twentieth Century* (New York: Oxford University Press, 1964) leaves a similar impression. Citing the reaction of the fundamentalist press to the 1926 meeting, Bailey writes that "cries of elation arose from the fundamentalists. . . . Perhaps in no major Protestant denomination in America did conservatives reign more triumphantly" (66). Leonard, *God's Last and Only Hope,* 70–71. In *Churches in Cultural Captivity,* 129, John Lee Eighmy comes close to Leonard with his conclusion that the 1925 statement "did not constitute a complete victory for the fundamentalists." In a highly nuanced interpretation that tries to refine the definition of fundamentalist, James J. Thompson Jr. argues that "many" rural Southern Baptists were attracted to Fundamentalism but few were active participants in the "movement." Thompson, *Tried As By Fire: Southern Baptists and the Religious Controversies of the 1920s* (Macon, Ga.: Mercer University Press, 1982), 156–57. In *Fundamentalism in American Culture,* 194, George Marsden declares that the Southern Baptist Convention "manifested substantial affinities to fundamentalism."

36. *RH,* 5 Jan. 1928, pp. 10–11; *RH,* 5 Jan. 1928, p. 10. Major accounts of nondenominational fundamentalist activities include the following: Dollar, *A History of Fundamentalism in America;* Stewart Cole, *The History of Fundamentalism* (New York: R. R. Smith, 1931; reprint, Westport, Conn.: Greenwood Press, 1971); and Brereton, *Training God's Army.*

37. Walter Russell Bowie, *Learning to Live* (Nashville: Abingdon Press, 1969), 9–81.

38. Bowie, *Learning to Live,* 83–139; "Offered by Judge Ben T. Crump and adopted by

the Vestry Oct. 10, 1921," in Papers of St. Paul's Church, Virginia Historical Society, Richmond; *SC*, 15 Oct. 1921, p. 5. For an example of praise for Bowie, see *RH*, 25 Jan. 1923, p. 7.

39. *SC*, 26 Aug. 1916, p.7; *SC*, 2 Sept. 1916, pp. 6–7.

40. *SC*, 30 Sept. 1916, pp. 5–8; *SC*, 28 Oct. 1916, pp. 5–6. Thomas H. Cragoe, "W. H. Griffith Thomas," in *Handbook of Evangelical Theologians* (Grand Rapids, Mich.: Baker Books, 1993), 67–82.

41. *SC*, 7 Oct. 1916, p. 7; *SC*, 14 Oct. 1916, pp. 7–8; *SC*, 11 Nov. 1916, pp. 6–7; *SC*, 4 Nov. 1916, p. 6; *SC*, 25 Nov. 1916, p. 9.

42. *SC*, 2 Aug. 1919, p. 9; Lucy Randolph Mason, *The Divine Discontent* (Richmond: Equal Suffrage League of Virginia, 1913). For the relationship between Fundamentalism and views about women, see Margaret Lamberts Bendroth, *Fundamentalism and Gender, 1875 to the Present* (New Haven, Conn.: Yale University Press, 1993) and Betty A. DeBerg, *Ungodly Women: Gender and the First Wave of American Fundamentalism* (Minneapolis: Fortress Press, 1990). *SC*, 29 July 1922, p. 5; *SC*, 20 Jan. 1923, p. 5.

43. *SC*, 3 Feb. 1923, pp. 5–6, 8; *SC*, 10 Feb. 1923, p. 5; Furniss, *Fundamentalist Controversy*, 164–65.

44. *SC*, 3 Feb. 1923, pp. 6–10; *SC*, 10 Feb. 1923, p. 5. Although Bowie did not agree with Grant's ideas, Bowie was a "modernist," a label which apparently carried much more emotional significance than that of "liberal." For Bowie's ideas, see Walter Russell Bowie, *The Road of the Star* (New York: Fleming H. Revell, 1922); *Some Open Ways to God* (New York: Charles Scribner's Sons, 1924); and *The Inescapable Christ* (London: John Murray, 1926).

45. Langbourne M. Williams to Dr. Ennion G. Williams, 28 Feb. 1923, Papers of the *Southern Churchman* Company; "Dr. Russell Bowie vs. the Southern Churchman," newspaper clipping, 1923, in the Bowie Papers; Langbourne M. Williams to Berryman Green, 28 Feb. 1923, Bowie Papers; *SC*, 17 Mar. 1923, p. 4; *PS*, 24 Jan. 1923, p. 1; *RCA*, 1 Feb. 1923, p. 2; *RNL*, 5 Feb. 1923, p. 4; *RNL*, 12 Feb. 1923, p. 4; *RNL*, 12 Mar. 1923, p. 2; *RNL*, 17 Feb. 1923, p. 1; *RNL*, 14 Mar. 1923, p. 1; William Edward Cox to Lewis C. Williams, 27 Feb. 1923, Papers of the *Southern Churchman* Company.

46. Murray M. McGuire, *The Faith of the Church: An Expression from a Layman* [Richmond: n.p., 1923]; Thomas Willcox, *Was Jesus Only a Good Man or Was He the Son of God?: A Layman's Views* (Richmond: n.p., [1923]); John B. Mordecai, *Some Modern Teachings: A Layman's Protest* (Richmond: n.p., [1923]). For a history of St. James's, see Minor T. Weisiger, Donald R. Traser, and E. Randolph Trice, *Not Hearers Only: St. James's Episcopal Church*, ed. Margaret T. Peters (Richmond: St. James's Episcopal Church, 1986).

47. *SC*, 28 July 1923, p. 6.

48. John B. Mordecai to President and Board of Directors, the *Southern Churchman* Company, 14 Sept. 1923, Papers of the *Southern Churchman* Company; Vestry Book, St. James's Church, 8 Nov. 1921, 5 Jan. 1922, 7 Feb. 1922, 28 Sept. 1922, 13 Oct. 1922, Papers of St. James's Episcopal Church, Virginia Historical Society, Richmond; Weisiger, *Not Hearers Only*, 55; Murray M. McGuire to Walter Russell Bowie, 14 Aug. 1923; Lewis C. Williams to Walter Russell Bowie, 20 Dec. 1923; E. Randolph Williams to Berryman Green, 17 Mar. 1924 in Papers of the *Southern Churchman* Company.

49. Walter Russell Bowie to Board of Directors, *Southern Churchman* Company, 14 Apr. 1924, Lewis C. Williams to W. R. Bowie, 23 Apr. 1924, W. R. Bowie to L. C. Williams 21 Dec. 1923, L. C. Williams to W. R. Bowie, 9 Jan. 1924, Ennion G. Williams to E. Randolph Williams, 22 Feb. 1924, Berryman Green to Lewis C. Williams, 22 Jan. 1922, Papers of the *Southern Churchman* Company.

50. Langbourne M. Williams to Lewis C. Williams, 15 Feb. 1926, Papers of the *Southern Churchman* Company; Langbourne M. Williams to Joseph B. Dunn, 26 Feb. 1926; Langbourne M. Williams to Lewis C. Williams, 28 Feb. 1927; Langbourne M. Williams to Lewis C. Williams, 19 Apr. 1927; Langbourne M. Williams to Lewis C. Williams 27 Apr. 1927. This interpretation of events is confirmed by Williams's niece, Maria Williams Sheerin, who unsuccessfully attempted to disguise his identity by referring to him as "Uncle Tom" "for purposes of confusion." Maria Williams Sheerin, *The Parson Takes a Wife* (New York: Macmillan, 1948), 12–15.

51. *SC*, 18 June 1927, p. 6; *SC*, 6 Aug. 1927, p. 6; *SC*, 25 Aug. 1928, p. 9; *SC*, 30 July 1927, p. 11; *SC*, 4 May 1929, pp. 12–13; *SC*, 9 June 1928, p. 5; *SC*, 24 Mar. 1928, p. 19; *SC*, 28 Oct. 1929, p. 15.

52. *SC*, 21 May 1927, pp. 5–6; *SC*, 4 June 1927, p. 1; *SC*, 5 Nov. 1927, pp. 6–7; *SC*, 26 Nov. 1927, p. 6; *SC*, 25 Oct. 1927, p. 5; *SC*, 29 Sept. 1928, p. 5; *SC*, 11 Feb. 1928, p. 5; *SC*, 23 Nov. 1929, p. 6; *SC*, 10 Aug. 1929, p. 14.

53. *SC*, 27 Oct. 1927, p. 5; *SC*, 12 Nov. 1927, p. 5; *SC*, 30 July 1927, pp. 5–6; *SC*, 25 June 1927, pp. 5–6; *SC*, 26 Jan. 1929, pp. 5–6; *SC*, 19 Nov. 1927, p. 6; *SC*, 26 Jan. 1929, pp. 5–6; *SC*, 5 Nov. 1927, pp. 6–7.

54. *SC*, 3 Sept. 1927, p. 5; *SC*, 24 Sept. 1927, pp. 6–7; *SC*, 2 Mar. 1929, p.7; *SC*, 20 July 1929, p. 6; *SC*, 9 Feb. 1929, p. 6; *SC*, 12 Jan. 1929, p. 5.

55. *SC*, 18 Feb. 1928, p. 2; *SC*, 10 Mar. 1928, p. 15; *SC*, 9 June 1928, p. 5; *SC*, 23 June 1928, p. 5; *SC*, 7 July 1928, pp. 12–13.

56. *SC*, 29 Sept. 1928, p. 11; *SC*, 28 Apr. 1928, p. 6; *VC*, Nov. 1927, p. 148; *VC*, Oct. 1926, p. 737; Bowie, *Learning to Live*, 139; Weddell, *St. Paul's Church*, 2:351–56; *RNL*, 16 Mar. 1927, p. 9; *SC*, 5 Nov. 1927, pp. 6–7, 13.

57. Bowie, *Learning to Live*, 126–27; Virginius Dabney, *Liberalism in the South* (Chapel Hill: University of North Carolina Press, 1932), 305.

58. Trollinger, *God's Empire*, 19–20.

59. Murray McGuire to W. Russell Bowie, 14 Aug. 1923, Papers of the *Southern Churchman* Company; *SC*, 9 June 1928, p. 6. Among those sensing the importance of lay activity among fundamentalists is Paul Carter, *The Decline and Revival of the Social Gospel: Social and Political Liberalism in American Protestant Churches, 1920–1940* (Ithaca, N.Y.: Cornell University Press, 1954), 54. William Trollinger, *God's Empire*, 7–9, also stresses the importance of the "grassroots" of Fundamentalism, particularly after defeats in the national and regional arenas. Bradley J. Longfield, *Presbyterian Controversy*, 5, portrays strife within Northern Presbyterianism as mostly "a conflict among generals." William Glass identifies a similar pattern among Presbyterians and Methodists in Glass, "Development of Northern Patterns of Fundamentalism in the South, 1900–1950," especially, 404–10.

60. Lewis C. Williams to Walter Russell Bowie, 21 June 1923, and Langbourne M. Williams to Walter Russell Bowie, 13 Apr. 1923, Papers of the *Southern Churchman* Company; *SC*, 10 Aug. 1929, p. 14. For an important standard historical treatment of the topic, see David Moberg, *The Great Reversal: Evangelism Versus Social Concern* (Philadelphia: Lippincott, 1972).

61. *RNL*, 4 Mar. 1924, p. 4; *RNL*, 11 Mar. 1924, p. 4. Willard B. Gatewood Jr., *Preachers, Pedagogues, and Politicians: The Evolution Controversy in North Carolina, 1920–1927* (Chapel Hill: University of North Carolina Press, 1966), 128–30, notes the role of University of North Carolina in fighting that state's proposed antievolution law.

62. *RH*, 5 Jan. 1928, p. 10. Marsden, *Fundamentalism and American Culture*, 179. In *The*

Divided Mind of Protestant America, 1880–1930, 62–65, 104–5, Ferenc Morton Szasz seems trapped by conventional categories. In writing about the South, he only briefly cites foes of Fundamentalism, suggests that they were few in number, and were largely overwhelmed. Among those emphasizing non-southern origins of Fundamentalism are Samuel Hill, "Fundamentalism and the South," 48–49, and William Glass, "The Development of Northern Patterns of Fundamentalism in the South, 1900–1950."

63. *RH,* 18 Jan. 1923, p. 2; McDaniel, *The Supernatural Jesus,* 206; McDaniel, *Seeing the Best,* 93.

64. *RH,* 25 Apr. 1901, p. 2; *RH,* 14 Jan. 1904, p. 8; S. C. Mitchell clipping "Some Mental Characteristics of Our Lord," *St. John's,* 23 Oct. 1901, Mitchell Papers, Library of Congress; E. C. Caldwell review of Henry Beech Carre, *Paul's Doctrine of Redemption* in *Union Seminary Review* 26, no. 4 (July 1915); 356–58; *PS,* 4 Dec. 1929, p. 2; H. D. C. Maclachlan, "Types and Ideals of Hebrew Prophecy," chap. 2, Maclachlan Papers; *Friendly Church Messenger,* May 1923, p. 20.

65. *RH,* 23 May 1929, p. 8; *VC,* Nov. 1927, p. 146; *VC,* Oct. 1926, p. 737; *RH,* 15 Dec. 1927, p. 3; McAllister, *Walter W. Moore,* p. 209.

66. Maclachlan, "The Sin of Duress," 749; Maclachlan, "False Prophets," Maclachlan Papers; Walter L. Lingle to Miss Louhan Anderson, 29 Sept. 1924, Lingle Papers; George W. McDaniel, *Seeing the Best,* 93–99; *RH,* 5 Jan. 1928, p. 23; *RCA,* 17 Jan. 1924, p. 2; *RCA,* 25 July 1929, p. 2; *PS,* 22 Apr. 1925, p. 2.

67. Maclachlan, "What Do Ye More Than Others," and "False Prophets," Maclachlan Papers; *RH,* 28 May 1925, p. 10; McAllister, *Walter W. Moore,* p. 209; *RCA,* 2 Aug. 1923, p. 2.

68. *RH,* 5 Jan. 1928, p. 11.

12. Avenues of Faith

1. *PS,* 6 Nov. 1929, pp. 3–4.

2. *RH,* 16 May 1907, p. 12; George W. McDaniel, *Seeing the Best* (Nashville: Sunday School Board of the Southern Baptist Convention, 1923), 162; *RNL,* 26 Feb. 1920, pp. 1–2.

3. *RH,* 12 June 1924, p. 23; *PS,* 8 Dec. 1926, p. 1.

4. C. Vann Woodward, *Origins of the New South, 1877–1913* (Baton Rouge: Louisiana State University Press, 1951), 448–52; Kenneth K. Bailey, *Southern White Protestantism in the Twentieth Century* (New York: Oxford University Press, 1964), 2–3; Samuel S. Hill, *Southern Churches in Crisis* (Boston: Beacon Press, 1968), 34–39. In *The Emergence of the New South, 1913–1945* (Baton Rouge: Louisiana State University Press, 1967), 196–210, George Tindall slightly qualified the notion of religious homogeneity and credited southern critic H. L. Mencken with popularizing the idea. U.S. Department of Commerce, Bureau of the Census, *Census of Religious Bodies: 1926* (Washington, D.C.: GPO, 1930), 1:523–24.

5. *RH,* 13 Sept. 1906, pp. 8–9.

6. John B. Boles, "The Discovery of Southern Religious History," in *Interpreting Southern History: Historiographical Essays in Honor of Sanford W. Higginbotham,* ed. John B. Boles and Evelyn Thomas Nolen (Baton Rouge: Louisiana State University Press, 1987), 542; Samuel S. Hill, *One Name but Several Faces: Variety in Popular Christians Denominations in Southern History* (Athens: University of Georgia Press, 1996), 2.

7. *CP,* 22 May, 1907, p. 1; *RH,* 13 Sept. 1906, pp. 8–9; *SC,* 26 July, 1913, p. 3.

8. H. Paul Douglass, *The City's Church* (New York: Friendship Press, 1929), 196.

9. Walter W. Moore to Walter L. Lingle, 27 July 1911, Lingle Papers, Presbyterian Historical Society, Montreat, N.C.

10. *SC,* 17 Apr. 1920, p. 13; Woman's Foreign Missionary Union of East Hanover Presbytery, "Seventeenth Annual Report," in "Minutes of Woman's Work in East Hanover Presbytery, Vol. 2, 1889–1918," 4 Apr. 1905, p. 2; *RH,* 14 Feb. 1924, p. 8; *RNL,* 8 Apr. 1918, p. 4; Dover Baptist Association, *Minutes of the One Hundred and Thirty-Seventh Annual Session* (Richmond: Clyde W. Saunders, 1920), 59; Dover Baptist Association, *Minutes of the One Hundred and Forty-Seventh Annual Session* (Richmond: Curtis Printing Co., 1930), 54.

11. Douglass, *The City's Church,* 226.

12. Baptist Council of Richmond, "Minutes of the Executive Committee, 1903–1929, "Annual Report," 1916, 255f, Virginia Baptist Historical Society, Richmond; *(St. Andrew's) Parish Record,* Easter, 1901, p. 12.

13. *PS,* 24 June 1925, p. 2; Ted Ownby, *Subduing Satan: Religion, Recreation, and Manhood in the Rural South, 1865–1920* (Chapel Hill: University of North Carolina Press, 1990), 129–36.

14. Baptist Council of Richmond, "Annual Report," 1916, 255; *PS,* 19 May 1920, p. 23; St. Paul's Vestry Book, 11 July 1927, p. 227, 229, Papers of St. Paul's Episcopal Church, Virginia Historical Society, Richmond; *RNL,* 31 Dec. 1925, pp. 1–2; Elizabeth Hayes Turner, *Women, Culture, and Community: Religion and Reform in Galveston, 1880–1920* (New York: Oxford University Press, 1997).

15. *SC,* 2 June 1928, p. 6.

16. Church Records, St. John's United Church of Christ (accession 34562 Miscellaneous Microfilm Reels 1146–48), W. H. Zimmerman to Max Linder, 2 Oct. 1911, "Protokoll Book, 1898–1920," insert following page 141, Archives Research Services, Library of Virginia, Richmond; *SC,* 29 July 1922, p. 5; *RH,* 23 May 1929, p. 8.

17. *RNL,* 15 Oct. 1901, p. 4; C. Luther Fry, "Changes in Religious Organizations," in Report of the President's Research Committee on Social Trends, *Recent Social Trends in the United States, Volume II* (New York: McGraw-Hill, 1933; reprint, Westport, Conn.: Greenwood, 1970), 1053.

18. *SC,* 9 Feb. 1924, p. 7.

19. *RH,* 10 Nov. 1910, p. 8.

20. *RH,* 18 Jan. 1923, p. 3; *SC,* 3 Jan. 1920, p. 9. *RH,* 25 May 1905, p. 2.

21. *RNL,* 10 June 1919, pp. 11, 20.

22. "Jesus Saviour," sermon, 5 June 1927, H. D. C. Maclachlan Papers, Disciples of Christ Historical Society, Nashville; *SC,* 7 Nov. 1925, p. 11; Lewis C. Williams to Walter Russell Bowie, 21 June 1923, Papers of the *Southern Churchman* Company, Virginia Historical Society, Richmond; *SC,* 16 Feb. 1918, p. 10.

23. *BRCA,* 2 May 1912, p. 9.

24. W. L. Carson, "The Only Cure for the World's Ills," sermon, 25 May 1924, W. L. Carson Papers, Presbyterian Historical Society, Montreat, N.C.

25. *RCA,* 25 July 1929, p. 2.

26. Virginius Dabney, *Liberalism in the South* (Chapel Hill: University of North Carolina Press, 1932), 262; *PS,* 2 Sept. 1925, p. 1; *CP,* 9 Sept. 1908, p. 5.

27. Maria Williams Sheerin, *The Parson Takes a Wife* (New York: Macmillan, 1948), 92–93.

28. *BRCA,* 30 May 1907, p. 11.

29. *BRCA,* 30 May 1907, p. 11; *SC,* 17 July 1926, p. 8.

30. Richard Hofstadter, *The Age of Reform* (New York: Random House, 1955), 23–26; *RH,* 22 Feb. 1906, p. 4; *RCA,* 28 Apr. 1921, p. 1; Walter Russell Bowie, *Some Open Ways to God* (New York: Charles Scribner's Sons, 1924), 43.

31. Edmund deS. Brunner, *Church Life in the Rural South* (New York: George H. Doran Co., 1923), 50, 99; James H. Madison, "Reformers and the Rural Church, 1900–1950," *Journal of American History* 73, no. 3 (Dec. 1986): 645–68; Jeffrey L. Gall, "Presbyterians, Warren Wilson, and the Country Life Movement," *Journal of Presbyterian History* 76 no. 3 (fall 1998): 215–31; Merwin Swanson, "The 'Country Life Movement' and the American Churches," *Church History* 46 (Sept. 1977): 358–73; J. Wayne Flynt, "Southern Baptists: Rural to Urban Transition," *Baptist History and Heritage* 16 (Jan. 1981): 24–31; Wayne Flynt, "One in the Spirit, Many in the Flesh: Southern Evangelicals," in *Varieties of Southern Evangelicalism,* ed. David E. Harrell and Martin E. Marty (Macon, Ga.: Mercer University Press, 1981), 37–40; James J. Thompson Jr., *Tried As By Fire: Southern Baptists and the Religious Controversies of the 1920s* (Macon, Ga.: Mercer University Press, 1982), 173–79.

32. Samuel Chiles Mitchell, "The Great Need of the Country Churches," *Baptist Union,* 1907 in the S. C. Mitchell Papers, Library of Congress, Washington, D.C.; *RCA,* 31 Mar. 1927, p. 2; *RH,* 8 Dec. 1927, p. 4; *RCA,* 9 Feb. 1928, p. 5; *RH,* 22 Dec. 1927, p. 4.

33. *RH,* 18 July 1929, 8–9, 13; Charles H. Hamilton and William E. Garnett, *The Role of the Church in Rural Community Life in Virginia* (Blacksburg: Virginia Polytechnic Institute, Virginia Agricultural Experiment Station, 1929). The Virginians thus conformed to a national pattern. In "Reformers and the Rural Church," 647, James H. Madison argues that elsewhere in the United States, "the outsiders were determined to remake rural churches in the image of the urban counterparts, even if the remaking uprooted traditional beliefs and values."

34. Fry, "Changes in Religious Organizations," 1019, 1021–22. Focusing on two congregations in *The Protestant Experience in Gary, Indiana, 1906–1975: At Home in the City* (Knoxville: University of Tennessee Press, 1992), James W. Lewis also concludes that churches succeeded in responding well to the challenges of urban life.

Selected Bibliography

Newspapers and Journals

Baltimore and Richmond Christian Advocate (Methodist), 1901–18.
Central Presbyterian (Presbyterian), 1900–1908.
Chesapeake Christian (Disciples of Christ), 1921–28.
Forward (Episcopal), 1920–21.
Friendly Church Messenger (Seventh Street Christian Church), 1921–28.
Labor Herald (Virginia Federation of Labor), 1924–28.
Labor Journal (Virginia Federation of Labor), 1922–24.
League Record (Presbyterian), 1916–24.
Presbyterian of the South (Presbyterian), 1909–10, 1913–29.
Religious Herald (Baptist), 1900–29.
Richmond Christian Advocate (Methodist), 1900, 1919–29.
Richmond Magazine (Chamber of Commerce), 1914–30.
Richmond News Leader, 1914–29.
Richmond Times, 1900–1902.
Richmond Times-Dispatch, 1903–14.
Southern Churchman (Episcopal), 1900–1929.
Square Deal (Richmond Central Trades and Labor Council), 1915–22.
Union Seminary Magazine (Presbyterian), 1900–1913.
Union Seminary Review (Presbyterian), 1913–29.
Virginia Churchman (Episcopal), 1922–28.

Manuscript Collections

Alderman Library, University of Virginia, Charlottesville
  Denny, Collins. Papers.
Bishop Payne Library, Virginia Theological Seminary, Alexandria, Va.
  Bowie, Walter Russell. Papers.
Disciples of Christ Historical Society, Nashville, Tenn.
  Maclachlan, H. D. C. Papers.
  Spencer, Jessie. Papers.
First English Evangelical Lutheran Church, Richmond
  Men's Bible Class. Papers.

James Branch Cabell Library, Special Collections and Archives Department, Virginia Commonwealth University, Richmond
Young Women's Christian Association. Papers.
Library of Congress, Washington, D.C.
Freeman, Douglas Southall. Papers.
Mitchell, Samuel Chiles. Papers.
Library of Virginia, Archives Research Services, Richmond
Munford, Mary-Cooke Branch. Papers.
St. John's United Church of Christ. Papers.
Virginia War History Commission.
McGraw-Page Library, Archives and Special Collections, Randolph-Macon College, Ashland, Va.
Trinity Methodist Episcopal Church. Papers.
Mary Grace Scherer Taylor, Richmond
Scherer, John J., Jr. Papers.
Presbyterian Historical Society, Montreat, N.C.
Carson, W. L. Papers.
Lingle, Walter L. Papers.
Magill, R. E. Papers.
Rare Book, Manuscript and Special Collections Library, Duke University, Durham, N.C.
Mason, Lucy Randolph. Papers.
Southern Historical Collection, Wilson Library, University of North Carolina, Chapel Hill, N.C.
Mitchell, Samuel Chiles. Papers.
Virginia Baptist Historical Society, Richmond
McDaniel, George White. Papers.
Virginia Historical Society, Richmond
Binford, Anna. Papers.
Brown, Ida Dorsey. Papers.
Chamberlayne, Churchill Gibson. Papers.
Crutchfield, John J. Scrapbook.
Ellett-St. Catherine's Alumnae Association. Papers.
Freeman, Douglas Southall. Scrapbook.
Grace and Holy Trinity Episcopal Church. Papers.
Munford Family Papers.
Price, Louise Fitzhugh. Papers.
St. James's Episcopal Church. Papers.
St. John's Episcopal Church. Papers.
St. Paul's Episcopal Church. Papers.
Scott Family Papers.
Seventh Street Christian Church. Papers.
Sheltering Arms Hospital. Papers.
Southern Churchman Company. Papers.
Valentine, Lila Meade. Papers.
William Smith Morton Library, Union Theological Seminary/Presbyterian School of Christian Education, Richmond

Cecil, Russell. Papers.
Moore, Walter W. Papers.

Minutes of Meetings and Conferences

Baptist Council of Richmond. "Minutes of the Executive Committee, 1903–29." Virginia Baptist Historical Society, Richmond.

Baptist General Association of Virginia. *Minutes of Annual Session,* 1900–1930. Virginia Baptist Historical Society, Richmond.

Dover Baptist Association. *Minutes of Annual Session,* 1900–1929. Virginia Baptist Historical Society, Richmond.

"Minutes of Woman's Work in East Hanover Presbytery." William Smith Morton Library, Union Theological Seminary/Presbyterian School of Christian Education, Richmond.

Presbyterian Ministers Association of Richmond, Virginia. "Minutes of the Meetings, 1900–1928." William Smith Morton Library, Union Theological Seminary/Presbyterian School of Christian Education, Richmond.

Richmond District Conference, Virginia Conference, Methodist Episcopal Church, South. Sessions, 1901–29. Archives and Special Collections, McGraw-Page Library, Randolph-Macon College, Ashland, Va.

Richmond Education Association, *Annual Report,* 1901–16. Virginia Historical Society, Richmond.

Richmond Ministerial Union. "Minutes of the Meetings, 1919–1928." Richmond Public Library, Richmond.

Richmond Preachers Meeting. "Minutes of the Meetings, 1900–1928." Archives and Special Collections, McGraw-Page Library, Randolph-Macon College, Ashland, Va.

Synod of Virginia, Presbyterian Church in the United States. *Annual Session,* 1899–1932. Union Theological Seminary/Presbyterian School of Christian Education, Richmond.

Virginia Annual Conference of the Methodist Episcopal Church, South. *Minutes of Annual Conference,* 1900–1930. Archives and Special Collections, McGraw-Page Library, Randolph-Macon College, Ashland, Va.

Virginia Conference of Charities and Correction. *Proceedings of the Annual Session,* 1900–1913. Library of Virginia, Richmond.

Government Documents

Bane, Frank. *Shall the Local Jail Be Abolished?* Richmond, 1922.

Richmond (Virginia) City Council. Special Joint Committee, Appointed to Investigate Official Conduct of Members of the Board of Police Commissioners and Members of the Police Force of the City of Richmond. Stenographer's Transcript, March–May 1915. Office of the City Clerk, Richmond.

U.S. Department of Commerce. Bureau of the Census. *Census of Religious Bodies: 1916.* Washington, D.C.: GPO, 1919.

———. *Census of Religious Bodies: 1926.* Washington, D.C: GPO, 1930.

———. *Fifteenth Census of the United States, Manufactures: 1929, State Series: Virginia.* Washington, D.C.: GPO, 1932.

———. *Fifteenth Census of the United States, 1930: Population.* Vol. 4. Washington, D.C.: GPO, 1930.

———. *Fifteenth Census of the United States: 1930, Population Bulletin, Second Series, Virginia.* Washington, D.C.: GPO, 1931.

———. *Financial Statistics of Cities Having a Population of Over 30,000: 1930.* Washington, D.C.: GPO, 1930.

———. *Religious Bodies: 1936.* Washington, D.C.: GPO, 1941.

———. *Thirteenth Census of the United States, 1910: Population. Statistics for Virginia.* Washington, D.C.: GPO, 1913.

———. *Wealth, Debt and Taxation: 1922.* Washington D.C.: GPO, 1924.

U.S. Department of Commerce and Labor. Bureau of the Census. *Census of Manufactures: 1905.* Pt. 2, Bulletin No. 44. Washington, D.C.: GPO, 1906.

———. *Census of Religious Bodies: 1906.* Washington, D.C.: GPO, 1910.

———. *Occupations at the Twelfth Census.* Washington, D.C.: GPO, 1904.

———. *Statistics of Cities Having a Population of Over 30,000: 1905.* Washington, D.C.: GPO, 1905.

———. *Wealth, Debt and Taxation: 1907.* Washington, D.C.: GPO, 1907.

U.S. Department of Labor. Bureau of Labor Statistics. *Vocational Education Survey of Richmond, Virginia.* Whole no. 162, misc. ser. no. 7. Washington D.C.: GPO, 1916.

Virginia State. State Board of Charities and Corrections. *Annual Report of the State Board of Charities and Corrections to the Governor,* 1908–21. Library of Virginia, Richmond.

Books, Articles, and Pamphlets

Abell, Aaron I. *The Urban Impact on American Protestantism, 1865–1900.* Cambridge, Mass.: Harvard University Press, 1943. Reprint, Hamden, Conn.: Archon, 1962.

Abernathy, Jack. *Living Monuments: The Story of Grace Covenant Presbyterian Church, Richmond, Virginia, 1790–1990.* Richmond: Grace Covenant Church, 1989.

Abrams, Ray H. *Preachers Present Arms: A Study of the War-Time Attitudes and Activities of the Churches and Clergy in the United States, 1914–1918.* New York: Round Table Press, 1933.

Addison, James Thayer. *The Episcopal Church in the United States, 1789–1931.* New York: Charles Scribner's Sons, 1951.

Allen, Frederick Lewis. *Only Yesterday.* New York: Harper & Brothers, 1931. Reprint, Harper & Row, 1964.

Alley, Reuben E. *Frederic W. Boatwright.* Richmond: University of Richmond, 1973.

———. *A History of Baptists in Virginia.* Richmond: Virginia Baptist General Board, 1973.

———. *History of the University of Richmond, 1830–1971.* Charlottesville: University Press of Virginia, 1977.

Anderson, James D. *The Education of Blacks in the South, 1860–1935.* Chapel Hill: University of North Carolina Press, 1988.

Ayres, Edward L. *The Promise of the New South: Life After Reconstruction.* New York: Oxford University Press, 1992.

Ayres, Edward L., and John C. Willis, eds. *The Edge of the South: Life in Nineteenth-Century Virginia.* Charlottesville: University Press of Virginia, 1991.

Bailey, Beth L. *From Front Porch to Back Seat: Courtship in Twentieth-Century America.* Baltimore: Johns Hopkins University Press, 1988.

Bailey, Fred Arthur. "Free Speech and the Lost Cause in the Old Dominion." *Virginia Magazine of History and Biography* 103, no. 2 (April 1995): 237–66.
Bailey, Kenneth K. *Southern White Protestantism in the Twentieth Century.* New York: Oxford University Press, 1964.
Baker, Ray Stannard. *Following the Color Line: American Negro Citizenship in the Progressive Era.* New York: Doubleday, Page & Co., 1908. Reprint, New York: Harper Torchbooks, 1964.
Baker, Robert. *The Southern Baptist Convention and Its People, 1607–1972.* Nashville: Broadman Press, 1974.
Barnes, William Wright. *The Southern Baptist Convention, 1945–1953.* Nashville: Broadman Press, 1954.
Barth, Gunther. *City People: The Rise of Modern City Culture in Nineteenth-Century America.* New York: Oxford University Press, 1980.
Bearss, Sara B., and Patricia D. Thompson. *Foster's Richmond.* Richmond: Virginia Historical Society, 1991.
Bendroth, Margaret Lamberts. *Fundamentalism and Gender: 1975 to the Present.* New Haven, Conn.: Yale University Press, 1993.
Bennett, Floyd S. *Methodist Church on Shockoe Hill: A History of Centenary Methodist Church, Richmond, Virginia, 1810–1960.* Richmond: n.p., 1962.
Berlin, Ira. *Slaves without Masters: The Free Negro in the Antebellum South.* New York: Oxford University Press, 1974.
Berman, Myron. *Richmond's Jewry, 1769–1976: Shabbat in Shockoe.* Charlottesville: University Press of Virginia, 1979.
Bernstein, Irving. *The Lean Years: A History of the American Worker, 1920–1933.* Boston: Houghton Mifflin, 1966.
Bethlehem Lutheran Church, Richmond, Virginia: 125th Anniversary. South Hackensack, N.J.: Custombook, 1977.
Blanton, Wyndam B. *Making of a Downtown Church: The History of the Second Presbyterian Church, Richmond, Virginia, 1845–1945.* Richmond: John Knox Press, 1945.
Blocker, Jack S., Jr. *American Temperance Movements: Cycles of Reform.* Boston: Twayne, 1989.
Boles, John B., and Evelyn Thomas Nolen, eds. *Interpreting Southern History: Historiographical Essays in Honor of Sanford W. Higginbotham.* Baton Rouge: Louisiana State University Press, 1987.
Bolt, Ernest C. *Ballots before Bullets: The War Referendum Approach to Peace in America, 1914–1941.* Charlottesville: University Press of Virginia, 1977.
Bowie, Walter Russell. *The Inescapable Christ.* London: John Murray, 1926.
———. *Learning to Live.* Nashville: Abingdon Press, 1969.
———. *The Road of the Star.* New York: Fleming H. Revell, 1922.
———. *Some Open Ways to God.* New York: Charles Scribner's Sons, 1924.
———. *Sunny Windows and Other Sermons for Children.* New York: Fleming H. Revell, 1921.
———. *Sunrise in the South: The Life of Mary-Cooke Branch Munford.* Richmond: William Byrd Press, 1942.
Boyer, Paul. *Urban Masses and Moral Order in America, 1820–1920.* Cambridge, Mass.: Harvard University Press, 1978.
———. *When Time Shall Be No More: Prophecy Belief in Modern American Culture.* Cambridge, Mass.: Harvard University Press, 1992.

Boylan, Anne M. *Sunday School: The Formation of an American Institution, 1790–1880.* New Haven, Conn.: Yale University Press, 1988.

Brandt, Allan M. *No Magic Bullet: A Social History of Venereal Disease in the United States since 1880.* New York: Oxford University Press, 1985.

Bremner, Robert H. *American Philanthropy.* Chicago: University of Chicago Press, 1960.

———. *From the Depths: The Discovery of Poverty in the United States.* New York: New York University Press, 1956.

Brereton, Virginia Lieson. *Training God's Army: The American Bible School, 1880–1940.* Bloomington: University of Indiana Press, 1990.

Brinson, Marion B., H. G. Haney, and G. Edwin Osborn. *A Century with Christ: A Story of the Christian Church in Richmond.* Richmond: Whittet & Shepperson, 1932.

Brownell, Blaine A. *The Urban Ethos in the South, 1920–1930.* Baton Rouge: Louisiana State University Press, 1975.

Brownell, Blaine A., and David Goldfield, eds. *The City in Southern History: The Growth of Urban Civilization in the South.* Port Washington, N.Y.: Kennikat Press, 1977.

Brownell, Blaine A. "Birmingham, Alabama: New South City in the 1920s." *Journal of Southern History* 38, no. 1 (February 1972): 21–48.

———. "Urbanization in the South: A Unique Experience?" *Mississippi Quarterly* 26 (spring 1973):105–20.

Bruce, Philip Alexander. *The Rise of the New South.* Philadelphia: G. Barrie & Sons, [1905].

Brundage, W. Fitzhugh. *Lynching in the New South: Georgia and Virginia, 1880–1930.* Urbana: University of Illinois Press, 1993.

Brunner, Edmund deS. *Church Life in the Rural South.* New York: George H. Doran, 1923.

Bryan, John Stewart. *Joseph Bryan: His Times, His Family and His Friends.* Richmond: Whittet & Shepperson, 1935.

Bryan, William Jennings. *In His Image.* New York: Fleming H. Revell, 1922.

Buck, J. L. Blair. *The Development of Public Schools in Virginia, 1607–1952.* Richmond: Commonwealth of Virginia State Board of Education, 1952.

Buckley, Thomas J. *Church and State in Revolutionary Virginia, 1776–1787.* Charlottesville: University Press of Virginia, 1977.

Buni, Andrew. *The Negro in Virginia Politics, 1902–1965.* Charlottesville: University Press of Virginia, 1967.

Burner, David. *The Politics of Provincialism: The Democratic Party in Transition.* New York: Alfred A. Knopf, 1968.

Burnham, John C. "The Progressive Era Revolution in American Attitudes Toward Sex." *Journal of American History* 59 (1962): 885–908.

Burton, Orville Vernon, and Robert C. McMath Jr., eds. *Toward a New South? Studies in Post-Civil War Southern Communities.* Westport, Conn.: Greenwood Press, 1982.

Cabell, James Branch. *Let Me Lie.* New York: Farrar, Straus & Co., 1947.

Calisch, Edward N. *Three Score and Twenty: A Brief Biography of Edward Nathan Calisch.* Richmond: Old Dominion Press, 1945.

Cannon, James, Jr. *Bishop Cannon's Own Story: Life As I Have Seen It.* Edited by Richard L. Watson Jr. Durham, N.C.: Duke University Press, 1955.

Carneal, Drew St.J. *Richmond's Fan District.* Richmond: Historic Richmond Foundation, 1996.

Carter, Paul A. *The Decline and Revival of the Social Gospel: Social and Political Liberalism in American Protestant Churches, 1920–1940.* Ithaca, N.Y.: Cornell University Press, 1954.

Cash, W. J. *The Mind of the South.* New York: Alfred A. Knopf, 1941.

Cauthen, Kenneth. *The Impact of American Religious Liberalism.* New York: Harper & Row, 1962.

Cecil Russell. *The Religion of Love.* Richmond: Presbyterian Committee of Publication, 1924.

Chafe, William. *The Paradox of Change: American Women in the Twentieth Century.* New York: Oxford University Press, 1991.

Chalmers, David M. *Hooded Americanism: The History of the Ku Klux Klan.* Garden City, N.Y.: Doubleday & Co., 1965.

Chatfield, Charles. *For Peace and Justice: Pacifism in America, 1914–1941.* Knoxville: University of Tennessee Press, 1971.

———, ed. *Peace Movements in America.* New York: Schocken Books, 1973.

Chenault, Frederick R. *The Broad Street Methodist Church, South and Community House.* Richmond: Whittet & Shepperson, 1923.

Chesson, Michael B. *Richmond After the War, 1865–1890.* Richmond: Virginia State Library, 1981.

Christian, W. Asbury. *Richmond: Her Past and Present.* Richmond: L. H. Jenkins, 1912.

Clapp, Elizabeth J. *Mothers of All Children: Women Reformers and the Rise of Juvenile Courts in Progressive Era America.* University Park: Penn State Press, 1998.

Clark, Norman H. *Deliver Us from Evil: An Interpretation of American Prohibition.* New York: W. W. Norton & Co., 1976.

Cohen, Warren. *Empire without Tears: America's Foreign Relations, 1921–1933.* New York: Alfred A. Knopf, 1987.

Cole, Stewart. *The History of Fundamentalism.* New York: R. R. Smith, 1931. Reprint, Westport, Conn.: Greenwood Press, 1971.

Connelly, Mark T. *The Response to Prostitution in the Progressive Era.* Chapel Hill: University of North Carolina Press, 1980.

Coontz, Stephanie. *The Way We Were: American Families and the Nostalgia Trap.* New York: Basic Books, 1992.

Couch, W. T., ed. *Culture in the South.* Chapel Hill: University of North Carolina Press, 1935.

Curry, Thomas J. *The First Freedoms: Church and State in America to the Passage of the First Amendment.* New York: Oxford University Press, 1986.

Curti, Merle. *Peace or War: The American Struggle, 1636–1936.* New York: W. W. Norton & Co., 1936.

Curtis, Susan. *A Consuming Faith: The Social Gospel and Modern American Culture.* Baltimore: Johns Hopkins University Press, 1991.

Cutchins, John A. *Memories of Old Richmond (1881–1944).* Verona, Va.: McClure Press, 1973.

Dabney, Charles William. *Universal Education in the South: Volume II.* Chapel Hill: University of North Carolina Press, 1936.

Dabney, Virginius. *Dry Messiah: The Life of Bishop Cannon.* New York: Alfred A. Knopf, 1949. Reprint, Westport, Conn.: Greenwood Press, 1970.

———. *Liberalism in the South.* Chapel Hill: University of North Carolina Press, 1932.

———. *Richmond: The Story of a City.* Rev. ed. Charlottesville: University Press of Virginia, 1990.

———. *Virginia Commonwealth University: A Sesquicentennial History.* Charlottesville: University Press of Virginia, 1987.

Daniel, W. Harrison. *History at the University of Richmond.* Richmond: W. Harrison Daniel, 1991.

Davidson, Elizabeth H. *Child Labor Legislation in the Southern Textile States.* Chapel Hill: University of North Carolina Press, 1939.

Davis, Arthur Kyle, ed. *Virginia Communities in War Time.* Vol. 7. Richmond: Virginia War History Commission, 1927.

Davis, Lawrence B. *Immigrants, Baptists and the Protestant Mind in America.* Urbana: University of Illinois Press, 1973.

Dayton, Donald W., and Robert D. Johnston, eds. *The Variety of American Evangelicalism.* Knoxville: University of Tennessee Press, 1991.

Dean, Talmage W. *A Survey of Twentieth Century Protestant Church Music in America.* Nashville: Broadman Press, 1988.

DeBenedetti, Charles. *The Peace Reform in America.* Bloomington: University of Indiana Press, 1980.

DeBerg, Betty A. *Ungodly Women: Gender and the First Wave of American Fundamentalism.* Minneapolis: Fortress Press, 1990.

D'Emilio, John, and Estelle B. Freedman. *Intimate Matters: A History of Sexuality in America.* New York: Harper & Row, 1988.

Dinnerstein, Leonard. *Antisemitism in America.* New York: Oxford University Press, 1994.

Dollar, George W. *A History of Fundamentalism in America.* Greenville, S.C.: Bob Jones University Press, 1973.

Donovan, Mary Sudman. *A Different Call: Women's Ministries in the Episcopal Church, 1850–1920.* Wilton, Conn.: Morehouse-Barlow, 1986.

Dorsett, Lyle W. *Billy Sunday and the Redemption of Urban America.* Grand Rapids, Mich.: William B. Eerdmans Publishing, 1991.

Douglass, H. Paul. *The City's Church.* New York: Friendship Press, 1929.

Doyle, Don H. *Nashville in the New South, 1880–1930.* Knoxville: University of Tennessee Press, 1985.

———. *New Men, New Cities, New South: Atlanta, Nashville, Charleston, Mobile, 1860–1910.* Chapel Hill: University of North Carolina Press, 1990.

Duke, Maurice, and Daniel P. Jordan, eds. *A Richmond Reader, 1722–1983.* Chapel Hill: University of North Carolina Press, 1983.

Dulaney, Paul S. *The Architecture of Historic Richmond.* Charlottesville: University Press of Virginia, 1968.

Dykeman, Wilma, and James Stokeley. *Seeds of Southern Change: The Life of Will Alexander.* Chicago: University of Chicago Press, 1962.

Eighmy, John Lee. *Churches in Cultural Captivity: A History of the Social Attitudes of Southern Baptists.* Knoxville: University of Tennessee Press, 1972.

Eisenberg, William Edward. *The Lutheran Church in Virginia, 1717–1962.* Roanoke: Trustees of the Virginia Synod, Lutheran Church in America, 1967.

Eliade, Mircea. *The Sacred and the Profane: The Nature of Religion.* New York: Harcourt, Brace & World, 1959.

Ellis, William E. *"A Man of Books and a Man of the People": E. Y. Mullins and the Crisis of Moderate Southern Baptist Leadership.* Macon, Ga.: Mercer University Press, 1985.

Ellyson, Belle Gayle. *The History of the Second Baptist Church, Richmond, Virginia: 1820–1970.* Richmond: Whittet & Shepperson, 1970.

Estep, William R. *Whole Gospel—Whole World: The Foreign Mission Board of the Southern Baptist Convention, 1845–1995.* Nashville: Broadman & Holman 1994.

Fass, Paula S. *The Damned and the Beautiful: American Youth in the 1920s.* New York: Oxford University Press, 1977.

Filene, Peter. "An Obituary for the 'Progressive Movement.'" *American Quarterly* 22 (1970): 20–34.

Fink, Leon. *Workingman's Democracy: The Knights of Labor and American Politics.* Urbana: University of Illinois Press, 1983.

Flynt, J. Wayne. *Alabama Baptists: Southern Baptists in the Heart of Dixie.* Tuscaloosa: University of Alabama Press, 1998.

———. "Dissent in Zion: Alabama Baptists and Social Issues, 1900–1914." *Journal of Southern History* 35 (winter 1968): 523–42.

———. "Religion in the Urban South: The Divided Religious Mind of Birmingham, 1900–1930." *Alabama Review* 30 (April 1977): 108–34.

———. "Southern Baptists: Rural to Urban Transition." *Baptist History and Heritage* 16 (January 1981): 24–34.

Foster, Gaines M. *Ghosts of the Confederacy: Defeat, the Lost Cause, and the Emergence of the New South, 1865–1913.* New York: Oxford University Press, 1987.

Fraser, Walter J., Jr., R. Frank Saunders Jr., and Jon L. Wakelyn, eds. *The Web of Southern Social Relations: Women, Family, and Education.* Athens: University of Georgia Press, 1985.

Freeman, Anne Hobson. "Mary Munford's Fight for a College for Women Co-ordinate with the University of Virginia." *Virginia Magazine of History and Biography* 78 (October 1970): 481–91.

Fredrickson, George M. *The Black Image in the White Mind: The Debate on Afro-American Character and Destiny, 1817–1914.* New York: Harper & Row, 1971.

Friedman, Jean E. *The Enclosed Garden: Women and Community in the Evangelical South, 1830–1900.* Chapel Hill: University of North Carolina Press, 1985.

Furniss, Norman, F. *The Fundamentalist Controversy, 1918–1931.* New Haven: Yale University Press, 1954.

Galishoff, Stuart. *Safeguarding the Public Health: Newark, 1895–1918.* Westport, Conn.: Greenwood Press, 1975.

Garrison, Winfred Ernest, and Alfred T. DeGroot. *The Disciples of Christ: A History.* St. Louis: Christian Board of Publication, 1948.

Gatewood, Willard B., Jr., ed. *Controversy in the Twenties: Fundamentalism, Modernism, and Evolution.* Nashville: Vanderbilt University Press, 1969.

———. *Preachers, Pedagogues, and Politicians: The Evolution Controversy in North Carolina 1920–1927.* Chapel Hill: University of North Carolina Press, 1966.

Gavins, Raymond. *The Perils and Prospects of Southern Black Leadership: Gordon Blaine Hancock, 1884–1970.* Durham, N.C.: Duke University Press, 1977.

Gee, Wilson, and John J. Corson III. *Rural Depopulation in Certain Tidewater and Piedmont Areas of Virginia.* Charlottesville: Institute for Research in the Social Sciences, University of Virginia, 1929.

———. *A Statistical Study of Virginia.* Charlottesville: Institute for Research in the Social Sciences, University of Virginia, 1927.

Gee, Wilson, and William H. Stauffer. *Rural and Urban Living Standards in Virginia.* Charlottesville: Institute for Research in the Social Sciences, University of Virginia, 1929.

Geisinger, Joseph F., ed. *History of U.S. Army Base Hospital No. 45 in the Great War.* Richmond: William Byrd, 1924.

Glasgow, Ellen. *Life and Gabriella.* Garden City, N.Y.: Doubleday, Page & Co., 1916.

———. *The Romance of a Plain Man.* New York: Macmillan Co., 1909.

———. *The Romantic Comedians.* Garden City, N.Y.: Doubleday, Page & Co., 1926.

———. *The Sheltered Life.* Garden City, N.Y.: Doubleday, Doran & Co, 1932.

———. *Virginia.* Garden City, N.Y.: Doubleday, Page & Co., 1913.

———. *The Voice of the People.* New York: Doubleday, Page & Co., 1902.

———. *The Woman Within.* New York: Harcourt, Brace, 1954.

Glenn, William N. *St. Andrew's Episcopal Church and Its Environs.* Richmond: Whittet & Shepperson, 1978.

Goldfield, David. *Cotton Fields and Skyscrapers: Southern City and Region, 1607–1980.* Baton Rouge: Louisiana State University Press, 1982.

———. *Region, Race and Cities: Interpreting the Urban South.* Baton Rouge: Louisiana State University Press, 1997.

———. *Urban Growth in the Age of Sectionalism: Virginia, 1847–1861.* Baton Rouge: Louisiana State University Press, 1977.

———. "The Urban South: A Regional Framework." *American Historical Review* 86, no. 5 (December 1981):1009–34.

Goodman, Susan. *Ellen Glasgow: A Biography.* Baltimore: Johns Hopkins University Press, 1998.

Gorrell, Donald R. *The Age of Social Responsibility: The Social Gospel in the Progressive Era, 1900–1920.* Macon: Mercer University Press, 1988.

Graham, Sarah Hunter. "Woman's Suffrage in Virginia: The Equal Suffrage League and Pressure-Group Politics." *Virginia Magazine of History and Biography* 101, no. 2 (April 1993): 227–50.

Grantham, Dewey W. *Southern Progressivism: The Reconciliation of Progress and Tradition.* Knoxville: University of Tennessee Press, 1983.

Green, Elna C. *Southern Strategies: Southern Women and the Woman Suffrage Question.* Chapel Hill: University of North Carolina Press, 1997.

Guild, June Purcell. *Black Laws of Virginia: A Summary of the Legislative Acts of Virginia Concerning Negroes from Earliest Times to the Present.* Richmond: Whittet & Shepperson, 1936.

Gusfield, Joseph. *Symbolic Crusade: Status Politics and the American Temperance Movement.* Urbana: University of Illinois Press, 1963.

Haber, Samuel. *Efficiency and Uplift: Scientific Management in the Progressive Era, 1890–1920.* Chicago: University of Chicago Press, 1964.

Hackley, Woodford B. *Faces on the Wall: Brief Sketches of the Men and Women Whose Portraits and Busts were on the Campus of the University of Richmond in 1955.* Richmond: Virginia Baptist Historical Society, 1972.

Hale, Thomas E., and Louis H. Manarin. *Richmond: A Pictorial History from the Valentine Museum and Deminti Collections.* Richmond: Hale, [1974].

Hall, Jacquelyn Dowd. *Revolt against Chivalry: Jessie Daniel Ames and the Women's Campaign against Lynching.* New York: Columbia University Press, 1979.

Hamilton, Charles H., and William E. Garnett. *The Role of the Church in Rural Community Life in Virginia.* Blacksburg: Virginia Polytechnic Institute, Virginia Agricultural Experiment Station, 1929.

Hamm, Richard F. *Shaping the Eighteenth Amendment: Temperance Reform, Legal Culture, and the Polity, 1880–1920.* Chapel Hill: University of North Carolina Press, 1995.

Hankins, Barry. *God's Rascal: J. Frank Norris and the Beginnings of Southern Fundamentalism.* Lexington: University Press of Kentucky, 1996.

Hankins, DeWitt. *The First Fifty Years: A History of St. Christopher's School, 1911–1961.* Richmond: St. Christopher's School Foundation, 1961.

Harlan, Louis R. *Separate and Unequal: Public School Campaigns and Racism in the Southern Seaboard States, 1901–1915.* Chapel Hill: University of North Carolina Press, 1958. Reprint, New York: Atheneum, 1969.

Harper, Keith. *The Quality of Mercy: Southern Baptists and Social Christianity, 1890–1920.* Tuscaloosa: University of Alabama Press, 1996.

Harrell, David E., and Martin E. Marty, eds. *Varieties of Southern Evangelicalism.* Macon, Ga.: Mercer University Press, 1981.

Harris, Carl V. *Political Power in Birmingham, 1871–1921.* Knoxville: University of Tennessee Press, 1977.

Harrison, Henry Sydnor. *Queed: A Novel.* New York: Grosset & Dunlap, 1911.

Harvey, Paul. *Redeeming the South: Religious Cultures and Racial Identities among Southern Baptists, 1865–1925.* Chapel Hill: University of North Carolina Press, 1997.

Hatch, Nathan O. *The Democratization of American Christianity.* New Haven, Conn.: Yale University Press, 1989.

Hatcher, Orie Latham. *Occupations for Women: A Study Made for the Southern Woman's Educational Alliance.* Richmond: Southern Woman's Educational Alliance, 1927.

———. *Rural Girls in the City for Work: A Study Made for the Southern Woman's Educational Alliance.* Richmond: Garrett & Massie, 1930.

Hawthorne, James B. *The Cloud of Witnesses and Other Sermons.* Nashville: Sunday School Board of the Southern Baptist Convention, 1908.

———. *An Unshaken Trust and Other Sermons.* Philadelphia: American Baptist Publication Society, 1899.

Heer, Clarence. *Income and Wages in the South.* Chapel Hill: University of North Carolina Press, 1930.

Heinemann, Ronald L. *Harry Byrd of Virginia.* Charlottesville: University Press of Virginia, 1996.

Hibbs, Henry H. *A History of the Richmond Professional Institute.* Richmond: Whittet & Shepperson, 1973.

Higham, John. *Strangers in the Land: Patterns of American Nativism, 1860–1925.* New Brunswick, N.J.: Rutgers University Press, 1955. Reprint, New York: Atheneum, 1971.

Hill Directory Company's Richmond Classified Business Directory. Richmond: J. L. Hill, 1930.

Hill, Samuel S. "Fundamentalism and the South." *Perspectives in Religious Studies* 13 (fall 1986): 49–55.

———. *One Name but Several Faces: Variety in Popular Christian Denominations in Southern History.* Athens: University of Georgia Press, 1996.

———. *Southern Churches in Crisis.* Boston: Beacon Press, 1968.

———. *The South and the North in American Religion.* Athens: University of Georgia Press, 1980.

Hobbs, Herschel. "Southern Baptists and Confessionalism: A Comparison of the Origins of the 1925 and 1963 Confessions." *Review and Expositor* 76 (winter 1979): 55–68.

Hobson, Barbara Meil. *Uneasy Virtue: The Politics of Prostitution and the American Reform Tradition.* New York: Basic Books, 1987.

Hofstadter, Richard. *The Age of Reform.* New York: Random House, 1955.

Hohner, Robert A. *Prohibition and Politics: The Life of Bishop James Cannon, Jr.* Columbia: University of South Carolina Press, 1999.

———. "Bishop Cannon's Apprenticeship in Temperance Politics, 1901–1918." *Journal of Southern History* 34 (February 1968): 33–49.

———. "The Prohibitionists: Who Were They?" *South Atlantic Quarterly* 68 (autumn 1969): 491–505.

———. "Prohibition Comes to Virginia: The Referendum of 1914." *Virginia Magazine of History and Biography* 75 (October 1967): 473–88.

———. "Prohibition and Virginia Politics: William Hodges Mann Versus Henry St. George Tucker, 1909." *Virginia Magazine of History and Biography* 74 (January 1966): 88–107.

———. "The Other Harry Golden: Harry Golden and the Cannon Scandals." *North Carolina Historical Review* 65, no. 2 (April 1988): 154–72.

Holifield, E. Brooks. *The Gentlemen Theologians: American Theology and Southern Culture, 1795–1860.* Durham, N.C.: Duke University Press, 1978.

Holli, Melvin. *Reform in Detroit: Hazen Pingree and Urban Politics.* New York: Oxford University Press, 1969.

Hopkins, C. Howard. *The Rise of the Social Gospel in American Protestantism, 1865–1915.* New Haven, Conn.: Yale University Press, 1967.

Hopkins, Richard J. "Are Southern Cities Unique? Persistence As a Clue." *Mississippi Quarterly* 26 (spring 1973): 121–41.

Hutchison, William R. *The Modernist Impulse in American Protestantism.* Cambridge, Mass.: Harvard University Press, 1976.

Isaac, Rhys. *The Transformation of Virginia, 1740–1790.* Chapel Hill: University of North Carolina Press, 1982.

Jackson, Joy J. *New Orleans in the Gilded Age: Politics and Urban Progress, 1880–1896.* Baton Rouge: Louisiana State University Press, 1969.

Jackson, Kenneth T. *The Crabgrass Frontier: The Suburbanization of the United States.* New York: Oxford University Press, 1985.

———. *The Ku Klux Klan in the City, 1915–1930.* New York: Oxford University Press, 1967.

James, Arthur W. *The State Becomes a Social Worker: An Administrative Interpretation.* Richmond: Garrett & Massie, 1942.

———. *Virginia's Social Awakening: The Contribution of Dr. Mastin and the Board of Charities and Corrections.* Richmond: Garrett & Massie, 1939.

J. L. Hill Printing Company's Directory of Richmond and Manchester, Virginia, 1900. Richmond: J. L. Hill, 1900.

James, William. *The Varieties of Religious Experience: A Study in Human Nature.* New York: Random House, 1902.

Johnson, Thomas Cary. *God's Answer to Evolution.* Richmond: Presbyterian Committee of Publication, 1924.

———. *Virginia Presbyterians and Religious Liberty in Colonial and Revolutionary Times.* Richmond: Presbyterian Committee of Publication, 1907.

Johnston, Mary. *Hagar.* Boston: Houghton Mifflin, 1913. Reprint, with an introduction by Marjorie Spruill Wheeler, Charlottesville: University Press of Virginia, 1994.

Jones, Anne Goodwyn. *Tomorrow Is Another Day: The Woman Writer in the South, 1859–1936.* Baton Rouge: Louisiana State University Press, 1981.

Katz, Michael. *The Shadow of the Poorhouse: A Social History of Welfare in America.* Rev. ed. New York: Basic Books, 1996.

Kelly, Balmer H. "'No Ism but Bibleism': Biblical Studies at Union Theological Seminary in Virginia, 1812–1987." *Journal of Presbyterian History* 66, no. 2 (summer 1988): 105–14.

Kennedy, David M. *Over Here: The First World War and American Society.* New York: Oxford University Press, 1980.

Kerr, K. Austin. *Organized for Prohibition: A New History of the Anti-Saloon League.* New Haven, Conn.: Yale University Press, 1985.

Kerr, Robert Pollok. *Will the World Outgrow Christianity and Other Interrogatives on Vital Themes.* Chicago: Fleming H. Revell, 1901.

Kessler-Harris, Alice. *Out to Work: A History of Wage-Earning Women in the United States.* New York: Oxford University Press, 1982.

Keve, Paul W. *The History of Corrections in Virginia.* Charlottesville: University Press of Virginia, 1986.

Kirby, Jack Temple. *Darkness at the Dawning: Race and Reform in the Progressive South.* Philadelphia: J. B. Lippincott, 1972.

———. *Westmoreland Davis: Virginia Planter-Politician, 1859–1942.* Charlottesville: University Press of Virginia, 1968.

Klaus, Susan L., and Mary Porter Johns Martin. *A Part of Us Forever: A Centennial History of St. Catherine's School, 1890–1990.* Richmond: St. Catherine's School, 1989.

Knight, Charles Louis. *Negro Housing in Certain Virginia Cities.* Richmond: William Byrd Press, 1927.

Knight, Josephine Augusta Clarke. *Symbols of the South: Education and Early Life in Richmond under Tutorship of Miss "Jennie" Ellett.* Richmond: Garrett & Massie, 1941.

Kousser, J. Morgan. *The Shaping of Southern Politics: Suffrage Restrictions and the Establishment of the One-Party South, 1880–1910.* New Haven, Conn.: Yale University Press, 1974.

Kuehl, Warren, and Lynne K. Dunne. *Keeping the Covenant: American Internationalists and the League of Nations, 1920–1939.* Kent, Ohio: Kent State University Press, 1997.

Kusmer, Kenneth L. "The Functions of Organized Charity in the Progressive Era: Chicago as a Case Study." *Journal of American History* 60 (December 1973): 657–70.

Laband, David N., and Deborah Hendry Heinbuch. *Blue Laws: The History, Economics, and Politics of Sunday-Closing Laws.* Lexington, Mass.: Lexington Books, 1987.

Larsen, Lawrence H. *The Rise of the Urban South.* Lexington: University Press of Kentucky, 1985.

Larsen, William. *Montague of Virginia: The Making of a Southern Progressive.* Baton Rouge: Louisiana State University Press, 1965.

Larson, Edward J. *Summer for the Gods: The Scopes Trial and America's Continuing Debate Over Science and Religion.* New York: Basic Books, 1997.

———. *Trial and Error: The American Controversy Over Creation and Evolution.* New York: Oxford University Press, 1985.

Leatherman, Carolyn H. "Richmond Considers a Free Public Library: Andrew Carnegie's Offer of 1901." *Virginia Magazine of History and Biography* 96, no. 2 (April 1988): 181–92.

Leavitt, Judith Walzer. *The Healthiest City: Milwaukee and the Politics of Health Reform.* Princeton: Princeton University Press, 1982.

Leonard, Bill. *God's Last and Only Hope: The Fragmentation of the Southern Baptist Convention.* Grand Rapids, Mich.: William B. Eerdmans Publishing, 1990.

Leuchtenburg, William E. *The Perils of Prosperity, 1914–32.* Chicago: University of Chicago Press, 1958.
Levine, Lawrence. *Defender of the Faith: William Jennings Bryan, The Last Decade, 1915–1925.* New York: Oxford University Press, 1965.
Lewis, James W. *The Protestant Experience in Gary, Indiana, 1906–1975: At Home in the City.* Knoxville: University of Tennessee Press, 1992.
Lindgren, James M. *Preserving the Old Dominion: Historic Preservation and Virginia Traditionalism.* Charlottesville: University Press of Virginia, 1993.
———. "'For the Sake of Our Future': The Association for the Preservation of Virginia Antiquities and the Regeneration of Traditionalism." *Virginia Magazine of History and Biography* 97, no. 1 (January 1989): 47–74.
Lingle, Walter L. *The Bible and Social Problems.* New York: Fleming H. Revell, 1929.
Link, William A. *A Hard Country and a Lonely Place: Schooling, Society, and Reform in Rural Virginia, 1870–1920.* Chapel Hill: University of North Carolina Press, 1986.
———. *The Paradox of Progressivism, 1880–1930.* Chapel Hill: University of North Carolina Press, 1992.
Logan, Rayford W. *The Negro in American Life and Thought: The Nadir, 1877–1901.* New York: Dial Press, 1954.
Longfield, Bradley J. *The Presbyterian Controversy: Fundamentalists, Modernists, and Moderates.* New York: Oxford University Press, 1991.
Lubell, Samuel. *The Future of American Politics.* 3d rev. ed. New York: Harper & Row, 1965.
Lubove, Roy. *The Professional Altruist: The Emergence of Social Work as a Career, 1880–1930.* Cambridge, Mass.: Harvard University Press, 1965.
———. *The Progressives and the Slums: Tenement House Reform in New York City, 1890–1917.* Pittsburgh: University of Pittsburgh Press, 1962.
Luker, Ralph E. *The Social Gospel in Black and White, American Racial Reform, 1885–1912.* Chapel Hill: University of North Carolina Press, 1991.
Lynd, Robert S., and Helen Merrell Lynd. *Middletown: A Study in Modern American Culture.* New York: Harcourt, Brace & World, 1929. Reprint, Harvest Books, 1956.
Lynn, Robert W., and Elliott Wright. *The Big Little School: Two Hundred Years of the Sunday School.* Nashville: Broadman Press, 1980.
McAllister, J. Grey. *The Life and Letters of Walter W. Moore.* Richmond: Union Theological Seminary, 1939.
McBeth, Harry Leon. "The Role of Women in Southern Baptist History." *Baptist History and Heritage* 12 (January 1972): 3–25.
McComb, David G. *Houston, the Bayou City.* Austin: University of Texas Press, 1969.
McComb, Louise. *Presbyterian School of Christian Education: The First Seventy Years.* Richmond: Presbyterian School of Christian Education, 1985.
McDaniel, Douglass Scarborough. *George White McDaniel.* Nashville: Sunday School Board of the Southern Baptist Convention, 1928.
McDaniel, George W. *The Churches of the New Testament.* Nashville: Sunday School Board of the Southern Baptist Convention, 1921.
———. *Our Boys in France.* Richmond: Baptist State Mission Board, 1918.
———. *The People Called Baptists.* Nashville: Sunday School Board of the Southern Baptist Convention, 1925.
———. *Seeing the Best: Sermons and Addresses.* Nashville: Sunday School Board of the Southern Baptist Convention, 1923.

———. *The Supernatural Jesus.* Nashville: Sunday School Board of the Southern Baptist Convention, 1924.
McDannell, Colleen. *The Christian Home in Victorian America, 1840–1900.* Bloomington: University of Indiana Press, 1984.
MacDonald, Edgar. *James Branch Cabell and Richmond-in-Virginia.* Jackson: University Press of Mississippi, 1993.
McDowell, John Patrick. *The Social Gospel in the South: The Woman's Home Mission Movement in the Methodist Episcopal Church, South, 1886–1939.* Baton Rouge: Louisiana State University Press, 1982.
Mack, Edward. *The Christ of the Old Testament: Studies in the Beginnings and Growth of Messianic Prophecy.* Richmond: Presbyterian Committee of Publication, 1926.
———. *The Preacher's Old Testament.* New York: Fleming H. Revell, 1923.
McKelvey, Blake. *The Urbanization of America, 1860–1915.* New Brunswick, N.J.: Rutgers University Press, 1963.
McKinney, John C., and Edgard T. Thompson, eds. *The South in the Continuity and Change.* Durham, N.C.: Duke University Press, 1965.
Maclachlan, H. D. C. "A Bourgeois Church in a Proletarian World." *Christian Century,* 22 April 1920, 9–12.
———. *Church and State.* Richmond: Richmond Press, 1910.
———. "The Church's Contacts with Socialism." *Christian Century,* 15 July 1920, 10–12.
———. "Is Tithing Christian?" *Christian Century,* 21 April 1921, 14–16.
———. *Memorial to the Honorable Council of the City of Richmond.* Richmond: Juvenile Protective Society of Virginia, 1913.
———. "Studies in Sin." *Christian Century,* 19 October 1922, 1289–92.
———. "Studies in Sin: The Sin of Duress." *Christian Century,* 14 June 1923, 746–50.
———. "Studies in Sin: Sinning at Long Range." *Christian Century,* 22 March 1923, 361–65.
———. "Studies in Sin: The Sins of Adolescence." *Christian Century,* 7 December 1922, 1515–19.
McLean, Francis H., and Hilda K. Mills. *Survey of the Social Agencies of Richmond Virginia.* Richmond: American Association for Organizing Family and Social Work, 1923.
MacLean, Nancy. *Behind the Mask of Chivalry: The Making of the Second Ku Klux Klan.* New York: Oxford University Press, 1994.
McLoughlin, William G. *Billy Sunday Was His Real Name.* Chicago: University of Chicago, 1955.
McMillen, Neil R. *Dark Journey: Black Mississippians in the Age of Jim Crow.* Urbana: University of Illinois Press, 1990.
Madison, James H. "Reformers and the Rural Church, 1900–1950." *Journal of American History* 73, no. 3 (December 1986): 645–68.
Magruder, F. A. *Recent Administration in Virginia.* Baltimore: Johns Hopkins University Press, 1912.
Mancini, Matthew J. *One Dies, Get Another: Convict Leasing in the American South, 1866–1928.* Columbia: University of South Carolina Press, 1996.
Mann, Etta Donnan. *Four Years in the Governor's Mansion of Virginia—1910–1914.* Richmond: Dietz Press, 1937.
Marchand, Roland. *The American Peace Movement and Social Reform, 1898–1918.* Princeton, N.J.: Princeton University Press, 1972.

Marsden, George M. *Fundamentalism and American Culture: The Shaping of Twentieth-Century Evangelicalism, 1870–1925.* New York: Oxford University Press, 1980.

———. *Understanding Fundamentalism and Evangelicalism.* Grand Rapids, Mich.: William B. Eerdmans Publishing, 1991.

Marty, Martin E. *Righteous Empire: The Protestant Experience in America.* New York: Dial Press, 1970.

Marty, Martin E., and R. Scott Appleby, eds. *Fundamentalism Observed.* Chicago: University of Chicago Press, 1991.

Mason, Lucy Randolph. *The Divine Discontent.* Richmond: Equal Suffrage League of Virginia, 1913.

———. *The Shorter Day and Women Workers.* Richmond: Virginia League of Women Voters, 1922.

———. *Standards for Workers in Southern Industry.* New York: National Consumers' League, 1931.

———. *To Win These Rights: A Personal Story of the CIO in the South.* New York: Harper & Bros., 1952.

May, Elaine Tyler. *Great Expectations: Marriage and Divorce in Post-Victorian America.* Chicago: University of Chicago Press, 1980.

May, Henry F. *The End of American Innocence: A Study of the First Years of Our Own Time, 1912–1917.* New York: Alfred A. Knopf, 1959.

———. *Protestant Churches and Industrial America.* New York: Harper & Row, 1949. Reprint, New York: Harper Torchbooks, 1967.

Mead, Sidney E. *The Lively Experiment: The Shaping of Christianity in America.* New York: Harper & Row, 1963.

Meagher, Margaret. *History of Education in Richmond.* Richmond: Works Progress Administration, 1939.

Meier, August, and Elliott Rudwick. "Negro Boycotts and Segregated Street Cars in Virginia." *Virginia Magazine of History and Biography* 81 (October 1973): 479–87.

Melosi, Martin. *Garbage in the Cities: Refuse, Reform, and the Environment, 1880–1980.* Chicago: Dorsey Press, 1981.

Melton, Julius. *Presbyterian Worship in America: Changing Patterns since 1787.* Richmond: John Knox Press, 1967.

Miller, Randall M., and Jon L. Wakelyn, eds. *Catholics in the Old South: Essays on Church and Culture.* Macon, Ga.: Mercer University Press, 1983.

Miller, Robert Moats. *American Protestantism and Social Issues, 1919–1939.* Chapel Hill: University of North Carolina Press, 1958.

———. "Fourteen Points on the Social Gospel in the South." *Southern Humanities Review* 1, no. 2 (summer 1967): 126–40.

———. "A Note on the Relationship between the Protestant Churches and the Ku Klux Klan." *Journal of Southern History* 32 (1956): 355–68.

Miller, Zane L. "Urban Blacks in the South, 1865–1920: The Richmond, Savannah, New Orleans, Louisville, and Birmingham Experience." In *The New Urban History: Quantitative Explorations by American Historians,* edited by Leo F. Schnore. Princeton: Princeton University Press, 1975.

Mims, Edwin. *The Advancing South: Stories of Progress and Reaction.* Garden City, N.Y.: Doubleday, Page, & Co., 1926.

Mintz, Steven, and Susan Kellogg. *Domestic Revolutions: A Social History of American Family Life.* New York: Free Press, 1988.
Mitchell, Broadus, and George Sinclair Mitchell. *The Industrial Revolution in the South.* Baltimore: Johns Hopkins University Press, 1930.
Mitchell, Mary H. *Hollywood Cemetery: The History of a Southern Shrine.* Richmond: Virginia State Library, 1985.
Mitchell, Samuel Chiles. "An Aftermath of Appamattox [*sic*]: A Memoir." Atlanta: mimeographed, 1954.
——. "The American Spirit in Education." *South Atlantic Quarterly* 8 (July 1909): 255–59.
——. "Phases in the Educational Movement of the Day." *Sewanee Review* 16 (January 1908): 18–25.
—— "Religious Education and Racial Adjustment." *Religious Education* 4 (October 1909): 316–23.
Moberg, David. *The Great Reversal: Evangelism versus Social Concern.* Philadelphia: Lippincott, 1972.
Moger, Allen W. *Virginia: Bourbonism to Byrd, 1870–1925.* Charlottesville: University Press of Virginia, 1968.
Moore, Walter W. *The Indispensable Book.* New York: Fleming H. Revell, 1910.
Muncy, Robyn. *Creating a Female Dominion in American Reform, 1890–1935.* New York: Oxford University Press, 1991.
Munford, Robert B., Jr. *Richmond Homes and Memories.* Richmond: Garrett & Massie, [1936].
Mussey, Mabel Hey Barrows, ed. *Social Hymns of Brotherhood and Aspiration.* New York: A. S. Barnes, 1914.
Negro Welfare Survey Committee. *The Negro in Richmond, Virginia.* Richmond: Richmond Council of Social Agencies, 1929.
Newby, I. A. *Jim Crow's Defense: Anti-Negro Thought in America, 1900–1930.* Baton Rouge: Louisiana State University Press, 1965.
Noll, Steven. *The Feebleminded in Our Midst: Institutions for the Mentally Retarded in the South, 1900–1940.* Chapel Hill: University of North Carolina Press, 1995.
Ochse, Orpha. *The History of the Organ in the United States.* Bloomington: University of Indiana Press, 1975.
Odegard, Peter H. *Pressure Politics: The Story of the Anti-Saloon League.* New York: Columbia University Press, 1928.
Odem, Mary E. *Delinquent Daughters: Protecting and Policing Adolescent Female Sexuality in the United States, 1885–1920.* Chapel Hill: University of North Carolina Press, 1995.
Odum, Howard W. *Southern Regions of the United States.* Chapel Hill: University of North Carolina Press, 1936.
O'Neill, William. *Divorce in the Progressive Era.* New Haven, Conn.: Yale University Press, 1967.
Osgood, Robert E. *Ideals and Self-Interest in America's Foreign Relations: The Great Transformation of the Twentieth Century.* Chicago: University of Chicago Press, 1953.
Ownby, Ted. *Subduing Satan: Religion, Recreation, and Manhood in the Rural South, 1865–1920.* Chapel Hill: University of North Carolina Press, 1990.
Patterson, James T. *America's Struggle against Poverty, 1900–1985.* Cambridge, Mass.: Harvard University Press, 1986.

Patterson, Michael S. "The Fall of a Bishop: James Cannon, Jr., Versus Carter Glass, 1909–1934." *Journal of Southern History* 39, no. 4 (November 1973): 493–518.

Pearson, C. C., and J. Edwin Hendricks. *Liquor and Anti-Liquor in Virginia, 1619–1919.* Durham, N.C.: Duke University Press, 1967.

Pell, Edward Leigh. *Four Feet on Fender.* New York: Dutton, & Co., 1917.

———. *The Life Worth While.* Richmond: Robert Harding, 1906.

———. *Our Troublesome Religious Questions.* New York: Fleming H. Revell, 1916.

———. *What Did Jesus Really Teach About War?* New York: Fleming H. Revell, 1917.

———. *Why I Believe in Jesus: A Personal Experience.* New York: Fleming H. Revell, 1926.

Phillips, Paul T. *A Kingdom on Earth: Anglo-American Social Christianity, 1880–1940.* University Park: Pennsylvania State University Press, 1996.

Pine Street Baptist Church. *Beacon on a Hill: A Brief History of One Hundred Years of Christian Service, 1855–1955, Pine Street Baptist Church.* Richmond: Pine Street Baptist Church, 1955.

Piper, John. *American Churches in World War I.* Athens: Ohio University Press, 1985.

Platt, Anthony M. *The Child Savers: The Invention of Delinquency.* Chicago: University of Chicago, 1969.

Pope, Liston. *Millhands and Preachers: A Study of Gastonia.* New Haven, Conn.: Yale University Press, 1942.

Prelinger, Catherine M., ed. *Episcopal Women: Gender, Spirituality and Commitment in an American Mainline Denomination.* New York: Oxford University Press, 1992.

President's Research Committee on Recent Social Trends, eds. *Recent Social Trends in the United States, Volumes I and II.* New York: McGraw-Hill, 1933. Reprint, Westport, Conn.: Greenwood Press, 1970.

Preston, Howard L. *Automobile Age Atlanta: The Making of a Southern Metropolis, 1900–1935.* Athens: University of Georgia Press, 1979.

———. *Dirt Roads to Dixie: Accessibility and Modernization in the South, 1885–1935.* Knoxville: University of Tennessee Press, 1991.

Pulley, Raymond H. *Old Virginia Restored: An Interpretation of the Progressive Impulse, 1870–1930.* Charlottesville: University Press of Virginia, 1968.

Rabinowitz, Howard N. *Race Relations in the Urban South.* Urbana: University of Illinois Press, 1980.

Rachleff, Peter. *Black Labor in Richmond, 1865–1890.* Urbana: University of Illinois Press, 1989.

Rice, Roger L. "Residential Segregation by Law, 1910–1917." *Journal of Southern History* 34 (May 1968): 179–99.

Rosen, Ruth. *The Lost Sisterhood, Prostitution in America, 1900–1918.* Baltimore: Johns Hopkins University Press, 1982.

Russell, Allyn C. *Voices of American Fundamentalism: Seven Biographical Studies.* Philadelphia: Westminster Press, 1976.

Ryan, Mary P. *Civic Wars: Democracy and Public Life in the American City during the Nineteenth Century.* Berkeley: University of California Press, 1997.

Ryerson, Ellen. *The Best-Laid Plans: America's Juvenile Court Experiment.* New York: Hill & Wang, 1978.

Ryland, Garnett. *The Baptists of Virginia, 1699–1926.* Richmond: Baptist Board of Missions and Education, 1955.

Salmond, John A. *Miss Lucy of the CIO: The Life and Times of Lucy Randolph Mason, 1882–1959.* Athens: University of Georgia Press, 1988.

Sandeen, Ernest R. *The Roots of Fundamentalism: British and American Millenarianism.* Chicago: University of Chicago Press, 1970.

Scanlon, James E. *Randolph-Macon College: A Southern History, 1825–1967.* Charlottesville: University Press of Virginia, 1983.

Schaffer, Ronald. *America in the Great War: The Rise of the War Welfare State.* New York: Oxford University Press, 1991.

Schiesl, Martin J. *The Politics of Efficiency: Municipal Administration in America, 1899–1920.* Berkeley: University of California Press, 1977.

Schlesinger, Arthur. *The Rise of the City, 1878–1898.* New York: Macmillan Co., 1933.

Scott, Anne Firor. *Natural Allies: Women's Associations in American History.* Urbana: University of Illinois Press, 1991.

———. *The Southern Lady: From Pedestal to Politics, 1830–1930.* Chicago: University of Chicago Press, 1970.

Scott, Mary Wingfield. *Houses of Old Richmond.* New York: Bonanza Books, [1941].

———. *Old Richmond Neighborhoods.* Richmond: Whittet & Shepperson, 1950.

Sears, Stephen W. *To the Gates of Richmond: The Peninsula Campaign.* New York: Ticknor & Fields, 1992.

Shattuck, Gardiner H., Jr. *Episcopalians and Race: Civil War to Civil Rights.* Lexington: University Press of Kentucky, 2000.

———. *A Shield and Hiding Place: The Religious Life of the Civil War Armies.* Macon, Ga.: Mercer University Press, 1987.

Sheerin, Maria Williams. *The Parson Takes a Wife.* New York: Macmillan Co., 1948.

Sherman, Richard B. "'The Last Stand': The Fight for Racial Integrity in Virginia in the 1920s." *Journal of Southern History* 54, no.1 (February 1988): 69–92.

Sibley, Marilyn M. *The Port of Houston: A History.* Austin: University of Texas Press, 1968.

Silver, Christopher. *Twentieth-Century Richmond: Planning, Politics, and Race.* Knoxville: University of Tennessee Press, 1984.

Simpson, William S., Jr. "1908-The Year Richmond Went 'Baseball Wild.'" *Virginia Cavalcade* 26 (spring 1977): 184–92.

Singal, Daniel. *The War Within: From Victorian to Modernist Thought in the South, 1919–1945.* Chapel Hill: University of North Carolina Press, 1982.

Sledge, Robert Watson. *Hands on the Ark: The Struggle for Change in the Methodist Episcopal Church, South, 1914–1939.* Lake Junaluska, N.C.: Commission on Archives and History, United Methodist Church, 1975.

Slosson, Preston William. *The Great Crusade and After, 1914–1928.* New York: Macmillan Co., 1930.

Smith, H. Shelton. *In His Image, But . . . : Racism in Southern Religion, 1780–1910.* Durham, N.C.: Duke University Press, 1972.

Smith, W. R. L. *History of the Baptist Home for Aged Women.* Richmond: L. H. Jenkins, 1922.

Smylie, James H. "The Roman Catholic Church, the State, and Al Smith." *Church History* 29 (September 1960): 321–43.

Solomon, Barbara Miller. *In the Company of Educated Women.* New Haven, Conn.: Yale University Press, 1985.

Sosna, Mort. *In Search of the Silent South: Southern Liberals and the Race Issue.* New York: Columbia University Press, 1977.

Spain, Rufus. *At Ease in Zion: Social History of Southern Baptists, 1865–1900.* Nashville: Vanderbilt University Press, 1961.

Stanard, Mary Newton. *Richmond: Its People and Its Story.* Philadelphia: Lippincott, 1923.

Starobin, Robert S. *Industrial Slavery in the Old South.* New York: Oxford University Press, 1970.

Storey, John W. *Texas Baptist Leadership and Social Christianity, 1900–1980.* College Station: Texas A & M University Press, 1986.

Strong, Josiah. *The Challenge of the City.* New York: Young People's Missionary Movement, 1907.

Sullivan, Mark. *Our Times: The United States, 1900–1925.* Vol. 4, *The War Begins, 1909–1914.* New York: Charles Scribner's Sons, 1932.

Swanson, Merwin. "The 'Country Life Movement' and the American Churches." *Church History* 46 (September 1977): 358–73.

Szaz, Ferenc Morton. *The Divided Mind of Protestant America, 1880–1930.* Tuscaloosa: University of Alabama Press, 1982.

Takagi, Midori. *"Rearing Wolves to Our Own Destruction": Slavery in Richmond, Virginia, 1782–1865.* Charlottesville: University Press of Virginia, 1999.

Tatum, Noreen Dunn. *A Crown of Service: A Story of Woman's Work in the Methodist Episcopal Church, South, from 1878–1940.* Nashville: Parthenon Press, 1960.

Taylor, Mary Grace Scherer. *Saints Alive!: A History of The First English Evangelical Lutheran Church, Richmond, Virginia, the First Hundred Years: 1876–1976.* Richmond: First English Evangelical Lutheran Church, 1976.

Taylor, Lloyd C., Jr. "Lila Meade Valentine: The FFV as Reformer." *Virginia Magazine of History and Biography* 70, no. 4 (October 1962): 471–87.

Teaford, Jon. *The Unheralded Triumph: City Government in America, 1870–1900.* Baltimore: Johns Hopkins University Press, 1984.

Teller, Michael E. *The Tuberculosis Movement: A Public Health Campaign in the Progressive Movement.* Westport, Conn.: Greenwood Press, 1988.

Thomas, Emory M. *The Confederate State of Richmond: A Biography of the Capital.* Austin: University of Texas Press, 1971.

Thomas, Hilah F., and Rosemary Skinner Keller, eds. *Women in New Worlds: Historical Perspectives on the Wesleyan Tradition.* Nashville: Abingdon Press, 1981.

Thompson, Edgar T., ed. *Perspectives on the South: Agenda for Research.* Durham, N.C.: Duke University Press, 1967.

Thompson, Ernest Trice. *Presbyterians in the South, Volume One: 1607–1861.* Richmond: John Knox Press, 1973.

———. *Presbyterians in the South, Volume Two: 1861–1890.* Richmond: John Knox Press, 1973.

———. *Presbyterians in the South, Volume Three: 1890–1972.* Richmond: John Knox Press, 1973.

Thompson, James J., Jr. *Tried As by Fire: Southern Baptists and the Religious Controversies of the 1920s.* Macon, Ga.: Mercer University Press, 1982.

Tilley, Nannie May. *The Bright-Tobacco Industry, 1860–1929.* Chapel Hill: University of North Carolina Press, 1948.

Timberlake, James H. *Prohibition and the Progressive Movement.* Cambridge, Mass.: Harvard University Press, 1963.

Tindall, George Brown. *The Emergence of the New South, 1913–1945.* Baton Rouge: Louisiana State University Press, 1967.

———. *The Ethnic Southerners.* Baton Rouge: Louisiana State University Press, 1976.

Torbet, Robert G. *A History of the Baptists.* Philadelphia: Judson Press, 1950.

Trachtenberg, Alan. *The Incorporation of America: Culture and Society in the Gilded Age.* New York: Hill & Wang, 1982.

Trattner, Walter I. *Crusade for the Children: A History of the National Child Labor Committee and Child Labor Reform in America.* Chicago: Quadrangle Books, 1970.

Treadway, Sandra Goia. *Women of Mark: A History of the Woman's Club of Richmond, Virginia, 1894–1994.* Richmond: Library of Virginia, 1995.

Trollinger, William Vance, Jr. *God's Empire: William Bell Riley and Midwestern Fundamentalism.* Madison: University of Wisconsin Press, 1990.

Troubetzkoy, Ulrich. *Richmond, City of Churches: A Short History of Richmond's Denominations and Faiths.* Richmond: Whittet & Shepperson, 1957.

Turner, Elizabeth Hayes. *Women, Culture, and Community: Religion and Reform in Galveston, 1880–1920.* New York: Oxford University Press, 1997.

Twelve Southerners. *I'll Take My Stand: The South and the Agrarian Tradition.* New York: Harper & Bros., 1930. Reprint, New York: Harper Torchbooks, 1962.

Tyler-McGraw, Mary. *At the Falls: Richmond, Virginia, and Its People.* Chapel Hill: University of North Carolina Press, 1994.

Vance, Rupert B. *The Human Geography of the South.* Chapel Hill: University of North Carolina Press, 1935.

Vance, Rupert B., and Nicholas J. Demerath, eds. *The Urban South.* Chapel Hill: University of North Carolina Press, 1954.

Wade, Richard C. *Slavery in the Cities: The South, 1820–1860.* New York: Oxford University Press, 1964.

Ward, Harry M., and Harold E. Greer, Jr. *Richmond during the Revolution, 1775–1783.* Charlottesville: University Press of Virginia, 1977.

Watkins, Rees. *The House of Happiness: A Ministry of Love.* Richmond: Woman's Missionary Union of the Richmond Baptist Association, 1981.

Weaver, Clarence E., ed. *Sketches of Richmond, Virginia, U.S.A.: Who's Who and What's What.* Richmond: Central Publishing, 1924.

Weber, Gustavus A. *Report of Housing and Living Conditions in the Neglected Sections of Richmond, Virginia.* Richmond: Whittet & Shepperson, 1913.

Weber, Timothy P. *Living in the Shadow of the Second Coming: American Premillennialism, 1875–1982.* Rev. ed. New York: Oxford University Press, 1979; Grand Rapids, Mich.: Zondervan, 1983.

Weddell, Elizabeth W. *St. Paul's Church, Richmond, Virginia—Its Historic Years and Memorials.* Richmond: William Byrd Press, 1931.

Weeks, William W. *The Face of Christ.* Nashville: Sunday School Board of the Southern Baptist Convention, 1927.

———. *The Heart of God.* Nashville: Sunday School Board of the Southern Baptist Convention, 1924.

Weisiger, Minor T., Donald R. Traser, and E. Randolph Trice. *Not Hearers Only: A History of St. James's Episcopal Church, Richmond, Virginia, 1835–1985.* Edited by Margaret T. Peters. Richmond: St. James's Episcopal Church, 1986.

Wheeler, Marjorie Spruill. *New Women of the New South: The Leaders of the Woman Suffrage Movement in the Southern States.* New York: Oxford University Press, 1993.

———. "Mary Johnston, Suffragist." *Virginia Magazine of History and Biography* 100, no. 1 (January 1992): 99–118.

White, Blanche Sydnor. *A Century of Service: A History of Bainbridge Street Baptist Church, 1857–1957.* Richmond: Whittet & Shepperson, 1957.

———. *First Baptist Church, Richmond, 1780–1955: 175 Years of Service to God and Man.* Richmond: Whittet & Shepperson, 1955.

———. *Richmond Baptists Working Together, 1780–1960.* Richmond: Richmond Baptist Association, [1961].

White, Ronald C., Jr. *Liberty and Justice for All: Racial Reform and the Social Gospel (1877–1925).* New York: Harper & Row, 1990.

White, Ronald C., Jr., and C. Howard Hopkins. *The Social Gospel: Religion and Reform in Changing America.* Philadelphia: Temple University Press, 1976.

Wiebe, Robert H. *The Search for Order, 1877–1920.* New York: Hill & Wang, 1967.

Williams, J. Paul. *What Americans Believe and How They Worship.* New York: Harper & Brothers, 1952.

Williamson, Joel. *The Crucible of Race: Black-White Relations in the American South since Emancipation.* New York: Oxford University Press, 1984.

Willingham, Elizabeth W. *The Life of Robert Josiah Willingham.* Nashville: Sunday School Board of the Southern Baptist Convention, 1917.

Wilson, Charles Reagan. *Baptized in Blood: The Religion of the Lost Cause, 1865–1920.* Athens: University of Georgia Press, 1980.

———. *Judgment and Grace in Dixie: Southern Faiths from Faulkner to Elvis.* Athens: University of Georgia Press, 1995.

———. "The Religion of the Lost Cause: Ritual and Organization of the Southern Civil Religion, 1865–1920." *Journal of Southern History* 46, May 1980: 219–38.

———, ed. *Religion in the South.* Jackson: University Press of Mississippi, 1985.

Wiltshire, Mollie Roberson. *A Century of Service: The History of Union Station Methodist Church, 1843–1943.* Richmond: Whittet & Shepperson, 1943.

Winsborough, Hallie Paxson. *The Woman's Auxiliary, Presbyterian Church, U.S.* Richmond: Presbyterian Committee of Publication, 1927.

Woodward, C. Vann. *Origins of the New South, 1877–1913.* Baton Rouge: Louisiana State University Press, 1951.

———. *The Strange Career of Jim Crow.* 3d ed. New York: Oxford University Press, 1974.

Woofter, Thomas J., ed. *Negro Problems in Cities.* Garden City, N.Y.: Doubleday, Doran & Co., 1928.

Writers' Program, Work Projects Administration. *The Negro in Virginia.* New York: Hastings House, 1940. Reprint, Winston-Salem: John F. Blair, 1994.

Zehmer, John G. *Old Richmond Today.* Richmond: Historic Richmond Foundation, 1988.

Zimmerman, Jane. "The Penal Reform Movement in the South during the Progressive Era, 1890–1917." *Journal of Southern History* 17 (November 1951): 462–92.

Theses and Dissertations

Armentrout, Donald Smith. "John Jacob Scherer, Jr.: A Type of Southern Lutheran." Ph.D. diss., Vanderbilt University, May 1970.

Bowden, William L. "History of the Cooperative Education Association of Virginia: An Analysis of a Community Development Agency and Its Practice of Adult Education." Ph.D. diss., University of Chicago, 1957.

Brinson, Elizabeth Stevens. "'Helping Others to Help Themselves': Social Advocacy and

Wage-Earning Women in Richmond, Virginia, 1910–1932." Ph.D. diss., Union Graduate School of the Union for Experimenting Colleges and Universities, 1984.

Bullock, Robert Hayden. "The Past Fifty Years of Presbyterianism in Richmond, Virginia." Th.D. thesis, Union Theological Seminary, 1943.

Cei, Louis Bernard. "Law Enforcement in Richmond: A History of Police-Community Relations, 1737–1974." Ph.D. diss., Florida State University, 1975.

Crumpton, Kenneth, Jr. "The History of the Lutheran Church in Richmond, Virginia, 1843–1965." Master's thesis, Lutheran Theological Southern Seminary, 1967.

Gignilliat, John L. "The Thought of Douglas Southall Freeman." Ph.D. diss., University of Wisconsin-Madison, 1968.

Glass, William. "The Development of Northern Patterns of Fundamentalism in the South, 1900–1950." Ph.D. diss., Emory University, 1991.

Headlee, Thomas J. "The Richmond Transit Strike of 1903." Master's thesis, University of Richmond, 1960.

Hoffman, Steven J. "Behind the Facade: The Constraining Influence of Race, Class and Power on Elites in the City-Building Process, Richmond, Virginia, 1870–1920." Ph.D. diss., Carnegie Mellon University, 1993.

Hohner, Robert A. "Prohibition and Virginia Politics, 1901–1916." Ph.D. diss., Duke University, 1966.

Hopewell, John Stanley. "An Outsider Looking In: John Garland Pollard and Machine Politics in Twentieth Century Virginia." Ph.D. diss., University of Virginia, 1976.

Leatherman, Carolyn Hall. "Richmond Rejects a Library: The Carnegie Public Library Movement in Richmond, Virginia, in the Early Twentieth Century." Ph.D. diss., Virginia Commonwealth University, March 1992.

Nadler, Samuel. "A History of the Instructive Visiting Nurse Association of Richmond, Virginia, 1900–1950." Master's thesis, Richmond Professional Institute of the College of William and Mary, April 1951.

Presley, John Carroll. "Samuel Chiles Mitchell: A Biography of a Southern Educator." Ph.D. diss., University of Virginia, 1992.

Sharp, Rebekah R. "A History of the Richmond Public School System, 1869–1958." Master's thesis, University of Richmond, 1958.

Index